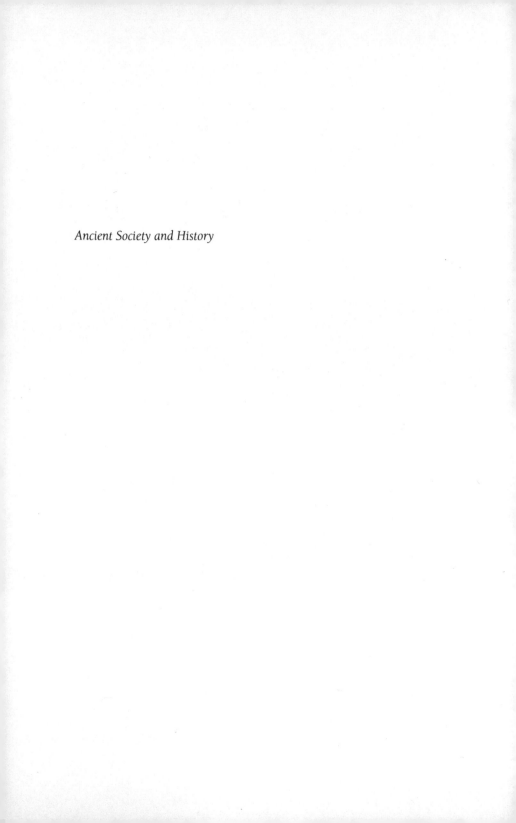

Ancient Society and History

Late Roman Spain

MICHAEL KULIKOWSKI

and Its Cities

The Johns Hopkins University Press
Baltimore and London

© 2004 The Johns Hopkins University Press
All rights reserved. Published 2004
Printed in the United States of America on acid-free paper
9 8 7 6 5 4 3 2

The Johns Hopkins University Press
2715 North Charles Street
Baltimore, Maryland 21218-4363
www.press.jhu.edu

Library of Congress Cataloging-in-Publication Data

Kulikowski, Michael, 1970–
    Late Roman Spain and its cities / Michael Kulikowski.
        p.   cm. — (Ancient society and history)
    Includes bibliographical references and index.
    ISBN 0-8018-7978-7 (hardcover : alk. paper)
    1. Cities and towns—Spain—History—To 1500.   2. Spain—
History—To 711.   I. Title.   II. Series.
    HT145.S7K838 2004
    307.76'0946—dc22

                                        2004001111

A catalog record for this book is available from the British Library.

a mi padre
por todos los años y todos los libros

Divina natura dedit agros, ars humana
aedificavit urbes.
—Varro, *De re rustica* 3.1.4

A culture, we all know, is made by its cities.
—Derek Walcott, "The Antilles:
Fragments of Epic Memory"

Contents

Illustrations

Preface

This book begins from three propositions. First, the political narratives and institutional history of many late antique provinces must be revisited in light of recent advances in source criticism. Many basic sources for the period have now appeared in new, improved editions and in some cases—that of Hydatius, for instance—the new edition has required fundamental changes, not least in matters of chronology. The now universal conviction that we must read evidence as text before we read it as source has altered our understanding of many authors, with the result that standard narratives of the period no longer seem to be as securely founded on the sources as they once did.

Second, discussions of late antique history that take their starting point in the third or fourth century tend naturally to underestimate the continuity of late antique institutions with those of the early empire. Thus, to understand late antique urbanism, one ought neither to assume a normative high imperial standard from which deviation represents decline, nor posit a third-century crisis that wipes clean the slate for late antiquity. Either assumption will miss how thoroughly conditioned late antique history is by the experience of the early empire, the period in which Spain became Roman, culturally and politically.

Third, and finally, at a time and in a place for which the archaeological evidence is more plentiful than the scant literary sources, we should interpret the literary sources against the background of the material evidence rather than trying to fit the archaeological record into a paradigm derived from the literary sources. That statement is uncontroversial for certain periods of ancient and early medieval history—archaic Rome, fifth-century Scandinavia, eighth-century central Europe—where written evidence ranges from the very scant to the nonexistent. But in most places where sufficient literary sources survive, they tend to retain their primacy in creating a historical framework, even if good archaeological evidence also exists in quantity. This book posits an alternative approach. It argues that the traditional narrative arc of Spanish history—from a period of romanization and urbanization, through a third-century crisis that destroys the city culture of the Antonine age, to a thoroughly rural late antiquity and early Middle Ages—cannot be sustained on the basis of the extant evidence. Instead, the evidence shows that the cities and their cultural and political world remained the chief motive force in Spain's late antique history. That conclusion, to my mind, is the inevitable result of reading the well-known literary evidence against recent archaeological findings.

The book's first three chapters look at the implantation of cities and city culture in the peninsula, the institutions that a city implies, and the continuity of those institutions into late antiquity, suggesting that late antique developments must be read in light of their roots in the early empire. The fourth chapter centers on the Diocletianic reforms and what those meant for the role of Spain within the Roman empire as a whole. The archaeological backdrop of late antique cities in the peninsula and the material evidence for the relationship between town and country are examined in chapters 5 and 6, which draw conclusions against which the succeeding narrative chapters can stand. Chapters 7, 8, and 9 present a revision of the political narrative of Spanish history from circa A.D. 400 to circa 500, the first segment of Spanish history since the Republican era in which it is possible to write narrative history. Chapter 10 presents the evidence, both archaeological and literary, for Christianity in Spanish late antiquity. The final chapters look at the confusion of the earlier sixth century, in the decades before King Leovigild founded a stable Gothic kingdom that brought much of the peninsula under the rule of a single power. The start of his reign inaugurates a new period in Spain's late antique history and one that has been much better served by scholarship than have the three centuries that preceded it. For that reason, it seems logical to conclude with him.

A book such as this could not have been written fifteen years ago. Only very recently has the archaeological record for Spanish late antiquity reached standards of reliability, and of independence from the historical sources, that make it a viable alternative category of evidence to the literary record. Only more recently still have modern studies of that material record been published in quantities large enough to allow an attempt at synthesis. The scholarship on Spain's Roman and late antique archaeology is scattered, and much of it does not circulate widely outside Spain and Portugal. I am sure that I have missed important studies. Yet this book will have served a large part of its purpose if it introduces an Anglophone audience to the work of great importance now being done across the Iberian peninsula. Certainly it could not have been written without that work.

One incurs many debts in a work of this scale. Some thirty pages of my dissertation on "The End of Roman Spain," defended in the summer of 1997, survive in chapters 7 and 8. Thanks are owed to its supervisor, T. D. Barnes, and to the other members of my dissertation committee, Walter Goffart and Alexander Callander Murray, for advice and encouragement both before and since. Thanks are also due to my thesis examiners Jonathan Edmondson, Leonard Curchin, and Mark Meyerson. Various people have helped shape this book and its contents over the years: Kim Bowes, Sebastian Brather, Palmira Brummett, Richard Burgess, Frank M. Clover, Craig Davis, Dimas Fernández-Galiano, Andrew Gillett, Geoffrey Greatrex, Kenneth Harl, Jocelyn Hillgarth, Lester Little, John Magee, Ralph Mathisen, Michael McCormick, Danuta Shanzer, David Wiljer, and Lea von Zuben Wiljer. My fellow participants in the colloquium on "Die spätantike Stadt—Niedergang oder Wandel?" organized by Jens-Uwe Krause and Christian Witschel in the Abteilung Alte Geschichte der Ludwig-Maximilians-Universität, Munich, inspired several last-minute changes.

Research for this volume was undertaken in part with grants from Smith College and the University of Tennessee. The Cartographic Services Laboratory at the University of Tennessee, under the direction of Will Fontanez, produced the maps and plans; Kathryn Salzer took the photographs. The interlibrary loan departments at Smith College and the University of Tennessee have handled a constant stream of exotic requests with patience and resourcefulness, while the ingenuity of UT's history librarian Anne Bridges has made it possible to acquire books otherwise inaccessible. Finally, no one living outside Spain can work successfully on its ancient history without the catalogues of Pórtico Librerías of Zaragoza, each a work of scholarly reference.

In a labor of this sort, one's personal debts are as numerous as one's professional. I have been lucky in the support of three generations of my own and my wife's family. I am not at all certain this book would have been written without their interest and generosity, and I am sorry that three who were there at its inception, Victor Kulikowski, Tomasz Wilk, and Opal Dye, have not lived to see its completion. My wife, Kathryn Salzer, has negotiated many a dirt track en route to a Roman ruin when she would rather have been looking at monasteries and has read many more drafts than conjugal duty requires. Any merit to be found in my prose I owe to my mother's early tuition. My greatest debt of all I owe to my father, without whose encouragement from earliest childhood I would not have become a historian, still less a historian of Spain. This book could be dedicated to no one but him.

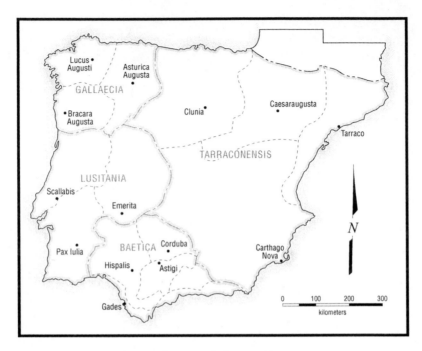

Spain, *conventus* boundaries and provinces before ca. 293

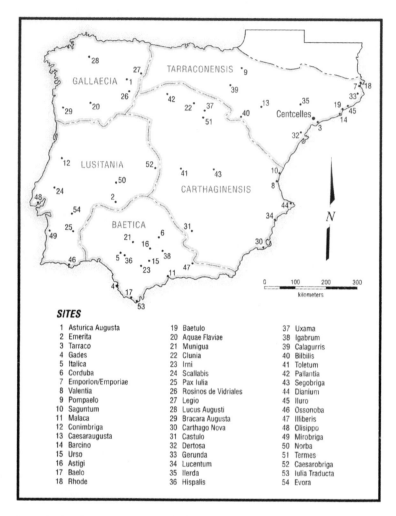

SITES

1 Asturica Augusta	19 Baetulo	37 Uxama
2 Emerita	20 Aquae Flaviae	38 Igabrum
3 Tarraco	21 Munigua	39 Calagurris
4 Gades	22 Clunia	40 Bilbilis
5 Italica	23 Irni	41 Toletum
6 Corduba	24 Scallabis	42 Pallantia
7 Emporion/Emporiae	25 Pax Iulia	43 Segobriga
8 Valentia	26 Rosinos de Vidriales	44 Dianium
9 Pompaelo	27 Legio	45 Iluro
10 Saguntum	28 Lucus Augusti	46 Ossonoba
11 Malaca	29 Bracara Augusta	47 Illiberis
12 Conimbriga	30 Carthago Nova	48 Olisippo
13 Caesaraugusta	31 Castulo	49 Mirobriga
14 Barcino	32 Dertosa	50 Norba
15 Urso	33 Gerunda	51 Termes
16 Astigi	34 Lucentum	52 Caesarobriga
17 Baelo	35 Ilerda	53 Iulia Traducta
18 Rhode	36 Hispalis	54 Evora

Spain, the Diocletianic provinces excluding Tigitania and the Balearics, and important cities

Late Roman Spain and its Cities

One

The Creation of Roman Spain

R oman Spain was a world full of cities, shaped by its hundreds of urban territories. This was every bit as much the case in late antiquity as it had been during the high imperial period. Students of late antiquity tend to lump Spain together with Gaul or Britain, as part of the western provinces generally, but the depth and breadth of Spanish urbanism meant it had far more in common with Italy or North Africa.[1] Spain was the Roman Republic's first great imperial venture overseas. Thus the Roman influence lasted longer and ran much deeper in Spain than in other parts of the Latin West. At the heart of that impact lay the cities and the political geography they created. The emperor Augustus consciously shaped the Spanish provinces around urban territories. Most Spanish *civitates* were not, as in Gaul, old tribal territories under a new administrative mask; they were small administrative units whose urban centers, within seventy years of Augustus's death, had gained privileged status under Roman law, as *municipia*. They were also the engine that drove the process by which Spain became Roman. For that reason, Spain's urban geography survived the disappearance of the empire that had brought it into being.

Between three hundred and four hundred cities dotted the Spanish landscape of the high empire. Apart from a few parts of the Gallaecian northwest, the Spanish provinces looked very similar to Italy after the Social War and the enfranchisement of Cisalpina. The unit that defined political, administrative, and social geography was the autonomous urban center and its dependent territory. Very few substantial centers of population lacked autonomy or were administered from some other city. The vast *civitates* of the Tres Galliae, within which several large towns might exist along with the administrative *civitas*-capital, simply did not exist in Spain, where the terms *civitas* and *municipium* were functionally interchangeable by the second century. It was, in consequence, the municipalities that knitted the peninsula together and that controlled it on behalf of the imperial government in which they participated. Most of these cities did not fall off the map in late antiquity, although they leave fewer traces in the historical record. Instead, they remained the essential units of control, not just for the imperial government and its various would-be successors, but also for local elites who maintained the Roman ideal of a political life based on the city until the days of the Córdoban caliphate.

Roman Conquest and Romanization

The Roman conquest of Spain took more than two hundred years, and by the time it was complete, Rome itself had undergone the profound change from republic to empire. The Roman Republic was drawn into the peninsula on account of its wars with Carthage, and so far as the Roman state and its leaders were concerned, Spain remained of purely military interest until the time of Augustus.[2] The wars against Hannibal began in Spain, when in 218 B.C. Gnaeus Cornelius Scipio landed with an army at the Greek city of Emporion, modern Ampurias in Catalonia. Their peninsular phase lasted until 206, when the younger Publius Cornelius Scipio, later called Africanus after his victory over Hannibal at Zama, expelled the Carthaginians from Spain. Scipio's victorious campaigns had driven deep into the Spanish interior, and in the valley of the Guadalquivir river, close to modern Seville, Scipio founded Italica as a settlement for his wounded veterans. Tarragona, a hundred miles down the coast from Ampurias and the Roman base after 217, would become one of Roman Spain's greatest cities. The years of fighting had brought with them not just the legions, but also

2

the train of civilians—camp followers and supply contractors—that trailed all Roman armies. The Spanish campaigns had also led to numerous encounters with indigenous peoples who had entered the Punic war as allies of either Rome or Carthage. Obligations to both nascent Roman communities and different peninsular groups soon made it impossible for the Roman state to withdraw from Spain even had it wanted to.

There is no reason to think that it did, given the competitive nature of Roman imperialism.[3] Roman politicians needed military successes abroad to enhance their status at home; Spain, with its numberless tribal units, proved an ideal environment for generals seeking glory. Moreover, the ongoing social struggles at Rome meant that at least some poorer citizens were happy to escape the city and seek opportunity abroad, whether in the ranks of the legions or in the civilian industries that followed them. The presence of these Roman civilians in turn perpetuated the military presence, since the protection of Roman citizens, either as necessity or pretext, required further wars. The nexus of these interests explains the ongoing Roman commitment to a Spanish conquest that carried on interminably after the younger Scipio's final victory over the Carthaginians in 206.

We need not trace in detail the phases of the Republican occupation of Spain—aptly described as "a random hunt for peoples to fight and booty to take home"—but it was through just such fighting that the Spanish provinces grew.[4] Rome acquired a Spanish empire that it barely administered, one that existed for the benefit of Romans in Italy. Spain was governed as occupied territory, no attempt was made to create a Roman environment, and local organizations could persist so long as local power was subservient to Rome. Already in 197 the Roman Senate had laid the foundations around which the future territorial organization of the peninsula would take shape, sending two praetors to Spain, each with his own *provincia,* the exact boundaries between which they were to determine for themselves.[5] The new provinces of Hispania Citerior and Hispania Ulterior, so-called on the basis of their distance from Rome, were centered on Tarragona and Córdoba, respectively, the former provided with the massive fortifications that defined the city right through the Middle Ages.[6] Despite vast territorial expansion and the introduction of a rudimentary taxation

3

system circa 179, little thought was given to the administrative shape of the Spanish provinces until the reign of Augustus. Rome's Spanish experience had profound effects on developments at Rome, and the Roman appetite for tribute certainly generated an important expansion in peninsular agriculture.[7] Yet Spanish integration into the Roman world was demonstrated in a more melancholy fashion, as the civil wars of the late Republic were fought on Spanish soil and local inhabitants suffered the grim consequences of picking the wrong side. The Roman attitude is made clear by the aftermath of Sertorius's revolt, which had been sustained in part with the help of Spanish allies: when Pompey celebrated his Spanish triumph in 71, he did so as conqueror of foreign peoples, the indigenous supporters of Sertorius, who remained aliens in the eyes of the Roman state. Again, only the reign of Augustus brought change.

In the years after Sertorius's defeat, the history of the Romans in Spain is entirely subsumed into the history of the Roman civil wars. Yet in a peculiar sense it was the civil wars between Pompeians and Caesarians that made Spain a normal part of the Roman world: the great traumas of the day convulsed its soil as they did other provinces, and Spaniards of every stripe were forced to take sides and reaped the harvest of their choice.[8] By the time Augustus won his victory at Actium there could be no doubt that the peninsula had become a part of the Roman world. In the north, among the Astures and Cantabri, there remained indigenous peoples unreconciled to Roman rule. But elsewhere the peninsula was at peace, and Augustus made it his first task to bring the far north into conformity with the rest. The emperor himself campaigned in the peninsula in 26 and 25 B.C., making it for a brief time the center of the Roman world. In the latter year, he declared a victory over the Cantabri that allowed him to close the doors to the temple of Janus at Rome.[9] This was no more than a propaganda victory, for campaigns continued in the Spanish north until Agrippa ended them decisively in 19 B.C. by massacring the Cantabrian warriors and resettling the survivors in the valleys where they would be easier to control. In this way the Augustan peace was extended to Spain and hostilities between Spanish natives and Roman armies ceased forever.[10] With the war won, Augustus imposed on Spain the new juridical and political shape that it would retain until the reign of

Caracalla at the beginning of the third century. Within this Augustan framework, Spain became Roman.[11]

The Augustan Reorganization of Spain

Augustus's policy recognized how diverse the peninsula remained after two hundred years of Roman presence in it. In those regions where a Roman model existed or where the native culture was already heavily urbanized, Spaniards had started to assimilate the Roman way of life. Caesar's victory over Pompey had reinforced these existing patterns, by planting prominent *coloniae* of Roman citizens on Spanish soil, carving out territories for these autonomous settlements from the *ager publicus* of which the provinces were composed. Some of these, like the new *colonia* at Córdoba, were imposed as punishment for having picked the wrong side in the civil wars, others were a reward for having backed the winner.[12] Either way, along with centuriation and citizens, these colonies brought Roman law and Roman juridical models into the heart of Spanish regions that had long known Romans as soldiers, traders, and publicans, though not perhaps as resident landowners. In the lower Ebro valley, the Mediterranean coast, and the great valley of the Guadalquivir, the population was accustomed to a Roman presence and open to a Roman way of life that it had already begun to adopt: according to Strabo, the inhabitants of the Guadalquivir valley had lost their own tongue and embraced Latin.[13]

Beyond this first Spain, however, there was another one where Romans were known only as soldiers on campaign or as tribute collectors.[14] Much of the west and southwest were like this, but so too was the Meseta and indeed even the hills and mountains that flanked the centers of Roman settlement along the coasts and river valleys. In these regions, the impress of Rome was hardly visible despite a century or more of subjection to the Roman empire, while the distant northwest had only just been subdued by force of arms and still operated according to a different, more or less tribal, set of rules. Augustus rebuilt the administrative shape of Spain to accommodate this diversity, while also creating a framework within which it could grow less pronounced.

The two existing *provinciae* of Citerior and Ulterior were remolded.

5

Beyond the Ebro valley and the Catalonian and Levantine coasts, Citerior remained largely devoid of cities and more or less without Roman settlement. To the old province, administered as it long had been from Tarragona, Augustus attached the strategically important area around the headwaters of the Guadalquivir in the Sierra Morena. Parts of the Gallaecian northwest, which had first come to the attention of the governors of Ulterior and had therefore been included in their *provincia,* were likewise attached to Citerior. In this way, a vast new Hispania Citerior was formed, soon to become more generally known as Tarraconensis after its capital. The old Hispania Ulterior, by contrast, was divided into two provinces, Baetica and Lusitania. The new division between Baetica and Lusitania ran roughly along the course of the Guadiana river, the Roman Anas, and marked the very real cultural boundary between the urban Spain of the Guadalquivir valley and the tribal Spain of present-day Extremadura and the Portuguese Alentejo.[15]

The Augustan administrative reorganization of Spain represented a rational assessment of regional differences within the peninsula, but it also served the more immediate political needs of the *princeps.* In the new Baetica, Augustus had a demilitarized province that could be safely entrusted to the Senate, thereby lending substance to his claim to have restored the Republic. From the time of the Augustan reorganization, which had certainly taken place before 13 B.C., Baetica was administered by a senatorial proconsul, while Lusitania and Citerior remained military provinces administered by the emperor through propraetorian and proconsular legates, respectively. The formal subdivision of Spain into different *conventus* was another product of the Augustan era. In Spain, as in some other Roman provinces, particularly in the East, *conventus* had developed around the communities of Roman citizens, who formed unofficial juridical groupings with which the provincial governor could deal and to whom he could dispense justice under Roman law.[16] The juridical component of the *conventus* was retained by Augustus, under whom the *conventus* of Spain were regularized as administrative districts of the Roman state. By the Flavian era, the fourteen Spanish *conventus* were fixed subdivisions of the provinces, centered on a city at which the provincial governor or his deputy could deal with the legal needs of Roman citizens.[17] The seven *conventus* in Tarraconensis, three in Lusitania, and four in Baetica not only integrated their territories by providing them with an economic and judicial focus, they also forced remote populations to travel into more developed areas in order to have their needs serviced, knitting the whole of the peninsula much more closely together.[18] In time, this fostered a communal spirit and we find both conventual councils and dedications to the *genii* of the different *conventus*.[19] In fact, the *conventus* were a successful enough means of organizing territory that we still find them in the fifth century after the provincial superstructure had disappeared.

Nevertheless, even with the new, smaller provinces and the new *conventus* within them, the Spanish land mass remained an enormous area to administer. Augustus seems to have decided quite consciously that the best way of providing for Roman control—and for conducting the census of the empire, which he made one of his foremost goals as *princeps*—was through a network of urban centers and assigned dependent territories, the *civitates,* which were everywhere the basic units of Roman administration.[20] The peninsula already sported many towns, both indigenous and Roman, but where these did not exist, Augustus hastened their creation. These towns were of very diverse origin and of very diverse status under Roman law. The *coloniae,* never more than thirty or so across the whole peninsula, were the deliberate creations of Roman governments, settled with Roman or Latin citizens, their territories carved from existing provincial territories. *Coloniae* shared the privilege of autonomous government over themselves and their dependent territories with another group of cities, the *municipia.* These were generally preexistent urban centers, some settled by Roman or Latin citizens, others old indigenous sites, which were granted privileged status by Rome and autonomous control over their territories. Apart from the privileged *coloniae* and *municipia,* the cities of the peninsula were stipendiary, which is to say tribute paying, and their inhabitants *peregrini,* foreigners in Roman law. Such stipendiary *civitates,* whether centered on a real urban settlement or not, were nonetheless an effective means of dividing and administering peninsular land, since they provided a focus with which the Roman state could interact. The Augustan era witnessed the foundation of many such peregrine cities, as well as more *coloniae* and *municipia* than had been created in the whole previous history of Roman rule in Spain. Some were created de novo, like the *colonia* of Augusta Emerita, modern Mérida, founded in 25 B.C. for veterans of the Cantabrian wars, or Barcelona, created on a virgin site in 9 or 8 B.C. The very name of Caesaraugusta, modern Zaragoza, testifies to the era of its foundation, while in the far northwest a string of stipendiary cities like Lucus Augusti, Bracara Augusta, and Asturica Augusta were founded to act as new urban centers for the recently conquered mountain tribes. At the same time, many existing towns were promoted to colonial or municipal status.

Within this Augustan system of provinces, *conventus,* and *civitates,* Spain became Roman; its inhabitants were transformed from the subjects of Romans into Roman provincials and participants in the Roman empire. This was hardly a conscious goal. Augustus, like Roman imperialists before him, had no special desire to turn his provincial subjects into Romans. However much Roman writers might conceive of Roman rule as bringing civilization to the conquered, the provinces existed to pay for the Roman state and an untaxed Roman Italy. If they could be administered cheaply and with a minimum of Italian manpower, so much the better. The co-optation of local elites was the easiest way to accomplish this end and one that bore rapid fruit in Spain. The three provinces required only a little over two hundred imperial officials to administer them in the centuries after Augustus, just governors and their small staffs, two subordinate legates in the vast province of Tarraconensis, and quaestors (in Baetica) or equestrian procurators (elsewhere) to oversee the collection of taxes and manage the income of imperial properties.[21] The rest of the work was done by the Spanish elites, who turned themselves into Romans as rapidly as they could.

They did so in order to secure their place within the new framework of society. All across the Roman world, the emperors could rely upon local elites to act as the basic units of government because those elites saw in Roman rule an advantage for themselves.[22] In Spain as elsewhere, the indisputable hegemony of Roman arms meant that the best way for local elites to maintain the power that they were accustomed to wielding locally was to become Roman. Doing so meant being able to exercise the old authority within the framework of the new

8

system.[23] The first step to becoming Roman was adopting a Roman way of life. In some cities, like Sagunto, local elites had adopted Roman titulature for local offices as early as the second century B.C.[24] Everywhere, the Latin language and Roman culture were necessary tools for the maintenance of power. This explains the spread of a Roman lifestyle, Latin literature, and Roman architectural tastes among the local elite. The most visible effect of this was that townscapes on the Roman pattern began to appear across the peninsula. In a few places, these were deliberate creations, ostentatiously Roman towns that could act as centers of Roman control, whether actual or symbolic. Astorga, Braga, and Lugo in the north fall into this category, even though they lacked privileged status. So, too, does Mérida in Lusitania, which lies on an open plain by the Guadiana river and, by replacing the fortified Republican site of Medellín, served as a monument to Roman prestige. In the middle Ebro valley, Zaragoza replaced the old fort at Celsa in the same way.

In these new foundations as well as in the older peninsular cities, much of the impetus to create a Roman townscape came from a mimetic impulse among local elites. Privileged towns had to live up to their status in physical terms, looking the part of Romans. In towns without a Roman status, or with the inferior Roman status of the *ius Latii*, local leaders worked to re-create themselves and their cities in the image of the ruling power.[25] This mimetic impulse produced the Augustan theater at Italica in Baetica, the lavish circus built during Augustus's reign at Lisbon on the Atlantic coast, and the large forum complex in the small town of Conimbriga in central Lusitania.[26] We can also see a steady diffusion of Roman styles into remoter areas, for instance, the triangle of cities—Clunia, Tiermes, and Uxama (Burgo de Osma)—that acted as the center of Roman urban culture in the northern Meseta. As one would expect, of course, the romanization of the townscape both began and took firmest root in regions that had for the longest time had a Roman presence, that is to say, the Mediterranean coast and the Guadalquivir valley, which were also the regions with the oldest pre-Roman urban traditions, whether indigenous, Greek, or Punic.[27] But the effects were felt everywhere in the peninsula, as recent archaeological discoveries are making ever clearer.[28]

The adoption of a Roman lifestyle was not in itself enough, however, because full participation in the political power of Rome required Roman citizenship. The attainment of Roman citizenship therefore became the foremost goal of local elites, because it allowed them to join in the political relationships of the larger Roman elite while at the same time maintaining their customary preeminence at home. Roman law distinguished different grades of citizenship rights. Even during the reign of Augustus, the full civic rights of the *civis romanus* were not very widespread in Spain, confined largely to immigrants from Rome and Italy or those natives who had gained access to citizenship through military service to Rome.[29] The less privileged status of the *ius Latii* was another matter. This juridical status had evolved from the rights originally granted to the Latin tribes of Italy in the fourth century B.C. and allowed participation in Roman civil law, the transaction of business according to Roman law, and the right of *conubium* or intermarriage with Roman citizens, as well as admission to full Roman citizenship through the tenure of local municipal office.

In the provinces, Latin rights were chiefly, or perhaps exclusively, granted to towns, often by the conversion of a stipendiary city into a *municipium iuris Latii*.[30] By the second century A.D., two grades of Latin right had been defined. In towns granted the *ius Latii maius,* the whole governing elite of a municipality, the curial order as well as their children, automatically gained Roman citizenship. In towns with the *ius Latii minus,* by contrast, an individual had actually to hold office in his town in order to acquire Roman citizenship.[31] The grant of either type of Latin right had important consequences for a community. On the one hand, it meant that a steady stream of full Roman citizens would emerge from the local elite, hastening the community's integration into the larger social world of the empire. Lower down the social ladder, it meant that local institutions, social and legal, would rapidly come to conform to the processes and forms of Roman law, inasmuch as the larger body of local citizens were able to use Roman law forms within their own community while their municipal elite, as Roman citizens themselves, would tend to administer justice and enforce rules according to Roman law.[32]

By the end of the Augustan period, the Latin right was distributed fairly widely among a substantial number of Spanish *municipia,* and a few more cities gained Latin rights under his Julio-Claudian successors. The existence of this slowly growing number of privileged communities no doubt spurred competition among non-privileged cities to attain the municipal status that brought Latin rights, at least until the Flavian era, when Latin rights were extended to the whole of the peninsula. In 73 or 74, during his tenure of the censorship, the emperor Vespasian issued what we call the Flavian municipal law, extending the Latin right to the whole of Spain.[33] This act of munificence was in part the reward for Spanish loyalty during the civil wars of A.D. 68–69. Those wars had begun in 68, when Ser. Sulpicius Galba, the imperial legate of Hispania Citerior, was invited by the rebel governor Vindex to take charge of the revolt against Nero because, as governor of Lugdunensis, Vindex commanded no legions himself. From the Roman citizens of the Spanish provinces, Galba raised a new legion, the Legio VII Galbiana, and marched on Rome.[34] After Galba's assassination at Rome, the legion he had created joined the cause of Vespasian and was renamed the VII Hispana, eventually playing an important role in the Flavian victory.[35] Vespasian's grant of the *ius Latii* to Spain was thus in part a reward for the service the Spanish provinces had done the new Flavian dynasty. It was also, however, a recognition of how deeply Spain had been integrated into the Roman polity since the days of Augustus, an integration attested by the speed with which Galba was able to raise the VII Galbiana.

It is not entirely clear how Vespasian's generosity was intended to be put into practice, and the subject remains a matter of controversy. Some have maintained that the grant was not universal, or that it existed *in potentia,* so that communities had to apply for a promotion that not all proved qualified to receive.[36] The likeliest hypothesis, however, is that Vespasian intended every Spanish stipendiary community— every *civitas* capital hitherto lacking privileged status under Roman civil law—to become a *municipium iuris Latii minus.*[37] Whether or not that was intended from the start, it was certainly the result of the Flavian grant and no clear exceptions exist, even in the most rural corners of Gallaecia.[38] Instead, it would appear that in the two decades after 73/74, Spain became entirely municipalized, its territory parceled out among a minimum of three hundred, and perhaps as many as four hundred, Flavian *municipia* with Latin rights.[39] There was clearly a time lapse between the general grant issued by Vespasian and

11

the promulgation of individual laws for the many new Latin communities in Spain. The earliest municipal charters we possess come from the reign of Domitian, but there is good evidence for various Spanish cities adopting the usages of Latin rights immediately, before a complete municipal constitution was delivered to them.

We now possess a copy of much of the Flavian municipal law from the Baetican town of Irni, thanks to the lucky discovery of its original bronze tablets in the 1980s.[40] The *lex Irnitana* complements the fragments of Flavian municipal laws long known from Salpensa and Málaga in the same province. Since the discovery of the *lex Irnitana*, fragments of several more Flavian charters have appeared, so that we now possess roughly two-thirds of the basic model law that was granted with local variations to all the Flavian *municipia* in Spain.[41] This basic municipal law was widely diffused across Spain, not only in Baetica but, as newly discovered fragments show, in Tarraconensis as well.[42] In the sections in which comparison is possible, there are slight differences among the different extant municipal laws. Space for local variation was clearly envisaged in the original form of the law, though how individual copies were composed and distributed remains unclear.[43] Regardless, the *lex Irnitana* and its various analogues laid down the structures of urban government and organized the way they would operate, creating at one stroke a remarkably homogeneous urban environment across the entire peninsula. The institutional life of the city described by the Flavian municipal laws was the basis of all future developments, remaining largely intact even in the later empire.

In the short term, however, the Flavian municipal law inaugurated a new and accelerated phase in the romanization of Spain. Vespasian's law gave the whole of the peninsula a status within Roman civil law for the first time and all of Spain's inhabitants became part of the Roman *res publica*. Municipalization brought inscription into Roman voting tribes and the acceleration of onomastic change in local society, Roman naming patterns replacing indigenous.[44] Because local officeholding brought Roman citizenship along with it, the Flavian municipal law meant the full integration of the Spanish elites into a political world centered on Rome.[45] In a variety of regions we can trace the gradual creation of mixed urban populations of Latin and Roman citizens, a process made inevitable by the promotion from stipendiary to municipal status, for instance, in a string of indigenous cities along the base of the Pyrenees, most of which were founded in the Augustan period and all of which were promoted under the Flavians.[46] The overall effect was to ensure that the co-optation of Spanish elites into a larger Roman elite took place juridically and en masse, rather than through individual grants of Roman status or merely through the mimetic adoption of Roman customs without a legal basis. At a fundamental level, the Flavian municipal laws created Hispano-Romans.

This is strikingly manifested by the increasing number of Spaniards at the center of imperial politics in the Flavian and Trajano-Hadrianic decades. The Flavians were as lavish with grants of senatorial rank as they had been with their grant of municipal status, and it was in large part thanks to Flavian adlections that Roman citizens from Baetica occupied the imperial throne in 97 and then again in 117.[47] By the reign of Hadrian as much as 25 percent of senators may have belonged to Spanish families.[48] The number of equestrians from Spain also grew equally rapidly, not just in Baetica but throughout the Spanish provinces.[49] In Baetica and in the cities of the Tarraconensian coast, Roman citizenship was already widespread under the Flavians, but in the course of the second century, certainly by the reign of Marcus, it became the norm for local elites throughout the peninsula. As a result, the *constitutio Antoniniana* of 212, which turned almost all the inhabitants of the empire into Roman citizens, had no revolutionary effect on the Spanish provinces. Every Spaniard of any consequence was already a Roman citizen.[50] And because the vast majority of the population had enjoyed Latin rights for five or six generations, they had used Roman law within the local community for nearly as long. The effect of the Antonine constitution was merely to extend the de facto enjoyment of Roman citizen *iura* to non-citizens traveling or dwelling outside their own *municipium*.

The Flavian municipal law thus had profound effects on the personal status, and therefore the social behaviors, of many Spaniards, but its impact on the broader institutional structure of Spain was just as important and certainly of longer-lasting significance. The municipalization of the peninsula that followed rapidly on Vespasian's grant of Latin rights placed every kilometer of Spanish land into a new juridical framework, as part of the *territorium* of a privileged city, whether a *colonia* or *municipium*. The organization and regulation of Spanish land that had begun with the creation of the three Augustan provinces was thereby completed in a more or less systematic fashion. Though their boundaries might already have been relatively well delineated, the transition to municipal status meant that every stipendiary city now fixed the borders of its *territorium* and thereby became a subdivision of the Roman provincial organization and thus of the Roman state. The relationship between a city, its territory, and the imperial government, not to mention the relationships among the various *municipia*, were now embedded in a single, fixed system of Roman law, with the boundaries between communities sanctioned by the emperor—hence their designation as *termini Augustales*.[51]

The integral link between city and country, assumed by Roman law, became the basic organizing principle of Spanish territory. Each municipal government ensured that the rural *territorium* of its city—the *universitas agrorum intra fines cuiusque civitatis*—rendered the tax revenue required by local government and by the Roman state.[52] In other words, the Flavian municipal law universalized the juridical and political aspect of the relationship of town and country, along lines that had already developed in those parts of Spain where Roman citizenship and communities with Roman law status had previously existed. The municipalization of Spain, its organization into hundreds of autonomous city territories, constitutes a vital distinction between the Spanish experience and that of, for instance, Gaul or Germany.[53] Because of the early and extensive promotion of Spanish towns to municipal status, the basic unit of political geography was smaller in Spain than elsewhere in the West.[54] We find almost no evidence for the *adtributio* of one urban site to another, politically more significant, site.[55] For the same reason, Spanish *vici* were much fewer than elsewhere in the West, and *pagi,* which were units of rural administration in some regions, in Spain designate only a subdivision of a municipal *territorium*.[56]

In consequence, Spain's political geography was fundamentally urban in a way that those of Gaul, Britain, and Germany were not, while the block grant of municipal status and concomitant Latin rights avoided the palimpsest of legal statuses that characterized the highly urbanized world of North Africa.[57] Even in Cantabria, Asturias, and

Galicia, where we find some evidence of *fora* acting as administrative centers for the predominantly rural population of the *civitas*, it is likely that such administrative units had municipal status.[58] In other words, by creating an indissoluble legal bond between hundreds of autonomous cities and their dependent rural territories, the Flavian municipal law ensured that the process of becoming Roman in Spain would take place according to fundamentally urban models, with the city and its elites the dominant force in society, even in marginal areas with a dispersed population.

Everywhere, the basic organ of local government was the *ordo decurionum*, analogous to the Senate at Rome. Government was thus essentially oligarchic, for oligarchy was a model well understood by Rome and encouraged among provincial subjects because it made for stability. Offices and responsibilities were shared out among the relatively small governing class and the annual magistrates of the city were elected from the *ordo*. In some parts of the peninsula, this model was entirely new. In others, it meant the adaptation of old styles of urban social relations to the new requirements of a Roman public life.

Regardless, the pressures to adopt a Roman way of life, to become Roman, were self-reinforcing in such an environment. The physically Roman framework of the new townscapes imposed an at least superficially Roman pattern on the course of daily life, which in turn encouraged further romanization of the physical environment. At the same time, and not coincidentally, we find the extension into the countryside of the Roman model of *urbs in rure*. Mediterranean-style villas began to spring up everywhere, concentrated, as in Italy, in the suburbs of the great cities and within easy road or river journey of them. The explanation of this is not far to seek, for the same men who furnished themselves with grand country retreats were also the magistrates and councillors of the local *municipia* and *coloniae*. The city thus became the great organizing device of the Spanish countryside and the pole around which a *territorium* of rural settlement—agricultural, industrial, or residential—revolved.

We can trace the spread of Roman behaviors, Roman onomastics, and Roman citizenship in the course of the second and third centuries A.D. by looking at the physical traces, architectural or epigraphic, that the process of becoming Roman left behind. Yet after the Flavian victory of 69, the peninsula knew almost continuous peace and considerable material prosperity until the beginning of the fifth century, with the result that its narrative history is very nearly a blank.[59] That Trajan and Hadrian were Spaniards is a point of some significance, but we do not on that account learn anything special about the life of Spain during their reigns. The later second century is just as barren of evidence: we know nothing about the revolt in 145 of Cornelius Priscianus save that it happened.[60] Under Marcus Aurelius, Mauretanian tribesmen raided across the straits of Gibraltar into Baetica.[61] In the civil wars that followed on the murder of Commodus in 192, the Spanish provinces threw in their lot with Clodius Albinus and consequently suffered from the vengeance of Septimius Severus, the eventual victor, whose general Tiberius Candidus campaigned in the peninsula against the partisans of Albinus.[62] In 238, at the very beginning of the third-century civil wars, the governor of Tarraconensis and future emperor Q. Decius Valerinus held Spain loyal to the emperor Maximinus when other provinces joined the senatorial opposition.[63] And, around 260 during the reign of Gallienus, barbarians from across the Rhine passed through Gaul into Spain and sacked Tarragona.[64] Apart from this there is silence, often the fate of peaceful lands in peaceful times.[65] At the heart of that peace and good order lay the Spanish cities and the Hispano-Roman elites that governed them. The institutions by which they did so were fundamentally the same ones with which their late antique descendants organized the political life of their own time. We can trace the survival of urban institutions best known in their early imperial incarnations into late antiquity, when the narrative of Spanish history first becomes accessible to us in the very last stages of Roman government in the peninsula.

Two

Urban Institutions in the Principate

Once it had taken root in the various parts of the peninsula, urban living had a dynamic of its own and came very rapidly to seem not only normal, but normative. By the end of the Flavian era, with the peninsula structured around its three hundred or four hundred *civitates,* every Spaniard lived within the *territorium* of one city or another, regardless of his own individual legal status.[1] After 212, a population composed entirely of Roman citizens dwelt in *civitates* within which no legal distinction was made between those who resided in the titular conurbation and those—the majority of the non-elite population— who lived in the countryside, whether in villages or more dispersed settlements. The result was a startlingly homogeneous political landscape, with several hundred autonomous urban centers structured like miniature Romes, governed by a variety of magistrates drawn from the local *ordo decurionum* and ruling over *civitas*-territories that were quite small by the standards of the Latin West.

This homogeneity is all the more surprising for having grown out of very diverse origins. Roman urbanism rested on different foundations in different parts of Spain, whether indigenous, Punic, or Greek in the south and the Ebro valley, or as a novelty in the center, the north, and the west.[2] Other differences went back to differing circumstances of foundation, whether as *coloniae* or *municipia* of Roman citizens, or as indigenous peregrine cities granted the Latin right along with promotion to municipal status. Despite this variety, the constitutional structure of the Spanish citizen *coloniae* was not dramatically different from those of the Flavian *municipia*, as the fragments of the *lex coloniae genetivae Iuliae* from Urso suggest, and whatever distinctions there had once been had disappeared by the third century.[3] During the second century, cities ceased to pay much attention to the titulature of status so that in all of third-century Spain we possess only one example of a city that retained its full early imperial titulature.[4] Regardless of their distant origins as *coloniae, municipia,* or stipendiary communities, most cities called themselves *civitates* or *respublicae* indiscriminately.[5] These basically similar cities were, with their territories, the fundamental units of organized existence and they were generally small enough that the Spanish landscape, unlike that of much of Gaul, really was defined by its network of cities. This Hispano-Roman urbanism was perhaps the most significant legacy of the early empire, because the city remained central to the life of Spain even after the monumental trappings that had accompanied its creation fell by the wayside and even after the imperial structure that had brought it into being disappeared. Spaniards, in other words, had internalized the desire to live together in towns.

What this meant is nowhere better illustrated than in the case of Munigua, located in the hills of the Sierra Morena and today 10 kilometers from the nearest paved road. This mountainous region just north of the Guadalquivir valley had not held much interest for Roman settlers, but was instead exploited for its mineral wealth. Some of the earliest materials found at Munigua are the remains of ironworks and, during the high empire, Munigua was a cult and administrative center for the mining encampments in the surrounding mountains. When the site was granted municipal status and Latin rights under Vespasian, the whole city was rebuilt to match its new status. Lavish, Roman-style houses and public buildings—forum, basilica, temple, baths—were built up the side of a steep hill, its western face shored up still further and supported by an enormous stonework capped by a large temple. Despite these impressive structures, early imperial Munigua probably had a tiny population, though it included the wealthy

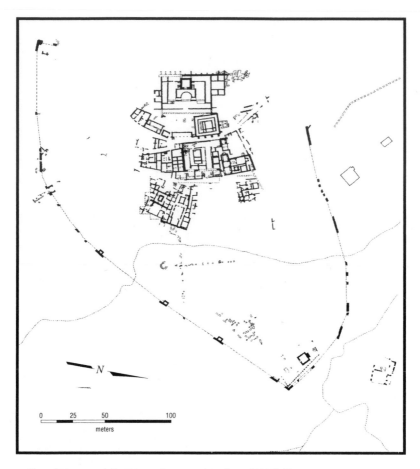

Plan of Munigua. (after Meyer, Basas, and Teichner [2001], 6)

owners of the townhouses around the forum that lay at the foot of the great hill.[6] The forum and much of the rest of the monumental city center had been built thanks to the munificence of the local worthy L. Valerius Firmus shortly after the site was granted municipal status.[7] An imposing sight even today, during the early empire Munigua was a powerful symbol of imperial prestige.

Yet whatever its symbolic importance in the early empire, Munigua was an isolated settlement in a zone where Roman urban habits had as yet made little impact and where the existence of Munigua itself did

The terrace and retaining wall of Munigua, viewed from the west. (K. Salzer)

little to alter that fact. In the later empire, however, when the mineral exploitation of the Sierra Morena had already gone into a terminal decline, this was no longer the case.[8] Perhaps toward the end of the third century, the site suffered widespread but not catastrophic structural damage that might best be attributed to an earthquake.[9] Rather than withering away into a ghost town after this shock, Munigua began to flourish as a center of habitation. Its population between the fourth and sixth centuries was larger than it had been during the high empire, as is suggested both by the size of the cemeteries and by the extensive reoccupation of the site to support a larger number of residents than previously.[10] The old *domus* to the east of the forum were repaired and some were subdivided into smaller units of habitation. Eventually, at least one of the Flavian *domus* was built over with new, smaller houses, which likewise sprang up all along the edges of the forum and the wide streets that had led up to the cult site on the top of the hill.[11] On one such street, laid out across all but a small sliver of the road surface, stands a series of small one-room buildings, perhaps poor houses, but more likely shops or stalls. The old symbolic shape of the city had dissipated entirely, but now a substantial number of people actually lived their lives there.

One can advance only one explanation for the arc of Munigua's history: when the city was built in the early empire, it was meant to control an economically important region that possessed only a small and scattered rural population in no way given to life in cities. The city was therefore inhabited only by those romanized elites whose job it was to manage the region's resources on behalf of the government. But by the later empire, even the highlands of Baetica had come to participate in the mainstream of Roman culture, with the result that urban living was now regarded as normal. The damaged site was rebuilt as a town for the satisfaction of the local population, no longer mountain-dwelling Spaniards, but Hispano-Romans living in a mountain town. Although there is no epigraphic evidence for the curial *ordo* and municipal magistrates of this later, more populous Munigua, their counterparts are known from other small cities across late antique Spain. A dramatic example of a Spanish town with a late imperial population substantially larger than that of its high imperial predecessor, Munigua illustrates just how deeply the habit of living in urban settlements at the

Early imperial street in Munigua with late antique shops built over it. (K. Salzer)

center of a municipal territory had become ingrained in Hispano-Roman society.

The Structure of the City

What gave the Roman city its defining importance were the institutions of social life that used the city as their stage. Living in a city, being a citizen, meant patterns of behavior that were self-perpetuating and also canons of self-representation and self-understanding that were passed on from generation to generation among the elite strata of society to which our sources give us the greatest access. The people who counted in society were tied to a place in which their names were prominently known; in which they were recognized as they walked the streets as being people worth knowing, people with influence, not necessarily just locally, but stretching out into the empire at large; in which their achievements might appear beneath a commemorative statue in some public place, or on a funerary monument outside the walls where passers-by could stop, think, and be impressed; and in which they could expect their children to witness ancestral importance and anticipate in turn the same honor and reverence for themselves.

The mechanics and institutions of town life varied from place to place, and municipal foundation charters represent an administrative ideal to which local practice need not always have conformed.[12] Nevertheless, the Flavian municipal law was widely distributed in the peninsula and the institutional features of urban life described in the *lex Irnitana* and its cognates are attested elsewhere in the archaeological and epigraphic record of the second and third centuries. Thus, although we cannot use our extant copies of the Flavian municipal law as an exact description of urban life as lived in any specific third-century place, this off-the-peg constitution does provide a broadly accurate description of the high imperial cities from which the late imperial world evolved.[13]

The municipal law describes an urban culture structured like a miniature Rome. The town's councillors are *conscripti,* just like Roman senators, because like senators they had their names inscribed in the album of their order. These *decuriones, senatores,* or *conscripti*—terms used interchangeably in the *lex Irnitana*—were the dominant social force in the town.[14] Though the Flavian municipal law does not phrase it so, this curial *ordo* was clearly hereditary and in origin made up of those families that had always produced the important men of the region.[15] The number of sitting councillors drawn from this oligarchy varied from place to place, often according to pre-Roman customs, so that at Irni we find the peculiar figure of sixty-three as the minimum strength of the curia.[16]

The need to keep the curia up to strength ensured that the councils were not completely closed orders, though some urban elites were clearly more open to new blood than others. In the old Augustan *colonia* of Tucci in Baetica, for example, the curial order was dominated by a single clan of Iulii for the first three imperial centuries, that is to say, for the whole period in which there is an adequate epigraphic record.[17] Barcelona was also an Augustan colony, but its curia showed a much greater willingness to co-opt outsiders.[18] Tucci was something of a backwater, off-the-main communications network of Baetica, while Barcelona was a successful port that had sucked the vitality from the older Roman towns of Baetulo and Iluro (modern Badalona and Mataró) nearby. One might therefore suppose that it was the degree of contact with the outside world that kept curias open, but this seems not to have been the case. Tarragona, Mérida, and Seville were all great cities, in constant contact with the rest of Spain and the empire, but though Tarragona had a rather closed and impenetrable urban elite, in both Mérida and Seville outsiders were frequently brought into the curia.[19]

Regardless of the size and composition of the curias, the basic institution of local government was everywhere the annual magistracies.[20] Not only did the magistrates see to the smooth functioning of the town itself, they also regulated the intercourse between the town and its dependent territory and provided the channel through which the imperial government communicated with the plurality of cities that made up the empire.[21] At the top of the local hierarchy were the chief magistrates, the *duumviri* at Irni, though the number, and hence the title, of these chief magistrates varied from city to city.[22] The chapter on duumviral duties is missing from the extant municipal laws, but these magistrates' chief task was to administer the proceedings of the council and to provide games. In theory, the duumvirs also had powers of jurisdiction within their *civitas:* slaves could be manumitted in their presence, they could appoint guardians for women and minors, and they presided over legal cases up to a certain financial value.[23] This judicial function became increasingly vestigial as time went on, and there is no unambiguous record of duumviral jurisdiction in or after the third century.

More important was the administration of council proceedings. This allowed the duumvirs to shape the affairs with which the curia would concern itself and that meant very real power. The framers of the Flavian municipal law had recognized as much when they laid out the duumviral responsibility to hear the voice of every councillor who wished to speak and not to dismiss the assembly before it had run its course.[24] Throughout the third century, we have records of decisions taken by vote of the curia and in each of these cases it was the chief magistrates who had guided proceedings to the point at which the vote was taken. Despite the trope of powerless and declining curias in the third and fourth centuries, we must remember that, whatever the deficiencies of curial power in the wider empire, within the town, the chief magistrates of the curia could shape the affairs of their fellows with real consequence.

Below the chief magistrates came the two aediles. According to the *lex Irnitana,* the aediles were "to have the right and power of managing the corn supply, the sacred buildings, the sacred and holy places, the town, the roads, the districts, the drains, the baths and the market, and of checking weights and measures; of managing the *vigiliae* when the occasion arises, and of seeing to and doing whatever else the decuriones or *conscripti* decide is to be done by the aediles."[25] This means that while the duumvirs led the government, the aediles saw to the practicalities of urban administration. Like the duumvirs, they possessed a certain limited jurisdiction, though there is no sign of its being exercised in the third century or later.[26] Beneath the aediles came the quaestors, responsible for urban finances, although relatively few quaestors are attested in Spain and some have thought that the office was not universal.[27]

The reward for all this office-holding was local power and public honors, but the essential ideological goal was service to the community. It was therefore essential that the right sort of person be chosen for the job. There were age and property restrictions for all public offices. Age thirty-five was the minimum for the duumvirate; to ensure that the largest number of the governing class had a chance to exercise its prerogatives, candidates for the duumvirate were prohibited from having held office for five years prior to their standing for election.[28] Once appointed, the magistrate was to swear an oath to "do properly whatever he may believe to be according to this statute and according to the common good of the *municipes*" and also to "restrain those whom he is able to restrain" from acting against the common good. For the duumvirs, this meant among other things making sure that everyone had their fair say in the council, and that everything that one of the *curiales* wished to have aired was duly aired before all of them.[29] The breach of this trust was actionable by the *municipium* and punishable by fines. There is no way of knowing how often such sanctions were necessary, but they are unlikely to have been very frequent given the generalized Roman respect both for social consensus and obedience to authority. As an incentive to consensus, magistrates were chosen by vote of the council, which is to say by their fellow citizens of high status.

Indeed, urban affairs were in general subject to vote by the curia and the regulations for correct voting procedure were both extensive and complex.[30] Decisions were not to be taken without a quorum of two-thirds of the councillors, while the disbursement of funds required a quorum of three-quarters.[31] If they were applied in practice, these rules would have often made a hard scrabble for votes necessary. On the other hand, many have doubted whether curial politics involved the genuine casting of free votes that represented an actual consensus. Such doubts become universal for the period from the third century onward. In reality, there is a false dichotomy at work in such questions. The manufacture of consensus in small, hierarchical societies does not require the same standards of freedom and impartiality as do modern democratic systems. The universal belief that those higher up the social hierarchy were necessarily representatives of the best interests of the community as a whole means that the modern obsession with free and uninfluenced decision making is meaningless. Patterns of patronage, clientage, and protection, however imperfect they look to modern eyes, do in fact produce consensus in relatively small and hierarchical societies. Throughout Roman Spain, as throughout the Roman world, curial leadership seems to have produced the sort of practical results that the elite community wanted, and which, so far as everyone was concerned, represented the best interests of the community as a whole.[32]

It would be strange if they had not done so, for working in the communal interest was precisely the burden of high status. It was what was expected of municipal elites in return for the honor of leading the community. Moderns tend to view public service and personal advantage as somehow incompatible, but the ancients did not. Public service was just that—service; indeed, it was service that some were duty-bound to render, and it happened that the benefits of this service were manifold. At the most basic level, public service was a marker and visible advertisement of social position. It helped fix one on the infinitesimally differentiated hierarchy of status. Each town had its municipal album in which the whole of the curial order was inscribed in very strict order of precedence. Thus, in our one extant example of such an album, from the provincial town of Timgad (ancient Thaumugadi) in North Africa, serving priests are listed first, followed by serving duumvirs, aediles, and quaestors, followed by ex-priests and ex-magistrates, followed by those members of the curial order who had not actually held office.[33] In Spain, as in Timgad, voting in council took place according to this list.[34] The most honored citizens cast their votes first, establishing the channels into which their social juniors fitted their own votes.

Communal occasions made the same point. The duumvirs were, in consultation with the decurions, to decide "how much should be spent for expenses on religious observances and games and how much on dinners which are offered to the *municipes* or the *decuriones* or *conscripti* in common."[35] Voted annually by the curia, sponsored by the *respublica,* and paid for out of municipal funds, festivals were not only a display of the urban unity of the city, but also served to enforce the demarcations of status within it by the minute gradations of physical positioning. Thus, when the town went to see games, each was expected to occupy the same assigned seat as always.[36] At a number of Spanish spectacular monuments the names of seat holders are inscribed for all to see.[37] This sort of status display is important in all societies, but much more so in relatively small communities in which information is communicated orally and in which public memory needs constant refreshing by visual display.

There is no doubt that this public memory was meant to extend through the generations. The honor of public service was service not just to one's contemporaries but to posterity as well, and the memory of visual display tends to be very strong. Yet unlike most medieval societies, which relied almost entirely on oral memory to preserve their recollections of the past, antiquity used the written word as well. Just as the names of serving councillors were inscribed in the municipal album, so the votes of the council were recorded in writing. The record was then read out to those who had voted its decision, and afterward deposited for the ages in the municipal archive.[38] Though this procedure had the effect of doubling the oral experience of the vote, thus fixing it more firmly in the memories of those present, it also spoke directly to posterity. One writes things down in the expectation of others reading, and the daily activity of the curia was in this way wrapped up in the lives of its own future. The same simultaneous concern for both present and future is visible elsewhere, equally embedded in writing. It was the curias that voted honors to the living and dead, both those from within their own number and those outside it. Again, the value of the permanent record was not just recognition in the present, but continued recognition by posterity.

We would expect this in the great imperial cities of the peninsula, and we duly find it in the fora of Tarragona and Córdoba and elsewhere where our catalogues of honorific inscriptions continue to grow with each new excavation. More telling, however, is the amount of good evidence for this attitude to public life that comes from very unlikely places. At the obscure Baetican town of Canama, known only from its epigraphy and a single reference in Pliny, we meet L. Titacius L.f. Quir. Lupus, who was voted both a public burial place and a pedestrian statue by the *ordo* of the city.[39] The example of Lupus is important. The text of an inscription, usually all that is still available to us, was itself only one component in a larger statement. The presence or absence of a statue was a visible marker of the importance of an inscription's dedicatee. The placement of a statue within the forum—the company it kept—was a coded statement of social position. The number and sort of honors voted also advertised the living social position of a man. They added bulk and weight to his presence, making him a larger figure in the perceptions of those around him.

Apart from that one inscription, we know nothing about the life of Titacius Lupus of Canama. But we must make the effort to imagine what we can. As the *conscripti* of Canama hurried to their senate chamber in the forum most would have walked past Lupus's statue; it would have served as a reminder, perhaps a subconscious one, of the man's importance, and we can imagine the deference this would have inspired when it came to debate. Lupus will have been an imposing presence in the town's little curia, a big fish in a small pond from our point of view, but perhaps an often decisive force in the daily lives of his contemporaries. We do not know whether Lupus had any sons, but if he did then they would have profited from the reflected glory of their father.[40] These are, again, the sorts of benefits that we struggle to quantify but that are nevertheless very real indeed, the benefits that come from being the son of the man to whom the town was obliged enough to erect a statue. If in our minds we multiply the number of men like Lupus, a handful in a small town like Canama, dozens in a metropolis like Tarragona, we can begin to imagine the impact that visual commemoration had on the lives of Hispano-Roman townsmen.

Lupus of Canama was honored by the curia of his town. The official context of the honor no doubt gave it a special burnish, particularly if it was placed in the municipal forum. But the public advertisement of honors was not solely confined to such official statements and we often cannot tell at whose expense the record of public honors was made. In the absence of official recognition, magistrates and decurions displayed their own public achievements, and private dedications probably outnumbered the strictly public ones. Thus, a *decurio collegii Aquiflaviensis,* one Iulius Aurelius Decoratus, and his sons, the aedile Iulius and the quaestor Marcus Aurelius, in 237 dedicated an altar to Jupiter Optimus Maximus in their hometown of Aquae Flaviae, the same town in which the famous chronicler Hydatius would much later serve as bishop.[41] We do not know where in Aquae Flaviae these Aurelii erected their altar, but it is not at all unusual to find honorific inscriptions taking the form of a religious dedication. Such dedications were both a form of thanksgiving and a formal statement of religious adhesion, and both the choice of deity and the format of an inscription could be very telling. Jupiter Optimus Maximus was the favorite capitoline deity in the Spanish northwest, where, in the early centuries of the empire, he played the same sort of integrative role that imperial cult played in Baetica and the northeast.

The altar of the Aurelii at Aquae Flaviae was therefore a conscious statement of *romanitas,* of belonging to a Roman dispensation of which they approved. For that reason, the choice of deity was supremely appropriate to this sort of inscription. Regardless of its religious content, the altar was as much as anything else an advertisement of the public honors of its dedicatees. At the same time as the Aurelii honored Jupiter, they also announced to all and sundry that the sons of one father had succeeded, at the same time, in beginning their climb up the municipal *cursus honorum.* Even though we do not know where this inscription was meant to be displayed, and thus cannot pinpoint exactly whom it was supposed to impress, it encapsulates an entire ethos and ideology of public service and public recognition for it, an example all the more striking for coming from the ends of the Roman earth.

Because of its religious content, the inscription also shows us how closely linked public service, *romanitas,* and religious observance were in the early centuries of imperial Spain. The same point emerges more clearly from the prominence of the imperial cult in much of the peninsula.[42] Membership in the municipal curia was the chief measure of local status, but a parallel measure lay in the public priesthoods, which stood either to the side, or sometimes at the top, of the hierarchy of municipal office. The imperial cult had been important in some parts of the peninsula since the time of Augustus, and at Tarragona cult to Augustus was established while the *princeps* was still alive. But it was the Flavian era that institutionalized imperial cult on a grand scale. The three basic priesthoods were the sevirate, the flaminate, and the pontificate. The first was normally confined to freedmen and hence well outside the *cursus* of the magistrate.[43] The flaminate and pontificate were identical local priesthoods, the former title found in Lusitania and Tarraconensis, the latter in Baetica.[44] Both demonstrated a very close connection to the imperial dynasty, and therefore, especially in the early days of the empire, advertised a prestigious and much coveted *romanitas* in those who held them.[45]

Because of the important political element in emperor worship, it is no surprise that *flamines* and *pontifices* were drawn from the ranks of the local *ordo* and had already held the chief magistracy in their towns. In a functional sense, the flaminate or pontificate crowned a magisterial career, and the sorts of public festivities that these priests were expected to sponsor mirrored this fact.[46] Yet the tenure of a priesthood also opened avenues to further advancement, since each of the three Augustan provinces had an imperial cult at the provincial level as well. Provincial cult was in origin confined to Roman citizens of equestrian status, but soon came to represent the highest honor to which local magistrates aspired.[47] By crowning a career in local service with a priesthood, one improved one's chances of leaping out into the wider world of provincial or imperial society, even if one came from a nowhere place like Consabura, a small *municipium* nestled in the Montes de Toledo.[48]

In this way, priesthoods were a means of personal advancement and a personal expression of loyalty to the imperial regime, but they were more than that as well. At the municipal level, the imperial cult was a communal expression of loyalty to the imperial regime and also an important psychological link to the wider world. Even in a small city with a circumscribed territory and a limited measure of real power, local decurions could participate in the fortunes of the larger world, of the empire as a whole, through the imperial cult. The psychological benefit of this phenomenon cannot be dismissed lightly—in an empire tied together only very loosely by administrative and bureaucratic links, potentially emotive symbolic actions could generate a real sense of community among vastly disparate people. By the third century, two hundred years of habit had become deeply ingrained and, regardless of whether there was any serious affective content in the ruler cult, it was widely understood that the towns participated in an empire, that the empire was a good thing, and that the safety of that empire depended on the well-being of the emperor.

The vast number of inscriptions formally dedicated by the curias to reigning emperors—or to deified imperial virtues like *Victoria* and

Concordia—shows this.[49] The number of third-century imperial dedications, relative to the epigraphic record as a whole, has been seen by
many as a sign of decadence, of the collapse of the independent spirit
of the curias and consequently a sign of a collapse into third-century
crisis. But there is another way to read the same phenomenon, as the
culmination of the long process of romanization that Spain had undergone since the days of Augustus. Curias had learned to conceive of
themselves as atoms within the larger empire of which the emperor
was the protector. By dedicating inscriptions to him, they were doing
their part to preserve not just their own *respublicae,* but also the greater
res publica of the empire as a whole. This task would no doubt have
seemed all the more pressing in the later third century, when a super-
fluity of emperors seemed incapable of coming to terms with one another. The dedications to each emperor in turn can be read as genuinely pious hopes for the good of the commonwealth, rather than as
mere servile flattery. It is in this context that we must place altars commemorating the *taurobolia* that were held at Córdoba for the safety of
Alexander Severus and not long afterward *pro salute imperii,* which is
to say, for the good of the empire itself; these altars are paralleled by
other dedications from the end of the century *pro salute* of the new
Caesars Constantius and Galerius.[50] In many ways, the imperial inscriptions are a sign not of curial decline but of curial vitality. Instead
of disintegrating in the face of political turmoil at the highest levels,
the curias chipped in as best they could to put things right.

Such demonstrations are to be expected in the great administrative
cities, the provincial and *conventus* capitals, and our expectations are
duly met.[51] On the other hand, we find the same sort of zeal elsewhere, which is more significant. As an example, we may take the important dossier of imperial dedications known from Barcelona.[52]
Barcelona was rich, but it was not an administrative center except of
its own *territorium.* Despite this, we find a large number of imperial
dedicatory inscriptions and a visible effort to stay up to date: an inscription dedicated to Probus notes his *damnatio memoriae.*[53] At
Seville, the expressive curial inscriptions from the first two centuries
of the empire peter out entirely in the third century, but imperial dedications survived into the fourth century, when we find a dedication
to Constantine as Caesar, voted by the *res publica Hispalense* and set up

in the old Republican forum of the city.[54] Barcelona was a great port
and no doubt got the latest news from the whole Roman world very
early, but in a minor provincial town like Acci, we find a similar dedication, this time to Carinus, which likewise records his eventual
damnatio.[55] At the small town of Elvira—the Roman Florentinum
Iliberritanum, or Iliberris—famous as the site of the earliest church
council in the West, third-century inscriptions raised *sumpto publico*
honored not just Gordian but also his wife Tranquilina.[56] Inscriptions
like this one are constantly being unearthed, and they demonstrate
that, even in the hinterland, curias were keen to take part in the world
of their day and anxious to get it right.[57]

The Decline of the Epigraphic Habit

Imperial dedications of the third century are by no means uncommon.
By contrast, the altar of the Aurelii of Aquae Flaviae, with its ostentatious respect for the ideology of office-holding, is a more unusual document because it comes from a period during which the epigraphic
dossier of Roman Spain shrinks very rapidly. The disappearance of the
Hispano-Roman epigraphic habit is notorious. It has traditionally
been equated both with a decline in the prestige and value attached to
the public offices that had hitherto been commemorated epigraphically and a more generalized third-century crisis. It is true that the sta-
tistics are stark: there are perhaps twenty thousand extant Latin inscriptions from Spain, from the Republican period until the Arab
conquest of 711.[58] Of these, less than a tenth date from after the year
250, with the vast majority falling within the bare century and half between Vespasian and the later Severans. This is, of course, a distribution of epigraphic evidence well known from all the western provinces
and indeed from most of the Roman world.

On the other hand, the Spanish case differs in several important respects. First, the sheer volume of Spanish inscriptions is, at its peak,
much higher than that in most parts of the Latin West. At the same
time, the precipitate disappearance of the epigraphic habit is much
more complete in Spain than in Italy, Africa, or even southern Gaul.
The Spanish case has thus been taken as an extreme example of trends
visible everywhere, and the loss of the epigraphic habit has been added

to the tally of third-century urban decline. Whereas at the start of the third century even a middling urban professional like the lawyer P. Gabinius Firmanus of Acci might, as a matter of course, have his career inscribed for posterity, by the middle of that century very few men outside the uppermost reaches of imperial service engaged in such behavior.[59] This, the theory goes, shows that either through loss of public spirit or lack of means, civic notables had ceased commemorating their achievements in stone. As a corollary, the decline in the habit of inscription is taken to correspond to a decline in the activities traditionally inscribed.[60]

Yet however ingrained such interpretations might be, they are too simplistic. Louis Robert long ago taught us to avoid seeing the loss of a means of describing civic participation as a loss of civic participation itself. He illustrated this by the fact that, despite the collapse of epigraphy commemorating euergistic acts in the eastern provinces, fourth-century patristic writings not only demonstrate the continuation of these euergistic behaviors, they also show the perpetuation of the very same language with which it had traditionally been appropriate to describe these activities.[61] Given that note of caution, we might ask whether the almost total disappearance in Spain of an epigraphic record by the middle of the third century actually reflects changes in the behaviors traditionally recorded, or merely a change in the one single behavior of inscription itself.

That there was a genuine move away from the habit of inscription throughout the Roman empire cannot be doubted. At different times in different places, and varying not just between provinces but within them, there was a quantitative drop in the number of inscriptions produced between the mid-second and the early fourth centuries and that drop was very often enormous.[62] Certain factors may serve to exaggerate the extent of epigraphic decline, in Spain as elsewhere. On the one hand, there was definitely a movement away from engraved inscriptions to painted ones, which have perished in much greater quantities.[63] On the other, the epigraphic sample is unscientific: chance and unprovenanced finds have always been common, while more heavily and continuously inhabited sites tend to leave fewer extant inscriptions than do those that went into a decline in the post-Roman centuries. At a site like Zaragoza, populous both in the Roman period and ever since, the constant reuse of any available building material has meant that we actually know of more local citizens from inscriptions found outside the town than we do from extant local inscriptions.[64] We must also reckon with the differing intensity of archaeology in the various Spanish regions.[65]

On the other hand, there had been pronounced regional variation in the quantity of inscriptions, even at the height of the inscribing trend. Some parts of the peninsula had adopted the habit of inscription with a great deal more gusto than had others. The river valleys and the coasts always produced more inscriptions than did the center and the north, but even in the latter regions there are striking exceptions, as the northwestern *conventus* of Braga, Lugo, and Astorga were far more epigraphically prolific than their neighbors in central Tarraconensis. Although it is fair to say that, on average, the inscribing habit died off in the first half of the third century, the rhythm of epigraphic decline was actually quite variable.[66] At the *conventus* capital of Cartagena, the inscribing classes changed their habits astonishingly early: within the town's quite substantial epigraphic corpus, almost no private or honorific inscriptions survive from after the Julio-Claudian era. More strikingly, the sort of imperial dedications that become common all over Spain in late antiquity are not found in Cartagena until after the Justinianic conquest in the sixth century.[67] At Cartagena, we are not looking at a faulty sample, but rather at a distinctive local variation from the Hispano-Roman norm.[68] At Tarragona, by way of contrast, the epigraphic habit of the early empire was never really lost, and local styles of inscription mutated quite organically into late imperial modes of official and imperial inscriptions.[69]

When all these caveats are heeded, it remains clear that the decline of the Spanish epigraphic habit took place over a long enough time span, and with so much regional variation, that it cannot be attributed to a single period of crisis, third-century or otherwise. Moreover, apart from the decline of epigraphy there is no positive evidence of a decline in civic institutions formerly commemorated in stone, merely the *ex silentio* argument from their relative absence of documentation. Crucially, the public areas of towns in which it had been normal to display commemorative inscriptions did not cease to be used. Nowhere in Spain is there a correlation between the decay of the fora and the disappearance of civic inscriptions. The loss of the epigraphic habit is therefore a symptom of decline only if we choose to privilege inscribing cultures over non-inscribing cultures. Historians nowadays strive to refrain from such value judgments, but how we account for the loss of the epigraphic habit without postulating crisis or making qualitative judgments about the health or sickness of a society is a more difficult question.

Finding an answer means looking at our evidence from an unfamiliar perspective. Rather than taking the second-century peak as the ideal from which all variation must represent decline, we have to observe the incidence of Spanish epigraphy across the whole of its Roman history. If we do this, we see that epigraphic commemoration of any sort is in fact a very limited activity, save during a 150-year period between the Flavians and the last Severans. Only in the chief towns of Baetica and those along the Mediterranean coast does a significant habit of inscription develop earlier, in the Augustan or Julio-Claudian era; only in the north and west does it continue well into the third century, as in the case of the Aurelii of Aquae Flaviae. The chronology of the epigraphic habit across the different Spanish regions, in other words, corresponds quite visibly to the period in which cities across the peninsula competed to make themselves look Roman.

The habit of epigraphic commemoration may therefore belong to the process of romanization and may represent a phase in the process of learning a new way to behave: epigraphic commemoration was one of the ways that Spaniards taught themselves to be Romans, because it helped implant and regularize the public, office-holding behaviors it memorialized.[70] Thus by the middle of the second century, the inscribed record of elite accomplishments was a normal part of the Hispano-Roman landscape. We must imagine the fora of all the newly monumental *municipia* dominated by the great bronze tablets of their colonial or municipal charters, but peppered with inscribed reminders of the local worthies who had built some of the town's public buildings and continued to provide their fellow townsmen with the amenities of a civilized life.

The inscriptions, in other words, advertised a particularly Roman sort of behavior at a juncture when such advertisement meant something. Inscription might advertise other things as well. It has been argued that, at least in a funerary context, the habit of inscription had specifically juridical content. That is to say, epigraphic commemoration was one of the ways in which both a deceased man and those who survived him advertised their access to the *iura privata* of Roman law, foremost among these the right to testation.[71] In both visual and legal terms, the fact of epigraphic commemoration was thus a definite marker of social status, while the roads in and out of every substantial town in the peninsula were lined with elaborate Roman-style tombs, their inscriptions advertising the achievements of the town's great families, who competed for status in death as they had done in life.[72]

On the other hand, once the status that was advertised by the fact of epigraphy became generalized, as it had in many parts of Spain well before the Antonine constitution of 212, the social utility of epigraphic commemoration declined. In fact, the advertisement of status that inscription had once served might well have become unpopular, as the extension of Roman citizenship status made it much less valuable as a way for Spanish elites to distinguish themselves from their social inferiors at the local level; those social inferiors were now universally citizens too, so the elite had to mark themselves off in some other way.[73] At a less theoretical level, it might be said that once Spaniards had internalized the habits of Roman thought and behavior that went along with the inscribing habit, the need to leave an inscribed record of such practices disappeared. After all, where things can be assumed there is no point in declaring them.[74] By the start of the third century, across the whole of the empire, everyone who counted for anything recognized everyone else who counted for anything as being Roman. This was the reason an Arab phylarch could become emperor of Rome, and it was the reason that artists all over Gaul felt able to reincorporate older Celtic motifs into the Roman media they worked.[75]

In much of Spain, this acculturation had taken place rather earlier than elsewhere. That fact may help account for the relatively early and remarkably complete disappearance of the epigraphic habit in Spain. Partial confirmation comes from the fact that the limited rebirth of an inscribing habit marks a similar phase in Spanish history, during which the inscription of an epitaph was an assertion, no longer of *romanitas,* but rather of Christianity.[76] This sort of social explanation of the loss of the epigraphic habit is useful because it takes us away from qualitative assessments of the past and states things in functionalist terms. More importantly—and unlike any variation on crisis models—the social explanation is flexible enough to account for the variable rhythm of epigraphic production and of epigraphic decline across the peninsula. Once we discard the automatic assumption that the disappearance of the inscribing habit attests the decline of urban institutions as a result of third-century crisis, it becomes possible to look at the evidence for those institutions in a new light, not as the last vestiges of disappearing institutions, but rather as the same institutions recorded in new, and frankly less accessible, ways.

Three

Urban Institutions in the Third and Fourth Centuries

Whatever its explanation, the third-century decline of the epigraphic habit among Hispano-Roman elites is a historical reality. It cannot have helped but change the means by which these elites interacted and reckoned their status relative to one another. On the other hand, the decline of the epigraphic habit serves to disguise the fact that the basic structures of municipal life remained fundamentally unchanged during the period in which inscriptions become increasingly uncommon. Municipal magistracies survived, as is shown by chance inscriptional finds from the later third and fourth centuries. Thus we meet the third-century duovir of Mérida, L. Antestius Pap. Persicus, who was also a *pontifex perpetuus* of the city and whose son Antestius Antianus undoubtedly followed him into the curia.[1] Another third-century magistrate, L. Iunius Iusti f. Gal. Severus, was twice duovir of Liria and also held the priesthood of his city twice.[2] A more important confirmation of the basic continuity of municipal institutions into the later empire comes from what might seem an unlikely source, the canons of a church council that met at Elvira in the Baetican *conventus* of Astigi, perhaps as early as 302 or 303.[3] Christianity ultimately worked very profound changes upon the urban life of Spain, but not until the middle of the fifth century did it do so with decisive force.

The canons of Elvira, by contrast, show the grave difficulties that the first generation of fourth-century Christians had in integrating their faith into a townscape and an urban lifestyle that still worked along the lines laid out in the Flavian municipal law.

The canons of Elvira are an important piece of evidence. For one thing, they show how far late third-century Christians had come from their apostolic roots in Jewish traditions. There is nothing here of the elaborate hypothesizing of the rabbinical Talmudic traditions nor any air of the parlor game that so frequently rises from Greek theology of the same period. Elvira addressed real problems faced by real members of the local Christian community. Many of those problems centered on the difficulty of reconciling the teachings of the church with the public responsibilities that urban institutions required. Thus, the nineteen bishops who had assembled at Elvira were called upon to rule about Christians who continued to perform their duties as *flamines* after baptism, and also about those who ceased to burn incense to the imperial genius but continued to offer gifts of other sorts.[4] The *flamines* whose activities so exercised the bishops were facing a problem well-known from the early Christian period—daily life in the world of the Roman city was impregnated with rituals that were, ostensibly at least, religious and dedicated to pagan deities of one sort or another. Even if to many of their practitioners such activities were more or less religiously neutral, a part of the background ritual that made up people's daily lives, to the committed Christian they were polluting commerce with demons. Many who thought of themselves as Christian, however, saw no contradiction in continuing with these habitual rituals while also professing their faith as Christians.

Against such seemingly lukewarm Christians, early councils repeatedly fulminated. From the city of Elvira itself we have evidence of a few pagan cults, to the local *genius* of the city, to the *manes,* to the very unusual Stata Mater, a minor goddess virtually unknown outside of Rome, whose specialty was putting out fires, and, of course, to the emperors.[5] We cannot know whether it was one of these specifically attested local observances that the episcopal legislation at Elvira condemned, but the canons confirm the continued vitality of such urban cult and of municipal priesthoods, which are not attested epigraphically in Elvira after the reign of Probus.[6] Similarly, the fact that the council prescribes perpetual excommunication for parents who marry their daughters to *sacerdotes gentilium* shows that *flamines* and *pontifices* remained desirable matches that some Christian parents were still eager to make.[7] This should hardly surprise us. Tenure of an imperial priesthood usually meant that one had reached the very top of the *cursus* in one's local municipal hierarchy and had thereby become one of the city's great men. The value of such priesthoods certainly continued deep into the fourth century and, at Tarragona, may have survived until its very end.[8]

The testimony of Elvira does not end with the pagan priesthoods, however, for the bishops found other urban institutions in need of regulation. They prohibited magistrates, and duumvirs in particular, from entering a church during the year in which they held office.[9] This prohibition is significant. On the one hand, it is based on the fact that no magistrate could avoid some measure of pollution by pagan ritual during the tenure of his magistracy; the best way to keep this pollution from affecting the whole Christian community was therefore to keep the magistrate out of church. On the other hand, the canon bears witness to the real powers that municipal magistrates still possessed at the start of the fourth century. The only possible explanation for the singling out of the chief magistrates, the duumvirs, for exclusion is because they still possessed some measure of coercive power that might inadvertently require them to condemn a fellow Christian.

The urbanism revealed by Elvira, then, was still centered on the same institutions of government that had directed Spanish town life since the first century or earlier. Many of the other canons of Elvira—from those regulating the relationship of masters and slaves to those condemning gambling, games, and mimes—all speak to a thriving urban environment in which quintessentially urban activities continue to flourish, thereby causing great consternation to the ecclesiastical authorities. One canon forbids participation in just the sort of festive processions documented centuries earlier in the *lex Irnitana*.[10] Though it is conventional to see the third and fourth centuries as an era in which municipal institutions declined dramatically, in time with the decline in the epigraphic evidence commemorating them, the canons of Elvira suggest a rather different reality.[11]

Elvira offers significant evidence to this effect in still another fashion, for it is clear that the Spanish bishops who gathered there conducted themselves very much as a meeting of a municipal curia or a provincial council would have done.[12] Here, in our first western church council, we can see how the procedures of Roman municipal government were adopted by and integrated into the context of Christian governance. The proceedings at Elvira are easily pictured from the record of them, the bishops sitting while their deacons and the crowd stood in attendance upon them.[13] Different bishops raised different questions that reflected their own pastoral experiences, while the organization of the canons reflects this procedure. Canons are not grouped together in any logically coherent structure but are instead scattered in clumps that rarely flow organically one from the other.[14] One can imagine someone raising a question about virgins, which prompted another question about virgins, and then a couple more, until one of the bishops said something to lead the whole gathering off in another direction, on to another batch of questions. In this respect, the procedure at Elvira reflects the internalization by the episcopal hierarchy of the governing habits of the municipal world in which they lived.

There are other points of connection as well. The decision-making process at Elvira was reactive, a reflection of Roman governmental practice more generally. Little attempt was made to foresee and forestall difficulties. Instead, problems were addressed as they arose, questions answered as they were asked. The fact that Roman government was so profoundly reactive accounts for the great frequency of contradictory rulings in the imperial law codes, a phenomenon equally evident in the corpus of early canon law. In other words, the form taken by the canons of Elvira demonstrates how thoroughly traditional urban institutions informed the behavior of the assembled bishops, in the same way that the contents of the canons demonstrate the vitality of those institutions themselves. The council of Elvira debated, voted, and issued decisions in precisely the same way that the town councils did in every town in Spain and had done since anyone could remember. In the final analysis, Elvira contradicts the still pervasive idea that Hispano-Roman city life effectively ended in the third century. It is one of history's small ironies that the Christian church—eventually the most powerful solvent of old urban habits—should leave its most important early traces in the peninsula with a memorial so thoroughly rooted in the old civic institutions of the Roman past.

Chance epigraphic finds and the canons of Elvira prove to us that the old curial institutions survived in Spanish cities into the fourth century. Later Christian documents tell the same story. In the year 400, nineteen bishops gathered in Toledo to put an end to the schism in the Spanish church caused by the condemnation of Priscillian. At the same time, they attempted to restrict the practice whereby churchmen continued to hold secular office in their towns.[15] Pope Innocent I deprecated the same practice and noted that some bishops continued in their curial duties, while others had not long before their consecration given shows in the amphitheaters for the delectation of their fellow townsmen. A bishop Rufinus and bishop Gregory of Mérida had gone so far as to argue in civil courts after they had risen to the episcopal dignity.[16]

All this evidence demonstrates the survival of the curias and the magistracies that *curiales* were expected to fill. Most curial powers seem to have remained intact as well, among them the important symbolic power of voting honors, even if such honors were now voted almost exclusively to the emperor or his representatives, as when the *ordo civitatis* of Málaga voted an equestrian statue to Q. Attius Granius Caelestinus, a *consularis* of Baetica during the reign of Constantine's sons.[17] More practical than this symbolic function was the continued power of the curias to control their own membership and elect their magistrates, and there is no Spanish evidence for the rise of *principales*, a social group within curias attacked in fourth-century legislation for oppressing their curial peers.[18] We do not know whether municipal elections took place according to the traditional procedures of local municipal laws or according to the modifications laid down in imperial laws, but if we have interpreted the relevant canon of Elvira correctly, then the magistrates whom the curia elected retained some coercive authority within their *civitates*.[19] As it happens, we possess a later fourth-century document that appears to confirm this view. The Luciferian *Libellus precum* gives an account of the Arian controversy from an ultra-rigorist position of orthodoxy and describes the tribulations of a Spanish Luciferian called Vincentius who fell afoul of his fellow citizens for insisting on remaining in communion with Bishop

Gregory of Elvira; as an alternative to mob justice, the judicial authority of the curial order was invoked.[20]

If these attestations to the continued importance of curial office were not enough, an important new power was granted to the curias during the fourth century. Since the time of Domitian, a previously unknown imperial official had begun to appear in the cities of the empire, the *curator reipublicae* or *curator civitatis*.[21] The circumstances in which this office evolved are obscure, but the *curatores,* at first senatorial or equestrian rather than municipal in rank, became the emperor's chief officials within the local city. *Curatores* were appointed for short terms of office, and perhaps mainly to cities in which the curia had failed to meet its fiscal obligations to the imperial government, though this supervision seems generally not to have been very thorough.[22] During the third century, when *curatores* first begin to be attested in Spain, the office came to be held increasingly by men of municipal rank, like two Aurelii who were curators at Italica in the 270s.[23] Then, during the reign of Diocletian, the curatorship was handed to the control of the curias, becoming another elective office within the cities.[24] In Spain, we know of other third-century *curatores* apart from the Aurelii, for instance, Q. Vibius Laetus, a duumvir of Córdoba who also held that city's curatorship.[25] The majority of known *curatores* held office in Baetica, whereas in Tarraconensis the name of only a single urban *curator* is extant, the fourth-century Messius Marianus.[26] He probably held his office as a result of election by his fellow *curiales* rather than as an appointee of the emperor.

Regardless of the precise origins of the urban curatorship, the *curatores* evolved into the chief financial officers of a city, supervising the various financial tasks for which the curia as a whole was legally responsible. One such responsibility was the oversight of civic lands; though these had been confiscated under Constantine and again by Valentinian and Valens, their revenues were later restored in large measure.[27] A more pressing responsibility was the tax burden of a city, and the *curator reipublicae* acted as interlocutor between the curia and the imperial government to which the revenue of taxation belonged. That the *curiales* were essential to the fiscal system of the post-Diocletianic empire is not open to dispute; indeed, the multiplication of provinces and their attendant imperial bureaucracy merely bound the cities more tightly into the system. On the other hand, the mechanisms for the collection and disbursement of tax revenues are matters of great, and perhaps insoluble, controversy.[28]

It is possible that *curiales* carried out most of the actual administrative work of the later imperial fiscal system, which would explain how the imperial government could maintain so small a bureaucratic establishment relative to the size of the tax-paying population.[29] If this was in fact the case, then fourth-century *curiales* would, under the direction of a *curator* chosen from among their own number, have kept the tax registers of the city and supervised the physical management of the renders from the land and poll taxes—the *iugatio* and *capitatio.* Whether the *curiales* actually collected those renders from individual taxpayers within their city's *territorium* or whether they instead managed revenues already collected by tax farmers is again a matter of controversy.[30] By the later fourth century, the state allowed the curias to retain and spend on municipal expenses a third of the revenue they collected from the *civitas*.[31] It likewise seems certain that individual members of the curia would, whether by appointment or by a vote within the curia, take charge of the empire's various indirect taxes, mostly those on the transport, storage, and transfer of goods. In Spain, we know the names of two such *curiales,* who are attested on a bronze *modius* discovered in the province of La Coruña at the turn of the last century. Potamius and Quintianus, whose *cura* was exercised between 367 and 375, evidently guaranteed the use of correct weights and measures by the inscription of their names.[32] Similarly, from 387 we have a record of a *horreus* perhaps destined for fiscal uses, being established in Tarraconensis.[33]

The *civitates* of Spain, like those across the empire however large or small, remained the basic unit of territorial administration and taxation, even if we will never have an entirely clear idea of how those taxes were gathered.[34] The importance of the curias in the financing of the Roman state is clear, inasmuch as the emperors could not do without them, a fact that accounts for the enormous title of the *Theodosianus* devoted to legislating on the need for *curiales* to remain in their condition and fulfill their duties. These laws are traditionally cited as evidence for precipitate urban decline in the later Roman empire—*curiales* no longer wished to serve and so the emperors acted with ever greater ferocity to keep them in their place.[35] Imperial laws are subject to all the usual distortions of normative sources, and impose on us a view of social phenomena that is unnecessarily *de haut en bas:* if one takes imperial legislation as a primary and privileged source of evidence, then the value of curial office does indeed seem to be in decline.

Yet it is possible to jump down from that bird's-eye view and instead look at the benefits that curial office brought, even in the fourth century. In doing this, we find a necessary corrective to the pessimism imposed by the codes. In the first place, to be a big man in the community never ceased to mean something. The modern West, committed at least in theory to egalitarianism, finds it easy to forget the importance of social position, but in deeply hierarchical societies rank is everything. Even if, as in the later Roman empire, the official hierarchy was relatively open, and one could thus aspire to raise one's social position, the social position one actually occupied still counted. The importance of rank is there to see in our Spanish sources, even at a very late date: it is present, for instance, in the fifth-century chronicler Hydatius's emphasis on the nobility of the Conimbrigan Cantabri, a nobility that made their abduction more shocking.[36] It is true that as time wore on, membership in the imperial hierarchy came to count for more than did membership in the municipal hierarchy. But to make that statement, and to acknowledge that many *curiales* sought greater prestige in imperial service of some sort, does not by itself invalidate the importance of curial office. The ability to lord it over one's peers and social inferiors is not a negligible benefit and that ability was not rendered invalid by the existence of still grander folk who could and did inflict the same treatment on the *curialis.*

Just as imperial office brought with it all sorts of perquisites, so curial office could be quite profitable. It is likely that the fiscal role of *curiales* as interlocutors between the imperial government and taxpayers or tax farmers provided quite a lot of scope for financial speculation, primarily on the difference between market prices and the government's fixed assessment of the value of a particular type of good.[37] Because this speculation involved mostly money of account rather than actual specie, it will have been less heavily affected by the reduced amounts of coinage circulating in Spain after the year 400.[38]

Moreover, if the settlement of barbarians in the provinces of the fifth-century empire really was managed by granting them shares of the state's tax revenues, then the curia's role in disbursing such revenues gave it a powerful social role as interlocutor between the state and the new, armed settlers.[39]

The social weight of curial membership and its financial opportunities were both quite real and perfectly compatible with the hyperbole of the law codes. They make sense of Salvian's famous statement that where there are *curiales,* there are tyrants to lord it over the many: *quae enim sunt non modo urbes, sed etiam municipia atque vici, ubi non quot curiales fuerint tot tyranni sunt?*[40] What in the hands of the monkish polemicist is a statement of condemnation is from our perspective a confirmation of the power and profitability of curial office. Salvian's revulsion is nothing other than an alternative perspective on the relationship of the *curialis* to the *civitas* long since attested by the Flavian municipal law, in which the responsibility of the curia for the municipal *territorium* is explicitly characterized as a source of revenue.[41] In other words, despite the fulminations of the *Theodosianus* against absconding *curiales,* things had not changed so very much. It meant something to lead the affairs of the locality. It meant something, socially and economically, to have charge of the finances of the *civitas.* It meant something to decide how fully one-third of the urban tax take would be spent. And it meant something to have access to the imperial bureaucracy, whether as a route for one's own career or as a set of contacts that would benefit one's station at home.

That men continued to fill these municipal positions into the later fifth century is shown by a papal letter of October 465, directed to the bishops of Tarraconensis. In it, Pope Hilarus mentions that the *honorati et possessores* of seven *civitates* in Tarraconensis—Tarazona, Cascante, Tricio, Calahorra, Briviesca, León, and the unidentified site of Varega—have written to him to put the case for Silvanus of Calahorra, against the opposition of the latter's episcopal colleagues.[42] That this group was at least partly composed of *curiales* is shown by the fifth-century *interpretatio* to a law of 408 that defines *honorati provinciarum* as *ex curiae corpore.*[43] Hilarus does not tell us why these *honorati* and *possessores* supported Silvanus, nor is there any record of his reply to them.[44] Silvanus clearly had powerful support, and we must assume that his tenure of the local episcopate was in some way advantageous to this ad hoc coalition. For although this group is regularly thought to represent some vestige of a provincial council, the absence of the chief cities of the province of Tarraconensis makes this impossible.[45] Similar considerations rule out any sort of conventual interpretation, and we are clearly dealing with men whose ambit is the *civitas*. With the exception of León, all of these towns lie within a relatively small part of western Tarraconensis along the main road up the Ebro valley to the Meseta and, again with the exception of León, none was a large or important *civitas*. The appearance of these men working in concert to defend the interests of a local bishop demonstrates the ongoing vitality of the curial community in the second half of the fifth century. It also shows that even tiny *municipia* like Cascante continued to exist into the later empire, along with their municipal governments, despite the fact that after the late second century one very rarely hears of them. Thus, at a time when the imperial government had more or less definitively abandoned Spain to its fate, the cities with their *curiales* and the other big men and landlords survived as the social group in control of life on the ground.

Thus far we have concentrated on the evidence for the survival of curial offices and curial functions through the third and fourth centuries and some that persisted into the fifth century as well. Other important curial roles are similarly well-attested in the later period, chief among them that of urban or provincial ambassador.[46] Civic embassies were a commonplace of life in the Roman world, and it was from the ranks of the decurions that ambassadors were chosen.[47] Embassies served specific tasks—petitions of one sort or another on behalf of the city in its corporate shape—as well as more general ones like offering honors to an emperor or merely waiting attendance on him. Just such superficially meaningless embassies had the essential function of tying cities symbolically into the larger imperial polity. Embassies between cities had similarly integrative functions, particularly as they tended to serve as opportunities for self- and mutual congratulation on the part of the cities concerned.

As with most subjects, the fourth century provides relatively little evidence for curial embassies, but we do have two clear examples of provincial embassies from the same period. The curia of Barcelona received a formal embassy from the province of Asia that arrived to dedicate a statue and inscription to the local native and former *proconsul Asiae* Nummius Aemilianus Dexter.[48] Similarly, the dedication to the *vicarius Hispaniarum* Flavius Sallustius in the forum of Trajan at Rome was in all likelihood presented there by a provincial or diocesan embassy from Spain.[49] The ambassadorial habit lasted long beyond the fourth century, as the career of Hydatius shows. As bishop of Aquae Flaviae, he famously took part in an embassy to Aëtius, while his chronicle is littered with the constant toing-and-froing of ambassadors in a fifth-century evolution of older habits.[50]

The personal access to the wider world of the empire that civic embassies fostered was one of the great benefits of curial membership. It put a town's ambassadors in contact with peers in other towns and with valuable contacts at the imperial court. In a world in which institutions of government were flexible, it was personal contact, characterized as friendship or more openly as patronage, that advanced one's career and allowed one to find work and advantage for one's own dependents. What the modern world calls networking was for the ancient world the only means of advancement. At its best, it could open the doors to a new career outside the hometown, to the provincial bureaus of imperial government. Or, if one were especially lucky, it might lead to a position in some other part of the empire altogether and bring with it the potential to spread a network of contacts that much further.

This brought advantage at home as well. It contributed to one's status within the home community, it made one more useful as a patron, and it opened up the possibility of attracting further clients, all of which meant becoming more important with respect to one's peers. The opportunities for gaining access to this much wider patronage grew dramatically after the third century, for the simple reason that the web of imperial administration became more complicated and varied in those years. Such access was not necessarily just a matter of lining one's pockets, though this was the standard reward and the one that imperial laws so regularly deplored. Rather, as the Priscillianist controversy of the later fourth century demonstrates, a network of contacts stretching into the palatine bureaucracy could literally be a matter of life and death.[51]

The Elites and the Lower Orders

With a discussion of municipal embassies, we exhaust the evidence for the persistence of the official functions of the *curiales* in the third and fourth centuries. Because of the collapse of epigraphic commemoration in third-century Spain, far less evidence survives than from earlier periods, though this does not mean the functions themselves disappeared. In the earlier, better-documented period, the behaviors that defined the curial class were not confined to the official contexts of office and administration and this fact, too, remained true of the late empire. Office-holding was a means of social display that established relative gradations of status only within a municipal elite. It could not articulate the relationship between the higher orders of society and their social inferiors. That relationship had to be manifested in a different fashion, though one that was equally public and visual. For the most part, municipal elites related to their social inferiors through the web of patronage and clientship endemic to Roman social relations.[52] The number of clients a man could command was an important measure of social prominence, because the ability to win favors for acquaintances and ease their passage through political life was a tangible witness to a man's own importance.

As importantly, the patron-client relationship acted as a necessary means of social support. Roman society looks superficially like one of very few premodern polities in which there was both a concept of the rule of law and also some approximation to its reality, but the exigencies of daily life made the protection of someone more powerful than oneself a necessary recourse. Not only could a well-connected patron provide otherwise inaccessible chances of profit and advancement, such a patron could also help deflect the crushing judicial machinery of the Roman state if one had the misfortune to come in contact with it. Patrons, for their part, had to be able to fulfill these roles, and their ability to do so affected the number of clients they could command. Success in this respect bred more success, and the whole system was self-perpetuating because there were strong incentives for both patrons and clients to pursue their respective ends with great vigor. The patron-client relationship therefore fed into the culture of display that we have already seen in the context of elite public service. Just as the commemoration of such service was a reinforcement of status, so the interaction of patrons and clients was a public ritual that allowed status to be constantly checked and evaluated.

The varieties of clientship were infinitely shaded. Within an *amicitia* that implied an ostensible equality of status and a *patrocinium* much more frankly unequal, the gradations of dependence and protection were manifold and subtle enough to evade any strict modern taxonomy. At the lower end of the scale, where the relationship was at its starkest and least euphemistic, clientage had a juridical component, explored in the writings of the jurists and formalized in imperial legislation, ever more strictly as the later empire wore on.[53] Both sorts of dependent relationship had very deep roots in Spanish soil, in both the city and the countryside, as is documented by the epigraphy of the peninsula. There is a rich laudatory vocabulary: *patrono indulgentissimo, patrono bene merenti, patrono optimo* (or indeed *patrono optimo et bene merenti*), and, best of all, *patronis merentissimis et felicissimis et prestantissimis et pientissimis.*[54] Most such examples come from the lower end of the social scale, where freedmen were legally obligated to their patrons in a way that free clients were not. But the evidence for patronage higher up the social scale is also to hand from the later empire. In his late fourth-century sermon on penitence, the bishop of Barcelona, Pacianus, appeals to his audience as a group of moderate, unindulgent people of middling means, and deliberately contrasts them to another richer audience, able to give banquets for their clients and retreat to the seaside to take their leisure. By evoking the pleasures of the social elite, he speaks directly to those of his audience on whom he wishes to urge moderation.[55] He enjoins his audience to refuse invitations to the banquets to which they might be invited when they are in a state of penitence.[56] In other words, he urges them to pass up the normal social interactions that went along with life in the Roman city.

The archaeological evidence bears out the importance of normal patronage relationships in the world of late antique Spain. At the heart of Roman patronage lay rituals of reception and attendance, which took place within a specially structured domestic environment. We have no description of these ceremonies from Spain itself, but they were precisely the sort of visibly Roman behavior that was portable and assimilable throughout the whole empire, as the domestic architecture of Spanish cities makes clear. Spain's great urban *domus,* like their counterparts elsewhere in the Roman world, were designed to facilitate and enhance the process of receiving clients. Although examples can be cited from any Hispano-Roman city in which even one urban *domus* has been thoroughly excavated, most such examples—for instance, the spectacular reception hall in the so-called Casa Mitreo at Mérida—come from the early imperial period, or were excavated in such a way that only the early imperial evidence has come to light.[57] We are, however, lucky to have a rather more useful example in the several *domus* partially excavated around the forum of Clunia.

Clunia had been an important city of the Arevaci and in the first century A.D. became the center of a Roman *conventus.* Clunia, like nearby Tiermes, is an important site for the archaeologist because the absence of late medieval and modern habitation has preserved more evidence from late phases of Roman habitation than tends to survive at sites that have been inhabited continuously since antiquity. Unlike Tiermes, Clunia was excavated before modern archaeological practices had become generalized in Spain and much information of value has therefore been lost. However, two *domus* near the forum of Clunia are well enough known to demonstrate the ongoing centrality of the patron-client relationship to the third-century city. One of these houses, originally built around the time of the city's rise to colonial status in the first century, was remodeled in the middle of the third. The public rooms which gave onto the forum were refloored with high-quality polychrome mosaics. The second *domus* was likewise remodeled in the third century, probably somewhat later than the first one, but with less expensive and less colorful geometric mosaics that were probably the work of a local atelier.

Clunia was by no means one of the great cities of Hispania, despite its juridical status as the head of a *conventus.* It enjoyed no special imperial patronage of which we are aware. Yet here, in the middle of the third century, the municipal elite are found remodeling their residences in precisely those portions that were open to public view and that were essential to the reception of clients and to the latter's attendance on their patrons. We can even detect the process of competition between the local worthies. There is some question as to the sequence of the renovations, but two scenarios are possible. If the high-quality mosaics of our first *domus* are earlier, we can view those of the second as an attempt by one neighbor to catch up with the conspicuous display of another, but constrained to use local rather than imported craftsmen in the process. If the local geometric mosaics are earlier, then we can envisage the same scenario in reverse, with one neighbor trumping the other's display by bringing in better craftsmen to prove how such things should be done. Either way, the relative quality of the mosaics in the two *domus* would have been as sure a measure of influence and power as was the number of clients who waited attendance in each.

Regardless of such speculation, this third-century redecoration is significant, and not just as an argument against the reflexive view of the third century as a period of urban decline. More important is the clear evidence it provides for the perpetuation of classical modes of behavior. The third-century owners of these *domus* made the conscious decision to concentrate their decorative expenditure on precisely those public areas where certain ritualized social activities were enacted, in particular, the reception of clients by patrons. The same phenomenon is known from other cities like Complutum, and in all these instances the architectural decisions made by municipal notables show us how they continued to behave publicly according to norms learned in the early centuries of romanization.[58]

The Lower Orders

We have so far been concerned almost exclusively with the upper reaches of Hispano-Roman society, with those who directed the affairs of the cities. The ways in which these people conceived of themselves and the world around them can very easily come to dominate any discussion for the simple reason that they are relatively well documented. Lower down the social hierarchy, it was *collegia* of various sorts that fostered the sense of communal identity that civic office and civic display fostered among the elites. Romans devoted enormous energy to giving the natural human impulse for association a quasi-official character. This is in part a function of the general Roman tendency to conceive everything in juridical terms—the concept of legal personality is, after all, a Roman invention. Because of this habit of conception, Roman people grouped themselves into associations—whether religious, social, or professional—that helped give them a sense of identity and purpose.[59] We may distinguish between official, state-sponsored associations and those that grew up independently, though in both cases the right of association was regulated by imperial law. On the other hand, both sorts of association were equally voluntary, at least until the fourth century, when compulsory associations of various sorts became more commonplace in the interests of imperial tax collection.[60]

In Spain we find evidence of various associations right down the social scale—more than a hundred from the peninsula during the Roman period.[61] Because the evidence for such associations is almost exclusively epigraphic, most of it comes from the second and third centuries, when the variety of the attested *collegia* is striking. At the apex of municipal society one finds the *collegia iuvenum,* usually patronized by leisured curial youth and mixing social, religious, and political functions.[62] At Complutum, it seems that a hugely expensive collegial building was built during the third century to serve one of the city's *collegia iuvenum.*[63] More commonplace were the social-*cum*-funerary associations—the *collegia* or *sodalicia tenuiorum*—that sometimes dominate the epigraphic record entirely in small towns from which few inscriptions survive.[64] These *collegia* ensured that the *tenuior* or *humilior,* having clubbed together with others of his status, would be given a decent burial by them when he died.[65] Funerary associations of this sort also existed still further down the social scale, among the servile population.[66] Like any more august body, a funerary *sodalicium* would have its members, constituted in this case by an entrance fee, enrolled in an album.[67] The funerary association could serve as a surrogate family, and we find the language of familial *pietas* adopted in precisely this context to suggest the bonds of duty that kinship would normally bring.[68]

Funerary *collegia* were thus one way in which the humbler sort of Hispano-Roman, whether servile or free, expressed his sense of legal and social belonging to a larger corporate body. Through such forms of association, even the lower strata of society participated in institutions that were fundamentally tied to Roman law and a Roman way of life, hence ultimately to the Roman state. In a similar way, one also finds professional associations across Spain, both of local traders and artisans and also of men in the service of the imperial government. There can be no doubt that part of the rationale for such associations was to give the group more effective weight in affairs than any single member would have exercised on his own. Professional associations could regulate who practiced particular trades locally, thus providing a measure of corporate protection to their members. Apart from that fundamentally economic role, however, it is quite clear that professional *collegia* also fulfilled the basic human pleasure in associating with others who share the same interests and experiences. We must not underestimate the social function of these *collegia*, nor the fact that they sometimes possessed an additional religious or funerary element as well.[69] Over time, the Roman state came to recognize the utility of such associations and worked to put them to use, particularly in such industries as served the *annona*.[70]

A whole set of inscriptions from Seville shows the importance of a variety of professional associations in the service of the state.[71] At Seville, one might reasonably suppose a severe decline in the *collegia* when the industrial production of Baetican oil for the *annona* declined toward the end of the second century, and indeed all our explicit testimony for *collegia* of the city in the service of the *annona* does come from before the early third century.[72] On the other hand, two laws of Constantine, addressed to a *vicarius* and a *comes Hispaniarum* in 324 and 336, respectively, speak of *navicularii* who are evidently engaged in the service of the *annona*. In keeping with the offices of their addressees, these laws take in the whole of Spain and do not make specific reference to Seville, or indeed Baetica, but the laws confirm the continued importance of such *collegia* in government service.[73]

As with funerary *collegia*, professional associations reached down to the lowest ends of the social scale, including the servile. Thus in 239, in the obscure little settlement of Segisama in the foothills of the Cantabrian mountains, an association of cobblers and textile workers—four slaves and seventeen freedmen—dedicated a bronze votive plaque to four men and a woman whom they took as their patrons.[74] Also toward the bottom of the social scale were the associations that performed various essential tasks for the city. *Fabri,* along with *cen-*

tonarii and *dendrophori,* are known from elsewhere in the Roman world as the *tria collegia principalia* of the cities, in large part because they were together responsible for firefighting. In Spain both *centonarii* and *fabri* are attested in major cities like Barcelona, Tarragona, and Seville.[75] At Tarragona, moreover, we know where their collegial meeting-house was located, as well as something of its sculptural and architectonic decoration, which was centered around a peristyle, in one side of which stood a small nympheum.[76]

The evidence from Córdoba, meanwhile, demonstrates the persistence of these associations down into the period when the epigraphic record shrinks so drastically. We first meet the *collegium corporis fabrorum* of Córdoba in 247.[77] A hundred years later its presence is again recorded: in 349, under the consuls Limenius and Catullinus, the *rectores* or presiding officers of this *collegium* dedicated a *tabula patronatus* to Julius Caninius, the patron of their association.[78] This little bronze tablet is fulsome in its language, and exactly similar to what one finds in such patronal *tabulae* of earlier periods. It is a useful caution against presuming that the absence or disappearance of epigraphic commemoration of an institution means the disappearance of the institution itself.

The social institution of the *collegia* impinged physically upon the townscape, because each had its own meeting hall in which members could gather. In this respect, each *collegium* mimicked the practice of the local curia in having a special locale in which to enact the business appertaining to its social role, thereby enhancing the sense of occasion and importance that attended the conduct of that business. The *fabri subidiani* at Córdoba, like the *fabri subaediani* elsewhere in the Roman world, were named after their meeting place. What may be a collegial building, though of *navicularii* not *fabri* or *centonarii,* is known from Faro, ancient Ossonuba.[79] The evidence for the survival of *collegia* and their social and economic roles into late imperial Spain is tantalizingly incomplete, but this is typical—after the third century, evidence for *collegia* is extremely limited throughout the Roman West, though what little does survive shows that professional *collegia* existed until the very end of the sixth century.[80] There is no reason to think that Spain was unusual in this respect, and we must imagine that its *collegia,* too, had a long life that is largely invisible to us.

Provincial and Conventual Institutions

The institutional phenomena at which we have so far been looking are all of a piece. Patronage, priesthoods, office-holding, and embassies all played a part in the coded ritual of membership in a governing elite that was recognizably the same across the Roman world, whether in Britain or Syria or Spain. Cooperative behavior fostered the sense of communal identity, but competition was every bit as important. That is to say, jockeying for position within the local curial order reinforced a sense of collective identity just as much as did joint dedications to members of their own number, joint petitions to emperors, or unanimous participation in the imperial cult. Lower down the social ladder, the urban *collegia* performed the same function, encoding membership in Roman society through a peculiarly Roman way of registering participation.

The social institutions found locally in every *municipium* in Spain were mirrored at the conventual and provincial levels, extending the boundaries of local society outward from the city into a wider world. What this meant is best illustrated by the example of Tarragona, which was provided with a huge imperial cult complex under the Flavians. Tarragona lies on the coast of modern Catalonia, just to the north of the river Francolí, the Roman Tulcis, that trickles down from the pre-littoral mountains of the interior. The *ager Tarraconensis* was rich in antiquity and supported the large rural population whose labors supplied the city.[81] The city was a Scipionic foundation, but it did not really begin to prosper until the late Republican period. The Republican and Augustan city lay mostly at the foot of a hill that had been enclosed within the Republican walls even though few structures were built on it.[82] After being made a *colonia civium romanorum* under Caesar, the city began to be monumentalized under Augustus, mostly out of local limestone. The civic forum, however, was rebuilt in marble, a judicial basilica was put up, and an impressive theater was built on a small rise between the forum and the port. Regardless of these Augustan precedents, it was the Flavian era that completely transformed the city.[83] The hill at the north end of the colony was subjected to an ambitious rebuilding project. At its peak, just inside the old Republican walls, a cult enclosure was built to house a temple, almost certainly of the imperial cult. To the south of this cult precinct, and slightly farther down the hillside, a second terrace was shaped to house a new forum. This huge space, 175 meters by 318 meters, was surrounded on at least three sides by a raised double portico, and it was only through this portico that one could enter the cult precinct beyond.[84]

On its western side, the forum was built up against the existing city wall. To the north and east, however, it had its own new walls, thus separating it physically from the other parts of the town that lay within the circuit wall. At the center of the forum there was probably a large garden. Around it, statues dedicated to the *genii* of the province's seven *conventus* were displayed, alongside honorific statues and other memorials to provincial notables. This statuary suggests that the new forum was built to serve as headquarters for the council of the *provincia Tarraconensis,* and it was probably here that the provincial *flamines* whose *cursus* have been so thoroughly studied displayed the records of their tenures of office.[85] The main duty of the provincial council was to elect these *flamines,* priests of the province's imperial cult, but it also served as a central meeting place for provincial notables to share and discuss their common interests. Provincial councils voted honors to the emperor in the manner of a municipal council,[86] and probably also voted to elect provincial patrons, who are known from several Spanish examples.[87]

The complex built to house this council required a tremendous expenditure of wealth and manpower, and its cost was in all likelihood borne by the emperor. The hill's upper terraces required substantial engineering work. Toward the top of the hill, the bedrock was shaved to create a level surface. Lower down, vast quantities of fill were hauled in to raise the level of the ground. This fill, of course, needed to be held in place, and a large retaining wall, 350 meters long and 20 meters high, was built for this purpose. Within a decade of this wall's having been built, it was put to a new use, as the northern wall of a brand-new circus. This was built during the reign of Domitian and occupied

(Facing page) Plan of Tarragona, showing the Flavian complex of (1) temple, (2) provincial forum, and (3) circus; the extramural cemeteries, and the extramural amphitheater. (after TED'A [1987])

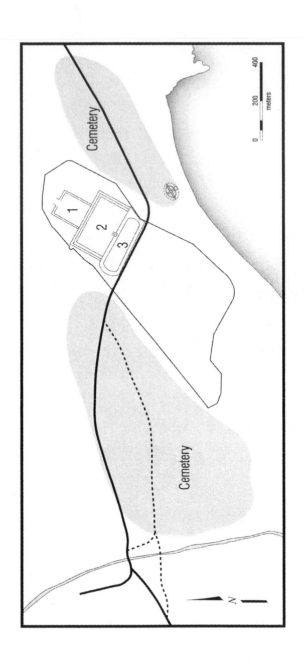

Cemetery

Cemetery

1
2
3

0   200   400
meters

N

a third terrace, running parallel to the provincial forum for its entire length so that the retaining wall of the forum became the foundation of the northern *cavea*—the stands—of the circus. The southern façade of the circus, meanwhile, functioned as the façade of the provincial cult complex as a whole, thereby articulating the relationship between the complex and the rest of the city. The façade of the circus—lying along the Via Augusta that here passed through town—presented the only opening into the provincial complex, and the provincial forum could be reached only by way of the corridors of the circus. The complex as a whole was so large that most of medieval Tarragona was contained within it, while entire blocks of the modern city are built into the vaults of the circus.[88]

From the late first century onward, therefore, the circus and the Via Augusta became the point of division between the new provincial center on the hillside and the old *colonia* in the lower town. From the upper stands of the circus, a staircase led to the midpoint of the south wall of the forum. Meanwhile, at the ground level of the circus, the same passages that controlled movement into and between the stands also led to two large, enclosed stairwells. These rose up inside the tow-

The *cavea* and vaulting of the eastern end of the circus at Tarragona. (K. Salzer)

The façade of the circus at Tarragona. These arches marked the division between the circus and imperial precinct of the city and the *colonia* below. (K. Salzer)

ers, which stood at the southeastern and southwestern corners of the forum. These towers, both partly extant, thus became the primary means of communication between the old colony and the provincial precinct.[89] The new cult complex was within the *colonia,* but deliberately not of it. The total effect was to separate the lower town, nowadays generally known as the Part Baixa, from a new upper town, the Part Alta. The provincial cult complex and the circus together made a strongly ideological statement in favor of imperial power, and their position was a visual metaphor for the way in which the imperial power of the province dominated the local power of the urban curia.

To those who saw it, Tarragona's provincial cult complex was no doubt a powerful stimulus to a psychological sense of *romanitas* and a sense of participation in a wider Roman empire. But who exactly did see it? The townspeople of Tarragona would never have been in any doubt as to their city's role in a much larger world. Right in their midst stood a constant reminder of that fact—it is by no means a coincidence that at Tarragona people were still putting up inscriptions to Italian emperors in the 470s, decades after the rest of Spain had given up on Italy as a foreign affair that had nothing to do with them.[90] Yet apart

61

from the citizens of Tarragona, who had to look at it every day, the provincial cult complex acted not upon Hispano-Romans in general, but only upon social groups that already felt a strong connection to the larger community of the empire—imperial priests who had found their way out of the local cult and onto the provincial stage, imperial officials attached to the provincial governor, and local dignitaries with business in the provincial capital. There is unambiguous evidence for priests of the imperial cult at Tarragona in the third and early fourth centuries and arguably for the very end of the fourth as well.[91] Literary evidence from elsewhere in coastal Tarraconensis would suggest the continuation of imperial cult much later into the fourth century,[92] while the physical environment of the cult center at Tarragona was largely undisturbed until the 440s.[93]

Despite all this, however, only a limited number of people can have been affected by the provincial institutions of Tarragona, while the provincial capitals at Mérida and Córdoba offer no more extensive evidence.[94] The evidence for conventual institutions is similarly limited. Throughout the Roman period, we hear much less about the *conventus* in the south of Spain than in the north and west. There they were the primary articulation of territory, particularly given the distances between the northwestern *conventus* and their provincial capital at Tarragona. No doubt for that reason, our most illuminating testimony for the *conventus* as a meaningful social unit in the later empire comes from the north, where in 222 Valerius Marcellus, a legate of the Legio VII Gemina, witnessed the hospitality pact between the legion and the *concilium conventus Cluniensis*.[95]

Such conventual *concilia* undoubtedly existed elsewhere in Spain, although it no longer seems likely that separate conventual fora existed in the *conventus* capitals.[96] With the exception of the one inscription from Clunia and a single dedication to the empress Iulia Mammaea from the *conventus* capital of Cartagena, we have no epigraphic record of conventual institutions in action during late antiquity.[97] In the fifth century, the *conventus* survived as territorial units and there are no fewer than seven references to them in Hydatius.[98] In none of these, however, does the word appear to have a social as well as a territorial dimension. As with provincial institutions, one wonders whether conventual institutions engendered a sense of community comparable to that created by the civic institutions of Spanish towns, or whether the *conventus* survived primarily as a means of designating geographic origin.[99]

None of this is to say that conventual or provincial institutions were unimportant or that they served no social function. The experience of imperial cult at the provincial level filtered back to the corners of the provinces, as those who had held provincial priesthoods returned home to live out their lives at the very head of the municipal *ordo*. Undoubtedly anyone who had traveled to Tarragona—or Mérida or Córdoba, where similar complexes existed—brought back word of the imperial presence there, even if they had not themselves gone as participants in provincial business. But as even so brief a sketch should show, the mechanisms for expressing provincial participation in empire were much fewer, and touched many fewer persons, than did those at the local, urban level. By the later second century, the elites of every corner of Spain had come to think of themselves as Romans, which is to say, to feel themselves to be participants in a Roman empire embodied in the person of the emperor. Yet they did so primarily as representatives of their own towns, where the symbols of that participation were more omnipresent and more deeply rooted than they were in any other place. For just this reason, the mechanisms of elite participation lasted locally with much more effect than they did across larger stretches of space. The creation of smaller, more manageable provinces by Diocletian did not change that fact. The memory of provincial boundaries was lasting, not least because these boundaries were preserved by the ecclesiastical administration of the Christian church. But the sense of community that survived at the level of the *civitas* in the post-Roman period seems not to have done so at the provincial level. The explanation is not far to seek—all the basic mechanisms of social and elite identity that came into existence during the Roman period were rooted in the city and the behavior of the city's leading social strata. When the empire ceased to exist, those institutions remained strong enough for the city to continue as the basic unit of political organization in the turbulent years that followed.

The urban institutions characteristic of the Roman city were implanted in Spain during the long centuries of romanization. The evidence presented in this chapter suggests that the institutions themselves long survived the decline of the epigraphic habit that makes them so much more difficult to trace in the later third and fourth centuries. This fact corroborates the evidence long known and increasingly acknowledged from elsewhere in the empire, particularly the eastern provinces. Most of the evidence for local institutions in late Roman Spain comes from one of two contexts, the imperial or the Christian. It is remarkably difficult to document any widespread effect of Christianity on the landscape or, indeed, the political world of Roman Spain before the fifth century. But the overwhelming impact of imperial government on fourth-century Spain is a phenomenon that impresses itself on us in numerous ways, both in the institutional reshaping of the Spanish provinces by Diocletian and in physical changes to Spanish townscapes. More than anything else, it is the revolution of Diocletianic government that accounts for the distribution of our fourth-century evidence and for the social changes which that evidence implies. If the urban institutions of the later empire were in large measure those of earlier decades, then the provincial framework within which they existed was quite profoundly different. And for that difference, Diocletian and his reaction against the troubles of the third century was primarily responsible.

Four

Diocletian and the Spanish Fourth Century

The reforms of Diocletian created the administrative boundaries that shaped Spain's late Roman history and outlived the imperial government there. These Spanish reforms were not unique, but rather one small part of an empire-wide reorganization that Diocletian undertook in an attempt to deal with the instability endemic to third-century government. For fifty years after the extinction of the Severan dynasty in 235, emperors and imperial aspirants came and went with what seems to us astonishing swiftness. Recent accounts have tended to downplay the traditional picture of an all-encompassing third-century crisis, afflicting politics, institutions, economics, and society all at once.[1] We can hardly doubt that the inflationary spiral of the period was severe and contributed to the weakness of individual emperors and the fragility of their relations with their soldiers and their subjects. Equally, however, the third-century crisis was primarily political. The effect of the rapid turnover of emperors was disastrous for the empire's governing elite, but also correspondingly limited.

Long periods of relative stability intervened between explosions of violence, and the effects of chaos at the very top of the imperial hierarchy were felt unevenly across the empire. The basic source of trouble was the cycle of foreign invasion and consequent usurpation and civil war that proved impossible to break for half a century. Its results were concentrated very heavily on the frontiers and in the frontier provinces.[2] The strength of the new Sassanian dynasty, installed at the Persian capital of Ctesiphon in 226 by the shah Ardashir, was perhaps the most important factor contributing to imperial instability in the third century: Alexander Severus was murdered in 235 precisely because of his failed invasion of Persia. The inability of successive emperors to win battles against the Persians, or to simultaneously defend the eastern frontier, the Danube, and the Rhine, encouraged mutinies among fractious Roman armies and usurpations from within them. Nevertheless, the western provinces were affected less badly, and for much less time, than were the provinces of the East. The civil wars from 235 to 253 did not impinge directly on the western provinces until the year 259 and the rebellion of Marcus Cassianius Latinius Postumus against Gallienus.

A Third-Century Crisis in Spain?

Postumus held some sort of military command on the lower Rhine, though in exactly what capacity is open to dispute.[3] He seems to have been provoked into rebellion by barbarian invasions. Some time around 260, groups of Rhine barbarians invaded the western provinces, and one invading army reached as far as Tarragona in Spain. Though these events were devastating, they were momentary affairs.[4] Postumus's success had more lasting results, a success he ensured with a dramatic victory over the Iuthungi shortly after taking the purple.[5] He very rapidly brought the whole of Gaul and parts of Raetia under his control, and by 261 had added Britain to his empire. Spain, too, recognized the new Gallic emperor, probably between 262 and 266. We possess three inscriptions, two from Tarraconensis and one from Baetica, which testify to his having been acknowledged there, though Lusitania was still loyal to Gallienus in 261 under its governor Clodius Laetus Macrinus.[6] Spanish officials had no real choice but to acquiesce in Postumus's usurpation. Between them, the Iberian provinces possessed only a single legion, the VII Gemina, stationed in northwestern Tarraconensis, its manpower dispersed across the north and its headquarters at León by now resembling a thriving town more than a legionary fortress.[7] There was no realistic possibility of opposing the seasoned armies of the Rhine frontier, and the usurpation of Postumus foreshadows the consistent pattern of the fourth and fifth centuries, when successful usurpation in Gaul brought the Spanish provinces into line as a matter of course.[8]

Despite the success of Postumus—who had, after all, been an able defender of the Rhine—the Spanish provinces seem to have been restored to the Italian emperors after Postumus's assassination in 269. Rather than dedications to the later Gallic emperors, we find a remarkable concentration of Spanish inscriptions honoring the Italian emperor Claudius II.[9] No longer attached to Gaul, Spain did not suffer during Aurelian's suppression of the Gallic empire in 274 and indeed not one battle of the century's many civil wars was fought on Spanish soil. Despite that fact, the third century is usually depicted as a catastrophic breaking point in Spanish history. The interpretation has deep roots in traditional historiography, which traces the integration of Spain into the Roman world under Augustus and the Julio-Claudians, a glorious explosion of romanized life in Spain under the Flavians and Antonines, and a spectacular new beginning in the fourth century, on a slate wiped clean by barbarian invasion and the internal malaise of the Hispano-Roman elites. This fourth-century Spain was wholly altered, the product of a stark ruralization brought on by a crisis that killed the glorious urbanism of the Flavian and Antonine era and left a new world where wealth, power, and culture resided in a rural environment divorced from cities, whose only role was to house imperial officials.[10]

This interpretation has held the field for more than half a century partly because of the tralaticious character of Spanish historical writing. More so than in most cultures of scholarship, ideas are reverently passed from study to study and generation to generation. This creates interpretative catenae in which ideas both good and bad gain plausibility by force of repetition. The picture of Spanish crisis in the third century derives from such habits, whereby a single piece of literary evidence for a barbarian invasion under Gallienus becomes the peg on which to hang every other piece of data.[11] Archaeology was particularly useful in this respect, because it could both confirm and extend the evidence of crisis. It was long the universal practice at Spanish sites to date all evidence of destruction—traces of fire, torn-down or rebuilt walls—to the third century and link it to the "Germanic" invasions.[12] A second invasion, unattested in the literary sources, was imagined and dated to 272, in order to account for destruction that could not be dated to 260.[13] With these assumptions in place, masses of material evidence seemed to confirm the written record for the very good reason that the material evidence was excavated, recorded, and published according to that record. The inevitable circularity of these arguments vitiates many a discussion of third-century Spanish history.

Material evidence can almost never be linked to precise historical events, and excavations conducted according to modern methodologies produce a very different picture of the Spanish third century, as we will see in the following chapter. They offer very little evidence for material decline during the political crisis of the third century. As to that political crisis, there is no reason to think that Spain suffered during it. The peninsula's incorporation into the Gallic empire was clearly a peaceful affair. More importantly, the barbarian invasions that loom so large in modern accounts are attested with nothing like the same significance in the ancient sources themselves.

Three ancient writers, all of whom derive their information from the same lost source, state that barbarians from across the Rhine penetrated Gaul, crossed the Pyrenees into Spain, and sacked Tarragona during the reign of Gallienus.[14] Another writer, later and less reliable but a Spaniard, maintains that some of these invaders remained in Spain for twelve years.[15] We might accept this latter notice as an authentic piece of local knowledge, but one of the earlier writers implies that the invaders moved on to Africa after the assault on Tarragona. Perhaps both accounts are correct: the invading army split, with part remaining active as bandits in the countryside for some years, the other part passing on to Africa. Either way, the evidence points to the passage of a barbarian army through a very confined corner of northeastern Tarraconensis. While no doubt traumatic and disruptive in the short term, this invasion is not enough to hang a century's worth of crisis upon. There is, in short, no reason to think that the Spanish provinces felt any great impact from the political disruptions of the third century.[16] On the contrary, Spain felt the effects of the crisis most strongly through Diocletian's reaction against it and the reforms that he instituted to forestall its repetition.

Diocletian

If the governmental crisis of the third century had barely rippled the surface of Spanish history, in other parts of the empire it had been very real indeed. Many a short-lived emperor had experimented with administrative or fiscal reforms that might restore stability at the center, but the habits of mutiny and assassination ingrained since the death of Alexander Severus cut short all such attempts. When Diocletian came to power, it was in circumstances little different from those that had brought any number of ephemeral contenders to the imperial throne. Yet through a combination of luck and persistence, Diocletian was able not only to keep hold of his throne, but to institute a series of reforms that, when continued by his ultimate successor Constantine, created what has rightly been called a New Empire.[17]

Diocletian seized power at Nicomedia in 284 after his predecessor Carus had been struck by lightning while on campaign against Persia and his young son Numerian had died in suspicious circumstances. In what looks like a well-organized coup d'état, Diocletian killed his potential rival, the praetorian prefect Aper, by his own hand, won the endorsement of the eastern army, and marched west to defeat Carus's elder son and co-emperor Carinus.[18] Diocletian succeeded to the line of soldier-emperors that followed on the collapse of Gallienus's regime in 268.[19] In part by following the lead of these predecessors, he managed to impose order and system on the whole of the empire. He did so by parceling out the tasks of government and reshaping its apparatus in ways that maximized imperial control. Diocletian's measures dealt with almost every facet of the imperial system. The currency and its mints were reformed.[20] The very large provinces of the high empire were divided into much smaller administrative units.[21] Provincial administration was reshaped, with civilian and military hierarchies systematically separated from one another for the first time.[22] The military was reformed to create a more responsive field army to replace the provincial legions, whose regional loyalties and inter-regional rivalries had helped make the mid-century civil wars so bloody.[23] And, most strikingly, Diocletian multiplied the imperial office by creating an imperial college.[24]

In all of these measures, Diocletian had been anticipated by one or another of his predecessors: more than one third-century emperor had tried to reform the currency;[25] in the vast provinces of the East, experiments with smaller provincial units went back to the middle of the century;[26] under Valerian and Gallienus, the de facto separation of military and civilian commands may have been attempted;[27] Gallienus had certainly created a mobile cavalry force capable of rapid response to crises;[28] and the appointment of co-emperors to ease the maintenance of control in far-flung corners of the empire had been tried not just by Valerian and Gallienus, but by the soldier-emperors like Carus who followed. However, the simultaneous enactment of all these reforms was novel, and, in the event, successful. In the short term, there can be little doubt that the most crucial point was the creation of an effective imperial college. From 285, Diocletian ruled with Maximian as one of two Augusti, while from 293 he was the senior member of the tetrarchy, a college of four emperors composed of two senior Augusti and two junior Caesars. This arrangement meant that there was always an emperor on hand in every part of the empire and rebellions could no longer brew in one place while the emperor was engaged in another. This system worked only so long as Diocletian was able to maintain control among his colleagues, but it provided the short-term stability that made other reforms possible. By the time Diocletian retired in 305, both internal administration and external frontiers had been put on secure enough footing that even two decades of intermittent warfare among the tetrarchs' successors did not precipitate a return to the governmental chaos of the mid-third century.

As a peaceful province far from the trouble-spots of empire, Spain had only a minor role in Diocletian's larger design, although even this minor role was carefully orchestrated. The multiplication of the imperial office had relatively little effect on Spain. Indeed, of all the tetrarchs, only Maximian ever set foot in the peninsula, though it is possible that his intention of spending some time in Córdoba prompted the construction there of the massive palace of Cercadilla.[29] Rather, it was Diocletian's division of the Severan provinces into many small

provinces that had the greatest long-term impact on Spain. The Diocletianic reform of the provinces more than doubled their total number and grouped them into regional dioceses administered by *vicarii*.
On the one hand, this simplified tax collection and thus made it easier to supply the army. On the other, the new provinces were too small
to give any single official a power base large enough to challenge the
emperor, an effect that was underscored by the separation of civilian
and military hierarchies so that the men who governed the provinces
were not also in command of provincial armies. The immediate effect
of this reform on the administration of Spain was enormous.

The New Spanish Diocese

In Spain as elsewhere, Diocletian grouped provinces together into a
diocese, under a diocesan *vicarius* resident in Mérida.[30] Within this
new diocese, the emperor maintained the Augustan provinces of Lusitania and Baetica with their capitals at Mérida and Córdoba, respectively. However, he divided the massive Augustan province of Citerior
in three: Tarraconensis, which retained Tarragona as its capital; Carthaginiensis, cut from the southeast of Tarraconensis with its capital at
Cartagena, but taking in a large swathe of the central peninsula and
the Balearic islands as well;[31] and Gallaecia, a region that had always
been somewhat different from the rest of Citerior and that was now
given its own capital at Braga in the far northwest.[32] As with so many
of Diocletian's reforms there were precedents for this one: Baetica had
been converted into an imperial province governed by an imperial
legate rather than a proconsul some time in the third century, while in
the early years of that century Caracalla had divided Citerior into a
nova provincia Hispania Citerior Antoniniana and a *Hispania superior,*
though these proved ephemeral.[33] Diocletian, however, went much
further than this, adding Mauretania Tingitana—essentially a small
stretch of the Moroccan coastline across the straits of Gibraltar—to the
five provinces carved from high imperial Spain. In the *Laterculus Veronensis*, a document of 314 that lists the provinces and dioceses of the
empire, these six Spanish provinces make up the Spanish diocese.[34]

Each of the Spanish provinces had its own governor, and in both
the old and the new provinces, Diocletian altered the status of the gov-

ernors. Indeed, it is possible that the administrative reforms in Spain began with a revision of official statuses: by 289 and before the subdivision of his province, the governor of Citerior had ceased to be a senatorial legate and had been replaced by an equestrian *praeses*.[35] A corresponding reform took place in Baetica and Lusitania at a date that we cannot determine precisely.[36] In fact, we do not know whether Baetica and Lusitania became equestrian provinces before or after neighboring Tarraconensis had been split in three, because the date of that provincial division, like that of parallel developments elsewhere in the empire, cannot be determined with any certainty. It is likely that Diocletian's whole program of provincial division and diocesan creation was implemented at a stroke in 293, but we cannot be sure.[37] It is, however, absolutely certain that the diocese of Spain had been created by 30 October 298, when the first diocesan *vicarius,* Aurelius Agricolanus, appears at Tangiers, ancient Tingi, in Mauretania Tingitana.[38]

Agricolanus is the first attested *vicarius Hispaniarum.* He appears not in Iberian Spain, but in Tingitania.[39] This point appears insignificant at first sight and has never been given much notice. In fact, however, it provides an important insight into the rationale behind Diocletian's reforms in the region. Every history of late Roman Spain takes as its subject the Iberian peninsula alone, and none gives more than a passing nod to Tingitania.[40] This is partly the result of Tingitania's invisibility in the narrative sources, but much more the result of modern political geography: modern history and the isolationism of Franco's Spain have conditioned us to think of the straits of Gibraltar and the Pyrenees as natural and inevitable frontiers, which they are not. Just as a common culture flourished on both sides of the Pyrenees during much of the Middle Ages, so too for more than half a millennium the straits of Gibraltar formed not a frontier but rather a highway between the Islamic cultures of Morocco and Andalucía. Diocletian was not alone in imagining Spain to include both the northern and southern shores of the straits of Gibraltar; the sharp definition of the frontiers of Spain is a more recent historical phenomenon. The question is why he took the administrative steps that he did.

There is a good deal of geographical logic to Diocletian's reform. In ancient times, Atlantic Mauretania consisted of little more than a coastal strip and a couple of river valleys that backed onto impenetrably forested mountains and uncultivable semi-desert. The Roman province of Tingitania was cordoned off from the rest of North Africa by the high ranges of the Rif and Middle Atlas. Coastal towns relied on marine industries, *garum* production at Lixus, for example, while in the interior Roman control never extended much beyond cultivable zones like the olive-growing region around Banasa.[41] Even this area of Roman occupation is consistently exaggerated on modern maps, and a graph of the region's rainfall patterns tells us all we need to know about Roman settlement in Tingitania.[42] Because of its aridity, and because east of Ceuta (ancient Septem) impassable mountains run almost to the Mediterranean shores, the provinces of Tingitania and Mauretania Caesariensis, to the east, were not contiguous and the zone between them had at best a nominal place within the Roman provincial system. The westernmost parts of Mauritania—the province of Tingitania—had since its inception been an outpost of Roman culture strictly coterminous with cultivable land, and more or less dissociated from the rest of Roman North Africa.

On the other hand, this Mauretanian oasis had always been readily accessible to Spain. The straits of Gibraltar are less than 15 kilometers apart at their narrowest point, and Tangiers, the capital of Tingitania, was a short sea voyage from Cádiz, Iulia Traducta, and Seville. It was, however, a long and inhospitable way from any town in Mauretania Caesariensis, and the single road that linked the two provinces seems to have had no Roman garrison or administrative structure to support its existence. Indeed, close ties between Tingitania and Spain had existed since the early empire, when the Claudian colonies of Tangiers and Lixus were administered from Baetica.[43] In A.D. 44, the governor of Baetica had actually been dismissed for failing to send Spanish corn to the army in Mauretania.[44] And both the Mauretanian king Juba and his son Ptolemy had held honorary magistracies in first-century Spain.[45] Proximity alone explains the closeness of these ties, and it likewise explains Diocletian's arrangements. The enclave that was Roman Tingitania could be administered far more effectively from Spain than it could be by an African vicar in distant Carthage.

Yet there may have been more than convenience to Diocletian's design, and it is possible to detect a strategic reason for attaching Tingitania to the other Spanish provinces as well. If the organizing principle of the Diocletianic reforms was imperial control, stabilizing the borders of the empire was every bit as important as binding the provinces more closely to the imperial center. Galerius and Diocletian campaigned in the East and on the Danube, Maximian and Constantius on the Rhine to precisely this end. In 296, for the same reasons, Maximian campaigned in Africa, probably from a Spanish base.[46] Maximian's efforts were accompanied by the redeployment of Roman garrisons within Tingitania, and they provide a logical explanation for the administrative link between Tingitania and the five Iberian provinces of Spain. Far from being a straggling appendage to the Spanish diocese, as is frequently imagined, Mauretania Tingitana may have been the point toward which other Spanish provinces turned, as a hinterland for Tingitania.

Across the empire, Diocletianic dioceses were oriented toward their respective frontiers. Frontier zones housed the troops that defended the hinterland, which in turn supported the life of the frontier zone with its tax revenues and its agricultural and industrial products.[47] The example of the Gallic dioceses and the Rhine frontier has been the most extensively studied. There, the vast peaceful interior of Gaul supported the military establishment in the Rhine provinces of Germania Prima and Secunda. Throughout the fourth century, these provinces protected the Gallic hinterland from the transrhenan incursions that had afflicted it in the third century. It is not impossible that Diocletian could have had in mind the raids of the Mauri across the straits of Gibraltar during the reign of Marcus Aurelius; they are, after all, recorded for us in a fourth-century text. If we posit that what the Rhine was to Gaul, Tingitania was to Spain, Diocletian's plans there become clear.[48]

At the accession of Diocletian, the three provinces of Roman Spain were a peaceful region. They were neither deeply affected by the third-century crisis nor had they played any part in worsening the crisis elsewhere in the empire. Spain had no external borders and had produced no usurpers.[49] None of this was true of Africa. Moorish tribesmen were a persistent nuisance there and Africa as a whole was a fertile source of civil disturbance and usurpation. Attaching European Spain to Tingitania simultaneously accomplished two objects. First, the Tingitanian *limes* was provided with a hinterland rich enough to supply its requirements. Second, the European provinces were safeguarded from any disturbances across the straits.

It requires real mental effort to visualize the Spanish diocese as an integral unit, conditioned as we are to generations of maps that illustrate late Roman Spain as the Iberian peninsula alone.[50] But if we do so, one of the supposed puzzles of fourth-century Spanish history disappears. For many years, scholars have affected surprise at the position of the Spanish diocesan capital, which Diocletian fixed at Mérida in Lusitania. However spectacular a city Mérida had become since the Augustan period, it is by no standard of measurement at the center of the Iberian peninsula, but tucked away at the highest navigable point on the Guadiana. On the other hand, if we remember that Tingitania was an integral part of the new organization, the choice of Mérida requires no special explanation: the city is central to the diocese as a whole. It stands directly on the main road between the northern *conventus* capitals and the ports of Seville and Iulia Traducta, both a short boat trip from Tangiers. As importantly, the only major road to traverse the peninsula diagonally across the Meseta started at Mérida and ended at Zaragoza in the Ebro valley, giving access in turn to the Pyrenean passes and the Catalonian coast. What is more, Mérida was situated at a point equidistant between the two small garrisons of Diocletianic Spain, one centered in the mining districts in the Cantabrian mountains and one on the frontier in Tingitania. This point is worth noting, since one of the vicar's main tasks was seeing that the army got its full share of state resources.

Mérida was the ideal site from which to administer a diocese that straddled the straits of Gibraltar and supported a frontier zone south of Tangiers in Mauretania. Recent work has suggested that parts of Spain, particularly the cities of the northwest, were reorganized to supply the *annona militaris,* which might partly account for the walls built around a large number of cities at the end of the third century.[51] The circulation of fourth-century coinage also suggests a connection with the *annona* and the pattern of military garrisons, though their precise interaction is poorly understood. Although these studies have all suggested the integration of Spain into the supply of the Rhine frontier, it is equally possible that Spain's role within the *annona* was directed southward, toward Tingitania.[52] Unfortunately, as little hard evidence supports the Tigitanian hypothesis as does the Rhine hypothesis.

Literary sources for Tingitania are extremely sparse, while archaeological evidence from Morocco is virtually nonexistent after the third century.[53] There is, however, evidence that food-producing establishments at Tangiers shrank considerably at the very end of the third century.[54] This might suggest new Spanish sources of supply, eliminating the need for local industries, though it is by no means probative evidence.[55] Even so, modern political geography should not blind us to the fact that Tingitania had a real place in Diocletian's conception of Spain, and that rulers of the postimperial period concurred: Byzantine governors and Visigothic kings strove very hard to maintain the Diocletianic legacy and keep the African and European parts of the Spanish diocese together, and it was the presence of Gothic garrisons on both sides of the straits that first suggested the possibility of invasion to Spain's Arab conquerors.

The Roman Army in Fourth-Century Spain

The Spanish diocese created by Diocletian was peaceful and, for the most part, demilitarized. A great deal has been written about the army in late Roman Spain, but only two sources have genuine value for the topic.[56] One is the famous *Notitia Dignitatum,* in several chapters of which Spanish troops appear. The other is a letter from the emperor Honorius to certain Spanish troops that is now preserved in a tenth-century codex from Roda among a miscellany of documents having to do with the city of Pamplona.[57] Both sources document the existence of Roman garrisons in fourth-century Spain, and the *Notitia* gives some impression of their disposition, but both are fraught with textual difficulties that make their evidence very difficult to deploy.

The transmitted *Epistula Honorii* consists of three sections of different provenance and date—a prefatory incipit, the letter proper, and a short explicit—the text of which is so hopelessly corrupt as to make no sense at all without emendation. The letter is addressed to at least four units of *comitatenses,* the mobile field army of the late empire, stationed in Spain. It either holds out to these soldiers the promise of *augmentum dignitatis* upon the successful fulfillment of their duty, or else grants them this as a reward for work already done. In other words, some sort of transfer or demobilization is envisaged but we cannot tell whether this was a hazy promise or a real commitment. The obscurity of the main text is exacerbated by the prefatory incipit, which claims to explain how the letter was brought to Spain, but is in fact a late addition without evidentiary value. Without the testimony of the incipit, the letter lacks any context that might allow us to emend its text with confidence, and previous attempts at emendation have read far more into the text than is actually there.[58] We can derive only one certain piece of information from the *Epistula Honorii,* that some time during the reign of Honorius (395–423) units of *comitatenses* were stationed in Spain. This confirms the testimony of the *Notitia.*

At first, the *Notitia Dignitatum* seems to be considerably more informative than the *Epistula.* It is a long list, nearly two hundred pages in the standard edition, divided into eastern and western sections that tabulate both the civil and military hierarchies of late Roman officialdom in rough order of precedence.[59] The *Notitia* gives the impression of great completeness and, along with the late Roman law codes, it is our main source for reconstructing the administrative structure of the late empire. Unfortunately, the precise nature and purpose of the extant *Notitia* are open to wildly divergent interpretations, and the question of dating is if anything more involved still. It seems obvious that lists of imperial offices and, especially, the deployment of troops, must have existed in quantity during the later empire, and their content will no doubt have resembled that found in the *Notitia.* It is, however, not at all clear that everyday working copies would have looked much like the extant *Notitia,* which is a lavishly illustrated copy of a deluxe Carolingian copy of a late Roman original. What that original was for is an almost insoluble question, because no late antique comparanda exist. Though we know that palatine bureaus maintained records of the imperial establishment, it is difficult to believe that copies kept for actual use were provided with the costly illustrations that grace the extant document. To complicate matters further, the information in the extant *Notitia* is of wildly divergent date, not just between the eastern and western halves of the document, but within the western half itself.

In consequence, there are as many different interpretations of the

Notitia as there are scholars who have written on it. Two recent proposals, equally plausible and only loosely compatible, have serious implications for the value of the information that the *Notitia* provides on Spain. One proposal would see our text as an essentially antiquarian document, cobbled together in the 420s from existing official lists, with the ideological motive of stressing the unity of eastern and western empires at a time when that unity had sunk to a very low ebb.[60] The other would suggest that the extant *Notitia* is a deluxe version of a working text originally designed at the eastern court of Theodosius before his campaign against the usurper Eugenius in 394.[61] Regardless of these theories, it is clear that the western portion of the document underwent a long series of progressively overlaid revisions until at least 419 and possibly much later, but because these revisions were not carried through systematically, doublets and contradictions abound. We cannot determine how many such alterations have impinged upon the base text, nor are there any criteria with which we can distinguish between original material and later corrections, or between corrections of different date. Only those entries that are confirmed by outside testimony can be placed in an identifiable context and dated, and no extrapolation can be made from these to unconfirmed entries. As a result, the extant *Notitia* cannot be used as evidence for the chronology of the deployments it shows, nor as independent confirmation for other sources that are not themselves dated precisely.[62]

These insoluble textual difficulties severely limit the value of the *Notitia* as evidence for the military establishment in Spain.[63] The text shows five separate groups of troops in Spain, some *comitatenses* belonging to the field army, others explicitly called *limitanei,* and still other troops under the direct command of the western *magister militum.* Sixteen units of *comitatenses,* under the command of a *comes,* appear in peninsular Spain, and another four units appear in Tingitania, under a second *comes.*[64] Also in Tingitania under the command of this second *comes* are three cavalry *vexillationes* attached to the field army, as well as eight units of *limitanei.*[65] In peninsular Spain, finally, there appear six units of garrison troops under the direct command of the distant *magister militum in praesenti.*[66] Because of the chronological difficulties of the *Notitia* as a whole, there are very substantial difficulties with dating the presence of these units in the peninsula.

Perhaps the fewest complications are presented by the garrison troops within the peninsula itself. These consisted of the Legio VII Gemina at León under a prefect, the cohort II Flavia Pacatiana at Paetaonium (Rosinos de Vidriales), the cohort Lucensis at Lucus Augusti (Lugo), the cohort Celtiberae at Iuliobriga (Retortillo), the cohort I Gallicae at Veleia (Iruña), and the cohort II Gallicae at the otherwise unknown *cohortem Gallicam*.[67] These garrisons were of long standing—the Legio VII Gemina is the same legion formed by Galba in A.D. 68 and subsequently returned to Spain by Vespasian—and some archaeological confirmation for the disposition of troops shown by the *Notitia* comes from a series of three bridges built in the vicinity of Veleia during the late third or fourth century, which might represent the construction skills of the cohort stationed there.[68] Given the antiquity of the Legio VII itself, it is generally assumed that the dispositions recorded in the *Notitia* reflect a very old state of affairs maintained by Diocletian and preserved throughout the fourth century. That is plausible, although not all the units attested in Spain after the first century are accounted for in the *Notitia* and, strictly speaking, we cannot tell whether the document actually reflects the disposition of one single date, or if so, what that date was.[69]

The other Spanish units in the *Notitia* are more obscure. The text describes two separate forces in Tingitania, all under the command of a *comes Tingitaniae*. The *comitatenses* and their attached cavalry vexillations are not associated with any particular sites, which is what one would expect from units of the field army.[70] The *limitanei,* on the other hand, form a line of garrisons running just to the south of Tangiers and Ceuta, well to the north of the Roman settlements in southern Tingitania.[71] For this reason, it is often wrongly asserted that in the late empire, the Roman frontier in Tingitania contracted into a tiny coastal territory around the straits of Gibraltar taking in Tangiers, Ceuta, and Lixus, but excluding important cities like Banasa and Volubilis.[72]

This error is rooted in two separate misconceptions. The first is a tendency to vastly exaggerate the earlier extent of Roman administration in Tingitania, so that it becomes possible to speak of a retreat from two-thirds of the Roman province. In fact, the late imperial garrisons remained within 100 kilometers of the southernmost centers of Roman population. The second misconception concerns the nature of imperial government in the province, which was centered on regions with a sedentary and agricultural indigenous population. This population had long coexisted with semi-nomadic and pastoralist neighbors, and the Romans continued this relationship, managing them through diplomacy backed with the threat of force. This was not a matter of keeping tribal groups outside the fixed boundaries of Roman control. Rather, Roman governments kept up a constant diplomatic activity that regulated the actions of tribes outside the agricultural regions that were actually administered by Roman officials. From Volubilis we possess a remarkable series of inscriptions that document the steady renewal of peaceful relations between the Roman governors of the settled population and the tribal leaders who lived nearby.[73] Roman garrisons were there to compel obedience when required and to demonstrate the Roman ability to apply that compulsion. The garrisons shown in the *Notitia* remained within easy reach of Volubilis, the southernmost city in Tingitania, and their deployment near the provincial capital at Tangiers implies administrative convenience as much as anything else. Nothing, at any rate, suggests a retreat from one set of defended positions to another. The date of the disposition of Tingitanian *limitanei* shown in the *Notitia* cannot be determined, but, like the garrison troops in the north of Spain, they may well date back to before the Diocletianic reforms.

The date and origin of the *comitatenses* and the cavalry vexillations in Tingitania are even more difficult, for their very existence is uncorroborated outside the *Notitia* itself.[74] Because units of Septimani appear in both the Tingitanian and the peninsular Spanish lists, it is possible that all the *comitatenses* listed for the Spanish diocese were initially sent there as a single group. If that were the case, we would be closer to a date for the comitatensian establishment in Spain, since the peninsular units—eleven *auxilia palatina* and five *legiones comitatenses*—do offer some evidence of their date.[75] Two of these units, the Ascarii seniores and Ascarii iuniores, had been part of the eastern army when the original text of the extant *Notitia* was first compiled but had been incorporated into the western army some time thereafter.[76]

We have evidence of this troop transfer because the administrator who revised the western list to show the Ascarii as western units made no corresponding deletion in the eastern list.[77] Consequently, the transfer of the Ascarii must have been effected after the initial redaction of our text of the *Notitia,* whether that took place in 394 or at some other date.[78] That fact, in turn, allows further hypothesis. The *Notitia* lists troops in order of seniority; the Ascarii are the most senior *auxilia* in peninsular Spain and the other units follow them in the lists. This should mean that all the *comitatenses* listed as stationed in the peninsula went there at the same time as the Ascarii, that is to say, after the redaction of the extant *Notitia.*[79] That, in turn, suggests a date after the accession of Honorius.[80] That would seem to confirm the evidence for Spanish *comitatenses* in the *Epistula Honorii,* although the two documents need not refer to precisely the same units.[81]

When all is said and done, the evidence for the army in late Roman Spain is not very substantial. If all the troops listed in the *Notitia Dignitatum* as being in Spain were there at the same time—and there is no guarantee of that—we could estimate their paper strength at about six thousand men in the European provinces of Spain and about the same again in Tingitania.[82] Such estimates involve too many variables to be very helpful, however, and we have little way of knowing what role the army played in the political life of fourth-century Spain. As throughout the post-Flavian period, the narrative of Spanish history remains obscure in the fourth century. We know that on the death of Constantius I, the Spanish provinces passed to his successor Constantine along with Britain and Gaul.[83] For a few years after 350, Spain was ruled by the usurper Magnentius.[84] Throughout the century, the province made a usefully distant place in which to exile politically dangerous opponents.[85] Apart from these isolated data, we hear nothing of political life in Spain between the Diocletianic reforms and the period of civil war that began in 407. Only with the events of that war does it become possible to write the narrative history of Spain, in those years when imperial government began to disintegrate in the peninsula. During the civil war, in the year 409, Vandals, Alans, and Sueves crossed the Pyrenees and invaded the Spanish provinces. Most studies take the events of 409 as the end of Roman Spain. This is nonsensical. The reign of Diocletian had revolutionized the nature of Roman government and altered the face of imperial politics. The Roman empire had always been a political institution, but after Diocletian, the empire was more and more defined by its bureaucracy. As contemporaries realized, the empire itself was a function of imperial office-holding: it existed where imperial officials existed and it is their disappearance, not the transient impact of barbarian invasion, that marks the end of Roman Spain.

Imperial Office-Holding and the Effects of Diocletian's Reorganization

The success of Diocletian's Spanish reorganization is confirmed by how little his successors tampered with it. Fourth-century emperors were not loath to change their predecessors' administrative arrangements and the Diocletianic and Constantinian bureaucracy evolved continuously at least into the reign of Constantius II.[86] New provinces were created quite regularly, particularly in the eastern half of the empire. In Spain, by contrast, we know of only two changes in the 150 years after Diocletian during which Roman emperors ruled Spain. Some time between 369 and the end of the fourth century, the Balearic islands were separated from Carthaginiensis and formed into their own eponymous province.[87] Also, in the 380s, the usurper Magnus Maximus created a new Spanish province of his own, carving it out of Tarraconensis, perhaps in the western Pyrenees.[88] This province seems to have been suppressed by Theodosius along with its creator and it had no lasting impact on the political geography of Spain.

Instead, the Diocletianic provinces remained more or less unchanged until Spain ceased to be part of the empire. The men who governed them are little known: in the period between Diocletian's reforms and the year 420, we know the names of sixteen *vicarii Hispaniarum* but can trace the careers of only six of them; in the same period, we hear of just over twenty provincial governors, though during that time there were six times as many governors as there were vicars.[89] The sample is too small to allow for meaningful prosopographical study, but we can trace the gradual inflation in the rank associated with Spanish governorships: both Baetica and Lusitania advanced from praesidial to consular status in the middle of the fourth century.[90]

The greatest impact of these governors and vicars was undoubtedly the enormous staffs that they maintained—at least a hundred for each governor, and perhaps as many as three hundred for the vicar, not counting the various supernumeraries constantly inveighed against in the laws of the period.[91] The early Roman empire was probably not as lightly administered as many believe, but there can be no question that the fourth century witnessed a vast expansion of the imperial bureaucracy.[92] In the cities where these officials resided, their day-to-day presence could mean regular interference in local affairs.[93]

This does not, on the other hand, seem to have reduced the importance of the *civitas* to administration at the local level. We have already seen how the municipal offices of the early empire survived into the fifth century, and there is no evidence that the number of Spanish *civitates* had shrunk in the fourth century.[94] The small number of *civitates* listed in high medieval ecclesiastical sources reflects divisions of the seventh century, at the earliest, and by no means shows that old urban administrative boundaries had disappeared in the late Roman period.[95] On the other hand, it does seem that the expansion of imperial government created a new understanding of what it meant to be part of the empire, to participate in its governance, and to hold power within it. More and more, rank and power came to be linked explicitly to holding imperial office so that one's place in the emperor's bureaucratic hierarchy, or one's relationship to it, came to be the organizing principle of life. Curial office-holding did not cease to have its value, but imperial office brought far greater status and far greater opportunity for profit. Indeed, the equation of office-holding with rank and status became so entrenched that a lack of access to high imperial office was a real grievance for the Gallic aristocracy by the end of the fourth century and a factor that contributed to the support for Gallic usurpers.[96]

This equation of status with imperial position is particularly important to understanding how Spain ceased to be part of the Roman empire in the fifth century. The centrality of imperial office created a worldview in which the empire was coterminous with its bureaucracy. Where people held imperial office there was an empire; where they did not, there was not. This attitude becomes visible in the fifth century, when the pressures of barbarian settlement and barbarian gov-

ernment led people to question what it meant to be Roman.⁹⁷ For
the most articulate Gallo-Roman of the fifth century, it was the ability
to hold imperial office and the existence of an imperial official hierarchy that marked the boundaries of the Roman empire. When office-
holding ceased in a region, so too did imperial rule.⁹⁸ Yet in Spain as
elsewhere, the bureaucratic classes carried the institutional life of the
empire into the post-imperial period.⁹⁹ The centers in which they con-
gregated—the great imperial cities of the fourth century—remained
central to the life of the fifth and sixth centuries. These cities had
achieved this centrality in a very physical way, for Diocletian's revolution in government not only altered the institutional and administrative framework of the Spanish provinces, but also profoundly affected
the material culture of the peninsula's cities.

Five

Change in the Spanish City

The third and fourth centuries brought very substantial changes to the physical landscape of Spain, certainly as much as they did to the peninsula's social landscape. A few small cities shrank dramatically or disappeared altogether, while the largest cities grew substantially. By the end of the second century, new works of monumental public architecture had largely ceased to be put up in the cities, but throughout the peninsula, the countryside came to be much more densely occupied while luxurious country residences appeared in large numbers. These changes have generally been analyzed in terms of a third-century crisis that destroyed the classical world of the Flavian and Antonine period, leaving in its place a Spain wherein decayed cities survived only as administrative centers. Because of these effects of the crisis, the argument runs, Spain suffered a profound process of *ruralización*, so that the part of Spanish society that mattered lived in the countryside by preference and ruled from there.[1] These same changes, however, can be explained equally well as a natural evolution beyond the period of Spanish romanization, with later, further change under the impact of the Diocletianic reforms. Any discussion of the evolving urbanism of the later empire must depend almost entirely upon archaeological evidence, which poses certain problems for the historian.

The archaeological record of Spain and Portugal has grown tremendously in recent decades, and archaeology now offers a more substantial body of evidence than do the few textual sources with which historians have traditionally worked. Not all of this archaeological evidence is of the same quality, and most Spanish site reports published before the 1980s raise real difficulties. The reasons for this vary, but the chief problem has been the use of textual evidence to determine the course of excavation or shape its results. In themselves, archaeological sites reveal relative chronologies through the relationship of different strata to one another. These relative chronologies can be converted to absolute dates by precisely dateable material remains found within a particular stratum, for instance, coins or distinctive ceramic types. If, however, absolute dates are borrowed from textual sources and assigned to the relative chronology of the specific assemblage, a step of pure assumption is introduced into the record of the material evidence. If, for one reason or another, an assemblage dated in this fashion comes to be accepted as a paradigm for a particular type of site in a particular region (with the result that other, comparable assemblages are dated by reference to the original), a single, hypothetical relationship between the material record and the chronology preserved in the extant texts can dominate whole libraries full of material evidence.

This pattern has been played out repeatedly in Spain, where a few dates drawn from the very sparse literary evidence—the invasion of *Mauri* under Marcus, the "Frankish" invasion of circa 260, the invasions of 409, or the conversion of the Goths in 589—have been used both to date sites excavated without due care for the stratigraphy and to fix the date of sites that provide only relative chronologies. When material evidence dated in this fashion is deployed by historians, the effect is to create circular networks of evidence, which are self-authenticating because archaeological results framed on historical premises are used to corroborate and explain historical processes. One cannot correct for such distortions unless the basis of a particular chronology is made explicit by the excavator, something that has become normal practice in Spain only in the course of the past two decades. Where the assumptions that lie behind the published chronology of an excavation are undetectable, the historian cannot safely use that excavation as evidence for change over time in the Spanish city. It is not merely a matter of applying incomplete material evidence with all due care or avoiding its blatant misapplication. On the contrary, where chronological assumptions are inexplicit, and where the publication of specific finds is not detailed enough for the reader to check, the greatest care in the world will not allow us to circumvent the distortion inherent in the available evidence.

Escape from this trap has only recently become possible, thanks to the advances made during the past twenty-five years of archaeological research in Spain.[2] More and more sites have been excavated on their own terms and dated according to purely archaeological criteria. A corresponding trend toward the very complete publication of sites allows the material record to speak for itself, by allowing readers to follow an excavator's analysis of the evidence uncovered.[3] The total quantity of such evidence is still restricted to fewer sites than one would like, and these are unevenly distributed both geographically and in terms of their relative importance in the Roman period. Site reports in which the interested reader can follow the stages of excavation, documentation, and inference are likewise still a minority of those available. Nevertheless, this restricted sample is now sufficiently independent of the textual sources that it does not merely confirm their evidence. It therefore demands that historians bring it to bear on their readings of late Roman Spain.[4] The correlation of this material record to the narrative of events is limited, where it exists at all. But it allows us to pursue certain fundamental questions about Spanish late antiquity from perspectives impossible even a short time ago.

Third-Century Cities

At the heart of the old views of urban decline lies the idea that an economic crisis in the third century effectively destroyed both the ability and the will of Spain's urban elites to care for the infrastructure of their cities. There can be no doubt that the Roman world as a whole suffered serious monetary crisis in the third century, a crisis that must have had a severe economic impact, even if the precise nature of that impact is not always clear. The question, however, must be how far this monetary crisis, and any consequent economic disruption, af-

fected Spain. The debasement of silver *denarii* and *antoniniani* across
the whole empire during the third century is a well-known phenomenon, with precedents during the reigns of Commodus and the Severans, but reaching epidemic proportions after 260. The debasement
of coins, consequent inflation, and subsequent official devaluations
ruined the token bronze coinage of the early empire and destroyed any
fixed relationship between silver and the undebased gold coinage still
used for donatives. The result of all this was the pricing of goods in
money of account, *denarii communes,* which could be exchanged at
variable rates against the circulating billon (silver-washed base metal)
coinage. Because of constant reminting and retariffing, usually at debased standards, the whole fiduciary structure of the Augustan monetary system broke down from the 250s onward.[5]

The effect of this collapse on daily life is very hard to trace, however. In Spain, as throughout the Roman West, the phenomenon of
coin hoarding is well attested in the third century. Because hoards are
found from one end of the peninsula to the other, they are of no use
in plotting specific local crises. Indeed, the phenomenon of hoarding
is less significant than the failure to recover the hoarded items.[6] In
third-century Spain, as elsewhere in the third-century West, many
people thought it worthwhile to secret away their wealth as insurance
for better times—better times which, for them, never came. That in
itself is powerful evidence for social disturbance in the third century,
even if the contents of Spanish hoards are open to widely different interpretations, making their value as evidence for the economy very
hard to judge.

The content and likely deposition dates of some hoards seem to
suggest that the peninsula—or at least the north and east of the peninsula, which has been best studied—experienced the same sort of monetary changes as did the rest of the Roman world. Coin hoards from
Tarraconensis, for instance, seem to show a very strong tendency to
hoard the best coinage available.[7] However, other studies suggest that
the distinction between good and bad coin, which we make on the
basis of metal content, was not made with the same regularity by
Hispano-Romans, and that the debasement of the metal content of the
coinage, particularly after the year 260, did little to change patterns of
coin use.[8] More important, it is not possible for us to correlate changes

in the quality of the coinage with the economic life of Spanish provincials. Though the disappearance of a viable token coinage would seem a priori to have made life more difficult for Spanish provincials, we lack any data for measuring how much more expensive life became in third-century Spain. Some have suggested that Spain was spared the worst experience of inflation because, lacking a substantial garrison, military salaries paid out in floods of debased coin were not central to the economy.[9] Certainly, Spaniards did not lose the habit of transacting business in coin, and were it not for the phenomenon of hoarding itself, we would have little evidence for a peninsular economy in crisis.

The evidence for peninsular trade might actually suggest the reverse. Commerce at the local level, particularly in foodstuffs, is unlikely to have been much affected by the currency crisis of the period. Industrial production for local markets, still relatively little studied, shows signs of continuity and even expansion, for instance, with the potters of the little settlement at Tomoví, not far from Tarragona, whose local wares achieved a very wide distribution within the *conventus* during this era of supposed economic contraction.[10] Much of the tableware of Zaragoza, meanwhile, was supplied from the third until the early sixth century by local ateliers from farther up the Ebro valley, in what is now La Rioja.[11] The systematization of the typologies of late Spanish *sigillata,* now in progress, will no doubt offer much more certain evidence along these lines.[12]

However, it is the wider world of long-distance commerce that provides the most easily traceable evidence. Here, the evidence is mixed. In the early empire, the olive groves of the Guadalquivir valley produced vast quantities of oil with which the army on the German frontier was kept supplied. This Baetican oil industry declined precipitously in the later second century, once oil became available elsewhere.[13] On the other hand, late antique Spain remained the empire's primary manufacturer of *garum,* the pickled fish relish that graced the table of every Roman with any pretense to taste. Recent excavation has shown that the industry existed over a much greater area than had once been suspected: *garum* factories have now been discovered as far north as the gulf of Roses on the Catalonian coast, while the manufacturers along the Gallaecian and Cantabrian coasts expanded their production in this period.[14] *Garum* production increased steadily from the third to the end of the fourth century, so that older buildings of various types were converted into fish-sauce factories, and the industry as a whole prospered into the fifth and even the sixth century.[15]

As the example of *garum* shows, the disappearance of the Baetican oil industry is not basis enough to diagnose a more general economic crisis. Spain's capacity to import commercial products from elsewhere also shows little sign of crisis during the era of gravest monetary instability. Instead, the third century seems to have witnessed a continuous growth in the commercial contacts between Spain and the outside world. Imports into the peninsula had always been channeled through a few key points, often though not always the chief civil and military cities of a region. The clearest evidence comes from Tarragona and its environs, where imported ceramics have been studied in greater depth than elsewhere. At Tarragona, the overwhelming majority of material came from Africa Proconsularis and Byzacena by the second quarter of the third century, and in ever growing quantity.[16] During the third century, Africa became the grain supplier for the whole Roman West, not least Spain, where in the coastal towns, cheap African grain seems to have driven Spanish supplies off the market entirely. The same phenomenon is witnessed in inland cities, though not on such a dramatic scale.[17] Extensive trading contacts with the Roman East, particularly Syria and Asia Minor, are also attested for the first time in the third century, and the quantity of this trade increased over the next two centuries. Again, the phenomenon is most noticeable in the great cities of the coast, or at inland trading cities like Mértola, an important port for two Lusitanian *conventus* capitals, Pax Iulia (Beja) and Mérida.

The fact that Spanish trade continued unabated and in some aspects grew during a century that is characterized as suffering from acute economic crisis might suggest that the crisis itself was less severe than is traditionally thought, at least in Spain. We cannot, in consequence, use the assumption of a third-century economic crisis to explain change in the Hispano-Roman town. Spain entered the third century as a highly urbanized region, its many cities conforming to the standard patterns of Roman public architecture, most of them with a full complement of the public structures that made up the ancient Roman city: fora, theater, amphitheater, public baths, and perhaps a circus. In partial consequence of this satiety, the third century witnessed relatively little in the way of monumental construction. More specifically, private patronage of new public amenities seems to have disappeared to a large extent. This fact is frequently taken as a sign of urban decline, or at least of the loss of public spirit among urban elites.[18] In fact, however, private curial euergetism was never particularly widespread in Spain, and a model derived largely from the experience of the Greek East should not be taken as normative for the peninsula.[19] While some Spanish monuments were the products of local euergetism, many others were derived from outside patronage whether private or imperial—investment in public monuments was one reason that cities sought patrons so avidly.

Cities that had enjoyed vast external patronage from the beginning had never developed the habit of local or private euergetism, or, where they did, it was supplementary to outside patronage. The Lusitanian capital at Mérida is a good example of this phenomenon.[20] Built for the veterans of Augustus's Cantabrian wars, the city was designed on a grand scale from the very beginning. It had not one but two large fora, one of which may have been the provincial forum, each presided over by several temples. The patronage of Agrippa gave the city an intramural theater and that of Augustus an amphitheater from almost its very foundation, though it was probably Flavian patronage that marmorized the latter monument.[21] By comparison with these enormous projects, local efforts seem puny. Beside the colonial forum, at the intersection of the *cardo* and *decumanus maximi,* a new forum began to be built in the Julio-Claudian period in very close imitation of the forum of Augustus at Rome. This so-called *foro de mármol* may well have been the work of the local curia. Similarly, we know of only two private dedications of temples, one a temple of Mars, the other a mithraic complex. Both date from the second century and may have been inspired by the new burst of imperial patronage that the city enjoyed under Trajan and Hadrian.[22]

Much less is known about the original sources of urban growth in Tarragona, though the theater was perhaps a donation of Augustus.[23] The creation of the vast Flavian provincial complex of the upper town inspired the construction of the amphitheater down by the seashore,

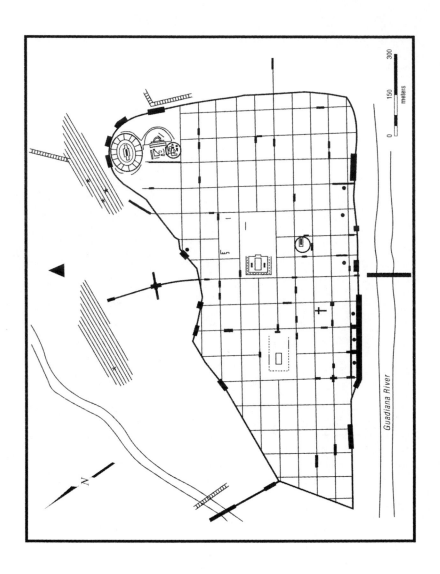

Guadiana River

N

0   150   300
     meters

at the expense of a local *flamen,* but thereafter whatever euergistic impetus existed seems to have diminished.[24] Smaller cities could experience similar good fortune. Because two of its native sons reached the imperial purple, the city of Italica was transformed into a regimented expanse of marble and public buildings by their patronage. Not only did the emperors refurbish the old Republican forum, they created an entire *Nova Urbs* beside the old one. The quality of the construction techniques in the new city did not match their impressive scale, however, and the new amphitheater and forum were badly damaged by soil subsidence before they had even been completed.[25] At Seville, an important city but not a provincial capital, we find the collective euergetism of corporations and *collegia,* and one of the city's fora may well have been specifically dedicated to the collective activities of the urban *collegia.*[26] On the other hand, we find little of the ostentatious private euergetism famous from elsewhere in the Roman world.

Italica is the single grandest example of what external patronage could lavish on a city. Where that sort of patronage could be counted on, there was no incentive for municipal elites to take much of a hand. In such circumstances, the curia and the curial elites did not take as their primary mark of status the creation of monumental buildings for their cities, in part because they could not hope to compete with the patronage offered by outsiders. It was therefore mainly in small cities, where external patronage was at best extremely limited, that the urban elite took upon itself the task of monumentalizing the city.[27] A good example is the unimportant *municipium* of Aurgi, modern Jaén. There we meet C. Sempronius Sempronianus, twice duumvir and perpetual pontifex, and his daughter Sempronia Fusca Vibia Anicilla, who together donated, entirely at their own expense, both a public baths and the conduits for its water.[28] It was chiefly in cities like Jaén, or in those like Sagunto with a famous history but no special role in the imperial era, that local elites internalized the notion that to spend lav-

(*Facing page*) Plan of Mérida, showing the chief public monuments and the street grid. The thicker lines represent sections of wall and street that are extant. The area of the Morería lies just to the west of the bridge over the Guadiana. (after Mateos and Alba [2000], 145)

ishly on public works was both a marker of social status and a necessary function of possessing it.[29] In such places, competitive expenditure functioned in parallel to the competition for local office, because like that competition, euergistic works helped establish one's social position in relation to one's peers.

At a higher level, euergetism also fueled the ongoing competition between different towns to look more Roman than did their neighbors. In the days before the Flavian municipal law, such construction not only brought prestige, but also increased the potential for an advancement in juridical status by looking the part of Roman. After the grant of municipal status, adorning one's city meant raising the status of that city within the province, which in turn raised one's own status as a member of the elite of a leading city.[30] Yet however beguiling this picture of rough-and-tumble competition to lavish expenditure might be, we are not justified in taking private euergetism as a measure of the health of the cities or of the public spirit of their curias.[31] In fact, the second- and third-century cessation of monumental construction by private individuals brought the whole of the peninsula into line with the long-standing habits of the most important cities.

Monumental construction did not cease altogether in the third century, and more traces of it are being discovered as old assumptions about the era's crisis are revised. The provincial forum at Córdoba, for instance, probably acquired a new temple in the course of the third century, while the townscape as a whole was maintained in more or less its Flavian aspect.[32] The fate of existing public monuments, in particular the disuse of theaters across the peninsula, is frequently taken as another expression of urban decline. The traditional approach maintains that, with the third-century economy in crisis, inflation either emptied municipal treasuries or made their contents worthless, thereby destroying the ability of curias to look after the monuments of their cities. Here, however, one must attribute alterations to the townscape to changing tastes. The theater was never especially popular in Spain, having been widely introduced in the Augustan age and then diffused in the long process of romanization that followed.[33] As long as the building frenzy of the early empire continued, theaters kept being put up. Once every city of importance had a theater, their symbolic value declined and some fell into disuse. At Tarragona, the theater, which had been rebuilt in marble only a few decades earlier, had probably ceased to be used by the end of the second century.[34] In the south, one of the first and largest theaters in the peninsula, built by the younger Balbus at his hometown of Cádiz, likewise stopped being used in the second century, as did the Augustan theater at Cartagena.[35] There are exceptions to this general rule: Mérida's theater was eventually rebuilt in the Constantinian era, while the architectonic remains of the theater at Córdoba suggest a redecoration of the *scaenae frons* in the second century.[36] But a further rebuilding of the *scaenae frons* with new Asian capitals in the fourth century would seem to signify an alteration in the purpose of the monument, inasmuch as parts of the theater had already been dismantled and reused elsewhere at this point.[37] On the whole, however, theatrical spectacles seem simply to have died off in the second and third centuries, when their social function as emblems of *romanitas*, and still more of participation in the *pax Augusta*, had ceased to matter.[38]

That this does not imply straightforward urban decline is demonstrated by the fates of other spectacular monuments.[39] With amphitheatrical spectacles gaining consistently in popularity, the disuse of urban theaters often coincided with improvements to the amphitheater.[40] At Tarragona, the more decorative furnishings of the theater were appropriated to embellish the amphitheater, which underwent dramatic redecoration under Elagabalus, probably in 221.[41] The monument was well-used in the third century, as is demonstrated both by the archaeology and by the martyrdom of Fructuosus there in 259.[42] Under Constantine, it was restored or remodeled.[43] Elsewhere, theaters were modified to accommodate gladiatorial spectacles. The Tiberian theater at Zaragoza, which had been redecorated under the Flavians and again under Trajan, was transformed in this way during the third or early fourth century, its orchestra and the first two rows of its *imma cavea* filled in with sand, the necessary absorptive medium for gladiatorial shows. The local taste for such spectacles seems to have lasted into the sixth century, given that new sand floors continued to be laid down until eventually the fifth row of the *imma cavea* was covered over.[44] With a few exceptions—the case of Segobriga is the only certain one—amphitheaters remained in constant use from the third through the fourth and fifth centuries.[45] It took the gradual conversion to Christianity, and the transformation of Christian cult into the central social activity of the urban population, to make any serious impact on the popularity of amphitheatrical spectacle.[46]

The circus was a similarly popular spectacle, if one that fewer cities could afford, and the sponsorship of circus games is much better attested in Spanish euergistic inscriptions than are other forms of spectacle.[47] Enjoyment of the circus, moreover, went unchallenged by the adoption of Christianity.[48] Thus people kept going to the circus at Toledo not just throughout the fourth century, but well beyond it. The Toledan circus was large, more than 400 meters long, and probably built on the model of the circus at Mérida. Much of the Toledan evidence was destroyed by unpublished digs of the 1960s, but in the one corner where a stratigraphy could be salvaged, there is no evidence of destruction from before the tenth century.[49] Obviously there is no question of its original function surviving at that point, but it had probably continued in use as a spectacular site through at least the fifth century. In the same way, the circus at Valencia may have been repaired during the fourth century, though by the sixth century small houses were built on the arena floor after a period of disuse, perhaps quite a long one.[50] No trace of a circus has yet been discovered at Zaragoza, but it would be surprising if so important an early imperial town had not possessed one and there is literary evidence for the celebration of circus games in the city as late as the start of the sixth century.[51] At that point, the fact that a chronicler felt the subject worth mentioning suggests that the holding of circus games had become a rare treat. Yet it is striking that even in the early 500s, the tastes of the Zaragozan population should still have run to so traditional an urban spectacle as the circus.

The contrasting fates of the different sorts of urban spectacular monument give the lie to any simple understanding of urban transformation in terms of decline. Changing taste will have determined the use or disuse of older buildings as much as anything else. One point that would seem to make this very clear is the haste with which disused monumental space within the city was reappropriated for other ends. At Tarragona, late antique buildings of uncertain purpose were put up beside the theater soon after it and its attendant nympheum had gone out of use.[52] Valencia, which seems to have experienced a fairly widespread recession in the 270s, was swiftly rebuilt thereafter.[53] Lérida is among the least known of Spain's major cities, not just in the late Roman period but in the early empire as well. Here too, however, there are signs of active urban construction during the late imperial period. Some time in the course of the third century, a major flood of the river Segre destroyed one of the city's Augustan-era buildings. On the fluvial sediment that the flood left behind, a new late antique building was put up, some time before the reign of Valentinian II. Too little of this building has survived to conjecture about its uses, but the very fact of its construction is important.[54] For a long time, fourth-century Lérida was relegated to the status of a ghost town on the basis of the famous correspondence between Ausonius of Bordeaux and Paulinus of Nola.[55] That view is no longer tenable. Lérida, like Tarragona and Córdoba, provides evidence for the steady reconstruction of public urban spaces throughout the late imperial period.

Much of this work will necessarily have involved the curias very deeply. From the very beginning, the chief practical duty of curial magistrates was the supervision and upkeep of the urban infrastructure, as the Flavian municipal law makes clear. The aediles, in particular, were responsible for the upkeep of roads, drains, and baths.[56] Within specified limits, the duumvirs and the curia could compel labor service from those within the city's *territorium* for the carrying out of public works.[57] The whole curia, meanwhile, was meant to authorize public spending on buildings and repairs.[58] Other duties were just as important. The curia had to approve the demolition or remodeling of buildings in town and residents could not tear down buildings they had no intention of replacing.[59]

The sorts of problem this kind of curial oversight engendered are well illustrated in the city of Sagunto, where a new circus was put up in the second century in a period when the city was flourishing thanks to the export of its local wines.[60] The circus was eventually built to the north of the city on the flat alluvial plain alongside the river Palancia, but the precise choice of site was peculiar. It required cutting right across the suburban extension of the city's *cardo maximus*, which led from the bridge over the Palancia to the monumental center of the Augustan town and thence to the Via Augusta.[61] We can explain the odd position of the circus in only one way. The whole of the suburban plain was dotted with private residences, and the owner of one such residence would appear to have exercised sufficient influence to keep the new construction off his own property. Even though a shift of a mere 50 meters would have preserved the old road system intact, at least one Saguntine citizen carried enough weight to bend the public interest to his own ends.

This was the sort of situation in which all the markers of status and influence that loomed so large in Roman social relations would have come into play. The debate in the curia would have been furious and the victor would have appeared all the more powerful when the debate was won, his own private interest triumphing over the best interests of the community as a whole. Although the case of the Saguntine circus is quite early, it offers a clear-cut example of the importance that curial decision making might have. Spanish curias continued to play this role in late antiquity, responding to the changing needs of local citizenry. The finest example of this phenomenon may be the city of Emporiae, modern Ampurias in Catalonia, doubly important because it was for many years seen as paradigmatic of urban collapse.

The site of Ampurias had been inhabited for centuries, both as the chief center of the indigenous Indiketes and later as the westernmost Greek colony in the Mediterranean. The earliest Greek town, known as the palaiopolis, was built on a small offshore islet, now the *barrio* of Sant Martí. By the third century B.C., a large Hellenistic town, which scholars call the neapolis, had grown up on the mainland. This Greek *emporion,* which still gives the city its name, had a substantial Roman population from the end of the third century, when the Scipios used the town as their base during the second Punic war.[62] But the site was completely transformed after Caesar planted an enormous *colonia* immediately to the west of the neapolis, on what had once been the indigenous town of Indica. This new *colonia* covered nearly 25 hectares, much more than comparable provincial towns, and the population of the region never grew large enough to make use of the newly built-up area.[63] Economic recession during the Julio-Claudian period led to the gradual abandonment of the neapolis and then its deliberate amortization. The work was done with care, so that wells and pits that could have posed a danger were deliberately filled in and sealed. Over the course of the second century, the neapolis of Ampurias became a suburban field, rapidly covered by the sand and earth swept in by the region's tramontana winds; by the fourth century, the structures of the neapolis were no longer visible above the soil and the residents of the late Roman city began to use the area as a cemetery.[64] Yet the same curia that had so carefully decommissioned the Hellenistic neapolis soon found itself unable to keep up the costly and otiose fabric of the vast *colonia,* and by the end of the second century a large part of the population of Ampurias may have been living in the palaiopolis.

This population was not, it should be stressed, a cringing remnant, insulating itself from the glorious classical past it had abandoned. Large numbers of silos built in the area between the *colonia* and the palaiopolis between the second and the fourth centuries attest to the importance of the city as an entrepôt for grain.[65] Imported luxury goods of the third through fifth centuries are abundant, and the municipal elite of the fourth century could afford to bury its dead in the finest Italian sarcophagi.[66] As importantly, aerial photography suggests the existence of a very large suburban area, perhaps given over to industry or market gardening. The density of population at late antique Ampurias is further suggested by the vast number of graves that have been found. These no longer form a strict *corona funeraria* around the city, but instead spread across a wide zone including the whole of the old neapolis and the suburbs for a long way in all directions. The remaining inhabitants of the palaiopolis, for their part, maintained the old Roman tradition of avoiding intramural burial until the seventh century.[67]

The example of Ampurias is important both for its substance and for the methodological lessons it provides. The abandonment of Hellenistic and Caesarian Ampurias was once attributed to destruction by barbarian invasions of the third century.[68] Modern archaeological methods have established a chronology that proves the old view impossible. It allows us to see how urban landscapes changed over time, as local responses to local needs. The clear signs of deliberation in the abandonment of the classical section of the town demonstrate continued oversight by the municipal authorities whose job it was to provide that oversight—the curia. It is still perfectly legitimate to characterize the abandonment of both the neapolis and the Roman city as decline, if we take the classical Roman city as our ideal and claim that life, even a wealthy life, lived in the walled and unplanned palaiopolis could not possibly have been as good as life in the orthogonal majesty of the Caesarian *colonia.* But contemporaries appear not to have seen things the same way. Instead, Ampurias's complex life cycle shows us a provincial urban elite consciously deciding to abandon their classical townscape, without any apparent ill effect either to their own prosperity or to the role of their city in the local power dynamic. One might suspect that other oft-cited cases of Spanish urban collapse—Iluro and Baetulo, for instance—would prove to be less straightforward in light of new and careful excavation.[69]

The amortization of Ampurias's neapolis is one example of the way in which the natural leaders and lawful representatives of the urban citizenry strove to maintain their towns in the way that people wanted them maintained. Not only was this part of the legal responsibility to their fellow townspeople as outlined in the municipal foundational charters, it was also a responsibility to the Roman state, as the late antique law codes show us.[70] The archaeological record preserves the physical manifestation of these responsibilities, in the practical work of maintaining aqueducts and water supplies as well as street surfaces. Evidence of the latter activity is not always easy to find, and archaeologists have only recently begun to look for it, but it does certainly exist, as has been shown for Mérida.[71] At Valencia as well there are clear signs of fourth-century maintenance of streets in such a way as to raise the level of the street surface considerably above that of the original flagstones, while one of the chief water distribution sites, immediately to the south of the *decumanus maximus,* appears to have been kept up for active use until the tenth century.[72]

Bath complexes, on the other hand, were more subject to changing tastes and behavioral patterns than were other amenities.[73] To be sure, in one or two places new bath complexes may have been put up in the third century or even later, but that was not usual.[74] More frequently, older public bath complexes were kept in use into the later period, thus almost certainly at curial expense. The baths found at Campo Valdés in Gijón on the Asturian coast, once regarded as the Roman city of Gigia, were built in the second century and used until the end of the fourth.[75] A huge Flavian bath complex at the very apex of the hill on which Segobriga was built actually seems to have been redecorated during the fourth or fifth century, though only the ongoing excavation will clarify the chronology.[76] The only public baths known from Braga seem to have had a similar longevity.[77] Elsewhere, the habit of public bathing may have fallen off somewhat. At Zaragoza, it is likely that bathing ceased to be communal and public and shifted instead to the baths of private estates in the countryside around the city.[78] At Toledo, the public baths built outside the city walls at roughly the same time as the circus went out of use in the course of the fourth century, when its large *natatio* was filled in and built over with what were probably residential buildings.[79] Similarly at Valencia, the old public baths in the plaza de la Almoina appear to have gone out of use during the third century.[80]

Because private baths continued to exist within cities, the decline of the big public complexes during the fourth and fifth centuries probably reflects not generalized urban decline, but rather a change in the way the specific rituals of bathing were performed: tastes had shifted toward a more intimate bathing experience, perhaps with invited guests whose companionship was congenial, and not in the full view of one's fellow citizens.[81] Developing Christian attitudes toward nudity only accentuated such changes, so that by the fifth century, bathing was a ritual performed almost exclusively in private baths with one's chosen and invited peers.[82] On the other hand, the persistence of communal bathing into the fourth century is vouchsafed not just archaeologically, but also in the sermon on penitence delivered in the 380s or so by Bishop Pacianus of Barcelona. In it, he urged the penitents in his audience to refuse invitations to the baths, as such "luxurious delights" are not for those meant to be mourning their sins.[83]

The Walling of Cities in Late Antiquity

The foregoing sketch suggests that in the third and fourth centuries Spanish curias worked consistently at their foremost practical function, no longer the construction of vast new structures, but rather the upkeep or suitable redesign of those that already existed. It is a picture that emerges from archaeological evidence uncovered without reference to paradigms of crisis and decline drawn from the literary sources. There is, however, one very large exception to the general absence of new construction in late antiquity. As has long been recognized, Spain experienced a golden age of wall-building between the third and the early fifth centuries.[84] The interpretation of this phenomenon, however, has long been tied up in general discussions of urban decline: in the crisis years of the third century, endemic insecurity caused walls to be thrown hastily up around the cores of shrunken towns. Indeed, walls became a potent symbol of crisis, and the existence of town walls was regularly used to document the passage of third-century barbarians through regions where they are otherwise unattested.

Here again, however, recent advances in Spanish archaeology have made old views untenable. Archaeologists are no longer willing to insist that wall-building and invasions must be linked, nor to reflexively date Spanish city walls to the third century.[85] Indeed, the fundamental difficulty of dating town walls without extensive stratigraphic excavation is now widely recognized.[86] Most walls continue to be dated typologically, rather than by controlled excavation along their foundations, and while typological dating can work very well for pottery, sculpture, and decorative architecture, it is a very blunt instrument for larger structures like fortifications in which function rather than style is the primary engine of change.[87] In fact, even where solid dating criteria are available, these rarely provide more than a *terminus post quem* and offer no means of telling how long after that date a particular wall was actually built.[88]

These general difficulties can be illustrated by some examples. The Lusitanian city of Conimbriga has some of the best preserved walls in the whole peninsula, but despite the systematic excavation of the site, they have been dated variously to the mid-third century, the tetrarchic era, and the fifth century. At Norba Caesariensis, modern Cáceres, the extant Almohad wall has visibly Roman foundations, but assertions of second- or fourth-century dates have no basis in excavation.[89] The extant walls at Seville were long assumed to be those of the Roman city, but recent research has shown them to be Almoravid with certain Almohad reconstructions, so that only recourse to the Arabic literary sources allows for the hypothetical reconstruction of the Roman wall circuit.[90] In a reverse of the situation at Seville, excavation at Aquae Flaviae (modern Chaves) has only just shown that the medieval walls of the city lay on Roman foundations, perhaps of the third century.[91] The walls of Barcelona, once dated reflexively to the reign of Gallienus, are now thought to be early fifth century.[92] Even dates that are thought to be quite clear are not: at Gerona, for example, it is confidently stated that ceramic finds beneath the floor of one of the wall's towers show that the wall was built in the last two decades of the third century on Republican foundations. What those ceramics actually show, however, is a much wider window of possibility, roughly 220/230 to 300, while the confident assertion of the more precise date is another fossil of the supposed Frankish invasion.[93]

Zaragoza is a more complex example of the controversies that walls can provoke. There is undoubtedly a great deal of patching to the city's wall, and bits of this are clearly late Roman. For a long time, these visibly late Roman remains were identified as a second city wall, put up in haste because of fear of invasions. Later excavations showed that there was certainly a wall around the city going back to the Augustan era, probably built by the same legionaries who are recorded as constructing the road from the new colony of Zaragoza to Pompaelo, modern Pamplona. Only recently has it become clear that this Augustan wall, formed of a core of *opus caementicium* faced with large granite blocks, is in fact one and the same wall as the supposed late imperial wall.[94] It is just that over the course of four hundred years, a good deal of repair work, rebuilding, and modification became necessary. In some spots, the wall was substantially thickened during the second century, for instance along the 80-meter stretch that survives at San Juan de los Panetes and remains one of the most impressive sights in the city to this day. At other places, however, the Augustan wall remained more or less unchanged throughout the history of the colony.[95]

When all is said and done, only seventeen of the more than forty Spanish city walls that have at one time or another been dated to the third or fourth century can be said with real confidence to do so.[96] That number is nevertheless quite significant in a period when monumental construction had largely ceased. If chronological problems force us to discard the correlation between wall-building and barbarian invasion, we must still ask whether a more generalized social crisis does not account for the construction or the reconstruction of so

The Roman walls of Zaragoza. (K. Salzer)

(*Facing page*) Plan of Zaragoza, showing the Tiberian forum at the intersection of the *cardo maximus* and *decumanus maximus,* the bridge over the Ebro, and the theater. (after Beltrán and Fatás [1998], 21)

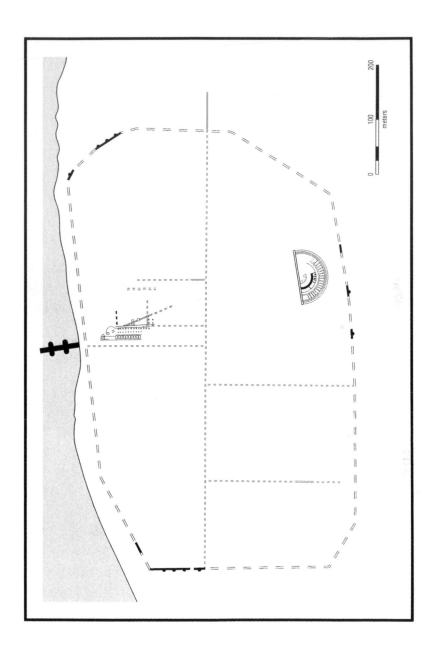

0   100   200
meters

many city walls in late antiquity. One traditional reason for seeing town walls as a reflection of crisis is the supposed signs of haste in their construction. These are always the same—the use of gravestones or spolia from older public monuments in the fabric of new or repaired walls. This evidence is not quite so strong as it might seem. Mausolea and public monuments tended to be made of stronger materials than were private dwellings, while gravestones were ideal building blocks, as they were often carved out of very hard stone. Although we often find these materials reused in city walls, we virtually never know the circumstances in which they became available for reuse. Gravestones are imagined as having been plucked off the carefully tended tomb of a beloved ancestor in a moment of crisis, but they might just as well have come from disused corners of the cemetery that no one could be bothered to weed.[97]

Untended graveyards are hardly unusual in our own world. We should not find it so hard to imagine them in the Roman world as well, and as it happens, we have evidence: in fourth-century Zaragoza, no sign of the first- and second-century cemetery to the north of the city along the bank of the Ebro remained visible. The cemetery had already gone out of use by the third century; many of its standing funerary markers were carried off for use elsewhere, while the memory of the graveyard's existence was lost.[98] At a recently excavated necropolis on the northeast road out of Mérida, a complex that included more than five lavish mausolea of the late first or early second century was dismantled down to its foundations in the third and fourth centuries. All the structural remains of the mausolea, both inscriptions and anepigraphic marble, were then reused haphazardly in the construction of poor-quality fourth-century tombs, more than fifty of which have been discovered within the excavated area.[99] We do not know the circumstances that allowed such despoliation to take place; perhaps the mausolea had belonged to families that no longer existed. Regardless, any discussion of wall-building must bear in mind this very liberal attitude toward the reuse of old materials, and not just gravestones.

Milestones were similarly tractable and it is not at all uncommon to find examples that were turned around and re-engraved on their reverse, or flipped over with the new inscription carved into the newly exposed epigraphic field. Alternatively, bits of the old inscription might be retained while other parts were re-engraved with the name and titulature of a different emperor in a sort of lithic palimpsest.[100] Such processes of reuse had been going on long before the late imperial period, as at Tiermes, where the walls of the early imperial Casa del Acueducto were constructed in part with brick reused from still earlier buildings.[101] Modern scholars see the extant remnants of antiquity as a complete parcel in common need of preservation. To contemporaries, however, they were the material of daily life, every bit as given to obsolescence as our own disposable fabrics. Thus when a piece of stone no longer served a purpose, it was reused, not because people could not afford to use something new, but because there was no need to preserve something old and perfectly serviceable immediately to hand.

The presence of spolia from cemeteries or old monuments is not, in other words, a necessary sign of poverty or haste and if we cannot maintain that late imperial walls were built in a hurry, then it becomes more difficult to view them as a direct response to crisis. What is more, although walls are intrinsically defensive structures, only one Spanish example shows deliberate elaboration of its tactical defenses. One gate in the late antique wall of Gerona was clearly built with an eye to defense. Traditionally called the Porta Rufina, near the modern Plaça de Sant Domingo, this gate involved a complicated approach in the shape of a dog's leg that made it impossible to advance on the gate itself without being exposed to flanking attack on both sides.[102] Elsewhere, the styles of Spanish walls conform to normal late imperial models, with protruding towers, either round or square, spaced fairly close together.[103] The model for such walls was military, but architectural innovations were quickly diffused and the existence of a special "Spanish legionary style" has been disproved. There is certainly no positive evidence for the involvement of military engineers or legionary labor being used in the construction of Spain's late Roman walls, though one cannot rule out the possibility that soldiers stationed in the northwest were employed in the process.[104]

If neither the fabric of the walls nor their design allows for simplistic crisis models, then we must suggest alternative explanations for the upsurge in wall-building from the later third century onward. Better control over commerce between a town and its *territorium* is a plausible alternative explanation, though not one attested explicitly in our evidence.[105] Status competition among cities is both a plausible explanation and one that the evidence can sustain.[106] Indeed, late imperial wall-building might in some cases be an extension of older forms of monumental construction, a city finding that the absence of a town wall might derogate from its prestige, particularly if a more prominent neighbor had one. Walls were something new over which cities could compete. After all, the older public monuments were still there. There was no need to build a second amphitheater, but a city wall offered new opportunity for display available to a new generation. It is easy to forget that by the middle of the third century many generations had passed since the great buildings of the past had been put up. Roman culture reverenced tradition, but it is a natural human instinct to want visible accomplishments of one's own, not merely those of one's parents. Walls could be one such monument, even if in places this meant tearing down older constructions.

As it happens, we have at least one case in which the city wall possessed an aesthetic dimension. The Roman settlement at modern Gijón was housed on the small peninsula that is now the Cimadevilla neighborhood. When the city was given a wall, some time between the late third and the fifth centuries, the whole of the peninsula was enclosed. This new wall was made to a high standard out of well-hewn sandstone blocks, but considerably greater care was put into the construction of the gate that stood astride the neck of the peninsula, and especially to its façade. That is to say, the greatest expenditure of time and money was lavished on the most visible point of the new wall, which suggests that at least some element of public display was involved in the construction of late antique walls.[107]

Another explanation would place the late third-century walls in the context of the Diocletianic reforms, as part of the integration of the Spanish diocese into the wider system of the *annona militaris*.[108] In this view, the walling of cities represents an imperial initiative, aimed at providing secure storage depots for produce and at guarding the routes along which *annona* traveled. This theory gains a certain plausibility if one imagines that walls were too costly for cities to finance out of their own resources, a calculation that has been made for Romano-British walls.[109] Whether this *annona* was destined for the

Rhine, as proponents of the theory suggest, or Tingitania, as is equally plausible, certain problems obtrude. For one thing, there is almost no evidence for the specific Spanish role in the *annona,* though it must have had one.[110] For another, the concentration of Spanish town walls in the north and northwest is problematical, insofar as much of the provincial *annona* would have had to come from southern Lusitania and Baetica, where late imperial walls are scarce.

Despite these reservations, both status competition and the administration of the *annona* are worth considering as alternatives to crisis in the explanation of late imperial walls. If nothing else, wall-building is no sign of urban decay. On the contrary, it demonstrates continued vitality inasmuch as the outlay of cash and manpower required to build a wall was considerable. Even if much of the unskilled labor was extracted from the inhabitants of a *civitas* as a *munus,* the skilled work involved was extensive and costly and the construction of town walls is inconceivable, with or without imperial subsidy, if curias really had become impoverished thanks to a third-century crisis. Town walls, regardless of the practical ends they may also have served, belong to the same world of civic display and construction as the old monuments of the early empire. But they were a new fashion in monumentalism, appropriate to an age that already possessed a full complement of the monuments that had accompanied the early years of romanization.

The Fourth- and Fifth-Century Townscape

The fashion for wall-building bridges the third and fourth centuries in Spain and gives the lie to old models of third-century urban crisis. In the course of the fourth century, however, a substantial gap seems to have opened up between those cities in regular receipt of imperial patronage and those without such benefits. For the most part, the division falls between the new provincial capitals created by the Diocletianic reforms and the peninsula's other cities. While the imperial cities prospered thanks to the presence of the imperial administrators and the wealth they brought with them, and other cities profited from the patterns of late antique trade, most Spanish cities may simply have ticked along in their third-century state, their buildings and streets growing slowly but steadily shabbier. These divergent patterns of urban development are increasingly evident from an archaeological record that can no longer sustain a single, monochromatic picture of decline.

The benefits that an imperial presence could bring to a city are strikingly illustrated in the epigraphy. The most famous examples are the Constantinian inscriptions of Mérida. The city's theater was restored some time between 333 and 335, which was unusual given the general disuse of theaters across the peninsula since the second century. At Mérida, a new *versura* beside the stage was built in the third, or more probably, the fourth century, while fragmentary inscriptions attest to the whole monument's restoration.[111] The slightly later restoration of Mérida's circus is attested in one of the most famous Latin inscriptions from Spain, from between September 337 and April 340. In it, the *comes Hispaniarum* Tiberius Flavius Laetus commands that the circus, which had crumbled through the ravages of the years, be repaired for a new age flowering under the happy rule of the victorious emperors Constantinus, Constans, and Constantius. The direction of the works lies in the hands of the *praeses* of Lusitania, Julius Saturninus, and consists of the reconstruction of columns, the addition of new decorative sculpture, and the addition of decorative waters to the monument, perhaps by means of filling the *euripus* that separated spectators from the arena itself.[112] Two other inscriptions from the circus likewise commemorate the victorious emperor Constantine II. The overall effect was to advertise the glory of the emperor, the power of his officials, and the physical effect that their patronage and protection had upon the city.[113]

How deeply the changes wrought by imperial patronage of Mérida went is difficult to say. The few residential structures known from within the late antique city seem to confirm its vitality, although the modern street plan and modern habitation make it difficult to excavate entire ancient buildings, let alone whole *insulae,* and the evidence of isolated structures in different parts of the city are not easy to synthesize.[114] Although one excavation seems to show severe disrepair within a fourth-century *domus,*[115] most suggest a booming fourth-century city that underwent substantial construction within the contours of the surviving first-century street plan.[116] The so-called Casa-

Basilica, located in the southern part of the city near the theater and amphitheater, was rebuilt according to the fashions of the day, with the patio around the *impluvium* extended and apses appended to the two main rooms off the eastern side of the peristyle's *ambulacrum*. Interestingly, the owner of this particular house seems not to have been particularly wealthy, inasmuch as the rubble-built construction is of a fairly low grade and the floors of the original second-century *domus* were retained wherever possible in the process of remodeling. Despite this, there was a clear attempt to keep up with changing fashions, while the new construction also meant the encroachment on previously public space by the new apses of the *domus,* a phenomenon documented elsewhere in the city.[117]

At a northwestern site very close to the city wall, a porticaded street flanked by more than one *domus* has been partially excavated. Although one of the houses is too badly preserved for any clear conclusions to be possible, the other was rebuilt with a new absidal hall during the fourth century.[118] Indeed, it is not until the latter part of the fifth century that one begins to find evidence for the decay of residential buildings within the walls of Mérida. The *domus* just mentioned, for instance, seems to have gone out of use, and some time between the fifth and the seventh centuries much of the street beside it was taken over with domestic constructions so that only the center of the old city street remained open. By contrast, other residences continued in use during that late period, as, for instance, the lavish *domus* in a porticaded street very near to the *decumanus maximus*, which continued to be occupied not just through the fifth century but even into the seventh.[119]

All the foregoing information comes from scattered excavations around Mérida. The single excavation to have taken place on a larger scale within the city is that of the Morería, a zone that runs for roughly 200 meters along the western wall of the ancient city.[120] Within the 12,000-meter-square excavation are the remains not just of the city walls, but of six Roman *insulae,* two of them known in full. The results from the digs in the Morería seem to confirm patterns of occupation known from the unconnected digs elsewhere in the city.[121] The remains of thirteen *domus* have been discovered, some of them enormously rich. At the so-called *casa de los mármoles,* the fourth-century structure sported its own private baths and a large marble peristyle with exquisite marble latticework between its columns. No full site report has appeared, but from the published remains, it would appear that the fourth century witnessed improvements and renovations not just to this *domus* but throughout this part of the city. Although the whole section of the Roman city uncovered in the Morería digs seems to have suffered very badly during the fifth century, perhaps from one of the many wars of the period, the fourth-century evidence demonstrates not merely the perpetuation of the high imperial infrastructure but rather a far-reaching renovation and improvement to the domestic architecture of the city. This suggests a major influx of new wealth, which must surely be explained by Mérida's promotion to the capital of the Spanish diocese and the consequent presence of a large governmental establishment from the later third century onward.

Other fourth-century cities similarly display the largesse that imperial officials were accustomed to dole out. At Lisbon, for instance, the governor of Lusitania, Numerius Albanus, restored the *thermae Cassiorum* in 336,[122] though only Tarragona, predictably enough, rivals Mérida for the richness of its epigraphic testimony. Under the tetrarchs, Julius Valens dedicated an inscription commemorating the construction of an unidentified *porticus Ioviae*.[123] Soon thereafter, the *ordo Tarraconensium* recorded its gratitude to Constantine for his reconstruction of the city's amphitheater.[124] Later in the century, Marcus Aurelius Vincentius, *vir perfectissimus* and *curator reipublicae,* restored the *thermae montanarum*.[125] Serious doubts have been raised about the substance of inscriptions that record the restoration of buildings *vetustate conlapsas,* inasmuch as the exaggeration of decay gave rhetorical weight to even small repairs by a patron.[126] Septimius Severus's claim to have rebuilt completely the Hadrianic Pantheon is the best-known example of such hyperbole, but there are very early Spanish examples of just such rhetorical exaggeration.[127] With imperial restorations in particular, the ideology of reconstruction is inextricably linked to the emperor's role as protector of the empire and, from the third century in particular, the restorer of lost Roman values. This means that this sort of inscription may not reflect the actual scale of the work it purports to record. Yet even if that is the case, these inscriptions occur in precisely those cities where the emperors and their representatives were most active, that is to say, in those cities that prospered most in the course of the fourth century.

Tarragona had been dominated by its imperial monuments since the first century, and the maintenance of the city's infrastructure may have depended on imperial subsidy from well before the fourth century.[128] The city was physically divided into an imperial sector in the Part Alta and an older colonial sector in the Part Baixa. A tension between the needs of the provincial complex and the colonial center below is not recorded, but the archaeological evidence makes it probable that by the fourth century, if not necessarily before, the imperial part of the town was better maintained than the rest of the city, suggesting greater investment. Indeed, the Part Baixa of Tarragona may have become entirely residential by the middle of the fourth century, with both colonial forum and theater abandoned or built over.[129] The Part Alta, by contrast, retained its older, monumental shape throughout the fourth and much of the fifth century.[130]

Recent excavations in Tarragona have concentrated on the circus and the provincial forum in the Part Alta and have shown that both retained their public character into the fifth century. The circus was never amortized and its *caveae* were not transformed into a residential district until the twelfth century, after the start of the Reconquista, when houses in the interior of the circus began to shape the city blocks that remain to this day. Positive evidence for fourth- and fifth-century use of the circus is lacking, but the monument's careful preservation suggests the continuation of games in it.[131] Moreover, if the circus experienced the same patterns of use and preservation as the provincial forum above it, then it did in fact remain an important public space beyond the late imperial period. For its part, the evidence of the forum is as unambiguous as archaeological evidence can be. The access towers that had led from within the *cavea* of the circus to the southern corners of the forum continued to be the main routes of passage between the Part Alta and the Part Baixa until the third quarter of the fifth century, when one tower was turned into an ash pit that clogged the stairwell entirely.[132]

Other changes away from the old monumental shape of the forum likewise only began to be visible well into the fifth century. Around the year 440, the marble paving stones in at least one part of the forum had been torn up and carted off. We know this because a refuse pit was dug on the site, its formative layers reaching below the level at which the marble paving stones lay.[133] There is no indication of whether this dump was a communal pit for several residences or whether it belonged to a single urban *domus*. Nor, for that matter, can we tell whether this amortization affected the whole forum—in another sector the despoliation of the marble paving stones seems to have come at least thirty years later, while in a third sector the marble slabs that ran along the outside of the precinct wall do not appear to have been removed for reuse until the last quarter of the fifth century.[134] Nevertheless, the reuse of some of the marble flagstones and the formation of the rubbish pit suggest the creation of a residential sector in one part of the forum.[135] By contrast, the northeastern corner of the forum functioned as an outdoor bazaar until the 440s.[136] It is entirely possible, moreover, that the famous inscription to Anthemius and Leo from 472 was originally put up in the provincial forum, in which case at least part of that space retained its old purpose even after the emperors had ceased to pay any regard to Spain whatsoever.[137]

The fact that Tarragona maintained its urban structure until the middle of the fifth century should come as no surprise in an imperial center of such long standing. In other cities, the late antique privileging of imperial over other forms of authority had a transformative rather than a preservative effect. This emerges with great clarity in the palace and administrative complex of Cercadilla in Córdoba, the most important archaeological discovery in Spain for decades.[138] The construction of this vast palace was the catalyst for the gradual evolution of classical Córdoba into a shape it retained throughout the Gothic and early Islamic periods. Córdoba had been an important Roman settlement since the second century B.C., but the Republican city was very small and Caesar destroyed it because of its loyalty to Pompey. The city was remade de novo under Augustus, with an entirely new street grid and new city walls enclosing 78 hectares.[139]

Outfitted with two large fora and the full complement of public buildings, including an intramural amphitheater and the recently discovered theater, the city was supplied with water from a very great dis-

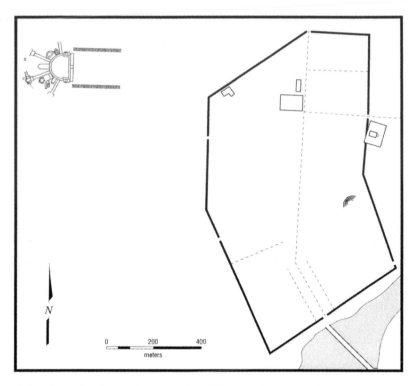

Plan of Córdoba, showing the relationship of the city walls to the Guadalquivir river and to the palace of Cercadilla in the northwest. (after Hidalgo [1996], 16)

tance by the aqueduct of Valdepuentes, so that the waters of the Guadalquivir itself were preserved for irrigation and transport.[140] During the reign of Tiberius the old colonial forum was augmented with a second, dependent forum, while under Claudius and Nero, another large plaza and temple complex was built over and around the eastern gate of the city.[141] This eastern complex extended outward beyond the walls of the city and included a circus in a complex that may have inspired the Flavian reconstruction of Tarragona.[142] Under Domitian a new and very complex aqueduct was built to bring clean mountain water in from the Arroyo Pedroche to the northeast of the city, and the volume of water carried by the city's aqueducts may have sustained as many as fifty thousand inhabitants.[143] Decorated with nearly a hundred different types of marble from all over the Roman world, the monumental fabric of the Flavian city seems to have remained largely unchanged until the end of the third century, when imperial intervention decisively altered the course of its development.

In the last decade of the third century, a large administrative complex—now known as the palace of Cercadilla—was constructed just outside the walls of the city, roughly 500 meters from the northwest corner of the city wall and somewhat further from the nearest gate.[144] This new palace rivaled the city itself for its splendor and importance and was large enough to require the expropriation and destruction of actively occupied suburban dwellings.[145] The ground of the site sloped naturally southward toward the banks of the Guadalquivir, and to build a monument on such a scale required not just the terraplaning of the site, but a good deal of earth-moving to create a flat terrace on which to build. The end result, however, had the desired effect of both scale and power. If one approached the city from the west, the new palace lay off to the left of the main road in a massive hulk dominating the skyline beyond the circus.[146]

The complex could not be entered from the west, but had to be approached from a single point coming away from the city to the east. One walked down a long plaza, lined on both sides by low rows of barracks, before reaching a rectangular hall, flanked on each side by looming towers. This was the only way into the monument and, on passing through, the visitor was faced with a semicircular garden through which he had to pass even to begin approaching the functional sections of the complex. The semicircle was formed by a cryptoportico, the ends of which were sealed off by the main entry hall. The cryptoportico itself rose a meter or so above the level of the garden, and articulated the symmetry of the space to the visitor.[147] Within it lay subterranean workshops, but these the visitor never saw. Instead, he was surrounded by an arcaded walkway, off which there was a hemisphere of doorways leading into a whole array of buildings at whose function he might only guess. Crossing the garden, up the short flight of stairs, he might be admitted into the large basilica that

(*Facing page*) Detail plan of the palace of Cercadilla. (after Hidalgo [1996], 21)

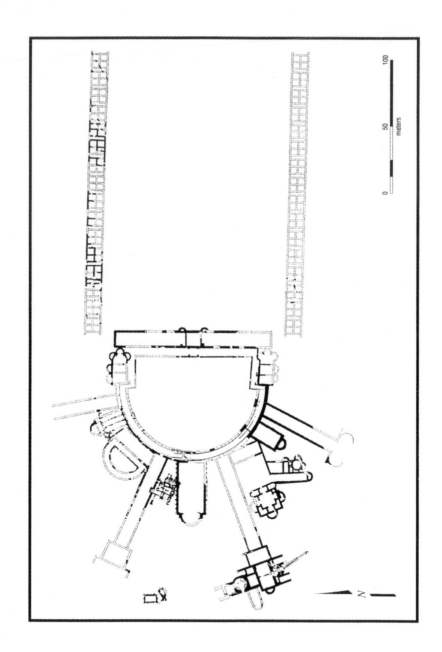

meters

0   50   100

stretched back from the exact center of the semicircle's circumference. Or, if business was less formal or less important, he might be led down to the right or left along the arcade, into one of the other, smaller basilicas that lay at symmetrical points of the compass in both directions. Other buildings, too, the purpose of which is less clear, were also arrayed off the portico, but not all of them were accessible from it. The contrast between different levels of public and private space would have been strikingly clear. Behind the first array of buildings lay others, some private quarters, others baths, others rooms whose function we cannot identify. Some were reached along corridors, running like spokes off a wheel from the portico. Others could be reached only after passing through several different spaces; thus off to the north of the great central basilica lay a small, private bath complex, to which the most important of guests might be admitted along with the chief resident.

The decoration and the amenities of the Cercadilla were no doubt the best that the age had to offer, and some of them may well have come from the site of the disused theater of the *colonia*.[148] However, centuries of use as a quarry after the sixth century, not least for the great caliphal palace at Medinat al-Zahra, have made it all but impossible for us to reconstruct this. It is unclear just how far beyond the arcaded portico the various structures to which it gave unity extended. What is certain, however, is that these structures could not otherwise be reached from outside. Cercadilla as a whole was turned inward, and offered to the outside world a blank, brick face, no doubt all the more imposing for its impenetrability. One could enter through only one passage, flanked by impressive testimony to military might, and after that one's progress was checked at every turn, not just by the scale, but by the articulation of the site as well.[149]

The question of whom this was all for is a vexed one. The monument's excavator believes Cercadilla to be the palace of Maximian, built at Córdoba as a residence from which the Augustus could conduct his African campaigns of the 290s, and architecturally comparable to Diocletian's palace at Split or Galerius's at Gamzigrad.[150] Unfortunately, however, Maximian's residency in the peninsula is unattested, and we know enough of his itinerary for any substantial missing period to be unlikely.[151] It is more likely that the new palace was indeed an imperial project, but that it was constructed as a residence for the governor of the new tetrarchic province of Baetica.[152] Only imperial impetus can account for the destruction that the complex was allowed to cause to the environs of the city, particularly the diversion of one of the city's aqueducts to supply the new palace. No fourth-century *privatus* could have achieved that feat, and the creation of Cercadilla is entirely in keeping with the enormously expanded role of the emperor in the later empire. The palace outlined for all to see the status of the emperor and his government in the new tetrarchic dispensation. No longer within the city, the emperor's representative in Baetica occupied a symbolic if not literal fortress outside it, a little city all his own, to which those who sought the emperor's patronage must betake themselves.

Throughout the whole of the fourth and at least the first half of the fifth century, the palace at Cercadilla was an active administrative monument, undergoing occasional repair, but never anything to suggest its abandonment as the heart of imperial government on the ground. Its most central architectural element, the great cryptoportico that articulated the whole vast space, was repaired at the start of the fifth century after the foundations had been somewhat damaged by subsidence. Although this repair was made with much poorer quality materials, its design deliberately imitated the tetrarchic fabric of the building.[153] This maintenance of the great palace at Cercadilla meant the sustenance of its social role as a psychological presence that hovered on the outskirts of the urban world, overshadowing the old city's own importance.

For this reason, Cercadilla caused severe changes to the infrastructure of the old city. Third-century Córdoba had been a thriving city, many buildings of the period have been discovered, and some would see it as having been gripped by a building boom.[154] The demand for architectonic materials was at any rate large enough for a new atelier of capital-sculptors to spring up.[155] But the decades after the construction of Cercadilla brought massive changes to this picture. High imperial Córdoba had been ordered as a dense network of buildings separated by roughly equidistant public spaces along the line of the *cardo maximus,* which ran north, after a slight dog's leg, from the southern gate of the city on the banks of the Guadalquivir. The northernmost of these fora was the oldest in the city, built in the Augustan period on the site of the Republican forum. Further south, near the monumental zone of the theater and amphitheater, lay another forum and, at the highest point within the walls, lay another plaza often called the provincial forum because of the number of togate statues found there, probably representing provincial priests.[156] This southern forum had already undergone substantial changes in the third century, though whether these represent the construction of a new public temple or a new private *domus* is a matter of dispute.[157] It is clear, however, that in the latter part of the fourth century, this forum ceased to be used in any official capacity, probably being converted into one or more private houses, as were the various plazas that surrounded the theater.[158]

The plaza and temple around the city's eastern gate were likewise built over by residences. The eastern circus had gone out of use by the end of the second century.[159] Thereafter, the great Neronian temple on the calle Claudio Marcelo was dismantled, and the whole of its podium was rebuilt as an urban *domus,* so that only the colonial forum at the northern end of the main *cardo* remained in active use, now serving as the space in which imperial dedications were chiefly displayed. On a less grand scale, some of the *decumani minores* near the provincial forum were covered over with low-grade housing in the fourth century.[160] Though public buildings continued to be maintained and restored, the city's population began to cluster closer to the river, perhaps because of the reduction in the amount of water available from the main aqueducts after the creation of Cercadilla.[161] All these changes altered the spatial layout of the city to some degree, and some, like the dismantling of the great temple, would have had a substantial effect on its visible outline. The concentration of urban life nearer the river accelerated dramatically in the post-Roman period, when the cathedral and the Gothic ducal residence both lay astride the old *cardo maximus* at the southern end of the city, where, in due course, the great mosque of Córdoba would replace them. Regardless, it seems certain that the main catalyst for these fundamental changes to the townscape was the creation of the new imperial space on the outskirts of the city.

Mérida, Tarragona, and Córdoba all attest to the impact that imperial government had on Spanish cities in late antiquity, and parallel evidence almost certainly awaits discovery at the peninsula's other provincial capitals, Braga and Cartagena.[162] Barcelona, briefly the residence of a usurping emperor at the start of the fifth century, seems to have undergone major construction at precisely that time.[163] Other cities, mainly those with important commercial functions, prospered during late antiquity without any visible signs of imperial patronage. Portus Illicitanus, modern Santa Pola on the Mediterranean coast of Alicante province, is a good example. Here, the growth of African imports to the eastern coast of Spain from the third century onward appears to have led to a late antique building boom. Remains of several *domus* decorated with mosaics are known, one of them probably built during the Constantinian era, and several warehouses have also been excavated.[164] The island of Tabarca immediately off Portus Illicitanus may have served as the town's deep water harbor, with goods being transhipped there and brought to the mainland in shallow-draft vessels; there was certainly an important *garum* industry there during the third and fourth centuries.[165]

Both the port and its mother town, Illici, seem to have done well into the fifth century.[166] But at the Portus, there are no positively documented signs of habitation after the later fifth century, which may suggest that the site was largely abandoned. If so, the cause is likely to have been the silting up of the port, as the modern shoreline is now 500 meters from where it stood in the Roman period. Another local site may have taken the place of Portus Illicitanus in the regional supply network, as there are clear signs of fifth- and sixth-century commercial buildings and extensive remains of imported goods a short way up the coast at modern Benalúa.[167] Until the later fifth century, however, Portus Illicitanus was a major coastal center and a prosperous one, and we should not find it at all surprising that it was chosen by Majorian as the naval staging point for his Vandal expedition.[168]

Other sites on the eastern coast display similar prosperity. Recent excavations in the port of ancient Sagunto, the modern Grau Vell, have unearthed a great deal of late imperial evidence. These include not just the usual ceramics, which are found at most sites on the east coast and attest to the intensity of trade with Africa between the third and sixth centuries, but also the remains of a late imperial tower, domestic constructions of various sorts, and the remains of a Constantinian-era mural that decorated one of their walls.[169] Underwater prospecting, moreover, has confirmed the vast quantity of imported material that passed through the port, which begins to decrease dramatically only after the 450s.[170] Other sites on the east coast show parallel developments, not least Barcelona, which experienced major building works in different parts of the city during the fourth century. These involved the appropriation of quite a lot of formerly public space, and the edges of many streets were built over with residential or perhaps commercial buildings. All this construction was not a reaction against earlier crisis or urban decline. Instead, the almost total absence of disused or destroyed building materials on sites with new fourth-century construction suggests that preexisting structures were carefully dismantled and their salvageable materials put into service in the new buildings.[171]

Port cities along the eastern coast were not the only places to benefit from late antique commerce. The position of Mértola, the ancient Myrtilis, on the river Guadiana allowed it to serve as the port of the *conventus* capital at Pax Iulia, modern Beja. Thanks to this role as an entrepôt for imported goods, Mértola's importance grew during the later empire. A luxurious bath complex was built over part of the old forum, perhaps in the later third century, and the city was walled at around the same time. Towering as it does over the Guadiana, Mértola was already an easily defensible site, which suggests that the new wall was meant to reflect the city's prestige as one of the chief ports of Lusitania. Excavation has not been extensive enough to determine how long the city retained its late imperial aspect, but its commercial role lasted into the fifth and sixth centuries, by which point the old forum and baths had been converted into a Christian basilica and baptistery.[172]

Similarly prosperous sites existed along the northern coast, a region only starting to be understood archaeologically.[173] Gijón is the only city in which substantial archaeological evidence has been uncovered, and the site was clearly very prosperous, maintaining an active *garum* industry until at least the end of the fifth century, when the city's natural markets up the Atlantic coast of Gaul had ceased to consume the product on any substantial scale.[174] In the meantime, however, Gijón imported products from all over the empire right into the middle of the sixth century, not just from the Atlantic coast of Gaul, which one would expect, but also from North Africa and the eastern Mediterranean, particularly the region of Antioch.[175] This prosperity may have been a consequence of the tetrarchic reforms. In the third century, the coast of Asturias and Cantabria was already linked to the Mesetan interior by good roads that allowed the shipment of interior products to the coast and thence to the Atlantic trade; after Diocletian, the Spanish north and west may have become important to the supply networks of the *annona,* which brought with them the collateral trade visible in the archaeological record.[176]

Cities like Barcelona, Mértola, and Gijón all owed their fortune to trade, whether linked to imperial patronage or not. A late antique city that prospered for reasons that escape us entirely is Complutum, modern Alcalá de Henares, neither an economic nor an administrative center so far as we know. Complutum nevertheless underwent a renaissance of real significance in the fourth century. On the one hand, many private houses were decorated with the best mosaics fourth- and early fifth-century central Spain could provide.[177] On the other hand, heavy investment was made in the city's central public complex. Complutum was a relatively young city, in that its indigenous and Republican predecessor had been located on the Cerro del Viso, a defensible hilltop across the river Henares and some distance from the high imperial city, which stretched out along the alluvial floodplain where the small Camarmilla meets the Henares. This high imperial site was only occupied and built up during the Neronian or Flavian period, probably in connection with the elevation of the city from stipendiary to municipal status.

As was quite normal, the first-century city had its forum at the intersection of the chief *cardo* and *decumanus*. The eastern side of the forum lay along the *cardo* and the southern end was closed off with shops, but on the western side stood an *insula* that, most unusually, housed both the judicial basilica and a substantial bath complex, which shared a single structural wall though they did not communicate with one another. This western complex housed the administrative heart of the city and it was much improved in the very late third or, perhaps more probably, the early fourth century.[178] The basilica was rebuilt in heavy *opus caementicium* with a facing of marble and its columns may have been re-embellished as well, while the bath complex was amortized and turned into an annex of the basilica. Its three main chambers were converted into long halls on the same plan as before and the old *caldarium* retained its hypocaust flooring in a state of full repair. From the outside, this newly marble-clad and impressively decorated building presented a closed face along at least two sides, though it could be entered from its northern side off the *decumanus maximus*. All of this remodeling was commemorated with a grandiose inscription, now very fragmentary, along the lines of those which we have already seen in the imperial inscriptions at Mérida: buildings that had fallen into ruin were restored *per aevum*.[179] This grand gesture on the part of the curia of Complutum was thus phrased in the fashionable rhetoric of its age, but the whole project reflects a city with a great deal of money to spend on the expensive reform of its monumental and institutional center.

Cities like Complutum may well have been exceptional.[180] Without the restorative power of imperial patronage and without any special commercial position, many peninsular cities, even formerly prosperous ones, suffered real difficulties in the fourth century.[181] The clearest case is that of Zaragoza, one of Roman Spain's great cities and a vitally important strategic point at the best ford on the middle Ebro. Built by Augustus after the end of the Cantabrian wars, Zaragoza was from the start planned on a grand scale, with open spaces left among the *insulae* for the construction of spectacular monuments, and the centuriation structured in such a way that the *cardo maximus* of the city was precisely aligned with the bridge over the Ebro. The Augustan plan was completed under Tiberius at the same time as a new and grander forum was put up to replace the Augustan original.[182] At the southern end of this forum, beside the great Tiberian temple, lay a public building that probably housed the city's *curia;* if so, the large size of the structure, 25 by 16 meters, suggests a substantial curial body.[183] The city was intimately linked to the Julio-Claudian dynasty, so much so that Germanicus held the duumvirate in the colony. However, unlike so many of the larger Spanish cities, Zaragoza seems not to have undergone any major rebuilding under the Flavians; it was after all already a very grand city. For whatever reason—perhaps the closeness of its association with a defunct dynasty in the Flavian, Trajanic, and Hadrianic decades, during which other Spanish cities had very strong claims to imperial patronage—the Augustan grandeur of Zaragoza seems not to have been repeatedly renewed.

What accounts for this failure we are unlikely ever to know: the epigraphy of Zaragoza, which might tell us, is very poor by the standards of high imperial Spain. It was certainly not the result of any real economic crisis, since the second-century city thrived as a manufacturing center and until the fifth century it remained the point from which imported goods, particularly ceramics from Narbonensis and Africa, were distributed to the whole Ebro valley. Regardless of the reasons, however, the third century saw a general decline in the city's urban fabric. Although its basic shape remained unchanged and its public spaces continued to be used, certain measures vital for the quality of life in a Roman city seem gradually to have faded away. The sewerage system, in particular, suffered. A product of the Tiberian period, it relied upon a constant flow of water and the pull of gravity to carry runoff water and waste products out of the city and into the Ebro. But as with every Roman sewage system, Zaragoza's was liable to become blocked without constant attention. It is clear that it did not receive this, because during the third century, a few parts of the city's sanitary system had silted up, and by the end of the fourth century, the main sewers under and around the forum had done so as well.[184] Without waste being systematically flushed out of the city's commercial and institutional heart, the order and relative cleanliness of the classical Roman city would have been less apparent.

This is not to say that the public life of Zaragoza necessarily suffered. The commercial life of the forum lived on into the sixth century and its Tiberian fabric was maintained until the middle of the fifth. In the fourth century, moreover, there is positive proof of the forum's having retained the symbolic aspects of its institutional life. That is to say, it continued to be the heart of the city's public life, the place in which the curia met and regulated the life of the city. We may be sure of this because of the discovery of a statue of a fourth-century *conscriptus* on the site of the forum.[185] The togate statue was originally sculpted in the first century, but was reworked in the fourth to accord with the new aesthetics of the day—the sharp relief was smoothed and the contours of the body were softened. The statue is lacking its head but one imagines that one of the smooth and inexpressive faces that represent the fourth-century ideal sat atop it. Whoever this man was, he and his fellow *curiales* continued to meet in the Tiberian curial building, which demonstrates that the loss of certain amenities—in this case the sewage system—did not mean the end of the city's Roman institutional life. We have already seen evidence for the continued health of the city's public life in the conversion of the theater into an arena during the fourth century, when a layer of sand was laid in the monument, filling in the orchestra and the first two rows of the *ima cavea*.[186] Nevertheless, the example of Zaragoza suggests that without imperial patronage, a city's monumental life was liable to grow increasingly tatty as the fourth century progressed.

Zaragoza is a particularly striking case because of its size and importance. Smaller cities experienced similar fates. In the Castilian Meseta, Tiermes had been an important center of romanization together with Clunia and Uxama. Like Uxama, Tiermes was walled at some point after the mid-third century, but no other monumental construction can be detected there.[187] This absence of monumental construction does not necessarily mean a decline in population, however, as a stretch of ground near the city wall was rebuilt, to unknown purpose, some time in the third or fourth century.[188] The one private building in the city to have been excavated in its entirety, the so-called Casa del Acueducto, had a long late antique phase. The original *domus* was very large, put up in the mid-first century and remodeled some time in the next. The architects of this house created a hybrid of indigenous rupestrian architecture and the new Italian models then entering the Meseta, especially via the *conventus* capital at Clunia. Because the whole city of Tiermes lay on very uneven ground, the *domus* had to be built on different levels to accommodate the slope, and parts of it were cut into the soft sandstone of the site in the native fashion. This survival of indigenous rupestrian techniques is known from other cities in the Meseta, the similarly hilly town of Valeria in particular.[189] Unlike the houses of Valeria, however, the Casa del Acueducto at Tiermes would have looked just like an Italian urban *domus* from the exterior, both in the substance of its walls and in the shape of the structure as a whole. Its interior was somewhat irregular, loosely ordered around two *atria,* each with its own *impluvium,* and contained nearly thirty rooms in total, many of them decorated with wall paintings.

Centuries of plowing have destroyed the stratigraphy of the site, with the result that precise dates are impossible to come by. The material remains do, however, suggest a very intense occupation during late antiquity, with large quantities of imported *terra sigillata* the best indication of this. On the other hand, this habitation may have taken the form of a subdivision of the old *domus* into at least two separate buildings, sealed off from each other by new walls built into what had once been internal passages.[190] Because of the absence of stratigraphy, the excavators were unable to establish either the date or the sequence of these changes, but the evidence from Tiermes is important in two major respects. First, it demonstrates the simple fact that people went on living in even rather minor cities during late antiquity, a point worth observing given that the Meseta is often taken to be one of the most extreme examples of late antique ruralization in Spain. Second, the quantities of ceramics found in the Casa del Acueducto demonstrate that a change in the usage of a building—even a change that subdivided the interior plan of a grand *domus* that had once occupied an entire *insula* of a smallish town—does not necessarily mean economic decline. Even allowing for the fact that luxury and semi-luxury goods were more readily accessible in the later empire, the ceramics of the Casa del Acueducto are still important testimony to the attractions of a life lived in towns to late antique Spaniards.[191]

Zaragoza and Tiermes are useful illustrations that may well be more typical than is yet realized.[192] The first was a product of the Roman revolution, the second, like so many others, part of the phase of explosive romanization that created substantial towns across the whole peninsula during the first and second centuries. But, like the majority of Spanish cities, neither Zaragoza nor Tiermes benefited from continuous external patronage on a large scale. As a result, both continued to exist in more or less their early imperial shape throughout late antiquity, though gradually growing shabbier to the eye. In both cases, there can be little doubt that the urban infrastructure declined from what it had once been.

However, the unquestionable fact of physical decay during the fourth century is quite separate from the question of a larger decline of urbanism. Neither Zaragoza nor Tiermes provides any evidence for a decline of urban population, while at Zaragoza there is positive physical evidence for the continuation of the institutional life of the Roman city. Little Munigua tells a parallel story. Its monuments largely gone, the city grew in size during late antiquity.[193] These examples of physically decaying townscapes in the fourth century are probably the norm, though only a great deal more excavation will provide confirmation. The countless older site reports that found evidence of physical decay and monumental disuse in cities across the Spanish interior are probably not wholly in error; but it seems likely that the reflexive assigning of such evidence to the third century will have to be revised and that the fourth, not the third century, will prove to have been decisive in the running down of the urban infrastructure.[194]

We have been looking at the broad continuities of Spanish urbanism between the second and the fourth centuries, and the changes caused by the restructuring of imperial administration and consequent shifts in relative power during the fourth century. How these processes affected the demography of the Spanish provinces is an obvious question that allows for no easy answers. As we will see in the following chapter, the rural population does seem to have expanded during the third century, but we have almost no way of determining the absolute size of either classical or late antique urban populations. Some have tried to extrapolate population size from the capacity of spectacular monuments—on this reckoning, Cartagena would have had as many as thirty thousand inhabitants during the early empire, a figure that seems too large.[195] Another approach attempts to work out formulas for the size of an urban population on the basis of the surface area enclosed by town walls. On this model, Zaragoza would have had as many as six thousand inhabitants, Gerona perhaps two thousand, but these figures are approximate at best and fail to take into account the fact that rapid urban growth often led to very populous extramural suburbs. One such suburb is attested at Gerona, for instance, near the necropolis of Mercadal across the river Onyar from the city.

Population figures based on the size of cemeteries is likewise ambiguous. On the one hand, we know of many more third-century cemeteries than we do first- and second-century ones; in many places, new cemeteries came into use in the third century and went on to enjoy long periods of use, often over several hundred years.[196] At first glance, this would appear to be evidence for a growth in population, but as always, there are interpretative problems. For one thing, the third century witnessed a slow change in mortuary practice from cremation, with subsequent deposition of the ashes in cinerary urns, to inhumation. Inhumation cemeteries are much easier to detect than are the older cremation cemeteries, a fact that has almost certainly distorted our sample. Yet without a firm statistical basis on which to judge earlier funerary demography, it must remain possible that the new third-century cemeteries were simply the way in which a fairly constant population dealt with the exhaustion of useable space in existing mortuary areas. In other words, neither the absolute nor the relative size of urban populations in late antique Spain is at all clear to us. Until more reliable ways of measuring ancient populations are discovered, and in the absence of the sort of documentary evidence that exists in Egypt, we have to base our historical understanding of change in Spanish cities not on demography but rather on the patterns of changing use in the townscape. In the countryside, by contrast, patterns of settlement distribution may in fact allow us to speculate about demographic change, and to the Spanish countryside we now turn.

Six

Town and Country

In some ways, the rural environment of Roman Spain is more accessible to us than is the urban, because continuous habitation has rarely obscured rural remains in the way modern cities sit atop their Roman forebears. To be sure, the study of rural sites is complicated by the shortcomings of older site reports and by the reflexive dating of signs of destruction to the supposed invasions of 260–270.[1] Nevertheless, as more and more excavations and surveys are conducted by modern methods, it has become possible to move beyond the old historiographic paradigm in which third-century urban decline produces a massive shift in power and wealth to the countryside, which culminates in a brilliant fourth-century villa culture.[2] Spanish villas lie at the center of this model of *ruralización:* because so many luxurious late antique villas appear to have been built on virgin ground, they must necessarily represent the flight of elite population from the city to new country retreats. This approach rests on both a simplistic zero-sum model, in which any growth in the countryside must necessarily be matched by an equivalent decline in the towns, and on old and unreliable excavations, the results of which are slowly being superseded.

Perhaps the most important discovery of the past two decades has been that many Spanish villas, including those dated to the fourth century in the standard corpora, were actually first built in the third century or earlier.[3] These findings challenge old chronologies of population shift from city to country, but even without the introduction of this new evidence, the systematic analysis of the old, flawed sample has produced striking results. It suggests that the rise in the number of third-century rural sites represents not a shift of population from an urban locus to a rural one, but rather a more systematic use of available land than in earlier centuries. Probably as a result of population growth, settlement extended into areas that had hitherto been uninhabited. Population always remained densest where land was most fertile, but the steady occupation of marginal sites meant that far more land was in active use by the start of the fourth century than had been the case in the early empire. This interpretation derives from a pioneering spatial analysis of just one Spanish region, Extremadura, but other local surveys have subsequently reached the same conclusions.[4] In regions like the Guadalquivir delta, moreover, similar methods have documented a continuous and intensive exploitation between the first and fifth centuries.[5] It would thus seem that third- and fourth-century Spain had a far larger rural population than ever before, spread over not just the best land, but also land of very indifferent quality.

The revolutionary potential of modern techniques has been demonstrated by the extensive surface survey of a single microregion, the *ager Tarraconensis*.[6] A series of evenly spaced transects, 5 kilometers in length, has provided a more complete picture of rural settlement within the *territorium* of a single city than can regional spatial analyses conducted on the basis of published reports. The approach revealed many unsuspected results, for instance, a broad absence of settlement in the immediate extramural area, suggesting a zone exploited directly from the city. High-status rural residences were concentrated nearer to the city itself. The further one moved from the city, the fewer wealthy sites existed and population as a whole became sparser the closer one got to the prelittoral mountain chain. Indeed, rural settlement was at its densest in a ring around the city beyond the zone that was cultivated from the town itself. The economics of the microregion are also revealing; the further one moved from the city, the fewer imported ceramics were likely to be available, and this pattern of distribution grows more and more pronounced as the late imperial period progresses. Tarragona, as the directors of the survey recognize, is not the most representative city in Spain, and it is unclear how many of the survey's results can be extrapolated to the rest of the peninsula. No comparable study of the economic relationship between a city and its hinterland is available, and none would be possible without a similarly rigorous survey. On the other hand, the pattern of rural habitation revealed by the *ager Tarraconensis* survey does seem to be consonant with that which is known in less detail from elsewhere.[7]

Everywhere that research on the subject has been conducted, it would appear that rural population clustered predominantly around towns, and that where it did not, it lay along road or river routes that allowed rapid communication with the nearest urban center. A survey of the so-called Siberia Extremeña, a part of eastern Badajoz province largely unpopulated in the present day, uncovered extensive remains of Roman-era population, both high- and low-status, concentrated around cities, to be sure, but really reaching out wherever there were roads or rivers.[8] A similar pattern characterizes the corridor of cities running north from Mérida into Gallaecia and such proverbially unromanized sections of the peninsula as Asturias and Cantabria.[9] In other words, even in the most backward regions, the close link between city and *territorium* was maintained into the later empire, and the same relative distribution of rural population can be observed as in far more urbanized parts of the peninsula. What is more, rural sites appear to have prospered at the same time as their local city; the villa of Rabaçal in Portugal, with its spectacular octagonal peristyle, flourished in precisely the period that the nearby city of Conimbriga was experiencing a building boom under the tetrarchy, while the explosive growth of luxurious villas around fourth-century Mérida tells the same story.[10]

Unfortunately, both old and new interpretations of rural development are affected by a real evidentiary problem: third-century rural sites, which tended to be built of stone and on a large scale, are much easier to detect than early imperial sites, generally built of more perishable materials. Whereas older publications of villas frequently document only remains of the third century and later, modern excavations regularly discover that third- and fourth-century villas were actually built on top of early imperial settlements, the traces of which are much less easy to detect.[11] Examples of this phenomenon are now so widespread that we may be sure many villas hitherto regarded as new foundations of the third century have early imperial ancestors that escaped detection when they were first excavated.[12] If this is in fact the case, and rural habitation was more widespread in the early empire than we have realized, Hispano-Roman rural history will require far more extensive revision than the evidence presently allows.

Within the confines of the present evidence, however, it seems likely that the third and fourth centuries witnessed a steady growth in rural population, perhaps a reflection of a very general prosperity. To what extent this phenomenon revised the map of the early imperial countryside must remain in doubt, but no such doubt attends the growing expenditure of wealth in the countryside from the third century onward. The rural villa, built on the common Mediterranean peristyle plan, decked out in marble and mosaics, and loaded with statues and tapestries, had by the later third century ceased to be the preserve of the super rich and instead become a very widespread comfort of the Hispano-Roman elite. Hundreds of third- and fourth-century villas are preserved at least in part, built in every possible terrain and each one fancier than the next.[13] The world of the Hispano-Roman villa is best illustrated not by exhaustive cataloguing but rather by representative examples from among sites that have been both extensively excavated and thoroughly published.

The World of the Villa

Perhaps the most striking thing about Spain's late antique villas is their sheer scale, as illustrated by the three consecutive villas built on the Lusitanian site of São Cucufate in the *conventus Pacensis,* not far from Beja in modern Portugal.[14] São Cucufate lies at the border between the Portuguese regions of the Alto and Baixo Alentejo and suffers from soaking winters, scorching summers, and granitic soil that makes cereoculture possible only with the aid of irrigation. Vine and olive can prosper, but the whole region was very much underutilized during the early Roman period. At São Cucufate this fact is reflected in the simplicity of the original first-century structure, probably little more than a farmhouse from which the vineyards round about could be super-

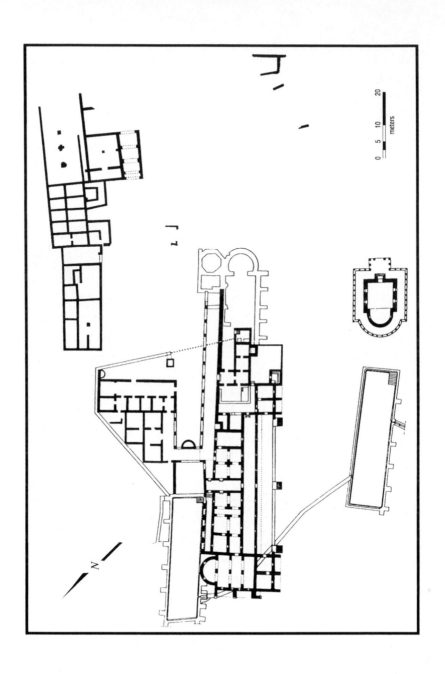

meters
0 5 10   20

Vaults of São Cucufate. (K. Salzer)

vised. In the second century, this structure was taken down and a new peristyle villa built over it with a large attached bath complex and a series of industrial dependencies. This villa was destroyed, perhaps by fire, at the start of the fourth century, and parts of it were sealed in beneath a layer of cinders. In the middle of the fourth century, these ruins were built over again, this time on the grand scale still visible today.

The excavators have characterized the designer of this third villa as an architectural genius and one cannot disagree with them.[15] Whereas both the earlier villas had accommodated themselves to the undulations of the rough terrain, the new villa was designed to dominate that terrain. It incorporated parts of the old second villa for structural support, but whereas the second-century residence had centered on a peristyle, the new fourth-century structure was a long, tall aulic villa. The western façade was flanked by two arched dependencies, per-

(*Facing page*) Plan of the villa complex at São Cucufate, showing the north and south cisterns, the main aulic villa, and the small temple. (after Alarção [1998], 29)

pendicular to the length of the main hall, while the entrance to the whole structure lay in the middle of the long façade. To reach it, the visitor had to ascend a massive podium running along the façade that had been built to emphasize the structure's careless disregard for the surrounding topography.

The eastern façade posed greater challenges to the fourth-century architect, since more of the second-century remains had to be accommodated there. The old baths were rebuilt with modifications and a latrine with twelve private compartments was put up. The hydraulics of this were particularly complex, as they had to maintain constant and separate flow of clean water both to supply the baths and to evacuate the toilets, a task made more difficult by the long droughts typical of the region. A large rectangular reservoir was built alongside the eastern façade to achieve this practical end, but was placed to simultaneously serve the aesthetic function of reflecting light up at the villa's eastern façade. Sunlight shimmering on the water emphasized the great length of the building and its rectilinear dominance over the rolling ground. A second reservoir lay several meters down the slope from the main, western façade and near it a small temple was built, probably on the remains of a much smaller second-century shrine. The villa itself was on two levels which between them offered more than 800 square meters of living space, a scale almost unknown elsewhere in Lusitania. This sort of display stressed the power of the villa owners to control the natural limitations of the site on which they had built.

Aesthetics, that is to say, had a social and ideological function as an advertisement of dominance. This was true not just of São Cucufate but of late Roman villas more generally. Rather than merely a place to live or work, the Roman villa was also an ideological expression of the society that created it. Villa design reflected the behavioral patterns that residents were supposed to display while dwelling in these places. The habit of display so central to Roman culture became more commonplace in late antiquity because, more so than in earlier periods, the appearance of luxury could be simulated by those unable to afford the real thing.[16] The display of luxury goods was an intrinsic part of domestic culture. In the villa environment, decoration underscored the ideological message of the villa itself, marking off public from private and creating a hierarchy of prestige among different rooms and sections of the house. Access to different areas within the villa was thus another way in which the status relationships of Hispano-Romans were visualized and enacted.

A particularly important site for illustrating the way in which late antique *domini* lived on their country estates is that of El Ruedo, at Almedinilla in the modern province of Córdoba.[17] Though the site has suffered from the vicissitudes of local politics, it was subject to a rigorous initial investigation.[18] This found much of its decorative schema *in situ* and its ongoing publication, though scattered, allows unparalleled insight into the residential environment of a fourth-century landowner. The villa at El Ruedo had a long history, but it was never one of the peninsula's most lavish sites. It is all the more revealing for that fact, as we can glimpse at El Ruedo an important late antique phenomenon often remarked outside the Spanish context—the filtering of generalized canons of elite taste down from the social strata of the senatorial aristocracy to an affluent, status-conscious, but by no means extraordinarily wealthy stratum of society.[19] In the late empire, even those who could not afford to ensconce themselves exclusively in gold and marble could and did manage to imitate the decorative mannerisms of those who could, and this is precisely what we find at El Ruedo.

During antiquity, the site fell within the territory of the town of Illiturgicola, a *municipium* of some importance in the hills of the Subbaetican cordillera southeast of Córdoba, from which we possess an ample epigraphic dossier.[20] The villa lies on a slight elevation overlooking the small river Almedinilla, a tributary of the larger Guadajoz, which itself flows eventually into the Guadalquivir. Well-supplied with water for agriculture and fishing and situated where it could catch every passing breeze in the intense Andalusian heat, the site perfectly fulfilled the classical criteria for a country residence. The deliberate planting of trees, documented around the residential structures, would have added both climatic and aesthetic comforts to the site. The villa was designed as a squarish block around a porticaded peristyle and is one of the earliest such designs known from Spain. The first phase of construction was probably late Julio-Claudian, but we can be sure that it received its definitive plan in the early second century, when the original patio was rebuilt as a peristyle and the residential area was extended to cover a full 1,350 square meters. Thereafter, successive *domini* remodeled their predecessors' works and a particularly major reconstruction can be dated to very near the year 300. Like earlier remodelings, this one left most of the structure of the old plan standing, thereby fossilizing several generations in the life of the building and making El Ruedo a good illustration of the way in which villas changed and grew over the years.

In the second-century plan, retained more or less unchanged until the end of the fifth century, the main entrance to the *domus* faced south and gave onto a *vestibulum,* or perhaps an atrium. A service entrance large enough to receive carts lay in the southwest corner of the block where it could not be seen from the main approach, and a third entrance may have given onto the private rooms to the east.[21] The villa block thus presented an imposing façade through which visitors, whether local *rustici* or more important guests, were all channeled through the entrance appropriate to their status. One imagines that few visitors got much further than the *vestibulum,* or the two *cubiculi* that flanked the corridor beyond it, from which one was afforded no glimpse of the life within—a snatch of peristyle down the corridor, but nothing beyond it.[22] Both the slight upward gradient of the house's interior and the placement of doorways off the main vertical axis of the building meant that no lines of sight penetrated from public areas to the private rooms in which the family of the *dominus* lived.

More prominent visitors entered this very different world by passing down the short corridor into the peristyle. There appears to have been no decoration to speak of in the public areas to the south of the peristyle, but the peristyle itself was lavish, 75 meters square and formed from as many as twelve columns of local sandstone.[23] In this one sees the economic compromises that a local *dominus* might have to make for a status display appropriate to his station: the *dominus* of the Antonine era could not afford, or did not have access to, columns of real marble. His third-century successors attempted to make good this deficit by putting in new capitals, basically corinthian, but carved of local material by a local atelier. In the major renovation at the start of the fourth century, the columns were covered in whitewashed stucco to imitate marble and the whole peristyle was remodeled to create an interior garden with a decorative water tank in its center.[24]

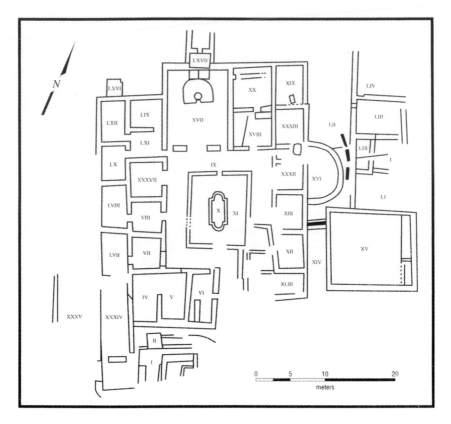

Plan of the villa of El Ruedo, Almedinilla. The Roman numerals are room numbers assigned by the excavators. (after Vaquerizo and Noguera [1997], plate 6)

In fact, the fourth-century remodeling was orchestrated to turn
plants and water into part of the villa's decorative schema, their interaction emphasizing the contrast of nature and artifice, and doing so at
relatively little expense. The centerpiece of this was a brand-new
nymphaeum, built through and beyond the rear wall of the second-
century *triclinium.*[25] The *triclinium,* the public dining room, was perhaps the most important part of a Roman villa, the focus of display at
the point where it could do most good, that is to say, in the entertain-
ment of favored guests. In the Antonine plan of El Ruedo, the importance of the *triclinium* was underscored by its marble, for though many

other rooms had limestone or stucco decked out to look like marble, only the *triclinium* boasted the real thing.[26] It is testimony to the conservatism of Roman taste and of aristocratic behavior that the *triclinium* remained as important to the fourth-century layout as it had been to the earlier plan. However, in remaking the villa to more modish canons of taste, the fourth-century *dominus* knocked out the back wall of the *triclinium* and put in a monument to running water. A small step, probably framed by columns, led into a water chamber, its walls painted with architectonic images and its floor paved with a local calcite that made a fair approximation to marble.

The dinner guests of the *dominus* could now enjoy the pleasant tinkling of water through the door behind them as they ate, all the time gazing at the household cook's artistry as it was displayed on a brand new *stibadium*. This podium, an important part of fashionable dining, was here made more striking by a fountain in its center.[27] Between the new garden in the peristyle and the *nymphaeum* off the *triclinium*, the public center of the villa was meant to strike the viewer with an impression of nature's tranquility harnessed by human skill, an impression that relied for its effect on the interplay of stone and mosaic, water and vegetation. But even here, we are struck by the need to obey the dictates of fashion on the cheap. The *stibadium* itself was made of brick, faced with opus signinum, and covered with a layer of stucco painted to imitate red marble. Moreover, the old mosaic of the Antonine *triclinium*, which had been partly broken to install the pipe that fed the fountain of the *stibadium*, was patched roughly rather than repaired.[28] The effect would have been horribly ugly and we must assume that the faults were covered up with perishable materials, rugs or mats of suitable quality. The whole fourth-century renovation is thus very revealing. We are continually struck by the lengths to which Roman elites would go in order to project an image of themselves as the possessors of the particular form of luxury that guaranteed their status. At El Ruedo, however, we see the limitations that hedged in such attempts and the compromises that maintaining the necessary façade might require.[29]

These limitations could in part be disguised by portable art, which decorated all the rooms beyond the peristyle, whether public or private. The sculptural ensemble of El Ruedo is the finest known from any Spanish villa and pride of place must go to the bronze *hypnos,* a masterpiece of Hadrianic bronzeworking, which decorates the cover of every publication on the site. Standing nearly a meter tall and sculpted in the round, it will have formed the decorative center of a room, perhaps the *triclinium* in which most of the statue was found.[30] If so, it was only one of several bronzes that looked down on the diners as they ate, for flanking the entrance to the *nymphaeum* are wall niches in which were found the attachments for two more bronzes, one of them probably a dancing hermaphrodite.[31]

The rest of the villa was filled with marble sculptures, mostly simple heads of divinities, herms of Dionysus, and difficult-to-identify goddesses. It also included several impressive sculptural groups, a large one of Perseus rescuing Andromeda and another of a satyr plucking a thorn from the foot of Pan.[32] The remains of several *kairoi* were also found and probably formed a group representing the four seasons.[33] Portrait art is less prominent, but the remnant of a bust wearing the *paludamentum* was found in the antechamber to the residential suite.[34] This would have carried a portrait head, perhaps of the *dominus,* perhaps of an ancestor, or perhaps merely of an artistic head that had caught the master's eye.[35] Fragments belonging to statues no longer extant abound and every room would have featured a panoply of artistry on which the eye could linger.[36]

The existence of so magnificent a collection in a villa otherwise relatively modest might seem to require explanation. More likely, however, the El Ruedo collection should be taken as testimony to how much we have lost elsewhere, an argument supported by the collection of Valdetorres de Jarama, a villa site not far from Madrid. Centuries of agricultural work have damaged the site badly enough that no stratigraphy could be recovered, but the octagonal plan is unique in Spain. Although no remains of mosaics or paintings have been found, the villa site at Valdetorres has yielded a rich sculptural collection which, like that of El Ruedo, was once displayed around its peristyle, perhaps about the year 400.[37] Among the numerous pieces of this important collection are the remains of four figures from a gigantomachy, two apollos and two giants, sculpted between the second and third centuries. The theme is extremely rare for sculpture in the round, and all four of the pieces would appear to have come originally from the same atelier in Asia Minor. Among the other pieces were a Roman Aesculapius of the third century, a Nubian boy sculpted in black marble, and a variety of other masculine figures. The site also turned up more than four hundred ivory fragments, mostly of decorative plaques that would have been fitted into wooden panels of walls or chests. Many of these ivories are geometrical or classicizing, for instance a high relief of a nymph pouring liquid from an amphora, but there is also an entirely unique plaque of a monstrous, lion-like animal, perhaps a manticore. These plaques are probably Egyptian—the manticore is certainly Coptic—and carved in the fourth or fifth century. If El Ruedo gives us a sense of what the middling sort of villa owner aspired to, then the sad fragments of Valdetorres can show us what it was possible to do with a larger budget.

Both the El Ruedo and the Valdetorres assemblages tell us something about the aesthetic tastes of late Roman landowners.[38] El Ruedo is particularly important, because its decorations survive in their architectural setting. After the reconstruction of the early fourth century, the villa retained its structural form, and presumably its function as a country residence, until at least the middle of the fifth century. There is no sign that, during that time, there was any major reconstruction or alteration of its decorative scheme. The tastes of our fourth-century *dominus* remained those of the generations that succeeded him. That is, the cultural forms associated with the aristocratic Roman existence not only remained relatively unchanging from the time that they first became dominant, but also outlasted the political structure of Roman rule within which they had been born. The dominant fact of these tastes is their basic Hellenism. Hellenistic canons of art and beauty were embraced by the Roman elites in the late Republican period, when their adoption was a matter of genuine controversy, but by late antiquity the repertoire of Hellenistic sculptural styles was the only one possible for those who aspired to appear as leaders of society.[39] Thus the pieces of sculpture that adorned El Ruedo were, with the single exception of the deliberately archaizing herm, firmly in the style of artists who had flourished in the fourth and third centuries B.C., and most were created on Hellenistic patterns in Greek ateliers of the first and second centuries A.D. Such pieces continued to take pride of place in the decorative schema of the Hispano-Roman villa centuries after they and their like had ceased to be actively produced.

Valdetorres, almost certainly later in date than El Ruedo, makes the same point still more strongly, but also raises interesting questions about the economics of the Roman art trade. One wonders how, around the year 400, a *dominus* went about acquiring the sculptural decoration for his residence, whether it was something one had actively to pursue as a collector, or whether it was possible to acquire such pieces from an art dealer, who could turn up and redo a villa in a particular style as an interior decorator might today. That question, in turn, raises another one, of whether the anti-pagan legislation of Theodosius stimulated the market in classicizing sculpture by making available supplies of statuary from closed temples. It is by no means far-fetched to see the collection of Valdetorres as having been amassed by some Spaniard who went east with the entourage of Theodosius and was able to indulge his taste for antiquities by means of looting temples in the wake of Maternus Cynegius.[40]

That hypothesis would certainly help account for the diversity of the Valdetorres collection in particular. As its excavators have pointed out, the sculptural assemblage must be understood as a collection in the modern sense of the word, that is to say, as pieces of artwork acquired from a variety of sources, disconnected from their original religious function and context, and grouped together for purely aesthetic reasons. At another level, however, such a collection formed a hoard, a heap of beautiful pieces whose function was to overwhelm by their quantity as much as by the admittedly very high quality of individual pieces. It is true that at El Ruedo at least the finest decoration was reserved for the private areas of the house, so that we ought not to underestimate the personal aesthetic aspects of the collection alongside the motives of status display. On these grounds, it has sometimes seemed possible to derive the intellectual and artistic outlook of a villa's owner from extant decorative remains, for instance, the Bacchic theme detected at El Ruedo.[41] But there are limitations to this approach.

First, there is the problem of the archaeological distance that separates us from the past choices of the villa's *dominus*. With very few exceptions, we possess only a very incomplete reflection of the houses in which the late Roman wealthy lived out their lives. Even our floor plans are frequently provisional, our understanding of architectonic decoration—the material used to decorate floors and walls and architectural features—is always fragmentary, and our access to the portable decoration that created a sense of luxury is generally nonexistent, because portable ornament has almost always been despoiled over the intervening centuries. Perishable features like screens, curtains, and hangings, which were as important in the definition of space as was the more permanent architectonic ensemble, have without exception disappeared. Even where such archaeological impediments are mitigated in one way or another, there remains a further obstacle between us and the ancient owner: we have no way of knowing whether a particular assemblage of space, buildings, and decoration reflects deliberate, or even passive, choice on the part of a particular owner or of generations within a single family. Nowhere in Spain can we connect a firm set of material remains to the mind or environment of a single individual. While a few names in mosaics or inscribed on domestic instruments like seals or brushes do survive from rural Spain, it is nowhere possible to state definitively that the extant name was that of the villa's owner. In the end, it is probably best not to read too much historical content into the artistic decoration, mosaic or otherwise, of late Roman villas.[42]

Thus while the artistic importance of Valdetorres de Jarama, El Ruedo, and their sculptural assemblages is beyond question, they may serve best as a general illustration of the sort of elite culture that dominated rural Spain throughout late antiquity. As a relatively modest site, El Ruedo demonstrates how far a single elite culture, bound up with the canons of the Hellenistic past, dominated Roman Spain, so that even those who lacked enormous disposable wealth strove to simulate the physical environment of those who did. The sculptural collection of Valdetorres, by contrast, may bring us into contact with one of the consequences of fourth-century political change. It is possible, as we have suggested, that the Valdetorres collection was brought together as a result of the release of vast amounts of eastern temple treasures by the anti-pagan activities of Theodosius and his Spanish followers. If the villa for which the collection was assembled was indeed built very close to the year 400, it is almost impossible to resist the inference that we have here a member of the Theodosian entourage returning from a hugely profitable tour of duty in the East and determined to display this fact in his native land. It is certain that Theodosian connections did bring considerable wealth into Spain, most famously the *missorium* of Theodosius, depicting the emperor in majesty and flanked by his sons and attendants, which was found near Mérida in 1847.[43] While the connection of Valdetorres to such trends must remain speculative, another Spanish villa should almost certainly be associated with the circle of Theodosius.

The villa of Carranque lies some 10 kilometers from the modern village of the same name, very near to the exact geographical center of the peninsula, on the banks of the river Guadarrama near the minor Roman city of Titulcia. Though Titulcia is barely known archaeologically, the villa at Carranque was the object of twelve uninterrupted years of excavation. The complex covered between 10 and 12 hectares and was situated at the intersection of the Toledo–Segovia and the Mérida–Zaragoza roads, both very important in the Roman period. The villa at Carranque stood astride this crossroads, and the footings of the bridge across the Guadarrama have recently been discovered.[44] Three buildings—the villa's *pars urbana,* a small *nympheum* at the topographical apex of the site, and a very large basilica—have been excavated in full, and now await detailed publication. The buildings are precisely contemporary with one another and dateable archaeologically to the Theodosian period, standing as some of the most impressive rural remains in Spain.[45]

The *pars urbana* has been called a palace by its excavator. In plan, it is a typical Mediterranean villa, facing down toward the banks of the river and taking advantage of the slight gradient sloping toward it. With its open design, it would have been very cold in a full Meseta winter, and thus its many hypocaust rooms were a necessity. The villa had two separate *triclinia,* probably for the graded reception of guests of different ranks. All of the public areas were decorated with extremely rich mosaics, including a neptune over which a fountain stood and a hunting scene that contains some of the most adventurous and unusual designs known from Spain. The exterior of the building was deliberately imposing, its chief façade looking toward the river and set off at each end by a tower.

The basilica was a still more impressive structure, its entrance facing west and giving onto a long patio. This patio was flanked on both sides by columnaded galleries that led into an elongated vestibule with two apsidal exedras. From the outer galleries one could also enter what may have been the site's original structure, a small, quadrilobal room in the northwest corner of the basilical complex. This has been interpreted as a mausoleum off which the basilical complex as a whole was eventually built, though that identification is by no means certain. Taken as a whole, the complex would have dominated the landscape on all sides, imposing its shape on the traveler even from some distance away. If one came up toward the complex from the river, it would have been necessary to pass directly between the palatial villa on the one hand and the gigantic basilica on the other. One could not have escaped the fact of being in the presence of one of the land's great men.

That impression was undoubtedly the point and there can be no question but that the owner of Carranque was a force to be reckoned with, perhaps at the very highest level of the Spanish aristocracy. Yet it has been suggested that we can identify Carranque's *dominus* more precisely as Maternus Cynegius, the companion of Theodosius, his praetorian prefect of the East and one of the architects of the Theodosian Christian revolution.[46] The evidence for this is circumstantial but suggestive. For one thing, the marble that decorates both villa and basilica was drawn from a variety of quarries in Egypt, mainland Greece, Chios, and Asia Minor, while one of the basilica's columns preserves the inscribed quarry-mark DNTH. This abbreviation has been plausibly expanded as *Domini Nostri Theodosii* and suggests that the marbles were taken from imperial quarries with official sanction.

As is the case of most villas, Carranque's portable decorations are almost entirely lost. But here again, a surviving fragment of a porphyry table suggests direct contact with the Roman East, as does a mosaic of the metamorphoses, the central panel of which depicts the legend of Piramus and Thisbe, otherwise unknown in the western provinces though not uncommon in the East.[47] The same mosaic bears an inscription identifying itself as the property of Maternus: *ex oficina mas[. . .]ni pingit Hirinius utere felix Materne hunc cubiculum.*[48] Given the Spanish background of the Theodosian clan—indeed the northern Meseta background, as Theodosius was himself from Cauca—the identification of Carranque's Maternus with Maternus Cynegius is attractive. On the other hand, the name Maternus is very common and the mosaic's highly erotic, if not actually pagan, theme is hard to reconcile with the violently Christian Cynegius who emerges from our literary sources.[49] When all is said and done, the evidence for imperial and eastern connections at Carranque is overwhelming, although the identification with Cynegius must remain open.

Still, doubts over the identity of its proprietor in no way diminish the importance of the site. It was specially designed to create the impression of unmatched power and that is precisely what it did. All fancy villas expressed power and status, and in Spain we have one of the richest corpora of villas in the whole Roman world. Nevertheless, the ideological significance of Carranque is almost surely greater than that of even the expansive remains of Torre de Palma or the fortress-like solidity of São Cucufate. The only rural site that can compare for its psychological impact with Carranque is the villa at Centcelles near Tarraco, a site at which an imperial connection has likewise been postulated. Centcelles, despite the vast attention given to the iconography of the splendid mosaics in its dome, remains little known archaeologically, and even its date is open to dispute.[50] If its proposed identification with a mausoleum, let alone the mausoleum or cenotaph of the emperor Constans, seems unlikely, a connection to imperial service is virtually indisputable, the elaborate mosaics perhaps illustrating the stages in the official career of the *dominus*.[51]

Like Centcelles, Carranque spoke not just to the neighboring locals, but rather to the whole of Spain. It advertised power and an imperial connection to each and every traveler who passed by it and, lying as it did astride a major highway, it would have been seen by far more people—and far more people of high status, for it was they who traveled most—than the average villa, howsoever monumental. Even if Carranque was not in fact the Spanish residence of Maternus Cynegius, it is certainly to be placed in his milieu, a product of the fourth-century impact of imperial office and patronage on the Spanish provinces and a way in which the profits and the connections of imperial service might bring wealth to one's home region and impose an entirely new face on a swathe of countryside.

Carranque is very much a fourth-century phenomenon, a product of the dramatic changes that the new centrality of imperial government brought to the later Roman world. In one respect, however, it is quite unusual: if the quadrilobal chamber within the basilica is correctly interpreted as a mausoleum, then it represents one of the very few high-status burials attested from a rural site in Spain. For the most part, our knowledge of rural burial practices is confined to the lower orders, about whose lives we know so little. The sections of villas that tend to be excavated are the so-called *partes urbanae,* the well-made domestic sections occupied by the *dominus* or his overseer. The *partes rusticae,* the industrial buildings and laborers' residences that were essential to a villa's existence, are intrinsically less interesting to the archaeologist.[52] As a result, we know relatively little about the lives of these laborers on the great estates of rural Spain, who are accessible to us only in death. Most villa sites have cemeteries associated with them, some on a very large scale, though few of these have been excavated with modern methods. There are distinct regional differences across Spain, especially inasmuch as parts of the Meseta retained indigenous habits of burial with grave goods well into the fourth, or even the fifth century, not the case in most of the peninsula.[53]

Despite the vast numbers of low-status burials known from Spain, presumably mostly the remains of agricultural laborers whether slave or free, almost no elite burials are associated with late Roman villa sites. Lead coffins known from the villa at Torre Llauder perhaps belonged to the family plot of the villa's owners, but apart from this single example, there is little else.[54] The distribution of our evidence for rural funerary practice is puzzling: given the vast number of known Spanish villas and the large number of rural necropoleis, the striking absence of high-status tombs or mausolea from the countryside cannot be explained simply as an accident of preservation. Instead, we must presume that high-status burials did not, as a rule, exist at rural villa sites, at least not until the seventh century.[55] We can account for this phenomenon in only one way: the men and women who owned the great villas of Spanish late antiquity were not buried near their rural residences because they continued to be buried in the urban cemeteries where their ancestors had been buried for centuries. This is no mere argument from silence. During the late antique centuries when high-status burials are virtually absent from rural sites, we continue to find luxurious sarcophagi, elaborate mausolea, and the whole panoply of funerary pomp and circumstance in urban cemeteries. Nothing better demonstrates the continued centrality of the city to the life of Spain than does the failure of the Spanish elites who built luxurious rural retreats to choose to be buried in them.

By taking the material evidence of the Spanish provinces as far as possible on its own terms, without attempting to fit it into paradigms derived in the first instance from the written sources, we uncover a picture of Spanish late antiquity very different from that found in traditional narratives. In particular, we find no sign of a devastating third-century crisis, whether the result of barbarian invasion or anything else. Nor, for that matter, do we find traces of a process of *ruralización* transforming the map of Spain. Instead, we find a broad continuity, in which the population and the exploitation of the countryside expand dramatically, along with the expenditure of wealth in the country. In the cities, it is the fourth, rather than the third, century that seems to have brought major structural change. That change is not easy to force into any historical model, though the increased impact of imperial government after the Diocletianic reforms must account for some of it. A key point is the absence of any sign of a flight to the countryside or a depopulation of the cities, either by their population as a whole or more especially by the elite segment of it. Neither the fate of urban monuments, nor the burial habits of Spanish elites, suggests any fundamental break with the period of romanization in the early empire, but rather an evolution from that past.

Methodologically, this is important. We now have far more archaeological evidence for Spanish late antiquity than we have traditional historical sources, and that material evidence is increasingly of a quality that allows it to function as an independent, autonomous source for understanding the Hispano-Roman past. In other words, the picture of late antique Spain that emerges from the material evidence should form the context within which we attempt to situate our narrative, rather than the reverse, which has long been the normal approach. The traditional historical sources for Roman Spain are few, and only become available for the very last decades of imperial rule there;

even then, we are dependent on just a couple of old warhorses like Orosius and Hydatius. If we are willing to accept that the material record can offer a picture of late Roman Spain with a substantially larger foundation than is provided by traditional written sources, it becomes possible to move beyond deeply rooted historical models and uncover what is potentially a more accurate picture of Spanish late antiquity. Certainly the narrative that will occupy us in the following chapters makes a good deal of sense against the background of historical change derived from the material evidence.

Seven

Imperial Crisis and Recovery

We can begin to study the historical narrative of Roman Spain only as the superstructure of imperial government begins to break down in the peninsula. During the four peaceful centuries that followed Augustus's organization of the Spanish provinces, only a handful of events are known to us. But beginning in the years of civil war at the start of the fifth century, Spain's history becomes traceable in some detail. It is a history of the process by which the Spanish provinces, and the Hispano-Roman elites who lived in the Spanish cities, ceased to be part of a larger state governed by a Roman emperor.

Between 406 and 418, Spain played an important role in the general imperial crisis of the early fifth century, first as part of the territory of the usurper Constantine III, later as the base of the general Gerontius and his imperial puppet Maximus. Then, after 409, the Vandals, Alans, and Sueves who had crossed the Rhine into Gaul in 405/406 invaded Spain and eventually settled in four of its five provinces. As a result of these developments, contemporaries outside Spain began to take an interest in the peninsula, thus placing it before the historian's eyes for the first time since the Roman conquest. Between the resolution of the crisis in 418 and the death of Majorian in 461 lie forty years in which the Spanish provinces remained generally subject to imperial government and continued to form part of the political calculus of the western empire. The death of Majorian, however, was also the end of Roman Spain.

The grounds for such a statement are straightforward and purely political. Indeed, political criteria are the only suitable yardstick for this sort of problem, for cultural change, whether material or intellectual, is both slow and impossible to quantify. After all, the Spanish intellectual world remained recognizably Roman until at least the seventh century, while change in the material culture of Roman Spain was both gradual and does not correspond to the political history of the peninsula in any helpful way. Political criteria, by contrast, are more useful, for the Roman empire had always been a political as much as a cultural phenomenon, and in the later empire, as we have seen, its political existence came to be coterminous with its administrative existence. Where imperial bureaucrats held office, the empire existed. Where they did not, it did not. Until the reign of Majorian, it was possible both for men to hold imperial office in Spain and for Spaniards to hold office elsewhere in the empire. After Majorian, both possibilities disappeared. When it was no longer possible to hold imperial office in Spain, Spain's existence as part of the Roman empire had come to an end.

This approach is validated by the fact that such fifth-century Romans as Sidonius Apollinaris used it themselves. Sidonius thought that Roman Gaul ended when the emperor ceded Provence to the Goths in 475.[1] Without the superstructure of office-holding and rank that went along with imperial authority, Roman Gaul ceased to be. We can readily apply Sidonius's analysis to Spain, though the peninsula lacked a Sidonius to articulate such a view on its own account. The same approach also helps make sense of the political dynamics of late Roman Spain at the same time as it points up the contrast between a late Roman and post-Roman period. It is, from one perspective, perfectly possible to argue that long before the reign of Majorian, Spain as a whole had been lost to any genuine imperial control, and that the peninsula into which Majorian briefly marched was no more than a Gothic hinterland, largely outside the control of everyone. But to say this ignores the fact that emperors up to Majorian clearly envisaged Spain as part of the empire they ruled, and determined, as time and circumstance allowed, to make their power felt. The vicissitudes of politics at ground level may have meant a fairly minimal level of imperial control, but that was a factor endemic to the fifth-century West. However intermittent, the continued participation of imperial officials and the government they represented in the political life of Spain did make a crucial difference. After the death of Majorian, imperial office-holding became impossible in a Spanish diocese to which emperors no longer appointed officials.

The first narrative history of Roman Spain that one can write is therefore the narrative of its disappearance. That we can do so at all is largely thanks to the chronicle of the Spanish bishop Hydatius, on whom we grow progressively more dependent as the fifth century moves along. Until about 418, he is one among several sources for the history of Roman Spain. For the next decade he is the main source. After 429, he is to all intents and purposes the only one, for one can glean very little from the minor theological writers of the fifth and sixth centuries.

Hydatius and His Chronicle

Given our dependence on him, it is a good thing that Hydatius's accuracy has repeatedly been vindicated in comparison to other fifth- and sixth-century chroniclers.[2] But even though it is easy enough to turn a history of fifth-century Spain into a paraphrase of Hydatius (and many have done so), an approach to his chronicle requires greater care. The man himself had an interesting life. He was born around the year 400 in the *civitas Lemica,* near the modern Xinzo de Limia in the extreme south of Spanish Galicia. At the age of six or seven he was taken on a pilgrimage to the Holy Land, where he met luminaries like John of Jerusalem, Theophilus of Alexandria, and, most important, Jerome, whom he reverenced for the rest of his life. For the next two decades we know nothing about Hydatius's life, but in 428, at a very young age, he was elected bishop of Aquae Flaviae, modern Chaves in the north of Portugal. He spent the rest of his life as a man of great local standing, an ambassador to the general Aëtius in Gaul, and a director of the episcopal campaign against Priscillianists in Spain. We do not know when he conceived the idea of continuing Jerome's chronicle down to his own times, but he did not begin writing the text that has come down to us until 457 or 458, and possibly somewhat later. The chronicle, at any rate, ends in 468, and Hydatius died shortly thereafter.[3]

There are many different avenues of approach to Hydatius's chronicle. We might study it as an integral text and look at its literary aspects as part of the new Christian genre of the chronicle. Given recent advances in our understanding of the chronicle genre, this approach to Hydatius has by no means been exhausted.[4] What is more, it has already allowed us to take a more nuanced approach to Hydatius's chronicle as a source for the history of his times. The essence of the chronicle form is that each year is marked out according to the author's chosen system of reckoning, and one or two events of outstanding importance are attributed to each year. On the other hand, events of one year are presented much as are the events of any other, and the conventional means of signaling the importance of different facts are absent.[5] This difficulty is particularly acute in Hydatius, who with the lone exception of the Gothic campaign of 456 never presents any event as being of greater significance than any other. Similar problems arise from Hydatius's geographical limitations. Hydatius mostly records events in Gallaecia and he includes both purely local and more general information with no change of emphasis, which lays a trap into which the modern historian can easily walk. Gallaecia was not Spain. We cannot simply extrapolate from conditions in Gallaecia to the rest of the Spanish provinces, or imagine that the confusion that reigned in the one place was also the rule elsewhere.[6]

Still, in recognizing that Hydatius concentrates heavily on Gallaecia, we should not make the mistake of thinking him isolated and incapable of recording anything more than he actually does record. Too much can be made of the gaps in Hydatius's knowledge, and there is no reason to think that those gaps reflect the institutional decline of the Roman empire.[7] Judged by any modern standard, the information networks of the late Roman world were not good.[8] It is possible that the things Hydatius did not know are evidence for a growing gulf between Gallaecia and the rest of the Roman world, but we have no grounds for comparison. A fourth-century bishop in an obscure Gallaecian town is unlikely to have been much better-informed than was

Hydatius in the fifth century. Hydatius's sources of information, insofar as they are visible to us, were perfectly normal. News could come directly from the East via Seville, but for the most part Rome and Gaul were the centers from which information reached Gallaecia. It is possible that much of the Italian news that found its way to Hydatius was mediated through Gallic informants, since most of the sources he names are in fact from Gaul. There is, however, one explicit reference to direct contact between Rome and Gallaecia, when the Gallaecian deacon Pervincus brought back to Spain the anti-Priscillianist writings of Pope Leo I.[9] What is more, correspondence between Rome and Astorga in Gallaecia survives from the very years when Hydatius was writing.[10] The chronicle of Hydatius presents the historian with many difficulties, but the isolation and ignorance of the chronicler is not among them.

The way in which Hydatius presents his material, on the other hand, is a problem to be reckoned with. Hydatius, it has recently been shown, believed the world was going to end on 27 May 482.[11] In keeping with their specifically Christian generic content, most chronicles set out to place the events of human history in the framework of Christian time, to record the annual stages by which human history marched toward the second coming. Always on the lookout for signs of the *parousia,* chroniclers were both generically and, one suspects, temperamentally inclined to focus on the worst in the world around them. In Spain, the eschatological enthusiasms had a long history; the Spanish heresy of Priscillianism embraced asceticism in the face of the world's imminent end, and during the later fourth century a young Spaniard claimed first to be the prophet Elijah and later Christ himself, while his proclamation of the second coming won the support of at least one Spanish bishop.[12] For Hydatius, who knew the world would be ending within a few years of his writing, these eschatological tendencies were exaggerated. His chronicle was consciously a history of the world's last days, and it is filled with signs and portents of the end. Hydatius saw the world as a bleak and terrible place, and was at pains to make the reader feel the same despair of its goodness as he did himself. He constantly glosses events as pessimistically as he can and we must therefore always distinguish between the events that Hydatius records, and the way in which he strives to make his reader interpret them. We need not accept his interpretation as our own at every turn.[13] In writing the history of late Roman Spain it is often necessary to look at what Hydatius says while rejecting the way he says it.[14] When we do so, we realize that Spain in the early fifth century is much less the scene of post-Roman apocalypse and much more a normal part of the gradually dissolving western empire.

The Imperial Crisis, 405–413

That fact is demonstrated with great clarity by the invasion of Spain by Vandals, Alans, and Sueves in the autumn of 409. That episode, painted in the blackest of colors by Hydatius, was really just one episode in a series of interlocking invasions and civil wars that engulfed the regime of Honorius beginning in the year 405.[15] In the early fifth century, the real power in the Roman West was not the young emperor Honorius, but rather the general Stilicho, a friend of Honorius's father, the late Theodosius I, and regent for his son since 395. The first ten years of Stilicho's regency had been afflicted by constant tension with the successive governments of the eastern emperor Arcadius, and by repeated conflicts with the Gothic king Alaric, whom Stilicho only maneuvered into temporary quiescence by 405.[16] In that year, however, a large army of barbarians, led by a Gothic king called Radagaisus, invaded Italy from the other side of the Raetian Alps. It took more than a year to deal with Radagaisus, who was finally executed on 8 August 406.[17] While Stilicho was preoccupied with this very immediate threat to his government and the person of the emperor, problems multiplied elsewhere in the West. On New Year's Eve 405, a collection of Vandals, Alans, and Sueves began to cross the Rhine into Gaul, after overcoming the opposition of the emperor's Frankish allies on the right bank of the river.[18] The invasion may have begun near Mainz, and during 406 the invaders caused considerable damage to the northern provinces of Germania Prima, Belgica Prima, and Belgica Secunda, with Honorius's government completely unable to stop their progress.[19]

Because of this imperial failure, the provincials took matters into their own hands. At some unknown point in the course of 406, the usurper Marcus rose up in Britain in direct response to the barbarians in Gaul.[20] Marcus proved unpopular, as did his successor Gratian, and it was not until early 407 that a more successful usurper came to power in Britain.[21] This was Constantine III, supposedly a common soldier plucked from the ranks on the strength of his auspicious name.[22] Renaming his sons Constans and Julian in a grand propaganda gesture, Constantine quickly crossed the Channel to Gaul and won the support of most of the Gallic prefecture, Spain included, soon thereafter. Through some combination of force and treaties, Constantine halted the depredations of the Vandals, Alans, and Sueves, who remained confined to the three northern Gallic provinces until the summer of 409.[23] He regarrisoned the Rhine, restored imperial government to Trier, where the mint began to strike coins in his name, and, by early 408, occupied the whole of Gaul including the imperial city of Arles.[24]

At this point, however, Constantine faced a very dangerous threat from the Spanish provinces that had initially recognized him and accepted his administrative appointments.[25] Spain was the birthplace of the Theodosian dynasty, its founder having been born at Cauca, modern Coca in Segovia province. Though many Spaniards had gone east to profit from the Theodosian ascendancy, members of the family remained in Spain in the early 400s. Then, despite the acceptance of the Gallic usurpation by the Spanish provincial governments, two Hispano-Roman relatives of Honorius, Didymus and Verinianus, determined to wage war against Constantine. They did so as private citizens, rebels in a province whose government recognized the usurper.[26] Although two other relatives of Honorius, Theodosiolus and Lagodius, acquiesced in the usurpation, Didymus and Verinianus raised an army from among their servile dependents.[27] Early in 408, Constantine raised his son Constans to the rank of Caesar and dispatched him to Spain, where he took up residence in Zaragoza with his praetorian prefect Apollinaris and the *magister officiorum* Decimius Rusticus.[28] Constans's army was commanded by the general Gerontius, who fought two battles against the relatives of Honorius. The first, at an unknown location, was a victory for the Spanish rebels. The second, fought in Lusitania after Gerontius had called in reinforcements from Gaul, witnessed their decisive defeat.[29] Lagodius and Theodosiolus, who had taken no part in the rebellion, fled Spain, one seeking refuge with Theodosius II at Constantinople, the other with Honorius at Ravenna. Constans permitted one unit of his troops, the *Honoriaci,* to sack the *campi Pallentini,*[30] after which he left his army under the command of Gerontius and himself escorted Didymus and Verinianus back to Constantine at Arles in the autumn of 408.[31]

Constantine had not left Arles from the point in spring of that year when it fell to him, and his coins boldly trumpeted his own legitimacy as a member of the imperial college. Such assertions found no favor in Italy, where Stilicho set about gathering an army to send against the usurper.[32] Constantine was delivered from this threat by a new combination of Italian crises: the army that Stilicho had mustered at Pavia revolted on 13 August 408 and massacred its Stilichonian officials while Stilicho himself fell foul of Honorius, who had him executed on 22 August.[33] The imperial court immediately collapsed into an orgy of palace intrigue, and this ineffectual government soon found itself confronted by Alaric, whom Stilicho's death had inspired to resume raising havoc. The planned attack on Constantine was shelved, while the usurper sat patiently at Arles and let Honorius's position deteriorate to the point that he would welcome Constantine's assistance and turn the usurper's self-proclaimed legitimacy into the real thing. The chance had come by late in 408, around the same time that the Spanish rebellion was suppressed. Honorius acknowledged Constantine as his colleague and sent him an imperial robe. In January 409 Constantine and Honorius entered the consulate together as imperial colleagues.[34]

The year 409, then, opened propitiously for Constantine, but his triumphs soon came crashing down around him. Some time in late spring 409, Gerontius revolted in Spain and set up his own emperor.[35] This was Maximus, one of his clients and a *domesticus.*[36] Gerontius chose Tarragona as his residence, the mint at Barcelona immediately began producing issues in Maximus's name, and a major repair of that city's Augustan walls was undertaken, enclosing the original wall in a new one and effectively doubling its breadth.[37] Constans, newly raised to the rank of Augustus, set off for Spain to deal with his former subordinate and, faced with this attack, the rebel general responded with a powerful, though ultimately uncontrollable, weapon: he stirred up barbarians in Gaul against Constantine, barbarians who ended up invading Spain.[38]

These barbarians were some part of the group that had crossed the Rhine in 405/406, but beyond that not much can be said. The participation of the Vandal king Gunderic in both the Rhine crossing and the invasion of Spain in 409 demands the connection, but we do not know what rate of attrition the Vandals, Alans, and Sueves suffered in the years after the Rhine crossing, nor do we know how many of those who dwelt peacefully in northern Gaul between 407 and 409 responded to Gerontius's overtures.[39] For many years, estimates of barbarian numbers have been gradually adjusted downward, but the only work to specifically address the number of Spanish invaders remains overdrawn.[40] Based upon the observable effects of their passage, the whole force of barbarian invaders probably numbered no more than a hundred thousand, and quite possibly less, though there is no solid evidence either way. All we can be certain of is that Gerontius found a way to entice some of the barbarians whom Constantine had confined to the north of Gaul in 407 into mobilizing again and invading southern Gaul. He need not have convinced every Vandal, Alan, and Sueve and the Vandals, Alans, and Sueves he convinced need not all have been the same men who had crossed the Rhine in 405. But the damage these invaders wrought on Aquitaine was bad enough to produce an outpouring of shocked lamentations from across the region.[41]

Although we cannot accurately gauge how much of a blow this invasion dealt to Constantine's own authority, it may be significant that the famous British revolt against Rome, with its expulsion of Roman officials, took place precisely in 409.[42] Certainly both Gerontius's revolt and the British rebellion are reflections of the spiraling instability that had beset the western provinces since the beginning of the century. Gerontius was neither the first nor the last Roman general to deploy barbarians in the course of a civil war, but events exceeded his ability to control them. The war with Constans occupied all of Gerontius's attention, the passes over the Pyrenees were either neglected or (less plausibly) betrayed, and Spain as well as southern Gaul lay open to the barbarians.[43] So it was that Vandals, Alans, and Sueves were able to cross from Gaul to Spain, in an invasion that began on either 28 September or 12 October 409.[44]

This event would shape the course of Spanish history for the next two decades, but as far as the rival Roman commanders were concerned, their war took precedence over any attempt to deal with the newly active barbarians. Most of 410 was thus occupied by the campaigns of Constans against Gerontius, while Constantine advanced into Italy, reaching no further than the Po before being forced to retreat. He reached Arles at the same time as Constans, who had similarly been forced to retreat from his Spanish campaign.[45] Father and son conferred at Arles and decided upon a plan of action. Either late in 410 or early in the next year, the loyal *magister militum* Edobich was sent to the Rhine to secure Frankish assistance while Constans again set out to fight Gerontius. Gerontius and Constans met somewhere between the Pyrenees and Arles, where Constans was defeated, falling back to Vienne, which lay along Edobich's return route from the Rhine. At Vienne, Gerontius killed the young Augustus and then turned on Arles.

By the time Gerontius won this victory early in 411, the death of Alaric greatly improved the position of Honorius in Italy, with the result that his government finally mustered a response to the Gallic problem. Honorius's generals Constantius and Ulfila marched on Arles, which they found already besieged by Gerontius.[46] The latter's troops deserted to Constantius, Gerontius fled, and Edobich's relief force was routed by Constantius and Ulfila.[47] The end of Constantine followed very quickly thereafter. Faced with certain defeat, he retired to a church and had himself ordained.[48] The gates of the city were opened; Constantius and Ulfila entered victorious and took prisoner Constantine and his surviving son, the *nobilissimus* Julian. They were sent to Honorius in Italy and executed en route beside the river Mincio.[49] On 18 September 411, the usurper's head was displayed on a stake at Ravenna.[50]

Gerontius committed a dramatic suicide: besieged by his own soldiers, his last refuge in flames around him, he killed his faithful servant and his devout wife before falling on his dagger.[51] His client Maximus, bereft of all support, put aside the purple and departed to live among the barbarians who had by now partitioned much of Spain among themselves. The defeat of Constantine by no means ended the troubles of Honorius's government. The *comes* Heraclian revolted in Africa, cutting off the corn supply to Rome, while in Gaul the defeat of Constantine coincided with the usurpation of the Gallic aristocrat Jovinus, supported by the remnants of Constantine's regime as well as Burgundian and Alan kings.[52] Alaric's royal successor Athaulf proceeded to launch his Goths into the Gallic confusion as a *soi-disant* ally of Honorius. The usurpations of Heraclian and Jovinus were not suppressed until 413, at which point the relationship between Athaulf and Honorius's government began to deteriorate rapidly. These troubles in Gaul and Africa posed a continuing threat to Honorius's hold on the throne, in a way that the barbarian depredation of provincials did not. So long as such imperial crises remained unresolved, the Honorian regime could spare no thought for Spain.

The Invasion of 409 and the Reign of Maximus

The Vandals, Alans, and Sueves were able to invade Spain in September or October 409, thanks to a momentary lapse in Roman attention while the commanders on the spot were more concerned with fighting one another than with safeguarding the territory they controlled from the dangers of barbarian attack. Hydatius paints a bleak picture of the violence that these barbarians inflicted on the Spanish provinces in 409 and 410. This violence and the barbarian settlement in 411 are universally taken to mark the expunction of Roman power in Spain.[53] In order to understand events, however, we must be clear about precisely what Hydatius does and does not say. Let us therefore quote his testimony in full:

> As the barbarians ran wild through Spain with the evil of pestilence raging as well, the tyrannical tax collector seized the wealth and goods stored in the cities and the soldiers devoured them. A famine ran riot, so dire that driven by hunger humans devoured human flesh; mothers too feasted upon the bodies of their own children whom they had killed and cooked themselves; wild beasts, grown accustomed to feeding on the bodies of those slain by sword, famine, or pestilence, killed even those men who were quite strong and, feasting on their flesh, everywhere became brutally set upon the destruction of the human race. And thus with the four plagues of sword, famine, pestilence, and wild beasts raging everywhere throughout the world, the annunciation foretold by the Lord through his prophets was fulfilled.[54]

Thus the apocalypse as reported by Hydatius. His whole chronicle is a catalogue of horrors, but nothing else in it is painted in quite so black a shade. Cannibalism and rampaging wild beasts are perhaps literary tropes, symbols of a widespread destruction in keeping with the highly colored rhetoric of the passage.[55] In any case, the violence soon came to an end, as Hydatius himself describes:

> When the provinces of Spain had been overturned by the course of the aforementioned disasters, thanks to the mercy of God the barbarians turned to the establishment of peace. They divided the regions of the provinces for themselves to live in by lot. The Vandals and Sueves took Gallaecia, which is located at the western edge of the Ocean sea. The Alans obtained the provinces of Lusitania and Carthaginiensis, and the Siling Vandals Baetica. In the cities and strongholds those Spaniards who survived the blows of the barbarians who were ruling the provinces submitted themselves to servitude.[56]

These two passages form the whole of Hydatius's testimony for the years between 409 and 411 in Spain. What exactly do they tell us?

As we have already seen, the years 409–411 were the last years of the great civil war's Spanish phase. They were also the years in which Maximus, Gerontius's client and puppet, was the reigning emperor in the peninsula. Few have been willing to speak of a reign of Maximus amid the horrors described by Hydatius, but that very same testimony constrains us to do so. The narrative of Hydatius may be grim, and yet it also bears witness to the continuation of an imperial government in Spain. Who, after all, are the *tyrannicus exactor* and the voracious *miles* if not Roman officials and soldiers? In his entry for 410, Hydatius clearly shows the simultaneous presence of barbarian invaders and Roman government officials. What is more, his words make it clear that these were active in the very same parts of the peninsula. The barbarian scourge and the tax collector's impositions are parallel and simultaneous afflictions, which means that Roman government continued to function even in those regions that had been invaded by Vandals, Sueves, and Alans. Tax collection was the most visible activity of Roman officials, and wherever we find tax collectors, we can be sure the machinery of government was working. That is true even when, as in the Spain of the later fourth and fifth centuries, the sources of coined money are obscure and its supply was probably shrinking.[57] In the present case, the tax collectors of Hydatius must have served the government of Maximus, for no other emperor's writ ran in Spain.[58]

The extent of Maximus's authority thus becomes the next question. He had his capital at Tarragona and a mint at Barcelona, while during his reign a major construction project was undertaken on the walls of the latter city.[59] These facts have generally been taken as proof that after 409 only Tarraconensis remained subject to Roman administration and free of barbarians, while Carthaginiensis, Baetica, Lusitania, and Gallaecia ceased to function as provinces and became a no-man's land of competing barbarian groups. In fact, military convenience alone explains the choice of Maximus's capital. Maximus and Gerontius were concerned with the emperor Constantine and events in Gaul. Tarragona and Barcelona lay on the Via Augusta, along the main land route to Gaul, whereas the diocesan capital at Mérida was a very great distance away.[60] Moreover, just as Hydatius nowhere implies that Tarraconensis was spared by the invasion of 409, so he shows that the government of Maximus functioned in the same areas that the barbarians looted and plundered. It levied taxes and with them maintained the soldiers who were needed for the war against Constantine, and his coins have been found in Carthaginiensis as well as Tarraconensis.[61]

Although many have done so, we do not need to postulate a treaty between Maximus and the barbarian invaders to explain his ability to govern the Spanish provinces, and our sources actually exclude the possibility.[62] The explanation is simpler and structural: the barbarians might be armed and violent but there were not very many of them; they made up a tiny fraction of an Iberian population of five or six million. The Iberian peninsula is vast. Thousands of barbarians would have fitted comfortably into any one of the Spanish provinces, never mind the peninsula as a whole. Nor need we imagine that the invaders of 409 were looking for land on which to settle and farm. They could quite happily support themselves by raiding, and by the institutionalized extortion that all soldiers, Roman or barbarian, inflicted on the sedentary populations they happened to encounter. And save that both had to compete for the same revenues of the urban and rural populations, there was no way that a barbarian presence in the peninsula could constitute much of a threat to the government of Maximus and Gerontius.

Roman government, as we have seen, was centered on the cities, from which rural areas were administered and to which tax proceeds and requisitions in kind were brought from rural estates. Barbarians could interfere with the produce of rural *territoria,* but they rarely succeeded in taking cities and thus did not affect the basis of Roman administration.[63] In Spain, no cities fell to the invaders of 409 and, as Hydatius himself tells us, it was to their cities that the Hispano-Romans fled when barbarians were near.[64] They may also have sought refuge in fortified strongholds, *castella.* But *castellum* can be a synonym for *municipium* or can designate a smaller settlement within municipal territory, and if one reads Hydatius in this way then the mere fact of retreat into a town brought with it a measure of safety.[65] In the countryside, conditions were worse, though there is no a priori reason to think that a Vandal war band was more onerous a neighbor than a Roman garrison. The greater rural landowners could spare money for bribes and tribute, and some may have maintained private soldiers to defend them, but tenants and smallholders suffered.[66] The barbarians looted and murdered where they appeared, and disease and famine might follow in their wake. Yet neither disease nor famine affected the question of imperial control. The ancient world was notoriously prone to famine, and it is not uncommon to hear of plentiful supplies as little as fifty miles from scenes of mass starvation.[67] Just as notoriously, governments intervened only when their own limited interests were threatened. So long as the soldiers were fed, little else was of consequence, and if feeding the soldiers meant aggravating food shortage in the countryside, that was no more than the accepted cost of empire.

This traditional Roman response to subsistence crisis closely matches the picture drawn by Hydatius. The barbarians terrorized parts of the countryside, they ate or burned the crops and left the survivors to face death by hunger and disease, but they did not interfere with the machinery of Roman authority. Neither did they end the demands of the Roman authorities on their subjects, as Hydatius's references to the greedy tax collector and the ravenous soldier show. It is in this context that we may place the well-known testimony of Orosius, who tells us that some Romans preferred poverty and liberty among the barbarians to the burden of Roman taxes.[68] That such a choice might be necessary tells us a great deal about the lasting efficacy of Roman administration. We lack the hard evidence to speak with certainty, but everything we do know suggests that we should describe the years between 409 and 411 as the reign of Maximus. While we cannot gauge the true extent of its reach, it is very probable that his authority extended throughout the whole of the peninsula, even into those areas that had experienced barbarian raids. Those raids were traumatic, and sixty years later Hydatius described them in the bleakest way he could imagine. Nevertheless, they were localized and did nothing to stop Maximus from exacting from the provinces their customary dues.

Maximus reigned until 412, but the defeat and suicide of his patron Gerontius made the end inevitable. Orosius tells us that Maximus was deposed by the Gallic soldiers, who then moved on to Africa.[69] Maximus himself, meanwhile, went off to live among the barbarians. Prosper tells us that after laying aside the purple, Maximus was allowed to live because of his inoffensive character.[70] This explanation is not impossible, but a practical reason is more attractive. As we have seen, the deaths of Gerontius and Constantine III had not ended the problem of Gallic usurpation, and in 412 the generals of Honorius were not at leisure to pursue Maximus into the farthest reaches of Spain. As far as the imperial authorities were concerned the calculation was simple. Gaul, Italy, and Africa always had and always did take precedence over Spain, while usurpations regularly took precedence over barbarian invasions, because barbarians could always be mopped up as time permitted.[71] Under the circumstances of 412, Spain will not have looked like much of a problem and because no usurper reigned there, it could even be viewed as loyal to Honorius. Thanks to the barbarians, imperial control was only nominal, but nominal control was enough so long as the Spanish provinces supported none of the extant usurpers. Only when usurpations had ceased to menace Honorius did his government turn its attention to Spain and decide that its nominal loyalty was to be made a reality.

In the meantime, however, the peninsula seems to have been at peace. Even before his deposition, Maximus's authority had lapsed. So long as Gerontius and his army remained in Spain, the barbarians had confined themselves to plunder and raiding. But in 411, when the rebel general carried his campaign against Constans into Gaul, the invaders ceased merely to plunder and actually settled down to stay in the Spanish provinces in a move that preceded the deposition of Maximus by as much as a year.[72] With his general and campaign army gone, Maximus was unable to maintain control. The barbarians divided up the Spanish provinces without reference to Roman authorities and when Maximus fell in 412, his empire had already disappeared.

What the barbarian division of the Spanish provinces amounted to is a matter of great controversy, but it led to five years of peace and stability in which the Spanish barbarians were left to their own affairs by imperial generals whose attention was occupied elsewhere. Orosius tells us that the barbarians took up farming, though we should not necessarily believe him. His words are only the familiar biblical topos of beating swords into plowshares.[73] The same words, however, confirm what Hydatius reports in his chronicle: the Lord in his mercy turned the barbarians to peace.[74] We know very little about the nature of this peace, but we should reject certain possibilities out of hand. There have been efforts to make the division of the peninsula in 411 fit into a scheme of late Roman *receptio,* the bureaucratic process by which large groups of foreign newcomers were settled on Roman land by imperial officials.[75] But Hydatius is explicit on this point. The barbarians ceased fighting *domino miserante,* through God's agency. Then they *sorte ad inhabitandum sibi provinciarum dividunt regiones.* The word *sorte* in this passage is obscure, but the subject of *dividunt* is not. The barbarians made the division themselves, and they did so for themselves. The local population might have been involved, but Hydatius's language absolutely excludes the possibility of any participation by imperial Roman authorities.

But even with that established, we are no closer to knowing what the provincial division actually entailed. The word *sorte* causes difficulties, because grammatically it should be translated as "by lot." Yet the notion of a casting of lots seems so peculiar that all sorts of far-fetched solutions have been conjured up.[76] The idea that thousands of square miles were apportioned by a roll of the dice is in itself improbable, but we may raise some concrete objections as well. Most important, the division was unequal.[77] The Alans received two provinces, the Siling Vandals one, and the Asdings and Sueves shared a single province between them, a distribution that can hardly have been random. What is more, the most powerful group among the invaders received the most important of the Spanish provinces.[78] The whole problem is one of those instances where the testimony of our source is clearly at odds with all historical logic and there is no satisfactory way to resolve the question.

What we do know is that however they decided the case, in 411 the barbarians ceased fighting and turned to peace. The Hispano-Romans, meanwhile, submitted to the domination of the barbarians. Hydatius describes this regime as servitude. "In the cities and strongholds," he tells us, "the Spaniards who survived the blows of the barbarians who ruled the provinces submitted themselves to servitude."[79] Servitude, in Hydatius's language, need not have had a qualitative implication. The phrase is often used of the rule of a usurper, and Hydatius may mean only that Spain had no legitimate government in 411 because the barbarians and not the emperor ruled it.[80] We cannot know if Hydatius meant that the Spaniards' lot in life was worse under barbarian rule, and the contrast between the devastations of 409–410 and the peace he describes after the provincial division suggests the contrary. Despite this fact, the modern literature tends to paint a very black picture of the decade after 411 by extending across a whole decade the horrors that Hydatius ascribes specifically to 410.[81] This is bad history. Every piece of evidence we have—not just Orosius's biblical rhetoric, but the record of events in Hydatius—implies that the half decade between the settlement of 411 and the campaigns of Wallia's Goths in 416 was a period of peace in the peninsula. This peace allowed the imperial authorities to ignore Spain for half a decade after Maximus was deposed. Then, with all the usurpations suppressed and Honorian administration restored to Gaul, the general Constantius decided that the time had come for aggressive action in Spain. His intervention upset the five-year peace of the Spanish provinces and once again turned the Spanish barbarians to violence in 416.

The Imperial Reconquest under Wallia

Constantius seems to have conceived of the Spanish campaign because a convenient tool for his purposes was already at hand in the shape of the Goths. The revolt of Heraclian in 412 had cut off the African corn supply, which in turn made it impossible for Honorius's government to supply the Goths with the food subsidy that Athaulf had negotiated in return for helping to suppress Jovinus. When the emperor failed to fulfill his part of the bargain, Athaulf reacted promptly. Again taking up arms against Honorius, he captured Narbonne in 413, and in 414 married Galla Placidia, sister of Honorius and a hostage in the Gothic train since the sack of Rome. In the same year, the Roman nobleman Priscus Attalus was raised to the purple by a Gothic king for a second time. Though Heraclian was defeated early in 413, Honorius and Constantius now faced a new usurpation in Gaul, this one backed by Gothic arms. To deal with it, Constantius imposed a blockade on supplies to Narbonne in 415. This embargo forced Athaulf out of Gaul and into Spain, where he took up residence at Barcelona.[82] There the Gothic king was murdered by one of his followers and was succeeded by Sigeric, whose reign lasted a mere seven days before he too was killed.[83] Thereupon Wallia succeeded to the Gothic throne, having undertaken a purge of potential competitors.[84] Either late in 415 or by early in the next year, Constantius negotiated a treaty with the new king of the Goths. According to this treaty, the Goths would return Athaulf's widow Placidia as soon as they had been supplied with the 600,000 *modii* of wheat they required to feed themselves.[85] Before the end of the year the Goths were fighting in Roman service against the Vandals and Alans of Baetica and Lusitania.[86]

Even from so brief a narrative there follow important conclusions for the state of affairs in Spain. Athaulf's peaceful occupation of Barcelona suggests that the city opened its gates to him and allowed the Goths to take up residence there. Certainly there is no hint of violence, any more than there had been at Narbonne two years previously. More importantly, there is no sign of conflict between the Goths and the other barbarians who were living in the peninsula. Instead, the artificial food shortage that had forced the Goths into Spain was gladly made up by the Vandals, who sold the Goths grain at a usurious rate.[87] Clearly, the first concern of the Gothic king was to find a means of feeding his subjects. For this reason, it is universally asserted that Wallia attempted to cross to Africa with the idea of finding a country in which he could feed his people.[88] Perhaps he entertained thoughts of such an expedition, but we may be certain he did not attempt it. Orosius is our only source for this episode and though he speaks of a Gothic army trying to reach Africa, there is no hint that either Wallia himself or his Gothic followers as a whole were involved.[89] Wallia, Orosius says, "was terribly frightened at the judgment of God, since in the previous year, when a large army of Goths furnished with arms and ships strove to cross to Africa, it was struck by a tempest within twelve miles of the straits of Gibraltar, and died a wretched death. Remembering as well the disaster suffered under Alaric, when the Goths attempted to cross to Sicily and were miserably shattered and drowned in the sight of their own people, he made a most favorable peace with the emperor Honorius, giving up many noble hostages."[90]

Not a word, then, of the Gothic people attempting to cross from Cádiz to Africa, nor of Wallia leading them on this adventure. There is in fact no evidence that the Goths as a whole or their king ever left the vicinity of Barcelona in Tarraconensis. Standard accounts depict the whole Gothic people wandering down the Mediterranean coast of Spain before turning back in distress from a failed crossing at Cádiz. This has no basis in the sources. On the contrary, the failure of a Gothic army to get to Africa convinced Wallia that this course was not a viable option and recalled to his memory Alaric's ill-fated attempt on Sicily. On the other hand, buying grain from the Vandals at a *solidus* a scoop was not an arrangement that could be sustained in the long term. All that remained was peace with the emperor and, with peace, sustenance. The negotiations between Wallia and Constantius were carried out by a certain Euplutius, and are not normally localized because the whole Gothic people is envisaged as on the move to or from Africa. In fact, Euplutius's mission will have been played out in or near Barcelona, for Wallia and his followers never left coastal Tarraconensis. The correct reading of Orosius helps clarify our understanding of Constantius's policy toward the Goths in Spain. The continued inability of the Goths to feed themselves in the vicinity of Barcelona was probably a prolongation of the artificial scarcity that Constantius had used to force Athaulf out of Narbonne. By starving the Goths into a treaty, Constantius acquired for himself a Gothic army already in residence in Spain and easily persuaded into reconquering the Spanish diocese on the emperor's behalf. And so in 416 the imperial reconquest of Spain was launched by Gothic proxy.

Wallia's campaigns against the other barbarians in Spain are well-attested but little known.[91] One can say only that from late in 416 until some time in 418 the Goths fought against the Vandals and Alans, though not the Sueves, and succeeded in exterminating the Silings and virtually eliminating the Alans before Constantius called off the Gothic offensive.[92] Orosius was a close contemporary and Wallia's campaigns are the last political events he records.[93] His account, however, is vague and generalized, and Hydatius remains a better witness.[94] The latter's narrative has little color but it is explicit enough: Wallia's campaigns were undertaken with Roman authorization and directed against the Alans and the Siling Vandals in Lusitania and Baetica.[95] Wallia was immediately successful, and the Alan king Addax was killed in the fighting.[96] The Gothic campaigns in the southwestern provinces did not, however, extend into Gallaecia, as is frequently affirmed. The Gallic chronicle of 511, it is true, does imply a Gallaecian campaign of the Goths, but the chronicler is here entirely dependent on Hydatius, whom he would appear to have misunderstood. Hydatius himself says nothing about the Asdings or the Sueves in his account of these campaigns, save to tell us that the remnants of the Alans sought refuge with Gunderic's Asdings.[97]

For the better part of two years, then, Wallia's Goths undertook the work of imperial reconquest, stopping only when Constantius told them to in 417, just before he recalled them to Gaul.[98] The general's reasons for this move have engendered a great deal of speculation, most of which has correctly sought to explain Constantius's action by reference to the state of affairs in Gaul. Perhaps the most plausible view is that the Goths, as easily manipulable allies of the emperor, were settled in Aquitaine with the deliberate intention of discouraging further rebellion among the Gallo-Romans who had so recently supported both Constantine and Jovinus.[99] We need not enter the debate on the settlement here, but may note that by 418 Spanish affairs were in a satisfactory enough state for Constantius to leave them as they stood. Baetica and Lusitania had been emptied of their Vandal and Alan occupants, though the Asding Vandals, whatever Alanic remnants had fled to them, and the Sueves remained unmolested in Gallaecia. That

Constantius called off the campaign before these latter groups had been dealt with is sometimes explained as an attempt to maintain a balance of power among the barbarians, but this overlooks a more logical explanation, based on the administrative structure of the Spanish diocese.[100]

Emperors, as we have seen on more than one occasion, had no objection to a barbarian presence as such so long as the wheels of government continued to turn and revenues continued to flow. The goal of the Spanish reconquest would have by definition to be the reintegration of Spain into the imperial system, its administrative restoration as a functioning diocese. To bring this about, the most important step would be the reconquest and revival of the diocesan capital at Mérida in Lusitania. The Gothic campaigns had been concentrated on Lusitania, and on Baetica, which lies en route to it, while in the provincial capital of Baetica the administrative complex at Cercadilla was in active use in these years.[101] When the Alans had been cleared out of Lusitania, the diocesan vicariate could be restored at Mérida and the Spanish diocese could once again begin to function within the imperial system. Significantly, it is in these years that we once again find a *vicarius* attested in Spain.[102]

Gallaecia, by contrast, was of far less importance. As even its native son Hydatius can tell us, it truly did lie at the ends of the earth. In fact, it was precisely the sort of region that Roman governments had always been willing to let go of when necessity required it, as had been the case with transdanubian Dacia or Britain between the Hadrianic and Antonine walls. This is not to imply that the cession of Gallaecia was planned or indeed even admitted. Such cessions rarely were.[103] Nor does it imply that Constantius had not originally meant for the Goths to make a clean sweep. It does, however, mean that when circumstances suggested to him that the Goths would be of more use in Gaul than in Spain, the situation in Spain was favorable enough to allow such a transfer. Spain had been brought back into the fold of Roman administration. The diocese was once again functional.

In order to sustain the new dispensation, the Spanish diocese was probably garrisoned by a much a larger army than it had been in the fourth century and earlier. Though neither the *Epistula Honorii* nor the *Notitia Dignitatum* provides precisely dateable, or even intelligible, information, both demonstrate that at some point during the reign of Honorius there were *comitatenses,* units of the field army, in Spain. It seems likely that the *comitatenses* attested in the *Epistula* and the *Notitia* came to Spain at around the same time that Wallia's Goths withdrew, which is to say some time in 418.[104] A simple process of elimination makes this hypothesis fairly probable. A field army loyal to the legitimate emperor cannot have been stationed in Spain during the reigns of Constantine III and Maximus, during the half decade between Maximus's deposition and the beginning of Wallia's reconquest, or during the years of reconquest from 416 to late 417 when the only imperial army in Spain was Gothic. The years between Theodosius's death in 395 and the beginning of Constantine's usurpation in 407 are a possibility, though unlikely given the relative peace of the western provinces until at least 405.

This leaves us with only two small windows of possibility. The first is a brief moment in 412 around the time Maximus was deposed. It is just possible that the Gallic soldiers who deposed Maximus belonged to the units of the field army we find noted in one or the other of our documentary sources. This option cannot be ruled out altogether, yet it seems unlikely because Orosius implies that these soldiers moved straight on to Africa. The only remaining possibility is the period immediately after Wallia's reconquest, from early 418 onward, when we do in fact meet a high-ranking Roman general, the *comes Hispaniarum* Asterius, waging a war against a usurper and also against the Vandals in Gallaecia. The sources for these campaigns imply that Asterius led a force already present in the peninsula, rather than an expeditionary force sent in specially for the campaign, which would in turn suggest the sort of force depicted in the *Notitia* and the letter of Honorius. It is thus very possible that the field army described in the *Notitia* was sent to Spain at the same time as the Goths were recalled, and that two years later it was under the command of the *comes* Asterius. This same Asterius tried to complete the work of restoration begun by Wallia, but instead managed to undermine what the Gothic king had already accomplished.

The Squandering of Wallia's Achievement

When the Goths withdrew from Spain in 418, the Asding Vandals and Sueves remained undisturbed in Gallaecia. They had taken no part in the fighting against Wallia, and after the Gothic withdrawal they seem to have occupied themselves as peaceably as they had done since the sharing out of the provinces in 411, until imperial initiative once again broke the peace.[105] In 420, the *comes Hispaniarum* Asterius attacked the Vandals in Gallaecia and forced them to break off a war with the Sueves that had begun in 419 for reasons which Hydatius does not record. In the course of the fighting, the Vandal king Gunderic besieged the Sueves under their king Hermeric in the Erbasian mountains.[106] As Hydatius tells it, "the Vandals gave up their siege of the Sueves after the appearance of the *comes Hispaniarum* Asterius, and after some men under the *vicarius* Maurocellus had been killed in their flight from Braga, the Vandals left Gallaecia and crossed into Baetica."[107]

Despite many attempts to find deep policy in Asterius's actions, it looks rather more as if he simply seized his chance when the wrangling of two barbarian kings offered him an opportunity to finish off the work begun by Wallia.[108] If so, the campaign was a disaster. Instead of completing the reconquest that Wallia had started, Asterius reversed its results. The Vandals might have been content to be left to themselves in Gallaecia—the withdrawal of the Goths had prompted no action on their part, after all—but Gunderic was ready to fight back when attacked. Rather than defeating the Vandal king, Asterius inspired him to leave off fighting the Sueves and attack the Romans instead. Gunderic chased off Asterius, killed some of Maurocellus's men in Braga, and then marched on into Baetica.[109] As a result, a province that Wallia had reconquered for the emperor was invaded by the Vandals and the foundation of imperial government in the peninsula again became insecure. Although there is no evidence that such important centers as Mérida or Córdoba were threatened by the Vandals in Baetica, Gunderic's followers were now at large in the heartland of the Spanish diocese instead of confined to distant Gallaecia.

Despite this setback, however, Asterius was soon promoted to the rank of patrician.[110] This promotion is not the paradox it might seem, for although he lost to Gunderic, Asterius won a campaign far more important from the imperial point of view: he defeated a second usurpation of Gerontius's old client Maximus and sent the captured usurper to Ravenna, where he was led in triumph during the celebration of Honorius's *tricennalia* in January 422.[111] This usurpation almost certainly began in the second half of 419 and, given that Orosius attests Maximus's barbarian connection, one might suspect that Maximus seized the purple with the support of the Gallaecian barbarians, even though the sources are silent.[112] The involvement of Asterius in the suppression of Maximus is, by contrast, quite certain and can be deduced from a letter of the Balearic landowner Consentius to Saint Augustine, written between September 420 and March 421.[113] In it, Consentius describes Asterius's military command in language that can only refer to the suppression of a usurper.[114] The details of this campaign are beyond recovery, and we cannot be sure whether Asterius defeated Maximus in 420 or 421. Regardless, the singularly hapless usurper was once again deposed, and this time he was taken to Ravenna, where he graced Honorius's celebration of thirty years on the throne.

Asterius, for his part, was made *patricius* in succession to the great Constantius, who had become Honorius's imperial colleague in February 421. We know nothing else about Asterius's career, and he may have died soon afterward. His success against a usurper had real consequence for the unity of the empire and won him his reward. His failure against Gunderic, however, meant that at least part of the Baetican province that Wallia had restored was no longer securely in imperial hands. The next attempt at making good this loss came soon enough, a measure of how much more stable and efficient Honorius's government was in the 420s than it had been a decade before. In 422, the *magister militum* Castinus was sent to Spain to attack the Vandals in Baetica, leading both a Roman army and a force of Gothic auxiliaries.[115]

His campaign generated wide interest among contemporaries because it involved the Roman general Boniface, a hero of the Gothic war of 413 and, after the death of Constantius in 421, one of the most powerful men in the western empire. Boniface was to have joined the expedition of Castinus, but a quarrel between the two men caused Boniface to desert and go to Africa instead.[116] Even without the aid of

Boniface, Castinus's campaign was at first a great success. He ran the Vandals to ground and besieged them at an unknown site, where he brought them to the edge of surrender. Then, however, he ventured an open battle. His calculation was understandable enough. Set-piece battles were a Roman specialty and, with few exceptions, barbarians could not win them.[117] Hydatius regards Castinus as foolish for having risked an open battle, but he wrote with the benefit of hindsight. Under the circumstances, Castinus could quite reasonably have expected to win a decisive victory. But his calculation failed. When his Gothic auxiliaries deserted, he was defeated by the Vandals and forced to flee to Tarragona.[118] But then events at Rome supervened, with the death of Honorius and the usurpation of John. From the perspective of the imperial center, the Spanish situation was of secondary importance, as so often before. For that reason, it was many years before the retreat of Castinus could be made good.

Eight

The End of Roman Spain

astinus's defeat did not mean the cession of Spain to the barbarians, but it opened another period of imperial disengagement that made later attempts at restoration more difficult. The problem, as so often during the reign of Honorius, came from Spain's position on the imperial periphery: within a year of his defeat, Castinus and with him the whole of the western empire was diverted from the Spanish situation by far more pressing matters in Italy. When Honorius died in 423, his *primicerius notariorum* Iohannes seized the western throne, a usurpation in which Castinus himself had a hand.[1] The Spanish diocese, along with Britain, Gaul, and Africa, was neglected by John's subsequent administration, and it was quite some time before the imperial government, under the renascent Theodosian dynasty of Valentinian III, had the leisure to once again consider Spain. It found the situation there far more parlous than it had been fifteen years before, when Constantius had commissioned Wallia to fight his Spanish battles for him.

Spain in the Reign of Valentinian III

John's usurpation meant disturbance at the heart of the empire, while the subsequent struggles between Aëtius and Boniface for predomi-

176

nance at the court of Valentinian kept the focus of imperial politics squarely on Italy. In the meantime, having been stirred into action by the imperial government, the Vandals were not slow to take advantage of that government's distraction. From their base in Baetica, they sent expeditions to the Balearics and Mauretania Tingitana, and pillaged Cartagena in 425.[2] They sacked Seville in that same year, and it is almost certain that all of these raids were seaborne. Seville, after all, could be reached in seagoing vessels, and Cartagena was readily accessible to Baetica by sea, much less so by land. This fact would seem to suggest that the Vandal base lay in or near one of the main coastal towns of Baetica like Iulia Traducta, Cádiz, or Málaga. There is no real way of telling, though the exploits of 425 do provide our earliest evidence of the Vandal seamanship that was to become infamous as the fifth century wore on.

Gunderic's regime in Baetica was a matter of plunder and extortion, rather than the government of a subject province, for though we hear of the Vandals sacking cities, nowhere do they seem to have retained control of them. The case of Seville is decisive here, for having sacked it once in 425, Gunderic had to capture it again in 428. It was at Seville that Gunderic died in that same year, to be succeeded by his brother Gaiseric.[3] This Gaiseric, perhaps the greatest barbarian leader of the fifth century, was soon to become the chief threat to the peace of the Mediterranean.[4] He may have defeated an imperial army soon after his accession, but the evidence is not good.[5] Either way, he did not reign long on Spanish soil, for in May 429 he led his followers to Africa, where they soon carved out a Vandal kingdom that endured a hundred years.[6] The one sure fact we possess about this Vandal exodus is its date. Though the number of Vandals who sailed from Iulia Traducta is also reported, the figure of eighty thousand has more typological than historical significance and we need not accept it as genuine.[7] The assumption has long been that the whole Vandal people made the short journey from Baetica across the straits of Gibraltar to Tangiers and then proceeded overland to the African diocese.[8] However, between their embarkation in Spain in May 429 and the siege of Hippo in the spring of 430 a full year later, we know nothing at all of their movements.[9]

Two points must be made. In the first place, the journey overland from Tingitania to Africa is undocumented and all logic militates against it. We have explicit evidence for Vandal seamanship before 429/430, Vandal numbers are unknown and need not have required an impossibly large number of boats, and the land route from Tingitania to Caesariensis was largely uncharted. Late imperial itineraries show that travel east from Tangiers was normally by sea: *a Tingi litoribus navigatur usque Ad Portus Divinus.*[10] We should, if only out of common sense, presume a sea journey from Tingitania unless evidence against it can be cited. Second, there is the evidence of Hydatius already quoted. Hydatius tells us that the Vandals raided Tingitania in 425 after their attacks on the Balearics, Cartagena, and Seville, but his language may mean something more than that. Hydatius tells us that the Vandals *invadunt* Tingitania, and the verb *invadere* can mean not only to invade, but also to take possession of something. That, in fact, is its most common usage in the law codes of the late empire. Given that, we need to seriously entertain the possibility that Gunderic had in 425 established a forward base of some sort in Tingitania and thus occupied positions on both sides of the straits of Gibraltar. The project of invading Africa, in other words, may have been conceived some time before Gaiseric actually put it into practice in 429. This is admittedly speculative, but it allows the early Vandal kings a strategic intelligence for which they are not often given credit.

Regardless of such speculation, Gaiseric and his followers had left the European provinces of Spain by May 429 and within the year had abandoned Tingitania as well. The Suevic leader Hermengarius had attempted to capitalize on Gaiseric's departure and raid into Baetica, but Gaiseric's last act on Iberian soil was to defeat the Sueve at Mérida and watch him drown there in the Guadiana.[11] The later history of Gaiseric's reign does not concern us, but with the Vandal king gone, the Roman emperor was left with just a single group of barbarians on Spanish soil. After 429, imperial efforts would henceforth be directed against the Sueves, although no such efforts were made for quite some time on account of the sanguinary contests among Valentinian's generals. By 433 Aëtius had succeeded in eliminating his rivals and taking control of imperial policy. The rest of the 430s were taken up with a series of campaigns against Burgundians, Franks, Iuthungi, rebel Nori, and, repeatedly, the Goths.[12] Most of Aëtius's campaigns were essentially frontier wars, but the multiple campaigns against the Goths require some consideration.

By settling the Goths to serve imperial ends, Constantius had effectively created a new power group that could compete for influence within late Roman Gaul. The Gothic provinces retained their Roman governors, but a Gothic royal court with its attendant Gothic army cannot have helped but exercise a powerful influence on Gallo-Roman affairs. Theoderic's position was anomalous, for though he was a legitimate member of the Roman polity, he and his followers were outsiders in terms of the hierarchy of imperial office.[13] This meant that, though for the most part he acted within the Roman polity and tried to manipulate affairs as much as he could from within, he could sometimes choose, and was sometimes constrained, to act as an outsider and attack the imperial system to achieve his ends. Our evidence for these activities is limited and it is often difficult to know whether we are dealing with actions directed by the Gothic king, or instead the activities of independent Gothic bands.[14]

Nevertheless, the Goths sometimes proved disappointing allies for the imperial government: in 425, and again in 430, there was fighting near Arles, in 436 a siege of Narbonne was lifted by the general Litorius, and in 438 and 439 a full-scale war was fought.[15] Litorius again commanded, but when he was captured, the praetorian prefect Eparchius Avitus had to negotiate a truce, which in the end proved lasting.[16] In the sources, these battles have a peculiar air of normality about them, as if they troubled contemporaries very little. Despite them, contemporaries thought highly of Theoderic and regarded him as a generally loyal subject of the emperor. All these Gothic campaigns, however, had important consequences for the Iberian peninsula. The difficulties with Theoderic contributed to the persistent imperial neglect of Spain throughout the 430s. Then, from the end of the 439 war until his death more than a decade later, Theoderic remained a close ally of Aëtius and the imperial government in Gaul. As such, he became the main weapon of imperial policy in Spain in a series of campaigns that would involve the Goths more deeply in peninsular affairs than they had ever been hitherto.

We must emphasize that despite the continuous distraction of the imperial authorities, Spain remained remarkably peaceful for nearly ten years after Gaiseric led his Vandals out of the peninsula to Africa. During that decade, the Sueves continued to confine themselves to Gallaecia, while even in that province Romans seem to have retained the key positions.[17] The Suevic king at the time was Hermeric and he, like all the Sueves, has rather an unsavory reputation. He had been king since at least 419, and one is accustomed to seeing him portrayed as the first of a line of perfidious Suevic rulers whose first aim was to break any agreement into which they entered.[18] We may note that the evidence bears this out only in part. First, Hermeric is never once known to have acted outside Gallaecia. Second, even in Gallaecia, only four years of a nineteen-year reign were taken up with aggression against the locals.[19] That is still a lot of fighting, and it seems that in the last year of his reign, just before his abdication, Hermeric had once again been fighting with some of the Gallaecians.[20] But this is a far cry from the random savagery presented in modern histories, and, more important, a far cry from the terms in which Hydatius described the first years of barbarian occupation in the peninsula. More important still, we must remember that Hermeric in all his reign never once disturbed the peace of the other Spanish provinces. The assumption must therefore be that, with the Vandals gone and the Sueves fighting to assert themselves in Gallaecia, those other provinces returned to a more or less normal life.

The peace of the Spanish diocese was broken in 438. The cause was a change of leaders among the Sueves. Hermeric was a sick man, and he abdicated in favor of his son Rechila. Rechila took to the offensive, surely because the Suevic power base in Gallaecia had been secured by his father. In 438, he campaigned in Baetica, defeating one Andevotus and capturing his treasure.[21] The identity of this Andevotus is wholly uncertain. Some would have him a Roman general, others a Vandal chieftain who had remained behind after 429. More likely he was a powerful landowner or local aristocrat in Baetica.[22] Regardless, this first campaign of Rechila was a minor one, a prelude to more ambitious exploits to come. In the next year, 439, the Suevic king invaded Lusitania and took Mérida.[23] It was a rich prize in more senses than one. Mérida was the metropolitan capital of the Spanish diocese and from the point of view of a Roman administrator the most important city in Spain. The symbolic value of taking it from imperial hands would have been high, and it was rich in purely material terms as well, but Rechila seems to have entertained the grander ambition of conquering all Lusitania at the same time. We find him in that same year accepting the surrender of a Roman *comes* at Myrtilis, the modern Mértola, far to the south down the Guadiana river.[24] This official, the count Censurius, had earlier been one of numerous imperial envoys to the Sueves, and Mértola lay along one line of retreat from Mérida.[25] In 441 Rechila was in Baetica rather than southern Lusitania. He took Seville and thereafter, according to Hydatius, he brought Baetica and Carthaginiensis under his *potestas*.[26]

It is hard to know what that *potestas* or authority consisted in. It surely did not mean an occupation of the Spanish provinces in any systematic way. For one thing, there were not enough Sueves. Suevic *potestas* almost certainly consisted of an ability to exact tribute periodically, a tribute that differed only in name from the plundering raids that were a familiar part of barbarian policy. The geographical distribution of Rechila's campaigns is suggestive in this respect. They were understandably enough focused on the densely populated regions around centers of Roman administration. The attacks on Seville and Mérida are self-explanatory, while Mértola was a rich commercial center in the *conventus Pacensis* with close ties to the rest of the Roman world.[27] It thus seems likely that Rechila aimed not at occupying Roman territory but rather at eliminating Roman officials in the southern Spanish provinces. By doing so, he eliminated alternative sources of local power and direct competitors for the wealth and revenues of the regions. Hydatius tells us that, after 441, Rechila held Gallaecia, Lusitania, Baetica, and Carthaginiensis in his *potestas*. Yet in all his subsequent testimony he shows the Sueves based in the vicinity of Mérida, which was clearly the Suevic king's favored residence. In the other provinces, we should presume that Rechila's conquest was largely nominal, and consisted more in the ability to raid and collect tribute without the opposition of imperial authorities than in a physical occupation of territory.

Though Baetica and Carthaginiensis were not actually occupied, the imperial administration of these provinces does seem to have stopped. This may have occurred with the acquiescence, or perhaps even the connivance, of powerful provincial interests. In the same year that Rechila conquered Baetica there occurred the Sabinus affair, in which the bishop of Seville was evicted from his see and replaced un-canonically by another. There is reason to think that the expulsion of Sabinus was linked to the Suevic conquest, for when the Sueves were expelled from Baetica, Sabinus was restored to his see.[28] We might sus-pect that some provincials seized on the opportunities presented by the Suevic conquest to achieve their own ends in local politics. If this is so, the collapse of the imperial administration may not have been entirely unwelcome to at least some provincials. Indeed, the same thing is suggested by the eventual reaction of the imperial government to the Roman inhabitants of the regions conquered by Rechila between 439 and 441. That reaction, however, was half a decade in coming, for as always Spain came low on the list of imperial priorities. Rechila's ex-pansionary campaigns had coincided with years of extreme Vandal pressure on the empire, and it is quite possible that Rechila launched his attacks in the sure knowledge that the emperor would regard the Vandals as a greater threat and leave him be in Spain. If this is true, Rechila's calculation was correct and when the peace treaty of 442 put a temporary stop to Vandal aggression, a more immediately pressing problem than the Sueves had developed in Spain. In 441, the same year that Rechila took Seville, we hear of Spanish Bacaudae for the first time.

Who exactly the Bacaudae were has become a matter of controversy. Long regarded as organized groups of rebellious peasants, they are now sometimes seen as the semi-militarized clienteles of local strong-men, who were thereby enabled to stand to some extent outside the control of imperial government.[29] Unfortunately, the sources provide little support for this latter view and the Bacaudae are best regarded as the sort of well-organized bandits who were so general a feature of Ro-man provincial life.[30] Be that as it may, Bacaudae are mentioned spo-radically in Gaul in the fourth and fifth centuries but appear only briefly in Spain, in the 440s.[31] Their range of action was limited to Tarraconensis, and more precisely the upper and middle Ebro valley, but they were nevertheless a threat with which imperial authorities had to deal before any thought could be given to the Sueves. In the first place, unlike the Sueves, the Spanish Bacaudae operated in one of the most important regions of the Spanish diocese. Zaragoza sat astride the main crossing point of the Ebro and was the point at which all the peninsula's main interior roads intersected.

More important, Bacaudae did more than threaten to withdraw a given region temporarily from imperial control. Instead, whether they were revolting peasants or impractically independent landlords, Bacaudae threatened to overturn the whole basis of that control. That is, rather than merely cutting off revenues from imperial coffers, which barbarians might do when they occupied a region, Bacaudae threatened to do away with the structures of landholding that actually generated imperial revenue. And so Bacaudae were dealt with brutally. Two different Roman generals were sent to crush the Spanish rebels. In 441, Asturius slaughtered a large number of Bacaudae somewhere in Tarraconensis, while in 443 Merobaudes smashed a group that was based at Araceli, in the Basque country far from the Ebro valley.[32] These campaigns were apparently successful enough to satisfy imperial policy, though by its very nature rural resistance could not be stamped out completely and Tarraconensian Bacaudae reappeared in 449.[33] Nevertheless, the defeat in 443 was sufficient for a time and the imperial government experienced no trouble from Bacaudae when it undertook the next of its campaigns against the Sueves in Spain.

In 446 a certain Vitus, about whom we know nothing else, advanced into Carthaginiensis and Baetica in command of both Roman and Gothic forces: "Vitus was made *magister militum* and sent to Spain supported by the aid of a substantial army. After he had harassed the inhabitants of Carthaginiensis and Baetica, when the Sueves arrived there with their king, he fled driven by a pitiable terror when the Goths who had come to aid him in plunder were likewise defeated in battle."[34] This record of the campaign, though short, is also suggestive. In the first place, Vitus is described as harrying the inhabitants of Carthaginiensis and Baetica. It was, of course, the usual practice of late Roman armies to despoil the provincial territories through which they marched, and Hydatius is elsewhere quite explicit in reprehending the voraciousness of imperial soldiers.[35] As we have seen, however, there is some evidence that parts of provincial society in Baetica and Carthaginiensis had cooperated with the Suevic occupiers in 440 and 441 for their own ends. Vitus's campaign may confirm this interpretation, and his despoiling of the provincials may imply that, in the eyes of the imperial government at least, they had indeed colluded in the Suevic occupation and therefore needed to be punished. Regardless of this, Vitus's campaign was an abject failure. The Sueves defeated both the Roman general and his Gothic auxiliaries, and proceeded to plunder Baetica and Carthaginiensis.[36]

The Suevic army had marched from its base in Lusitania to deal with Vitus, which implies that, even before this campaign, Suevic *potestas* had not meant actual occupation of Baetica or Carthaginiensis. Despite Vitus's defeat, it seems likely that both provinces were restored to imperial control, even if they remained vulnerable to Suevic incursions. This interpretation is suggested by three points. First, in 449 the *comes* Censurius was again in Spain, this time at Seville, the second city of Baetica. He was assassinated there, for reasons unknown, by another commander who would later become a minister of the Gothic king Theoderic.[37] Second, the next imperial campaigns against the Sueves were fought not in Carthaginiensis and Baetica, but in Gallaecia and Lusitania, which implies the control of the provinces farther east. Finally, in 455 we find the Sueves attacking regions of Carthaginiensis that, we are told, they had previously returned to the Romans.[38] Not one of these points is strictly speaking probative, but their sum suggests that the campaign of Vitus succeeded in restoring imperial government in Baetica and Carthaginiensis. Either way, the Sueves themselves remained based in Lusitania.[39] It was there, in his residence at Mérida, that King Rechila died two years after his defeat of Vitus.[40]

Rechila was succeeded in August 448 by his son Rechiar, who inaugurated his reign with a plundering expedition in an unknown province, possibly Carthaginiensis or Tarraconensis.[41] Rechiar was to prove the most assertive of Suevic kings, and one who seems actively to have rejected imperial authority instead of just fighting to control a share of imperial territory. Rechiar has the distinction of being the first barbarian king to mint coins in his own name.[42] This is tremendously important. In the late empire, minting was a declaration of independence. Imperial usurpations were announced by the striking of coinage, without which there was no usurpation.[43] This principle would have been known to the barbarians. We possess many coins of the early fifth century struck in regions that had come under barbarian control, but they are coins struck in the name of the ruling emperor.[44] They were therefore advertisements of loyalty, demonstrating that these barbarian regions remained parts of the empire. Not just the Goths, whose general faithfulness no one questions, but even the Vandals, minted only in the imperial name until the very end of the century. We cannot, of course, know Rechiar's mind. But by placing his own monogram on the coinage, he was in effect declaring his withdrawal from the *imperium Romanum*. That, at least, is how any Roman contemporary would have understood his action.

Rechiar's father and grandfather had been opportunists. They had snatched at Roman territory close at hand when it seemed safe to do so. Rechiar was far bolder. The first action of his reign was a march to Toulouse, where he married a daughter of the Gothic king Theoderic late in 448.[45] The Goth seems to have been hedging his bets, rather than proclaiming any anti-imperial policy: Visigothic princesses had been married to Suevic and Vandal leaders in the past without causing the Goths the least hesitation in fighting against their peoples, and just such a Gotho-Suevic alliance had produced the patrician Ricimer.[46] Returning to Spain with his bride in February 449, Rechiar attacked certain Basques, but he was back in Toulouse again in July 449. This time, his return march coincided with a renewed outburst of Bacaudic activity: the Bacaudic leader Basilius invaded the small town of Tarazona, the center of a prosperous mining valley, and killed some imperial soldiers who had taken shelter in the church there.[47] Rechiar, we are told, joined the Bacaudic leader Basilius in pillaging the territory of Zaragoza.[48] Lérida, well to the east of Zaragoza and distressingly close to the provincial capital at Tarragona, was entered and some of its population seized soon afterward, but it is impossible to say whether this was the work of Basilius, Rechiar, or the two in combination.[49]

This is the last we hear of Rechiar until after the assassination of Valentinian III, when, as Suevic leaders were accustomed to do, he seized the opportunity of chaos within the Roman ranks to again attack some of the Spanish provinces. Between 449 and 455, however, the Sueves seem to have contented themselves with those provinces that were then under their control, that is, with Gallaecia and Lusitania. It is not impossible that it was Rechiar's father-in-law Theoderic, then on very good terms with the imperial government, who constrained him to good behavior. On the other hand, the Hun attack on the western provinces may have provided Rechiar or some of his followers with another opportunity to break the peace.[50] All in all, the emperor's Spanish provinces, Carthaginiensis and Baetica included, seem to have been relatively stable. Parts of inland Tarraconensis continued to suffer from Bacaudic uprisings, but these were dealt with soon after the defeat of Attila.

In 453 or 454, Frederic, brother of the new Gothic king Theoderic II, went to Tarraconensis and campaigned against the Bacaudae, apparently with success, for the name never appears again in Spain.[51] This campaign has a symbolic importance beyond its immediate effect. The Goths had intervened in Spain on behalf of the emperor before, but not since the days of Wallia three decades earlier had they done so under their own command. The Spanish campaigns since the Gotho-Roman peace of 439 had been undertaken by Roman generals, commanding joint Gothic and Roman armies. But now, in the very last years of Valentinian's reign, we first encounter the dynamic that dominates the final years of Roman Spain. Frederic fought the Bacaudae *ex auctoritate Romana,* but not under Roman command. The task of maintaining imperial control in Spain had been delegated to the Goths. During the reigns of Avitus and Majorian this pattern intensified, and Spain was kept part of the Roman empire by Gothic energies.

Avitus and the Last Roman Reconquest

Valentinian III was assassinated on 16 March 455, and, whether or not he had orchestrated the assassination, Petronius Maximus profited by it and declared himself Augustus on 17 March. His reign was not a happy one. The Vandal king Gaiseric used revenge for Valentinian as a pretext to sail on Rome and sack the city. Maximus was killed on 31 May as he tried to flee. During his brief reign Maximus had appointed a Gallic aristocrat and former praetorian prefect, Eparchius Avitus, as *magister militum* and sent him to the Gothic court at Toulouse, where Theoderic II, second son of the late Theoderic, had been king for nearly two years, having murdered his elder brother Thorismund in 453. Theoderic was a cultured man, much given to the habits of a Roman aristocrat, but he was also a man of great caution. In a reign of fourteen years, he would prove hesitant in flexing Gothic muscles: though confronted by no fewer than five imperial vacancies in the course of his reign, he never once acted without a great deal of prodding and persuasion. This makes his decisive action in 455 somewhat anomalous.

Avitus was still at Toulouse when the news of Maximus's death arrived there and the *magister militum* decided to take the purple himself.[52] We know far more about Avitus than other ephemeral emperors of the later fifth century because he had an able panegyrist in the person of his son-in-law, the poet Sidonius Apollinaris.[53] Sidonius suggests that it was Theoderic who urged Avitus to take the purple, and many scholars have therefore been inclined to view Avitus as a Gothic puppet. This is highly improbable, for Avitus was a well-connected member of the prickly Gallic aristocracy, and other sources imply that the Gallic army lay behind the proclamation. Indeed, his actual acclamation as emperor on 9 July 455 came at Arles, the administrative capital of Gaul for half a century and the seat of the *concilium* that bound the Gallic aristocracy together. Avitus may already have planned a coup that the death of Maximus made easier, or the Gallic army may have wished to present Italy with a fait accompli, but either way we must discard the idea of Theoderic as the power behind Avitus's throne. The Gothic king was convinced to lend his approval to an arrangement that was going to be carried through whether he liked it or not.

Avitus's brief reign lasted for less than two years, but it was of considerable significance for Spain. Under Avitus, the last concerted effort was made to reestablish complete imperial control of the peninsula, an effort that was rewarded by almost complete success. Avitus's first concern was understandably enough not the Sueves, but rather the securing of his own position. From Arles he proceeded to Rome, where he was accepted by the populace and designated consul for the following year.[54] In pursuit of his own imperial ends, Avitus might well have been content to leave the Sueves to their own devices, had their king Rechiar not taken matters further than was tolerable by invading Tarraconensis.[55] At the new emperor's behest, Theoderic launched a full-scale war against his brother-in-law Rechiar and put an end to the Suevic kingdom within the year.

Early in the autumn of 456, Theoderic led a large Gothic army into northern Spain and marched on Gallaecia. At least at the start of this campaign, he was accompanied by the Burgundian kings Chilperic and Gundioc, though whether they actually took part in the fighting that followed is open to question.[56] The march across Tarraconensis seems to have been unopposed, but on 5 October Theoderic brought Rechiar to battle near the river Urbicus, the boundary of the *civitas* of Astorga and about 8 kilometers from the city, right on the edge of Gallaecia. The Sueves were routed and a great many fled the battlefield, their king among them.[57] Rather than leave matters there, Theoderic determined to eliminate Suevic power entirely, cutting a swathe through the heart of Suevic territory. By the end of October he had advanced from Astorga in the foothills of the Cantabrian mountains to Braga in the far west and on 28 October, Theoderic sacked the city.[58]

Braga and its *conventus* had been the center of the Suevic polity since the first division of the Spanish provinces, and even though the Suevic kings had preferred to reside in Mérida since 439, the region around Braga would remain a Suevic stronghold for more than a century to come. The Gothic sack cannot have been too destructive, for Theoderic stayed on at Braga for several months, perhaps using it as a base from which to put down continued Suevic resistance in Gallaecia. Rechiar was captured at Oporto at the mouth of the Douro and taken back to Braga, where he was executed in December.[59] The location was no doubt deliberately chosen to impress upon both Sueve and Hispano-Roman that a new dispensation was at hand, even in the Suevic heartland. For Hydatius, certainly, Theoderic's conquest marked the end of the Suevic kingdom and his judgment is suitably lapidary: *regnum destructum et finitum est Sueuorum.*[60]

On the other hand, Theoderic himself seems to have been less sure of the situation. He advanced into Lusitania, wherein Suevic kings had chosen to reside for the previous twenty-five years.[61] The Gothic king apparently contemplated sacking Mérida, which may imply that he met resistance there, though whether this is the case, and if so, from whom, is impossible to tell.[62] Hydatius tells us that the city's patron saint Eulalia intervened, and the city's populace may have shared his views when Theoderic decided not to sack the city, but rather to set up his winter residence there. In the meantime, Gallaecia experienced the inevitable aftermath of a full-blown war, an outburst of banditry and the small-scale reorganization of survivors among the vanquished Sueves.[63] Theoderic, for his part, had achieved what he set out to do *cum voluntate et ordinatione Aviti imperatoris,* that is, destroy the Suevic kingdom and restore its provinces to Roman control. When Theoderic took Mérida, the diocesan capital of Spain was restored to the imperial government for the first time in fifteen years.

Avitus, meanwhile, had been less lucky. Driven from Rome in early autumn 456, defeated by Ricimer, and consecrated bishop of Placentia in October, he was murdered soon afterward by the general Majorian, who would himself become emperor a year later.[64] The news reached Theoderic early in 457 and in early April he set off to Toulouse, presumably to guard his own position in Gaul. He left behind him garrisons to enforce his settlement.[65] Hydatius puts the worst possible construction on their intentions, and it seems that a number of cities and fortresses in Gallaecia were sacked by the Gothic garrison. The looting would no doubt have appealed to the troops in and of itself, but this was no Gothic assault on the Roman provinces of Spain. The army's mission was explicitly to put down the remnants of the Sueves. As Hydatius himself admits, the Goths acted on imperial authority, and all the violence that Hydatius records took place in formerly Suevic territory. The Hispano-Roman provincials suffered at the hands of the Gothic army, but that suffering implied the restoration of imperial authority.[66] At the local level, we begin to see in these years the start of the patterns that would dominate Spain's post-Roman history, patterns of local notables in competition with small Suevic forces and the Spanish representatives of the Gothic king at Toulouse. The difference, in the years between 456 and 460, was that the Goths who kept the peace did so for the sake of the emperor and the imperial government. For Avitus, Theoderic had truly been what Sidonius later called him: *Romanae columen salusque gentis.*[67] The Gothic king had conquered Spain for Avitus, and the order he had established there was maintained under Avitus's successor Majorian.

Majorian

The months after Avitus's death were a time of confusion. In Spain, Theoderic strove to maintain the control so recently established. In the

northwest, the remnants of the Sueves had returned to their customary harassment of the Gallaecians, while different chieftains struggled
among themselves for supremacy. This was not on a scale to worry
Theoderic, who held the diocesan capital at Mérida and whose army
had suppressed potential opposition in the north. On the other hand,
Theoderic does seem to have been concerned to hold the south, for he
sent an army to Baetica in 458. We may suspect that it was the political machinations of the local urban elite that made the move necessary: it is at precisely this time that Sabinus, the exiled bishop of Seville, returned to Spain from Gaul and reclaimed his see from the man
who had displaced him around the time of the Suevic conquest twenty
years before.[68] Despite these disturbances, there can be little doubt
that Theoderic's regime was effective and that control of the Spanish
provinces lay in the gift of the Gothic king. And so when he was moved
to recognize Majorian as emperor, Theoderic could hand the new emperor control of the Spanish diocese in its entirety.

Nevertheless, Theoderic's recognition of Majorian was long in coming. Disturbed as the months after Avitus's death were in Spain, they
were considerably more so in Gaul and Italy. A complex cycle of political maneuvering began, involving not just Avitus's assassin Majorian, but a whole variety of local powers in Italy and Gaul, together
with an eastern court itself thrown into confusion by the death of the
emperor Marcian on 27 January 457. Behind Majorian stood the figure of the patrician Ricimer, though that relationship would soon fall
apart and it was Ricimer who brought Majorian's reign to a premature
end in 461. The first concern of Ricimer and Majorian was to concil-
iate various factions within Italy, which was a slow process. Although
the army acclaimed Majorian as Augustus in April 457, he did not formally take the purple until 28 December.[69] In the meantime, he seems
to have contented himself with the title of *magister militum* and an un-
defined constitutional mandate as he tried to rally together the breadth
of support he would need to rule effectively.[70]

Even after his official proclamation in December, his throne was not
secure, and the diplomatic efforts that eventually won him the support
of the whole Roman West continued right through 458 and into 459.
So long as the Italian situation was unstable, Majorian himself stayed
out of Gaul, and played opposing interests there off against one an-

other. Theoderic took no immediate action, but events forced his hand. On Avitus's death, the Burgundian king Gundioc had taken over much of the territory of Lyons with the active consent of the citizens. When Majorian's general Aegidius moved against Gundioc in 458, Theoderic was forced into opposing Majorian in order to support his Burgundian ally. By the following year, Theoderic had been defeated in battle and forced to submit.[71] Only then did the Gothic king give to Majorian the rule of the Spanish diocese that he had reconquered on behalf of Avitus three years before.

With the Gothic alliance secured, Majorian could plan to use Spain as the base from which to launch a major campaign against the Vandals. The local preparations for this campaign were presumably undertaken by the Gothic army that had been keeping the peace of the province. This army was commanded jointly by a Roman, the *magister militum* and *comes* Nepotianus, and a Goth, the *comes* Suniericus who had commanded the force sent to Baetica early in 459. It is difficult to be precise about the authority under which these two men were serving, and it is perhaps best to think of this force as an imperial army provided by the Gothic king.[72] The preparations for the African campaign will have taken up the winter and early spring of 460. Readying a major offensive could be a slow process, and both accumulating materiel and mustering the men was time-consuming and labor-intensive for those who had charge of it. The invasion fleet was mustered at Portus Illicitanus, on the Mediterranean coast between Cartagena and Valencia in the modern province of Alicante.[73] By May 460, Majorian was ready to come to Spain, presumably at the head of an army.

He almost certainly arrived by way of Aquitaine and Novempopulana rather than from Narbonensis, for he is attested at Zaragoza, which lies on the former route to Spain from Gaul, but not the latter.[74] If this was indeed the route he took, that in turn implies that the emperor came to Spain from the court of Theoderic at Toulouse, and may well have brought more Gothic soldiers with him. Regardless, he got no further than Tarraconensis when news of a heavy blow reached him. Traitors had warned the Vandals of his Spanish preparations and they struck preemptively, burning the fleet at its moorings in the bay of Alicante. Thwarted, Majorian turned and retraced his steps to Gaul.[75] In August of the following year, having demobilized his army in Gaul, he was arrested and executed by the patrician Ricimer at Dertona in the north of Italy.

Imperial Office and Political Life, 400–460

With the withdrawal of Majorian from Spain and his subsequent execution, Spain ceased to be part of a Roman empire, because none of the ephemeral claimants to the throne who followed him could secure their own positions in Italy and Gaul, let alone govern Spain. No imperial officials are attested in Spain after 460, and no Spaniards are known to have held imperial office after that date. The inference is clear: the end of Majorian severed the institutional links between Spain and the imperial government. In the half century before the death of Majorian, those links are repeatedly attested. It is important to bear that in mind and not to extend the Hydatian evidence for the chaotic state of Gallaecia to the rest of the peninsula. Despite the fact that imperial government in Spain was sometimes ineffectual, most of the Spanish provinces continued to function normally within the imperial administrative structure, though the cessation of the imperial coin supply to the peninsula must have had a serious impact on the fiscal aspects of that relationship.[76] Even where the imperial administration functioned badly, there was no notion that the Spanish provinces ceased to be parts of the empire.

Hydatius's chronicle contains very little administrative information, but one of his favorite themes illustrates the normal integration of the Spanish provinces within the imperial system quite well. Hydatius consistently gives great prominence to diplomacy, and records a large number of embassies in the years between 429 and 460, tracing and retracing their steps across the northern half of the peninsula, to and from Gallaecia.[77] We meet envoys from the Goths, from the imperial authority as represented by Aëtius, and from "Romans" more generally, all going to the Sueves. We meet Suevic envoys heading in the other direction, and, in opposition to the Sueves, we meet embassies from the Romans of Gallaecia. Hydatius, it is clear, had a special interest in the topic, and indeed he himself had once been part of a delegation to Aëtius.[78] Most of these embassies seem to have had no real end in view, and even fewer led to results of any importance. For these reasons, a dire interpretation is usually put on them, and by extension on fifth-century diplomacy in general, as visible signs of the emperor's inability to accomplish anything.[79] Yet that is not what the embassies actually tell us.

Internal diplomacy was a commonplace of Roman life under the empire, and had been since long before there were any half-autonomous barbarians settled on Roman soil. This diplomacy was the oil that kept administrative machinery running smoothly and kept the regions of the empire in touch with and tied to the imperial center.[80] Though no doubt of great importance at the local level, these embassies were mundane affairs and hardly worth recording in most of the historical sources that have come down to us. They bulk so large in Hydatius because he had been an envoy himself and took an interest in the subject, not because they were of unusually great importance for developments in fifth-century Spain. The embassies he records between Sueves, Goths, provincials, and imperial authorities were not identical to the traditional embassies of provincials to court, but they were a direct outgrowth of them and had largely the same purpose. They accomplished nothing earth-shattering because they were not meant to do so. Instead, they kept open the lines of communication. Importantly, they ensured that competing groups, Suevic or Gothic, imperial or provincial, knew more or less what the others were doing at any given time. The fifth-century scene was novel inasmuch as some of the groups involved in this internal diplomacy were able, and often willing, to fight the imperial authorities. On the other hand, the structure within which this diplomacy took place was the same as it had been in the fourth century and even earlier. In adapting themselves to it, the Goths and the Sueves expressed their intention of existing within the Roman polity.[81] In a very real sense, the Hydatian account of diplomatic affairs illustrates not the breakdown of imperial authority, but rather its relative continuity, because he shows us the integration of the various barbarian groups into the imperial system.

Hydatius's description of diplomatic activity is in fact a Spanish reflection of political change common to the whole Roman West. The game of political life was still played by the rules that the imperial government had written long before. What had changed was the ability of that government to dictate the winner. In the fourth century, the imperial government had had an overwhelming advantage in politics, and while certain of its representatives could be challenged or attacked, the state itself always won. By the middle of the fifth century, on the other hand, the imperial government met opposing interests, barbarian and provincial both, on more level ground. Across the Roman West, growing challenges to imperial authority helped propel major changes in the organization of society. One change that is particularly notable is the passage of effective government into the hands of soldiers. As the fifth century progresses, we have records of fewer and fewer civilian officials, and history comes to be made increasingly by the empire's *comites* and *duces*.[82]

Spain illustrates this trend quite starkly, for after 420 there is no unequivocal reference to a civilian official in the peninsula and we meet only *magistri, duces,* and *comites* in the pages of Hydatius.[83] Between 425 and 460 the chronicler records the *magistri* Asturius, Merobaudes, and Vitus, and the *comites* Censurius, Mansuetus, and Fronto.[84] The preponderance of military officials is made still more striking by the historic demilitarization of the Spanish provinces, and also by the lack of countervailing civilian institutions. The new militarization of society was shared by the Gallic provinces, but in Gaul, a new *concilium septem provinciarum* had been created in 418, at the same time that military men began more and more to dictate the future of the diocese. Spain had no similar institution, at least not one that was imperially sponsored. Indeed, changes in the urban landscape by the middle of the fifth century make it hard to imagine where any such council in Spain could have met—in Tarragona, for instance, part of the provincial forum had been stripped of its monumental pavement before 440 and people were living, working, and dumping their waste in a place where state business had until recently been conducted.[85] More and more, it seems, links between Spain and the imperial government were maintained militarily, or more precisely, by military men.

Because the Spanish evidence is so limited, we cannot tell whether these trends were more pronounced in Spain than elsewhere. On the other hand, the gradual militarization of the governing hierarchy is well known in Gaul, and there are suggestions of parallel developments in the two regions. Constantius had organized the settlement of 418 to temper the Gallo-Roman tendency to usurpation, not only settling the Goths in Aquitaine and setting up the *concilium septem provinciarum* in Arles, but also allowing Gallo-Romans to monopolize imperial office in Gaul.[86] The dominance of imperial government in Gaul by Gallo-Romans grew steadily, and it seems likely that a similar process took place in Spain. We have only two certain examples: the *comes* Asterius, attested in the peninsula between 419 and 421; and Flavius Merobaudes, poet, panegyrist of Aëtius, and in 443 *magister militum* in Spain. We know that Asterius was an in-law of a Tarraconensian priest named Severus, while Asterius's daughter was either the niece or the granddaughter of Severus's female relative Severa.[87] Since Severa was clearly not Asterius's wife, she must have been either the mother or the sister of his wife. But it is more than this marriage relationship that links Asterius to the Spanish context, for his own words would seem to attest blood relations in Tarraconensis as well.[88] That suggests that he was himself a Hispano-Roman, presumably an aristocrat, and certainly linked by marriage to a powerful clan of Hispano-Roman aristocrats. If this is correct, then we are perhaps justified in seeing a Spanish parallel to Constantius's well-attested Gallic policy.

Another hint of something similar lies in the possible family connection between this *comes* Asterius and the *magister militum* Asturius who fought the Bacaudae of Tarraconensis in 441.[89] That connection can only be speculative, for variations on the name Asterius are neither uncommon in the later empire nor confined to Spaniards.[90] On the other hand, our second Asturius was indisputably the father-in-law of Flavius Merobaudes, the poet and *magister militum,* who is our second definite example of a Hispano-Roman holding office in fifth-century Spain. Merobaudes was a native of Baetica and of good birth, and he left Spain to seek a career at Ravenna.[91] Though we do not know his age, he would have lived through the time of troubles at the beginning of the fifth century. His later *cursus,* everything that a member of the provincial nobility could wish for, illustrates that such careers remained possible in fifth-century Spain. We meet him first as *comes sacri consistorii,* then honored with either the patriciate or the honorary consulate for his skill as an orator.[92] Fragments of his panegyric to Aëtius are extant and form the best-known part of his legacy. On the other hand, Merobaudes's career illustrates the growing militarization of western society we have been discussing, for his final attested office is as *magister militum* in Spain in 443. When last we hear of him, he has been recalled from his Spanish command on account of palace intrigue at the court of Valentinian.[93] That fact is a significant reminder of the peninsula's integration into the wider political life of the western empire.

This political integration was maintained by Majorian, under whom it was still possible to hold imperial office in Spain: Sidonius writes of Magnus, a Narbonensian senator and soon praetorian prefect of Gaul, who held office as *magister* in Spain.[94] But just as Merobaudes is the last Spaniard whom we know to have held high imperial office, so Magnus is the last imperial official we know to have served in Spain. The Gregorius, *vir inlustris,* who was buried in 492 in a place of honor near the tomb of Saint Eulalia in Mérida may also have served the imperial government in his youth.[95] But after Majorian's death such possibilities ceased to exist, and we can no longer sensibly claim that Spain remained Roman. Instead, there begins a long century of political fragmentation to the most local of levels, a century of local communities in conflict with one another. The existence of imperial government in the peninsula, however intermittent, however debilitated, had made a very real difference to Spanish history and had provided a unifying element that disappeared with the emperor and his officials. The absence of this unity, and of any real impulse toward it, marks the aftermath of empire.

Nine

The Aftermath of Empire

O
ur scraps of evidence for the half century after the departure of Majorian from Spain record unconnected details that it is impossible to subsume within a single linear account. They show us a politically fragmented world, in which fundamentally local leaders—Hispano-Roman aristocrats, Suevic chieftains, or Gothic kings and their generals—might sometimes attempt to impose themselves at more than the local level. None of them met with lasting success, and it is fundamentally misleading to treat the later fifth century as the beginnings of a Visigothic Spain.[1] Not only was the Gothic presence in Spain limited in numbers and impact, but the historical dynamic of the period remained very much a product of Roman political traditions and of the institutional shape that centuries of imperial rule had imposed on the peninsula.

Goths, Sueves, and Provincials in Fifth-Century Gallaecia

Try as he might, Theoderic could not keep control of the whole Spanish diocese after 460. The Gothic army stayed on under the command of Suniericus and Nepotianus, who probably made their base at Mérida, the old diocesan capital that had served as Theoderic's own base during his stay in Spain.[2] Their attempts to maintain order were successful only briefly and both men were recalled by Theoderic in 462.[3] It is possible that Nepotianus had become too powerful for Theoderic's liking—the fact that Hydatius takes the trouble to record the general's death in Gaul two or three years after his departure from Spain suggests close ties to at least some Gallaecians.[4] Nepotianus was replaced by one Arborius, which indicates Theoderic's intention of holding on to the Spanish diocese; presumably he wished to use it as a negotiating tool with Majorian's successor as he had once done with Majorian. But the task proved impossible. When Arborius was recalled from Spain in 465, he is himself the only evidence for a Gothic army in the peninsula.[5]

The narrative of Hydatius now begins to document the anarchy it is often thought to show throughout its length. Even before Arborius's recall, Theoderic's generals had to fight both Suevic war bands under their own competing kings and also cities, perhaps led by their local councils, which resisted the Gothic army.[6] After 464, the representatives of the Gothic king were clearly no longer in control of events: in that year or the next we find Theoderic treating with the Sueves as equals for the first time since his campaigns against them under Avitus. He even returned the wife of the Suevic king Remismund, whom he had been keeping as a hostage.[7] The provincials were left to come to terms with the local situation as best they could, forging alliances and breaking them without interference from outside the province. The most the Goths could manage was ineffectual plundering.[8]

That, at least, is the picture that emerges from Hydatius, still our only source. Although he continued his account until 468, the order that was once observable in it disappears. There is little point in recapitulating Hydatius's last few pages as if their narrative tells a story—it does not.[9] Still less is there any point in pretending that the Hydatian evidence holds good for Spain as a whole. After 460, Hydatius records nothing of the Spanish world outside Gallaecia and the *conventus* of Scallabis in westernmost Lusitania. All the same, the historical patterns revealed by these last few entries of Hydatius do tell us something about the social dynamics of life in one post-imperial province, dynamics that may have existed elsewhere in the peninsula as well. The central point is the localism of the political relationships described in the last pages of Hydatius's chronicle.[10] We are confronted by a series of different Suevic groups, by different provincials, and by various representatives of the Gothic king.

With the Sueves, we meet a whole succession of named leaders—Maldras, Frumarius, Remismund, Rechimund—and we may be sure there were others whom Hydatius had no occasion to name. Some have sought to plot the constitutional position of these Sueves or to define the territories that each controlled.[11] Hydatius does not tell us enough to make these exercises profitable. We are, for example, told that on the death of Frumarius, Remismund united the Sueves *regali iure,* but this makes no difference to the behavior of the Gallaecian Sueves in general and there is little to distinguish years in which Remismund was the sole possessor of the royal title from the preceding years in which various men competed for the honor.[12]

The Hispano-Romans we meet are just as motley a bunch. Most are aristocrats of one sort or another, whether Palogorius, an envoy to Theoderic, the family of the Cantaber of Conimbriga, or Lusidius, the betrayer of Lisbon.[13] On the other hand, the social position of the informers Dictynius, Spinio, and Ascanius, responsible for the three-month imprisonment of Hydatius, is never described, though they were presumably prominent citizens of Lugo, or conceivably of Aquae Flaviae.[14] Among the Goths, Hydatius keeps the focus firmly on their peninsular generals, first Suniericus and Nepotianus, then Arborius, while in the background, the distant figure of Theoderic hovers in Gaul. It is usually quite hard to tell how much control Theoderic actually exercised over his generals, and how much control they in turn exercised over the other, unnamed Goths whom we meet in the narrative.

Despite this confusion of powers, historical patterns do emerge. First of all, the scene of action is distinctly focused on towns: the rivalries between various contesting groups enact themselves as struggles for the control of towns. This must reflect political realities rather than a deficiency in the Hydatian narrative, for Hydatius was quite capable of noticing rural conflicts when they impinged upon his story.[15] The focus on the conventual capitals at Scallabis and Lugo is likewise worthy of remark. The last pages of Hydatius would seem to confirm that what was at stake was control of actual nodes of administration, still functioning as such.[16] We must draw a similar inference from the fact that local Sueves made sure to kill the city governor of Lugo.[17]

Nevertheless, the measures taken and alliances made to ensure the control of towns are resistant to simple analysis. First of all, the urban population seems to have been thoroughly mixed, at least in parts of Gallaecia, and there is no question of barbarians in the country and Hispano-Romans in the towns.[18] The communal violence in Lugo at Easter 460 shows as much, for it was Sueves resident in the city who turned on their Roman compatriots during the festive season.[19] And despite the implications of this particular incident, conflicts seem only rarely to have been simple cases of Roman versus barbarian. The Goths sent to punish the Sueves of Lugo by Theoderic's generals were deterred by the Hispano-Romans Dictynius, Spinio, and Ascanius (and it was at the instigation of these three that the Sueve Frumarius took Hydatius captive shortly thereafter, and against their wishes that he later set the bishop free).[20] We find a similar alliance of Sueve and Hispano-Roman in 468, when the Sueves of Remismund took Lisbon only after Lusidius, one of its leading citizens, betrayed the city to them.[21] His motives are obscure, but his alliance with the Sueves was more than momentary: later in the same year, Remismund sent him to Italy as an envoy to the new emperor Anthemius.[22] Elsewhere, local rivalry is portrayed as arising between Hispano-Roman and Sueve. Thus we find the abduction of mother and children from the Conimbrigan family of the Cantaber in 464 or 465.[23] Even here, however, the outrage was possible only after the Sueves had entered Conimbriga *dolose,* and Hydatius's laconic statement may conceal a conflict among the Romans of Conimbriga into which the Sueves were drawn.[24] We are on somewhat firmer ground with the cases of the Aunonenses and the Aurigenses, who are both found in conflict with groups of Sueves. The location of Aunona, and whether it represents a region, or perhaps a town or village, is a matter of dispute, but Remismund's Sueves expended a great deal of effort in trying to capture it.[25] In the case of the Aurigenses, the inhabitants of Orense and its *territorium,* we know only that they suffered at the hands of the Suevic chieftain Rechimund in 460, shortly after the Easter massacre at Lugo that Hydatius records with such disgust.[26]

This incident brings us to the question of the Gothic role. The Lugo massacre took place while Majorian was still alive and Theoderic was still making serious efforts to hold the Iberian peninsula. The king's generals Suniericus and Nepotianus accordingly punished the Sueves for breaking the peace and Suniericus's capture of Scallabis in the same year should be read in a similar light.[27] Gothic generals could experience resistance from both Sueves and Hispano-Romans, not just in these instances, but as far back as 457, when Astorga, Palencia, and the fort at Coviacum had resisted Theoderic's army at a time when it was clearly in the service of the emperor.[28] In each of these cases, the Gothic intervention was satisfyingly punitive, but after the death of Majorian and the return of Suniericus and Nepotianus to Gaul, Gothic action became less effective and Arborius accomplished a good deal less than his predecessor. This change may have been a result of weakness. Though many scholars envisage them as commanders of permanent Gothic garrisons in southern Spain, the evidence of Hydatius is inexplicit, while the subsequent history of Gothic intervention in the peninsula suggests that the armies of the 460s were small expeditionary forces rather than an army of occupation.[29]

Despite this decline in his power to compel obedience, Theoderic remained the single most important figure in the local affairs of western Spain, at least psychologically. The provincials themselves recognized this, for though some might wage war against the Goths, others sent hopeful embassies to Theoderic as they had once sent embassies to Aëtius. These very embassies, however, give us a measure of how much things changed in the few years after Majorian's departure from Spain: in 460, the Goths had been willing to send an army to chastise the Sueves of Lugo for breaching the peace, but by 463 Theoderic did no more than send negotiators—Cyrila, Salla, Opilio, and others unnamed—all of whom are conspicuous by their ineffectuality.[30] Both Sueves and provincials solicited these embassies and were eager to have the ambassadors of the Gothic kings on their side, but the Sueves in particular seem to have been willing to disregard any arrangements they made as soon as the envoys turned their backs.[31] It nevertheless seems clear that, by 463 or 464, there had ceased to be any real prospect of effective Gothic intervention, and the repeated embassies between Gallaecia and Toulouse will have become comfortably *pro forma*. Indeed, one can imagine the Gothic ambassadors haranguing

Roman and Sueve alike about the need to keep the peace, knowing full well how little substance lay behind their words. Whatever the theoretical predominance of the Goths, matters were left to provincial Romans and provincial Sueves to settle for themselves.

This should come as no surprise. By the start of the 460s, two generations of Sueves had been born in Gallaecia and lived out their lives there. They had not known the wandering life of the 410s, let alone the forests of Germany. The Gallaecian Sueves were distinct from their Hispano-Roman neighbors, no doubt. Hydatius testifies as much, and people identified as Sueves survived to the very end of the sixth century, though it is impossible to say how such ethnic distinctions were maintained. Yet, however distinct these Sueves may have been, there was one thing they were not—foreigners. The Sueves whom Hydatius characterizes so unpleasantly were by 460 as native to the Gallaecian landscape as were their Hispano-Roman coevals. We falsify this essential point if we talk of Sueves in the 460s as "invaders." As far back as the 430s some of the people of Carthaginiensis willingly cooperated with the Sueves, at a time and in a context where those Sueves certainly were invaders.[32] In Gallaecia and northern Lusitania in the 460s, cooperation requires no special pleading by way of explanation. Sueves and Romans were neighbors, and just as one fights more readily with a neighbor, so, when circumstance requires, does one cooperate.

As importantly, by the second half of the fifth century, Roman and Sueve were equally native to the northwest of Spain. This helps to explain the extreme localization of the conflicts that we witness in the last pages of Hydatius's chronicle and accounts for our inability to find a simple explanatory pattern in them. Local Sueves and local Romans acted according to antipathies, rivalries, and calculations of interest that defy ethnic categorization and that had causes that are now totally obscure to us. No doubt the dynamics of local power frustrated outsiders at the time as much as they now frustrate our attempts at understanding them—hence the indiscriminate Gothic punishment of both Sueves and Romans in Lusitania after the collusion of Lusidius and some Sueves at Lisbon.[33] Compared to their Roman or Suevic neighbors, the Goths were outsiders. Recruiting them for one's own ends in a local squabble was highly desirable, but in the final analysis,

Hydatius shows us a Spanish north and west in which both violence and cooperation make little reference to the world outside the immediate neighborhood.

Euric, Alaric, and Tarraconensis

Evidence drawn from just eight years in a single chronicle is an uncertain foundation for generalization. Unfortunately, no comparanda against which we might test Hydatius survive from elsewhere in Spain, only general evidence for the institutional presence of urban curias in the later fifth century.[34] There are good reasons to doubt how far the Hydatian evidence reflects the wider Spanish experience. For one thing, the Sueves who were such an essential part of political life in Gallaecia and northwestern Lusitania were absent from the rest of Spain. This means that the sorts of conflicts that we see in Hydatius would have taken place within local Roman populations or between those populations and Goths from the kingdom of Toulouse, though we have no evidence to confirm that such conflicts did in fact take place. It is likely that the Goths remained as important to the whole of Spain as they did to Gallaecia, but the reality of Gothic control was probably minimal everywhere. After the recall of Arborius in 465, there is little evidence for a permanent Gothic presence south of the Pyrenees. Gothic kings might attempt to maintain control over a few chief cities like Tarragona or Mérida, and local powers might try to turn the Gothic presence to their own ends, but it was only after Alaric II's disastrous defeat at Vouillé in 507 that the Goths again made serious efforts to hold Spain. Until then, the Gothic kingdom remained a fundamentally Gallic power, for which Spain took second place to Gaul as it had so often done under the emperors.

The murder of Theoderic in 467 by his brother Euric did nothing to change that old pattern.[35] Although it is normally asserted that Euric launched a full-scale assault on the few western provinces still under imperial control immediately upon his accession, in fact he essayed no serious attacks on imperial territories before 471 and generally continued his elder brother's cautious policies. The last pages of Hydatius give no hint that the accession of Euric made a difference to interactions among Goths, Sueves, and provincials in Spain. Euric's policy changed after 471, when he crossed the Rhône and defeated an imperial army somewhere beyond Arles.[36] This conflict had been provoked by Anthemius, not Euric, but the Gothic king thenceforth took an increasingly aggressive stance, launching the annual raids into the Auvergne famously described by Sidonius and also seizing the main cities of Narbonensis along the Mediterranean coast. In 475 he took first Arles, then Marseilles, but returned them to the control of the emperor Nepos in exchange for the formal cession of the Auvergne. But when Nepos was driven from Italy, Euric retook the coastal cities of Narbonensis, perhaps feeling himself no longer bound by his earlier agreement. Thereafter, Euric was the undisputed master of southern Gaul, an uneasy neighbor to the Burgundians to the east and the confused mass of petty chieftains north of the Loire.

In the same period, the Gothic king also attempted to take and hold parts of Spain. Our evidence comes from the anonymous *Chronica Gallica a. 511.*[37] The chronicler states that, in the sixteenth year of the emperor Leo, "Gauterit, *comes Gothorum,* took possession of Spain by way of Pamplona, Zaragoza, and nearby cities. Likewise Heldefredus, with Vincentius the *dux Hispaniarum,* took possession of the coastal cities, after besieging Tarragona."[38] The chronicler's dating scheme is frequently eccentric, but seems to be more or less correct for the reign of Leo.[39] This allows us to place the campaigns of Gauterit, Heldefredus, and Vincentius in the year 473. To that same year, we may date Vincentius's promotion to *magister militum* and his expedition to Italy, on which he died. These brief notices are all we know of Spanish history between the end of Hydatius's chronicle in 468 and the 490s, but they show that in 473 Euric launched a concerted effort to capture the province of Tarraconensis.

The three cities named by the chronicler make it quite clear that Euric intended to hold the province: Tarragona was the provincial capital, and one in which only a year previously the consulate of Anthemius was being publicly recognized.[40] Pamplona was the key to the passes of the western Pyrenees, while Zaragoza on the middle Ebro sat astride the routes into the interior of the peninsula. The difficulty lies not in divining Euric's intentions, which are clear enough, but in determining what the king actually achieved. Most take a maximalist approach to the evidence, viewing the campaigns of Gauterit, Heldefredus, and Vincentius as marking the incorporation of Tarraconensis into Euric's Gothic kingdom. This interpretation is colored by three presuppositions. One is the notion that Euric was rootedly anti-imperial and committed to wresting from the emperor every inch of territory that he could; another is that the Gothic kings had the same ability to take and hold territory that the imperial government had once possessed; and the third is that, because Tarraconensis and the rest of Spain were securely part of a peninsular Gothic kingdom in the later sixth century, the campaigns of 473 were the moment when Spain came permanently under Gothic rulership.

None of these suppositions is correct. Euric's hostility to the imperial government was opportunistic and not in any way systematic, while none of the evidence at which we have been looking suggests that, in the years after Majorian's death, the Gothic kings were able to successfully control the parts of the Spanish peninsula that they had conquered in the 450s. Most importantly, we are always better off interpreting ancient evidence in the light of past developments rather than with the benefit of hindsight. Royal policy in Spain had generally amounted to a steady holding operation as Gothic generals were sent, with or without armies, to try to keep order among locals disinclined to listen to them. We can sense the essential weakness of the royal position in the fact that all Euric's armies had to invade Spain from Gaul. This implies that there was no Gothic army in Spain in 473, hence that earlier Gothic successes had proved momentary. There is no a priori reason to think that Euric's campaigns into Tarraconensis proved an exception to this rule. To the contrary, Alaric II's campaigns of the 490s into just those regions assaulted by the generals of his father suggest that Euric's conquests of 473 were every bit as impermanent as earlier ones.

One piece of evidence from elsewhere in the peninsula may shed light on Euric's behavior in Tarraconensis. There is a justly famous inscription from the bridge at Mérida, showing the Gothic noble Salla helping Bishop Zeno to rebuild the walls and bridge of the city in 483. The inscription is dated by the Spanish *aera,* and refers to itself as having been set up in the time of the mighty Gothic king Euric—*nunc tempore potentis Getarum Euricii regis.*[41] We have already met Salla as one of the many negotiators whom Theoderic had sent to the Sueves. Indeed, it was Salla who, on returning to Gaul from one fruitless Suevic embassy, found Theoderic dead and Euric king.[42] If Salla was in Mérida at Euric's behest in 483, then his association with Theoderic had not affected his prospects at the court of Theoderic's assassin. The inscription does not definitively show that Salla was Euric's military representative in Mérida, but the words of the inscription clearly show him to have been the subject of Euric.[43] That a Goth called Salla should have performed a traditional act of patronage at Mérida tells us something valuable about the interaction of Goth and Hispano-Roman at the local, urban level. It also demonstrates Euric's determination to hold the old diocesan capital of Spain, and in this way it may also be the key to the events of 473.

The evidence is slim and disconnected, but we can read Euric's actions much like those of his elder brother in the years after 456: by seizing and attempting to hold key Spanish cities, the Gothic king both kept an eye on events locally and also held bases from which it was possible to react to those events if it was necessary to do so. Sometimes, as at Mérida, the Gothic position could be maintained, not least because the king's representative found it possible to cooperate with a prominent local authority. Elsewhere, particularly where local powers were hostile, royal control was untenable and had to be asserted periodically by force. That analysis is borne out by the next extant evidence for later fifth-century Spain, several references in a set of marginal annotations to the chronicle of Victor of Tunnuna that have been dignified with the title of *Chronicon Caesaraugustanae* but are now more sensibly called the *Consularia Caesaraugustana*.[44] These annotations are at times enigmatic, always ambiguous, but demonstrate one point beyond any question: in the 490s, Tarraconensis needed to be retaken by the Gothic subjects of Euric's successor, Alaric II.

Euric died in 484 at Arles, possibly his residence in the later part of his reign, and his son Alaric II succeeded him at Toulouse.[45] Thereafter, Alaric's reign is very nearly a narrative blank, perhaps a reflection of general stability in Gaul. Tarraconensis, however, shows no signs of similar quiescence. The notices of the *Consularia Caesaraugustana* are controverted enough to require quotation in full. We are told that, in the consulate of Asterius and Praesidius, the Goths seized Spain.[46] Then, in the consulate of Paul, a man called Burdunelus was proclaimed tyrant.[47] In the following year, in the second consulate of Anastasius, the Goths "took up residence" in Spain, while Burdunelus was betrayed by his own men, sent to Toulouse, and there roasted to death in a bronze bull.[48] Six or seven years later, in the consulate of Cethegus, games were held in the circus at Zaragoza.[49] Two years after that, in the consulate of Messala, the city of Dertosa was taken by the Goths, while a tyrant called Peter was killed and his head sent to Zaragoza.[50]

None of these events can be dated with precision.[51] The marginal annotations with which we are concerned were correlated to consular dates that appear in the chronicle of Victor of Tunnuna. However, these correlations do not obey a systematic internal chronology of their own, and it is unclear whether the annotator realized that Victor's own chronology was faulty, leaving out several years entirely. This means that we cannot accept the consular dates of the annotator as correlating accurately to the *anno domini* dates implied by the consular dates in Victor. We are instead left with the relative chronology of the annotations and the rough guess that the first several notices correspond to the early 490s, while the last two belong to the middle part of the first decade of the sixth century. The content of the annotations is every bit as troublesome: taken on their own terms, they suggest a pattern of Gothic incursion, local resistance, local collaboration, and further local resistance, but they are more often interpreted as showing large-scale Gothic migration into, and settlement in, the peninsula.

The key passages are the most enigmatic: *Goti in Hispanias ingressi sunt,* which has been read as a record of migration, and *Gotthi intra Hispanias sedes acceperunt,* which has been read as a record of settlement. In the standard interpretation, the chronicle's notices record the popular migration of Visigothic tribesmen to Gaul, who were followed by their noble leaders only after the Gothic debacle at Vouillé. This approach has been complicated by the imprecise introduction of archaeological evidence. A famous set of row-grave cemeteries in the Castilian Meseta, identified as Gothic in the 1920s and 1930s when they were excavated, has been taken as proof that large numbers of Goths entered Spain and settled there at the end of the fifth and the start of the sixth century.[52] That is problematical. As we have seen, it is not legitimate to directly and uncritically associate material evidence with the few historical events recorded in the literary evidence. More damagingly, the very notion that material artifacts carry ethnicity, that a particular form of jar or buckle is "Gothic" and therefore must have been worn by a Goth, can no longer be sustained.[53] Thus, even if we could say that the Meseta cemeteries did beyond question hold the remains of Gothic immigrants to Spain, we could never be sure that they represented a movement of persons recorded in a literary source.

Instead, we must take the literary evidence on its own terms, which does not here suggest migration. It is essential, when dealing with a short and obscure text like the *Consularia Caesaraugustana,* to see its evidence in its entirety and not selectively. This means placing the phrase *Goti in Hispanias ingressi sunt* in the context of the chronicle's general Latinity, rather than trying to tease meaning from it in isolation. In late Latin, the verb *ingredior* frequently means "to enter into possession of," by extension from its basic meaning of "to enter"; this is, for instance, its most common meaning in the Theodosian Code. Within two lines of the phrase in question, the author of our annotations clearly uses the verb in precisely this sense: *Dertosa a Gotthis ingressa est.* No one has ever doubted the meaning of this phrase, namely, that a Gothic army captured the city of Tortosa. The previous use of *ingredior* needs to be read in the same way: the Goths, meaning a royal army, took possession of Hispania. That reading provides the key to the *Gotthi sedes acceperunt,* which should refer to Gothic garrisons placed on Spanish soil, perhaps for the first time since 456. There is, in other words, no question of a migration of a Gothic people here. Instead, the action belongs to the depressingly familiar pattern of Gothic intervention in Spain. This interpretation has the advantage of reading the chronicle's evidence in the light of past historical experience, rather than as a foreshadowing of the later Gothic kingdom. It also suggests that Euric's conquests in Tarraconensis had not been maintained, since they had once again to be fought over.[54]

That same conclusion emerges from the actions of the provincials that the chronicler records. As we have seen, a certain Burdunelus *tyrannidem assumit* in the 490s and thereafter the *tyrannus* Petrus was killed and his head displayed at Zaragoza; it has been suggested that the proclamation of the latter was accompanied by the circus games at Zaragoza noted by our sources.[55] Although our chronicler refers to them as tyrants, Burdunelus and Peter will have called themselves either *augusti* or *reges*. The word *tyrannus* was the standard late Roman locution for usurper. Our annotator uses it not only of Burdunelus and Peter, but also of the general Odoacer and of Athanagild, a later claimant to the Gothic throne, marking an explicit contrast between the illegitimate *tyrannus* and the legitimate *rex*.[56] Given that, it is impossible to tell whether Burdunelus and Petrus called themselves *augusti* or *reges* inasmuch as there are contemporary parallels for both uses.[57] Either way, the Spanish author's attitude toward them is quite clear: they were illegitimate claimants to positions to which they had no right.

Why the chronicler should have taken such a stance is beyond us, but it is a salutary reminder of the complexities of local politics. That is to say, we are not looking at a simple dichotomy of Goth and Hispano-Roman, but at Hispano-Romans of different political persuasions.[58] The same point is made quite forcibly by the fate of Burdunelus. The end to his usurpation came not with defeat in battle, but through the treachery of his own supporters, who handed him over to the representatives of Alaric II, presumably the Gothic garrison that had recently been installed in the region.[59] Petrus may have met the same end.[60] We are, in other words, looking at the continuation of patterns already discernible in the last pages of Hydatius—the messy betrayals and alliances engendered by the interaction of barbarians and provincials. Though the brief notices of the *Consularia Caesaraugustana* are drier and more obscure than those of Hydatius, they are visibly manifestations of the same phenomenon. The Goths, in the Tarraconensis of the *Consularia* as in the Gallaecia of Hydatius, were a new power, accommodating themselves to the vicissitudes of local politics just as local politics molded itself to their presence. We cannot know what inspired Burdunelus and Petrus to their proclamations, but it will not do to read their actions in the light of a simple dichotomy of Goth and Roman. Instead, their usurpations and their brutal fates offer us a further glimpse into the otherwise deep obscurity of the period.

Archaeology and History in Fifth-Century Mérida

Only one place in Spain offers the potential of an alternative avenue by which to penetrate the obscurity of the fifth century and cast light on its darker corners. Because Mérida is so central to the chronicle of Hydatius, we hear about it far more than we do any other Spanish city of the fifth century. Because the city has been subject to more regular and better-published excavation than have most other Spanish cities, we know quite a bit about its material record. It should therefore be possible to relate these two sources of information to one another, a procedure that underscores both the potential and the limitations inherent in using material evidence to illuminate the historical record. The most famous piece of evidence for the city's urban infrastructure in the later fifth century is the inscription that attests the work of Salla and Zeno in rebuilding the bridge over the Guadiana.[61] There is no archaeological trace of fifth-century work on the bridge, but there is much evidence of work on the city walls at roughly the same period.

For 50 out of the 200 meters of wall circuit uncovered in the excavations at the Morería, large granite blocks were built up in front of the original Augustan walls, effectively doubling their width.[62] In the interstices for which suitable blocks could not be found, column bases and funerary *cupae* were employed to fill in gaps. Several of the smaller gates were narrowed considerably, so that no more than a single cart could pass through at a time. This work was done quite deliberately. Spolia were trimmed specially for the task at hand and marble remains were systematically avoided, perhaps because marble resists fire less well than other available stone. Given the sheer quantity of granite deployed in these works, it is likely that large stretches of the old city cemeteries were denuded of their mausolea and grave markers, but the builders made special effort to use anepigraphic pieces.

In the stretch of wall preserved in the Morería, we thus have evidence of a public works project, one that was planned and conformed to a set of guiding principles, and one that therefore required supervision and considerable expense. It cannot have been the work of momentary crisis and, for that reason, we cannot connect it specifically to one of the attested attacks on the city. Because none of the reforms can be precisely dated on their own terms, neither should we attempt to connect them to a specific episode of reform such as that of Zeno and Salla.[63] But they must, clearly, be a response to the general situation attested in the chronicle of Hydatius before it breaks off, a situa-

Bridge over the Guadiana at Mérida. (K. Salzer)

tion in which repeated attacks on the city and its suburbs made necessary the general strengthening of defenses.

There is other, isolated testimony to work around the city walls in the fifth century, but the effects of fifth-century violence are best illustrated from the six Roman *insulae* excavated in the Morería.[64] All the houses show signs of damage from the fifth century, some of it severe.[65] The *casa de los mármoles,* for instance, suffered a fire that destroyed much of its northern section, while walls and roofs came down in several other houses. Three cadavers have been found from this period. Two lay beneath a pile of collapsed *tegulae,* but one was laid out carefully and represents the only certain intramural burial known from Mérida. One must presume that the dead man expired at a moment when transportation to a cemetery was impracticable. It is not possible to determine whether these various signs of destruction were simultaneous or whether they belong to several separate episodes.

Regardless, this section of the city experienced a hiatus in occupation for perhaps as much as a generation, probably because it was more exposed to potential hazard than were neighborhoods farther from the walls. It was, however, reoccupied during the sixth century and survived as an urban neighborhood into the Islamic period, preserving the old street plan as well as the old *insulae.*[66] In some of the *domus,* the new occupants leveled off the standing debris and put down packed-earth floors. In others, they dug down to the level of the last mosaic floor and lived on it as the previous owners had done. However, most of the houses were broken down into separate residences, rather than being used as single-family houses as designed, and the original peristyles were transformed into communal gardens or courtyards for the use of several families.[67] One should, however, note that this reconstruction of early imperial or fourth-century houses into multiple residences is paralleled in sites within the walls that offer no signs of destruction.[68]

The destruction that the Morería experienced in the fifth century was quite serious, if not total, and there are one or two other sites in the fifth-century city that may show some signs of collapse.[69] Much more extensive evidence comes from a suburban cemetery that probably housed the *martyrium* of Mérida's patron, Saint Eulalia. There, the fourth-century mausolea that had been built around the martyr's cult site were damaged, some perhaps razed to their foundations, during the fifth century; this damage may be paralleled at the nearby cemetery of Sta. Catalina.[70] As in the Morería, it is not certain that all this destruction was simultaneous. If it was, it suggests a brutal sack of the funerary suburbs. But it might equally pertain to a series of different episodes, and there is no archaeological basis for deciding the case.

Nonetheless, the archaeological evidence that survives from Mérida is very rich by the standards of the Spanish fifth century and Mérida is as yet the only peninsular site where the literary and the archaeological evidence can be brought directly to bear on one another. The careful repair of the city wall shows us the measures made necessary by the century's political instability. More importantly, the physical remains of the Morería show us quite graphically what the conquest of a city—so often noted in Hydatius without emphasis—meant in practice: the collapse of buildings on top of their inhabitants, the burning of houses, the smashing of ancestral mausolea within sight of defenders on the city's walls. We have likewise a vital reminder of the restrictions that enemy attack and siege placed on a city: householders trapped within the walls and forced to bury their dead far from the traditional cemetery. We cannot and should not suppose that the violence attested in the material record corresponds to one of the episodes that our single literary source happens to record—the fifth-century narrative is much too lacunose for that.[71] But the evidence does allow us to put flesh on the bones of one very specific narrative source, something that is impossible for us to do anywhere in the rest of the peninsula. We cannot, of course, extrapolate the material experience of Mérida to elsewhere in the peninsula, but it demonstrates the potential that material evidence excavated on its own terms can have for our understanding of Spanish history.

For the most part, by contrast, the material evidence offers not direct insight into a section of peninsular history but rather a parallel set of information that can illuminate trends in the historical record just as it is illuminated by it.[72] That is certainly the case with one of the most fundamental social transformations in the history of Spain, the dissolution of the old world of the Roman city and its replacement with a new Christian model of urbanism. That historical change, like the impact of imperial government in the fourth century, is readily apparent in the material record, but only implicit in the traditional historical sources. In the later fifth and sixth centuries, the old fabric of the peninsula's Roman cities was Christianized. The phenomenon was quite general and affected all the cities of Spain, regardless of their relative prominence during the fourth and earlier fifth centuries. Christianity had, of course, been a social factor of enormous significance since the start of the fourth century, in Spain as in the rest of the Roman empire. Yet however much that might have been the case, it is only in the later fifth century that the world of the Hispano-Roman city was remade on a Christian model.

Ten

The Impact of Christianity
in the Fifth Century

Perhaps the most revelatory consequence of treating the archaeological record as an autonomous source of evidence comes in our understanding of Spanish Christianity. If we take the literary evidence as normative, Spain appears to have been dominated by Christianity and its controversies from the very start of the fourth century. The tiny corpus of Hispano-Roman authors demands that inference and scholars have long accepted it. Taken on its own terms, however, the archaeological record suggests a very different story: the world of the fourth-century Spanish city was essentially that of the early empire, physically and socially. The church, its authority, and its social functions remained on the physical margins of the town. This physical marginality continued even as the role of the Christian hierarchy, particularly the role of the bishop within the urban community, grew in importance. Change came only in the middle or later fifth century, with the result that the old high imperial landscape disappeared forever.

The disappearance of imperial government and the presence of a new barbarian population may well have hastened such changes. But the physical Christianization of the landscape was the strongest catalyst for social change in Spain since the first trauma of Roman conquest. During the fifth century, Christianity dissolved the old urban environment and the old patterns of Hispano-Roman social behavior embedded in it. Christianity began as an extramural cult, patronized by urban Christians, but not within a town's walls. Over time, Christian belief and the need to participate in Christian rituals drew a larger section of each town's citizens to spend a larger portion of their lives outside the city walls. Eventually, this had a corrosive effect on the old townscape as its central monuments became less and less socially meaningful. As the classical townscape ceased to have social significance, it became disused or was reused, until finally it was appropriated by the church. Spanish towns were monumentalized again, but this time on a Christian pattern. The heart of the city returned to where it had been during the years of romanization, but where the old civic forum had lain there was now the city's main church instead.

Christian Origins

Pious hope places the origin of Spanish Christianity in apostolic times, but the earliest genuine evidence is literary and comes from the third century, when a letter of Cyprian testifies to the existence of several Spanish episcopal sees.[1] In a letter of 254, Cyprian, with thirty-six other bishops gathered in synod, addressed the schism that had emerged among Spanish bishops.[2] This had been triggered by the Decian persecution, which brought out in Spain the same sort of passions and controversies that persecution engendered in Christian communities everywhere. The basic problem was simple: how rigorous should the church be with those who had compromised their Christian beliefs in time of persecution? In Spain, the question centered on the treatment of the bishops Martialis and Basilides, one the bishop of Mérida, the other of León and Astorga, though it is impossible to know which bishop belonged to which see.[3] Having compromised with imperial officials during the persecution, they were deposed by their communities, which then elected new bishops, one Sabinus replacing Basilides and one Felix probably replacing Martialis.[4] When the deposed bishops, having made their case to the new Roman bishop Stephen, attempted to reassert their episcopal powers over their flocks, the newly elected bishops appealed—perhaps in person—to an African synod headed by Cyprian.[5] Another Felix, this one a Christian layman of Zaragoza, also wrote to the synod to defend the new bishops and corroborate the evidence of Martialis's and Basilides's apostasy. Addressing the congregations of the cities in question, Cyprian and his colleagues upheld the strictness of canonical teaching on this point and agreed that bishops who had lapsed into apostasy must indeed be treated as having become laymen, though we do not actually know what became of the Spanish clergymen named in Cyprian's letter.

In fact, the glimpse of Spanish affairs that the letter offers raises rather more questions than it can answer. While it tells us that certain congregations of Spanish Christians had regular relations with both Rome and Carthage, we know nothing about their size. Despite the tendency to treat the sees named in Cyprian's letter as the oldest and most important in Spain, there may well have been others of equal importance that he does not mention. The letter similarly tells us nothing about the number of Spanish Christians or what part, small or large, they formed of the population. Speculation on all these points is frequent, but there are no evidentiary grounds for it.[6] Nevertheless, within half a century of Cyprian's writing, many Spanish cities had Christian communities large enough to leave archaeologically visible traces, which seems to confirm the connection between Spanish and African Christianity suggested by the letter of Cyprian.[7] Another such connection lies in the Spanish zeal for martyr cult, a development for which Cyprian, by the example of his death, was himself inspirational.

One says zeal for martyr cult, rather than zeal for martyrdom, because it is virtually impossible for us to gauge the extent of persecution in Spain. Most of the records we possess for early Spanish martyrs are inauthentic, so that we can attest the growth of a martyr cult without being able to tell whether or not the martyr actually lived and died as his cult believed.[8] A good example is the case of Felix, bishop of Gerona, an important saint thought to have been martyred in the Diocletianic persecution. Despite the wide extension of his cult, the earliest witness to his existence is the story of his passion as told by Prudentius, whose *Peristephanon* also happens to be the first adequate evidence of Christian cult at Gerona.[9] Indeed, it is only in 404 that a bishop of the city is firmly attested, in a letter of Innocent I that reprimands a bishop Minicius for uncanonically ordaining a bishop of

Gerona.[10] The other great Spanish martyrs, Vincentius of Valencia and Eulalia of Mérida especially, are similar to Felix in this respect: despite the evidence of powerful cult, the evidence for the martyrs themselves is minimal.

One exception to this rule is Fructuosus of Tarragona, a victim of the Valerianic persecution arrested with his deacons Augurius and Eulogius on 16 January 259. Six days later, on 21 January, they were brought before Aemillianus, the *praeses* of Citerior. The simplicity of the Fructuosus narrative has long been considered the guarantor of its authenticity.[11] The narrative's miracles are limited to visions, its account of the judicial process is clearly based on autopsy or official transcript, and the behavior of Aemillianus is entirely plausible.[12] The *acta* of the soldier Marcellus, a centurion of the Legio VII who had thrown away his arms and military insignia because it was wrong for a Christian to bear arms, are similarly authentic, at least in their first recension.[13] Marcellus was executed at Tangiers in 298, after a brief inquiry by the diocesan vicar, not for his Christianity but for dereliction of duty. The *acta* of both Fructuosus and Marcellus serve to place Spanish Christianity into the general experience of the third-century empire, and the *passio Fructuosi* in particular makes a powerful narrative impact, but neither does much to illuminate the process by which Christianity developed in Spain because apart from the texts themselves we know nothing about the communities of Spanish Christians in which Fructuosus and Marcellus had dwelt.

Indeed, for most of the fourth century, the evidence for the role of Spanish Christianity is quite mixed. We have good records of the Christians' attempt to accommodate themselves to the world around them, but this same evidence suggests the persistence of a largely classical and non-Christian environment in the towns. The canons of Elvira are of course the most important such evidence. We have already seen what they tell us about the persistence of curial magistracies in the towns, but they also shed much light on the sorts of questions faced by the early Christians of Spain. Many canons were concerned with working through the sexual mores of Christian belief. Others moderated Christian observance for the sake of the communal good, hence the prohibition of fasting during the month of August so as not to disturb the harvest.[14] But it was the difficulty of modulating relationships with the non-Christian majority that most worried the bishops at Elvira, and the problem was not a new one: Cyprian had addressed the same question in his letter of 254, condemning Bishop Martialis for belonging to a non-Christian confraternity and planning to be buried in its cemetery rather than among his own Christian brethren.[15]

The bishops who gathered at Elvira early in the fourth century were drawn from all over the south of Spain and thus brought with them to the council the problems that they were experiencing in their own towns. The site of Elvira itself, however, might well have been carefully chosen: we have very little evidence of pre-Christian devotion in the city.[16] Juvencus, one of the earliest Christian poets whose work is extant, may likewise have been a local native.[17] That is to say, the Spanish bishops may have chosen to meet at Elvira because of the relative strength of the Christian community there by contrast to other religious groups. The need to seek out such moderate advantages was clearly real to the bishops. Taken together, the council's canons bear witness to a substantial Christian community that nevertheless felt itself threatened on all sides by the manifestations of a non-Christian past.

Similar evidence for the integration of fourth-century Christianity into an environment that was only partly Christian comes from the sermons of Bishop Pacianus of Barcelona. In his sermon urging penitence on his flock, Pacianus reproves the persistence of non-Christian practices within his congregation, which is to say among people who clearly considered themselves to be Christians. Not only does he repeat the strictures long since enunciated at the council of Elvira against those who continued after baptism to engage in sacrifice, presumably in the service of imperial cult, but he also refers to a more intriguing pagan cult that survived in Barcelona.[18] This was a pagan festival, perhaps known as the *cervalia,* which Pacianus characterizes all too vaguely as abominable and licentious. He refers to a tract he had written called the *Cervulus,* in which he attacked the entire disgusting festival.[19] In his sermon, although he gives no details of the festive rituals, he does complain that his efforts to stamp out the festival had in fact tempted a much larger part of the population to take part in it than would otherwise have done so. Pacianus feared that the practices of one part of his flock would infect all the others, as a small amount of yeast leavens the whole loaf.[20] If Pacianus is to be taken at his word, the people of Barcelona would not have known how to celebrate their local festival had his condemnations in the *Cervulus* not shown them the way, but this rhetorical flourish is no more than a blind, a bishop putting as good a face as possible on the continuing attraction of his flock to pre-Christian ritual. According to Jerome's *De viris illustribus*, Pacianus died at an advanced age during the reign of Theodosius, under whom most of his writings were composed.[21] In other words, as late as the 380s or 390s bishops faced the same difficulties in steering their flocks away from traditional practices as had confronted the council of Elvira, and they faced this problem not in the retrograde countryside, but in a vibrant Mediterranean seaport like Barcelona as well.

As this brief account of the literary evidence shows, we are well advised to be cautious in accepting the traditional view of an intense and early Christianization of Spanish society. However early and however broadly Christianity spread within the peninsula's towns, it coexisted with a very persistent non-Christian world fundamentally rooted in the institutional world of Roman urbanism. The best evidence for this is not the exiguous literary sources, but rather archaeology. In city after city, recent archaeological excavations suggest an exceptionally slow spread of Christianity into the townscape of the peninsula's cities. For nearly two centuries after identifiably Christian finds begin to appear, Christian cult appears to have been confined to its original home within the aureole of cemeteries that surrounded every Spanish city. The evidence for this phenomenon is striking, not merely for its substance but for the consistency with which it is attested across the peninsula.

The Physical Impact of Christianity: Tarragona, Zaragoza, and Valencia

The best starting place, as in so many things, is Tarragona, which possesses one of the largest late antique cemeteries known. More than two thousand of its graves were excavated during the early part of the twentieth century in the pious hope of discovering the tomb of Fructuosus, Tarragona's local martyr.[22] Evidence that did not further that project was destroyed without record, but the discovery of what was ostensibly the saint's tomb and the outbreak of the Spanish Civil War coincided to prevent further damage to the site.[23] More recently, a thorough reexamination of all the surviving evidence—including published reports, unpublished notes, and surviving artifacts—has clarified our understanding of the early Christian cemetery at Tarragona.[24] This has allowed for targeted modern excavation within the funerary zone of ancient Tarragona.[25] The earliest evidence for Christian burials comes from a funerary tract to the west of the city that had already been in use for decades before the first traces of Christian graves appear. This part of the cemetery lay, as Roman cemeteries tended to do, along a main road to the city itself, in this case the Via Augusta, which passed through Tarragona between the imperial complex of the Part Alta and the old *colonia* in the Part Baixa.

From these beginnings, the western cemetery continued to grow, perhaps a reflection of an increase in the local population during late antiquity. Thus the recent finds in the Parc de la Ciutat, a short distance to the east of the early Christian tombs excavated in the 1920s and 1930s and closer to the city walls, date from the end of the fourth and the fifth centuries, and lie over the remains of a suburban villa that had been abandoned in the second century.[26] As important as the simple growth of Tarragona's Christian cemetery was the monumental development of one part of it. Over monumental tombs, perhaps of the fourth century, a basilica was later built, its walls cutting right through existing sarcophagi.[27] The date of this earliest Christian basilica is uncertain, and will remain so because the early excavations were so poorly documented, but a fifth-century date is likeliest.[28] This first basilical structure was almost certainly built over a preexisting cult site, perhaps one associated with the veneration of a martyr, though there is no evidence to associate it specifically with Fructuosus.

A second early Christian cult complex at Tarragona was likewise extramural, lying a short distance to the north of the long-known palaeochristian cemetery and built around a secondary road, perhaps 4 meters wide, between the Via Augusta and the Francolí river.[29] The space to the west of this road was in use as a cemetery by the second century, but in the fourth century both sides of the road were built up in grand style. On the western side of the road, closer to the river, a large villa centered on a columnaded portico was built, with a small private bath attached. To the east of the road lay a substantial U-shaped complex of buildings arranged around a central square, the open end of which faced onto the road. Among the six buildings uncovered here, a Christian basilica occupied the entire northern edge of the complex. The southern edge was taken up by a long building with many small rooms, the purpose of which remains unknown. The short, eastern side of the complex was probably agricultural, built around a giant cistern that probably served to irrigate the fields beyond the complex.

The basilical section of the complex is unlike any other known from Spain. The triple-naved basilica was oriented toward the east, with a raised transept that provided a zone of privileged burials. The central nave ended beyond the transept in an eastern apse, while a counter-apse at the west end contained a large funerary monument. This monument was composed of two burial chambers, one larger and earlier than the second. This western end of the basilica was approached from an atrium, in which a columnaded ambulatory surrounded a central patio and fountain. Both the basilica and the ambulatory of the atrium were quite literally filled with tombs; the excavators uncovered more than 160 inhumations and estimate that the true number was over two hundred if allowance is made for parts of the complex where agricultural work has destroyed the ancient remains entirely. Because the whole structure was systematically despoiled of any useable stone in the course of succeeding centuries, almost no epigraphy remains from the site. The single exception is a complete dedication to a *beata Thecla*, a consecrated virgin from Egypt, who died at age seventy-seven at an unknown date.

The interpretation of the site is a mystery and its date difficult to fix. The villa is almost certainly fourth-century, while the basilical complex is perhaps somewhat later, dating to the first half of the fifth century and in continuous use for two centuries thereafter. This means that it is almost certainly later in date than the basilica known since the early years of the twentieth century, and although the two cemeteries were clearly part of the same general funerary environment in the suburbs of Tarragona, it is unclear whether the two burial zones were contiguous with one another.[30] It is thus possible that the basilical complex by the Francolí was an expansion of the city's original Christian cult complex, made necessary by the growing wealth and power of the church. The agricultural dependencies of the complex, which may have been used for its sustenance, certainly add weight to this interpretation. On the other hand, it is possible that the younger complex was an essentially private foundation by the owner of the villa that lay across the road from the basilica. The identity of that owner, and indeed of the church's dedicatee, is unknown.[31] Similarly, whether the complex was a monastery of some sort cannot be determined on the basis of our sources; if it was, then it would be the only archaeologically attested monastery in Tarragona.[32]

Because of the poor state of the extant remains and their current preservation within a modern parking garage, it is unlikely that archaeology will allow us to resolve the many questions that are raised by this long unsuspected complex. On the other hand, it does attest to the way in which Christian cult—whether monastic or secular— grew in the vicinity of Tarragona during the fourth and fifth centuries. Like the vast early Christian cemetery along the Via Augusta, the complex by the Francolí was extramural. Indeed, throughout the fourth century and for most of the fifth, there is no evidence for Christian cult sites within the walls of the city. That is to say, despite the evidence for a powerful church hierarchy at Tarragona, the metropolitan status of its bishop, and the church councils held there in 380 and again in 419, every archaeological indication suggests that the *locus* of Christian cult, and thus the residence of the Christian bishop and the venue of church councils, was extramural.

Only at the very end of the fifth century is there evidence of change. Some time between 475 and 525, the Part Alta underwent its first major structural change since the Flavian period. A large building with three parallel halls was built in the northeastern corner of the vast imperial complex, cutting through the walls of the old Flavian cult precinct and making use of their ashlar blocks.[33] Very near to the site of these architectural renovations, in a sector that now houses the cathedral, a liturgical jar and a fragment of a chancel screen from the early sixth century have been found, suggesting an older church near the medieval cathedral.[34] The new aulic building might thus have been an *episcopium*—the bishop's residence—put up next to a new, intramural church. Both structures were built at the highest point of the Part Alta, deliberately altering the shape of the imperial cult complex, with a symbolism that is impossible to miss. It cannot have been unintentional, and its impact is hardly lessened by the partial disuse of the old forum during the 440s or 450s. The old secular heart of Tarragona, the symbol of its relationship to the rest of the empire, was now the site of a Christian church.

Yet the date of this transformation is important. Even at Tarragona, that *genetrix piorum* among cities,[35] the secular townscape of antiquity remained dominant until the later fifth century, despite the continuously growing importance of Christianity among the city's population.[36] Christian cult at Tarragona had begun when the religion was proscribed by the emperors. It had therefore necessarily developed in the extramural funerary zone, away from the public life of the city. Perhaps more surprisingly, it had stayed there even when the emperors had long since become Christian and the public life of the Roman city was becoming a Christian public life. Only long after the old imperial townscape had already begun fundamentally to change, and only when the superstructure of imperial government itself had disappeared, did Christianity come to dominate the public heart of Tarragona.

That story, and its chronology, are paralleled throughout Spain, not least at Zaragoza. The Christian community of Zaragoza was one of the earliest to leave us some trace of its existence, in the shape of the Felix, *fidei cultor,* of whom Cyprian speaks.[37] By contrast, archaeological traces of the city's Christians first become visible at the start of the fourth century. As at Tarragona, this earliest site of Christian cult was extramural. The road that led south out of Zaragoza had not developed a large concentration of burials during the high empire. Instead, the main necropoleis of the city lay along the roads running west toward the Meseta and Mérida and east down the Ebro valley, while a smaller and older graveyard lay on the banks of the Ebro just north of the city wall. Though this last cemetery had ceased to be used long before the fourth century, the two main funerary zones had not. The eastern and western cemeteries, which date back to the era of second-century incineration graves, continued in use during the third century and indeed for many centuries thereafter, gradually becoming Christian cemeteries over the fourth and fifth centuries as Zaragoza became a Christian city.

It is striking, however, that the first Christian burials that we can detect come from the southern zone, which had little, if any, precedent as a funerary site.[38] While this suggests an early Christian aversion to resting in eternal peace among their pagan fellow citizens—a phenomenon also known at Toledo—it is striking how rapidly the southern necropolis became a burial site of great prestige.[39] The earliest Christian remains of the site, centered on a martyrium, date from the very early fourth century, around the time of the great persecution. By the 330s, the southern cemetery had become an ostentatious place to be buried, and for the rest of the fourth century and perhaps in the fifth as well, it was the preserve of a wealthy and status-conscious Christian elite. It was here that the stunning examples of Christian funerary artwork for which Zaragoza is famous were all displayed. The sarcophagi of Zaragoza, some of the finest known from the Latin West, have long been studied, although petrographic analysis has only now confirmed the dates and provenance of the most important of them. Made in Roman ateliers between the 330s and 350s, of Proconnesian and Parian marble, many of the sarcophagi—the famous *receptio animae* sarcophagus, for instance—are works of startling iconographic complexity.[40] While on the one hand these sarcophagi were tools of dogmatic pedagogy, on the other they were a very costly new means of status display for those Christians of Zaragoza who could afford the expense.[41] The sarcophagi belonged to precisely that class of *curialis* whose togate statues were still displayed in the fourth-century forum.[42]

It is interesting to see how this class of citizen seems to have monopolized the most desirable resting place in fourth-century Zaragoza. That burial *ad sanctos* was an increasingly valuable commodity of late antiquity is a well-known fact. Indeed, at most of Spain's early Christian churches, one can document the competition for interment as close as possible to the body or relics of the titular saint or martyr, a privilege soon guarded by the wealthiest and best-connected locals. At Zaragoza, this phenomenon is attested starkly and early. While the city's western and eastern cemeteries continued in use right through the sixth century—the latter expanding to cover 30,000 square meters during the fourth century—the southern cemetery around the local martyrium remained a more exclusive preserve. Even as the community came to consist entirely of Christians, the vast majority of Zaragozans continued to be buried where their ancestors had always been buried. The local elites, now Christian, had for their part discovered a new means of displaying status publicly.

We have no archaeological evidence with which to determine the identity of the martyr venerated in the southern cemetery of Zaragoza. While it is possible that the martyrium was dedicated to the deacon Vincentius, a native of Zaragoza who was martyred at Valencia, it is more likely that the earliest cult at Zaragoza was devoted to the mysterious eighteen martyrs of whom Prudentius sings in his *Peristephanon*.[43] What little is known of this martyr cult comes from Prudentius himself, but it is clear that it predated the cult to Vincentius because Vincentius and another native of Zaragoza, the confessor Encratis, are said to have been schooled for their own suffering by the example of the eighteen martyrs.[44] What is more, it is fairly clear that the Zaragozans possessed no relics of Vincentius when Prudentius wrote a few years after 400.[45] For these reasons, it is best to associate the early archaeological evidence for Christian cult at Zaragoza with the eighteen martyrs, presumably victims of the Decian or Valerianic persecution. We may doubt the historicity of these eighteen Zaragozan martyrs, especially as even what we know of the later Vincentius and Encratis is inauthentic.[46] But that is hardly the point; for its Christian citizens as for Prudentius, Zaragoza will have been a *patria martyrum* that even Rome and Carthage would scarcely be able to match when the martyrs rose up to greet Christ on the judgment day.[47] And while all the Christians of Zaragoza could take pride and comfort in the protection of these martyrs, only the better off among them would have enjoyed the benefits of burial *ad martyros*.

The existence of a vigorous martyr cult will no doubt have had a transformative effect on certain social activities. By 541, it was the communal faith in Vincentius's protection and the physical parading of his tunic round the city walls that finally ended the siege of the Frankish kings Childebert and Chlothar.[48] At the time of this siege, Christian cult had taken over the city center, impinging upon the forum of Tiberius, where the old curial building was turned into a church. As at Tarragona, however, we must notice how long this transformation of the townscape actually took. The earliest Christian cult at Zaragoza was extramural, and it stayed there for a century and a half or more after the end of the Diocletianic persecution.[49] This means that the church council held at Zaragoza in 380 to deal with the Priscillianist controversy, like those councils at Tarragona noted above, met outside the city walls.[50] That is to say that, at Zaragoza as at Tarragona, the impact of Christianity on the shape of the Roman town came long after Christian belief and ritual had become central to the spiritual life of the city.

We may thus be sure that, when the emperor Majorian marched from Toulouse into Tarraconensis and stopped at Zaragoza, he saw a city that remained remarkably similar to that of the third and fourth centuries, in its basic shape if not perhaps its visible monuments. We know very little about the archaeology of fifth-century Zaragoza, and almost no strata from the first half of the century have been uncovered. This probably implies the perpetuation of fourth-century norms, which as we have already seen were somewhat reduced by the standards of earlier centuries: the sewers were not maintained, public baths had ceased to serve a social function, and the public gardens by the southeastern wall had been torn up. The amphitheater, by contrast, remained a public monument that continued to attract enough spectators to make its upkeep worthwhile.[51] The forum continued to be used as the commercial and administrative heart of the city during the fourth century, and there is no reason to think it had gone out of use during the first half of the fifth.[52]

In the second half of the century, however, the forum, like the city as a whole, underwent substantial changes that may have dramatically altered what it looked like. A wide variety of disconnected excavations have unearthed signs of landfill and terraplaning, the terracing and leveling of old foundations, and new buildings put up using spolia from earlier structures.[53] The pavement of the forum was breached and, in some spots, rubbish pits were dug. If *curiales* continued to meet in their old assembly hall, they did so in a forum now more or less earthen floored and presumably dotted with structures whose occupants we know only from their trash. On the other hand, a grain silo dug below the level of the old paving suggests that as late as the end of the sixth century the forum's commercial function survived the dismantling of most of its physical characteristics, a fact that continued to be true into the Arabic period.[54]

Like the silo, the later fifth-century changes to the townscape of Zaragoza do not necessarily imply clear-cut decline, because change on so large a scale requires both initiative and money. What they do imply is the disappearance of any social role for the old Roman shape of the town. The extramural martyrial complex continued as a cult center, and the famous *receptio animae* sarcophagus remained on display into the seventh century, when it was reinscribed with a new funerary litany.[55] But now, for the first time, there is evidence for intramural cult as well. The unmistakable remains of a Visigothic-era chancel screen were found precisely on the site of the great curial building on the southern edge of the Tiberian forum; this means that a church, with its liturgical separation of congregation from officiating priests, had been installed in what had once been the institutional heart of the Roman city.[56] We have no clue as to the dedicatee of this church, nor do we have evidence for an *episcopium* within the walls, as we do at Tarragona. The symbolism of our evidence is thus not so great as it is in Tarragona, but the practical point remains identical: by the sixth century, and for the very first time, a Christian monument rather than an administrative building stood at the center of a city.

At both Zaragoza and Tarragona, then, we can clearly observe the rhythm of urban change, if not necessarily its precise chronology. Christianity did ultimately act with tremendous transformative power on the townscape, but only gradually. The basic structure of Roman urbanism, implanted so long before as both a physical and an ideological reality, was very strong. Christian cult was for hundreds of years an extramural affair, as Christian burial remained until after the *Reconquista*. But Christian cult gradually drew the urban population more and more frequently outside the old network of streets and buildings that the pre-Christian town had used constantly. As social life was ever more focused on the church, so people spent more time at or around the church, which is to say away from the forum and the great intramural buildings. Eventually, the forum and its appurtenances ceased to have any use. And then, when the heart of the city was no longer occupied by the public function it had once possessed, the Christian activity that had acquired that public function moved to occupy physically the old heart of the city. Thus, by the time the Gothic king Leovigild found himself in control of the whole peninsula, the coins minted in his name at Zaragoza—or Cesaracosta as they have it—were minted in a city that was physically dominated by the structures of the church.

Wherever the evidence is available, it speaks to similar rhythms of change. The earliest baptistery known at Seville was extramural, built in a high imperial cemetery that lay above the ruins of some Republican or Augustan portuary buildings. Although the baptistery cannot be reliably dated, its *piscina* underwent three clear phases of development, corresponding with the gradual shift from adult to infant baptism.[57] At Cartagena, the extramural cemetery at San Antón had a long Christian phase, lasting from at least the fourth through the sixth centuries. On the other hand, there is as yet no sign of when—before the fourteenth century, at least—Christian cult sites began to make an impact on the intramural area.[58] At Complutum, a cult site existed about 2 kilometers to the east of the city and was associated with the martyrs Justus and Pastor by the end of the fourth century, when Paulinus of Nola and his wife Terasia buried their dead infant there *ad sanctos* some time between 389 and 393.[59] These martyrs are mentioned soon thereafter in Prudentius's *Peristephanon,* but it is not until the seventh century that they reach their definitive legendary form as a pair of holy children executed by the legendary tetrarchic governor Datianus.[60] Very little excavation has taken place at this martyrial site, but it is clear that over time the ecclesiastical complex that grew up in this distant suburb of Complutum became the chief center of population in the region: it was the core of medieval Alcalá de Henares, as it is now the center of the modern city.[61]

At Valencia, both of the city's traditional cemeteries appear to have become Christian in the course of the fourth century, but it is not possible to localize the site of the earliest Christian cult with any certainty.[62] The extramural site still occupied by the medieval monastery of La Roqueta may have housed the city's first *martyrium.*[63] The earliest extant parts of La Roqueta are Romanesque, but test trenches have uncovered burials that are probably of the late third or early fourth century, and also glass vases of an early fifth-century type.[64] This evidence is too slender to allow for certainty. It is, however, consonant with what we know from other cities about the location of early Christian cult sites. If the identification of La Roqueta with the first Christian site in Valencia is correct, its dedicatee will probably have been the Zaragozan Vincentius who was believed to have been martyred at Valencia.

By the later sixth century, Valencia's episcopal seat sat atop the monumental Flavian forum, appropriating the *curia* and other structures for its own use.[65] When this appropriation of the civic heart of the city by the church began is much harder to say; it was certainly not before the later fifth century and probably after a major fire had damaged the standing buildings quite badly.[66] Excavations in the modern Plaza de Almoina, which sits on top of the high imperial forum of the city, have uncovered structures and funerary monuments that are clearly late antique. One of the structures is a long building, divided into three naves, the central one of which finishes in a horseshoe apse. To the south of this apse, in a spot colloquially known as the Cárcel de San Vincente, lay a smaller church, centrally planned in the shape of a cross. The foundations of this building cut across remains of the fifth century, and it is likely that the small church is a sixth- or seventh-century memorial to a site associated with the local hero Vincentius.[67] Taken together, the evidence would appear to suggest the gradual development of a complex of several ecclesiastical buildings on the site of the old forum. The difficulty comes in knowing when these structures began to be built, as the chronological evidence is very limited. The poorer burials in the zone almost certainly predate the extant remains of the church, which perhaps belong to the middle of the sixth century, but a fifth-century date for the earliest burials remains open to question.[68] A series of interments, some of them collective, which surround the basilical structure, and which have also been found in the calle del Mar, are certainly of a later date.[69] Some of these were put up with care, perhaps in the later sixth or the seventh century, and

(Facing page) Plan of La Almoina, Valencia, showing the several ecclesiastical buildings that grew up over the forum of the Roman town around a memorial to Saint Vincent. (after Albiach et al. [2000], 75)

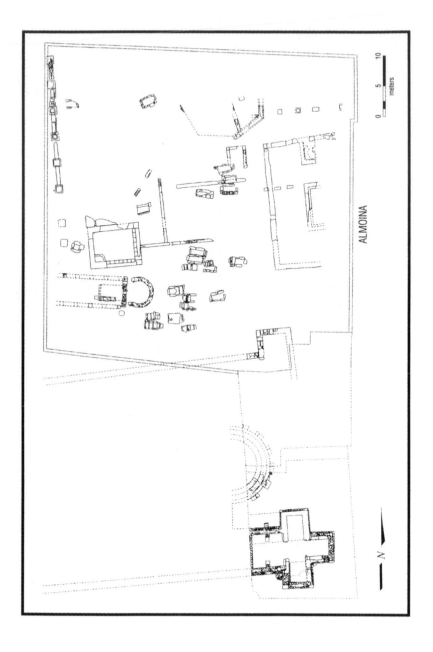

ALMOINA

0 5 10
meters

N

demonstrate the way in which important families eventually shifted their preferred burial spaces from the older Christian cemeteries outside the city walls.[70]

If the earliest burials in La Almoina really do belong to the fifth century, a point that may never be resolved satisfactorily, then they would be very significant indeed. They would, in fact, represent the only certain case of a genuine intramural necropolis of fifth-century date from anywhere in Spain. Intramural burial or burial within the *pomerium* had been a form of pollution in traditional Roman practice. As a consequence, it is generally cited as one of the profoundest changes that Christianity wrought on the classical civilization of Rome.[71] The old but still most cited work on the Christianization of Spanish cities likewise makes intramural burial the especial characteristic of a late antique transformation that began in the fourth century.[72] But the intramural cemeteries that one finds most frequently cited are either not in fact intramural or based upon old excavations of which no extensive record was published and no verifiable trace remains.[73] By contrast, those cities from which recent and well-published data is available seem never to have lost their old habit of extramural burial. Tarragona, Ampurias, and Zaragoza are the best-known examples, but even in marginal places, the distinction between the town and the suburban funerary zone remained unbreakable.[74]

It must remain possible that Valencia forms an exception to this pattern, that here we have a precocious example of a change that overtook other cities either not at all or only after the old Roman townscape had lost all social significance. On the other hand, it is possible that the first burials at La Almoina have been dated too early and that Valencia fits into the pattern of Christianization that is beginning to emerge from the better-known cities of the peninsula.[75] Indeed, apart from the difficulties over chronology, the city does seem to have followed the pattern of Christian development that we have now come to expect from elsewhere in the peninsula: the city's earliest Christian cult began in the extramural zone, perhaps at La Roqueta, and remained there for quite some time.[76] Time and again, this pattern of development is confirmed by well-excavated and well-dated archaeological evidence, and the two large cities that offer variations—Barcelona and Mérida—also prove the general rule.

Barcelona and Mérida

At Barcelona, the first solid evidence for an intramural church comes from the late fifth century at the earliest, but its placement within the townscape is the most important thing. A Christian basilica, its annexed baptistery, and an episcopal palace were built into four *insulae* in the northeastern corner of the city, a space delineated by a minor *cardo* and *decumanus,* the *intervallum,* and the wall of the city itself.[77] The complex preserved as much of the preexisting *insulae* as was consonant with opening up a public reception space in the episcopal palace; in consequence, it is not at all clear whether the transformation of the *insula* would have made any noticeable difference to the exterior façade of the city block. The baptistery, however, was built out over part of the *decumanus minor* between two of the *insulae* that were appropriated for the complex.

At the time of its construction, the whole of the basilical site was remarkably marginal to the ground plan of the Roman city. Although it eventually evolved into the heart of the city, and indeed sat beneath the city's comital palace and Romanesque cathedral, the basilical complex was originally very much on the edge of Roman Barcelona.[78] This fact may reflect an earlier implantation of intramural Christian cult in Barcelona than in Tarragona or Zaragoza. In those cities, the church did appropriate the old central public space of the city, but only after that public space had ceased to exercise its old social function. At Barcelona, by contrast, it would seem that the Roman town plan still retained its importance when the first intramural church was built, with the result that this church had to be built on the periphery of the street grid out of respect for its old significance. It is, unfortunately, impossible to date the construction of the basilica of Barcelona with any precision, which makes its place in the historical process we are discussing less clear than it might be.[79]

Mérida, like Barcelona, demonstrates the diversity of urban change in fifth-century Spain without contradicting the general patterns established by such sites as Tarragona and Zaragoza. As at Tarragona, the suburbs of Mérida had always encompassed large funerary zones and the roads out of the city were dotted with mausolea and necropoleis, many of which have been located though few have been well-

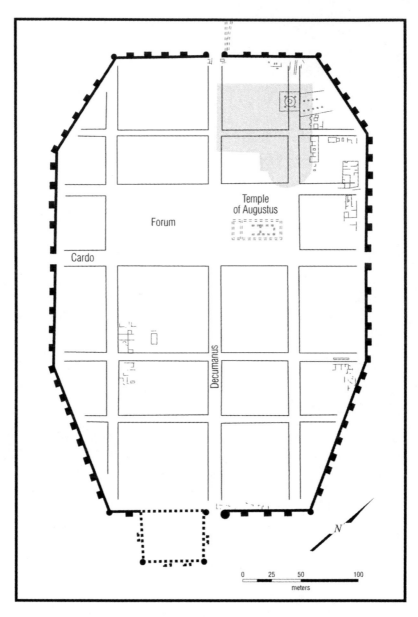

Plan of Barcelona showing the walls of the city and the position of the early Christian complex in the northwest corner of the city, underneath the modern cathedral. (after Gurt and Godoy [2000], 427)

excavated or published.[80] We know that Mérida boasted a Christian community quite early, since it was to the city's bishop that Cyprian addressed his famous letter in the third century. On the other hand, the first material traces of this community do not become visible until much later. Only two dated Christian inscriptions, both fragmentary, survive from before the fifth century and it is not possible to trace a Christian cemetery before the second quarter of the fourth.[81]

At that point, two Christian cemeteries become archaeologically visible, and given that their excavated portions lie barely 200 meters apart, it is entirely possible that they represent only a single site. Both lay to the northeast of the city, not far from the road to Medellín, and contained a mixture of elaborate mausolea and simpler, though still quite well-made, tombs. Neither shows any sign of non-Christian precedents, which suggests that at Mérida, as at Zaragoza, the emerging Christian community chose to bury its dead apart from the pagan cemeteries of the past. The less well-documented of these sites lies under the modern *barriada* de Santa Catalina, but the better known site is preserved beneath the extant church of Santa Eulalia.[82] The fabric of this church is fundamentally Romanesque, though much altered over the centuries, but it stands atop a sixth-century basilica that had itself been built over a cemetery filled with tombs and three large mausolea. One of these mausolea, eventually enclosed within the sanctuary of the basilica, was regarded by early Christians as housing the remains of Eulalia herself and served the function of a *martyrium* or *cella memoriae*.[83] The argument for regarding this mausoleum as Eulalia's *martyrium* is very strong, inasmuch as the archaeology shows it to have been the most prestigious structure on the site, while its architectural details match those described in the seventh-century lives of the bishops of Mérida.[84]

Eulalia's supposed mausoleum, what we may for convenience call her *martyrium,* lay in a suburban plot not very far from the city's eastern gate that had been inhabited almost since the city's foundation. Given that four very different *domus* occupied the site consecutively, the property must either have changed hands several times or belonged to a family with very changeable tastes. The latest of these houses had been abandoned by the end of the third century. Parts of its structure may have begun to crumble away, but others were still standing when the site was transformed into a cemetery, seemingly at the start of the fourth century. This was not an unusual fate for suburban *domus* that had outlived their usefulness; part of the suburban property on which the so-called Casa del Anfiteatro was built was also appropriated as a cemetery toward the end of the third century, while at Ampurias the suburban landscape exhibited a constantly shifting pattern of residential, agrarian, and funerary uses during late antiquity.[85]

The earliest funerary structure on the site of Santa Eulalia was put up some time in the early fourth century, almost certainly before the 340s.[86] This was a mausoleum, oriented east-west with a shallow apse at its eastern end and, probably, a bench around the walls of the interior. Separating the main part of this mausoleum from the apse stood two columns, between which lay the only interior space in which no inhumations took place. The rest of the mausoleum, however, was filled with graves, both in the apse and beyond it, and it was this mausoleum that the Christian community of Mérida regarded as holding the remains of the saint. Another mausoleum, preserving the foundation and thus the rectangular shape of a room in the old Roman *domus,* was more or less contemporary with Eulalia's martyrium to its east. Between these two structures a third, extremely elaborate mausoleum was put up at a somewhat later date at a right angle to Eulalia's martyrium, oriented north-south with an apse at its southern end and a stairway down to a richly ornamented crypt at the northern end.

This second absidal mausoleum, clearly the tomb of a local dignitary, suggests that the practice of burial *ad sanctos* was already popular at Mérida during the middle or late fourth century. Certainly a great many other tombs were dotted among these impressive structures, and most of these seem to have belonged to persons of relatively high social status. Whereas most early Christian cemeteries in Spain consisted of simple inhumations under roof tiles or broken amphorae, those in this part of Mérida were built out of marble or a combination of brick and marble, or else the bodies were laid in expensive marble sarcophagi. One tomb, built up against the walls of the third, absidal mausoleum, preserves the remains of a rich mosaic over its brick surface, another sign of the deluxe nature of the site. The growth of this cult site from the fourth to the fifth centuries cannot be traced as

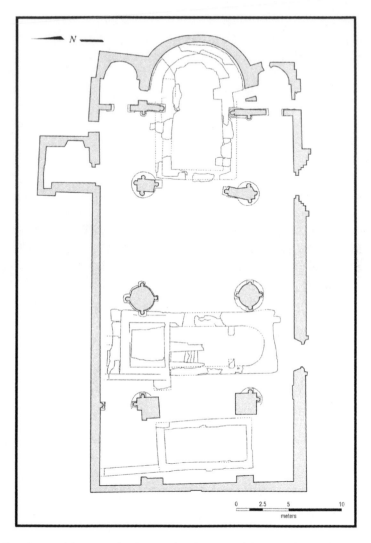

Plan of Sta. Eulalia at Mérida, showing the placement of the original mausolea in relation to the walls of the extant church. The extant church is Romanesque, but its plan largely corresponds to that of the late fifth-/early sixth-century basilica. (after Mateos [1999], 51)

broadly as one would like because, despite the thorough excavation of the later basilica, little similar work has been possible in its immediate vicinity.[87] Yet as is shown by the mosaic-covered tomb, the environs of Eulalia's *martyrium* remained a popular spot for the city's Christian elite to seek a final resting place.

At some point in the second or third quarter of the fifth century, however, various mausolea and some of the tombs at the site were very badly damaged, perhaps even razed to their foundations, so that only the crypt of the second absidal mausoleum remained undisturbed when the basilica was built at the end of the century. The damage, which may be paralleled at the nearby cemetery of Sta. Catalina, is complete enough to rule out any natural process of disuse and must reflect an episode of violent destruction. The excavators of the site have placed this evidence in the context of the raid on Mérida in 429, mentioned by Hydatius when he describes the death of the Suevic king Hermengarius.[88] The argument involves special pleading, and there is no archaeological reason for connecting the destruction with Hermengarius, rather than any of the other attacks that the city suffered during the fifth century.[89]

Despite the leveling of many old structures, the site continued to be an important cemetery, probably without any hiatus. Many of the extant tombs, perhaps including the one covered in mosaics, date from after the sacking of the site, and it is clear that the crypt of the absidal mausoleum was restored to use with a new, shallower staircase running down into it. Perhaps at the very end of the fifth century, more likely at some point early in the sixth, the whole site was rebuilt as a basilica. The date depends upon whether the epitaph of a *vir inlustris* called Gregorius—found *in situ* within what had been the second absidal mausoleum and dated to the year 492—was already standing when the basilica was put up around it or whether Gregorius was laid to rest in the nave of a newly built basilica. The archaeological evidence offers no guide and the problem is insoluble.[90]

The figure of Gregorius, however, is important. As we have suggested, it is possible that Gregorius represents the last known Spaniard to have served in an imperial government.[91] Be that as it may, the burial of a *vir inlustris* in what is likely to have been the premier Christian cemetery of Mérida during the very last decade of the fifth century demonstrates as little else could the continuing local dominance of the urban elite. Though Gregorius's tomb is one of the very few to have been preserved *in situ,* it is significant that at both the basilical cemetery and the nearby cemetery of Santa Catalina there is never any evidence for low-status burials. So far as we can tell, the Christians buried in both places came entirely from the upper strata of society, if not exclusively from the urban elite then at least from among those with substantial wealth. We do not know where Mérida's Christian poor were buried; one imagines they went on using the low-status cemeteries of centuries past.[92] Méridan Christianity, or at least its most prestigious locus near the supposed *martyrium* of the patron saint, was the exclusive preserve of the notables.

Mérida, for all its exceptional status as diocesan capital and for all the exceptional wealth of its known Christian cemeteries, belongs to the increasingly familiar pattern. Despite aprioristic statements to the contrary, Mérida need not have had an intramural church much earlier than the time at which one is first documented, which is to say in the literary sources for the sixth century.[93] Before that, the Christian life of the city is likely to have been concentrated in the extramural zone, as it was elsewhere in Spain. The famous bishop Zeno, whose restoration of the city's walls and great bridge in concert with the *dux* Salla we have already had occasion to examine, still belonged to a world in which Christianity lay at the physical margins of the city, however important it might be to the city's public life. Wherever there is evidence, the same pattern presents itself: the gradual spread of Christian sites from the margins to the heart of the city, even if, as at Barcelona, this meant re-creating the heart of the city in a place where it had not lain in the imperial period.

The pace of this change seems to have varied from city to city, but it was evidently slow, whether in the capital cities of Tarragona and Mérida or in an interior town like Zaragoza, which had long since left behind its years of greatest prosperity.[94] It is still casually assumed that all great cities must have had an intramural church by the end of the fourth century.[95] Yet it is a remarkable fact that nowhere in Spain has such a church been positively identified. In this respect, the archaeological evidence offers us an interesting context for our literary evidence. It gives one pause to imagine Hydatius, a great man in his community of Aquae Flaviae, celebrating Mass not in the very center of his city, but in an episcopal complex located somewhere outside the walls. The many councils of bishops may likewise not have been as physically central to the landscape of the town as their centrality to the extant literary evidence would suggest. The archaeological evidence would thus seem to cast doubt on one of the long-standing topoi of Spanish—and indeed not just Spanish—historiography.

Churchmen in Fifth-Century Spain

The later fourth century is widely held to have witnessed a shift in both moral authority and actual power away from municipal or imperial officials and toward officials of the church, a shift that is attested physically in the movement of ecclesiastical buildings into the cities. The material evidence demonstrates a rather different chronology away from the old topography of power to a new, Christian one. That might in turn lead us to question our literary evidence for the role of churchmen in fourth- and fifth-century Spain. If we do so, we find that the topographic primacy of urban patterns fixed during a long imperial past is mirrored in the political reality of the fourth and fifth centuries: so long as representatives of the imperial government survived, they were the chief source of authority around which public life—including the public life of the church and the Christian faithful—revolved.

An early example comes from the mid-fourth century, when Spain, with the whole of the Roman West, was caught up in the Arian controversies. Ossius, bishop of Córdoba, had been an early influence on the beliefs of the first Christian emperor Constantine, and his denunciation of Bishop Potamius of Lisbon in 355 led to an audience with Constantius II in which the Baetican bishop was constrained to endorse the homoean theology favored by the emperor.[96] Potamius, the first known bishop of Lisbon, was a somewhat earlier convert to the homoean theology, and the names of Ossius and Potamius stand together as the authors of the creed of Sirmium.[97] Despite the eventual coercion of most western bishops into conformity with imperial theological policy, Potamius was an unusually enthusiastic supporter of Constantius's creed.[98] We catch a glimpse into his motives from the Luciferian *Libellus precum,* written in 383 or 384 by the Roman priests

Marcellinus and Faustinus and addressed to the emperors Valentinian, Theodosius, and Arcadius.

The *Libellus* is a tendentious history of the Arian controversy, attempting to prove that the extreme rigorism associated with Lucifer of Cagliari was the correct way of dealing with those who had besmirched themselves by contact with Arianism. According to the *Libellus,* Bishop Potamius had apostasized from orthodoxy to Arianism when offered a *fundus fiscalis.*[99] One need not be convinced by this slander to find plausible the relationship between bishop and imperial hierarchy that it implies. As far as the authors of the *Libellus* were concerned, Potamius was induced to apostatize by the promise of an imperial tax farm. The acceptance of such a grant would have locked the bishop into the imperial system by providing him, and his church, with a direct financial stake in it; anyway, too principled resistance could be dangerous, as a supporter of the Spanish Luciferian Gregory of Elvira found to his cost.[100] Even though the source of our information is tendentious, one ought not to be unduly surprised at the apostasy of Potamius in the political context of the 350s, when coercion was the norm. Nor, in the political world of the Constantinian empire, is the deference of a bishop like Potamius to imperial authority particularly unusual.

On the other hand, we find a similarly deferential relationship between episcopate and imperial authority in an important source of the early fifth century. Toward the end of the year 420, a pious layman called Consentius wrote to Saint Augustine from Minorca to recount the convoluted story of a monk called Fronto whom he had sent on a mission to detect heresy in Tarraconensis.[101] After Fronto uncovered what he took to be a heretical plot, he accused a woman named Severa and her relative, the priest Severus, of heresy before the episcopal tribunal of Titianus, bishop of Tarragona and provincial metropolitan. The accused had powerful relatives. Severa was either the mother or sister of the wife of the *comes Hispaniarum* Asterius, and Severus could likewise claim *affinitas* with Asterius.[102] Threatened by Fronto, Severus wrote to Asterius for help, and the *comes* actually broke off his campaign against the usurper Maximus in order to come to Tarragona and defend his relative. When Fronto refused a summons to the count's *praetorium,* having claimed sanctuary in Titianus's church, Asterius and his retinue came before the bishop's court, which they proceeded to dominate. The count's retainers urged the tribunal to condemn Fronto as a slanderer and several of the bishops responded by leading the crowd in demanding the death penalty for Fronto. One bishop, Agapius, tried to strangle Fronto in full view of all those present, only stopping after a sharp reprimand from Asterius. The *comes* himself then questioned Fronto at some length, but became convinced that there might be something in the monk's accusations. With that, he decided to leave his relations to their own affairs rather than compromise his own spiritual safety, and returned to the war he was fighting.

The Fronto narrative has great intrinsic interest, both as the only first-person account of a late antique court case and as the most circumstantial source for any aspect of fifth-century Spain. In the present context, however, what requires comment is the relationship of the *comes* Asterius to the episcopal court in which he found himself. Such ecclesiastical tribunals, conventionally called *episcopales audientiae,* had been given legal status by Constantine, who granted vast powers of jurisdiction to bishops.[103] The reign of Julian eliminated these privileges and they were restored much more cautiously by later Christian emperors, who restricted the competence of ecclesiastical courts to religious questions.[104] Even if the precise demarcation between secular and religious jurisdiction remained ill-defined, there can be no question that the case of Severus and Severa was appropriate to an episcopal tribunal. Given that, the deference shown to Asterius by the bishops gathered at Tarragona is very striking. The whole tenor of Asterius's dealings with the bishops demonstrates a sense of effortless superiority not at all in keeping with traditional ideas of growing episcopal power in the fifth-century West. The evidence of Potamius, in its turn, would suggest that fifth-century developments were less distinct from the habits of the fourth century than is sometimes thought. The frequent, and sometimes frantic, appeal to imperial authorities that one finds in the chronicle of Hydatius is further evidence for the fifth-century persistence of old habits.

Yet the chronicle of Hydatius also reveals a world in which the bishop was more and more central to the life of the community, making decisions and leading delegations that might once have been purely curial responsibilities. The inscription of Salla and Zeno on the bridge at Mérida is a manifestation of the same phenomenon. This sort of shift in the traditional exercise of urban power from the curia to the bishop is well-known and much studied in the late antique West generally. Its chronology is unclear. In Spanish cities, municipal office persisted deep into the fifth century, as stray references in the literary sources demonstrate. There must therefore have been a period, perhaps stretching to decades, during which municipal and episcopal authorities functioned simultaneously, whether in concert or in competition. All the same, the episcopal authority ultimately became predominant in the cities of Spain and bishops completely dominate our sixth-century evidence.

The Evidence of the Priscillianist Controversy

Clearly a change of dramatic proportions in the larger social world of Spain, the gradual shift in the locus of authority within the city was in other ways not so revolutionary. It did not, for instance, alter the dominant role of the urban center within its *territorium,* as we can see from a consideration of Priscillianism, Spain's only indigenous heresy before the Adoptionist controversy of the Carolingian era and the best-documented ecclesiastical conflict in Spanish late antiquity. The new vein of ascetic religiosity that emerged in the 370s around the figure of an aristocratic layman called Priscillian is first attested in the politically most important part of the peninsula, the easternmost corner of Lusitania around Mérida and the *conventus Cordubensis.* Priscillian's message of extreme asceticism soon became tremendously influential.[105] He called upon his compatriots to renounce totally the blandishments of the secular world, a renunciation that the very fact of their baptism demanded of them. In study of the scriptures, canonical and apocryphal, the Christian finds the spiritual sustenance that he or she requires, and that sustenance is best imbibed far from the distractions of the world. Indeed, physical retreat from the town is the best assurance of spiritual well-being, and the contemplative necessities of true Christianity require extended withdrawal from the world. There is more to Priscillian's teaching than such a précis suggests, but its other aspects—a fascination with demonology and numerology, for instance—are merely methods by which the ascetic and contemplative ideal is to be explicated and achieved.

When Priscillian's message began to be heard in Córdoba and Mérida, what might have been mere ascetic eccentricity came to be regarded as a dangerously threatening heresy.[106] Bishop Hyginus of Córdoba first raised the alarm, but it was Bishop Hydatius of Mérida who in 380 spurred into action his episcopal colleagues elsewhere in Spain. A council met at Zaragoza in that year. We do not know who presided, or why Zaragoza, so far from the site of the controversy, was chosen, but twelve bishops from Aquitaine and the Spanish provinces attended.[107] We possess competing accounts of the council and the extant canons reflect only a small amount of the business it undertook.[108] The bishops gathered at Zaragoza condemned a number of specific ascetic practices, but the first Priscillianist tractate, perhaps a confession of faith presented by Priscillian to the council, implies that the most important charge laid against Priscillian was that of sorcery.[109] On the other hand, Priscillian could count on a great deal of episcopal support, not least from the bishops Instantius and Salvianus, of unknown sees, who would later consecrate him bishop, and it remains unclear whether anyone was actually condemned at Zaragoza.[110]

After Zaragoza, the Priscillianist bishops counterattacked, using as a pretext an unnamed charge brought against Hydatius of Mérida by one of his priests. Instantius and Salvianus went to Mérida to assert themselves against Hydatius and perhaps to consecrate a successor to him, but they were beaten by the urban mob and driven out of town.[111] Despite this setback, they consecrated Priscillian to the vacant—or perhaps new—see of Ávila in Lusitania, a consecration in which the metropolitan, Hydatius of Mérida himself, took no part for obvious reasons.[112] Hydatius and his allies, chief among them Ithacius of Ossonuba (modern Faro), appealed to the emperor Gratian, forcing many followers of Priscillian into hiding. Priscillian and his closest supporters, however, set off for Rome to put their case before the pope, setting in train the sequence of events that would ultimately end with Priscillian's execution for sorcery by the emperor Magnus Maximus.[113]

We need not trouble ourselves here with the arid theological controversies that raged on after Priscillian's death and even after the schism engendered by his death had ended. The council of Zaragoza, however, reveals a great deal about the evolving role of bishops in relation to their territories. At one level, of course, the controversy that erupted during and after Zaragoza was genuinely theological, although there is an interesting disjunction between the teachings of Priscillian as revealed in the works attributable to his pen and the points on which his critics most insisted. There is likewise a strong case to be made for the conflict's entanglement in the politics of gender, because of Priscillian's dangerously liberal attitude toward the spiritual and intellectual competence of women.[114] Yet because the conflict became so rapidly politicized from 380 onward, drawing in more and more participants, it was increasingly difficult for those involved to moderate their positions without losing face. Positions hardened, new causes of grievance were found, and we must not take the later developments of anti-Priscillianist concerns as normative for the earliest stage of the controversy.

Instead, the canons of Zaragoza are the surest guide to what was disturbing in Priscillian's behavior, and it was behavior not belief that mattered first. Disturbing aspects of Priscillian's thought—the charges of heresy and sorcery—were products of a burgeoning polemic, detected or invented only after the opposition to Priscillian had already arisen. The initial opposition to Priscillian articulated itself on much less intellectual grounds. The extant canons of Zaragoza, as transmitted in the seventh-century *Collectio Hispana,* reflect only a tiny portion of what transpired there.[115] Since the council was clearly a scene of violent controversy that left neither Priscillianist nor anti-Priscillianist bishops satisfied, we should probably regard the transmitted canons as the topics on which the gathered bishops were able to reach a modicum of consensus. It is by no means far-fetched to think that what made it into those minutes were just those canons that could command more or less universal assent, while the order and relative vehemence of the extant canons will reflect the ebb and flow of the council's own debates.[116]

Almost all the canons are concerned to censure actions that derogate from the authority of bishops: the first treats women's reading of scripture in the company of strange men, the third the failure to take the Eucharist within the church, the eighth episcopal regulation of the age at which women might take the veil. The seventh canon is phrased vaguely, but condemns those who take the title of teacher without proper qualification—presumably episcopal status—and may well be a direct response to Priscillian, who did indeed take the role of an authoritative pedagogue, as we know from the sermons among his tractates.[117] The second and fourth canons, however, are the most important inasmuch as they localize the derogation of episcopal authority in a geographical context. That is to say, they tell us where the bishops were afraid of losing their authority—in the countryside. The second canon instructs that during Lent *ab ecclesiis non desint nec habitent latibula cubiculorum ac montium* nor *ad alienas villas agendorum conventum causa non conveniant.* The fourth canon makes the same point for Advent: *nulli liceat de ecclesia absentare nec latere in domibus nec sedere ad villam nec montes petere nec nudis pedibus incedere sed concurrere ad ecclesiam.*[118] Twice the bishops returned to what was virtually the same topic, twice they tangled with the problem of those who absented themselves from the church. And while in the fourth canon urban *domus* are included in the prohibition, the real fear, twice repeated, is of meetings held in places potentially outside the reach of the bishops: the fastnesses of Spain's mountains and the scattered villas where episcopal control depended on the goodwill and cooperation of the landowner.

The Priscillianist controversy occurred at a relatively early stage in the history of Spain's Christianization.[119] The specific powers of bishops and the shape that their authority was to take within the Christian community had not yet been ossified in any standard form. The bishops who met at Zaragoza clearly had very great differences of opinion over the orthodoxy of Priscillian's theological views—there was certainly not enough consensus to condemn either the man or his views explicitly, so that Priscillian could deny that any condemnation had been issued while his opponents could insist that it had. But what all the bishops could agree upon was the threat that unsupervised rural Christianity posed to their own urban power. If they were the shepherds of their flocks, then they must make sure that those flocks were herded into the churches and not allowed to stray into the mountains outside the protective, controlling reach of the shepherd's crook.

That is to say, the bishops who approved the canons of Zaragoza were responding to a profound challenge to the traditional relationship of town and country that they, as good Roman townsmen drawn mostly from local elites, instinctively felt it necessary to perpetuate. The city's *territorium* had been controlled from its urban center ever since the peninsula had been given a Roman political geography. The town's magistrates could command not just respect but also obedience to the limits of the town's *territorium*. The bishops who met at Zaragoza were drawn from the elites to whom such obedience was due; some came to the episcopate directly from municipal magistracies, others continued in their curial duties while in office.[120] Their role as Christian leaders, in other words, was an outgrowth of their role in the social life of the Roman town. From their point of view, the control of rural religiosity by an urban episcopate was the only form a properly disciplined Christianity could take.

This is not to say that Priscillian himself was some sort of avatar of ruralism or, still less, that his beliefs appealed to a covert social movement in the countryside against the urban civilization of Rome.[121] The mere fact that Priscillian's chief supporters were themselves bishops locates his movement as much in the towns as in the countryside, while the failure to condemn Priscillian outright at Zaragoza shows that there was real sympathy in parts of the episcopate for the man's asceticism. What there was no sympathy for was the practice of that asceticism outside the reach of the urban bishops—one of the few things that those who met at Zaragoza could all agree upon. If one wishes to, it is possible to take the rather clear-cut social challenge of rural asceticism and interpret it as a more abstract dialectic of public and private.[122] Yet in the Priscillianist conflict, abstraction into theology and disciplinary theory followed on what was at first a relatively simple matter of power: those who had power in the conventional *locus* of Christian cult, the towns, saw a challenge to that power that it was necessary for them to suppress.[123]

The conflict is exemplified in the fundamental differences of taste and style between Priscillian himself and Ithacius of Ossonuba. On the figure of Ithacius, Sulpicius Severus is scathing: *fuit enim audax, loquax, impudens, sumptuosus, ventri et gulae plurimum impertiens. hic stultitiae eo usque processerat ut omnes etiam sanctos viros quibus aut studium inerat lectionis aut propositum erat certare ieiuniis, tamquam Priscilliani so-*

cios aut discipulos in crimen arcesseret.[124] Now Ithacius is the villain of Sulpicius's story and he could hardly have painted a less flattering picture.[125] If one reads behind the Sulpician hostility, however, Ithacius emerges as a normal scion of the late Roman elite, convivial (*loquax*), secure in the power of his social position (*audax*), and fond of the luxuries to which his social position naturally entitled him (*sumptuosus, ventri et gulae plurimum impertiens*). Nothing was more natural than for such a man to viscerally detest the ostentatiously ragged Priscillian, whose behavior mocked his own high birth and whose evident success with noble ladies undermined not only conventional propriety but public order.[126]

Priscillian himself clearly understood this point, for in his third tractate he gives us a cruel parody of Hydatius of Mérida's speech to the council of Zaragoza. Hydatius had condemned the reading of apocryphal literature, saying "condemn what must be condemned, read not what is superfluous."[127] Priscillian recasts the bishop's objection: "condemn what I don't know, condemn what I don't read, condemn what I do not pursue because I pursue torpid leisure."[128] The point is well made. Hydatius is too much the Spanish aristocrat to be a proper Christian. There could be legitimate disagreement on the place of the apocrypha in the study of divine revelation. There could likewise be legitimate disagreement as to the admissibility of ascetic practice into the developing observances of Spanish Christianity. Just such disagreements no doubt kept these topics out of the transmitted canons of Zaragoza. By contrast, the sort of challenge that Priscillian posed to the assembled bishops was not controversial. His brand of uncivilized asceticism took the Christian community out of the towns and into the country, where the bishops could not control it, and in so doing it mocked the conventions of urban life to which the bishops accommodated themselves because they were a product of them. Hydatius's reaction to Priscillian was extreme, and the intensity with which he pursued his vendetta ultimately brought him down. But though his episcopal colleagues expressed themselves with greater temperance, they clearly shared his and Ithacius's views. Those views reflect the integration of the Spanish episcopate into the urban world of its time and its resistance to anything that might threaten the traditional power of that urban world over the lands around it.

It would thus appear that the threat which Priscillian posed to the episcopal hierarchy of Spain, at least initially, was not so much a matter of asceticism per se, but rather of the way in which his asceticism challenged the traditional social order into which the Spanish episcopate had integrated itself. At one level, the Priscillianist controversy can be viewed as an episode in the relationship between town and country in Roman Spain, in that followers of Priscillian posed a threat to the control that the fundamentally urban elite of the Spanish episcopate exercised over their rural dioceses in the same way that municipal elites had always dominated the territories of their towns. To interpret the Priscillianist controversy in this way is not necessarily to endorse the bishops' fears or to imply that their interpretation of the situation was correct. Indeed, the reaction of the bishops who met at Zaragoza presupposed something that we cannot take for granted—that the countryside which they were concerned to dominate was in fact a Christian environment by the 380s. Rather than accepting that episcopal assumption, we are constrained to ask what evidence there actually is for rural Christianity in fourth-century Spain.

The Evidence for Rural Christianity

No one would dispute that Christianity was a basically urban phenomenon in its earliest incarnation. Such literary evidence as we have suggests that even in the sixth and seventh centuries, the countryside of Spain had still barely been touched by Christian practices, that the rural communities had merely added Christianity to their repertory of local rites and practices.[129] Homely spirits, whether malevolent or benign, were the constant companions of rural society and they lived on to populate the invisible world that the Christians saw around them: the council of Elvira recognized that Christian landowners might be lynched by their rural dependents if they attempted to demolish non-Christian idols;[130] the bishops who gathered at Zaragoza to combat the threat of the ascetic Priscillian condemned him in part for his participation in the pagan rituals of the countryside;[131] traditional curse tablets are now known from clearly Christian contexts;[132] and at the very end of the sixth century, Martin of Braga found it necessary to deprecate the local custom of burning tapers at crossroads, little dedications in just that region where the peculiar, half-Romanized cult of the *lares viales* had been strongest.[133]

On the other hand, individual landowners could manage their estates with a freedom impossible within the communal environment of the towns, and this meant that a monumental Christianity appeared much sooner in the countryside than in the towns. Villas and large rural properties came to be dotted with little churches and baptisteries so that even the strangest rural structures might be turned into churches.[134] In other places, local landowners might sponsor the creation of monasteries on their lands.[135] Sometimes these new churches were part of an attempt to resacralize a non-Christian cult site as a place of Christian worship: thus a complex that included both a baths and a temple at Edeta, modern Llíria, had its *caldarium* converted into a Christian basilica some time in the fifth century.[136] Likewise at Can Modolell near modern Mataró, the site of an abandoned *mithraeum,* perhaps once part of a larger villa complex, was terraplaned and rebuilt toward the end of the fifth century, and the fragments of an early Christian altar found at the site suggest that it was a church of some sort that was put up as a means of deliberately resacralizing the spot in a Christian mold.[137]

The beginnings of this process cannot generally be dated to before the end of the fourth century, when the Spanish countryside began to be reimagined as a new network of Christian sanctity. Unfortunately for our understanding, problems of dating are pervasive and not just because so much material evidence continues to be dated from the narrative evidence rather than on its own terms.[138] Many rural sites, in Spain as elsewhere in Europe, have been in continuous agricultural use since the Middle Ages, if not since Roman times, and centuries of plowing make uncontaminated stratigraphy very unusual. We are thus frequently constrained to date rural Christian sites in rough typological terms on the basis of the overall assemblage of materials rather than from uncontaminated strata. Most of the better excavated sites lie in Baetica and Lusitania, where the visible impact of rural Christianity was much greater than in the north. They give us some sense of the paths that rural Christianization might take, but they do nothing to establish a paradigm that probably does not exist.

At a very few sites, the establishment of Christian cult looks like a communal decision rather than the work of a *dominus* imposing his religion on his lands. One such site is Gerena, 24 kilometers north of modern Seville.[139] The site, well supplied by ground water, had sustained a Roman population from very early, probably in the service of both oleoculture and the mines of the Sierra Norte, which lies just at hand. There is no sign of this settlement having had any juridical status—it was a rural camp or village and if it was dependent upon a nearby villa, then the *domus* has not been found. Some time in the late fourth or early fifth century, a basilica was built at Gerena, just outside the low wall of the village. The basilica was a long rectangle, divided into three naves, with three separate chambers at their heads. The narthex served as a baptistery, with separate internal divisions so that the actual baptismal chamber, in which the font is still extant, was separated from the rooms in which neophytes could await their initiation. This baptistery was a later addition to the original basilica, and though separated from the basilica internally, viewed from the outside the whole complex would have appeared as a single rectangular whole. Neither basilica nor baptistery is fancy. The foundation walls are made from the same limestone rock on which the foundations rest, while whatever decoration there once was has since disappeared. Within the confines of these limitations, the inhabitants of Gerena appear to have followed the basic fashions of Christian worship observable throughout the peninsula. On the one hand, they wanted to be buried inside the church, to be closer to the sainted dead. On the other, the universal move toward infant baptism is eventually evidenced by the remodeling of the baptismal font from a deep cruciform plan to a later shallow tetraconch.[140]

Gerena's baptistery suggests the close association of rural church-building with a baptismal function, which is attested with great frequency at villa sites and which we must assume reflects the owner's zeal for converting his tenants or *coloni*. Perhaps the best example of this phenomenon—and certainly one of the very earliest—is found at the villa of Torre de Palma in the Alto Alentejo.[141] The villa complex of Torre de Palma is the largest known from Spain, consisting of not just two contiguous villas—one built around an atrium, the other around a larger peristyle—but also the largest villa rustica yet uncovered. The site was badly damaged by its early excavators, but recent reexcavation has clarified matters to a certain extent. The middle of the fourth century appears to have witnessed a flurry of building activity, perhaps a reflection of sudden wealth or promotion on the part of the *dominus*.[142] A second bath complex was built to the southwest of the residential villa, at the opposite end of the site from the original second-century baths, and to these new baths was attached a *domus* built around a small tetrastyle atrium.

At the same time, a large basilica was also put up, its construction technique very similar to that of the baths and the new *domus*. It probably dates to the middle of the fourth century, because the date suggested by several *nummi* of Constantius II found in the plaster of the floor has now been confirmed by carbon 14 dating.[143] In the sixth century, the original basilical structure was renovated to form a long rectangle, with an apse at each end, although the original floor was preserved. A baptistery was also associated with the original fourth-century church, though only much later, perhaps in the seventh century, did it achieve the seven-room structure that it displays today. In the same period, the sixth-century basilica was much expanded, with a second double-apsed basilica laid end-to-end with the first one. Within an elongated rectangle, there were now two separate liturgical zones, with four apses between them, and an attached baptistery that could be approached either from within the older basilica or from the exterior of the building. From very simple beginnings, Torre de Palma grew piecemeal into a liturgical complex of great intricacy.

The villa at Torre de Palma illustrates not just the baptismal aspects of rural Christianity, but also the way in which a rural *dominus* could use the reconstruction of his property along new Christian lines to reconfigure the entire site in a more sumptuous fashion. A similarly labor-intensive process of Christianization is visible at the villa of El Saucedo, where the original plan was carefully retained, while the walls of the basilical hall were dismantled to within 50 centimeters of the ground before the structure was rebuilt as a church. This involved creating new partitions of space in the interior, closing up at least one doorway and putting in a new one in order to have the basilical space communicate with a new baptistery, in which a cruciform *piscina* was installed. A new mosaic was likewise put in the exedra of the old basilica, but on the whole the new church imitated as closely as possible the external decorative features of the old *domus*.[144]

At most rural sites, we must be content with much less straightforward evidence for the physical Christianization of the landscape. Thus at the villa of Monte da Cegonha, near the town of Vidigueira 13 kilometers from modern Beja, an impressive villa was put up on the remains of a much less impressive building in the third or fourth century, while a large new bath complex incorporated other parts of the older building. The northern hall of the basilica comprised a small Christian basilica with a baptistery built into one of its two sacristies. A large necropolis developed around this basilica, both inside and outside its walls, spanning perhaps four centuries of use. It is, however, impossible to know whether the basilica was an integral part of the fourth-century remodeling of the villa or whether it was installed in one part of the villa after the site had lost its original residential function. That is to say, we cannot tell whether the *dominus* of Monte da Cegonha was a deeply pious Christian who installed a church on his lands at a precociously early date in the fourth century, or whether the basilica was a later development making use of preexisting monumental architecture for a new religious purpose. Although the most recent scholars to work on the site favor the former interpretation, nothing in the material evidence itself is probative.[145]

The complex of São Cucufate, which like Monte da Cegonha lies not very far from Beja, poses similar problems. During the lavish fourth-century renovation of the site, a small temple was put up just beyond the second of the site's two cisterns.[146] This tempietto has few typological parallels in Spain and was clearly non-Christian in origin. At some point in the lifespan of the villa it was converted into a Christian church and became the center of a necropolis from which some eighteen inhumations have been uncovered. The date of these inhumations is not entirely clear, but may be early fifth-century. Although the excavators suggest that the development of a Christian site around this temple is a sign that the villa had ceased to serve in its residential capacity, there is no probative evidence for this point.[147] Both Monte da Cegonha and São Cucufate provide evidence for the way in which villa sites were physically transformed by the adoption of Christianity, but they also illustrate the difficulties that beset attempts to define the chronology of this process.

There are a great many Christian basilicas at Spanish rural sites, and most pose similar problems.[148] Insofar as these constraints allow for meaningful generalization, the monumental Christianization of the Spanish countryside would appear to have begun in earnest during the last decades of the fourth century, but to have proceeded with much greater speed and ease than it did in the cities. That is not to say that Christian belief spread more easily in rural than in urban Spain; indeed, the reverse is likely to have been the case if our literary sources can be believed. And of course, in the countryside as much as in the cities, we have no way of gauging the size of the Christian population or of knowing what percentage of the population as a whole it made up. At the end of the fourth century, that population remained very mixed, and Potamius of Lisbon gives us the typology of an urban population which, however schematized, probably reflects the world around him, with its *milites, Iudaei, gentiles, christiani, proselyti, clarissimi senatores, nobiles iudices, nautae, servi.*[149]

By the end of the fifth century, that picture had changed dramatically. In the course of the later fourth and the fifth centuries, the countryside of Spain began to be marked by a network of Christian cult sites. In the towns, Christianity was clearly the dominant religion by the end of the fourth century, if not necessarily the only one. But Christian cult and the authority of Christian leaders was not nearly so complete as is often believed. The authority of the imperial government was something to which the Spanish bishops showed suitable and necessary deference, while the Spanish episcopate maintained many of the social assumptions of the age-old Roman municipal life, if for no other reason than that many bishops were drawn from Spain's urban elite. The physical persistence of the old Roman townscape reflects the tenacity of established urban behaviors that took a very long time to change despite the adoption of Christianity by the society as a whole. It was not until the very end of the fifth century that the Spanish town began to be fundamentally Christian in social, political, and physical terms.

In the decades after imperial government disappeared from Spain, churches moved from the margins to the center of the Spanish townscape, doing so because the old Roman town plan had finally ceased to have any great social significance. This was the culmination of a process by which episcopal authority and power came to replace that of the municipal elite of the curia in the affairs of the town. The re-building of the bridge at Mérida under the patronage of a Gothic count and the city's bishop is emblematic of this change, as is, from the op-posite perspective, the burial beside Saint Eulalia's tomb of the last im-perial *vir inlustris* known from Spain. Whether we turn to the mater-ial or the literary evidence, our record of sixth-century history is substantially poorer than it is for the fifth. The transition to a world in which the Christian church—its leaders, its rituals, and its build-ings—dominated the social world of Spain was, as the material evi-dence shows, much slower and substantially later than is traditionally thought. But it had to a very large extent taken place by the start of the sixth century, and was a basic fact of peninsular life in the many con-fusing decades before a Gothic king came close to uniting Spain's cities and provinces under the rule of a single man once again.

Eleven

The Earlier Sixth Century and the Goths in Spain

The growing Christianization of the physical and social world of the fifth and sixth centuries is undoubtedly their most significant feature, with church power extending into the void left by the decay of older forms of urban authority. The old municipal institutions did not simply disappear. Some continue to be attested where sources exist, and in much of the peninsula, political life devolved to the level of the *civitas* in the absence of any more effective power. For this reason, it is very difficult to impose any shape on the history of the Spanish provinces as a whole during the first seven decades of the sixth century. They were a continuation of the confused pattern of local developments that we have seen in the later fifth century. Only with the accession of the Gothic king Leovigild does Spanish history develop a certain unity once again. Most of our evidence for the earlier sixth century deals with the activity of Gothic kings and derives from the very late sixth or the seventh century, when a Gothic kingdom encompassed almost the whole of the peninsula. That fact has consequences: the Gothic kings bulk far larger in our sources than they did in the history of the peninsula as a whole, with the result that we can all too easily retroject late sixth- or seventh-century Gothic strength into the earlier parts of the sixth century. But to do so is misleading.

For the Spanish provinces, the sixth century opened much as the previous one had closed. The Gothic kings may have claimed hegemony over the peninsula, but there is little evidence that such claims were widely accepted. Even in Tarraconensis, Gothic control was precarious, as the campaigns against the "tyrants" Burdunelus and Petrus had shown.[1] The church council of Agde, held in 506 under King Alaric's patronage, provides similar evidence of this weakness.[2] The council met on 10 September 506, under the presidency of Caesarius of Arles.[3] As a council of Nicene bishops within the Gothic kingdom, the bishops who met at Agde set about confirming the authority of earlier councils and creating a uniform discipline for the kingdom's church.[4] Though twenty-four bishops, eight priests, and two deacons represented most of the churches of the Gothic kingdom, they counted no Spaniards among their number. Provisions were made for a further council in the following year, at which Spanish *confratres* might attend, but their total absence from Agde is telling.[5] That it caused concern at all suggests that royal claims to Tarraconensis, and perhaps to Spain as a whole, were broadly known and acknowledged, that the Spanish *confratres* were regarded as belonging to Gothic kingdom; at the same time, their absence from Agde itself suggests that Spain, Tarraconensis included, lay outside the Gothic kingdom in practical terms.[6]

Spain and Theodoric the Great

This situation only changed with the great upheaval of 507, when Alaric's monarchy was overthrown on the battlefield of Vouillé. Thereafter, Gothic kings were forced first to reside in Spain while attempting to reconquer Gaul, then to make Spain their chief field of activity. Alaric's downfall was rapid. During 506 and 507, he and the Frankish king Clovis edged toward war.[7] The Ostrogothic king Theodoric, brother-in-law of Clovis and father-in-law of Alaric, sought to downplay the causes of dispute and forestall the outbreak of open conflict, calling on the Burgundian king Gundobad to help him restrain his neighbors.[8] He promised Alaric support, but only if he sought arbitration, and threatened Clovis with war if he did not show similar restraint.[9] Alaric and Clovis met on an island in the Loire river, but failed to patch up their differences, and so Theodoric's efforts came to naught.[10] Clovis marched south, Gundobad chose to stand with Clovis, and Theodoric's fear that the Visigoths were not up to the fight proved fully justified.[11] Alaric's kingdom stood behind him and Apollinaris, the grandson of Sidonius, headed a contingent of Arvernian aristocrats in the battle against Clovis.[12] The Frankish and Gothic armies met near the town of Poitiers, far to the north of Toulouse, at a site called *Voglada, Vogladum,* or the *campus Vogladensis,* traditionally identified as Vouillé.[13] There, as the laconic annotations of the Zaragoza *Consularia* tell us, "King Alaric was killed in battle by the Franks and the kingdom of Toulouse was destroyed."[14] Clovis and Gundobad converged on Toulouse, which they sacked before Gundobad pursued Alaric's successor into Spain.[15]

The Gothic's king's grown son Gesalic, the offspring of a concubine, had been elected at Narbonne after Frankish and Burgundian occupation definitively closed Toulouse to him. Thereafter, he retreated into Spain to regroup, but we do not know if Gesalic was present at Barcelona when Gundobad besieged it.[16] Gesalic probably had his young half-brother Amalaric in tow, for the two were not yet seen as rival claimants to the Gothic throne and Gesalic would serve as Amalaric's regent for a short time.[17] Meanwhile, the conquerors continued their operations in Gaul. Gundobad probably returned to Burgundy before the onset of the winter of 507/508, but the Franks seem to have been engaged in fighting at Carcassonne and Clovis's son Theuderic marched on Clermont via Albi and Rodez.[18] After taking possession of the Gothic royal treasure, or at least some part of it, Clovis retired to Bordeaux, where he spent the winter of 507/508.[19] In the spring, he marched back to Tours via Angoulême, where he overcame a Gothic garrison before joining Theuderic back in Paris later in the year.[20] Despite these wide-ranging campaigns, Clovis's hold on the formerly Gothic lands was precarious and only in the following decade was the region brought firmly under Frankish control.

The failure of Theodoric the Ostrogoth to prevent the conflict between Alaric and Clovis can only have wounded his pretensions to lead the barbarian West, while the sudden friendliness of the Roman emperor Anastasius toward Clovis raised the specter of a Frankish alliance with Constantinople.[21] Theodoric therefore decided to make good the threats that he had uttered not long before.[22] In the summer of 508, an Ostrogothic army crossed the Alps into Gaul, where it inflicted a punishing defeat on a mixed force of Franks and Burgundians that had been besieging Arles for some time.[23] Theodoric himself now came to Gaul and his general Ibba occupied Narbonne.[24] During 509, the warfare among Ostrogoths, Franks, and Burgundians dragged on, but it soon became secondary to the problem of the Visigothic succession.[25]

In the immediate aftermath of Vouillé, Theodoric had acquiesced in the succession of Gesalic; certainly until 510 or 511 there is no sign of contact between Theodoric and his grandson Amalaric and it is likely that, during those years, Theodoric regarded Gesalic as an ally and de facto regent for Amalaric.[26] The new Visigothic king made his residence at Barcelona, where there are obscure hints of faction and division at his court.[27] By 511, however, a serious breach had opened between Gesalic and Theodoric. The problem was one of power, exacerbated by the demands of blood kinship. Gesalic was Alaric's bastard by a concubine. He had no blood ties to Theodoric and, if recent studies of barbarian kinship are correct, his maternal kin group is likely to have profited more from his accession than any Ostrogothic connections.[28] Meanwhile a legitimate heir, who happened to be Theodoric's own grandson, remained available. One need not appeal to any abstract principles of legitimacy to explain Theodoric's growing hostility. A very pragmatic goal—his own dominance of Visigothic affairs—existed alongside any such principles. Thus, despite his initial acquiescence in Gesalic's succession, and despite the acceptability of Gesalic to at least some of the Visigoths, Theodoric determined to replace him with his half-brother.

Either in 510 or early 511, Theodoric's general Ibba forced Gesalic to flee to Africa, where the Vandal king Thrasamund declined to do more than give him money and send him on his way.[29] Gesalic returned to Gaul and tried to regain his position, but Ibba again defeated him. He then spent a year or so in Aquitania, and we hear nothing of any Frankish support.[30] Here is the proof, if any was needed, that the Frankish conquest of southern Gaul was by no means complete: Gesalic's ability to linger a full year in Aquitania suggests the survival of Gothic parties still loyal to the old dynasty of Alaric and hostile to the new predominance of the Italian Goths. After gathering his strength in the course of that year, Gesalic made one final attempt to regain his throne, but was defeated by Ibba 12 Roman miles from Barcelona, evidently still the chief Visigothic residence under the Ostrogothic protectorate. The defeated king fled yet again, this time to Burgundian territory.[31] He was captured and executed soon afterward. The identity of his killers is unknown, but none of our sources—Spanish, Gallic, or Italian—register the slightest regret at his passing.

Instead, the chroniclers regard Theodoric as the ruler of the Visigoths until his own death at the start of 526. Of Amalaric we hear nothing for as long as his grandfather lived. The young king was presumably a cipher, though it is not clear how Theodoric controlled Spain for most of his regency; only late in the reign do we hear of the Ostrogothic nobleman Theudis as the royal proxy in Spain.[32] Theodoric had sent Theudis to Spain as a military leader, but the general swiftly went native. He married a Hispano-Roman woman from among whose clients he was able to field a private army. So entrenched did Theudis's position grow that Theodoric feared his revolt or usurpation. Through intermediaries, he attempted to cajole Theudis into returning to Ravenna, only to meet with consistent refusal. There was nothing Theodoric could do to compel him, but Theudis made his king's position less embarrassing by loyally paying up the tribute owed annually by Spain.[33]

At the time of Theodoric's death, however, we have no record of Theudis or his activities. Instead, Amalaric was finally enabled to rule on his own account. Theodoric's death might have triggered a succession crisis if the great king's Italian successors had attempted to maintain the control over the Visigoths that he had himself exercised. Instead, on Amalaric's initiative, his government and that of his cousin Athalaric and his aunt Amalasuntha parted company on good terms.[34] The kingdoms of Visigoths and Ostrogoths were divided, Amalaric taking the territory to the west of the Rhône, Athalaric that to the east. Athalaric "truthfully and equitably" returned the Visigothic royal treasure to his cousin.[35] As importantly, Ostrogoths who had married Visigothic women and Visigoths who had married Ostrogothic women were freely allowed to choose their allegiance, a choice that presumably meant relocation within the freshly divided territories and may have been necessary to clarify tax obligations.

In other matters, however, Amalaric was not so fortunate. At the very start of his reign, in order to ward off the danger of Frankish attack and perhaps as a counterbalance to both Theudis in Spain and the Ostrogothic government in Italy, Amalaric had married the Frankish princess Clothild, a daughter of Clovis and hence sister to four reigning kings. The marriage went badly, Amalaric's Arianism sitting ill with the orthodox Clothild. He battered her, she called upon her brothers for help, and in 531 Childebert of Paris marched to Narbonensis, where he defeated Amalaric. The fate of the latter is not entirely clear. We have three sources, each of which tells a different story: Procopius locates the battle in Gaul and has Amalaric die in it; the Zaragoza *Consularia* has Amalaric flee Narbonensis, only to be killed at Barcelona by a Frank named Besso; while Gregory of Tours has him die at Narbonne, murdered by his own men, after a failed attempt at flight.[36] Procopius is perhaps the least reliable of our sources, but there is little to choose between them. What is clear is that Amalaric's reign came to a sorry end in 531. His followers fled to Spain and joined Theudis, who now became king of the Visigoths in turn. Just what this meant for the life of the peninsula is problematical: as in the years between the death of Alaric in 507 and that of Amalaric in 531, so under Theudis the extent and nature of Gothic royal authority in Spain is not easy to gauge.

The Extent of Gothic Rule in Spain, 507–531

The evidence for Gothic administration in Spain after Vouillé is limited to two letters of Cassiodorus and a few lines of Procopius.[37] As we have argued, royal control of Spain under Euric and Alaric was limited to a continuous military effort to hold a few key Spanish cities and there was probably no substantial Gothic immigration to Spain before the death of Alaric. With the flight of Gesalic and Amalaric from Gaul, Gothic kings began to reside in Spain, but royal activity, and the kings' primary interests, remained focused on Gaul: Gesalic, after all, made his bid to regain the Visigothic throne not in Spain but in Narbonensis; Amalaric is positively attested in only two cities, Barcelona and Narbonne; and we know that during Theodoric's protectorate the Goths regained parts of Narbonensis and Aquitania Prima.[38] All this suggests that, between Vouillé and the death of Amalaric, Spain took second place to Gaul in the calculations of the Gothic kings, as it had always done in the calculations of Roman emperors, even though the kings had been forced by circumstance to reside south of the Pyrenees.

That Gallic orientation helps make sense of the limited evidence for Gothic administration in Spain. Procopius states that Theodoric, having possessed himself of the Visigothic treasure, returned to Ravenna but continued to send generals and armies to Gaul and Spain, ordering these territories to pay an annual tribute. Some part of this was given out as a donative to the armies of both Ostrogoths and Visigoths, with the result that the two peoples became one, dwelling in the same lands under the leadership of the same man.[39] Though we cannot push Procopius's language very far, the dominance of the Ostrogothic partner that he implies is corroborated by the imitative coinages of Spain from this period, which were minted on the Ostrogothic standard.[40] Under Ostrogothic hegemony, Spain and Gaul were treated collectively and as essentially military possessions and sources of revenue. Where and how this tribute was collected is unclear, but at least at the start, Theodoric attempted to reimpose Roman administration: Liberius became praetorian prefect in Gaul some time after 508, holding the post until after Theodoric's death.[41] At the same time, a certain Gemellus is attested as *vicarius praefectorum* in Gaul, a position that implies the reimposition of long-standing mechanisms of tax collection and administration.[42]

If the evidence for Gaul is thus fairly strong, two of Cassiodorus's *Variae,* addressed in the mid-520s to the *comes* and *vir spectabilis* Liuverit and the *vir inlustris* Ampelius, suggest a similar attempt to regularize Ostrogothic government in Spain.[43] Precisely what offices the two men held is not clear, and the duration of their stay in Spain need not have been long. In the earlier of the two letters, Liuverit and Ampelius are charged with making the journey to Spain to correct financial abuses and impose order on government.[44] According to Theodoric, the Spanish provincials were subject not to the orderly exactions of the public tax rolls but to the capricious whim of the tax collectors. While these tax collectors defrauded the treasury, the Spanish taxpayers were failing to pay what they owed. Liuverit and Ampelius were to establish accurate weights and measures, and no official was to extract more in tribute than was then paid into the royal coffers. The second letter, directed to the two men when they were already in Spain, deals with the illicit diversion to Africa of Spanish grain destined for Rome.[45] Theodoric informs Liuverit and Ampelius that two inspectors, Catellus and Servandus, are on their way to look into the incident; in the opening of the letter, he implicitly condemns Ampelius and Liuverit by comparison to the *vir spectabilis* Marcianus, who had seen to the grain supply in a praiseworthy manner.

The subtext of both letters is revealing. Both glow with the old rhetoric of imperial legislation, but the real concern is the smooth supply of Spanish tribute to Rome and Ravenna. That is to say, once we penetrate behind the Cassiodoran verbiage, we are not at all far away from Procopius's assessment of Ostrogothic rule in Spain as essentially military and exploitative. Marcianus's rank of *spectabilis* might imply that he was *vicarius* in Spain as Gemellus was in Gaul, but neither Liuverit nor Ampelius appears to have exercised regular administrative appointments in Spain.[46] Despite holding the illustrissimate, Ampelius was not the praetorian prefect of Spain, an office that existed only very briefly after 526 when the separation of Ostrogothic and Visigothic realms made it necessary. Then, we meet the Spanish prefect Stephen, whose rise and fall at the hands of Amalaric struck the Zaragoza annotator as interesting.[47] In other words, before Amalaric's sole reign only the dubious case of Marcianus attests to a regular administrative superstructure in Spain.

The *Variae* do, by contrast, attest quite a number of lesser officials, including the *vilici* of public estates, the managers of the *cursus publicus,* and the *conductores domus regiae.*[48] The mention of *telonei,* here meaning customs dues levied on overseas shipping, suggests the existence of *telonarii* to collect them, while a reference to duties imposed on overseas traders must refer to the old *collatio lustralis.*[49] Theodoric's instructions thus assume a network of minor officials to see to the government's needs, although the functional relationship of these minor officials to their imperial models is not always clear. The *domus regia* was presumably the same office as the *domus dominica* of the *Breviary,* formed out of lands that had once belonged to the imperial *res privata,* and Theodoric proposed to pay its *conductores* a salary to reduce the chances of peculation. The existence of such offices is important evidence for a fairly high level of administrative complexity, but there are problems of interpretation, particularly with the *domus regia*.

On the one hand, it is not at all difficult to imagine that a record of the estates that constituted the local holdings of the *res privata* had been preserved in the half century since the disappearance of imperial government. After all, the basic continuity of Roman landholding at the level of the *fundus* is attested in a substantial stretch of northern Tarraconensis into the 550s and the seventh-century Visigothic laws are adamant about preserving ancient boundaries.[50] On the other hand, it is considerably harder to understand how those lands had been maintained as a collectivity across fifty disturbed years and therefore how the Gothic government proposed to extract its dues from them. Two possibilities suggest themselves. One is that the basic mechanisms of imperial government in Spain had been substantially maintained in the fifty years since the death of Majorian, either to the benefit of the kings of Toulouse—which seems unlikely given what we have seen of their weakness in Spain—or to the benefit of the local *potentiores*. If the latter, one might speculate that what Theodoric castigates as the failure of the landowners to pay their accustomed dues was in fact the resistance of *possessores* to paying tax and tribute on lands that had been free from imperial exaction for more than fifty years. But a second interpretation is equally plausible: the *Variae* show us Theodoric trying to impose on Spain a system of royal, subimperial government that had at this point disappeared there. Such attempts had been feasible in Italy, where palatine offices survived uninterrupted through the reign of Odoacer into the Ostrogothic period. But in Spain, after fifty years, the exactions demanded by the Ostrogothic king may have seemed substantively new.

We can read the evidence either way, depending on how we conceptualize institutional change in the post-imperial period more generally. Our documentary record is peppered with lacunae, but in between them we find attestations of fiscal and administrative institutions with traditional nomenclature but signs of functional difference; to take a Spanish example, the financial officials of the seventh-century *leges Visigothorum* are described in much the same language as those of the Theodosian Code, or indeed those of the *Variae,* but they do not seem to work in the same way.[51] We are therefore left with the fundamental interpretative question of whether the gaps in our evidence represent ellipses in which Roman governmental institutions continued to exist and to evolve without our being able to watch them do so, or whether in some of these gaps lurk stages at which the institutions simply ceased to function, only to be re-created when political circumstances allowed. The Spanish evidence cannot answer a question central to the debate on the transformation of the Roman world. The royal officials in Spain who appear in the *Variae* certainly existed, but knowing what precisely they did and to whom they answered is another matter.

It is just as difficult to determine the extent of the territory over which the Ostrogothic king's officials were able to exercise their functions. On the minimalist approach favored throughout the present study, one might limit Ostrogothic administration to the *civitates* of Tarraconensis in which Gothic kings or their officials are explicitly attested, which is to say the territories of Barcelona and Gerona. The enigmatic figure of Theudis, however, may suggest that Ostrogothic administration extended beyond the small part of Tarraconensis in which it is explicitly attested. Theudis, whose nephew Hildibad eventually became king in Italy, was a powerful figure in his own right.[52] He found the Spanish environment congenial, married locally, and created his own power base on the foundation of his wife's wealth and estates, warding off Theodoric's suspicions by faithfully rendering up the Spanish tribute year in and year out.

There is no explicit testimony as to Theudis's favored residence, nor of the location of his wife's vast estates, but his later sphere of activity as king may provide grounds for speculation. Unlike Gesalic and Amalaric, or the generals of Euric and Alaric before them, Theudis is found not in the cities of coastal Tarraconensis, but rather in Carthaginiensis. Indeed, we have no explicit attestation of his personal presence anywhere outside the city of Toledo, where in 546 he promulgated the sole piece of royal legislation extant from the decades after Alaric's promulgation of the *Breviary*.[53] This fact may mean that Theudis regarded Toledo as his chief residence, a choice inexplicable in terms of the political geography of the imperial period—not only was Toledo never a provincial capital, it had never even served as the center of a *conventus*.[54] One might instead explain Theudis's choice of residence on the theory that he chose to reside as king in the region where he had the strongest local support.[55] If this was in fact the case, and if we can retroject this evidence to the reigns of Theodoric and Amalaric, then we might imagine Theudis making his base in northern Carthaginiensis while Amalaric and his court remained in coastal Tarraconensis. If so, the Spanish taxes that eventually found their way to the Gothic armies would have been collected from a territory that included not just the chief cities along the coast of Tarraconensis, but also the Spanish interior as far as the middle Ebro valley and the Meseta of New Castile.

The evidence of church councils confirms this impression. Amalaric was invoked in the prayers at the second council of Toledo, held in May 527. A letter of Bishop Montanus of Toledo, appended to the conciliar acta in the *Collectio Hispana,* deals with disputed ordinations in the regions of Carpetania and Celtiberia, which is to say in the western part of Tarraconensis and the north of Carthaginiensis, and threatens to involve the king in the dispute.[56] Participation in the councils of this period again suggests the same conclusion. Only one bishop from outside Carthaginiensis or Tarraconensis can be shown to have attended any council held in Spain while Theodoric, Amalaric, and Theudis reigned.[57] It is true, of course, that ecclesiastical jurisdictions did not always march in step with political boundaries, and bishops of Rome continued to insist upon viewing all the churches of Spain as a single entity. Nevertheless, the testimony of the early sixth-century councils is consonant with the other literary evidence.[58] It suggests that Theodoric, Amalaric, and Theudis ruled a Spanish kingdom consisting of substantial parts of Tarraconensis and Carthaginiensis, as well as a strip of the old Narbonensis, but not necessarily much else.

Goths in the Material Evidence

No literary evidence allows us to extend the scope of Gothic administration or overlordship outside Tarraconensis and Carthaginiensis until late in the 540s, and the lack of any reference to Córdoba, Seville, and Mérida under Theodoric and Amalaric is a significant silence. To be sure, one or two funerary inscriptions from Baetica bear philologically Germanic names and a few artifacts that are traditionally described as "Visigothic" are known from the early sixth-century province.[59] Neither fact is at all compelling. The bearers of Germanic names need not necessarily be identified as Goths and, even if they were Goths, their isolated burials tell us nothing about a larger Gothic presence in the region. Other archaeological evidence is still more fraught with peril, and by contrast to their evident role in the political history of the peninsula, the Gothic impact on Spain's material record is both minimal and impossible to chart with any precision. It is increasingly acknowledged that whatever impact the Goths did have was long-term, not immediate, and not directly linked to any particular historical event.[60] The material culture commonly described as Visigothic—the perfect little northern churches at San Juan de Baños or San Pedro de la Nave, for instance—are products of a much later period than that with which we are concerned, a seventh-century kingdom in which it is impossible to separate out "Gothic" from "Roman" elements in the cultural fusion.[61] Indeed, before the rise of a new Spanish material culture in the seventh century, separating out any specifically Gothic element in the Spanish landscape is virtually impossible. It is, of course, true that some of the cultural and political trends reflected in the material record must have been stimulated by the presence of Gothic power in the peninsula, not least the changes to the townscape of Mérida, at which we have already looked.[62]

But it is nonetheless difficult for us to go much beyond that level of generalization. Any attempt to specify a precise Gothic impact on the local material record, much less to locate Gothic populations, is hemmed in by crippling methodological problems. At the center of these is the question of how we detect ethnicity in the material record. Ethnicity is, after all, a social construct. Though it has biological and linguistic elements, its meaning derives from the interaction of living people, while the material record preserves only the imperishable artifacts of the dead. There can be no question that some such artifacts played a role in signifying ethnicity among people while they were alive. The problem lies in whether the same artifacts are intrinsically diagnostic of ethnicity when separated from the social interactions during which they were displayed. Put another way, can specific artifacts, taken out of context, be used to determine the ethnicity of their owners? Traditional archaeological practice assumes that material objects do carry ethnicity in this way. Particular types of artifacts, generally elements of personal adornment found in a funerary context, are thought to determine the race or ethnicity of the person with whom they were buried. Once that assumption has been made, it becomes possible to trace the interaction of ethnic and racial groups on the basis of material finds and to trace the movement of populations on the same basis.[63] Yet even the material possessions one takes to one's grave do not establish identity in quite so clear-cut a manner, as recent theoretical studies of the archaeology of ethnicity have shown.[64]

Because ethnicity is neither purely biological nor purely material, any understanding of it requires access to the human perceptions that define it. These cannot be derived from the material traces alone, but must be teased out of the juxtaposition of those traces with the literary sources of the era. By means of that juxtaposition, it is in theory possible to make statements about the reflections of ethnicity in the material record, for example, that in a given zone of contact between Romans and barbarians, particular assemblages of artifacts are likely to be representative of a certain barbarian ethnic group.[65] There are, unfortunately, very few regions and eras in which this sort of statement is possible within the limitations of our written and material sources.[66] Still more problematical is our inability to extrapolate beyond such specific instances. Personal artifacts are portable and they change hands with great ease. Just because a certain form of artifact signifies a particular ethnicity in one place and at one time does not mean that it carries the same ethnic meaning with it to other places at other times. Fashions change more readily than do perceptions of self, and those who take a fancy to wearing outlandish clothing do not transform their ethnicity by so doing. In other words, the extrapolation of ethnic conclusions on the basis of material evidence alone excises the vital element of living human perception, and thereby renders any such conclusions suspect. As a result, the traditional ascription of ethnicity to particular forms of artifact is methodologically unsound; it allows us to locate and follow ethnic groups in the archaeological record, but only because it presumes far more from the material evidence than can actually be inferred from it.

In the Spanish context, certain cemeteries have long been characterized as Visigothic because of the personal ornaments found in them.

The ascription of a Visigothic ethnicity to particular types of brooches, clasps, and belt buckles has permitted analysis of the peninsula's Gothic history in terms of the distribution of these types, with a Gothic presence detected wherever such artifacts are present.[67] The four cemeteries held to be archetypically Visigothic lie in the Castilian Meseta at Duratón (Segovia), Castiltierra (Segovia), El Carpio del Tajo (Toledo), and Herrera de Pisuerga (Palencia).[68] With their origins dated to the early sixth century, these cemeteries have tended to be the norm against which other Spanish cemeteries are judged.[69] The distribution across Spain of artifact types found in these cemeteries, meanwhile, is used to trace the spread of Visigothic population out of the Meseta and into other provinces.[70]

The difficulties with such interpretations of the material evidence run deeper than the methodological reservations already voiced. For one thing, the chronologies of our "Visigothic" cemeteries are extremely insecure. None has been excavated with modern techniques and all our information has to be derived from early twentieth-century site reports that contain faulty site plans, offer only lacunose coverage of finds, and often fail to correlate grave goods to specific graves.[71] Worse still, it is almost impossible to determine from the information at our disposal whether any particular assemblage came from a sealed context. Additionally, our evidentiary base is not as full as it seems at first: though the fact is rarely acknowledged, fewer than half the graves in our supposedly Gothic cemeteries contain any grave goods at all, let alone types considered ethnically diagnostic. What is more, the highly differentiated typology of Spanish ornamental artifacts that has been constructed in recent years, though its relative chronology is almost entirely secure, depends very heavily on assumptions and dates drawn from the literary record for its absolute chronology.[72]

These difficulties have very real consequences for our understanding of Spain's Visigothic history. At a high level of generalization it remains possible to interpret the Mesetan cemeteries in an ethnic fashion.[73] One can do so because it is impossible to deny that these cemeteries and a few others preserve ornamental forms very distinct from those that were commonplace in most of late antique Spain, aquiliform brooches only the most aesthetically striking among them. That is to say, at least a few of the people who were buried in these

Mesetan cemeteries favored fashions that differed significantly from the preexisting norm. Given that fact, and assuming that the sixth-century date of these ornamental forms is substantially correct, then it is indeed logical to view these Mesetan cemeteries as belonging to a population distinct from the Spanish norm. Because we know from the literary sources that outsiders called Visigoths did settle in Spain during the fifth and sixth centuries, we might well accept that the people buried in the Mesetan cemeteries represent these Gothic incomers.

Yet even with so minimalist a statement, there are serious problems. First, until a proper stratigraphic excavation is conducted in a cemetery of the Mesetan type we will have no guarantee that the typological dating of existing examples to the sixth century is correct. If it is not, then the case for identifying the cemeteries as Gothic grows much weaker. Second, and more seriously, the habit of inhumation with personal ornaments was a surprising novelty in the Spanish Meseta but it was equally unknown in southern Gaul, the region from which the literary sources tell us the Spanish Visigoths came. The Visigothic kingdom in Gaul is famously invisible archaeologically.[74] This latter consideration has prompted some scholars to attribute the Mesetan cemeteries to another ethnic group, perhaps Balkan or Danubian, which entered Spain in the company of the Visigoths, though there is not, in fact, any evidence to support such a hypothesis.[75] On the other hand, were the paradigm of ethnic ascription not so deeply ingrained, one would not find it difficult to interpret these cemeteries as an indigenous development within Mesetan society, in the same way that the development of the Gallic *Reihengräber* civilization no longer seems susceptible of an ethnic interpretation.[76] In the face of so many methodological and practical reservations, the safest course of action is to refrain from precise judgments. If one wishes to, it is possible to regard the Mesetan cemeteries as the product of a new population in the region, whose habit of burying its dead with certain types of personal ornament gradually grew more common, at the same time as ornament types themselves became more homogeneous during the seventh century. Beyond this level of generalization, however, we cannot go. Even if we accept that our four Mesetan cemeteries are, broadly speaking, Visigothic, that does not mean that any particular person buried with a certain set of artifacts positively was, or positively was not, a Goth.

Outside of the Meseta, where no substantial late antique cemetery has ever been excavated, the problem is compounded: stray objects, deprived of any archaeological context, tell us nothing at all about the ethnicity of a population.[77] Fashions are easily transmitted, individual items of dress even more so. The presence in Baetica of a brooch that might be interpreted as "Gothic" in a Mesetan context does not necessarily imply that its Baetican wearer was a Goth. By the same token, the absence of "Gothic" brooches in a region does not necessarily mean an absence of people whom contemporaries would have recognized as Goths. In other words, the scattered stray finds that make up the bulk of this sort of evidence cannot be used to chart the ethnic mixture of sixth-century Spain.

We cannot use a half dozen decontextualized brooches to maintain that there was a sixth-century Gothic presence in Baetica.[78] In the same way, the discovery in a cemetery a few miles from Complutum of several "Gothic" trilaminate brooches, perhaps fifth-century in date, does not mean that the city received an important Gothic garrison in the fifth century.[79] When all is said and done, the material evidence for the presence or absence of Visigoths in fifth- and sixth-century Spain is too limited and too uncertain to tell us any more about the peninsula's purely Gothic history than we already know from the literary evidence. The correlation between the archaeological evidence and ethnicity is just not strong enough to permit it. Ultimately, the creation of the new artistic, architectonic, and liturgical culture that we call Visigothic was not a matter of ethnic transmutation, let alone ethnic migration. On the contrary, it was a product of political triumph, of the success with which Leovigild's Gothic monarchy imposed itself on very nearly the whole peninsula, thus creating an environment in which a new, relatively uniform culture could spread.[80]

The Silent Decades, 531–565

If we know relatively little about the reigns of Theodoric and Amalaric in Spain, then we know still less about the sole reign of Theudis. With the murder of Amalaric in 531, Theudis became king in his own right.

It is unclear how much of the Gothic population actually felt itself subject to him, but a very large portion of the Gothic nobility must at least have acquiesced in his rule, for we hear of no rivals for the Gothic kingship during what proved to be a remarkably long reign—perhaps as much as seventeen years, though here the chronological defects of our sixth-century sources become crippling.[81] Our scant sources record only three episodes in Theudis's reign, despite its length: the successful repulsion of a Frankish invasion of Tarraconensis by the royal general Theudisclus; at least one attempt—a spectacular failure—by the king himself to expel the imperial garrison of Ceuta in Tingitania; and his assassination late in the 540s, followed by the accession of the same Theudisclus who had defeated the Franks.

On none of these events are the sources very illuminating, although the Frankish invasion is at least well-attested. Gregory of Tours, unsurprisingly, took a strong interest in the event, but his overwhelming concern was to document how the tunic of the martyr Vincentius, rather than any human agency, raised the siege of Zaragoza, assuring us incidentally that the Frankish kings conquered most of Spain and brought untold loot back to Gaul.[82] From a Spanish perspective, we have only the brief statement of the Zaragoza *Consularia,* from which derive the versions in both the long and short forms of the *Historia Gothorum* traditionally attributed to Isidore. These Spanish notices show that, whatever role we attribute to the intervention of the blessed Vincentius, it was the general Theudisclus who drove the Franks out of Spain with great slaughter.[83] Theudisclus's success was total, and there is little evidence that the Frankish incursion had any permanent effect on the Spanish north.[84] The date of the episode is uncertain, though the chronology of the Frankish monarchy makes the earlier part of 541 likely.[85]

The expedition against Ceuta in Tingitania came some time thereafter.[86] Theudis led a Gothic army to take the city from the soldiers who occupied it and who had previously expelled a Gothic army from it. This earlier Gothic force is puzzling, for we have absolutely no indication of when or how it had come to be resident in the city. From Procopius, we know that Belisarius ordered his subordinate John to take Ceuta in 534, in the course of the Vandal war, and that the city was captured.[87] The Procopian narrative does not tell us from whom the city was captured or imply that the city resisted the Byzantine force sent to take it, and it is most unlikely that Ceuta was in Gothic hands in 534, when there is no hint of Gothic royal authority outside northern Spain. Given this, one might suspect that Ceuta was for most of the later fifth and early sixth centuries a *civitas* much like those of southern Spain, effectively independent under the leadership of its local elites, who then acquiesced in the Byzantine takeover.

That would in turn suggest that the Gothic garrison of Ceuta, which Isidore says was expelled before Theudis's expedition, had been installed only after John captured the city in 534, thereby provoking Gothic interest. After Belisarius had shattered the Vandal kingdom, Theudis would hardly have viewed a Byzantine presence in Ceuta with equanimity. He may well have been trying to preempt any Byzantine action in Spain by installing a garrison on the Tingitanian side of the straits. We will never know exactly when it happened, but this expedition is the first Gothic intervention in southern Spain attested since the middle of the fifth century. Regardless of dates, the Gothic force was expelled from Ceuta by *milites,* the standard Isidorian term for imperial soldiers, prompting Theudis to attempt the city's recovery.[88] The expedition was a disaster and the Gothic army decimated by a sally of the defenders, supposedly after the Goths had laid down their arms in deference to the solemnities of Easter Sunday.[89]

There can be little doubt that this failure destroyed a substantial part of the support that Theudis had hitherto commanded. He was killed soon afterward, to be replaced by a man with a better claim to military leadership, his former general Theudisclus, the victor of the Frankish campaign of a few years earlier.[90] While he lived, however, Theudis had clearly satisfied enough of the Gothic military to maintain his position without our hearing of challenges to it. It was not merely the Gothic nobles who supported him either. His sole extant law suggests that within such territory as he controlled, he was worth petitioning for legal judgments in Roman law courts. Theudis's law regulated the workings of the law courts, limiting in particular the *suffragia* that could be paid to judges to induce them to hear cases.[91] The form of the law suggests that it was issued in response to an inquiry, perhaps from a petitioner aggrieved at the size of the *sportula* demanded by one judge or another. Regardless, Theudis appears to have laid down general principles of legal conduct on the part of judges, commanding that his law be included in the lawbook of his predecessor Alaric II. The inclusion of the law in the *Breviarium* shows that it was intended for application in such municipal courts as used that text. In the process, it testifies to the at least partial diffusion of the *Breviarium* within the sixth-century Gothic kingdom. That diffusion, and the fact of the law itself, serves to demonstrate a fairly generalized acknowledgment of Theudis, in his role as Gothic king, as a legitimate source of law for the kingdom at large.[92]

As with so much of sixth-century history, these hints and fragments are suggestive rather than clearly demonstrative, but from them we may safely draw one substantive conclusion: in the years before the murder of Theudis, the Gothic monarchy existed in the provinces of Carthaginiensis and Tarraconensis as it had in Gaul during the later fifth century; that is to say, it was a territorial government acknowledged as such by both the military followers of the king and the general population of the cities and their *territoria*. How closely that kingdom was administered by the royal court is beyond our capacity to discover. It is possible that the level of governmental control described in the *Variae* of Theodoric's reign was maintained under Amalaric and Theudis, but there is no way of telling.

In the large part of the peninsula that fell outside the Gothic kingdom, the control of territory and the administration of justice will have been entirely in the hands of local elites, without any higher authority standing above them. An examination of Cassiodorus's *Variae* has already shown that many of the institutions of Roman government survived the demise of imperial authority. They can only have done so at the municipal level, in the hands of local elites, whether curial or senatorial. Where there is no early sixth-century evidence for Gothic royal government—which is to say in three of the peninsula's five Diocletianic provinces—power and the direction of public life must have devolved into the hands of local *potentiores,* however one defines that group. Even within the Gothic provinces, the cooperation of such local elites was of course essential to the successful rule of the Gothic kings; Theudis, in particular, seems to have stabilized his hold on the Gothic throne by associating himself to the interests of a part of the indigenous aristocracy through his alliance with the powerful family of his wife, and until the reign of Leovigild, no ruler came close to re-creating the governmental superstructure that had existed under the emperors.

The evidence for contact with the larger Mediterranean world corroborates this picture of political localism. Contacts, both ecclesiastical and secular, were by no means infrequent. We have the letters of Popes Symmachus and Hormisdas in the 510s that suggest that the churchmen of the peninsula continued to prosecute jurisdictional disputes among themselves despite the disappearance of a governmental framework that would have made strict hierarchical relationships easier to control. The letter of Hormisdas, meanwhile, shows that the bishop of Rome expected that Spanish bishops might have to deal with eastern clerics and, in the midst of the Acacian schism, he is anxious that they not have any contact with schismatics.[93] Greek inscriptions, not just from Mérida but now in increasing quantities from the port at Mértola, likewise attest to ongoing contacts with the East.[94] This eastern connection is confirmed later in the sixth century, when the *Vitas Patrum Emeritensium* show frequent traffic between the eastern empire and Mérida, though very little between Mérida and the rest of Spain until the reign of Leovigild.

Martin of Dumium's career in Gallaecia is similarly instructive.[95] The fact that a man from Illyricum should be able to come from nowhere to rally and organize the Gallaecian episcopate is testimony not just to Martin's own remarkable character, but also to the ease with which non-Spaniards could penetrate and settle in the peninsula.[96] From Martin's story we can also see that Chararic, the Suevic king whom Martin eventually befriended, was in frequent enough touch with Gaul to send to Tours for a cure to his son's illness. Yet at the same time, the localism of Martin's mission, and its total failure to make any impact outside Gallaecia, attest to the basic fragmentation of jurisdiction and political units in the Spain of the sixth century.[97] Indeed, none of the known contacts between Spain and the rest of the Mediterranean or European world are systematic, nor do any of them take in more than one small part of the Iberian peninsula. Frequent marriages among royal Visigoths and Franks do not alter this impression, for they were essentially dynastic alliances among families rather than diplomatic relations between kingdoms.[98]

275

This political fragmentation was much exacerbated by the assassination of Theudis and the succession of Theudisclus. Theudis had successfully defended his hold on power for a very long time, but the failed expedition against Ceuta was his undoing. News traveled fast in the sixth-century Mediterranean and no Spaniard of any importance, whether Goth or Hispano-Roman, could have been unaware of Justinian's policy toward the barbarian *regna* of the west.[99] Given that the attack on Ceuta might so easily have provoked a violent response from the emperor, it is unsurprising that a proven general seemed a wiser choice for the Gothic throne than the aging and defeated king. Theudisclus had, after all, driven two Frankish kings out of Spain in the not too distant past. His reign, however, was to be less spectacular. He ruled for no more than a year or so and was killed among friends at Seville while deep in his cups.[100] One Agila was named king in his place, though we do not know when or where his acclamation took place.[101]

Agila clearly lacked the extent of the support that Theudis, and perhaps Theudisclus, had commanded before him. Almost immediately, he determined to launch a campaign against the city of Córdoba. Failing to take the city, he moved on to Mérida, the first time a Gothic king can be shown to have taken an interest in the great capital city since the reign of Euric.[102] Agila arrived at Mérida only to find that a rival candidate for the throne had appeared to his rear: the acclamation of a Gothic nobleman called Athanagild had taken place at Seville, some time between 549 and 551.[103] The war between Athanagild and Agila seems to have flowed back and forth in the stretch of Baetican territory between Seville and Mérida over a period of half a decade or so.[104] In the course of the fighting, Athanagild decided to call upon the Byzantine emperor for assistance. This succor arrived, no earlier than 552, in the shape of a substantial Byzantine army, possibly under the command of the aged administrator Liberius, a man with a long-standing knowledge of Gothic affairs.[105]

The Byzantines in Spain

Athanagild's request for aid will have caused much rejoicing at Constantinople. Justinian was nothing if not an opportunist and had regularly exploited rivalry within the chief families of the barbarian *regna* as pretext for imperial intervention. In Africa and Italy, opportunism had masqueraded as defense of dynastic legitimacy.[106] In Spain, some other justification would have to have been found, inasmuch as Athanagild was clearly a rebel against Agila. The sources allow no room for speculation, but the army that Justinian dispatched did indeed allow Athanagild to best his rival Agila, if not decisively. The war between the rival Goths dragged on for several years, until Agila's supporters decided the issue by assassinating their king and declaring for Athanagild.[107] The imperial forces had used the intervening period to establish themselves more firmly in the south of the peninsula, perhaps only now occupying the vicinity of Cartagena.[108] At this point, their erstwhile protégé Athanagild turned on them, but found them impossible to dislodge. Instead, at an unknown date before 565, he concluded a pact with Justinian that attempted to regulate the boundaries between imperial and royal territory in Spain.[109] In the meantime, and until 568 or 569, the merest outline of peninsular affairs becomes obscure.[110]

As is not the case with the Goths, the material record provides useable evidence for the Byzantine interlude in the sixth-century southeast, though not very much of it because several of the potentially most informative sites are either barely excavated or excavated very badly. One such site is the Alcudía of Elche, the small acropolis of the imperial city of Illici. Because of the Dama de Elche, a famous and possibly forged Iberian statue, the Alcudía was the subject of intense and early archaeological interest that was not to the site's benefit. Although very late antique walls survive at the site and there are numismatic remains of both the Justinianic and late Visigothic periods, no stratigraphy was ever recorded. The few excavated remains to have been published were rigidly linked to a chronology based entirely on the literary sources: a Franco-Alamannic invasion, an Alanic invasion, a Visigothic invasion, and the like.[111] As a result, we can be reasonably sure that there was a fortified settlement and a Christian basilica on the Alcudía during the sixth century, but nothing more.[112] We cannot say to whom this fortress pertained or how the political vicissitudes of the period affected the lives of the inhabitants of the fertile vega round about.

The case of the Alcudía is sadly typical and there are only two sites in the presumed zone of Byzantine occupation where modern excavations have added substantially to our understanding. One of these sites is Cartagena—Carthago Nova, or Carthago Spartaria as it had now come to be called—the grandest city in the emperor's Spanish territories, though not necessarily the capital of a Spanish province.[113] The other, long-unsuspected, site was very minor indeed. A Roman *municipium,* the name of which remains unknown, stood on a site now called El Tolmo de Minateda, about 10 kilometers southeast of Hellín in the province of Albacete.[114] Though the upland site was long known to have been an Iberian settlement, it was not until heavy rains in 1988 exposed much of the hillside that the extent of Roman-era material was realized.[115] Though establishing stratigraphies has been difficult, it seems that materials of the Augustan period went into the construction of a new city wall some time during late antiquity and a reused inscription mentioning duovirs guarantees the municipal status of the Roman site.[116] The late antique wall has long since collapsed, but the extant mounds of ashlar blocks suggest that it was as much as 9 meters high. Though no date can be established for the original erection of the wall, it seems clear that the walls were extensively repaired in the sixth or seventh century. Definite remains of residential structures from the seventh and eighth centuries also survive within the walls, while the fortified area likewise possessed an industrial sector in which the remains of warehouses and an olive press have been found.

At the south end of the hillside there is a high outcropping of rock, referred to as an acropolis by the excavators. This was separated from the rest of the walled town by a secondary wall and dotted with cisterns, presumably to help it withstand a siege. The defensive purpose of the whole late antique site can hardly be doubted and El Tolmo was indeed ideal strategically, controlling access from the coastal region around Cartagena to both the southern Meseta and upper Andalucía. At the time of the Arab conquest, it was important enough to be included in the famous *pactus Theodomiri* and even today it sits at the juncture of three modern *autonomías.*[117] But while it is tempting to conjecture a relationship between the sixth-century development of the site and the Byzantine presence on the coast, we are not justified in doing so with any sort of precision. We can probably say that the fortifications at El Tolmo do reflect the stimulus to defensible habitation that came with the political instability of the Byzantine conquest. But whether the inhabitants of El Tolmo fell within the Byzantine province, the control of a Gothic king, or neither, we are unlikely ever to know.

No such doubts attend the case of Cartagena, although it remains among the least known of all Spain's great ancient cities. Impediments to exploration are rooted in the city's modern history and go beyond the usual problem of continuous habitation since antiquity. Because Cartagena has been strategically important throughout the modern period, its shoreline has been heavily filled and regularized since antiquity, while the city's present-day military establishments keep large areas of the ancient site off limits to archaeological inquiry.[118] Nevertheless, the city's Roman remains reach back before the Augustan era, to at least Caesar's grant of colonial status in thanks for the city's support against the Pompeians. Yet Cartagena seems not to have experienced the monumental embellishments that graced so many Spanish cities under the Flavians and Antonines and its failure to follow the early imperial trends observable elsewhere in the peninsula may have something to do with the strength of old, pre-Roman, traditions: the very early disappearance of its epigraphic habit is notorious.[119] One would expect that the city's promotion from *conventus* to provincial capital under Diocletian would have made a large difference to the prosperity and topography of the city, but it is very difficult to document this. The Byzantine occupation, by contrast, brought dramatic changes.

The construction of a new, late antique wall near the port of the city, cutting off much of the old, Augustan town, has now been called into question.[120] Scattered rescue excavations within the Augustan perimeter suggest continued habitation right through to the seventh century.[121] It does remain probable that the existing city wall was repeatedly reinforced during late antiquity and the Byzantine period may have seen substantial residential construction within the city. New houses were built, standing at a different angle to the old street plan, which suggests its substantial redefinition.[122] During the fifth century, the *cavea* of the old theater had been filled in and the leveled site used as a market. On top of these fifth-century remains, a new residential

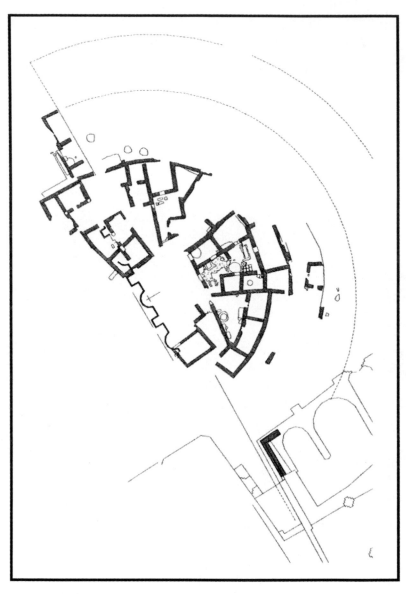

Byzantine residences and common area built over the theater of Cartagena and conforming to the arc of the *cavea*. (after Ramallo and Ruiz [2000], 315)

neighborhood grew up after 550. Like the fifth-century shops, the sixth-century houses conformed to the shape of the theater's *cavea*. Thus several separate buildings, probably one-room dwellings, and a larger storehouse were disposed around a triangular common area that housed a communal oven.[123]

These insights into the urbanism of Byzantine Cartagena suggest the same sort of changing approach to the use and disposition of urban space as is visible elsewhere in the peninsula from the end of the fifth century. The old Roman shape of sixth-century Cartagena had disappeared, but a new and not unprosperous townscape emerged under the occupation of revived imperial government; certainly the need for coinage was such that small bronzes bearing Greek value marks were minted in the city during its Byzantine decades.[124] On the other hand, Cartagena was probably rather better off than other cities within the Byzantine sphere of influence in Spain and its success did not have much of an impact beyond the city and its immediate vicinity, as shown by the important survey of ceramic distribution in the Vinalopó valley.[125] Apart from at Cartagena itself, intraregional trade appears to have to declined dramatically at those coastal sites that are thought to have fallen within the zone of Byzantine occupation. Inland, only the strategic site at Lorca shows as much evidence for imported goods as does Cartagena.[126] Cities that had old trading ties to the eastern provinces maintained them, but the Byzantine occupation of North Africa more or less ended commercial contacts between that province and Spain. On the whole, it would appear that the latter half of the sixth century witnessed a general retardation of the trading capacity of cities in the Byzantine province, while such imports as did arrive tended not to travel very far inland.[127] Despite these changes to economic patterns at the local level, the evidence suggests that the Byzantine impact did not reach very far beyond the coastline. On the contrary, the real revolution in Spanish history came with the dramatic conquests of the Gothic king Leovigild.

Spain before Leovigild

Because the evidence for the years between the deaths of Theudis and Athanagild is so lacunose, it has been subject to a wide variety of speculative interpretation. For those who believe in a Hispano-Gothic kingdom dating firmly to the fifth century, this period represents a stage of disintegration and rebellion against the authority of the Gothic state.[128] Even those who are less certain about the scale of Gothic power tend to approach the period in terms of local attitudes toward Gothic rulership. A bewildering number of contradictory hypotheses therefore exist, attributing political, ethnic, and/or religious motivations to rival Goths, Byzantines, and Spanish cities or aristocracies and tracing out the putative relationships between them.[129] The fact of the matter is that we know too little to attempt such things with any measure of plausibility and must instead strive to place as small a burden of hypothesis on the sources as possible.

By the end of Theudis's reign, we can postulate a Gothic military presence along the routes between the Meseta and the straits of Gibraltar, without which the raid on Ceuta would have been impracticable. This Gothic military presence is unlikely to have been welcome in a region whose local elites had been effectively independent since the 460s or 470s. Indeed, one might speculate that the sudden and severe instability that afflicted the Gothic ruling elite after the later 540s was provoked in part by the challenges of dominating a region that had previously lain outside the Gothic orbit. More certain is the fact that the opposition of southern cities like Córdoba exacerbated tensions within the Gothic nobility itself. Theudis, Theudisclus, and Agila intruded themselves upon a Spanish south where they were not welcome and where they proved totally incapable of imposing themselves as an acknowledged superior authority. This meant that, whatever their intentions might have been, they became one more local power among those already on the spot, the same fate that befell Athanagild's erstwhile Byzantine associates. The imperial presence proved no more congenial to certain noble families of Carthaginiensis than Agila's was to the citizens of Córdoba—it was, after all, the arrival of the Byzantines that prompted Isidore's father to relocate the family to Baetica, where the young Isidore was born.[130]

The reign of Athanagild is particularly revealing of the difficulties that all these groups had in imposing themselves on the Spanish political map. There is no sign that Athanagild ever made his power felt outside the corridor between Baetica and Toledo and perhaps Zara-

goza, and even there, the cities of Seville and Córdoba objected stren-
uously to the royal presence.[131] The sort of local urban acquiescence
that was necessary for the Gothic monarchy to function was totally absent. We can be sure of this because Seville, which had been the initial site of Athanagild's revolt against Agila, soon ceased to be subject
to him. There is no reason to think that the citizens of Seville and Córdoba were working in concert with each other in their opposition to
Athanagild. On the contrary, we seem to be witnessing the continuation of incoherent warfare among basically autonomous cities with no
ingrained tradition of subordination to the Gothic king and no incli-
nation to experience Gothic rule. In fact, it is quite possible that the
hemorrhage of Gothic royal power under Athanagild was more extensive than is suggested by the evidence of conflict in the peninsular
south. That is to say, the sort of independence that most of southern
and western Spain had enjoyed under Theodoric, Amalaric, and Theudis may now have become the norm in Tarraconensis and Carthaginiensis, where previously royal rule had been strong.

That possibility is at least suggested by events in the years after
Athanagild's death, when, in order to wield any control over Spain, the
Narbonensian nobleman Liuva had to appoint as co-ruler his brother
Leovigild. Athanagild died at Toledo, probably in 568, and the aftermath of his passing underscores the weakness of his rule. For five
months after his death, according to Isidore, no one claimed the
Gothic throne, a fact that has elicited frequent expressions of puzzle-
ment from scholars.[132] It need not, because the abeyance of the Gothic
royal title fits well with the minimal testimony of the sources. Athanagild came to the throne as a rebel and was accepted half-heartedly and
faute de mieux. In the course of his reign, the authority of the Gothic
monarchy bled away. More than that: Athanagild was so weak that the
Gothic kingship became an irrelevance to the Gothic nobility itself, to
the point that no one troubled to murder him. When he finally died
of his own accord, no Gothic noble could be bothered to claim his
royal title.[133]

A claim was eventually made, though not by any Spanish Goth. Instead, a man called Liuva was proclaimed king at Narbonne, across the
Pyrenees in Gaul.[134] No one appears to have challenged this proclamation, but neither do the Goths in cispyrenean Spain seem to have

paid it much attention. They, in other words, had fallen quite comfortably into the now habitual pattern of Spanish politics, as contented with an autonomous local existence as were the citizens of Seville and Córdoba against whom Athanagild had fought in vain. No one challenged Liuva's claim to the royal title, but for that title to have substance, force was necessary. The date of Liuva's acclamation is unclear, but must be either 567 or 568.[135] At first, there is no sign that the new king took much of an interest in Spain and there is no evidence that his authority was accepted there save in the passive sense that it went unchallenged. It may well have been this point that inspired the great novelty of Liuva's reign: the appointment of a co-king. Among the Visigoths we know of only one previous instance of such co-rulership, the joint rule of Theoderic II and his younger brother Frederic in the 450s. In that case, however, Frederic was unquestionably the subordinate of his elder sibling, whereas both Isidore and John of Biclar make it clear that Liuva associated Leovigild to himself as an equal. That Leovigild was immediately assigned the Spanish provinces—*regnum citerioris Hispaniae,* as John puts it—suggests that Liuva's main concern was to make real the claims of his family to a Gothic kingship drained of all content during the time of Athanagild.

The aftermath of Leovigild's proclamation has often been treated. Though the absolute chronology of his reign is not always secure, the sequence of events is easily discernable and need not be rehearsed at length here. Leovigild married Athanagild's widow Goiswintha, thereby arrogating to himself whatever residual loyalty there might have been toward the dead king.[136] He then spent the decade of the 570s conquering the Iberian peninsula city by city, whether from local authorities or, in the deep south, from Byzantine soldiers.[137] In 569 or 570 he raided and despoiled the territories of Basti and Málaga. In the next year, he conquered the city of Asidona from its Byzantine garrison. The year after that, he turned to Córdoba. When the death of Liuva left Leovigild as sole king, he swiftly associated his children Hermenegild and Reccared to the throne, but proceeded in his conquests by taking the region of Sabaria. In 573 or 574, he invaded Cantabria and occupied its chief city, Amaia. Working west from there, he was ready by 575 or 576 to invade Gallaecia and attack the Suevic king Miro, whom he reduced to the status of tributary. Perhaps in the next year, Leovigild seized Orospeda. Evidently to commemorate these signal successes, Leovigild built a new city and named it Reccopolis after his younger child. His elder son Hermenegild, married to a Frankish princess and sent to Seville to keep an eye on the recently conquered south, quickly rebelled against his father in one of the most discussed episodes of Visigothic history.[138]

For the next several years Leovigild not only campaigned successfully against his eldest son, but also found time for much else: he occupied part of the Basque country and founded another city there; he sent troops into the region around Sagunto where the monastery of Saint Martin was sacked; and he did away with the Suevic kingship of Miro and his short-lived successors Eboric and Audeca. When Leovigild died in 585 or 586, he was succeeded peaceably by his younger son Reccared. Under Reccared's rule the stability of the monarchy was much solidified by the conversion of the kingdom to orthodox Christianity at the third council of Toledo. With this dramatic act of political theater, the Hispano-Roman episcopate agreed in effect to underwrite the monarch's authority.[139] A new era had dawned in the political history of both the Gothic kingship and of Spain itself, a new beginning made possible only by the strenuous violence of Leovigild and his conquests.

One can, if one wishes, interpret his campaigns as the suppression of widespread rebellion within a legitimate Gothic kingdom. That is, after all, the position taken by John of Biclar: *Leouegildus . . . provinciam Gothorum, quae iam pro rebellione diuersorum fuerat diminuta, mirabiliter ad pristinos reuocat terminos.*[140] John wrote at a time when Leovigild's son Reccared reigned with the consent of the Gothic nobility and the peninsular episcopate. When Isidore wrote his *Historia Gothorum*, the ideological basis of Gothic kingship had developed further still, and Isidore was himself the greatest exponent of that ideology. It is only natural that both he and John should conceptualize the decades before Leovigild as a period of deviation from a norm of Gothic royal hegemony. But the events that John and Isidore record do not bear out the interpretations they place on them.

John's own words make clear the sheer diversity of the opposition to Leovigild, which took more than a decade to suppress and required the systematic conquest of more than two-thirds of the peninsula's land mass. Leovigild was no beleaguered king suppressing rebellions on all sides. Rather, he was a canny warrior who carved a new kingdom for himself out of a series of disunited cities and regions that were not in the habit of accepting any authority above the local. It is the novelty of Leovigild's authority that explains the difficulty we have in tracing an institutional continuity between fifth- and early sixth-century Gothic kingship and the monarchical institutions described in the *lex Visigothorum* of the seventh century. Much as Leovigild might picture himself as the restorer of a venerable Gothic monarchy, and much as John and Isidore might portray him in those terms, his efforts created something new because they introduced Gothic monarchy as a novelty to most of the peninsula. In this way, his reign brought to an end the immediately post-Roman phase of Spanish history.

Twelve

The New World of the Sixth Century

T he social and physical landscape of the Spain that Leovi-gild drew together under his rule is obscure, much more so than that of earlier periods. The literary evidence, almost entirely ecclesiastical, allows certain inferences about the life of a few specific places, chiefly Mérida and the parts of rural Cantabria in which the monk Aemilianus was active. Yet this is undoubtedly the period in which the medieval map of Spain was being drawn. In place of the several hundred *civitates* of the imperial period, we find a new and simpler ecclesiastical geography. The *Nomina hispanarum sedium,* which probably has a seventh-century base text, shows us about eighty episcopal *civitates,* roughly the same number attested in the conciliar records of the seventh century.[1] The seventh century, in other words had very nearly arrived at the world of the twelfth-century *Liber censuum,* with its sixty-seven Spanish cities. This is a far cry from the Spain of the Antonine Itinerary, which lists more than a hundred *civitates* even while leaving out at least a third of the peninsula's land mass.[2] It is beyond our power to recover when this drastic simplification of the Spanish administrative map took place.[3] In the middle of the fifth century, Spain was still working within the recognizable, and very small, limits of the imperial *civitates.*[4] By the seventh century, the landscape resembled that of contemporary—or indeed also imperial—Gaul, while the bronze municipal laws of defunct cities made their way into the shops of metal workers to be melted down.[5] How that transformation took place we cannot say.

Archaeology, for its part, is not a great deal more enlightening for the course of the Spanish sixth century. The archaeology of the sixth through eighth centuries is relatively immature and until recently attracted no interest beyond documenting a Visigothic and Byzantine presence in the peninsula. This perspective has begun to change, but problems intrinsic to sixth-century material evidence make it resistant to interpretation. For one thing, traditional means of establishing site chronology cease to be feasible: the typology of African *terra sigillata* grows vaguer from the middle of the fifth century and becomes useless after the middle of the sixth century, when African imports to Spain decline to statistical insignificance.[6] The only coins found with any regularity are bronzes of Theodosius and his sons, the last to reach the peninsula in quantity and therefore in circulation for a very long time. Typologies of church plans and the items of personal adornment sometimes found in graves are no substitute. Worse, there is a near total absence of monumental building in the manner of earlier centuries, including even the earlier part of the fifth. Rubble or wooden structures of indeterminate, squarish shape are much harder to interpret than are well-understood types of the late imperial era.

As the tradition of monumental construction fades and ceramic imports from Africa shrink to a nullity, we lose the yardsticks by which we have traditionally measured economic and social prosperity. Sixth-century Spain looks impoverished by the standards of earlier centuries, and it is very difficult for us to characterize these changes as anything other than an absolute decline. The hints and whispers of the material evidence suggest that the last remnants of classical urbanism disappeared from the Spanish landscape by the end of the sixth century. The cities no longer looked much like they had in the early fifth century and before, while the social behaviors that had taken the Roman cityscape as their background had more or less ceased in favor of church-centered activity. No great crisis is necessary to explain these changes, and the countryside seems to have changed rather less than the cities.[7] Nevertheless, if the sixth century witnesses quite definitively the end of classical urbanism in Spain, that by no means implies the disappearance of a new sort of city life—what we may call early medieval urbanism—which kept the city, its demographic concentrations and its ability to organize the territory around it, as the dynamic motor of Spanish life.

The Life of the Cities

We can only make sense of sixth-century political history in terms of the cities over which Frankish kings, Gothic nobles, and Byzantine generals fought, hoping thereby to master the territory at whose heart the city still lay. The ecclesiastical sources for the later sixth century give a similar impression of fundamentally city-based power structures. The question thus becomes what a sixth-century Spanish city was like, inasmuch as it no longer looked like or functioned as a fourth- or early fifth-century city had done. The centrality of the church to the physical shape of Spanish cities is perhaps the most important aspect of sixth-century urbanism. At Córdoba, a traveler crossing the great bridge over the Guadalquivir would have been confronted immediately by the church of Saint Vincentius, which lay under what is now the oldest section of the Great Mosque. By the early seventh century, the landmarks of the city will have been almost entirely Christian and Vincentius's church was just one of several churches.[8]

The sense of ecclesiastical dominance of urban society is reinforced by the fact that what little public building took place centered entirely on the construction of churches. Few early Christian churches in Spanish towns are accurately dated, and much of what is considered fifth- or sixth-century may equally well belong to the seventh, with the result that the archaeological remains alone are not yet enough to speak safely about trends in church-building. The epigraphic evidence does, however, seem to suggest just such a trend in the course of the sixth century. Indeed, at least a part of the new Gothic nobility had internalized the patronage habits of the old Roman elite, as the famous inscription of Gudiliuva shows. In it, this *vir inlustris* recounts how he built three churches at his own expense, one dedicated to Stephen the protomartyr, another to Saint John the martyr, and a third to Saint Vincent of Valencia. This was the work of a lifetime, for the first church was consecrated in 594 under Reccared, the last under King Witteric (r. 602/603–610), from whose reign the inscription dates. Two generations of bishops at Acci were Gudiliuva's partners in this patronage, Bishop Paul dedicating the last church and Bishop Lilliolus the earliest.[9]

Even if Gudiliuva belongs to the new Gothic kingdom of Leovigild and Reccared, his sort of lay patronage was part of a long Spanish tradition.[10] On the other hand, bishops are generally more prominent in the sixth-century record than they had ever been in the past, and for the first time episcopal years enter dating formulas.[11] The most prominent example is the career of Bishop Justinian of Valencia, whose episcopate lasted for eleven years around the 540s. Justinian presided over a church council, the *acta* of which are preserved in the *Collectio Hispana,* though the council was not of any great importance.[12] For that reason, it goes unnoticed in the bishop's extant epitaph, in which he celebrates his achievements as a builder of new churches and restorer of old ones, a munificent patron of festivals and tireless preacher, and an instructor of virgins and monks, who wrote much that would instruct future generations.[13]

This portrait is interesting for how carefully it delineates the image Justinian wanted to project. Twenty years earlier, Bishop John of Tarragona's epitaph commemorated his life as a preacher of great faith and a defender of the poor.[14] Justinian of Valencia's epitaph goes much further than this. While on the one hand he displays himself as a learned Christian teacher—and indeed the very first words of the epitaph declare him to have been a *pius praeclarus doctor*—he also revels in the role of aristocratic patron. This is not just a matter of pious Christian building projects, although there were clearly a number of those and some have thought it possible to detect one of his monastic foundations at the Punta d'Illa de Cullera.[15] Justinian also wished to be remembered for the festivals he put on, an important testimony to the way in which the hierarchy of the local church had, by the middle of the sixth century, taken over the roles that had formerly belonged to municipal patrons.

Far and away the most spectacular evidence for episcopal patronage, however, comes from Mérida, from which we possess extensive literary evidence in the shape of the *Vitas Patrum Emeritensium,* an anonymous work of the mid-seventh century that narrates the lives of a series of the city's bishops.[16] Its accuracy in topographical detail has now been proved by excavation, and its narrative details probably deserve similar credence.[17] The *Vitas* present the bishops of Mérida as absolutely central to their city's public and monumental life, and this presentation would seem to be reflected independently in the archaeological record. Much effort was concentrated on the shrine of Saint Eulalia, the site of a massive construction project at the end of the fifth or the beginning of the sixth century.[18] Eulalia's mausoleum was incorporated into the sanctuary of a new basilica, the new sanctuary apse enclosing that of the old mausoleum precisely. The sanctuary as a whole was unusually elongated in order to embrace the whole of the saint's mausoleum: no part of Eulalia's *martyrium* was allowed to lie beneath the nave of the basilica where the feet of laymen trod.[19] Between the sanctuary and the nave was a narrow transept, from the southern side of which stairs led down into the episcopal crypt. That transformation was significant. Burial close to the martyr had always been a privilege, but it now became more privileged still, so that only the bishops of Eulalia's church would enjoy interment so close to her own sacred remains. That sense of privilege was underscored above ground as well, for the transept, and thus the sanctuary beyond it, were separated from the nave by either an arcade or a wall.[20] The liturgical separation of congregation from the officiating priesthood, so characteristic of the fully developed Visigothic liturgy, clearly had Hispano-Roman precedents.[21]

If the construction of the basilica of Eulalia represented a reshaping of Christian community in such a way as to underscore episcopal power, the new basilica preserved as much of the old Christian cemetery as possible, so much so that the walls of the building were slightly misaligned with one another in order to limit damage to old tombs as much as possible. The foundations of the arcades in the nave did damage a few burials, but the basilica also incorporated and reused the crypt of one of the earliest mausolea. Immediately beside the staircase down to that crypt stood the raised tomb of the *vir inlustris* Gregorius, who died in 492. The tomb of Gregorius was the only raised funerary structure to stand within the nave of the basilica. Given this mark of honor, second only to that of the bishops themselves, it is possible that

Gregorius was a major patron of the church, perhaps contributing a large sum toward its construction. Indeed, he and one of the city's bishops may have collaborated in the construction of the basilica, in the same way that Bishop Zeno and the *dux* Salla had in 483 jointly patronized the repair of Mérida's walls and the bridge over the Guadiana. If that were so, then the very fabric of the basilica attests to the persistence of municipal leadership in the hands of the episcopate and the local elite together. That may be excessively speculative, but Gregorius's burial in so privileged a spot demonstrates the importance of both the man himself and his family, which would have gained status from so visible a recognition of his claim to burial *ad sanctos*.

Nevertheless, Gregorius's epitaph is the exception in a body of evidence that stresses the importance of ecclesiastical, rather than lay, authority in sixth-century Mérida. As the *Vitas Patrum* show, the Méridan church possessed a great deal of intramural property by the middle of the sixth century. The main episcopal church and its adjacent baptistery would appear to have been located near the old provincial forum, along with the episcopal palace and the residence of a Gothic *comes,* and there were at least three other intramural churches as well. Unfortunately, we cannot confirm this evidence from the *Vitas* on archaeological grounds because although a great many seventh-century sculptural and architectonic remains are known from this part of the city, none have been found *in situ*.[22] The extramural zone around Eulalia's basilica does, however, demonstrate a great deal of costly investment by later sixth- and seventh-century bishops. Because the site has been in continuous liturgical use since the twelfth century and remained an active funerary monument until 1837, most of its sixth-century decoration has disappeared. However, enough remains embedded in the Romanesque fabric to show that consecutive late antique bishops redecorated or rebuilt their church for the sake of their own and their martyr's glory, for instance by rebuilding the small apses on either side of the sanctuary with the newly fashionable horseshoe arches of the seventh century.[23]

Eventually, Eulalia's new basilica became the center of a grand episcopal complex. Excavation in the Sta. Catalina neighborhood, about 200 meters from Eulalia's basilica, has revealed an enormous building put up in the middle of the sixth century after the area had ceased to be used for burial.[24] This sixth-century structure was centered around an apsidal hall oriented toward the east, off which long symmetrical wings depended. These wings consisted of porticaded corridors 17 meters in length, each of which gave onto a central patio lying between them. Typologically similar to structures known in Gaul, Italy, and Africa, the building has been identified with the *xenodochium*, or traveler's hospital, known from the *Vitas Patrum* to have been built by Bishop Masona toward the end of the sixth century.[25] Though this identification cannot be proven, it is highly probable given how faithfully the *Vitas* appear to reflect the actual topography of the city. Even if the identification is not correct, the building is almost certainly part of the same episcopal complex as the basilica of Eulalia. Taken together they add new weight to the image of episcopal might that the sixth-century literary sources suggest.

Church patronage is the most visible aspect of sixth-century urbanism, in part because it is difficult to know how much of the monumental structure of the old Roman cities remained in place. Much was clearly still standing, but we do not know what sort of shape it was in, and the evidence grows progressively worse as the century progresses. Certainly there is scattered evidence for the preservation, and even the restoration, of urban monuments in parts of Spain.[26] In many places, city walls were well kept up and some may even have been renovated in substantial ways. Thus at Gerona, the Porta Rufina with its elaborate defenses may well date from the later fifth or the sixth century.[27] But the example of Gerona is not isolated. At Tarragona, for instance, one of the towers of the old Republican wall was filled in and sealed up to restore its structural integrity some time in the later fifth or sixth century.[28] In both these examples, the introduction of expressly defensive reforms is testimony to the disturbances of the century. Times had changed since the late imperial period, when an effective imperial government had ensured peace and when city walls served a symbolic as much as a practical purpose. It is no accident that across the street from the church of Saint Vincent at Córdoba, and with it flanking the bridge over the Guadalquivir, there stood a fortified palace traditionally identified as the residence of the Gothic *comes*.[29]

Still, not all our evidence for sixth-century urbanism can be explained in terms of church patronage and urban defensibility. At least

The reuse of public space: monumental architecture in the forum of Segobriga sub-divided for late antique residences. (K. Salzer)

in some places, other urban monuments were kept up as well. At Aurgi, for instance, the monumental arch that protected the spring that watered the city was still standing in the tenth century when the Arab historian al-Himyari described it.[30] More impressively, the theater at Zaragoza was still in use as an amphitheater in the later fifth and early sixth centuries, an urban spectacular tradition that only died off some time between 540 and 560.[31] At that point, the arena was abandoned, a walled graveyard was installed above what had in the distant past been the orchestra of the theater, and small residential buildings were put up over the *cavea*. Around these spread a rubbish tip, which covers the larger part of the excavated area. Similar patterns are attested at Lisbon. Although we do not know when the first-century theater went out of use, during the fifth or sixth century its *vomitoria* were being used as residences.[32] In this corner of Lisbon, as in the theater of Zaragoza, then, the transition from the classical to the medieval landscape was complete by the end of the sixth century.

There was still an urban population, indeed an urban population that dwelt in parts of the town that had not previously been residential, and nothing would suggest urban abandonment. In fact, the new

residential sector inside the Zaragozan theater continued to be inhabited until the eleventh century, when the whole of it was razed and ter-
raced to create an Islamic-style house and attached shop.[33] At the
same time, however, this example shows us how far the people of Zaragoza had traveled from their Roman past. The population buried its
dead within the city walls and it no longer patronized the urban activities of the Roman past. Indeed, the last remnants of the urban social behaviors of Roman times would seem to have disappeared.

Complutum offers complementary evidence for the desuetude of
the imperial townscape. On the one hand, it seems likely that high-
status urban *domus* were still being put up in the middle of the fifth
century.[34] On the other hand, the forum and the administrative buildings around it had certainly been demolished by the beginning of the
sixth.[35] The standing buildings were taken down with some care and
the site was systematically terraplaned before new structures—perhaps houses, though no full description has been published—were
put up using the spolia of the older buildings.[36] Complutum, in other
words, experienced a transformation from its classical to its postclassical urban topography in the course of the later fifth century. As at
Zaragoza, however, there is no sign of population decline and the site
of the old imperial city continued to be occupied. What is more, the
Roman tradition of strictly extramural burial was clearly maintained
and the city's older cemeteries continued in use, though they faced
competition from the rather distant martyrial site dedicated to the
saints Justus and Pastor. Yet before the seventh century, there is no reason to believe that this cult site formed the center of Complutum or
that it had overtaken the old imperial city as the chief site of local population. Instead, we have the by now familiar contrast between an urban center, gradually losing its classical shape, and an extramural
Christian cult site in which the power of the local ecclesiastical establishment was concentrated.

The monumental zones of Tarragona, by contrast, present less
clear-cut evidence. The sixth-century development of martyrial cult to
Fructuosus on the floor of the old extramural amphitheater clearly
ended the celebration of games there.[37] Yet as late as the 610s, King
Sisebut could reproach Bishop Eusebius of Tarragona for his love of
ludis teatriis faunorum.[38] These games cannot have been held in the

amphitheater and may therefore have taken place in the old circus, the only one of the city's spectacular monuments still likely to have been intact at the start of the seventh century. It is often thought that, alongside these indisputable changes to the monumental topography of the city, Tarragona also experienced a dramatic shrinking of population in the later fifth and sixth centuries, a view based on the changes to its cemeteries. The early Christian cemetery of the city along the Via Augusta is generally regarded as having remained in use until the seventh century, but only as a high-status site from which low-status burials had effectively disappeared. If true, this pattern might be interpreted as evidence for a few wealthy families clinging to traditional patterns of burial in a city that no longer housed a substantial population.[39] Unfortunately, the excavations of the 1920s and 1930s will not safely bear this interpretative burden, because precisely the poorest graves were least well documented. Only modern excavation in undisturbed sections of the cemetery will decide the point, but it seems likely that the still prevalent notion of seventh-century Tarragona as a ghost town will need to be revised, in the same way that the old picture of the city as virtually abandoned in the fifth century has now been thoroughly discredited.[40] In the long run, a picture of an inhabited, perhaps even wealthy, but distinctly postclassical urbanism is likely to emerge.

We have a useful comparative case in Ampurias, a city that had lost its classical shape as early as the second century. Despite the abandonment of most of the Hellenistic and Roman city during the later first and second centuries, Ampurias remained a commercially active urban center right until the Arab conquest. The population dwelt in the old fortified palaiopolis and its size and density are attested by the number of surrounding cemeteries. The continued use and reuse of urban space even in a period as late as the sixth century is illustrated in just these cemeteries, particularly one excavated recently after ancient remains were discovered during the opening of a new road up to Sant Martí.[41] The dig was conducted in a spot that had been an extramural cemetery in the early imperial period, over which warehouses were built when the cemetery had stopped being used. In the fourth century, when the warehouses had been abandoned for some time and perhaps after their remains were no longer visible above ground level, the site was again taken over by a graveyard. Then, in the sixth century, a major program of demolition and rebuilding was undertaken. All the structures standing on the site, both funerary and otherwise, were leveled and the site was terraplaned. On this artificially leveled surface, a whole series of buildings was put up, their foundations of different heights on account of variations in the depth of the subsoil. Though the precise purpose of these new buildings cannot be determined, they add to the evidence of Ampurias's having continued to thrive as a center of local habitation, however far removed this may have been from the classical Roman city that had existed on the spot for so short a time.

The example of Ampurias is particularly valuable inasmuch as it draws us away from a reflexive belief in the traditional picture of urban shrinkage. Barcelona, the sixth- and seventh-century remains of which have not yet been published in detail, suggests a similar decomposition of the classical townscape: the old *insulae* were broken down into new, smaller city blocks, the streets both old and new paved with disused roof tiles, the fourth-century *domus* subdivided into tiny cottages, but the whole remained populous and, by the standards of the time, wealthy.[42] A site like Ampurias, however, is for now better documented than more important neighbors like Barcelona. It provides positive evidence for the survival of a successful, if postclassical, Spanish urbanism, and thus a guide to understanding the physical changes that are documented in those other Spanish cities where sixth-century evidence is only just beginning to emerge from the general obscurity.

It shows how important it is to distinguish fundamental changes in the manner of urban life from the fact of urban living itself. Thus, although Zaragoza would appear to have lost the last vestiges of its Roman townscape by the middle of the sixth century—in the sense that however many Roman buildings were still standing, the last lingering social aspects of that townscape were no more—there is no reason to think that the number of people who lived in the city declined or that the city underwent any sort of urban shrinkage. It might have done so, of course, and we might be inclined to think that it did given the sheer poverty of the later sixth-century evidence. But to assert as much in the absence of evidence is to make a qualitative judgment that has much to do with modern biases in favor of classical urbanism and nothing to do with the empirically observable material evidence.

The Sixth-Century Countryside

Whether the disappearance of the classical townscape in the sixth century has rural parallels is very much an open question. The really epochal transformation of the Spanish countryside had come with the spread of villa culture and the attendant intensive exploitation of the land in the third and fourth centuries. The adoption of Christianity, and the deliberate Christianization of the landscape by landowners or villagers, had done no more than alter the structures of the villa properties. It certainly did not signal the end of the Spanish villa culture of the third and fourth centuries. Determining when particular villas ceased to be occupied in a traditional late Roman fashion is one of the great methodological challenges that confront archaeologists of the peninsular countryside, a task complicated by the same dwindling of dateable material that afflicts the sixth-century city.

The villa of Baños de Valdearados demonstrates the problems we face. The *domus* of the villa was clearly occupied in its fourth-century plan until well into the sixth century, with neither the subdivision into smaller rooms nor the reconstruction as an industrial site that is found in some Spanish villas. By the middle of the sixth century, however, imported goods disappear. This may suggest that the owner abandoned the site, leaving behind an empty shell to decay over the centuries. But Baños de Valdearados might just as easily have been occupied for several more decades, the residents making do with the last imported furnishings to reach the site and eking these out with local products that we are unable to date.[43] Although present methodologies cannot detect habitation later than the middle of the sixth century, that does not necessarily mean that such habitation did not exist. In other words, our evidence for abandonment is negative—the absence after a certain date of imported ceramics—but no positive data exist to confirm the fact of abandonment. Before the ninth or tenth century, the villa had collapsed and disappeared from view, because the burials that lay above its foundations have no stratigraphic relationship to

them. The medieval people who buried their dead at Baños de Valdearados did so in what was to them an open field.[44] But we may never be
able to date the beginnings of that slow decay that eventually finished
Baños de Valdearados off. Instead, we must come to terms with this
gradual fading off into nothingness of the old classical past, without
sharp barriers or markers for us to put a finger on.

That is the case across the whole of Spain. The vague chronological parameters offered by Baños de Valdearados are typical of the
peninsula as a whole, though some sites offer more positive evidence
than do others. Thus at the villa of Saucedo, in the modern province
of Toledo near Talavera de la Reina, the *pars urbana* had been remodeled on an entirely new plan in the fourth century, and in the sixth the
great hall of the villa was converted into a church, its baptismal font
making use of the still-functional plumbing of the original design. A
coin find suggests that it was not until the very late seventh or even
the eighth century that the building ceased to be actively occupied as
a residence.[45] If Saucedo offers positive evidence of long survival,
other sites offer positive evidence of an earlier decline. At the villa del
Pesquero near Mérida, for instance, there is no trace of any habitation,
primary or secondary, after the fifth century, and the site was neither
visibly Christianized before its abandonment nor did it become a rural
church at any time thereafter.[46]

At Torre de Palma, it seems clear that after the middle of the fourth
century there were no more large construction projects. By the sixth
or seventh century, the villa's formal rooms were taken over by hearths
and other low-status accretions, while it is likely that whole sections
of the old *domus* had fallen down.[47] On the other hand, the villa of
Torre Águila not far from Mérida appears to have continued as the luxurious center of a large agricultural zone as late as the eighth century;
while a necropolis grew up around the site's basilica, there is no hint
of the villa's having been abandoned or subdivided, and it is likely to
have remained the residence of some local notable throughout the period of the Visigothic monarchy.[48]

A more common phenomenon was for the luxurious *pars urbana*
of the villa to undergo a gradual conversion into an industrial zone, as
at Torre Llauder in the Catalan Maresme. In the Severan era, the villa's
Augustan floor plan was completely rebuilt around an *atrium* and im-

pluvium, while at the start of the fourth century, in accordance with contemporary fashion, the *triclinium* was remodeled by the addition of a large apse that cut into the Severan bath complex that had stood beyond the wall of the older *triclinium.* Probably some time in the fifth century, however, most of the rooms that surrounded the *triclinium* were converted to industrial purposes. A room off the atrium with a fine mosaic floor was converted into a grain store and, in a phenomenon well known from the period, holes were punched in the floor to provide bases for large dolia.[49] Another room was subdivided with walls laid down on top of an old mosaic, the columns of the peristyle were removed, and by the sixth century only the *triclinium* retained its fourth-century characteristics. Every other room in the old *pars urbana* had been converted to agricultural or industrial use. Meanwhile, a brand-new complex of workshops was built to the west of the old *pars urbana,* probably in the course of the sixth century. This agricultural phase seems to have continued uninterruptedly into the Carolingian era, with no trace of disruption during or after the Arab conquest.[50]

Sixth-century Torre Lauder would scarcely have been recognizable as the same place it had been a hundred years earlier. Instead of a Roman villa, it may have resembled much more what we think of as a village. Indeed, villa sites may generally have come to look more and more like rural villages. One sign of this is the proliferation of graveyards at a small distance from the places where people lived. The site of the villa at Almedinilla, at which we have already looked, demonstrates what seems to be a fairly regular pattern. Some time in the course of the later fifth century, much of the old *pars urbana* was rebuilt. New walls were put in, and an industrial, perhaps metallurgical, function is suggested by various hydraulic emplacements and a large oven.[51] Not far from the old *pars rustica,* nearly two hundred graves were discovered in a necropolis that we know to have extended much beyond the excavated areas. The dead were of all sexes and ages, many of them infants, and were interred over a period of roughly two hundred years.[52] What had once been a rural residence seems to have become instead an industrial village that buried its workers in the areas round about it.

At the complex at El Bovalar, in the Catalan province of Lleida, we can actually document the evolution of a medieval village from its late antique roots.[53] The earliest structure on the site was a rural church, probably built in the fifth century. The villa to which the church belonged has not been yet been discovered, though it is difficult to explain an isolated rural church without a residence someplace in the vicinity. Regardless of that, the church at El Bovalar prospered in the fifth and sixth centuries and was redecorated in fine style in the latter century. At the same time, a village sprang up around the church, some of its houses even making use of the church's standing walls as supports. There is evidence of agricultural work in the shape of various farm implements, and though no plows were discovered, many tools associated with the harvesting of grapes were found. The villagers kept a variety of animals, mostly cattle and sheep or goats, but not many pigs. Each small house had its own materials for carding wool, which suggests that this was the primary economic activity here. The mixture of industry and agriculture that characterized this tranquil ensemble appears to have continued until some point in the eighth century, when a fire may have obliterated it entirely. The site therefore provides a rare example of continuous occupation from the sixth century into the period of the seventh-century Gothic kingdom.

Its integration into the life of that kingdom is well documented numismatically, for El Bovalar's inhabitants were active users of the *trientes* that seventh-century Gothic kings minted in great quantities at a bewildering variety of mints.[54] The coins of El Bovalar are significant. Because they are not directly associated with the site's church and do not derive from a single hoard, they demonstrate the monetization, and presumably the commercial activity, of a site in the Spanish interior at a date when most imagine an autarchic and protofeudal countryside mired in incipient serfdom.[55] Against the background of such traditional assumptions, the evidence from El Bovalar comes as something of a shock, even if we cannot retroject its evidence for seventh-century monetization back to the sixth century or generalize from El Bovalar to the rest of the peninsula; until more sites similarly bereft of monumental remains are excavated, we will have no way of knowing how unusual El Bovalar actually is. Nevertheless, the total absence of sixth-century trade goods at El Bovalar seems to confirm the evidence of rural sites across the peninsula.

So far as we can tell, there was a genuine quantitative decline in the trade capabilities of rural Spain from the fifth century onward. One can multiply impressionistic examples from across the peninsula, but the few rigorous studies that have been undertaken all tell the same story. In the coastal and prelittoral zones of Tarraconensis, a wide variety of imported luxury ceramics reached far beyond their point of entry at Tarragona itself during the third, fourth, and early fifth centuries. After the middle of the fifth century, however, there was a dramatic falling-off of imported ceramics at places like Puig Rodon and Roda, even though these sites, one on the coast and one easily accessible to it, continued to import a large amount of food staples as witnessed by the quantity of amphorae found there. At similar sites further inland, like the villa at Vilauba or the once important city of Gerona, imports had followed the same patterns as those at Tarraco in the fourth and early fifth centuries, but after the middle of the fifth century not only luxury goods but all imports diminished dramatically.[56]

Both the *ager Tarraconensis* survey and the detailed study of ceramic distribution in the Vinalopó valley reach clearly confirmatory conclusions.[57] Not only did imports into Spain decline in absolute terms during the first half of the sixth century, the penetration of these imports into the countryside from their points of entry was minimal where it was not nonexistent. Such conclusions are not universally applicable, and even within these areas some sites defied the general rules.[58] But whatever the exceptions, the general tenor of the surveys is unmistakable: from the start of the sixth century, imported goods declined precipitously from an already reduced fifth-century base, and most rural sites ceased to use imports altogether.

It is unclear whether we should interpret these changes as a sign of decreasing contacts between the city and the countryside, or as a more general sign of decreasing wealth and consequent ability to purchase imported goods. Regardless, a few correctives to uniformly grim interpretations now exist, for instance a brand-new bath complex built in the suburbs of Mérida during the sixth, or perhaps the seventh, century.[59] Better known is the site of Pla de Nadal, in the modern province of Valencia. Here, a perfectly Vitruvian villa appears actually to have been put up for the first time in the sixth or perhaps even the seventh century.[60] The archaeological interest of the site is increased by the existence there of columns and decorative friezes *in situ,* something otherwise unknown from this period. The basic structure of the villa is aulic, with perpendicular rooms at either end of the main hall. From the exterior the building would have looked very much like a smaller version of the more famous São Cucufate.

The great interior rooms of Pla de Nadal communicated with each other via horseshoe arches and much of the structure was built out of dolomite, a technique documented in this region at earlier periods. The upper story of the villa was built from wood, of which many carbonized remains survive. More surprisingly, the decorative architecture—including some rather abstracted corinthian capitals—was purpose-built for the site out of local stone rather than being reused from the spolia of a classical building. This is highly unusual and a reminder that even at so late a date as the seventh century there were still some people who wished to dwell in the Roman style of the Spanish past and that the craftsmen necessary to service these desires did in fact exist.[61] These craftsmen must almost certainly have been supplied by the nearby city of Valencia, one small piece of evidence against a rigid disjunction between sixth-century city and country.

Sixth-Century Urbanism and the Problem of Interpretation

The material evidence of the sixth century is suggestive, but it does not allow for many firm conclusions. The physical world of the imperial period had disappeared, Spanish communities were progressively less connected to the larger Mediterranean world, and there was almost certainly less wealth in circulation than previously. At the same time, the basic shape of the peninsula remained that which the imperial centuries had created: the cities of the later empire remained the centers of population for the post-imperial world. The economic ties with their *territoria* had almost certainly weakened, as our evidence for the distribution of goods shows. But the dominance of the Spanish city over the surrounding countryside, one of the primary creations of imperial government, survived.[62] That, at least, is the only way we can account for the literary sources of the sixth and seventh centuries, which still envisage their world as centered on the city. News, gossip, orders—the human interactions that make life happen—all these things came from the cities, however small and impoverished those might seem to us, or might have seemed to a Hispano-Roman of the third century. Political life was still lived against the backdrop of the city and the sixth-century countryside is as politically invisible as it had been in the fourth and fifth centuries.

The chief literary works of the period all confirm this impression. The life of the sixth-century saint Aemilianus, the Spanish San Millán, was lived within the narrow confines of the Sierra de Cantabria and the Sierra de la Demanda, though his hagiographer Braulio of Zaragoza deliberately implies a much wider field of action.[63] Braulio's *Vita* provides precious insight into the life of late antique Cantabria, before the conversion of the Visigothic kingdom to orthodoxy in 589.[64] Aemilian's long career was played out far from the great cities of Roman Spain, in a region traditionally regarded as the least urbanized of the whole peninsula. Yet even here, if Braulio is to be trusted, the lives of the local populace were centered on cities. Their social interactions and their power relationships had their gravitational center not in the countryside, as one might have expected, but rather in the public world of the city.

The *vita* of Aemilian distinguishes carefully between three existential spaces—the city, the country, and the wilderness. Aemilian spends his early life trying to flee the countryside for the wilderness.[65] He does so because the townspeople keep trying to find him and have him exercise his sanctity in the place where the lives of the worldly take place, that is to say, in the cities.[66] Braulio's life abounds in familiar topoi, both literary and historical. Aemilian dwells forty years in the wilderness, but however far he flees, the fame of his sanctity pursues him. Finally, Didymus of Tarazona, the bishop within whose diocese Aemilian's wilderness retreat fell, was compelled to pursue the saint, drag him—perhaps metaphorically, perhaps not—from his solitude, and have him ordained a priest in his own village of Vergegium.[67] Didymus, in other words, employed the familiar means of dealing with an unauthorized holy man that we see time and time again throughout the history of the early church. But all did not work out as Didymus hoped. Aemilian began to systematically alienate the property of the church at Vergegium, which caused Didymus to dismiss him from his post. That outcome might well have been Aemilian's intention, and for the rest of his life he was permitted to dwell at his oratory near Vergegium and enjoy the contemplative life for which he had so long striven.[68]

As is so often the case with saints' lives, it is hard to localize the various miracle stories that accompany Aemilian's long life. It is more or less impossible to apportion Aemilian's various miracles between his forty years as a hermit, his short period as a priest, and his retirement at his oratory at Vergegium. It is clear, however, that Aemilian's Vergegium existed between two urban poles, one at Tarazona, where Didymus was bishop, and the other at Amaia in the Sierra de Cantabria.[69] Aemilian may have dwelt in the wilderness, but it was in the cities that his fame spread. It was from the cities that people sought his aid, and equally from the cities that the secular clergy attempted to impose their control on the saint. The conflict between the active and contemplative life dramatized in Braulio's *vita* is also a conflict between city and country. In the context of a saint's life it is to be expected that the contemplative, rural life should win out. Part of Aemilian's holiness no doubt derived from the remoteness of his residence—liminality was an important component of eremitical sanctity.

As much recent study has shown, the wilderness was an alternative locus of power and authority to the city-based, and thus essentially social power of the bishop; this was very much the danger that fourth-century bishops had diagnosed in Priscillian and had led to his death. Hermits could provide an alternative source of spiritual power because they lived in a world consciously different from the public world of the cities. In a functional sense, the otherness of the hermit's world created his greatest social utility to the people around him. By his very nature, he represented a source of rural power unavailable in the social world of the city. For the hermit to exercise power in this way, however, there must also be something to which he provides that alternative. In other words, the rural world of the hermit implies the urban world of the bishop in the city. The relationship is in part a product of the hagiographical genre, with its roots in the urban world of the fourth-century Mediterranean. Yet what the *vita Aemiliani* shows us, with remarkable specificity, is that the same situation prevailed in sixth-century Cantabria. Intentionally or not, Braulio shows us a world where the normal run of important social relations takes place in the cities, even in remote Cantabria. Aemilian exists outside this world, and the people who seek him are city folk who return to their urban milieu upon being cured. Braulio's *vita* records a seemingly endless stream of visitors from the city of Amaia.[70] The social atmosphere of the city, a city's social constructions and social differentiations, is evident throughout the *vita,* in which the one thing the townsfolk have in common is their need of Aemilian and the miraculous cures he provides them. Sick and diseased people are brought from Amaia to Aemilian—no small distance, one might add—and then return to city. That we have to do with a real city is made clear by the titles certain men bear.

We may leave aside the various senators and the mysterious *senatus Cantabriae* that appears several times before meeting its doom at the hands of Leovigild.[71] The nature of this senate has never been adequately explained and the existence of the senatorial title need not imply a thriving city life. On the other hand, the *curialis* Maximus whose daughter Columba Aemilian exorcises is another matter altogether. The curial office is necessarily urban and we cannot dismiss it as mere elegant variation on Braulio's part, for he is scrupulous in his nomenclature. Admittedly, alongside the curial Maximus, we meet the *senator* Honorius whose haunted *domus* almost certainly lies on a rural estate.[72] Nevertheless, it is striking that even in the mountain fastnesses of post-Roman Cantabria men still took up seats on city councils, with all that this implies for the vitality of the idea of the city in sixth-century Spain.

We derive the same impression from the chronicle of John of Biclar, who wrote some time shortly after 590. John was an orthodox Christian of Gothic parentage who had been educated at the imperial court at Constantinople, and on his return spent a decade in disfavor at Barcelona during the religious conflicts of Leovigild's later reign. With the conversion of Reccared, John became a valuable asset to the newly orthodox monarchy and ended his days as bishop of Gerona, a post he took up some time after 589 but before 592. His chronicle is in essence the story of the conversion of the Visigoths from heresy to orthodoxy and it must form the basis for any study of Leovigild's reign. Much less attention has been given to the evidence John provides about life in the Spain of his era and the relationship of city and country in the years before the Iberian peninsula was united under a Gothic king. If one reads John with an eye to social history, one is immediately struck by a single fundamental point: despite the hundred years that have passed since the last imperial administrators were active in the peninsula, Spain remains a world of cities. Leovigild's reign is for the most part the story of a conquest, the process by which he imposed the rule of a Gothic monarch on a whole series of independent polities, Hispano-Roman, Byzantine, and Gothic. That conquest, however, is almost entirely a conquest of cities—it is John's assumption that taking a city means ipso facto the taking of a region. This is in itself significant, for it implies that the Spanish cities of the post-Roman period retained the same sort of importance they had had in the Roman period, that is to say, as administrative and governmental centers, control of which brought with it control of their dependent territories.

Precisely the same conclusion can be drawn from Frankish accounts of the warfare between Goths and Byzantines, while hints in other late literary sources imply a similar importance in the ideological and political role of cities.[73] Thus the notion of a ruling elite based on the old Roman curia, explicitly documented in the *vita Aemiliani,* survived a very long time. In a seventh-century Visigothic formula, for instance, we read of a Gothic noble marrying a girl *de stirpe senatus.*[74] As late as the eighth century, under Umayyad rule, the leading Christians of Córdoba described themselves as senators and their ruling body as a curia; this self-representation was not entirely a fantasy, and it seems that, under the emirs, the Christian communities of al-Andalus were in fact governed by a ruling elite descended, at least in a distant way, from the old curias.[75]

The problem for the modern historian lies in understanding what this all means. As the material evidence suggests, there can be no question of any genuine continuity of the social behaviors implied by the classical cityscape into the later sixth and seventh centuries. Too little of the infrastructure associated with those behaviors survived for them to do so and a place like Amaia had no doubt always been tiny and undeveloped, even if it had the legal trappings of a city that the existence of *curiales* implies. Yet despite the changes to the city's physical and social shape, Spanish political life—the engines that turned the course of events—remained fundamentally resident in the cities. This is testimony to the basic strength of institutions implanted in the cities during the early empire, so that in the absence of the world system that created the Hispano-Roman city, the cities themselves and the paradigm of their power survived. The fact of the matter was that, in the absence of a superstructure of imperial or royal government, social and political organization became localized, and it did so at the level of the city. The locus of power to direct affairs did not, in other words, devolve to a rural environment as it did in so much of Europe north of the Alps and Pyrenees. Just as there is no evidence for a profound transfer of power from city to country in a third-century crisis, so there is no reason to believe that the passing of empire meant a passing of the city's centrality to the organization of peninsular affairs.

The protofeudalism of Visigothic Spain is a cherished topos of Spanish historiography, sustainable because so little evidence survives. Perhaps the seventh century really did bring with it a move toward a rural, agricultural, and military organization of society that we know from the contemporary Frankish world. If so, there are no obvious sixth-century antecedents and the Arab conquest arrested the process completely. The Umayyad armies brought with them an elite outlook that was as basically Greco-Roman in its assumptions as that of the fifth- and sixth-century Goths had been. The early governors and the emirs thought in terms of a political world organized by cities. Whether or not profound changes had started to take place in Gothic society behind the impenetrable obscurity of the seventh century, Islamic Spain was everywhere a world shaped by the political control of cities. The point is significant for the broader sweep of Spanish history.

If, as this book has suggested, Spain's heritage of Roman urbanism did not die in late antiquity, if the basis of Spanish political society remained urban throughout the post-Roman centuries, then old paradigms of Spanish history will eventually need to be reconsidered. The transformation of Spain into a society where political power resided in the countryside will have to be relocated, perhaps to the period of the *Reconquista,* when Castile and León were linked far more closely to the cultural world of northern Europe than they had ever been in the past. Such large-scale implications need not concern us here, but it is worth pointing out that they exist. Instead, we may conclude with a glance at the epigraph to this book. The 1992 Nobel laureate tells us that a culture is made by its cities. That fact is not historically inevitable, nor has it always been the case in the historical past. Cultures have been made by their peasants and by their landlords, in other words, by their countryside. Spanish late antiquity has been placed in that latter camp. But as the foregoing chapters have argued, its politics and its people were fundamentally urban. Spanish history in late antiquity is inextricable from Spanish urbanism; Spain's culture was indeed made by its cities.

Appendix 1

The *Epistula Honorii*

The text of the *Epistula Honorii* appears in the manuscript as follows
(periods represent punctuation marks above the line between words,
while colons represent two off-set points, one on the line and one
above it):

Incipit . sacra honorii imperatoris . quam de roma detulit
militie . urbis pampilonensis . cum sauiniano patricio quidem
tempore erede prelatus in spaniam profectus est . ob infestatione
diuersarum gentium barbarorum : honorius imperator glosus perpetuus
triumfator . semper agustus : Uniuersis militibus nostris . senioribus
iunioribus (5)
speculatoribus . ac britanicis . gaudentes sanctissimi . comilitones nostri
conmunium remuneratione meritorum et omnis iuxta exultatione
gaudentes . his enim maxime est splendor . inluxtris . qui pari cunc
tos luce perfudit : A quos uos magnifice comites . hac magistri
utriusque militiae ad similitudine nostre clementie constituti : Consti (10)
tuta sit . uobis stipendia galliganarum . que constitutioni uestre
porreximus ut eandem uis esset forma uirtutis . quibus exellens . una
deuotio est . proinde instructissimi in eque nobis cuncta subdita sit
In spania et amplica congruum et dignitatis augmentum que
serenitas nostra aurias prestiterit usibus gratanter agnoscimus : (15)
Ut ubi <ubi> uiuendi . degendique . tempus extiterit omni alacritate atque
uirtute abeatis ospitiiis obsequamini quapropter fore quidem confidi

mus . ut muneris resolutis incitet . potius quam restinguat ardore*m* :
Obtamus conmilitones n*ostros* per multos annos uene agere et alia
manu bene ualete : am*en* (20)

The same text, with commentary, appears in "The *Epistula Honorii,
Again*," *Zeitschrift für Papyrologie und Epigraphik* 122 (1998): 247–52.

Appendix 2

Magistrates of Late Roman Spain

This table shows the definitely attested magistrates of late Roman Spain, from the accession of Diocletian until the fifth century, with their dates, full names, and attestations. Less secure cases are listed in *PLRE* 1: 1080; 1089–90.*

A) Diocesis Hispaniarum
(a) *Vicarii*†

298, 30 Oct.	Aurelius Agricolanus	*Passio Marcelli*
306/337	Q. Aeclanius Hermias	CIL 2: 2203 = CIL 2²/7: 263
324/326 (?)	Septimius Acindynus	CIL 2: 4107 = RIT 97; Saquete (2000)
332 (?), 15 July	C. Annius Tiberianus	CTh. 3.5.6‡
341, 7 April	Albinus	CTh. 11.36.5
355/376	Sextilius Agesilaus Aedesius	CIL 6: 510 = ILS 4152
357 (?)	Clementinus	*Coll. Avell.* 2: 33–38
before 361	Flavius Sallustius	CIL 6: 1729 = ILS 1254
363, Jan.	Volusius Venustus	Amm. Marc. 23.1.4
365, 8 Sept.–366, 25 Nov.	Valerianus	CTh. 1.16.10; 9.1.9
369, 14 May–370, 1 June	Marius Artemius	CTh. 11.26.1; 8.2.2; IRG 1: 87
383, 27 May	Marinianus	CTh. 9.1.14; Symm., *Epist.* 3: 23–29
395, 27 July–397, 18 Dec.	Petronius	CTh. 4.6.5; 4.21.1; 4.22.5; 12.1.151

399, 29 Aug.–before 400, 9 Dec.	Macrobius	CTh. 16.10.15^S; 8.5.61
401, 10 Sept.	Vigilius	CTh. 1.15.16
420	Maurocellus	Hyd. 66

(b) *Comites*

316, 4 Dec.–317, 19 Jan.	Octavianus	CTh. 9.1.1; 12.1.4
332, 17 Oct.	C. Annius Tiberianus	CJ 6.1.6
333, 4 May–336, 19 May	Severus	CTh. 8.12.5 + 11.39.2; 8.18.3; 13.5.8

(B) Baetica
(a) *praesides*

306/312	Octavius Rufus	CIL 2: 2204 = CIL2²/7: 261
before 324	Faustinus	CTh. 9.9.2; CIL 2: 2205 = CIL2²/7: 264

(b) *consulares*

337/361	Decimius Germanianus	CIL 2: 2206 = CIL2²/7: 265
350/375	Usulenius Bro . . .	*HEp.* 8: 180
357, 28 Aug.	Q. Attius Granius Caelestinus	CTh. 9.42.3
368/371	Taunacius Isfalangius	Amm. Marc. 28.1.26

(C) Hispania Citerior
(a) *praesides*

286/293	Julius Valens	*AE* 1929: 233 = RIT 91
288/289	Postumius Lupercus	CIL 2: 4104 = RIT 92

(D) Hispania Tarraconensis
(a) *praesides*

312	Valerius Julianus	CIL 2: 4105 = RIT 94
316, 6 May	Julius Verus	CTh. 2.6.1
324/326	Badius Macrinus	CIL 2: 4106; 4108 = RIT 95, 96

(b) *correctores*

before 382	Paulinus	Aus., *Par.* 26.9–12§

(E) Lusitania
(a) *praesides*

285/305	Aemilius Aemilianus	*HEp.* 5: 81
293/305	Aurelius Ursinus	CIL 2: 5140
c. 300/c. 320	Caecilianus	CIL 11: 831 = ILS 1218
315/319	C. Sulpicius —s	CIL 2: 481

336	Numerius Albanus	CIL 2: 191 = ILS 5699
337/340	Julius Saturninus	AE 1927: 165
before 362	Vettius Agorius Praetextatus	CIL 6: 1777; 1778; 1779 = ILS 1258; 1259

(b) *proconsules*

| 382/383 | Volventius | Sulp. Sev., *Chron.* 2.49.1 |

(F) Gallaecia
(a) *praesides*

| before 338 | Aco Catullinus | CIL 2: 2635 |

(G) Tingitania
(a) *praesides*

| 291 | M. Aurelius Cletus | Villaverde (2001), 394 |

*Balil (1964) and Chastagnol (1965) are the basic studies.
†M. Aurelius Consius Quartus was *vicarius* at an unknown date in the fourth century: CIL 6: 1400 = *ILS* 1249.
‡See Barnes (1982), 145, n. 17, for the date.
§The title of *corrector* may be poetic license for *praeses*.

Notes

Abbreviations

Note: Journal abbreviations follow *L'Année philologique* except as noted.

AAC	*Anales de Arqueología Cordobesa*
AE	*Année Epigraphique*
AEspA	*Archivo Español de Arqueología*
AHDE	*Anuario de Historia del Derecho Español*
Ant. Crist.	*Antigüedad y Cristianismo* (Murcia)
BAGRW	R. J. A. Talbert, ed. *Barrington Atlas of the Greek and Roman World*. Princeton, 2000
BRAH	*Boletín de la Real Academia de Historia*
BSAA	*Boletín del Seminario de Estudios de Arte y Arqueología* (Valladolid)
CAR	*Cuadernos de Arquitectura Romana*
CCH	Gonzalo Martínez Díez, ed., *La colleción canónica Hispana*. 6 vols. to date. Madrid, 1965–
CCSL	Corpus Christianorum, Series Latina
CICM	José Luis Ramírez Sádaba and Pedro Mateos Cruz. *Catálogo de las inscripciones cristianas de Mérida*. Cuadernos Emeritenses 16. Mérida, 2000
CIL	Corpus Inscriptionum Latinarum

CILA	Corpus de Inscripciones de Andalucía
CLA	*Codices Latini Antiquiores*
CLRE	Roger S. Bagnall, Alan Cameron, Seth R. Schwartz, and K. A. Worp, eds. *Consuls of the Later Roman Empire*. Atlanta, 1987
CNA	*Congreso Nacional d'Arqueología*
CSEL	Corpus Scriptorum Ecclesiasticorum Latinorum
GCS	Die griechischen christlichen Schriftsteller der ersten Jahrhunderte
HEp.	*Hispania Epigráfica*
ICERV	José Vives. *Inscripciones cristianas de la España romana y visigoda*. Barcelona, 1942
IG	*Inscriptiones Graecae*
IHC	Emil Hübner, ed. *Inscriptiones Hispaniae christianae*. Berlin, 1871. *Supplementum*. Berlin, 1901
ILER	José Vives, *Inscripciones latinas de la España romana*. 2 vols. Barcelona, 1971–72
ILPG	Mauricio Pastor Muñoz and Angela Mendoza Eguaras. *Inscripciones latinas de la provincia de Granada*. Granada, 1987
ILS	H. Dessau, ed. *Inscriptiones Latinae Selectae*. 3 vols. Berlin, 1892
IRC	*Inscriptions romaines de Catalogne*. 5 vols.
IRG	*Corpus de Inscricións romanas de Galicia*. 4 vols.
IRVT	Josep Corell. *Inscripcions romanes de Valentia i el seu territori*. Valencia, 1997
MCV	*Mélanges de La Casa de Velázquez*
MEC	Philip Grierson et al., eds. *Medieval European Coinage*. 2 vols. to date. Cambridge, 1986–
MGH	Monumenta Germaniae Historica
AA	Auctores Antiquissimi
LL	Leges
SRN	Scriptores Rerum Merovingicarum
MM	*Madrider Mitteilungen*
NAH	*Noticiario Arqueológico Hispanico*
PL	Patrologia Latina
RABM	*Revista de la Biblioteca, Archivo y Museo* (Madrid)

RGA	*Reallexicon der germanischen Altertumskunde*
RIT	Géza Alföldy. *Die römischen Inschriften von Tarraco.* Madrider Forschungen 10. 2 vols. Berlin
SHHA	*Studia Historica, Historia Antigua*
TED'A	Taller Escolar d'Arqueologia
TIR	*Tabula Imperii Romani*

Chapter 1. The Creation of Roman Spain

1. Most recently, Liebeschuetz (2001), 74–94.
2. The literature on pre-Roman and Republican Spain is enormous. For the pre-Roman period, there are convenient English summaries in Harrison (1988) and Fernández Castro (1995), both with basic bibliographies. Republican history is accurately sketched in Richardson (1996), 1–149. For Spanish geography, see Cary (1949), 231–43, and, in more detail, Way (1962).
3. For Roman imperialism, see Harris (1979); (1984); Mattingly (1997); and, with particular reference to Spain, Richardson (1986). For what follows, see esp. the diverse works of P. A. Brunt ([1965]; [1978]; [1990], 433–80).
4. Richardson (1996), 56.
5. In the early stages of Roman imperialism, the word *provincia* meant the sphere of action of a Roman magistrate overseas and had no necessary territorial connotation, but the assignment of two *provinciae* in Spain in 197 began the conceptual shift from a functional to a territorial definition of the word *provincia.*
6. See Hauschild (1983); (1993a), with the historical sketch of Carreté, Keay, and Millett (1995), 26–38. Much less is known about Republican Córdoba, but see the articles in León (1993a).
7. Thus the difficulties of fighting in Lusitania forced the shift from the unwieldy manipular legion to the famous organization by cohort (Goldsworthy [1996], 35), while the extraordinary appointment of Scipio Aemilianus to a second consulate in 134, with the express goal of putting an end to the Celtiberian wars, signaled the beginnings of the constitutional upheaval that eventually brought down the Republic (Astin [1967], 125–60). For Roman taxation as a stimulus to local agriculture, see Keay (1990); Edmondson (1990).
8. Thus a town such as Cádiz in Baetica, with its loyalty to Caesar, could produce such a family as that of Cornelius Balbus, who already in 40 B.C. had become Rome's first foreign-born consul, on whom see Rodríguez Neila (1992).
9. Brunt (1963).
10. On the conquest, Syme (1970); Alföldy (1996).

11. There is a good overview in Alföldy (1996) and stimulating essays on the Augustan project in Bendala (1990); (1998).
12. On the differing origins of the Caesarian colonies in Baetica and the consequences thereof for relations between Roman and native, see Fear (1996) with the comments of Haley (1997).
13. Strabo 3.2.151.
14. For the military as a stimulus to romanization, see Le Roux (1982); Alonso and Fernández Corrales (2000).
15. See Cortijo (1993a).
16. On the origins of *conventus,* see Burton (1975); Lintott (1993), 54–69; Galsterer (2000), 346–48.
17. The *conventus* boundaries of Spain are the subject of endless and probably insoluble dispute, as is the question of whether *conventus* boundaries corresponded precisely with provincial boundaries. The standard accounts are Albertini (1923), 83–104, and Estefania (1958), but see the new boundaries used in those volumes of CIL 2^2 that have appeared so far.
18. Curchin (1994) for the social effects of the *conventus* organization. The fourteen *conventus* capitals were Tarragona, Cartagena, Zaragoza, Clunia, Astorga, Lugo, and Braga in Tarraconensis; Santarém (Scallabis), Beja (Pax Iulia), and Mérida in Lusitania; and Córdoba, Écija (Astigi), Seville, and Cádiz in Baetica. See map 1, and for greater detail, *BAGRW* 24, 25, 26, 27.
19. A list of inscriptions attesting conventual offices and institutions appears in Albertini (1923), 104.
20. In general, Bowman (1996). *Res Gestae* 8.2 for the census, with Edmondson (1990); Navarro and Magallón (1999) on the role of cities in the Augustan plan for Spain.
21. Abascal and Espinosa (1989), 206; Ojeda (1999).
22. Brunt (1976).
23. For a complex assessment of this process in Gaul, see Woolf (1998); for Spain, Curchin (1990b).
24. Ortiz de Urbina (2000), 83–90.
25. Adoption of Roman culture could be an important condition for gaining status under Roman public law, or for promotion from one such status to another: Sherwin-White (1973), 225–36.
26. Alarção and Étienne (1977), 28–38.
27. The network of pre-Roman urbanism is well brought out in Bendala (1994).
28. Compare Alföldy (1987) with id. (1999) to see the difference that a decade's worth of archaeological and epigraphic discoveries makes to an assessment of romanization in the southern Meseta.

29. For the role of the military in the process of romanization, see Roldán (1974); (1976); (1993); Le Roux (1982); Alonso and Fernández Corrales (2000).
30. Mentxaka (1993), 39–63, has a discussion and very full bibliography of recent controversy on how Latin rights were granted.
31. On the content of the Latin right, see Sherwin-White (1973), 108–16; García Fernández (2001) for a historical overview.
32. *Lex Irn.* 93; Lintott (1993), 132–45.
33. D'Ors (2001) argues that, in strictly legal terms, this was not a legislative act, but rather the extension of the existing Augustan municipal law to Spanish stipendiary communities.
34. For the Vindex episode, see Brunt (1959).
35. As the VII Gemina, it was eventually returned to Spain, where its northern headquarters at Legio would in time evolve into the medieval capital city of León: Vittinghoff (1970).
36. See Mentxaka (1993), 39–63, with references, for the debate.
37. Pliny, *NH* 3.30: *universae Hispaniae Vespasianus imperator Augustus iactatum procellis rei publicae Latium tribuit.* The *iactatum* should almost certainly be read as *iactatae* to modify *Hispaniae*.
38. The controversy arises from the relative absence of physical urban centers in the peninsular northwest and north: if a *civitas* had no urban center, could there be a *municipium?* If not, was the *ius Latii* granted to *civitates* with essentially rural populations, which became "virtual" *municipia* without a physical center, or was it simply not granted to areas without the physical infrastructure to create *municipia?* For the problematics, one may consult Abascal and Espinosa (1989), 72–73; Richardson (1996), 188–219; Ortiz de Urbina (1999); (2000), 34–56, 123–26; Castillo (1999), with references to the recent literature; Pérez Losada (2002), 325–41, for Galicia. Ortiz de Urbina (2000) is the most up-to-date compendium of the evidence. The issue is complex and far outside the scope of the present book; here I follow the opinions of Alföldy (1999), who rightly points out that the parts of Spain still lacking definite examples of Flavian *municipia* are precisely those in which the least archaeological work has been done.
39. Alföldy (1999) proposes a figure of circa thirty *coloniae* of Roman citizens and three hundred *municipia* with Latin rights for the post-Flavian period and, following id. (1987), 27–30, outlines appropriate criteria for identifying *municipia;* the total number of Spanish *municipia* can be raised to nearly four hundred if Pliny's lists of Spanish *civitates* and *populi* are deployed without corroboratory evidence for their transition to municipal status, as by Abascal and Espinosa (1989); Albertini (1923), 105, counts 513 *civitates* from Pliny; Ptolemy shows only 248 *poleis* in the second cen-

tury A.D. Galsterer (1971), 37–50, 65–72, was much too conservative in its numerical estimates, as the epigraphic discoveries of recent years have proved repeatedly.

40. Lucky in a literal sense as well: the recovery of the various bronze tablets from private hands after their clandestine excavation was an enormous achievement on the part of the Spanish authorities: see Fernández Gómez and del Amo (1990).

41. For most purposes the edition in González Fernández (1986), with translation and commentary, is more than sufficient, but there is a diplomatic transcription in Fernández Gómez and del Amo (1990). The *lex municipii Salpensiani* is edited most conveniently in CIL 1963 = *ILS* 6088, the *lex municipii Malacitani* in CIL 1964 = *ILS* 6086, but see also Spitzl (1984). On the *lex Villonensis,* see González Fernández (1993). González Fernández (1990), 16–134, presents critical editions of the *lex Irnitana,* along with the other fragments of municipal charters and the *lex Ursonensis,* a Flavian-era copy of the original foundation charter of the Caesarian colony of Urso. Mangas (2000), 83, and id. (2001), 28, offer a table showing graphically which chapters of the municipal law survive from each of the ten copies known fragmentarily. For the text of additional fragmentary municipal laws, see Stylow (1999); González Fernández (1999a).

42. For the new fragment from Duratón, in the province of Segovia, ancient Tarraconensis, see Hoyo (1995) = *HEp.* 6: 855.

43. The long debate over whether there was a model law from which local exemplars were derived appears to have been solved in the affirmative by the appearance of a fragment of a municipal law in which spaces have been left blank to accommodate local variation: Fernández Gómez (1991); Castillo (1999), 272, with references to debate.

44. Generally see Wiegels (1985). For onomastic change in Oretania, González Román (2000).

45. Rodríguez Neila (1999).

46. Navarro and Magallón (1999).

47. On the accession of Trajan, see Syme (1958), 1–44; and on Hadrian, Birley (1997), 77–92.

48. See Étienne (1966a) and more generally Caballos (1990).

49. Alföldy (2000a), 453–56; Caballos (1999) tabulates the evidence.

50. See Curchin (1990a), 75.

51. Curchin (1994), 90, and Le Roux (1994), 39–43, with references to the epigraphic evidence; Augustan precedents for Lusitania, Edmondson (1990); Alarção (1990).

52. See Corbier (1991). The definition of the *territorium* is from *Dig.* L.16.239. For the careful delineation of territory at even the microtopographical level, see the bronze tablet from Fuentes de Ropel in Zamora province: *HEp.* 2: 733; 8: 502.

53. Lintott (1993), 129–45, for a comparative overview.
54. As opposed to the between three hundred and four hundred *civitates* of Spain, only 114 *civitates* are listed for the Tres Galliae and the Septem Provinciae in the late fourth-century *Notitia Galliarum*. For the earlier imperial Gallic evidence, Drinkwater (1983), 103–14; Wightman (1985), 94.
55. For the general concepts, Laffi (1966); for Spain, Rodríguez Neila (1975).
56. Curchin (1985) and Le Roux (1992–93) are preferable to Cortijo (1993b), which relies on African and Gallic comparanda more than the extant Spanish evidence. Pérez Losada (2002) is excellent on the *autonomías* of modern Galicia. For the need to evaluate the evidence of individual provinces according to their own criteria, Alföldy (1987), 26–27; Bowman (1996).
57. See in general Gascou (1982a); (1982b).
58. Alföldy (1999).
59. The many attempts at a narrative should be greeted with caution. Most, e.g., Balil (1967) and Montenegro Duque et al. (1986), are no more than general histories of the empire with extrapolation in the direction of Iberia.
60. The sole evidence is *Fasti Ostienses* = *AE* (1936): 98: *De Cornelio Prisciano in sen(atu iudicium) / (cor)am factum quod provinciam Hispaniam hostiliter / (inqu)ietaverit.*
61. *Hist. Aug., V. Marci* 21.1. Standard accounts of this invasion are lurid and largely imaginary. See instead Arce (1981).
62. Herodian 3.7.1; 3.8.2; CIL 2: 4114 = *RIT* 130, with Cepas (1997), 15. See Birley (1988), 121–28, on the war with Albinus.
63. See Syme (1971), 192, 195–96. The Valerinus should perhaps be read as Valerianus: Alföldy (1969), 57–58 *contra,* Kienast (1996), 204–8. See now also the reattribution of a milestone from Cercedilla in central Spain to Maximinus and Maximus: *HEp.* 5: 550.
64. Victor, 33.3, Eutropius, 8.8.2, and Jerome, s.a. 2280 (ed. Helm, 221); Oros., *Hist.* 7.41.2.
65. For the evidentiary consequences of the imperial peace, see Millar (1986). More recent phases of Spanish history have displayed a similar phenomenon: during the latter part of the reign of Charles V of Habsburg "the government ran so smoothly . . . that it almost seems as if for twenty or thirty years the country had no internal history" (Elliot [1964], 156).

Chapter 2. Urban Institutions in the Principate

1. For the numbers, see chapter 1. As noted there, whether the *civitates* of northern Lusitania and northwestern Tarraconensis were assimilated to the municipal structure of the rest of the peninsula remains unclear, though the views of Alföldy (1999) seem most convincing. Regardless,

these regions remained peripheral to the experience of most of Spain.

2. On the pre-Roman roots of urbanism in Baetica, see the synthesis of Fear (1996), with Haley (1997).

3. The *lex Ursonensis* (*ILS* 6087 or González Fernández [1990], 19–49; a bronze tablet with part of the hitherto missing text was recently discovered: Mangas [2001], 19) was granted to the new veteran colony at Urso, modern Ossuna, in 44 B.C. when Mark Antony was consul, but the extant version, which preserves about a third of the text, dates to the Neronian or Flavian period and cannot represent the pristine Julian text, since it contains a reference to the Augustan province of Baetica. Throughout the first and early second centuries, the distinctions between *municipia* and *coloniae* were gradually eliminated de facto: Galsterer (1971); Ortiz de Urbina (2000), 68–70.

4. CIL 2: 3394 from Acci in Tarraconensis, just over the border from Baetica.

5. The term *res publica* originally connoted civic autonomy. See Alföldy (1977), 12–14; Ortiz de Urbina (1999). There is a list of Spanish cities called *reipublicae* in CIL 2: 1161. For African comparanda, Gascou (1979).

6. For which see Grünhagen and Hauschild (1983); Hauschild (1984); Hauschild and Hausmann (1991). Houses 1 and 6 are published in detail by Meyer (2001), house 2, the most revealing on the site, by Teichner (2001).

7. Chicarro (1972–74), 336–37, with commentary in Melchor (1993), 446.

8. Domergue (1990), 309–13, for the mines.

9. *Pace* Pérez Centeno (1999), 412–13, an earthquake is not positively demonstrated, although it has been postulated in almost every publication of the site and there is now evidence for a major third-century earthquake at Córdoba that might be related to the Muniguan evidence: Monterroso (2002a). House 2, which preserves the only reliable stratigraphy in the monumental zone of the city thus far published, shows that this damage took place toward the last couple of decades of the third century, much later than was maintained in early publications; a secure *terminus post quem* is provided by *terra sigillata Africana* C and by late third-century *antoniniani*: Teichner (2001), 262–67.

10. The evidence for late antique Munigua has not been published systematically, but see Grünhagen and Hauschild (1983). On the funerary archaeology, see Raddatz (1973) and Vegas (1988). The chronology is now established by Teichner (2001) which, along with Meyer (2001), offers the first comprehensive treatment of three residential buildings over the centuries.

11. See plan, Teichner (2001), 269, and Meyer (2001), 91–100, for the subdivision and building-over of houses 1 and 6.

12. Mackie (1983), iii.
13. Jones (1964), 724, for the homogeneity of urban constitutions across the third-century empire.
14. *Lex Irn.* 30, 31.
15. Abascal and Espinosa (1989), 167–70; Mangas (1996), 40–46.
16. *Lex Irn.* 31. See Curchin (1990a), 21–23, for pre-Roman roots.
17. González Román (1991a).
18. For instance, one Domitius Maternus who, though a native of Aquincum in Pannonia, was made a member of Barcelona's curia by vote of its members: CIL 2: 6153. A more exceptional case was that of L. Lucretius Severus, a native of Córdoba, who was granted citizenship in the nearby town of Axati and simultaneously raised to the decurionate: CILA, Sevilla 1: 207.
19. Alföldy (1984) with Saquete (1997), 162–63, on Mérida, and Rodríguez Neila (1999), 56–62, for Baetica generally.
20. Mentxaka (1993) is an excellent commentary on the relevant *capitula* of the *lex Irnitana*. There is a short and sensible overview in Mangas (2001).
21. Inspection of the *territorium: Lex Irn.* 76. Relationship to imperial government: *Lex Irn.* 85. The distribution of such imperial pronouncements as that found on the *Tabula Siarensis* shows that the relationship worked.
22. Thus *quattuorviri* are frequently attested, but there is some dispute over whether these refer to the local duumvirs and aediles collectively or whether they represent an unusual sort of collective chief magistracy: see, inter alia, Torrent (1970), 74, and Curchin (1990a), 33. Other anomalous titles also appear here and there—we find decemvirs, praetors, and censors at different towns across the peninsula, while there is even an octovir attested from Norba. These anomalies tend to predate the Flavian era, which suggests a certain standardization of local government after Vespasian: see Curchin (1990a), 36–40.
23. *Lex Irn.* 28, 29, 84.
24. Ibid., 39, 43.
25. Ibid., 19 (trans. Crawford in González [1986], 182). All translated quotations from the *lex Irnitana* in this chapter are those of Crawford.
26. E.g., *Lex Irn.* 26, 50, 63–69, 84.
27. The job of the quaestor is described at *Lex Irn.* 20 as the "the collecting, spending, keeping, administering, and looking after the common funds of the *municipes* of that *municipium* at the discretion of the *duumviri*," and also the supervision of the public slaves of the *municipium* (trans. Crawford in González [1986], 182). Many fewer colonial and municipal quaestors are attested in Spain than are other officials. The explanation for this fact varies. It may be that the *duumviri* oversaw financial responsibilities in many places and that, where this was the case, the quaestorship did not exist.

28. *Lex Irn.* 25, by inference from the minimum age of the *praefectus* to be appointed by a duumvir who finds himself compelled to absent himself from the city. For personal wealth as a qualifier for municipal service, see Curchin (1983). Gaps between terms of office: *Lex Mal.* 54.
29. *Lex Irn.* 39.
30. The main section on voting procedure is among the missing parts of the *lex Irnitana* but can be supplied from *Lex Mal.* 51–59.
31. *Lex Irn.* 31, 70, 79.
32. For extended treatment of this in terms of public monuments, see chapter 5.
33. Chastagnol (1978).
34. *Lex Irn.* 40.
35. Ibid., 77.
36. Ibid., 81.
37. E.g., the third-century inscription of M. Valerius Cassianus from the amphitheater at Italica: CILA, Sevilla 2: 515; or the seats of the Fabii Seneciones from Italica's theater: *HEp.* 4: 690.
38. *Lex Irn.* 41.
39. *EE* 8: 91; Pérez Centeno (1999), 406.
40. On curial children, Rodríguez Neila (1999), 48–52.
41. *Iovi Optimo Maximo . . . Pro Salute Sua et suorum Iulius Aurelius Decoratus Decurio colegii aquiflaviensis Iulius . . . aedilis et Marcus Aurelius filiorum suorum Decurio colegii Aquiflaviensis . . . Quaestor V.S.L.M. perpetuo et Coroliano Cos VIII Idus Iunias* (Rodríguez Colmenero [1997], 264).
42. In general, Étienne (1958).
43. This also limited its distribution to areas where prosperous freedmen were numerous, thus Baetica in particular: Rodà (1988).
44. It is likely that the Republican-sounding title of *pontifex* was retained in Baetica so as to avoid the offensively authoritarian connotations of the title *flamen imperialis* in a senatorial province: Étienne (1958), 231–34. *Contra,* Castillo (1988).
45. Much ink has been spilled on whether imperial cult contained a genuinely religious component, or whether it was a simple oath of loyalty, a political expression of dynastic politics, rather than a religion in any emotive sense. This is perhaps unfair, for ancient polytheism was very capable of accommodating wide varieties and degrees of worship, which were all meaningfully religious. Religious feeling is not quantifiable, hence the futility of the attempt of Hoyo (1988) to measure the religiosity of different social strata.
46. See CIL 2: 5523 = CIL 2²/7: 221 = *ILS* 5079 for the duties that a *flamen* would undertake.
47. See Étienne (1958), and for Tarraconensis, where the phenomenon is best attested, Alföldy (1973).

48. As did the provincial *flamen* L. Domitius M. Fil. Serg. Dentonianus (Alföldy [1973], 69).
49. E.g., *RIT* 58; *RIT* 344, 347. See generally Arce (1986b) and the very complete collation of third-century evidence in Cepas (1997), 110–33.
50. CIL 2²/7: 233, 234, 235; CIL 2: 1171; CIL 2²/7: 260a. On the Republican forum of Córdoba, the site of many important new epigraphic finds, see Campos and González (1987) and Campos (1993).
51. See, for instance, the conventual dedication to Iulia Mammaea of CIL 2: 3413 = Abascal and Ramallo (1997), no. 44, or the dedication to Gallienus made in 261 by Clodius Macrinus, propraetor of Lusitania, and just as quickly withdrawn when the province went over to Postumus: Ramírez et al. (1993). A brand-new inscription, probably of the *concilium provinciae* of Baetica to the reigning emperor and mentioning a hitherto unknown governor, Usulenius [Bro . . . ?], from circa 350–375, is published in *HEp.* 8: 180, with a reading superior to Stylow (2000).
52. CIL 2: 4505–7, 6153. See also Mariner (1973).
53. CIL 2: 4507.
54. Campos and González (1987).
55. CIL 2: 3394.
56. CIL 2: 5505, 2070. Another inscription is dedicated to Probus: CIL 2: 2071. Thus it is the case that at many minor sites the only attestation of third-century activity comes from imperial dedications, for instance, at Consabura, near modern Consuegra in the foothills of the Montes de Toledo, where the curia honors Philip the Arab (CIL 2: 3073).
57. See, for instance, the dedications to Gallienus and to one of his sons from Ercavica in the *conventus Caesaraugustana:* Osuna Ruiz (1976), 29; Alföldy (1987), 67.
58. At present, the corpus of Latin inscriptions from Spain is more scattered than it should be. Hübner's CIL 2 and supplement are now very old, as is his *IHC* and its supplement, while Vives's *ILER* is unreliable, and not all the new evidence is registered in the *Année Epigraphique* or *Hispania Epigraphica* (though the latter journal suffers more from irregular publication than from lacunae). The best editions of many inscriptions are still to be found in the local corpora of modern Spanish provinces or of individual cities. The most recent of the former include the *Inscriptions romaines de Catalogne* and the *Corpus de inscricións romanas de Galicia,* while the standards for the latter were set by Alföldy (1975). The excellent second edition of CIL 2 (on which see Edmondson [1999]) will eventually be published in fourteen parts and should subsume all of the foregoing.
59. *ILPG* 77.
60. Liebeschuetz (2001), 11–19, restates this traditional idea of epigraphic decline as evidence for the loss of civic behaviors.
61. Robert (1960), 570–71, and *passim.*

62. See the basic works of MacMullen (1982) and Mrozek (1973), the charts and tables of which latter are especially illuminating despite the limitations of his samples. The methodological comments of Rouiché (1997) and Witschel (1999), 60–84, are highly pertinent.
63. See *AE* 1989: 422, for a Spanish example of this.
64. Beltrán and Fatás (1998), 52.
65. Andalucía, for instance, was for years grossly underrepresented in the epigraphic record, as in the material record as a whole, because the region had no modern tradition of provincial archaeology; yet in the post-Franco era, Andalucía has produced nearly all the most dramatic epigraphic finds. There is an important *bilan* in Mayer (1997). See also the exhaustive catalogues of new finds in the *chroniques* published in the *REA* for 1975, 1979, 1982, and 1989.
66. In the same way that the rhythm of epigraphic growth had been: Edmondson (2002).
67. Abascal and Ramallo (1997), 26–52.
68. The city had similarly been precocious in adopting Italian-style architectonic decoration: Ramallo (1999).
69. Alföldy (1975).
70. For this phenomenon in Gaul, Woolf (1998), 77–105; the closely parallel development of monumental inscription and municipalization itself is underscored in Häussler (2002).
71. Meyer (1990)—the one difficulty being that Spanish funerary inscriptions tend to advertise their *ex testamento* status much less than those of, say, Africa or Gaul.
72. The spread of Roman burial habits as another index of romanization is studied illuminatingly by von Hesberg (1993).
73. There is a parallel here to the generalized late imperial trend, whereby the citizen/non-citizen dichotomy came to be replaced by the *honestioris/humilioris* dichotomy.
74. This is the same reason that reference to a city's constitutional status is so rarely found in inscriptions put up for local consumption, where the intended readership already knew their town's status. Such references are normal only in inscriptions put up by a *municipium* or an individual *municeps* outside the native city: see Alföldy (1987).
75. For this "Celtic Renaissance" see MacMullen (1965) and for an attempt to see similar processes at work in Spain, Marco Simón (1988).
76. Galvao-Sobrinho (1995).

Chapter 3. Urban Institutions in the Third and Fourth Centuries

1. Curchin (1990a), n. 350.
2. CIL 2: 6014.
3. All the manuscripts of the *Collectio Hispana,* the seventh-century canon

law collection that transmits the only text of the council (edited at CCH 4: 231–68) that we possess apart from epitomized excerpts, record that it was *Constantini temporibus gestum tempore eodem quo et Nicaena synodus habita est* (CCH 4: 234). Despite that ascription, however, and as Duchesne (1887) showed, the total absence of any reference to persecution requires the council to have met before 303; the problem of date is effectively insoluble, but the date of 300–302 adopted by Salvador (1998) for his prosopography of southern Spain is sensible. Doubts cast on the authenticity of the council and its canons by Meigne (1975) and Superbiola (1987) are dispelled in Sotomayor (1991), with important notes on the textual transmission in idem (2000).

4. Elvira 2–4, 55.
5. Pastor (1988).
6. CIL 2: 2071 = CIL 2²/5: 622a–c.
7. Elvira 17.
8. Inn., *Ep.* 3.7 (PL 20: 485–93), where the *coronati* may well have been provincial priests.
9. Elvira 56: *Magistratus vero uno anno quo agit duumviratum, prohibendum placet ut se ab ecclesia cohibeat.*
10. Elvira 57 and *Lex Irn.* 40.
11. The best introduction to Hispano-Roman urbanism, Abascal and Espinosa (1989), makes precisely this assumption.
12. Hess (1955) rightly points out the dependence of conciliar practice on secular Roman models, but lays excessive emphasis on the senatorial rather than municipal precedent, which was surely more familiar to the vast majority of those present.
13. CCH 4: 241: *residentibus etiam XXVI presbyteris, adstantibus diaconibus et omni plebe, episcopi universi dixerunt . . .*
14. The illogical order of the canons formed a major part of the spurious arguments of Meigne (1975) against the authenticity of the council.
15. I Toledo 8 (= CCH 4: 331–32): *Si quis post baptismum militaverit et chlamydem sumpserit aut cingulum, etiamsi gravia non admiserit, si ad clerum admissus fuerit, diaconii non accipiat dignitatem.*
16. Inn., *Ep.* 3.7 (PL 20: 485–93).
17. CIL 2: 1972. See also the *tabula patronatus* put up at Córdoba by the *ordo* of Tipasa in honor of Flavius Hyginus, the former governor of Mauretania Caesariensis in the late fourth or early fifth century: CIL 2: 2110 = CIL 2²/7: 276. Hyginus was thus almost certainly a native of Córdoba.
18. See references at Jones (1964), 3: 230 n. 41, with Norman (1958).
19. For imperial laws, see, e.g., *CJ* 10.32.2; *CTh.* 12.1.8; 12.1.84. For coercive authority, Elvira 51 and p. 4, above.
20. *Coll. Avell.* 2: 74; see Fernández Ubiña (1997).
21. On which see Burton (1979), with the attestations listed in Duthoy (1979).

22. Galsterer (2000), 358–60.
23. CIL 2: 1115.
24. Jones (1964), 728.
25. CIL 2: 2207. See also the Iulius Ho . . . , a curator from third-century Seville (CIL 2: 6283).
26. CIL 2: 4112 = *RIT* 155, dedicated to the *praeses* of Tarraconensis for his restoration of some baths.
27. Jones (1964), 732–33, with references.
28. Goffart (1974).
29. Durliat (1990), 11–94, which is too categorical in reading the vocabulary of the late Roman economy—*terra, possessio,* and *possessor*—as purely abstract and fiscal, ignoring the many instances when our sources, both legal and otherwise, only make sense if the vocabulary is read literally.
30. Id. (1990) would have the actual collection of taxes left to tax farmers, themselves sometimes *curiales* and sometimes senators, who were considered as *possessores* when acting in their fiscal capacity as tax farmers.
31. Jones (1964), 732–33; Durliat (1990), 11–94.
32. *AE* 1915: 75 = *ILER* 5836.
33. CIL 2: 3222 = *ILS* 5911. Arce (1986b), 221–23, disputes the fiscal context.
34. As is recognized by Ward-Perkins (1998), though denied for no good reason by Liebeschuetz (2001).
35. Restated in Liebeschuetz (2001), 19–22.
36. Hyd. 225. The fact that the Lusidius who betrayed Lisbon to the Sueves was a notable of the city similarly increased the gravity of his action: ibid., 240.
37. Durliat (1990), 75–84. The tirade of Salvian, *De gub.* 5.17, though not cited by Durliat, makes specific reference to just this practice: *illud est gravius, quod plurimi proscribuntur a paucis, quibus exactio publica peculiaris est praeda, qui fiscalis debiti titulos faciunt quaestus esse privatos.*
38. On which see, briefly, Harl (1996), 158–86.
39. This is the theory of Goffart (1980), which, though probable for Ostrogothic Italy, is much less well-documented in the other provinces.
40. Salv., *De Gub.* 4.18.
41. *Lex Irn.* 76.
42. Hil., *Ep.* 16 (Thiel) = PL 58: 17. The reading *Varega* may be an error for *Vareia,* but the identification of that site with modern Varea is not entirely certain: see *TIR* K-30: 236 and *BAGRW* 25: C3, with the discussion of Castellanos (1999), 67–68.
43. *CTh.* 1.20.1. On the *interpretationes,* see Matthews (2001).
44. Larrañaga (1989) is the best account of the controversy, with full references to the ample bibliography.
45. E.g., Thompson (1982b), 177. Castellanos (1999), 21–25, regards this coalition of *honorati* as purely informal.

46. Jones (1964), 763–64.
47. Millar (1977), 375–84; *Lex Irn.* 44–47; for other Spanish evidence, Abascal and Espinosa (1989), 124–26.
48. CIL 2: 4512. Mayer (1992); (1996) argue persuasively for the identification of this Aemilianus Dexter with the Dexter that Jerome, *DVI* 132, names as the son of the city's Bishop Pacianus, but the relationship cannot be proven and the name is not uncommon.
49. *ILS* 1254.
50. Hyd. 88, for his own ambassadorial role, with pp. 192–93, below.
51. On the political development of the Priscillianist controversy, see chapter 10.
52. For this, see MacMullen (1974), 57–127, and the collection of essays in Wallace-Hadrill (1989).
53. See esp. *CTh.* 12.1, with Krause (1987). These juridical aspects of clientage were in time taken over as normative in the legislation of the Visigothic kings, while the informal, consensual, and euphemistic *amicitia* of higher-status citizens remained uncodified: Kienast (1984) and King (1972), 159–89.
54. See CIL 2: 1198 s.v. *patronus.* The last example is CIL 2: 5812.
55. Pac., *De paen.* 10.1.
56. Ibid., 11.1.
57. Hernández Ramírez (1998) provides a good introduction to the *domus* architecture of Mérida with recent bibliographies. On the Casa Mitreo, a short introduction in *Mérida: Patrimonio* (1999), 59–64, with the bibliography at Hernández Ramírez (1998), 244–45.
58. See the catalogue of the urban *domus* of Complutum with bibliography in Rascón (1995), 61–94.
59. Waltzing (1895–1900) and Kornemann (1901) remain the basic studies.
60. The fiscal purpose of such associations is made explicit in *CTh.* 12.1.179, although Teja (1973) seeks to minimize the incidence of *collegia* in the later empire.
61. The basic work on Spain is Santero (1978), an exceptionally valuable work of reference with one conceptual problem: the author assumes that the record of associations is identical to their incidence, which is to say that he does not distinguish between the habit of inscribing records of association on stone and the habit of association itself. The fact that the vast majority of our attestations of associations come from precisely those years in which the epigraphic habit was at its peak means that one cannot safely say that the second and third centuries were the apogee of the associative habit.
62. Jaczynowska (1970), with Santero (1978), 95–104, on Spain.
63. The *termas de Hippolytus,* so-called because of their mosaic decoration, lie in the extramural zone to the north of high imperial Complutum. The grounds on which the complex should be identified as a collegial build-

ing—rather than, say, the baths of a suburban villa complex—have not been published at length, although the identification is presented as certain in Rascón (1995), 79–85; (1999).

64. In general, see Santero (1978), 61–93; as an example of how large funerary associations can bulk in the epigraphic record, Jiménez Cobo (2000), 39–45.

65. These arrangements are attested archaeologically as well, inasmuch as the distribution of graves into small groups at a recently excavated necropolis at Mérida may well be a reflection of funerary *collegia* at work: Ramírez and Gijón (1994); also Estévez (2000b).

66. For instance, the public slave of Tarragona whose colleagues saw to his burial some time during the third century: CIL 2: 4163 and 6071 = *RIT* 370: *Dis manibus Q. Arato vernae Tarragonanensi posuerunt Porcius Paris et Q Urbicus collegae merenti.* Domestic slaves might form similar associations, though these are less well-known: Santero (1978), 82–86.

67. We possess six early imperial inscriptions from Cabeza del Griego, all of the same college of the *sodales Claudiani*. One of these, CIL 2: 5878, is a fragment of the album of the *collegium*. Such associations could also see to the proper burial of members who died far from home, like M. Sallustius Felix of Dertosa, *peregre defuncto* in an unknown place: CIL 2: 4064, undated. They might likewise provide a support network for those who had left their places of origin behind for new residences, like two natives of Uxama dead at Segovia and buried there at the expense of their *sodales*: CIL 2: 2731, 2732, the second-century epitaphs of A. G. Pompeius Mucro and A. Valerius.

68. See, for instance, the Porcius Gaetulus who was *pius in collegio,* a dedicated member of the family constituted by his funerary association, in the early years of the third century: CIL 2: 1976.

69. E.g., the funerary inscription dedicated at Iluro by the professional *collegium urbanum:* CIL 2: 3244.

70. On the Spanish side of this, Santero (1978), 134–41.

71. CIL 2: 1163, 1168, 1169, 1180, 1182, 1183, all more or less second-century and mentioning *navicularii, scapharii,* and *lyntrari.*

72. For the decline of the *annona,* Remesal (1997).

73. *CTh.* 13.5.4; 13.5.8. On the *navicularii* of Seville, Chic (1999).

74. CIL 2: 5812.

75. E.g., *Fabri:* Barcelona: CIL 2: 4498; Tarragona: CIL 2: 4316 = *RIT* 435. *Centonarii* at Tarragona: CIL 2: 4318 = *RIT* 436; Seville: CIL 2: 1167.

76. Koppel (1988).

77. CIL 2²/7: 188.

78. CIL 2: 2211 = CIL 2²/7: 332: *Limenio et Catullino Conssulibus V Idus Apriles Iulio Caninio Patrono merentissimo principatus ob splendorem domus tuae patrone honorificentissime offerimus tibi cuncti tesseram patronatus fabri*

subidiani quem libenti animo iubemus suscipi offerentes rectores Clodius Augendus Curiatius Innocentius Iunius Germanus. See Salvador (1998), 61–62.

79. Gil Mantas (1993), 522.

80. Thus at the start of the fifth century, an inscription from Benevento records the repair of a collegial meeting hall (CIL 9: 2998), while the letters of Gregory the Great record a *corpus saponarium* at Naples in 599: *Ep.* 9.113.

81. See Carreté, Keay, and Millett (1995).

82. Though note Piñol (1993).

83. For what follows, see the slightly dated state of the question in TED'A (1989a), 435–48, or the Castilian version in TED'A (1989b), 150–82. To this should be added the evidence of engineering from Aquilué (1993); the study of decoration in Pauliatti and Pensabene (1993); and the study of the forum portico in Güell et al. (1993).

84. See Pauliatti and Pensabene (1993) and Güell et al. (1993); the monumental stairs leading from the center of the north wall of the forum into the cult precinct have now been discovered, as has a smaller access stair at the southwest corner of the cult precinct: Peña (2000).

85. Trillmich (1993) disputes the strict typological division between civic and provincial fora in the Spanish provincial capitals. On the *flamines,* Alföldy (1973).

86. CIL 2²/7: 254.

87. These include a patron of the three Spains and the two Mauretanias: Alföldy (2000a), 19. Provincial patrons appear for the first time in third-century Spain, but the evidence is not always clear cut: thus the badly preserved text of CIL 2: 1972 seems to show the *ordo* of Málaga voting to honor as a patron the *consularis* Castinus, with the consent of the whole province. But whether this patronage is of the province or just the city of Málaga is unclear. On the whole, the phenomenon of provincial patronage is much less well understood than that of municipal patronage, with which it shares its distinctive vocabulary: Ventura and Stylow (1993) with full citation of the evidence.

88. See Dupré et al. (1988); Piñol (2000).

89. For the circulation of traffic between circus and provincial forum, Dupré et al. (1988).

90. CIL 2: 4109 = RIT 100.

91. CIL 2: 6083 = RIT 86, from the reign of Philip; AE 1930: 148 = RIT 156 and AE 1930: 150 = RIT 87 from the later third century; and CIL 2: 4102 = RIT 89; CIL 2: 4105 = RIT 94; and CIL 2: 4106 = RIT 95, the latter three from the same statue base in Tarragona. For the later fourth or early fifth century, the case depends upon one's reading of the word *coronati* in Inn., *Ep.* 3.7 (PL 20: 485–93), which chastises Tarraconensian bishops for having entered the episcopate directly from the life of the curia.

92. Pac., *De paen.* 5.2, of Barcelona.
93. TED'A (1989a).
94. The fifth-century evidence of Hydatius may suggest the continuation of provincial councils as the decision-making bodies from which ambassadors were sent; certainly, he speaks often enough of envoys coming from or going to "the Gallaecians," a phrase that might well be interpreted as signifying a provincial council, though that leaves open a whole array of questions over how the council was constituted and where, given the Suevic occupation of Braga, the council met.
95. CIL 6: 1454 = *ILS* 6109.
96. The existence at Zaragoza of two fora, one colonial, the other conventual, which has seemed likely to become conventional wisdom—see, e.g., Beltrán and Fatás (1998), 22; Jiménez Salvador (1998)—must now be rejected: Hernández Vera and Núñez (1998).
97. CIL 2: 3413 = Abascal and Ramallo (1997), no. 44.
98. Hyd. 93, 172, 189, 197, 213, 243, 244. The usage in 196 is obscure.
99. As we find with the description in 400 of the bishop Exuperantius as *de Gallaecia, Lucensis conventus, municipii Celenis:* I Toledo, a. 400 (CCH 4: 327).

Chapter 4. Diocletian and the Spanish Fourth Century

1. Witschel (1999) is a very thorough attack on the notion of crisis in this period.
2. For the narrative of imperial politics in the third century, the best account is now Potter (1990), 3–69.
3. I. König (1981), 53–54, with survey of older literature; Drinkwater (1987), 25–26.
4. Aur. Vict. 33.3; Eutr. 9.8; Jer., *Chron.* s.a. 264 (Helm p. 221). Drinkwater (1987) shows that far more lasting damage was done to Gaul by barbarian raids during the reign of Aurelian in 274 than by the invasions of 260.
5. Bakker (1993).
6. Macrinus's loyalty to Gallienus is attested in a recently discovered inscription from Mérida: Ramírez Sádaba et al. (1993). The inscriptions of Postumus are, in Tarraconensis: CIL 2: 4919, 5736; and in Baetica: CIL 2: 4943; all are dated by the consulates of Postumus, themselves a matter of hypothesis: Drinkwater (1987), 116.
7. Vittinghoff (1970).
8. It has, however, been argued that the scarcity of the Gallic emperors' coinage militates against Spain having been administratively incorporated into their empire, regardless of what the literary sources say: Cavada (1994).
9. Tarraconensis: CIL 2: 3833, 3834, 3737, 3619, 4879, 4505 = *IRC* 4: 24; Baetica: CIL 2: 1672 = CIL 2²/5: 79.

10. E.g., Montenegro et al. (1986). The origins of this approach lie in the 1940s, when the crisis-based contrast between high and late empires most eloquently expressed in Michael Rostovtzeff's *Social and Economic History of the Roman Empire* (1957; first pub. 1926) seemed self-evident, as shown by the volume titles enshrined in the original *Cambridge Ancient History*—"The Augustan Empire," "The Imperial Peace," "Imperial Crisis and Recovery"—given classic, modern statement by Alföldy (1985). In the 1960s a residually Marxist view of class struggle (encapsulated in the subtitle of Balil [1970]: amenaza exterior y inquietud interna) elaborated and deepened the preexisting notion of third-century crisis, while scholars of both left and right accepted these essentially determinist views of second- and third-century Roman history.

11. The "Frankish" invasion took center-stage in the 1950s—Taracena (1950); Tarradell (1955); Balil (1957); Sánchez Real (1957)—but is still the symbol of third-century crisis in the countless works of J. M. Blázquez, e.g., (1964); (1976); (1978); (1987) and many studies of Hispano-Roman history, e.g., Balil (1959–60); (1965); (1967); Tarradell (1977); Tsirkin (1987); Carr (2002). There is an overview of the historiography in Cepas (1997), 18–24.

12. Ramos Folques (1960); Almeida (1977). And the approach persists: Blázquez and García-Gelabert (1993); Carrillero et al. (1995).

13. Taracena (1950), demolished by Sagredo (1987). As an example of how far the process of explanatory extension can go, Gonzalbes (1986), 13, makes the Frankish invasion the reason for the third-century destruction of the old province of Tingitania.

14. Aur. Vict. 33.3: *Francorum gentes direpta Gallia Hispaniam possiderent vastato ac paene direpto Tarraconensium oppido, nactisque in tempore navigiis pars in usque Africam permearet;* Eutr. 9.8: *Germani usque ad Hispanias penetraverunt et civitatem nobilem Tarraconem expugnaverunt;* Jer., *Chron.* s.a. 264 (Helm p. 221): *Germanis Hispanias optinentibus Tarraccon expugnata est.* The episode clearly derives from the lost *Kaisergeschichte,* but Victor's reference to Franks is an anachronism: Barnes (1996b) with Geuenich (1997), 18, 37–42, for the parallel case of the Alamannic name.

15. Oros., *Hist.* 7.41.2: *etiam sub Gallieno imperatore per annos propemodum duodecim Germanis evertentibus exceperunt.* See Drinkwater (1987), 73–75.

16. Cepas (1997), 15–16, is the most sensible treatment available.

17. In the title of Barnes (1982).

18. For the narrative, Williams (1985).

19. Syme (1971), for the source problems of the period; good narratives in Christol (1997) and Watson (1999).

20. Carrié (1994).

21. Seston (1946), 334; Barnes (1982), 224–25.

22. On the late imperial administration, it is highly unlikely that anything will ever replace Jones (1964), which suffers mainly from a synchronic approach that disguises the extent of administrative change over time. For those—remarkably few—points on which Jones requires adjustment, see Martin (1995).

23. For the problem, see Hartmann (1982), 89–94; for the solution, Hoffmann (1969–70), which is good on the Diocletianic reforms, though unreliable for the period after Constantine for the reasons explained in Kulikowski (2000c).

24. Barnes (1982), 3–9.

25. Harl (1996), 125–57, with Drinkwater (1987), 210–14.

26. Potter (1990), 63 n. 194.

27. Drinkwater (1987), 25–26.

28. Ritterling (1903).

29. Barnes (1982), 56–60, for Maximian's itinerary. A fragmentary poem preserved in a contemporary papyrus refers to Maximian as the Iberian Ares: Page (1941), 544, no. 135. For Cercadilla as the palace of Maximian, Haley (1994) and Hidalgo (1996), with the objections raised in Arce (1997). See pp. 116–19, below.

30. This is shown by the *Laterculus* of Polemius Silvius. A long and wholly otiose controversy over the (unfounded) possibility of Seville having been the diocesan capital was finally laid to rest by Étienne (1982), reprising the arguments he had made earlier in Étienne (1966b).

31. At some point after 369 the Balearics were parceled off from Carthaginiensis and made into their own province of Baleares.

32. The standard treatment for the late imperial provinces is Albertini (1923), 117–26, though for Gallaecia one should consult Tranoy (1981) and Alföldy (2000a).

33. For Baetica, Alföldy (1995); for Tarraconensis, Alföldy (2000a), *passim,* with Alföldy (1969), 49–50, 106–8.

34. For the date, see Barnes (1996a), 550. In a text of this sort, only a diplomatic transcription can be used safely. One appears in Barnes (1982), 202–3. For Spain, the text reads: *Diocensis hispaniarum habet provincias numero VI. beticam. lusitaniam. kartaginiensis. gallecia. tharraconensis. mauritania tingitania.*

35. The last known senatorial legate was M. Aurelius Valentinianus, *vir clarissimus, leg. Augg. pr. pr.,* who held office under Carus. Postumius Lupercus (CIL 2: 4104 = *RIT* 92) was the first equestrian governor, a *vir perfectissimus, praeses Hispaniae Citerioris.* The *praeses* Julius Valens (*AE* 1929: 233 = *RIT* 91) cannot be dated securely.

36. Baetica had remained a senatorial and proconsular province under the Severans (CIL 8: 12442, 21451), but became an imperial province in the third century: Alföldy (1995). An *agens vices praesidis,* Aurelius Julius, ap-

pears in 276 in Italica, but this need not imply that a reform had been implemented. The first securely attested *praeses Baeticae* is Octavius Rufus, between 306 and 312. A recently discovered inscription shows that Lusitania was still governed by a *legatus Augustorum pro praetore* under Gallienus (Ramírez Sádaba et al. [1993]), while the first *praeses* is attested between 284/293 and 305 (either Aemilius Aemilianus: Saquete et al. [1993] = *HEp*. 5: 81 or Aurelius Ursinus: CIL 2: 5140).

37. For the arguments in favor of 293, see Barnes (1982), 225. The objections to a tetrarchic date raised by Noethlichs (1982) and Migl (1994), 54–68, falter on a consideration of imperial politics between 305 and 314: if dioceses existed in both East and West in 314, as the Verona List shows that they did, then they must have been created before the breakdown of the tetrarchy.

38. In the *Passio Marcelli,* for the text of which see Lanata (1972). There are two recensions of the *Passio.* In the earlier and presumably more authentic version, Agricolanus appears at Tangiers. In the second, he appears at León in Gallaecia.

39. The forms *Tingitana* and *Tingitania* tend to be used interchangeably to refer to the single Diocletianic province. More properly, *Tingitana* should occur in compound with Mauretania, *Tingitania* when the word stands alone.

40. Arce (1982), 46–47; Le Roux (1982), 373–77; even a treatment of the organization of Spanish territory in late antiquity leaves the province out: Revuelta (1997).

41. There is a large literature on Tingitania of very variable quality. For an overview one can still do worse than Carcopino (1943), though it is dated in parts and was always tendentious in others. The best short appreciation of Roman policy in Tingitania is Frézouls (1980).

42. This was acutely observed as long ago as Mann (1974), 528. Carcopino (1943) is particularly hyperbolic on the extent of Roman occupation, as is the relevant map in Cornell and Matthews (1982), 172–73.

43. See Hamdoune (1994), 81–87.

44. Curchin (1990b), 61.

45. Gil Farrés (1966), nos. 1629 and 1642–43; CIL 2: 3417 = *ILS* 840.

46. See Barnes (1982), 59: Maximian's campaign in Spain is attested by *P. Argent.* 480, though whether this refers to European Spain or Mauretania Tingitana is open to question. Regardless, the imperial residency in Spain was brief and by 297 Maximian was fighting in Mauretania Caesariensis in Africa proper. He was based at Carthage from that year until 299.

47. Scholarly approaches to Roman frontier studies have changed a great deal in the past decade and a half. Whittaker (1994) is now basic.

48. However, if Spaul (1997) is correct about the sleepy peace of Tingitania, some other explanation must be sought.

49. There is no reason, *contra PLRE* 1: 163, to believe that the usurper Bono-sus was a Spaniard: the evidence of *Quadr. tyr.* 14.1 comes in perhaps the least authentic life in the *Historia Augusta.*

50. Note one laudable exception: Vicens Vives (1986), map 20.

51. See Fernández-Ochoa and Morillo (1991); (1992); (1997); (1999). For extended discussion of town walls, pp. 101–9, below.

52. Little material evidence of Spanish *annona* has been documented in Gaul or the Rhineland after the decline of the Baetican oil industry at the end of the second century. The literary evidence for a Spanish role in the fourth-century *annona* is confined to the highly rhetorical Claud., *In Eutr.* 1.404–11.

53. Villaverde (2001) collects every possible shred of primary evidence for late antique Tingitania: it is a meager haul; for the epigraphy, see Villa-verde (2000).

54. Ponsich (1982), 809.

55. The slight evidence for fourth-century Spanish ceramics found on both sides of the straits of Gibraltar is collected in Bernal (1997).

56. For most of the past fifty years, the military history of late antique Spain has been entangled in discussion of a supposed internal frontier or *limes* in the peninsula, garrisoned by Diocletian to protect the province against the uncivilized tribesmen of the Basque and Cantabrian north or from in-ternal peasant rebellions: Grosse (1947), 25; Barbero (1963); Vigil and Barbero (1967); Barbero and Vigil (1971); Blázquez (1974); (1976); (1980); Domínguez-Monedero (1983), 115–16; Sanz (1986), 225–26; Tudanca (1997). Once the theory of a *limes* took hold, a specific burial rite involving inhumation with grave goods and small knives was imag-ined to represent these Germanic *limitanei*: Palol (1958); (1964); (1970), since repudiated by Palol (1987), but renewed by Pérez Rodríguez-Aragón (1996). Although there had always been dissenters, e.g., Arce (1980); Le Roux (1982), 394–95, the theory's absurdity was only fully demonstrated by Fuentes Domínguez (1989), 169–86, to which the reader is referred both for the evidence and as a case study of collective scholarly delusion.

57. The codex is now in the library of the Real Academia de la Historia de Es-paña in Madrid (Codex 78, Bibl. Acad. Hist. Madrid). Its contents were first published in Lacarra (1945), 266–75. The best treatment of the man-uscript is Díaz y Díaz (1979), 32–42. A diplomatic text of the *Epistula* ap-pears with commentary in Kulikowski (1998) and is reproduced in ap-pendix 1 for those readers who wish to grapple with the unreadable text for themselves.

58. Since Lacarra's *editio princeps,* there have been four editions of the *Epis-tula,* two plausible (Jones [1964], 3: 36; Sivan [1985]), one neither diplo-matic nor plausible (Gil [1984], 185–88), one a work of fantasy (De-

mougeot [1956]). Arce (1999) is the most recent, and reasonable, treatment. With a source both unique and patently corrupt, a diplomatic transcription is the only adequate defense against reading one's own scholarly prejudices into the text.

59. Seeck's is the standard text. A new Teubner edition is forthcoming from S. Ireland, as is a translation and commentary by P. S. Brennan in the Liverpool Translated Texts for Historians series.

60. Brennan (1995).

61. Kulikowski (2000c).

62. Ibid.

63. Arce (1999) would have us dismiss it altogether.

64. Spain: *Occ.* 7.118–34; Tingitania: *Occ.* 7.135–39.

65. *Vexillationes: Occ.* 7.206–9. *Limitanei:* 26.11–20, explicitly so described, despite being under the command of a *comes* rather than a *dux limitis.*

66. *Occ.* 42.25–32. The military status of these troops is controversial. They are usually described as *limitanei* by modern scholars, though unlike the eight units in Tingitania they are not explicitly described as such in the *Notitia.* This identification imports into Spain the old-fashioned view of *limitanei* as an inferior grade of hereditary soldier-farmer, of little military consequence by comparison to *comitatenses,* even though Isaac (1988) showed that the title *limitaneus* meant nothing more than a soldier under the command of a *dux limitis* and had no qualitative connotation.

67. See García y Bellido (1976), 80 with fig. 21, and/or Marot (1999b), 150, for a distribution map.

68. Llanos (1978), 176–77.

69. The *ala Parthorum,* recently attested in two inscriptions of circa 70–150 from Herrera de Pisuerga, is absent from the *Notitia: HEp.* 7: 561–63. The *Notitia* clearly signals a change in deployment at *Occ.* 42.30, which shows a *tribunus cohortis Celtiberae, Brigantiae, nunc Iuliobriga,* but we cannot tell whether the *nunc* is a late correction introduced into the base text some time during its working life, or a piece of recent information included at the moment of first drafting. Epigraphic evidence from the army camp at Cidadela (*BAGRW* 24: C1) in the modern province of La Coruña suggests that the unit was stationed there until the 270s at the very least: Caamaño (1989); Caamaño and Fernández (2000).

70. *Occ.* 7.135–39: *Intra Tingitaniam cum viro spectabili comite: Mauri tonantes seniores, Mauri tonantes iuniores, Constantiniani, Septimani iuniores. Occ.* 7.206–9: *Intra Tingitaniam cum uiro spectabili comite Tingitaniae: Equites scutarii seniores, Equites sagittarii seniores, Equites Cardueni.*

71. Ibid., 26.11–20 shows an Ala Herculea at Tamuco, the Cohort secunda Hispanorum at Duga, the Cohort prima Herculea at Ad Lucos, the Cohort prima et Ityraeorum at Barrensis, the Cohort Pacatianensis at Paca-

tiana, the Cohort tertia Asturum at Tabernae, and the Cohort Friglensis at Friglas. The identification of most of these sites is disputed, but see *BAGRW* 28.

72. The view derives from Carcopino (1943), 231–58. Euzennat (1989) gives a far more nuanced account of the evidence.

73. There is a large literature on Roman relations with the tribal peoples of Mauretania Tingitana: see Frézouls (1980) with the copious bibliography in Christol (1987).

74. Some have declared that this small army must be a late and makeshift response to crisis, since one unit, the Constantiniani (*Occ.* 7.138) may have been a *legio pseudocomitatense*, i.e., a unit transferred from garrison duty to the field army. There is no reason to object to the inference, but it can be no more than that.

75. *Auxilia* (*Occ.* 7.119–29): Ascarii seniores, Ascarii iuniores, Sagitarii Nervii, Exculcatores iuniores, Tubantes, Felices seniores, Inuicti seniores, Victores iuniores, Invicti iuniores Britones, Brisigavi seniores, Salii iuniores Gallicani. *Legiones* (*Occ.* 7.130–34): Fortenses, Propugnatores seniores, Septimani seniores, Vesontes, Undecimani.

76. Ascarii seniores and iuniores (*Occ.* 5.166–67 = *Occ.* 7.119–20 = *Or.* 9.24–25). For that matter, so had one of the vexillations in Tingitania, the Equites Sagittarii seniores (*Occ.* 6.84 = 7.208 = *Or.* 8.30).

77. Hoffmann (1969–70), 28, demonstrated that duplications in the army lists of the *Notitia* represent troop transfers.

78. *Pace* Hoffman (1969–70), 25–31, we cannot date the transfer more precisely to 410, as shown in Kulikowski (2000c).

79. There remains the possibility that we have before us a thoroughgoing revision that hides a transfer to Spain of the very senior Ascarii at some point after the other units were already in the peninsula, and there is a further complication in the shape of the commander of these units, the *comes Hispaniarum* (*Occ.* 7.118). There had been *comites* in Spain under Constantine, but these were civilian officials equivalent to *vicarii* and different from the military commander shown in the *Notitia*. The only other early attestation of a *comes Hispaniarum* comes in the chronicle of Hydatius (Hyd. 66) in the year 420, though other such *comites* appear later in his chronicle. The parallel between the *Notitia* and Hydatius has encouraged many to date the presence in Spain of the units in *Occ.* 7 to 420 on the evidence of Hydatius. This is unjustified. It is entirely possible that the reference to a *comes Hispaniarum* in the *Notitia* is the earliest extant reference, and thus the post may date to any point after 395.

80. The units are unlikely to have been deployed to Spain in the peaceful decade between 395 and 407, or in the embattled years of usurpation after that year. We might therefore suggest that they were sent to Spain only after the restoration of peace in 417. See p. 171–72 below. The date of

388 suggested by Fuentes Domínguez (1997a), 367, and placed in connection with the usurpation of Magnus Maximus, is impossible.

81. We are certainly not justified in pooling the evidence of the documents, using one to fill in the lacunae in the other, as does Jones (1964), 3: 36.

82. This is the estimate of Le Roux (1982), 390.

83. Proved by Christol and Sillières (1980); see also Barnes (1982), 197–98; Arce (1982), 23–24. There is no justification for the old view that Spain rallied to Maxentius.

84. This is controversial (e.g., Arce [1982], 25–26; Montenegro et al. [1986], 342) though it should not be. Several milestones, largely concentrated in Gallaecia, commemorate Magnentius and his brother, the Caesar Decentius. Magnentius: CIL 2: 4744; 2: 4791; 2: 4765; 2: 4840 = IRG 4: 38; IRG 3: 18; HEp. 1: 562a; HEp. 5: 539; Gorges and Rodríguez-Martín (1997). Decentius: CIL 2: 4827; 2:6221; IRG 3: 14; 2: 4692 (Cartama, Baetica). There may also be one milestone of Magnentius from Tarraconensis, but the reading is dubious: IRC 1: 164. There is, however, a funerary inscription from Tarraco that is dated by the consulate of Decentius and Paulus: RIT 943. The coinage of Magnentius and Decentius is also relatively well-attested at Spanish sites of the mid-fourth century: see, e.g., Carrobles and Rodríguez (1988), 97–104. It is possible that Spain resumed allegiance to Constantius after his victory at Mursa, but the evidence is ambiguous. Zos. 2.53.3, merely states that Magnentius was unable to flee to Mauretania through Spain.

85. Julian, for instance, exiled the Alamannic king Vadomarius to Spain after his arrest for treasonable correspondence with Constantius: Amm. Marc. 21.4.6. Gratian, for his part, exiled the bishop of Parma to the "farthest reaches of Spain": Mansi, *Concilia* 3: 628.

86. See Vogler (1979).

87. The *termini* are established by the *Breviarium* of Festus (369), in which the province does not appear, and the *Laterculus* of Polemius Silvius (circa 395), in which it does.

88. The province is attested by only a single milestone, now preserved in a church at Siresa in the modern province of Huesca, which records the repair of a road by Antonius Maximinus, perhaps the first *consularis et praeses* of a *nova provincia Maxima*. The inscription has been much-published (CIL 2: 4911; Beltrán [1954]; AE 1957: 311; AE 1960: 158). The reading *novae provinciae Maximae primus consularis et praeses,* first proposed by Chastagnol (1966), 286, is plausible but at best conjectural.

89. A full list of imperial officials, with attestations, appears in appendix 2. See also Vilella (1992).

90. Lusitania: praesidial in 337 (inscription of Julius Saturninus in Chastagnol [1976], 261), consular by 362 (*terminus ante quem* for governorship of Vettius Agorius Praetextatus, see appendix 2 for full attestations). Bae-

tica: praesidial on 12 December 337 (*CTh.* 11.9.2, to Egnatius Fausti-nus), becoming consular during reign of Constantius II (353–361, CIL 2: 2206 = CIL 2²/7: 265, Decimius Germanianus).

91. For the figures, see Jones (1964), 373–77, 592–96.

92. Among many recent studies of early imperial administration, Nelis-Clé-ment (2000) shows just how interventionist early imperial government might be in the provinces; older views are synthesized in Lintott (1993).

93. See, e.g., *Coll. Avell.* 2.33–39, for the intervention of the *vicarius* in the case against the Spanish theologian Gregory of Elvira and, ibid., 73–74, for the *consularis* of Baetica intervening in the church politics of Cór-doba.

94. *Pace* Arce (1982), 101, Roldán (1975) does not demonstrate this, nor even claim to.

95. The twelfth-century *Liber censuum* of the Roman church lists sixty-seven *civitates* in Spain, which correspond very roughly to the seventy or so episcopal sees known from seventh-century church councils (a list ap-pears in Orlandis [1987], 218–19). But earlier church councils, espe-cially Elvira (CCH 4: 239–41), show that many of the smaller Flavian *civitates* survived into the ecclesiastical organization of the later empire, while the sixth-century *parrochiale Suevum* likewise shows a closer cor-respondence between church organization and the old *civitates* (CCSL 175: 411–20; David [1947], 19–44). When they disappeared is un-known, but the later fifth or the sixth century is the likeliest hypothesis.

96. See esp. Stroheker (1948).

97. The difficulties that contemporaries faced in answering this question are well illustrated by the incompatible theses of Harries (1992) and Teitler (1992), as well as the discussion of Elton (1995).

98. This is the irrefutable thesis of Harries (1994), based on the testimony of Sidonius Apollinaris. The attitudes made explicit by Sidonius are im-plicit in the actions of the Gallic aristocrats surveyed in Stroheker (1948); Matthews (1975); and Mathisen (1984).

99. For which see MacMullen (1964).

Chapter 5. Change in the Spanish City

1. See, e.g., Fernández Ubiña (1981); Montenegro et al. (1986), with the historiographical survey of Cepas (1997), 24–27. Strong arguments against the old interpretations, e.g., Gutiérrez (1993) or Gurt et al. (1994), have not yet filtered into general discussions of the fourth and fifth cen-turies.

2. During the later 1980s in particular, municipal enthusiasm and schol-arly advances tended, by a fortunate accident, to coincide. As a result, digs of the late 1980s were both generally well-conducted, and also well-funded and well-published. Sadly, the 1990s saw much less coordinated

excavation in Spanish cities, a result of a general decline in political support—and hence of public money—for archaeology. Many of the contributions to the *Actas* of the twenty-fifth national archaeological congress, held in Valencia in 1999, deal with the implications of these changes. For the particularly lamentable demise of Tarragona's Taller Escolar d'Arquelogia (TED'A), which in the late 1980s conducted and published the best archaeological work ever undertaken in Spain, see Mar and Ruiz (1999).

3. Until the early 1990s, one could count the number of well-dug and well-published sites on the fingers of one's hands, but now there are too many to cite; one must nevertheless single out the pioneering work on the forum at Ampurias (Sanmartí [1984]) and the three Memòries d'Excavació by the TED'A ([1987]; [1989a]; [1990]) for blazing a trail now more generally trod. Some sites, of course, continue to be dug and published on archaic lines. The prolific literature on the Iberian and Roman site at Castulo is all more or less useless, as the site has been dug according to rigid preconceptions about the historical context and its contents published so as to be inseparable from the excavator's assumptions, themselves often completely opaque.

4. Few historians have noticed Spanish archaeology's new independence from historical assumptions and even the most iconoclastic accounts of late Roman Spain, e.g., the excellent García de Castro (1995), continue to use the material evidence as an occasional supplement to textual sources. No scholarly histories have followed the lead of two brilliant works of *vulgarisation*, Bajo Álvarez (1995) and Ripoll and Velázquez (1995).

5. Summary treatment in Harl (1996), 125–57.

6. Wightman (1985), 195.

7. Hiernard (1978); Balil and Martín (1979); Gurt (1985); Medrano (1990). But Abascal (1994) argues against extrapolating too far from coin finds to historical interpretation.

8. Cavada (1994).

9. Ibid.

10. Revilla (1994).

11. Aguarod and Mostalac (1998) provides excellent summaries of the extensive work recently done on northern Spanish ceramic production, of which Paz (1991) is essential.

12. Tovar (1997).

13. Remesal (1997).

14. Catalonia: Nolla and Nieto (1982); other important works cited in Gorges (1992), 104 n. 83. Gallaecia and Cantabria: Fernández Ochoa (1994a); (1994b).

15. Thus an early imperial bath complex at Torreblanca del Sol was turned

into a *garum* factory in the fourth century: Puertas Tricas (1986–87). At Málaga, part of the disused theater was even taken over for this purpose: Rodríguez Oliva (1993). Nolla and Nieto (1982) show that the factory at Rosas probably continued in active use until the end of the sixth century. See also Ramallo (1989), 140; Reynolds (1993).

16. Aquilué (1992), esp. the evidence of the rubbish pit from c/ Caputxins 33 cited on p. 27, which dates from between 225 and 275.
17. E.g., Pérez Centeno (1999), 75, with references.
18. Abascal and Espinosa (1989), 187–88; Melchor (1999). Indeed, if one uses private euergetism as the yardstick of urban health, then one must date the onset of urban decay to the first Antonines, as does the otherwise excellent Mangas (1996). Cf. Pérez Centeno (1999), 422–32.
19. Veyne (1976) remains the classic study of euergetism, but Alföldy (1994) has some useful observations on how far Roman *beneficia,* rooted in the patron-client relationship, diverged from Hellenistic *euergesia.* The epigraphic record of euergetism from Spain is tabulated in Melchor (1993), revised in id. (1999).
20. Saquete (1997).
21. Nogales (2000) suggests that the original amphitheater of the city was substantially smaller than the monument now extant. There is some controversy as to whether the city wall of Mérida initially enclosed these two monuments or whether the extant wall in the vicinity of the theater and amphitheater was a later, perhaps Flavian, addition. See esp. Mateos (1994–95).
22. There is a good introduction to the monumental development of Mérida in Velázquez (1998).
23. Alföldy (1994), 65.
24. Alföldy (1997), 62–67.
25. The introduction by García y Bellido (1960) remains useful, to be supplemented by Luzón (1975) and the collective work by Luzón and others (1982). The literary evidence for Hadrianic Italica is treated in Syme (1964).
26. This possibility is based on the mass concentration of collegial inscriptions from the city in just the one spot, for which reason the zone is now called the *foro de corporaciones* by archaeologists. If it is likely that this collegial forum was maintained and patronized by the *collegia* that met there, there is also evidence for a specific dedication by a *collegium,* perhaps that of the *centonarii,* of a temple to Liber Pater: Campos and González (1987); Campos (1993).
27. Saquete (1997), 167.
28. CIL 2: 3361 = CIL 2²/5: 30.
29. CIL 2²/14: 374, for the donation of the Saguntine forum by C. Baebius Geminus. See Melchor (1999).

30. For euergetism as a means of inculcating Roman, urban behaviors in Spanish municipalities, see Mackie (1990).
31. Goffart (1974), 91–94, is properly skeptical of idealizing early imperial euergetism as unrewarded altruism.
32. Carrillo et al. (1995a); Ventura (1996), 147.
33. Jiménez Salvador (1993).
34. Mar, Roca, and Ruiz (1993).
35. Cádiz: González, Muñoz, and Blanco (1993). Cartagena: Ramallo and Ruiz (1998), 122.
36. Márquez (1993); (1998a), 190–92; in general, see the exhibition catalogue of Ventura et al. (2002).
37. Monterroso (2002a). The theater may have been damaged in a third-century earthquake and never rebuilt.
38. Jiménez Salvador (1993).
39. An up-to-date chart of extant spectacular monuments in Spain appears in Ramallo (2002), 117.
40. In general, see the articles collected in Álvarez and Enríquez (1994).
41. Alföldy (1997), 68–85.
42. Vianney and Arbeola (1987); Beltrán and Beltrán (1991); Mar, Roca, and Ruiz (1993); Pérez Centeno (1999), 23, with further references.
43. *RIT* 98–99 and see p. 30, below.
44. Beltrán Lloris (1993). A similar conversion took place in the theater at Sagunto: Hernández Hervás et al. (1993).
45. As is acknowledged by Sánchez-Lafuente (1994), very few excavations have been conducted in such a way as to provide *termini ante quem* for disuse. The amphitheater at Segobriga is the only site where there are positive signs of a late third- or early fourth-century abandonment in favor of residential use. See also Almagro and Almagro (1994).
46. See Teja (1994); (2002).
47. See Melchor and Rodríguez (2002), 155–56.
48. Teja (2002).
49. The circus at Toledo is—along with that at Mérida—the earliest known from the peninsula. The 1964 excavation by Marcelo Vigil collected vast quantities of material, never published, and destroyed the stratigraphy of nearly the whole site, so that the professional excavation undertaken in 1982–83, published in Sánchez-Palencia and Saínz (1988), was badly limited in what it could achieve. More recent excavations have been able to document only Islamic-era finds within the old Roman circus: Sánchez-Palencia et al. (1996); Sánchez-Palencia and Saínz (2001).
50. Overview of the site in Ribera (1998), with greater detail on the ceramic chronology in Ribera (2001).
51. *Cons. Caes.* 85a (= CCSL 173A: 27): *Caesarauguste circus expectatus est.*
52. Ruiz (1993), 112.

53. The disuse and destruction of residential buildings in Valencia is attested mostly from older excavations, not all of which inspire great confidence. But the sheer number of sites within the city that appear to show late third-century disturbance is probably decisive: Blasco et al. (1994); Albiach et al. (2000).

54. Junyent and Pérez (1994).

55. A prejudice still evident in the generally excellent Pérez Almoguera (1996), which despite its ostensible publication date, actually dates to 1991. Ausonius, *Ep.* 21, *Ad Paulinum* 58–59: *aut quae deiectis iuga per scruposa ruinis arida torrentem Sicorim despectat Ilerda.* This description is colored beyond recognition by Ausonius's desire to goad Paulinus into a response, and is contradicted by Ausonius's own *Professores* 23.4, which shows his Burdigalan friend Dynamius setting out his stall as a teacher in the Spanish city.

56. *Lex Irn.* 19.

57. Ibid., 83.

58. Spending: ibid., 79, 82–83.

59. Ibid., 62.

60. On the circus, Hernández Hervás et al. (1995); Pascual (2001). For the Saguntine economy, Aranegui (1993).

61. Hernández Hervás et al. (1995).

62. For the pre-Caesarian site, Sanmartí et al. (1990).

63. Aquilué (1984); Sanmartí (1984); Marcet and Sanmartí (1989); Mar and Ruiz (1990); (1993).

64. The cemetery, which is unambiguously fourth-century and later in date, has no archaeologically visible relationship to the remains of the neapolis, suggesting that when the fourth-century graves were dug, the old buildings were buried and invisible above ground: Nolla (1992).

65. Llinàs et al. (1992) and (1997), 28–29.

66. Nolla (1993), 217–18; Nolla et al. (1996). Ampulles of Saint Menas suggest a pilgrimage commerce with the East: Almagro (1952), 51–52, and Almagro and Palol (1962), 40, with full discussion in Palol (1992a).

67. Nolla (1995).

68. For the old view, see Almagro (1951), 50–54, reiterated in Almagro (1998), which ignores the findings of the past twenty years.

69. The near-simultaneous Republican foundations of Iluro (Mataró) and Baetulo (Badalona), both in the old *conventus Tarraconensis,* are usually said to have begun a precipitous decline under the Flavians that turned them into ghost towns by the third century: Prevosti (1981a) and (1981b) were pioneering works of spatial analysis in their time, but are based entirely on much older site reports, while more recent works, e.g., Clariana (1996), retain the old interpretative paradigms. Both Iluro and Baetulo require the sort of ground-up reevaluation on the basis of new excavation that Ampurias received in the 1980s.

70. See the laws collected in *CTh.* 15.1.
71. E.g., in the digs at c/ San Salvador and c/ Almendralejo, no. 2: Barrientos (1998b); Sánchez Sánchez (2000). Overview of the Méridan evidence in Mateos (2000) and Alba (2001).
72. Albiach et al. (2000), 67–69.
73. Mora (1981) is a good, though dated, catalogue of known bath complexes from all periods; Fernández Ochoa and Zarzalejos (2001) is an up-to-date account of the later empire, which serves chiefly to show how little is known.
74. Astorga, Castulo, and Conimbriga, none certain: Fernández Ochoa and Zarzalejos (2001), 29. Castulo has been extensively, though badly, excavated, while Astorga is only just beginning to be understood archaeologically: Amaré (2002a); (2002b).
75. Fernández Ochoa, García, and Uscatescu (1992). It is clear that we can no longer identify Gijón with Ptolemy's Gigia, as the latter would appear to lie on the Mesetan side of the Cantabrian range, while Gijón is coastal: Fernández Ochoa (1997), 261, with references to the debate.
76. The evidence of date is at present confined to the typology of a large mosaic laid in the *frigidarium* at a late date. No site report has yet appeared, but there are notices in Almagro and Abascal (1999a) and (1999b) and a popular introduction in Abascal, Almagro, and Lorrio (1997).
77. Martins and Delgado (1996). None of the baths of Mérida are well enough dated for us to fit them into these patterns: Barrientos (1997).
78. Aguarad and Mostalac (1998), 11.
79. Rojas (1996).
80. Blasco et al. (1994); Marín Jordá and Ribera (1999).
81. The private baths of Barcelona have not been published in full, but there were many of them, with costly mosaics, in the fourth century: Gurt and Godoy (2000), 429–32.
82. For Spain, see Fornell (2001) and García Entero (2001). The primary evidence for fifth-century bathing is of course the famous letter of Sidonius, *Ep.* 2.9.
83. Pac., *De paen.* 10.2.
84. The single best discussion of the topic is Fernández Ochoa (1997), 249–59, which updates both the catalogue and analysis of Fernández Ochoa and Morillo (1991); (1992), and the useful anecdotal survey of Hauschild (1993a).
85. However, Hauschild (1994b) still regards walls as solely defensive structures and therefore dateable to three main periods of crisis in Spanish history: the late Republic, the reign of Marcus, and the era of "Germanic" invasions in the third century.
86. Except in the far north of the peninsula, little systematic progress has been made beyond the classic study of Richmond (1931) and its continuation in Balil (1959–60).

87. As already pointed out in Petrikovits (1971). In many places, walls that are visibly medieval are assumed without the slightest evidence to rest on late antique foundations, e.g., at Faro, a site more or less untouched by systematic modern archaeology: Gil Mantas (1993), 537.

88. Thus at Tiermes, a coin of Gordian III corresponds to the foundation-level of the wall and provides the *terminus post quem* of 238/244, but beyond that it is impossible to tell: Fernández Martínez (1980).

89. Pérez Centeno (1999), 282; Fernández Ochoa and Morillo (1992), 321–22.

90. Campos (1993), 194–95.

91. Rodríguez Colmenero (1999), 61–64.

92. Járrega (1991); Granados and Rodà (1994).

93. Nolla and Nieto (1979), where the dates suggested by the ceramics are narrowed down by appeal to the literary sources. The former author, it should be noted, has since disavowed a belief in the destruction of the city by third-century invasions—Nolla (1984), 175–77; (1988)—but retains the old date for the wall.

94. For the old view, see Richmond (1931), 98, and Beltrán Martínez (1976), 34. For the modern interpretation, Beltrán Lloris and Fatás (1998).

95. A parallel case to Zaragoza is Mérida, where the number of wall circuits has been debated for years. It now seems relatively clear that there was only ever a single circuit, conceived in the Augustan period and periodically rebuilt, with neither a later expansion from a small core, nor a retraction as a result of third-century crisis: Hernández Ramírez (1998), 23–60; *contra,* Mateos (1994–95).

96. See the surveys of Fernández Ochoa and Morillo (1991) and (1992), of which there is a very summary sketch, in English, in Fernández Ochoa and Morillo (1997). The only Spanish city wall that it is possible to date with absolute confidence is the Republican circuit at Tarragona: Hauschild (1983); (1984–85); (1993a).

97. The assumption is persistent: Palol (1992b).

98. *Necrópolis de Zaragoza* (1991); Aguarod and Mostalac (1998), 15.

99. Ramírez and Gijón (1994).

100. In a good example from the modern province of Gerona, new imperial names were engraved directly on top of the old ones, the name of Constantine replacing that of Galerius, Claudius II becoming Theodosius I: Casas (1982–83). A similar case has recently come to light from near the villa of Torre Águila in Badajoz province: Gorges and Rodríguez (1997) = *HEp.* 7: 152, wherein a Constantinian milestone was reinscribed with the name and titulature of Magnentius.

101. Argente et al. (1984), 64.

102. On the Porta Rufina, see Serra-Ràfols (1927–31) and Nolla (1988).

103. See Johnson (1983) for a basic introduction.

104. Fernández Ochoa and Morillo (1991); (1992); Fernández Ochoa (1997); Fuentes Domínguez (1996).
105. But see the suggestions of Spaul (1997) on Tingitania.
106. Rebuffat (1974).
107. Fernández Ochoa and Morillo (1994b); Fernández Ochoa (1997).
108. Fernández Ochoa and Morillo (1991); (1992); (forthcoming); Fernández Ochoa (1997).
109. Wacher (1998).
110. The one piece of evidence is Claud., *In Eutr.* 1.404–11, which alludes to Spanish corn supplying Rome in moments of emergency.
111. It is clear that the construction of one *versura*, or antechamber, to the east of the *pulpitum*, and the incomplete work on a second one to the west, must date after the Trajano-Hadrianic work on the theater. The palaeographical evidence of the brick stamps on the materials for the new construction suggests a later fourth-century date, though certain anomalous features force this into the realm of hypothesis. The evidence is well-published in Durán (1998), in which, along with Durán (1999), there also appears an extended and prosopographically unlikely attempt to make the creation of the *versurae* the work of Quintus Aurelius Symmachus.
112. Text at Chastagnol (1976), 268: *Florentissimo ac beatissimo saeculo favente felicitate et clementia dominorum imperatorumque nostrorum Flav. Claudi Constantini maximi victoris et Flav. Iul. Constanti et Flav Iul. Constantis victorum fortissimorumque semper augustorum circum vetustate conlapsum tiberius Flav. Laetus v.c. comes columnis erigi novis ornamentorum fabricis cingi aquis inundari disposuit adque ita insistente v.p. Iulio Saturnino p.p.L. ita conpetenter restituta eius facie splendidissimae coloniae Emeritensium quam maximam tribuit voluptatem.* Chastagnol argues convincingly that *aquis inundari* cannot refer to the filling up of a 30,000-square-foot monument with water but must instead commemorate some sort of decorative additions. See also Humphrey (1986), 373–75. From his funerary inscription, we know of a late fourth- or early fifth-century Emeritan charioteer named Sabinianus: *CICM* 51, although Arce (2001b); (2002c) argue, somewhat implausibly, that the *auriga* of the inscription is figurative, not literal.
113. There is not a great deal of archaeological evidence with which to flesh out the epigraphic testimony, but see Montalvo et al. (1997) and Sánchez-Palencia et al. (2001) for what little has been documented of the late antique circus. There is good reason to think a priori that the promotion of the city to the status of diocesan capital would have had a dramatic effect on the city's shape, but the late stages of the city's plan remain to be explicated. Though we can localize two fora in the city, one presumably the colonial, the other the provincial, their late antique stages are entirely unknown. Again, although a major reconstruction of

the city's walls has been postulated, its date is impossible to confirm archaeologically: Mateos (1995a), 131–35.

114. The series of *memorias* published under the title *Mérida: Excavaciones Arqueológicas,* which has appeared irregularly since 1997, provides the best record of these excavations. For a state of the question, see Palma (1999b) in the third volume of the series.

115. Barrientos (1998a).

116. Mateos (1995a); Alba (2000). One change to that street grid in the fourth century can be documented, when a new street was cut through an *insula* beside the *decumanus maximus,* thereby cutting through one old *domus* and prompting the construction of new houses: Mateos (1992), 57.

117. Durán (1991), although it is not archaeologically possible to place this reform in relation to the construction of the *versurae* of the theater as is done in Durán (1998); (1999). For the encroachment of a new building into the portico of a public street after 360/361, see Barrientos (2000a), with a possible nearby parallel in Estévez (2000a). Other definite examples in Ayerbe (1999) and Palma (2001).

118. Barrientos (1998b).

119. Mateos (1992), 63; (1995a).

120. There is a general overview in Alba (1997), but the site as a whole awaits full publication.

121. Alba (1998); (1999).

122. CIL 2: 191, on which see Andreu (2001).

123. *AE* 1929: 233 = *RIT* 91.

124. *RIT* 98–99.

125. CIL 2: 4112 = *RIT* 155.

126. Thomas and Witschel (1992).

127. In the Vespasianic CIL 2: 1956, one Junia Rustica repaired some public porticoes at Cartima that she claimed had fallen into disrepair with age, thus necessitating her munificence, even though the structures can hardly have been more than a couple of decades old when she put up the inscription.

128. Ruiz (1993).

129. The evidence needs careful handling, however: although the upper town of Tarragona has been the subject of extensive, high-quality modern excavation, for the lower town we are almost entirely reliant upon old data that was excavated under the assumption of severe urban crisis in the third century, or the early twentieth-century reports of Serra Vilaró, which record monumental remains without noting their context or the circumstances of their excavation; from these it is possible to document the existence of monuments, for instance, an honorific arch of probably Augustan date (Dupré [1994]), but little or nothing of their history. The supposed disuse of the colonial forum is possible, but the evidence

comes from old site reports in which it is impossible to check the assumptions and statements of the excavators. The same thing is true for the date of the disuse of the theater (see Mar, Roca, and Ruiz [1993]). Nevertheless, the sum of the evidence from haphazard excavations undertaken in the Part Baixa over the past century is consistent, and the scant but important recent work seems to confirm old assumptions, though in a very restricted excavation area: Adserias et al. (1997); Macias (2000).

130. See pp. 57–62, above.

131. "Excavacions arqueològiques Tarragona" (2000), 64, and Ruiz and Mar (2001) are very cautious: some of the vaults beneath the *cavea* of the circus may have been reused as domestic spaces by the fifth century, though that is uncertain. Excavations of the Plaça de la Font, which lies entirely within the arena of the old circus, uncovered nothing to suggest an end to its spectacular use before the sixth or even the seventh century.

132. Carreté and Dupré (1994).

133. TED'A (1989a).

134. Aquilué (1993), 97.

135. Late alterations to the southwestern corner of the precinct suggest similar changes: Vilaseca and Diloli (2000).

136. Sánchez Real (1969); López (1993).

137. *RIT* 100: *B.F.S dd(ominorum) nn(ostrorum) Leonis et Anthemi Augg(ustorum)*, where the initial abbreviation has been expanded either as *bonum factum saluti* or *beatissimo felicissimo saeculo*. Rovira (1993) suggests the provincial forum as the original provenance of the inscription, but it was not found *in situ*.

138. The first widely accessible report, Márquez, Hidalgo, and Marfil (1991), already underlined the site's importance. That we even know of this tetrarchic palace is something of a miracle. Because it lay within the rail yard of the old city train station, it was undisturbed by the enormous expansion of modern Córdoba until the 1980s, when the decision to tear down the old station and replace it with one that could accommodate the new high-speed AVE trains brought the site to light. Sadly, the same construction has since destroyed the most important parts of this amazing complex, and we are only lucky that there was enough time to excavate the site properly before its destruction.

139. Carrillo et al. (1995a).

140. Ventura (1993), 154; Moreno et al. (1997).

141. Jiménez Salvador (1994) for the eastern plaza and its temple. Márquez (1998b) is now the best introduction to the public plazas of Córdoba; Márquez (1999) shows how small architectonic remains can demonstrate the existence of certain public buildings within the city.

142. Murillo et al. (2001). This circus had ceased to be used and was turned into a quarry for stone by the end of the second century. The late imperial circus of the city lay to the west of the walls.

143. Ventura (1996), 39. The remains of a third aqueduct have now been discovered: Hidalgo (1999).

144. All the material evidence is in keeping with a late third- or early fourth-century date, but the one piece of epigraphic evidence fixes the construction between 293 and 305: Hidalgo and Ventura (1994); Hidalgo (1996), 141–47.

145. Underneath one of the trichora were discovered the remains of a suburban *domus,* only recently redesigned at the time of its destruction to make way for the new complex.

146. The site of the circus to the south of the palace has not been definitively proved, though it is made virtually certain by nineteenth-century cartographic evidence and remains uncovered in unofficial excavations: Hidalgo (1999). The circus probably existed long before the palatine complex at Cercadilla—the consensus would appear to be second-century—but it is possible that the two constructions were contemporary.

147. The structure was also essential architecturally, since it was the main mechanism for supporting the terrace by which the site was terraplaned. At the southern end, the cryptoportico needed to be more than 6 meters deep.

148. Monterroso (2002b).

149. There is a possibility, for which see Hidalgo (1999), that a passage connected the southeastern corner of the cryptoportico to the northern face of the western circus, but that must remain conjectural, inasmuch as a full 200 meters separate the sites of the two monuments.

150. Haley (1994); Hidalgo and Ventura (1994); Hidalgo (1996), 151–56.

151. The objection is raised by Arce (1997). For Maximian's itinerary, see Barnes (1982), 56–60.

152. The attempt of Marfil (2000) to make Cercadilla into an episcopal palace is impossible, given a date of construction before the Great Persecution.

153. Hidalgo (1996). New fifth-century mosaics in the north basilica reflect a similar inability to replicate the decorative features of the fourth-century original.

154. León (1993b). A large peristyle *domus,* known as the *domus* of Gaius after one of its presumed owners, lay alongside the *cardo maximus* of the city. It was remodeled in the third century and occupied in its third-century shape until the very end of the fifth century: Ventura and Carmona (1992).

155. Márquez (1993).

156. This identification is not entirely certain: Márquez (1998b).

157. Ventura (1991); Ventura et al. (1993); Carrillo et al. (1995a); León (1993b).

158. Carrillo et al. (1995b), 49.
159. Murillo et al. (2001).
160. Carrillo et al. (1995b).
161. Ventura (1996), 147. For the restoration of an unknown monument, see CIL 2²/7: 321.
162. Our archaeological understanding of both cities remains sadly wanting. For Braga, see Martins and Delgado (1996), where it is suggested that the city did undergo a period of general reconstruction during the late third and early fourth centuries, and Díaz Martínez (2000) for the fifth century and later. For the limited evidence of Cartagena, see Ramallo (2000) and pp. 279–81, below.
163. Járrega (1991); Granados and Rodà (1994); Gurt and Godoy (2000).
164. Sánchez, Blasco, and Guardiola (1986), 29–44.
165. Sánchez Fernández (1991); Márquez, Molina, and Sánchez (1999).
166. The latter site has not been fortunate in its excavators and the basic text, Ramos Fernández (1975), is worthless. Reynolds (1993) is thus necessarily tentative in all his statements about the city of Illici itself.
167. Reynolds (1993), 15.
168. P. 191, below. One should note the distinct contrast between the prosperity of Portus Illicitanus and nearby Dianium, modern Denia, a coastal site very similar to Portus but seemingly lacking in the same late antique structural remains, though it did share in the same general pattern of imports as Portus: see Gutiérrez Lloret (1988).
169. For the ceramics, López Piñol (1991). For the mural, Guiral and Mostalac (1991). Fortifications: Barrachina et al. (1984).
170. Berto (1991). Numerous coin finds from the mid-third through the fifth centuries have a chronology similar to that of the ceramics: Gozalbes (1999).
171. Granados (1987), 356.
172. The best introduction to the archaeology of Myrtilis is Torres and Macias (1993).
173. A ground-clearing exercise that summarizes the known evidence and can act as a basis for further research is Fernández Ochoa and Morillo (1994b).
174. In this it was similar to many other points on the Cantabrian coast: Fernández Ochoa (1994a); (1994b). For Atlantic trade between Gijón and northern Europe, see Fernández Ochoa and Morillo (1994a).
175. Much of the ceramic evidence comes from a rubbish deposit that accumulated in the bath complex of Campo Valdés after its abandonment in the late fourth or early fifth century: Fernández Ochoa, García, and Uscatescu (1992).
176. Fuentes Domínguez (1996); Fernández Ochoa (1999); Fernández Ochoa and Morillo (1999), 103–5. Unfortunately, the evidence of the *annona* in the north and west—the number of late third- or early fourth-

century walls in the region, the presence of troop detachments noted in the *Notitia Dignitatum,* the quantity of contemporary milestones—is largely circumstantial. A possible literary reference to the *annona* in the Spanish north is Claud., *In Eutr.* 1.404–11, but Claudian should almost never be read too literally.

177. We know less about these *domus* than we would like to, because all were unearthed in rescue operations that devoted themselves mainly to the mosaics, rather than to the plans of the *domus* or the stratigraphies of the site; all evidence for date has therefore to come from the typologies of the mosaics, which show a concentration in the three-quarters of a century between the tetrarchic and Theodosian periods, though a few fall significantly outside that range: Fernández Galiano (1984a); (1984b), with the summaries and bibliographies of Rascón (1995), 61–94. Rascón (1995), 55–57, gives an inventory of excavations carried out between 1984—when Alcalá de Henares established a body for the planned exploration, excavation, and protection of its archaeological heritage—and 1993, but the results of these excavations are available only in summary form in Méndez and Rascón (1989a); Rascón (1995); (1999). A publication that would allow the reader to see the specific evidence on which the excavators have based their conclusions is badly needed.

178. See Rascón (1995) with the modified conclusions of Rascón (1999).

179. Rascón (1995), 112. Although he argues that the inscription demonstrates a genuine episode of destruction in the history of the city, it is much likelier to be yet another example of the restorative and renovative rhetoric so essential to the self-advertisement of the late Roman elite.

180. Though note the intriguing suggestion that the fourth century witnessed the very first development of urban environments and their habits in parts of the Spanish interior, particularly the southern Duero valley: Barraca (1997).

181. There are strong parallels in northern Gaul: Wightman (1985), 235.

182. Mostalac and Pérez (1989), 137–44; Hernández and Núñez (1998).

183. The best introduction to early imperial Zaragoza is now Beltrán Lloris and Fatás (1998), 23–33, to be supplemented by the new evidence of Hernández and Núñez (1998).

184. Mostalac and Perez (1989), 104–13, with the stratigraphy and the finds, paralleled in the recent excavations of Hernández and Núñez (1998); see also Aguarod and Mostalac (1998), 11–12, which prefers an earlier date than the ceramic remains warrant.

185. Aguarod and Mostalac (1998), 22–23.

186. Beltrán Lloris (1993). This conversion was probably accompanied by the amortization of the public gardens and the *nymphaeum* that lay alongside the theater: Aguarod and Mostalac (1998), 28.

187. Uxama, according to its chief excavator, had a rich urban life in the later

Roman period (García Merino [1995], 12), but the evidence has not been published. The first substantial report on the city's wall deals with the remains of a wall-tower: García Merino and Sánchez (1998).

188. Argente et al. (1984), 197–291; Casa et al. (1994).
189. Fuentes Domínguez (1991).
190. Argente and Díaz (1994).
191. The first stratigraphic sequence established in the lower Guadalquivir valley, at the urban site of Celti, suggests a similar sequence of occupation: Keay, Creighton, and Remesal (2000).
192. The first serious work on the Roman public buildings of Coimbra in Portugal, the ancient Aeminium, seems to show a similar chronology in the late fourth or the early fifth century, though there is no sure *terminus post quem* for the disuse of the site: Carvalho (1998), 162–74.
193. See pp. 18–23, above.
194. Fuentes Domínguez (1997b) implies as much, even if basing the conclusion on many older, and only partially reliable, site reports.
195. Ramallo and Ruiz Valderas (1998), 84.
196. A well-known example is Tarragona, where the zone between the walls and the river Francolí, once occupied by suburban villas, began to be used as a cemetery during the third century and continued as such for nearly two centuries: full references at Pérez Centeno (1999), 25 n. 89.

Chapter 6. Town and Country

1. Reports on the important remains of the huge villa complex at Els Munts, roughly 12 kilometers from Tarragona (Berges [1969–70]; [1970]) are almost impossible to use as evidence for precisely this reason. Recent excavations in the residential quarter of the complex do seem to confirm a bad fire during the third century, though with no further chronological precision: Tarrats et al. (1998). Els Munts is by no means the only example we might cite. The standard corpus of Hispano-Roman villas, Gorges (1979), is now more than two decades old and suffers from the limitations of its sources, as does its only serious rival, Fernández Castro (1982). Any revision of the corpus of Spanish villas would have to carefully separate sites at which reliable stratigraphies exist from those—the majority—where little more than the plan is securely known.
2. The view remains persistent, in both the scholarly literature and the textbooks: Rodríguez Oliva (1994); Richardson (1996): "the breakdown of the system"; Montero Vallejo (1996), 65–108.
3. Gorges (1992) is an indispensable guide to the publication of rural sites between 1968 and 1990. The implications of recent work on rural sites are well-explored in Fernández Galiano (1992c), written for a popular audience, despite its eccentric insistence that many sites that we call villas were in fact temples.

4. The work of Fernández Corrales (1988) represents a methodological advance over the cataloguing approach to rural habitation in Prevosti (1981a); (1981b) (summarized in Prevosti [1991]) and Ponsich (1970); (1974); (1987); (1991), still used in, e.g., Carrillo (1991). The conclusions of Fernández Corrales are confirmed for other parts of the peninsula by Aguilar, Guichard, and Lefebvre (1992–93) and, with less methodological rigor, Gómez Santa Cruz (1989); González Conde (1987); Salinas de Frías (1992–93).

5. Escacena and Padilla (1992).

6. Keay (1991b); Carreté, Keay, and Millett (1995).

7. It is also consonant with the results that Carr (2002) extracts from the extensive surveys documented in Ponsich (1970); (1974); (1987); (1991).

8. Aguilar and Guichard (1993).

9. Alonso, Cerrillo, and Fernández (1992–93); Salinas (1992–93); Fuentes Domínguez (1996).

10. On Rabaçal, see Pessoa (1991); (1995). For the *territorium* of Mérida, see in particular the remains of Torre Águila: Rodríguez Martín (1995a); (1995b).

11. On this among other difficulties, see Sillières (1993). Examples of the phenomenon are widespread, e.g., the villa de Pesquero near Mérida, where a fourth-century mosaic of Orpheus was laid over a second-century polychrome mosaic with a geometric design, which had in turn been laid on top of a simple undecorated floor of the first century (Rubio [1988]; [1991]); or the villa of El Saucedo in the *conventus Emeritensis,* where a simple early imperial plan was rebuilt on an enormous scale with a double-apsed basilica and a private bath complex (Bendala et al. [1998], with summary of findings and full bibliography of earlier site reports). A more complex example is that of La Sevillana, also in Extremadura, where a small first-century *domus* lies on a rise underneath what became a late Roman baptistery and accompanying necropolis. This *domus* was abandoned in the late first or second century, while later owners built a new and luxurious complex half a kilometer farther along the banks of the Zújar, where the topography allowed much greater opportunity for expansion and where remains of the fourth century now lie under the local reservoir: Aguilar (1991); Aguilar and Guichard (1993).

12. A point made forcefully in Aguilar, Guichard, and Lefebvre (1992–93) and Aguilar and Guichard (1993), 40–46.

13. The villa of Torre de Palma (Monforte, Portugal) is the largest villa site in the Iberian peninsula. Unfortunately, destructive excavations in the 1950s and 1960s limit our understanding of the villa's history before the construction of a basilica on the site in the fourth century: Maloney and Hale (1996).

14. These were blessed with an exemplary excavation and the thoroughgoing publication of Alarção, Étienne, and Mayet (1990).

15. Ibid., 87.
16. Maguire (1999) is essential here. Stucco could disguise the fact that a villa's walls were made of packed mud rather than stone; plaster could imitate marble; or decorations in cheap material could imitate genuine luxury goods, as in the case of a well-known glass ring from Zaragoza that copies a costly intaglio made of precious stone: Ortiz Palomar (1992).
17. There is a preliminary synthesis in Vaquerizo (1994b), superseded by Vaquerizo and Noguera (1997), as well as a variety of specialist studies cited below. The English account in Vaquerizo and Carrillo (1995) is summary.
18. Vaquerizo (1990); Vaquerizo and Noguera (1997), 25.
19. Maguire (1999).
20. CIL 2: 1637–59 or CIL 2^2/5: 251–72; CIL 2: 5472 = CIL 2^2/5: 286.
21. Atrium: room I on the plan. Exigencies of excavation have meant that the eastern part of the site is known only sketchily.
22. The *cubiculum,* room VI, and a hypothetical counterpart across the corridor, might have served as a waiting area or cloakroom, but was more likely a store for the agricultural renders of the local *rustici.*
23. Rooms IX, XI. There were certainly eight columns, perhaps as many as twelve.
24. Room X. In the renovation, the old mosaic was retained in the ambulatory, but a low wall filled in the intercolumnar space of the peristyle and sealed in the lower portions of the columns. The outside of this little wall was stuccoed and painted, the inside faced with *opus signinum,* thus setting off the peristyle from the patio. The tank, which had a rounded apse at each end, served both as an ornament and as a reservoir from which to water the garden.
25. *Triclinium:* room XVII; *nymphaeum:* room LXVII.
26. See Vaquerizo and Noguera (1997), 60–77.
27. This was fed from the *nymphaeum* by an underground lead pipe that continued on underneath the floor of the *triclinium* and issued into the tank of the peristyle.
28. The original mosaic was simple, but of high quality: Vaquerizo and Noguera (1997) substantially modifies the preliminary publication of the El Ruedo mosaics in Hidalgo Prieto (1994).
29. Financial embarrassment may also lie behind the decision not to rebuild the *exedra,* with its fine mosiacs (room XVI), and to make only minor changes to the rooms that lay to the west of the peristyle, in the corner beside the *triclinium* (rooms LXI, LIX, LX, and LXII). This small suite of bedrooms lay off an anteroom with a particularly fine mosaic, and was decorated with wall paintings. The largest of the three rooms, probably a *cubiculum* in the strict sense of a bedroom, was partly dug into the hillside on account of the gradient and in it the fourth-century *dominus* installed a hypocaust floor, the only one in the villa and useful for the chill of winter evenings.

30. Vaquerizo (1994a); Vaquerizo and Noguera (1997), 150–59.
31. This was not found *in situ,* but certainly belonged to the villa: the torso was bought by the Junta de Andalucía on the commercial antiquities market, but one of its missing arms was uncovered in the *triclinium* at El Ruedo: Vaquerizo and Noguera (1997), 160–65.
32. Vaquerizo and Noguera (1997), 118–23 and 124–29, respectively.
33. Ibid., 180–89.
34. There is a single portrait, of Domitian remodeled from a portrait of Nero: ibid., 106–11.
35. Ibid., 116–17.
36. The complete catalogue can be found in ibid., 105–210.
37. In the archaeological circumstances, dating must be more tentative than usual. The basic studies are Puerta, Elvira, and Artigas (1994); Carrasco and Elvira (1994); Arce, Caballero, and Elvira (1997); as well as the popularizing Elvira and Puertas (1988).
38. Morand (1994) is an exhaustive study of the tastes of Spanish villa owners based almost entirely on mosaic evidence.
39. On the Republican debate, see esp. Gruen (1992).
40. But note that Bravo (1997) plays down the significance of Spaniards in the Theodosian entourage.
41. Some have seen this Dionysiac or Bacchic theme as signifying a cult site: Fernández Galiano (1992a); (1992b).
42. The debate stems from the attempt of Fernández Galiano to identify an otherwise unattested phenomenon, the pagan monastery, with many of our rural villas, working in particular from a mosaic, which he identifies as depicting Cadmus and Harmony, at the villa of La Malena in the Ebro valley. The debate may be followed in Fernández Galiano (1992a); (1992b); (1992c) and Arce (1992a); (1993).
43. See Almagro-Gorbea et al. (2000), which reprints in full A. Delgado's 1849 publication of the spectacular silver dish.
44. Dimas Fernández Galiano, personal communication.
45. The main publication of the site is Fernández Galiano (2001), which supersedes id. (1998). Many of the mosaics are well reproduced, in color and on a larger scale than in the main publications, in Bajo Álvarez (1995), 22, 26–27, 42–43, 98–99.
46. Fernández-Galiano (1998); García Moreno (2001).
47. Arce (1986a).
48. *AE* 1989: 470bis, where Le Roux conjectures *masculini* or *masclini* as the correct reading of *mas*[. . .]*ni.* Mayer and Fernández-Galiano (2001), 121, propose *masuriani.*
49. Arce (1993), 268–70, rejects the identification for this reason and on general methodological grounds. He is probably right.
50. Centcelles suffered badly from neglect for much of the last century and,

for the study of its iconography, the colored plates of Domenech (1931) preserve detail since lost.

51. The most extensive modern treatment of the mosaics is Schlunk (1988), who first suggested the identification of the monument with the mausoleum of the emperor Constans, killed while fleeing the usurpation of Magnentius in 350. This view was worked out in detail by Arbeiter (1989), and defended against criticism in id. (2002). However, the arguments against the identification in Arce (1994); (2002a) seem decisive, and they make it very clear that Centcelles as a whole is a hypertrophied villa, not a mausoleum or cenotaph. But there are no probative grounds on which to choose between Arce's view of the cuppola mosaics as illustrations of an episcopal investiture, and those of Warland (2002), reading the same images in a secular context.

52. Carrillo (1993) has useful observations on the preference for excavating the luxurious domestic parts of villas rather than the vital industrial appurtenances. The practice badly skews our sample, because we know far more about the distribution, layout, and construction of the *partes urbanae* than we do about the *partes rusticae,* even though, as Cerrillo (1995) rightly stresses, the *domus* at most villa sites was less important than the various industrial buildings that surrounded it. The typological division between *pars urbana* and *pars rustica* is not rigid, even within a relatively small part of the peninsula. At some sites, for instance at the villas El Pesquero and Torre Águila near Mérida, the residential parts of the villa complex are separated from their industrial sections, at Torre Águila by a wall at least a meter high (Rodríguez Martín [1988]), while at Los Términos in modern Cáceres province, a site possibly connected to the great north-south route of the via de la Plata, the *domus* and the enormous industrial zone of the villa were separated by an arroyo that can turn into a substantial stream when in spate (Cerrillo [1983] and Cerrillo et al. [1991]). At other sites in the same region, by contrast, industrial and residential functions were integrated into the same part of the complex, as at the villa at La Cocosa (Aguilar and Guichard [1993], 19), or the villa of La Sevillana in eastern Extremadura, where a large double-apsed building was built along the entire length of the main residential building. Although apsidal buildings are normally identified as *exedrae* or churches, this structure was actually a storehouse, never laid with mosaics, completely unarticulated in its interior, and discovered with fragments of storage *dolia* still in place. Along with this rare example of an industrial building incorporated into the main domestic structure, La Sevillana also sported a number of outbuildings devoted to the agricultural exploitation of the property (Aguilar, Guichard, and Lefebvre [1992–93]; Aguilar and Guichard [1993], 79–80). The differences may depend upon patterns of residency. Where the *dominus* was in residence for much of the year, his *do-*

mus might sensibly be separated from the commercial or industrial parts of the site; where the owner was often absent, the residential part of the villa, perhaps generally occupied by the owner's bailiff, was just as easily placed at the functional center of the site.

53. Fuentes Domínguez (1989). Mesetan grave goods tend to consist of local ceramic ware, cheap jewelry, and small knives. In general, Spanish rural cemeteries tend to lack the great variety of grave forms that give urban cemeteries much of their interest.

54. The coffins, which disappeared in 1927, were found in the necropolis of Bòbila, which was probably associated with the villa at Torre Llauder rather than the town of Iluro (modern Mataró): see Clariana and Járrega (1994).

55. And they remained rare then, though see Gil and González (1977) for an example.

Chapter 7. Imperial Crisis and Recovery

1. Harries (1994).
2. Burgess (1993), 6–10.
3. The best biography of Hydatius is Burgess (1993), 3–6.
4. The chronicle is only just beginning to be studied as a literary genre in its own right, rather than a mere quarry of historical data. One consequence of these studies has been a new and salutary emphasis on the milieus of our late antique chroniclers, and of the *Tendenzen* of the works they produced. Much of the best work in this respect has been a series of editions that collectively replaces many parts of Mommsen's *chronica minora:* Favrod (1993); Placanica (1997); and, most important, Burgess (1993) and Cardelle de Hartmann's editions of Victor, John of Biclar, and the *Consularia Caesaraugustana* in CCSL 173A. For interpretation, Muhlberger (1990) is fundamental, as are the essays collected in Croke and Emmett (1983) and Clarke (1990), while Arce (1995) demonstrates how a literary appreciation of chronicles can affect our factual understanding of the past.
5. Muhlberger (1990), 8–47.
6. Ibid., 245–56, notices some of the problems of extending Hydatius's Gallaecian testimony too far.
7. He was unable, for instance, to discover the date of the deaths of Jerome or of John of Jerusalem, and he did not realize that Cyril directly succeeded Theophilus at Alexandria: Hyd. 97, 53. See Thompson (1982b), 147–48, for extended comment on Hydatius's ignorance.
8. See Lee (1993). Vilella (1989), while potentially useful, is methodologically ill-conceived, since its attempt to express external contacts with late antique Spain statistically assumes the a priori significance of certain dates, 409 prominent among them; Vilella (2000) seems to suggest

that the forthcoming Spanish volume of the *Prosopographie chrétienne* will suffer from the same problems.

9. News via Seville: Hyd. 97, 170; Gallic sources: ibid., 65, 137, 143; Pervincus: ibid., 128.

10. We possess the reply of Pope Leo I (PL 54: 677–92) to a letter from Thoribius, the bishop of Astorga, the contents of which are suggested not only by Leo's reply, but from an earlier letter of Thoribius to Hydatius and Caeponius that is also extant (PL 54: 693–95).

11. This is demonstrated at length by Burgess (1989), 155–93, and restated with excessive brevity in both Burgess (1993), 9–10, and Burgess (1995).

12. Prisc., *Tract.* 2.6. On Bishop Rufus and the charismatic Spaniard, Sulp. Sev., *VMart.* 24.1–2.

13. The persuasiveness of Hydatian rhetoric is demonstrated by Matthews (1975), 332, where the modern historian adopts Hydatius's voice wholesale.

14. That is to say, we should adopt the attitude toward Fabius Pictor avowed by Polybius, *Hist.* 3.9.5: "My opinion is that, while not treating his authority as negligible, we should not regard it as final, but that in most cases readers should test his statements by references to facts themselves" (trans. Paton, with modification).

15. There are countless modern narratives of the period, most of which depend on one another rather than directly on the primary sources. The best are Seeck (1913), 377–90; (1920), 42–50; Demougeot (1951), 376–96; Courtois (1955), 38–58; Stevens (1957); Stein (1959), 16–25. Among more recent treatments, only Matthews (1975), 307–20, Arce (1988), and Drinkwater (1998) actually come to grips with the sources rather than relying on earlier modern literature. The narrative that follows is abridged from Kulikowski (2000b), wherein the points of controversy are treated at length.

16. For Stilicho and Alaric, see Cameron (1970), 156–88, and Heather (1991), 199–213.

17. Both dates and details of the invasion appear in the Copenhagen Continuation of Prosper's chronicle (= MGH AA 9: 299).

18. The traditional date for the Rhine crossing is 31 December 406, but Kulikowski (2000b) shows that Prosper 1230 (= MGH AA 9: 465) must be an error for 31 December 405. The Rhine crossing is recounted anecdotally in Greg. Tur., *Hist.* 2.9, which preserves fragments of the fifth-century account of Renatus Frigeridus, but offers no dates. We do not know what caused these invaders to appear on the Rhine when they did, and there is no evidence for the view of Heather (1995) that they were fleeing the expansion of the Huns, or for that of Drinkwater (1998) that they were splinters from the great army of Radagaisus.

19. Mainz is cited first by Jerome, *Ep.* 123.15, in a list of cities sacked by the invaders. The itineraries in Schmidt (1942), 17–18; Demougeot (1951), 385–87; and esp. Courtois (1955), 44–47, depend upon the wholly unreliable evidence of late hagiographies, toponymy, and coin hoards.

20. Zos. 6.3.1 shows that Marcus's usurpation was a response to the Rhine crossing, while Olymp., frag 12 (Müller) = 13.1 (Blockley) places it in 406.

21. Olymp., frag. 12 (Müller) = 13.1 (Blockley), with Soz. 9.11.1 for Gratian.

22. Soz. 9.11.2; Oros., *Hist.* 7.40.4.

23. This can be established on the basis of Jerome, *Ep.* 123.15 (= CSEL 56: 92), which shows that when the letter was written at Bethlehem very late in 409 or early in 410, Jerome had no definite knowledge of a barbarian presence in southern Gaul, but a very detailed record of their depradations in the north. See Kulikowski (2000b). Constantine's battles are attested by Zos. 6.3.2, his treaties by Oros., *Hist.* 7.40.4, while his first coins (*RIC* 10.144) proclaim him *Restitutor Rei Publicae*.

24. Zos. 6.3.3; *RIC* 10.146–47. Drinkwater (1998) demonstrates a period of cohabitation in the winter of 407/408 between a Constantinian government in Lyon and an Honorian one in Arles, before the conquest of the latter by Constantine, recorded in Zos. 6.2.3–4.

25. Oros., *Hist.* 7.40.5, says that Constantine sent *iudices* to Spain who were received there obediently.

26. This recognition by the Spanish authorities explains the failure of such troops as were in Spain to oppose the army of Constans, and is therefore, *pace* Arce (1999), not evidence against the existence of the units described in the *Notitia Dignitatum*.

27. Soz. 9.12.1.

28. Ibid., 9.11.4; Zos. 6.4.1. Greg. Tur., *Hist.* 2.9 (= MGH SRM 1: 56) shows that shortly after this date Constans had his court in Zaragoza. The name of Decimius Rusticus, later attested as *ex officiorum magistro* in Gregory, is almost certainly hidden in the lacuna at Zos. 6.4.2: Paschoud (1989), 32.

29. Soz. 9.11.4–9.12.1; Oros., *Hist.* 7.40.6–8. Sozomen, following Olympiodorus, places both battles in Lusitania. Orosius, on the other hand, states that the brothers set up their defenses in the Pyrenees after crossing the peninsula unopposed, but he does not place the site of the second battle specifically. Zos. 6.4.3–4 is muddled, introducing Lusitanian troops (which, *contra* Paschoud [1989], 33–34, at no time existed) in place of a battle in Lusitania. Certainty is impossible and any solution requires discarding part of either Orosius or Sozomen. Some sort of Pyrenean defense is entirely possible, perhaps conducted at a strong point like Clausurae, modern Les-Cluses in the French Pyrenees, on which see Castellvi (1995).

30. See Soz. 9.12.1; Oros., *Hist.* 7.40.7–8: Orosius describes the *Honoriaci* as *barbari*, but given their title they were clearly a regular unit of the Roman army. *Contra* Paschoud (1989), 33, there is no reason to equate them with any of the several units of Honoriani in the *Notitia Dignitatum*. The *campi Pallentini* were presumably the region of Palantia, modern Palencia in the Meseta (*BAGRW* 24: G2), in a region with a large number of sumptuous villas, for which see the distribution map in Fernández Castro (1982), 42, with the references in her index.

31. This too is fraught with controversy. Orosius (*Hist.* 7.40.9–10) and Sozomen (9.12.3) both record that Constans left his own soldiers (Orosius makes them the *Honoriaci*) to guard the Pyrenean passes in defiance of an old custom whereby local *rustici* had that duty. One cannot simply dismiss this out of hand, as it is recorded in two independent sources, but the information is inexplicable. Who these traditional guardians were can only be guessed at, for there is not a shred of evidence. They were obviously not regular troops, and after Constans had beaten Didymus and Verinianus there is no conceivable reason for his having garrisoned the passes.

32. *RIC* 10.143–49.

33. *Excerpta Sangallensia*, s.a. 408 (= MGH AA 9: 300).

34. Zos. 5.43.2; Olymp., frag. 12 (Müller) = 13.1 (Blockley). The consulate of Honorius seems not to have been accepted outside Constantine's own *pars imperii*, but the evidence for it is good: *IG* 14: 2559 (Trier).

35. Gerontius's motives are obscure. It is possible that his rebellion prompted Constantine to make Constans Augustus and send him to Spain. It is equally possible that the promotion of Constans and the replacement of his praetorian prefect Apollinaris by Decimius Rusticus (Zos. 6.13.1) worried Gerontius enough that he felt driven to revolt.

36. The status of Maximus vis-à-vis his sponsor is the subject of endless controversy. Maximus appears as *pais* and *domestikos* in Olympiodorus and *oikeos* in Sozomen. For Gregory of Tours (*Hist.* 2.9 = MGH SRM 1: 56), he is *unum e clientibus suis*, while Orosius (*Hist.* 7.42.5) contents himself with a *Maximus quidam*. That Maximus was allowed to live after his patron's suicide may argue against their blood kinship, and, *pace* Gurt and Godoy (2000), 436, he was certainly not a freedman.

37. Residence: Soz. 9.13.1. Coins: *RIC* 10: 150–51; Marot (1997). Walls: Járrega (1991); Gurt and Godoy (2000), 426–28.

38. Zos. 6.5.2.

39. *Add. Prosp. Haun.*, s.a. 406 (= MGH AA 9: 299); Hyd. 63.

40. Jones (1964), 194–96, has a good discussion of the problems that face the historian trying to reckon barbarian numbers. García Moreno (1985) puts the number of Spanish invaders at two hundred thousand, but he makes much play with the famous figure of eighty thousand Vandals in

the headcount taken by Gaiseric in 429. Unfortunately, this figure is no more trustworthy than any other numbers that appear in the ancient sources: Goffart (1980), 231–34.

41. See Roberts (1992) on the evidence of, in particular, Orientius.
42. Zos. 6.3.3. The literature on this event is huge and uneven. A long series of articles on the subject by E. A. Thompson, with full references in Thompson (1982a), is basic, as are Bartholomew (1982) and Muhlberger (1983).
43. Oros., *Hist.* 7.40.9 blames the *Honoriaci* for betraying the passes. Soz. 9.12.6 says merely that those who were to have been guarding the passes failed in their duty. If Gerontius was as wholeheartedly occupied in fighting Constans as the sources imply, it is no wonder that he wasted little effort on garrisons.
44. Hyd. 34.
45. Soz. 9.12.6.
46. Olymp., frag. 16 (Müller) = 17.1 (Blockley).
47. Soz. 9.13.3.
48. Ibid., 9.15.1.
49. Olymp., frag. 16 (Müller) = 17.1 (Blockley); Soz. 9.15.2–3; Greg. Tur., *Hist.* 2.9 (= MGH SRM 1: 56).
50. *Cons. Const.*, s.a. 411 (= Burgess [1993], 243).
51. Soz. 9.13.4–7.
52. For Jovinus, see Scharf (1993).
53. E.g., García Moreno (1976); Arce (1988), 110: "La invasión desastrosa y apocalíptica del 409 d.C. en España."
54. Hyd. 40: *Debaccantibus per Hispanias barbaris et seuiente nihilominus pestilentiae malo opes et conditam in urbibus substantiam tyrannicus exactor diripit et milites exauriunt. Fames dira crassatur adeo ut humanae carnes ab humano genere ui famis fuerint deuoratae; matres quoque necatis uel coctis per se natorum suorum sint paste corporibus; bestie, occisorum gladio fame pestilentia cadaueribus adsuatae, quosque hominum fortiores interimunt eorumque carnibus paste passim in humani generis efferantur interitum. Et ita quatuor plagis ferri famis pestilentie bestiarum ubique in toto orbe seuientibus, predicte a domino per prophetas suos adnuntiationes implentur.* Translation from Burgess (1993), 83, with modifications.
55. Cannibalism also appears in the account of Olympiodorus, who records that the famine that afflicted Spain during the Vandal invasion was so bad that one woman ate all four of her children in succession, after which her neighbors stoned her to death (Olymp., frag. 30 [Müller] = 29.2 [Blockley]). This has the circumstantial detail of an authentic anecdote, true or not, while Hydatius's statement is rhetorical flourish. The two accounts need have no relationship to one another.
56. Hyd. 41: *Subuersis memorata plagarum crassatione Hispaniae prouinciis*

*barbari ad pacem ineundam domino miserante conuersi, sorte ad inhabitan-
dum sibi prouinciarum diuidunt regiones. Calliciam Vandali occupant et
Suaeui sitam in extremitate Oceani maris occidua. Alani Lusitaniam et Carthaginiensem prouincias et Vandali cognomine Silingi Beticam sortiuntur.
Spani per ciuitates et castella residui a plagis barbarorum per prouincias dominantium se subiciunt seruituti.* There is a long-standing crux in the translation of this passage, which follows from the reading of *sitam* as *sita* in
Mommsen's original edition and requires that the Asdings and Sueves be
settled at a site in the far west of Gallaecia. Burgess's edition restores the
correct reading of *sitam,* but his translation (Burgess [1993], 83), is so
conditioned by traditional readings that he gives *Calliciam . . . sitam in
extremitate . . . occidua* as "that part of Gallaecia which is situated on the
very western edge of the Ocean." In fact, Hydatius is merely telling his
readers where the whole province of Gallaecia lies, i.e., on the western
edge of Spain, by the ocean.

57. The monetary economy of later fourth- and fifth-century Spain is a problem without easy solution. As in the third century, the Spanish provinces
were probably undersupplied with coin (Cavada [1994] for the third,
Sienes [1999] for the fourth century). Much of the coin that entered the
provinces must have had a military purpose, but its circulation is not yet
fully understood, and no one has yet explained how the economy functioned after the last substantial influx of coined money entered Spain
during the reign of Honorius. See Figuerola (1999) for discussion and
bibliography.

58. The revolt of Gerontius had severed Spain from Constantine III's regime,
just as Constantine's had taken Spain, Gaul, and Britain from that of
Honorius. The theory of Raña (1988) according to which Priscus Attalus
exercised a brief rule in Spain independently of the Goths, is based upon
a mistranslation of Orosius.

59. Soz. 9.13.1 tells us that Tarragona was Maximus's residence, while we
have three series of bronze and silver coins from the Barcelona mint (*RIC*
10: 150–51, 351; Marot [1997]). The situation of the mint does not necessarily imply that Barcelona was Maximus's capital, *pace* Gurt and Godoy (2000), 437. Walls: Járrega (1991).

60. A point recognized by Ripoll (2000), 378.

61. Marot (1997).

62. Belief in a treaty is very widespread, e.g., Reinhart (1952), 299; Stroheker (1972–74), 596; Orlandis (1987), 25–26; Collins (1995), 18.
Schmidt (1933), 109, envisaged "ein Vertrag mit der kaiserlichen Re-
gierung," without specifying which emperor he had in mind, while
Schmidt (1944), 22, instead describes a treaty between the invaders and
the legitimate government of Honorius, in which view he is followed by
Torres (1977), 48. But Hydatius never so much as hints at a treaty and
the passage of Orosius often cited in support (*Hist.* 7.43.14) actually

concerns the conquest of the Silings and Alans by Wallia's Goths. See n. 94, below.

63. Elton (1996), 82–86.
64. Hyd. 41.
65. For the use of *castellum* for *municipium*, Rodríguez Colmenero (1999), 13; more generally, Revuelta (1997), 135–38.
66. Sanz (1986) compiles the evidence for private armies in late Roman Spain.
67. Garnsey (1988), 3–88.
68. Oros., *Hist.* 7.41.7: *inveniantur iam inter eos quidam Romani, qui malint inter barbaros pauperem libertatem, quam inter Romanos tributariam sollicitudinem sustinere.*
69. Ibid., 7.42.5: *Maximus exutus purpura destitutusque a militibus Gallicanis, qui in Africam transiecti, deinde in Italiam reuocati sunt, nunc inter barbaros in Hispania egens exulat.* The identity of these Gallic soldiers is unclear. They might be Maximus's own imperial corps, some sort of *schola palatina* that Orosius describes as Gallic because they had originally come from Gaul in the army of Gerontius and Constans. On the other hand, they might be the remnants of Gerontius's own force who, having mutinied against their general and forced him to commit suicide, returned to Spain and deposed his emperor. Or, finally, they might be a unit of Constantius and Ulfila's army sent to Spain by the Honorian generals precisely in order to dispose of Maximus. There is no way to decide the matter, but regardless of their origins, the Gallic soldiers who deposed Maximus had clearly returned to the allegiance of the legitimate emperor Honorius. After dealing with Maximus, they were redeployed to Africa, perhaps in order to fight the usurper Heraclian, and by 417, when Orosius was writing, they had been called back to Italy.
70. Prosper 1245 (= MGH AA 9: 466): *Maximo in Hispania regno ablato vita concessa eo quod modestia humilitasque hominis affectati imperii invidiam non merebatur.*
71. Elton (1996), 44.
72. The narrative of Hydatius contrasts a period in 410, when the provincials suffered under the exactions of Maximus's government, with one in 411, when the Roman civil authority ceases to be mentioned, even though Maximus continued to reign until 412. This inference may be confirmed by the internal chronology of Hydatius, who places the division of Spain (Hyd. 41) before the fall of Constantine (ibid., 42) though dating both events to 411.
73. Oros., *Hist.* 7.41.7: *barbari exsecrati gladios suos ad aratra conuersi sunt.* Torres (1971), 59, takes the words literally.
74. Hyd. 41. See n. 56, above.
75. Burns (1992), restated in Burns (1994), 251–69.

76. Thus Thompson (1982b), 155, argues that the only means of avoiding conflict between the different barbarian peoples was to leave the outcome to chance. More frequently, the lot is taken as just another example of primitive savagery.

77. Denied by, e.g., Torres (1977), 50, who argues that the lots were equal and proportionate to the numbers of barbarians involved—on what source he bases his population estimates is unclear.

78. Hyd. 60 refers to the *Alani, qui Vandalis et Sueuis potentabantur,* which probably just means that the Alans were more powerful than the Vandals and Sueves, not that they were ruling over them, as Burgess (1993), 87, translates the phrase.

79. Hyd. 41: *Spani per ciuitates et castella residui a plagis barbarorum per prouincias dominantium se subiciunt seruituti.*

80. This is the force carried by Salvian's famous lines about slavery and freedom under the barbarians (*De Gub.* 5.22): *malunt enim sub specie captivitatis vivere liberi quam sub specie libertatis esse captivi.*

81. See, e.g., Oost (1968), 109, who uses Hyd. 40–41 to describe the period *after* the deposition of Maximus, or García Moreno (1985), 32, where notices drawn from throughout the chronicle are taken to describe the situation of the 410s.

82. Prosper gives the consular date for this as *Honorio X et Theodosio VI,* i.e., 415. This must be correct despite Hydatius's placing the same events in 416, since the Paschal Chronicle (Bonn, 572) states that the news of Athaulf's death reached Constantinople on 24 September 415.

83. There are two anecdotes extant about Athaulf's murder—that a Gothic retainer called Dubius avenged Athaulf's earlier murder of his old master by killing the Gothic king (Olymp., frag. 26 [Müller] = 26.1 [Blockley]), and that a Goth called Everwulf murdered Athaulf because the king was in the habit of mocking his small stature (Jord., *Get.* 163 = MGH AA 5: 100). See Pampliega (1996–97).

84. Prosper 1257 (= MGH AA 9: 46): *regnumque eius* [i.e., *Athaulfi*] *Wallia peremptis qui idem cupere intellegebantur invasit.*

85. Olymp., frag. 31 (Müller) = 30 (Blockley).

86. Hyd. 52: *succedens Vallia in regno cum patritio Constantio pace mox facta Alanis et Vandalis Silingis in Lusitania et Betica sedentibus adversatur.*

87. According to Olymp., frag. 29 (Müller) = 29.1 (Blockley), the Vandals named the Goths *Truli* on this occasion because they bought grain at the rate of one *solidus* to the *trula.* Wolfram (1988), 26, regards *trulo* as an archaic term of derogation, equivalent to our *troll,* but Olympiodorus ought to be taken at his word, as by Heather (1991), 6 n. 5.

88. E.g., Schmidt (1933), 460; Seeck (1920), 59; Bury (1923), 1: 202; Stein (1959), 267; Oost (1968), 138; Gonzalbes (1981), 29–30; Orlandis (1987), 29; Wolfram (1989), 170. The assertion is colored by the notion

expressed by Seeck (1920), 64, in which Africa "solange für die Germanen das Ziel der heißesten Wünsche war," an idea echoed almost verbatim in Ripoll (2000), 375. Collins (1995), 19, appears to believe that the Visigothic attempt on Africa was made in 418 rather than 415.

89. Isidore, *HG* 22, is not an independent witness, being wholly derived from Orosius. His statement that Wallia himself attempted the crossing to Africa is only a misunderstanding of his source.

90. Oros., *Hist.* 7.43.11–12: *hic* [sc. *Vallia*] *igitur—territus maxime iudicio Dei, quia cum magna superiore abhinc anno Gothorum manus instructa armis navigiisque transire in Africam moliretur, in duodecim milibus passuum Gaditani freti tempestate correpta, miserabili exitu perierat, memor etiam illius acceptae sub Alarico cladis, cum in Siciliam Gothi transire conati, in conspectu suorum miserabiliter arrepti et demersi sunt—pacem optimam cum Honorio imperatore, datis lectissimis obsidibus pepigit.*

91. Hyd. 52, 55, 59–61; Oros., *Hist.* 7. 43.13–14; *Chron. Gall. 511* 33 [562], 35–36 [564–65] (= Burgess [2001b], 96); Sid. Ap., *Carm.* 2.362–65.

92. It is to this period, specifically late in 416, that one should date the difficulties experienced by Orosius in getting to Gallaecia. See Severus of Minorca, *Ep.* 4.1: *Qui* [sc. *Orosius*] *postquam transvehi ad Hispanias, sicut desiderabat, nequivit, remeare denuo ad Africam statuit.* The date is established in Bradbury (1996), 25.

93. Oros., *Hist.* 7.43.15: *itaque nunc cottidie apud Hispanias geri bella gentium et agi strages ex alterutro barbarorum crebris certisque nuntiis discimus, praecipue Valliam Gothorum regem insistere patrandae paci ferunt.*

94. One point on which Orosius is not in the least bit ambiguous has nevertheless frequently been misinterpreted. One often reads that the Alans, Vandals, and Sueves against whom Wallia was sent were themselves bound by treaties to Rome (e.g., Díaz Martínez [1993], 318). But what Oros., *Hist.* 7.43.10–14, actually says is *Deinde Vallia . . . pacem optimam cum Honorio imperatore, datis lectissimis obsidibus pepigit . . . Romanae securitati periculum suum obtulit, ut aduersus ceteras gentes, quae in Hispanias consedissent, sibi pugnaret et Romanis uinceret. quamuis et ceteri Alanorum Vandalorum Sueborumque reges eodem nobiscum placito depecti forent mandantes imperatori Honorio.* This can only mean that the Alans, Vandals, and Sueves had hoped to obtain a treaty with the empire and instead found themselves confronted by a Gothic army in the imperial service.

95. Hyd. 52: *Vallia . . . Alanis et Vandalis Silingis in Lusitania et Betica sedentibus aduersatur.* There is not the slightest evidence that Wallia fought in the capacity of *magister militum,* as suggested by Seeck (1920), 62.

96. Hyd. 55: *Vallia rex Gothorum Romani nominis causa intra Hispanias caedes magnas efficit barbarorum.* Ibid., 59: *Vandalis Silingi in Betica per Valliam regem omnes extincti.* Ibid., 60: *Alani, qui Vandalis et Sueuis potentabantur, adeo cesi sunt a Gothis ut extincto Addace rege ipsorum pauci qui superfuer-*

ant oblito regni nomine Gunderici regis Vandalorum, qui in Gallicia resederat, se patrocinio subiugarent. There is no way of telling in what sequence or locale these campaigns were fought, and there is no record of individual battles. One might deduce from the order of Hydatius's account that the Alans were the first object of the Gothic offensive. Since the Alans, as he says, were more powerful than the Vandals and Sueves, it would have been logical for the Goths to have dealt with them first. On the other hand, Hydatius records the defeat of the Silings before that of the Alans, so the matter cannot be resolved. The death of Addax is well attested but a reference to the capture and death of a Vandal king Fredbal found in the extant text of Hydatius is to be rejected as a late, and unfounded, interpolation: Burgess (1993), 55.

97. *Chron. Gall. 511* 36 [565] (= Burgess [2001b], 96): *Iubente Constantio intermisso bello, quod intra Galleciam supererat, reuersi Gothi ad Gallias sedes accipiunt a Tholosa in Burdegalam ad Oceanum uersus.* This entry can easily be derived from a conflation of Hyd. 60 (*Vandalorum, qui in Gallicia resederat, se patrocinio subiugarent*) and Hyd. 61 (see next note).

98. Hyd. 61: *Gothi intermisso certamine quod agebant per Constantiam ad Gallias reuocati sedes in Aquitanica ad Tolosa usque ad Oceanum acceperunt.* Prosper 1271 (= MGH AA 9: 469): *Constantius patricius pacem firmat cum Wallia data ei ad inhabitandum secunda Aquitanica et quibusdam civitatibus confinium provinciarum.*

99. Kulikowski (2001).

100. Advocates of the balance of power theory explain that the Goths could simply not be allowed to become as powerful as they would have done had they been permitted to complete the reconquest of Spain: Schmidt (1933), 461; Reinhart (1952), 37; Oost (1968), 153. Burns (1994), 270–71, suggests that the Asdings and Sueves were preserved as pools of manpower and recruits.

101. See Marquéz, Hidalgo, and Marfil (1991) and Hidalgo (1996).

102. This is Maurocellus, attested in 420: Hyd. 66, although the fact that we find him in command of troops casts some doubt on whether he can actually be a diocesan *vicarius*.

103. Or as Mann (1974) points out, the withdrawal of Roman government in such regions was not conceptualized as the cession of territory.

104. We are not, it should be stressed, considering the garrison units described in chapter 42 of the western *Notitia*. These units, all but one of which were stationed in Gallaecia, cannot possibly have survived the decade of usurpation and warfare after 407, and, as we saw in chapter 4, there is no way of knowing for certain whether they had even still existed in 395.

105. The barbarian bandits whom we meet in 419 in Aug., *Ep.* 11*.2.5 were almost certainly Goths and active in Tarraconensis.

106. Hyd. 63: *Inter Gundericum Vandalorum et Hermericum Sueuorum reges certamine orto Sueui in Erbasis montibus obsidentur ab Vandalis.* The site has not been identified, though Florez (1789), 218, was inclined to equate the Erbasian mountains with the Arvas, between León and Oviedo, a reasonable guess entirely beyond confirmation. Torres (1977), 61–62, has an extensive and inconclusive discussion. The name *Erbasus* is perhaps derived from the *Narbasoi* noted in Ptolemy 2.6.48, who have not themselves been localized with any certainty: Schulten (1936).

107. Hyd. 66: *Vandali Sueuorum obsidione dimissa instante Astirio Hispaniarum comite et sub uicario Maurocello aliquantis Braga in exitu suo occisis relicta Gallicia ad Beticam transierunt.* The language of Hydatius is more than usually opaque here. The narrative thrust of the passage suggests that it was Vandals who were killed at Braga, and this is the view of most commentators, among them Stein (1959), 269; Schmidt (1942), 26; and Bury (1923), 1: 208. The syntax, however, requires that the dead men be Romans under the command of Maurocellus. The obscurity would be alleviated by expunging the preposition *sub,* for then the text could indeed be taken to record a Vandal defeat, but the word is securely attested and I therefore adopt the translation given here. (Note that no rendering of the passage can make it refer to Vandals killing Sueves, as one finds in Reinhart [1952], 38, and García Moreno [1989], 50). *Pace* Villaverde (2001), 284–85, Maurocellus cannot be a Tingitanian official.

108. With variations, Bury (1923), 1: 204; Schmidt (1933), 110; (1942), 26; Stein (1959), 267–69; Jones (1964), 188; Stroheker (1972–74), 597; and O'Flynn (1983), 73, all see the campaign as a Roman attempt to protect the Sueves and thus preserve the balance of barbarian power in the peninsula.

109. Hyd. 66.

110. Greg. Tur., *Hist.* 2.9: *cum autem Asterius codicillis imperialibus patriciatum sortitus fuisset.* The notice must date from between Asterius's campaign in Baetica and the Spanish campaign of Castinus in 422.

111. Though the most complete account of this usurpation comes from the highly unreliable *Chron. galla. 452,* 85 (= Burgess [2001a], 76), on which see Muhlberger (1990), 146–51, it is confirmed by the much better testimony of the Ravenna Annals, s.a. 422 (= Bischoff and Koehler [1939]) and Marcellinus Comes, s.a. 422 (= MGH AA 11: 75).

112. Barbarian support for the usurpation is widely accepted, e.g., Seeck (1920), 63; Stein (1959), 269; Mayer (1993). For a demonstration of the chronology, see Kulikowski (2000a): the usurpation must have begun some time after 417, because when Orosius wrote Maximus was still in exile among the Spanish barbarians (Oros., *Hist.* 7.42.5), while the relative chronology of the Gallic chronicler, placing the usurpation in rela-

tion to a solar eclipse and subsequent comet, suggests the second half of 419: *Chron. Gall. a. 452, 77*–89 (= Burgess [2001a], 75–76).

113. Aug., *Ep.* 11*.4.3–12.2, for the date of which see Kulikowski (2000a).

114. Aug., *Ep.* 11*.7.3: *uir illustris Asterius comes cui tanti exercitus cura et tanti belli summa commissa est.* The proof comes in a comparison of this phrase with the wording of Oros., *Hist.* 7.42.1–3, on the suppression of Constantine III, of which Consentius's words are a direct echo. See Kulikowski (2000a). The only adequate treatment of this ecclesiastical conflict on which *Ep.* 11* centers is Van Dam (1986), but Kulikowski (2002) treats it in depth.

115. Hyd. 69: *Castinus magister militum cum magna manu et auxiliis Gothorum bellum in Betica Vandalis infert; quos cum ad inopiam ui obsidionis artaret adeo ut se tradere iam pararent, inconsulte publico certamine confligens auxiliorum fraude deceptus ad Terraconam uictus effugit.*

116. Prosper 1278 (= MGH AA 9: 469): *Hoc tempore exercitus ad Hispanias contra Wandalos missus est, cui Castinus dux fuit. qui Bonifatium virum bellicis artibus satis clarum inepto et iniuroso imperio ab expeditionis suae societate avertit. nam illo periculosum sibi atque indignum ratus eum sequi, quem discordem superbientemque expertus esset, celeriter se ad Portum urbis atque inde ad Africam proripuit.*

117. Elton (1996).

118. Hyd. 69: *quos* [sc. *Vandalos*] *cum ad inopiam ui obsidionis artaret adeo ut se tradere iam pararent, inconsulte certamine confligens auxiliorum fraude deceptus ad Terraconam uictus effugit,* which does not imply that the "contingent . . . des Visigoths passa aux Vandales pendant la bataille," as Stein (1959), 275, would have it.

Chapter 8. The End of Roman Spain

1. Prosper 1282 (= MGH AA 9: 470): *Honorius moritur et imperium eius Iohannes occupat conivente, ut putabatur, Castino, qui exercitui magister militum praeerat.*

2. Hyd. 77: *Vandali Baliaricas insulas depredantur quique Carthagine Spartaria et Spali euersa et Hispaniis depredatis Mauritaniam inuadunt.*

3. Ibid., 79: *Gundericus rex Vandalorum capta Ispali cum impie elatus manus in ecclesiam ciuitatis ipsius extendisset, mox dei iudicio demone correptus interiit; cui Gaisericus frater succedit in regno.*

4. The portrait of Gautier (1951) remains well worth reading.

5. *Chron. Gall. a. 452* 107 (= Burgess [2001a], 77): *XX ferme milia militum in Hispaniis contra Vandalos pugnantium caesa.* I suspect that this entry is actually a misdating of Castinus's defeat by Gunderic in 422.

6. Hyd. 80: *Gaisericus rex de Beticae prouinciae litore cum Vandalis omnibus eorumque familiis mense Maio ad Mauritaniam et Africam relictis transit Hispaniis.*

7. The figure is reported by Victor of Vita, *Hist.* 1.1.2, but see Goffart (1980), 231–34. For Iulia Traducta as the point of departure, Greg. Tur., *Hist.* 2.2.
8. E.g., Courtois (1955), 160–62; Bourgeois (1980), 216. Gonzalbes (1981), 30–32, would prefer their disembarkation at Ceuta.
9. The siege of Hippo is reported by Possidius, *Vita Augustini* 30. The epitaph from Altava (Marcillet-Jaubert [1968], 101–2 [no. 147]), which is often cited as evidence for the Vandal passage from Tingitania to Caesariensis, is inexplicit and its *barbari* are as likely to be local *Mauri* as anything else.
10. It. Ant. 9 (Cuntz, 2).
11. Hyd. 80: *qui* [sc. *Gaisericus*] *priusquam pertransiret, admonitus Heremigarium Sueuum uicinas in transitu suo prouincias depraedari, recursu cum aliquantis suis facto predantem in Lusitania consequitur; qui aud procul de Emerita . . . maledictis per Gaisericum caesis ex his quos secum habebat, arrepto, ut putauit, euro uelocius fugae subsidio in flumine Ana diuino brachio precipitatus interiit.*
12. Sid. Ap., *Carm.* 7.233–34; *Chron. Gall. a.* 452 106, 118 (= Burgess [2001a], 77–79); Hyd. 85, 88, 99, 102; Prosper 1322 (= MGH AA 9: 475). For the hegemony of Aëtius in general, Bury (1923), 1: 240–313; Stein (1959), 317–50.
13. Given this, the interpretative model of resistance and collaboration of, e.g., Courcelle (1964), Loyen (1963), or Thompson (1980), is particularly misleading in a history of the fifth-century West, as is the assumption that all Romans were necessarily closer to one another than any Romans were to the Goths, so that any Roman who helped the Goths was a collaborator; such interpretations are a legacy of the Second World War and misrepresent fifth-century conditions entirely.
14. It is usually possible to argue both sides according to taste in every instance, since the sources are so intrinsically ambiguous. The standard accounts of Wolfram (1988), 172–81, Thompson (1982b), 38–57, and Heather (1996), 181–215 fit the scanty evidence into their authors' larger theories of Gothic society and none of the three are especially reliable. For example, Hyd. 82 (*Per Aetium commitem aud procul de Arelate quaedam Gothorum manus extinguitur Anaolso optimate eorum capto*) is generally taken to refer to a Gothic chieftain acting quite independently of King Theoderic, though the inference is speculative. Similarly, Wolfram (1988), 175, supposes that Theoderic himself ordered the Gothic betrayal of Castinus in 422, though Hydatius breathes no word of it.
15. Arles, 425: Prosper 1290 (= MGH AA 9: 471) with Loyen (1943), 40. Arles, 430: Hyd. 82. Narbonne: Prosper 1324 (= MGH AA 9: 475); Sid. Ap. *Carm.* 7.246–47.
16. War: Prosper 1333, 1335 (= MGH AA 9: 476); Hyd. 108; Sid. Ap. *Carm.* 7.300–303, with Loyen (1943), 47–50. And peace: Prosper 1338 (=

MGH AA 9: 477); Hyd. 109; Sid. Ap. *Carm.* 7.308–9; *Chron. Gall. a. 452* 123 (= Burgess [2001a], 79).

17. Hyd. 81: *plebem qui castella tutiora retinebat.*
18. The panegyrical account by Torres (1977), 57–81, is exceptional, though no less distorted.
19. Hyd. 81, 86, 91.
20. Ibid., 105: *Sueui cum parte plebis Calleciae cui aduersabantur pacis iura confirmant.*
21. Ibid., 106: *Hermericus rex morbo oppressus Rechilam filium suum substituit in regnum; qui Andeuotum cum sua quam habebat manu ad Singillionem Beticae fluuium aperto marte prostrauit magnis eius auri et argenti opibus occupatis.*
22. See, e.g., García Moreno (1989), 56; Salvador (1998), 31; and *PLRE* 2: 86. García Moreno (1982), 230 n. 15, indulges in an unfettered flight of fancy on this point. Isidore, *HG* 85 (= MGH AA 11: 300), has *Andevotum Romanae militiae ducem.* This we may ignore, in favor of the evidence of Hyd. 106: when describing officials, Hydatius invariably gives their office, and when describing barbarians, he normally specifies Sueve, Vandal, or Goth, so we may suspect that Andevotus belonged to neither category and was therefore a Hispano-Roman of some importance.
23. Hyd. 111: *Rechila rex Sueuorum Emeritam ingreditur.*
24. Ibid., 113: *Censurius comes, qui legatus missus fuerat ad Suevos, residens Martyli obsessus a Rechila in pace se tradidit.*
25. His earlier contact with the Sueves is noted at ibid., 88 and 103, and he reappears in the year 449 (ibid., 131).
26. Ibid., 115: *Rex Rechila Hispali obtenta Beticam et Carthaginiensem prouincias in suam redigit potestatem.*
27. See Torres and Macias (1993) and chapter 5 in this book. An unusually large number of late antique Greek inscriptions are preserved at Mértola, suggestive of its important connections to the wider empire.
28. See p. 190, below.
29. All known sources for the Bacaudae are collected and translated in Sánchez León (1996a). The classic treatment of the Bacaudae is Thompson (1952), which retains its original value. For recent work treating Bacaudae as primarily a peasant phenomenon, Bravo (1983); (1984); (2000). For the alternative approach, Van Dam (1985), 9–56, and Okamura (1988). The history of the controversy is summarized at length in Sánchez León (1996b), which offers no new interpretations of its own.
30. The apt criticisms of Drinkwater (1989); (1992), with a firm grounding in the sources, are essential here.
31. Hyd. 117, 120, 133–34, 150. Whatever the merits of its arguments for Gaul, Van Dam (1985), 49–53, misstates both the course of events in, and the geography of, Spain. Drinkwater (1992), much more convincing

than Van Dam on fifth-century Bacaudae, is similarly inapplicable to Spain.

32. Hyd. 117, a. 441: *Asturius dux utriusque militie ad Hispanias missus Terraconensium caedit multitudinem Bacaudarum.* Ibid., 120, a. 443: [*Merobaudes*] *breui tempore potestatis suae Aracellitanorum frangit insolantiam Bacaudarum.* It is possible that Mer., *Pan.* 1, frag. 2A.23 contains a reference to this campaign: Clover (1971), 37–38. For the location of Araceli, Sayas (1985).

33. Hyd. 133–34.

34. Ibid., 126: *Vitus magister utriusque militiae factus ad Hispanias missus non exigue manus fultus auxilio, cum Carthaginienses uexaret et Beticos, succedentibus cum rege suo illic Sueuis, superatis etiam in congressione qui ei ad depredandum in adiutorium uenerant Gothis, territus miserabili timore diffugit.* The language of Hydatius requires us to see the Goths as a separate unit under his command.

35. Ibid., 40, but in general see MacMullen (1963), 77–98.

36. Hyd. 126: *Sueui exim ilas prouincias magnas depredatione subuertunt.*

37. Ibid., 131: *Per Agiulfum Spali Censurius iugulatur.* Despite the doubts of *PLRE* 2: 34, 39, the identification of this Agiulf with the Aioulfus who later accompanied Theoderic II on his Spanish campaign is very likely.

38. Hyd. 161: *Sueui Carthaginienses regiones quas Romanis rediderant depredantur.* Hydatius's language here is open to two contrasting interpretations and cannot be pressed too hard. It can, of course, mean that the Sueves attacked regions of Carthaginiensis that they had returned to the Romans at the same time as they retained other regions of Carthaginiensis for themselves. On the other hand, it may simply mean that the Sueves attacked those parts of Carthaginiensis that they had returned to the Romans, which were the only parts they had taken.

39. There is no reason to think that they were recognized by the imperial government. Ibid., 163 speaks of a *iurati foederis promissa,* which contrasts with his usual use of *pax* to describe agreements with the Sueves, but this is as likely to be elegant variation as it is to indicate an official treaty with the imperial government.

40. Ibid. 129.

41. Ibid.: *Rechila rex Emerita gentilis moritur mense Augusto; cui mox filius suus catholicus Rechiarius succedit in regnum . . . Obtento tamen regno sine mora ulteriores regiones inuadit ad predam.* Burgess (1993), 99, translates *ulteriores regiones* as "farthest reaches [of Gallaecia]." This reading equates the regions assaulted by Rechiar with the *sitam in extremitate Oceani maris occidua* mentioned in Hydatius's account of the initial provincial division in 411. This is probably not correct, since it is hard to understand why Rechiar should need to assault the one region of the peninsula that had been firmly under Suevic control since the initial conquest. Everything

hinges on how one reads *ulterior,* which, if a provincial designation, could mean Gallaecia or Lusitania, or, if merely a descriptive adjective, should mean far away from Mérida, and therefore Carthaginiensis or Tarraconensis. One cannot tell.

42. *MEC* 1: 77–80.
43. Drinkwater (1994).
44. *MEC* 1: 1–80; *RIC* 10: 450–70.
45. Hyd. 132: *Rechiarius accepta in coniugem Theodori regis filia auspicatus initio regni Vasconias depredatur mense Februario.*
46. Gillett (1995).
47. Hyd. 133: *Basilius ob testimonium egregii ausus sui congregatis Bacaudis in ecclesia Tyriassone foederatos occidit.* Tarazona is not one of the better known towns of Roman Spain and most of the evidence we have for urban life there comes from the third century: see Mora (1981), 61, and Bona and Nuñez (1985).
48. Hyd. 134: *Rechiarius mense Iulio ad Theodorem socerum profectus Caesaraugustanum regionem cum Basilio in reditu depredatur.*
49. Ibid.: *Inrupta per dolum Elerdensi urbe acta est non parua captiuitas,* which supplies no clear agent for the attack.
50. This is the logical inference from ibid., 147, a. 452/3: *Ad Sueuos Mansuetus comes Hispaniarum et Fronto similiter comes legati pro pace mittuntur et optinent conditiones iniunctas.* If peace had been broken and reimposed, this presupposes recent Suevic aggression, certainly between 449 and 451, and most plausibly in 451 given the concentration of imperial forces on the threat posed by Attila.
51. Ibid., 150: *Per Fredericum Theuderici regis fratrem Baucaude Terraconenses caeduntur ex auctoritate Romana.*
52. For dates and attestations, Burgess (1987). On the reign, Harries (1994), 54–81, and Stevens (1933), 19–35.
53. The career of Avitus is largely to be reconstructed on the basis of Sid. Ap., *Carm.* 7.
54. *CLRE* 447. But he was never recognized by the eastern emperor Marcian.
55. Hyd. 163: *omni iurationi uiolata Suaeui Terraconensem prouinciam, quae Romano imperio deseruiebat, inuadunt.* Avitus's reign had been inaugurated by the usual diplomatic exchanges with the Suevic king, and Hyd. 165 records a second Gothic embassy and a second Suevic attack on Tarraconensis before Avitus and Theoderic were actually persuaded to attack Rechiar: *Legati Gothorum rursum ueniunt ad Sueuos; post quorum aduentum rex Sueuorum Rechiarius cum magna suorum multitudine regiones prouintiae Terraconensis inuadit.*
56. The Burgundian contingent is attested at Jordanes, *Get.* 231, and Hyd. 179 speaks of a *multitudine variae nationis* accompanying the Gothic king. However, Gundioc was already back in Gaul at the time of Avitus's death,

and I am not convinced that either Burgundian king actually crossed the Pyrenees with Theoderic.

57. Hyd. 166: *Mox Hispanias rex Gothorum Theodoricus cum ingenti exercitio suo et cum uoluntate et ordinatione Auiti imperatoris ingreditur; cui cum multitudine Sueuorum rex Richiarius occurens duodecimo de Asturecensi urbe miliario ad fluuium nomine Vrbicum III non. Octubris, die VI feria, inito mox certamine superatur. Caesis suorum agminibus, aliquantis captis plurimisque fugatis ipse ad extremas sedes Gallaciae plagatus uix euadit ac profugus.*

58. Ibid., 167: *Theuderico rege cum exercito ad Bracaram extremam ciuitatem Galleciae pertendente V kal. Nouembris, die domenico, etsi incruenta, fit tamen satis maesta et lacrimabilis eiusdem direptio ciuitatis.*

59. Ibid., 168: *Rechiarius ad locum qui Portum Cale appellatur profugus regi Theuderico captiuus adducitur.* Ibid., 171: *Occiso Rechiario mense Decembri.*

60. Ibid., 168.

61. Ibid., 171: *Occiso Rechiario mense Decembri rex Theodoricus de Gallacia ad Lusitaniam succedit.* Burgess (1993), 109, distorts the sense of the passage when he translates *succedit* as "withdrew."

62. Hyd. 175: *Teudericus Emeritam depredari moliens beatae Eulaliae martyris terretur ostentis.*

63. Ibid., 172: *In conuentus Bracarensis latrocinantum depredatio perpetratur.* The Sueves who remained *in extrema parte Galleciae* set up one Maldras as their king (ibid., 174), but as events would show, he had none of the unchallenged authority possessed by Rechiar and his royal predecessors.

64. See Burgess (1987); *contra*, Mathisen (1985); (1991).

65. Hyd. 179: *Theudoricus aduersis sibi nuntiis territus mox post dies paschae, quod fuit II kal. Aprilis, de Emerita egreditur et Gallias repetens partem ex ea quam habebat multitudine uariae nationis cum ducibus suis ad campos Galleciae dirigit; qui dolis et periuriis instructi, sicut eis fuerat imperatum, Asturicam, quam iam praedones ipsius sub specie Romanae ordinationis intrauerant, mentientes ad Sueuos qui remanserant iussam sibi expeditionem, ingrediuntur pace fucata solita arte perfidiae . . . Palentina ciuitas simili quo Asturica per Gothos perit exitio. Vnum Couiacense castrum tricesimo de Asturica miliario a Gothis diutino certamine fatigatum auxilio de hostibus et obsistit et praevalet.*

66. Modern scholars are accustomed to see this Gothic action in Gallaecia as exceptionally brutal, but the violence of soldiers toward civilians was neither novel nor peculiar to the Goths because of their barbarism. Throughout the history of the empire Roman garrisons had imposed just as violently on the provincials on whom they were quartered: see MacMullen (1966), 194–97, and idem (1963), 77–98.

67. Sid. Ap., *Carm.* 23.71.

68. Hyd. 185: *Gothicus exercitus <cum> duce suo Cyrila a Theodorico ad Hispanias missus mense Iulio succedit ad Beticam.* Ibid., 187: *Sabinus episcopus Ispalensis, post annos XX quam certauerat expulsus, de Galliis ad propriam redit ecclesiam.*

69. Auct. Prosp. 455.8 (= MGH AA 9: 492).
70. Harries (1994), 82–102, is very good on the sensitivity needed to build a lasting political coalition in the later fifth century.
71. Hyd. 192, s.a. 459: *Legati a Nepotiano magistro militiae et a Sunerico comite misi ueniunt ad Galletios nuntiantes Maiorianum Augustum et Theudoricum regem firmissima inter se pacis iura sanxisse Gothis in quodam certamine superatis.* This campaign was probably won by Aegidius and corresponds to that mentioned by Paulinus of Perigueux, *VMart.* 6.111–12. See Loyen (1943), 82.
72. Nepotianus was probably a Roman general who transferred his allegiance to Theoderic only after Majorian was killed, refusing to recognize his successor as did many other Roman commanders at the time. Hyd. 192 leaves open the possibility that Nepotianus was one of Majorian's generals; ibid., 196 shows Suniericus and Nepotianus as joint commanders of a Gothic army (*Pars Gothici exercitus a Sunierico et Nepotiano comitibus ad Galleciam directa*), while Nepotianus was eventually relieved of his post on Theoderic's orders (ibid., 208: *Nepotianus Theuderico ordinante Arborium accipit successorum*). For a different view on Nepotianus, see Burgess (1992), 25.
73. *Chron Gall. a. 511* 71 (= Burgess [2001b], 98); Mar. Avent., s.a. 460 (= Favrod [1993], 64). Both Gallic sources believe Illici to be very near to Carthago Nova, and this has misled some commentators into thinking that the fleet was mustered in the port of the latter city. However, Portus Illicitanus is archaeologically attested as a major port into the later empire: see Sánchez, Blasco, and Guardiola (1986).
74. *Cons. Caes.* 23a (= CCSL 173A: 10).
75. Hyd. 195: *Mense Maio Maiorianus Hispanias ingreditur imperator; quo Carthaginiensem prouinciam pertendente aliquantas naues, quas sibi ad transitum aduersum Vandalos praeparabat, de litore Carthaginiensi commoniti Vandali per proditores abripiunt. Maiorianus ita a sua ordinatione frustratus ad Italiam reuertitur.* There is a universal tendency to extend the emperor's march all the way to Cádiz, based ultimately on Procopius, but Hydatius's *Carthaginiensem . . . pertendente* implies that he never got beyond Tarraconensis and Procopius's account at *Bell.* 3.7.4–14 is fantasy, start to finish.
76. See Mendes Pinto (1999) for the problem; Marot (1999a) for some of the ways local communities might deal with the failure of the coin supply.
77. See Gillett (2003).
78. Between 429 and 460, Hydatius devotes a full 10 percent of his entries to the record of embassies, Hyd. 88, 92, 103, 147, 153, 163, 165, 170, 186, 192. Hydatius went to Aëtius in 432, ibid., 88: *Censorius comes legatus mittitur ad Sueuos supradictu secum Ydatio redeunte.*
79. Orlandis (1987), 33–46; García Moreno (1989), 49–67. This pessimism about imperial capabilities is also evident in Harries (1994), 24–25.

80. See Millar (1977), 363–463.
81. These issues are discussed with great authority by Gillett (2003), chapter 2, though he starts from the assumption, not accepted here, that the arrival of the Sueves, Goths, or other barbarians automatically meant the end of imperial authority in a region.
82. A glance at the fasti in *PLRE* 2: 1274–80 will make this clear.
83. The last is the *vicarius* Maurocellus (Hyd. 66).
84. Asturius: Hyd. 117 (*dux*), 120 (*magister*); Merobaudes: ibid., 120; Vitus: ibid., 126; Censurius: ibid., 88, 91, 103, 113, 131; Mansuetus: ibid., 147; Fronto: ibid., 147, 163.
85. TED'A (1989a), with pp. 113–14, above.
86. This was remarked long ago by Sundwall (1915), but is best treated in Stroheker (1948), 43–83, with Matthews (1975), 329–51.
87. Aug., *Ep.* 11*.4.3: *post autem cum adversum me Severus illustris atque praecelsi vir, affinis sui, Asterii comitis viribus niteretur, id egit, ut mulier memorata [sc. Severa] ad neptis suae Asterii comitis filiae, potentissimae feminae auxilium convolaret.*
88. Ibid., 11*.11.8: *Severi autem et ceterorum fidem, quamvis aliqua mihi consanguinitate iungantur, tamen certum est fidei meae obesse non posse.*
89. Asturius: Hyd. 117, 120, with *PLRE* 2: 174–75 (Astyrius).
90. *PLRE* 1 lists four genuine Asterii, *PLRE* 2, twelve, and *PLRE* 3, a mere three.
91. Sid. Ap., *Carm.* 9.297; Hyd. 120; with *PLRE* 2: 756–58, and Salvador (1998), 89–91. See also Clover (1971), 8, who maintains that Merobaudes was not a Spaniard by birth.
92. For the *comitiva*, CIL 6: 1724. On the problem of his patriciate, Barnes (1975) with Cameron (1976) on honorary consulates.
93. Hyd. 120: *Mox nonnulorum inuidia perurgente ad urbem Romam sacra preceptione reuocatur.*
94. Sid., *Carm.* 15.155–57: *ille magister / per Tartesiacas conspectus splenduit urbes / et quibus ingestae sub temporae praefecturae / conspicuus sanctas reddit se praesule leges.* *PLRE* 2: 700 (Magnus 2) suggests that this was the *magisterium officiorum* but the only time a palatine official such as the *magister officiorum* could have been in Spain was during the brief journey of Majorian there, a journey that did not, of course, make it as far as Baetica.
95. Mateos (1999), 142 = *CICM* 37: *Gregorius vir inlustris famulus dei vixit lvi menses v requievit in pace die xvi kalendas nobembre era dxxx.*

Chapter 9. The Aftermath of Empire

1. As it is in all the multivolume histories of Spain, e.g., Orlandis (1987). A short but excellent exception is Salvador (2000b).
2. The evidence is Hyd. 196, which shows that Suniericus and Nepotianus were based outside Gallaecia.

3. Ibid., 207, 208, 226.
4. Ibid., 218.
5. Ibid., 226.
6. Ibid., 201: *Suniericus Scallauim, cui aduersabatur, optinet ciuitatem.*
7. Ibid., 222, s.a. 464/5: *Legatos Remismundus mittit ad Theudoricum, qui similiter suos ad Remismundum remittit, cum armorum adiectione uel munerum directa et coniunge quam haberet.*
8. Ibid., 244: *Gothi circa conuentum pari hostilitate deseuiunt; partes etiam Lusitaniae depraedantur.* Though here is one of those instances wherein *Gothi* may mean "some Goths" rather than "the Goths."
9. Both Thompson (1982b), 161–87, and García Moreno (1989), 68–73, are sensible transcriptions of Hydatius.
10. The post-Majorianic entries are 196–247, occupying five pages in the Burgess edition.
11. Torres (1977); Thompson (1982b), 166–68.
12. Hyd. 219 for the accession of Remismund. Ibid., 225, 227, 236, 237, 240 all fall into the pattern of more or less random local violence without reference to the Suevic king that characterizes the years before Remismund became the sole bearer of the royal title. By contrast, the hostilities between the Sueves and the people of Aunona appear to have been directed by Remismund: ibid., 229, 235, 243.
13. Respectively, Hyd. 215, 225, 240.
14. Ibid., 196.
15. E.g., Andevotus at ibid., 106.
16. The struggles over Lugo and Scallabis are shown at ibid., 194, 196, 201, 215. Of the other cities that appear in Hydatius's narrative, only Conimbriga is fought over as fiercely as the two conventual capitals.
17. Ibid., 194: the Sueves kill some Romans *cum rectore suo honesto natu.*
18. *Pace* Thompson (1982b), 171.
19. Hyd. 194.
20. Ibid., 196.
21. Ibid., 240. Burgess (1993), 121, is wrong to take *qui illic preerat* to mean that Lusidius was "governor of the city." The phrase merely implies his prominence, for when Hydatius wanted to talk of a city's governor he used the word *rector* (e.g., Hyd. 194).
22. Ibid., 245.
23. Ibid., 225.
24. The sacking of Conimbriga, in 466 or 467, allows even less opportunity for explanation: ibid., 237. In explaining such conflicts, however, local disputes now obscure to us are surely more plausible than the mere stupidity of the Roman inhabitants, which is sometimes adduced, e.g., by Thompson (1982b), 171.
25. Hyd. 229, 243.

26. Ibid., 194.
27. Ibid., 196, 201.
28. Ibid., 179.
29. The internal evidence of Hydatius does not show what, e.g., Thompson (1982b), 188–90, claims it does. Generations of Gothic leaders had to fight to impose their control over different chunks of the southern peninsula, which rather undermines the notion of an effective Gothic occupation of Baetica from 458 to "the arrival of the Moors in 711, some two and a half centuries later."
30. See, respectively, Hyd. 215–16, 233, 235. Opilio had been sent to Spain by Euric, who succeeded his elder brother in 467, as shown by Gillett (1999).
31. This, however, may reflect Hydatius's anti-Suevic bias as much as the truth of the matter.
32. P. 182, above.
33. Hyd. 240.
34. I.e., the letter addressed by Pope Hilarus to the *honorati* and *possessores* of Tarraconensis in 465: Hil., *Ep.* 16 (Thiel) = PL 58: 17, on which see p. 47, above.
35. For this date over the traditional 466, see the arguments of Gillett (1999). The murder is attested in Hyd. 233–34; *Chron. Gall. a. 511* 74 (= Burgess [2001b], 98); Mar. Avent., s.a. 467.
36. *Chron. Gall. a 511* 76 (= Burgess [2001b], 99); with Gillett (1999), 26 n. 86. Euric's defeat of Riothamus, king of the Bretons, which is sometimes seen as belonging to the same policy of aggression, is likewise undateable. The *terminus post quem* is Sidonius's election as bishop in 469/470, because Sidonius's *Ep.* 3.9, written when Riothamus was still king, was composed before the episcopal election.
37. The argument of Gillett (1999), 36–38, for a Spanish origin is refuted by Burgess (2001a).
38. *Chron. Gall. a. 511* 78–79 (= Burgess [2001b], 99): *XVI. Gauterit comes Gothorum Ispanias per Papilonem Cesaraugustam et uicinas urbes obtinuit. Heldefredus quoque cum Vincencio Ispaniarum duce obsessa Terrachona marithimas urbes obtinuit.*
39. I.e., his reckoning of the regnal years for Leo's reign begins correctly from the equivalent of A.D. 457 and introduces no observable error thereafter.
40. CIL 2: 4109 = *RIT* 100.
41. *ICERV* 363 = *CICM* 10: *solberat antiquas moles ruinosa vetustas / lapsum et senio ruptum pendebat opus. / perdiderat usum suspensa uia per amnem. / et liberum pontis casus negabat iter. / nunc tempore potentis Getarum Ervigii (recte Euricii) regis, / quo deditas sibi precepit excoli terras, / studuit magnanimus factis extendere nomen, / veterum et titulis addit Salla suum / nam postquam eximiis novabit moenibus urbem, / hoc magis miraculum patrare*

non destitit. / construxit arcos, penitus fundabit in undis / et mirum auctoris imitans vicit opus. / nec non et patrie tantum creare munimen / sumi sacerdotis Zenonis suasit amor. / urbs Augusta felix mansura per scla. longa / novate studio ducis et pontificis. / era dxxi. The inscription is not extant and is known only from a corrupt eighth-century manuscript, but Vives (1938) proves that the original belonged to the fifth-century reign of Euric, and not the seventh-century reign of Ervig.

42. Hyd. 233: *Per Theodoricum Salla legatus mittitur ad Remismundum regem Sueuorum; qui reuersus ad Gallias eum a fratre suo Euerico repperit interfectum.*

43. The assertion of König (1980), 223, that there was an established *ducatus Emeritense,* has no foundation in the sources.

44. Named the *Chronicon Caesaraugustanae* by Mommsen and printed at MGH AA 11: 221–23, this "chronicle" has regularly been associated with the *historiola* of Maximus of Zaragoza known from Isid., *DVI* 33, though as Collins (1994) shows, the identification is impossible on grounds of genre and content. The text is a series of annotations to a compilation of chronicles consisting of Prosper's abridged Eusebius–Jerome with the continuations of Prosper, Victor of Tunnuna, and John of Biclar. The annotations survived to modern times in two late sixteenth-century manuscripts, both copies of a single original. One of these is still extant as MS Escorial & IV 23, while the other was destroyed during the Spanish Civil War. These annotations were clearly made in Tarraconensis, though the assignment to Zaragoza is extrapolation from the erroneous identification of the annotations with Maximus's *historiola.* The new edition in CCSL 173A prints the annotations where they belong, alongside the text of Victor, and accepts their derivation from a single, or perhaps two, *consularia.*

45. *Chron. Gall. a. 511* 83 (= Burgess [2001b], 99): *VII. Mortuus est Eorichus Arelate et ordinatur filius suus Alaricus Tholosa.*

46. *Cons. Caes.* 71a (= CCSL 173A: 22): *His consulibus Goti in Hispanias ingressi sunt.*

47. *Cons. Caes.* 74a (= CCSL 173A: 23): *His consulibus, Burdunelus in Hispania tyranidem assumit.*

48. *Cons. Caes.* 75a (= CCSL 173A: 23): *His consulibus, Gotthi intra Hispanias sedes acceperunt et Burdunelus a suis traditus et Tolosam directus in tauro aeneo impositus igne crematus est.*

49. *Cons. Caes.* 85a (= CCSL 173A: 27): *His consulibus, Caesaraugustae circus expectatus est.*

50. *Cons. Caes.* 87a (= CCSL 173A: 27): *His consulibus, Dertosa a Gotthis ingressa est. Petrus tyrannus interfectus est et caput eius Caesaraugustam deportatum est.*

51. It is very difficult to derive *anno domini* dates from the *Consularia;* certainly those given by Mommsen in his edition are no more than guess-

work, however often they may be quoted as established fact. The difficulty, however, is intrinsic to the source. We may presume that the extant *Consularia* survives in more or less its original form, as a series of marginal annotations keyed to the consular years of Victor of Tunnuna, beginning with the year 450, and to the first regnal year of John's chronicle. Victor's focus was almost exclusively eastern and African, and the Spanish annotator thus supplemented Victor's entries with material more interesting to a western, Spanish audience. Where he could, for the years 462 and 463, he tried to supply gaps in Victor's consular fasti, though he did not realize that Victor omitted eight years entirely (445, 452, 472, 478, 481, 493, 503, 547). With few exceptions, our annotator's sources are unknown. For a brief period covering the years between 460 and 463, he had available to him an accurate source for western affairs that used a consular chronology: the annotations on Majorian and the consuls for 462 and 463 are supplied correctly. Elsewhere, the annotator clearly lacked any source that he could correlate reliably with the chronologies of Victor and John: where he can be checked, he is inevitably wrong. This problem is exacerbated by deficiencies in the chronological schemata of Victor and John themselves. Victor omits eight years from his chronology, while because John began his chronicle after Justinian's indefinite suspension of the consulate, it has never been possible to determine with certainty with what year A.D. he wanted his imperial and royal regnal chronologies to begin. Now, where the defective chronologies of our sources are sytematic, it is possible to correct them. In the present case, there is no way to derive a system from the errors in the *Consularia*. The effect of this for the modern historian is limiting: where the annotator can be checked, he is almost without exception wrong. There is no reason to think him more reliable where he cannot be checked. The *Consularia* therefore requires a minimalist approach: where its information is unique and cannot be checked against more reliable external evidence, it can be used only according to the internal relative chronology rather than tied to an absolute chronology derived from other, more reliable, sources.

52. The work that established the "Gothic" identity of these cemeteries was Zeiss (1934). The connection between the cemeteries and the *Consularia Caesaraugustana* was made by Abadal (1960) and remains an article of faith for the most recent student of the Meseta cemeteries, Ripoll (1998a); (1998b).

53. The fundamental arguments are those of Brather (2000); (2002), but in general see pp. 266–71, below.

54. Dertosa, the strategic point at which the Ebro leaves the prelittoral mountain chain for the coastal plain, may well have been one of the *maritimas urbes* that Euric's generals seized in 473.

55. Arce (2001b).

56. *Cons. Caes.* 70a (= CCSL 173A: 22): *Hoc consule Odoacrus tyrannus a Theoderico rege interfectus est;* ibid., 144a (= CCSL 173A: 47): *Agilane mortuo Athanagildus, qui dudum tyranidem assumpserat, Gotthorum rex efficitur.* On the general usage, see Neri (1997).

57. For instance, the Moorish *dux* who made himself emperor some time during the fifth century: *AE* 1945: 97. For Gaul, see Fanning (1992).

58. It is unclear why Escribano and Fatás (2001), 126–28, present Burdunelus as a rebellious Gothic chief and Petrus as Roman aristocrat.

59. The linking of the *Gotthi . . . sedes acceperunt* and the *Burdunelus a suis traditus* with an *et* should suggest a meaningful connection between the two events.

60. Although the annotator places the Gothic capture of Dertosa and the death of Petrus in the same year, he does not link the two notices grammatically as he does in the notice of Burdunelus's death and the Gothic garrisons.

61. Vives (1938) and p. 205, above.

62. Alba (1998).

63. *Contra,* Mateos (1999); (2000), 505.

64. Barrientos (2001) appears to show work near the exterior base of the wall in the northeastern corner of the circuit, at the modern c/ Concordia.

65. Alba (1998); (1999).

66. Alba (1998).

67. Alba (1999).

68. Sánchez Sánchez (1997); Palma (2000).

69. E.g., Barrientos (2000b).

70. For the destruction at Eulalia's shrine, Mateos (1999); the evidence for Sta. Catalina is frequently asserted, but has not been published extensively enough to be checked, though see Montalvo (1999). Sánchez Sánchez (2001) on the burials in the c/ Travesía Marquesa de Pinares follows Mateos in attributing damage to the funerary zone to Suevic sack, while admitting that the archaeological evidence offers no proof.

71. *Contra,* Palma (1999b).

72. Fuentes Domínguez (1997b), esp. 488, is rare in recognizing as much and saying so explicitly.

Chapter 10. The Impact of Christianity in the Fifth Century

1. There is a good overview of scholarly approaches to early Spanish Christianity in Teja (2000). Jorge (2002), 87–91, illustrates the accumulation of legends around fictional early bishops from Lusitania.

2. Cyp., *Ep.* 67. For discussion, Teja (1990).

3. As proved by Clarke (1971).

4. Cyp., *Ep.* 67 does not explicitly state that Felix replaced Martialis, but the paralellism with Sabinus and Basilides makes it almost certain that this was in fact the case.

5. The letter of the synod is addressed to the priest Felix and the *plebes* of León and Astorga, and to the deacon Aelian and the *plebs* of Mérida. The fact that the appellant bishops Felix and Sabinus are not themselves the addressees of the letter, and that at *Ep.* 67.6 the verb *asserere* is used of the appeal of Felix and Sabinus in contrast to the *scribere* used of the appeal of the addressees, suggests the physical presence of the two bishops at Carthage.

6. Such speculation depends not on the nonexistent evidence, but rather on one's position in the great debate over the scale and chronology of Christian conversion in the Roman empire. The fundamental question is whether Constantine, the first imperial convert, was part of a very wide body of Christians so that, by converting, he merely recognized a historical inevitability, or whether, by contrast, Constantine was a revolutionary who created a pattern of conversion that might not have existed without him. The first option is the view of Barnes (1981) and argued in many of the author's other works. The second, more traditional, view is restated by the important critique of Cameron (1983), pursued, with more than one factual error, in Cameron (1993). The positive evidence for a very slow move to a generalized Christian society is presented in Lane Fox (1986) and MacMullen (1984). The observations on the function of Christian epigraphy in Galvao-Sobrinho (1995) are valuable, but our sample is too faulty for the distribution of epitaphs to serve as a marker of Christianization.

7. The similarities are mostly those of liturgical and funerary architecture, e.g., the use of sigma-shaped *mensae* at Cartagena: Berrocal and Laiz (1995), but note also other small points like the citation in the sixth Priscillianist tractate of Luke 20.34–36 in the form also cited by Cyprian (on which see Chadwick [1976], 213).

8. See in general Castillo Maldonado (1999); Gurt et al. (1994), 169–71.

9. *Peristeph.* 4; other attestations, all seventh-century save for Greg. Tur., *Glor. Mart.* 91, are summarized in Castillo Maldonado (1999), 520.

10. Inn. I, *Ep.* 3 (= PL 20: 485–93), responding to the decisions of the first council of Toledo.

11. The key study is Franchi dei Cavalieri (1959).

12. Aemillianus asked Fructuosus whether he was aware of the emperor's orders to sacrifice and when the bishop said that because he was a Christian he did not know the emperor's orders, Aemillianus gave him every chance to comply, explaining that if the gods are not worshiped then the emperors are not respected. Aemillianus also failed to shift the deacon Augurius and finally gave up. His final exchange with Fructuosus has a

real ghoulish wit: Aemilianus: *Episcopus es?* Fructuosus: *Sum.* Aemilianus: *Fuisti* (Musurillo [1972], 176–85).

13. See Lanata (1972); García Gallo (1983).

14. Elvira 23, with Lomas (1993).

15. Cyp., *Ep.* 67.6.

16. Pastor Muñoz (1988). Third-century imperial cult is attested by inscriptions to Gordian III (*ILPG* 32) and Probus (*ILPG* 33).

17. A suggestion cautiously endorsed in Sotomayor (1994), 545.

18. Pac., *De paen.* 5.2.

19. Ibid., 1.2.

20. Ibid., 8.1.

21. Jerome, *DVI* 106.

22. Serra-Vilaró (1948) summarizes the findings of his excavations.

23. del Amo (1979–89) reminds us of how much the early excavations destroyed; Carreté et al. (1999) is more charitable.

24. del Amo (1979–89).

25. Particularly in a hitherto undisturbed portion of the cemetery that lay under the modern Parc de la Ciutat: TED'A (1987); see now also Bea and Vilaseca (2000); García Noguera and Remolà (2000) for further portions of the city's enormous funerary zone.

26. TED'A (1987), 125.

27. Serra-Vilaró (1948), 35.

28. del Amo (1979), 281–84, for the revision of Serra-Vilaró's too early dating. Third-century gravestones that seem to display Christian iconography of loaves and fishes may belong to the basilical site, but their precise provenance within the cemetery is unknown. The earliest Christian inscription found *in situ* (*ICERV* 189 = *RIT* 944) dates only from 393, at which date the area of the basilica had been used for burials for many decades.

29. For this extremely important site we must rely on the preliminary reports of Mar, Roca, and Ruiz (1996) and López i Vilar (1997); (2000).

30. There is disagreement among the excavators on this point: Mar, Roca, and Ruiz (1996) would see this complex as an extension of the first Christian cult site of Tarragona. López i Vilar (1997) rejects any direct connection.

31. López i Vilar (1997) speculates that the *beata Thecla* whose inscription was found at the site may have been its dedicatee, but that is to make too much of too little evidence.

32. There is a reference to the monastery of the monk Fronto in Tarragona in Aug., *Ep.* 11* and the epigraphic testimony of *ICERV* 278 = *RIT* 939, in which the mid-sixth-century bishop Sergius dedicated a second extramural monastery, a fact that presupposes the existence of an earlier one.

33. Aquilué (1993), 97–107.
34. Hauschild (1994a).
35. The phrase comes from Prud., *Peristeph.* 4.22.
36. Not that the population was entirely Christian: even as late as the early fifth century, a somewhat unusual headstone from the city's eastern cemetery uses a series of phrases—*mater infelicissima, dis manibus*—which had gone out of general use many decades earlier to be replaced by more thoroughly Christian formulas. At the time of its inscription, a headstone of this sort can only have been a very public affirmation of paganism: Alföldy (1992). A similarly late pagan inscription from Segovia, Hoyo (1998), is regarded as a forgery in *HEp.* 8: 389.
37. Cypr., *Ep.* 67.
38. One must, of course, remember that signs of earlier burials—particularly incineration burials—may either have been missed in older excavations or may still await discovery.
39. It seems that a new, Christian cemetery developed to the west of the circus at Toledo during the fourth century, where the city's Vega Baja has produced a great many uncontextualized Christian finds, in contrast to the old necropolis of the city that lay to the east of the circus: see Rojas and Villa (1996) and Carrobles (1999).
40. Fine, large color photographs appear in Escribano and Fatás (2001), 91–108.
41. The most recent study is Mostalac (1994).
42. P. 125, above.
43. *Peristeph.* 4 is dedicated to the eighteen martyrs, *Peristeph.* 5 to Vincent. *Peristeph.* 5.505–12 locates the resting place of Vincentius on the coast, presumably at Valencia, the site of his martyrdom.
44. Ibid., 4.105–8.
45. Ibid., 4.93–96 would seem to show that Zaragoza possessed no relics of Vincentius's body, and so had to worship a spot at which, according to legend, he had suffered a nosebleed before his martyrdom. By the 540s, Gregory of Tours attests to the cult of Vincent at Zaragoza, where the townpeople now believed themselves to possess the saint's tunic (*Hist.* 3.29), while by the seventh century, a church of Saint Vincent is attested by the poems (Eug., *Carm.* 10) of the seventh-century bishop of Toledo, Eugenius, himself a native of Zaragoza. For the date of Prudentius's Spanish hymns, Lana (1962), 42–43.
46. The earliest layer of the Vincentius legend, that referred to by Augustine in *Serm.* 274 and versified by Prudentius, is unlikely to be earlier than the mid-380s (Castillo Maldonado [1999], 47).
47. The premise of *Peristeph.* 4 is the competition among Christian cities to see which can claim the largest number of martyrs at the Second Coming.

48. Greg. Tur., *Hist.* 3.29.
49. Arce (1979), who though working solely on the basis of conjecture insisted that the supposed churches of Saint Vincent and of the eighteen martyrs must have been located extramurally where the palaeochristian cemetery lay, has thus been proved right. Excavations in the Plaza de la Seo (see Mostalac and Pérez [1989]), under the Tiberian forum that had long been conjectured as the site of the church of Saint Vincent, have found no trace of Christian cult earlier than the sixth, or perhaps even the seventh, century.
50. This first council of Zaragoza, which drew bishops from both northern Spain and southern Aquitaine, was held *in secretario* (CCH 4: 292: *Cesaragusta in secretario residentibus episcopis*). The phrase does nothing to help us locate the council, since its precise meaning is unclear. It may refer to a concrete place, by parallel to its usage in contemporary legal language, in which case it will have been the council chamber or audience room of the bishop, or it may be a mere abstraction that simply refers to the fact of the bishops' meeting: see Lewis and Short, s.v. Either way, the translation of Vives (1963), 16, "in the sacristy," is impossible. For the identity of the bishops attending, Chadwick (1976), 12–13.
51. See p. 95, above.
52. *Contra,* Hernández and Núñez (1998).
53. There is an accurate summary in Aguarod and Mostalac (1998), 67–74, but see the several reports by Casabona, Delgado, and Galve, listed in Aguarod and Mostalac's bibliography, for details.
54. Mostalac and Pérez (1989), 115–16. For the early Arabic period, see ibid., 117–21, and note the fact that *solidi* of Justin II were still in circulation in the seventh- and eighth-century town.
55. There is a transcription and linguistic analysis by J. F. Mesa Sanz in Aguarod and Mostalac (1998), 86–87.
56. Casabona (1990) and Aguarod and Mostalac (1998), 79–80.
57. Bendala and Negueruela (1980), who tentatively propose a fourth-century date for the initial construction of the *piscina* and a late seventh- or early eighth-century date for its final modification.
58. Excavations have now conclusively disproved the old theory that an early Christian church lies beneath the disused Gothic cathedral: Ramallo and Ruiz (1996–97); (1998); Ramallo (2000), 603.
59. Paul. Nol., *Carm.* 21.
60. Castillo Maldonado (1999), 514, for citations and map of the eventual distribution of their cult.
61. Méndez and Rascón (1989a); Rascón (1995); (1999); Sánchez Montes (1999).
62. Ribera and Soriano (1987); Blasco et al. (1994); Ribera and Soriano (1996).

63. Soriano (1995).
64. Ribera and Soriano (1987); (1996).
65. On the Republican and Flavian forum, see, briefly, Marín, Piá, and Rosselló (1999); for the fourth and early fifth centuries, Albiach et al. (2000), 63–69.
66. Albiach et al. (2000), 68, but one awaits the publication of a full stratigraphy.
67. Soriano (1994). There is a popular account of the excavation, with color photographs of the musealized site, in Rosselló and Soriano (1998).
68. Escrivà and Soriano (1989). Ribera and Soriano (1996), 199, for the evidence of ceramic dates. Albiach et al. (2000) refines the chronology.
69. Ribera and Soriano (1996), 196, suggests that most of the c/ del Mar burials are early Islamic, with the exception of one larger mausoleum.
70. Color photographs of these mausolea at Rosselló and Soriano (1998), 46. Others of these collective tombs seem to have been built in haste, with a similarly casual deposition of the bodies in them, and it has been suggested that they might reflect a period of exceptionally high mortality, perhaps one of the epidemics of the sixth century: Ribera and Soriano (1987).
71. See esp. Fevrier (1974); for Spain, Revuelta (1997), 67–68.
72. García Moreno (1977–78); Barral (1995); restated in Liebeschuetz (2001), 89, and, with only slight reservations, in Fuentes Domínguez (1997b), 492–93.
73. To the first group belong Mérida and Segobriga, to the second Barcelona, Roda, Iluro, Clunia, and Veleia.
74. Thus the supposedly late antique burials in the underground aqueduct of Tiermes have now been shown to be ninth-century or later: Argente (1993); while at ancient Saldania, the modern La Morterona about 64 km north of Palencia, the late antique cemetery lay outside the wall, in the spot now called Las Animas, and it was not until the city disappeared entirely beneath the soil, perhaps in the seventh century, that burials in the formerly intramural zone can be documented: Pérez and Abasolo (1987); Pérez Rodríguez-Aragón (1990).
75. Mateos (1999), 184, would appear to share these doubts, and Ribera and Soriano (1996), with its better-documented typology of the interments, is less insistent on a fifth-century date than earlier publications.
76. As is recognized by Soriano (1990).
77. See Granados (1987); (1995); Granados and Rodà (1994). Bonnet and Beltrán (2000a) corrects older reports, showing that what had previously been regarded as the basilica was in fact the episcopal hall, and that the basilica itself remains unlocalized, beneath the present-day cathedral.

78. The evolution began at the end of the sixth or the start of the seventh century, with a massive redesign of the whole complex on a far more monumental scale: Bonnet and Beltrán (2000a), 470–86; (2000b).

79. Extant fragments of *tituli picti* (*IRC* 4: 310 = *HEp.* 6: 161) from the baptistery are palaeographically of the late fifth or the sixth century, but there is no way of determining the chronological relationship between the *tituli* and the original construction of the church.

80. This is beginning to change: Ayerbe and Márquez (1998).

81. *CICM* 26, a. 381; 65, a. 384; a few other inscriptions may be fourth-century: *CICM* 17; 20; 24; 25; 48; 51; 63; 64; 163.

82. For Santa Catalina, see Caballero and Mateos (1991); Mateos (1995b), 309–10; Montalvo (1999).

83. Mateos (1999) is the final site report, superseding Caballero and Mateos (1991); (1992); (1995). The work is a model of how archaeological evidence should be presented—its first chapters report on the finds as they were excavated in strictly descriptive fashion without imposing the author's assumptions or analyses on them. Their interpretation in strictly material terms is then presented and only then does the author allow himself a more general interpretation with reference to literary evidence and hypotheses drawn from it. With these latter interpretations it is necessary to take issue, as the next several notes will show; that it is possible for one to do so on the basis of the published evidence demonstrates the virtues of the report.

84. Much of the narrative of the famous *Vitas Patrum Emeritensium,* an anonymous chronicle of the city's bishops written early in the seventh century, takes place around the ecclesiastical complex that included and surrounded the church of Saint Eulalia. (The nominative *Vitas* is correct; however, the antiquarian ascription of the work to a seventh-century deacon named Paul has been dismissed as unfounded by Maya Sánchez in her definitive edition of the work.) *VPE* 5.5 (ed. Maya Sánchez, 59) mentions Bishop Masona's prayer before the main altar of the church, under which the remains of Eulalia herself rested. *VPE* 4.10 (ed. Maya Sánchez, 45–46) notes the interment of Bishop Paulus and his nephew and successor Fidelis in the same crypt, near to the saint herself. *VPE* 5.13 (ed. Maya Sánchez, 98) describes the death of the deacon Eleutherius. The remains of the sixth-century basilica built above the fourth-century mausoleum match the church described in the *Vitas* at every point where it is possible to check: the apse of the basilica lies directly above the apse of the old mausoleum, which was entirely enclosed within the basilica's sanctuary although this produced a highly unusual elongation of its shape; the basilica was constructed with a crypt directly before the sanctuary; and the epitaph of a deacon [H]eleutherius was

found *in situ* in the nave of the basilica. The identification of the archae-ologically attested basilica with that described in the *Vitas* would there-fore appear to be proved.

85. The phenomenon seems to be quite generalized at Mérida: Feijoo (2000b). Mateos (1995a), 130, with Palma and Bejarano (1997), for the Casa del Anfiteatro. Above, pp. 98–100, for Ampurias.

86. This is implied by the presence of coins from that decade within the bases of the earliest tombs on the site, though because there is no undis-turbed stratigraphy anywhere on the site, the date is not absolutely cer-tain.

87. See now Sánchez Sánchez (2001) for early Christian burials in the nearby c/ Travesía Marquesa de Pinares; other burials belonging to the same cemetery in Nodar (1997a); (1997b).

88. Hyd. 80: [Heremigarius] *aud procul de Emerita, quam cum sanctae martyris Eulaliae iniuria spreverat, maledictis per Gaisericum caesis ex his quos secum habebat, arrepto, ut putavit, euro velocius fugae subsidio in flumine Ana di-vino brachio precipitatus interiit.*

89. Mateos (1999), 186–87, the only time the author indulges in special pleading. The material evidence he provides without bias shows that the damage is likely to belong closer to 450 than 429.

90. While admitting that the material remains themselves do not allow the inference, ibid., 159–60, does accept the Gregorius epitaph as a *termi-nus ante quem* for the construction of the basilica.

91. See chapter 8.

92. But see Bejarano (1998) and Márquez Pérez (1998) for consideration of the problem.

93. Mateos (1999), 184.

94. For the evidence of Córdoba, see Marfil (2000).

95. Mateos (1992); (1995a); (1999), *passim.*

96. On Ossius, see De Clerq (1954).

97. Hil. Arel., *Syn.* 3 (PL 10: 482); Phoeb., *Contra Arianos* 3. For the career of Potamius, see Montes Moreira (1969), on which Conti (1998) and Jorge (2002), 106–9, are largely dependent.

98. For the unpopularity of the new imperial theology in the West, Barnes (1993), 109–35.

99. *Coll. Avell.* 2.32: *Potamius Odyssiponae civitatis episcopus primum quidem fi-dem catholicam vindicans, postea vero praemio fundi fiscalis, quem habere con-cupiverat, fidem praevaricatus est.* The *fundus* here is almost certainly to be interpreted in a fiscal rather than a literal sense, thus referring to the tax renders of one or several imperial estates, rather than the properties them-selves.

100. Ibid., 2.73–76. A priest called Vincentius was threatened with beating by Bishop Hyginus of Córdoba and one Bishop Luciosus, of an unknown

see, for remaining in communion with Gregory, on whom see Salvador (1998), 103–5.

101. Aug., *Ep.* 11*, on which there is a very large bibliography. Van Dam (1986) and Kulikowski (2002) are the most complete treatments. For the date, Kulikowski (2000a).

102. Severa was either grandmother or aunt of Asterius's adult daughter (*Ep.* 11*.4.3: *ut muliera memorata* [sc. *Severa*] *ad neptis suae Asterii comitis filiae, potentissimae feminae auxilium convolaret*). Since she was clearly not the mother or the sister of Asterius himself, she must have been the mother or sister of his wife. On the basis of her name she was also a blood relation of Severus, and the most economical deployment of evidence would therefore make Severus either uncle or brother of Asterius's wife.

103. *CTh.* 1.27.1 (of 318); confirmed and clarified by *Const. Sirm.* 1 (of 333). On episcopal *audientiae,* see Gaudemet (1959), 229–52; Selb (1967); Cimma (1989); and Harries (1999), 191–211.

104. Particularly by means of Julian's abrogation (*Ep.* 436A–438C) of Constantinian legislation that allowed just one of two contending parties to move a dispute into an inappellable, episcopal court. For later restrictions, *CTh.* 16.2.23; *CJ* 1.4.7 (of 398); *CTh.* 16.11.1.

105. In an uncial manuscript of the fifth or sixth century (*CLA* 9: 1431), we possess eleven Priscillianist tractates, many or all of which may descend from the pen of Priscillian himself.

106. Sulp. Sev., *Chron.* 2.46.8.

107. Despite having been an early opponent of Priscillian, Hyginus of Córdoba—a staunch enough defender of orthodoxy to have physically attacked one of Gregory of Elvira's supporters not too long before (*Coll. Avell.* 2.73–75)—is notable by his absence from Zaragoza. Sulpicius Severus claims that the council at Zaragoza reprimanded Hyginus for his unwillingness to excommunicate heretics: *Chron.* 2.47.3.

108. Sulpicius maintains that the council condemned Priscillian and several others, while Priscillian insists that he had it on the authority of a bishop Symposius who had attended the gathering that no one had been condemned by name. It is impossible to decide the matter, for though the canons of the first council of Toledo, held in the year 400, do imply that a condemnation was issued at Zaragoza, extant canons of Zaragoza make no explicit mention of Priscillian or indeed any other named churchman.

109. Prisc., *Tract.* 1.28 (Schepss 23–24). The date of the first tractate is impossible to fix on internal evidence, and can only be dated on external grounds by appeal to individual hypotheses about the development of the controversy.

110. Sulp. Sev., *Chron.* 2.46.

111. Prisc., *Tract.* 2.49 (Schepss 40). It is impossible to know precisely what transpired here. For different hypotheses, see Chadwick (1976), 31–33, and Burrus (1995), 51–53.
112. Sulp. Sev., *Chron.* 2.47.4.
113. Chadwick (1976) remains the best narrative.
114. Burrus (1995).
115. The accounts of Zaragoza in Sulpicius Severus and the first Priscillianist tractate are incompatible with each other, but they are both evidence for much discussion, and perhaps legislation, not reflected in the transmitted canons.
116. For the patterns of conciliar minutes, see Burrus (1995), 30–33, which develops the ideas of Laeuchli (1972) on the significance of the original debate to the final form of conciliar *acta.*
117. There is no justification for assuming in the absence of internal evidence, as does Burrus (1995), that the sermons preserved within the Priscillianist corpus date from the period after their author's consecration as bishop—indeed, the seventh canon of Zaragoza is strong evidence that Priscillian had indeed preached prior to his consecration.
118. See the commentary of Bowes (2001).
119. Montenegro (1983); Burrus (1995).
120. As shown by the slightly later testimony of Inn., *Ep.* 3.7 (PL 20: 485–93), which may even suggest that some had held a pagan priesthood before their episcopal consecration.
121. Van Dam (1985), 90–91; Barbero (1963).
122. As does Burrus (1995), though much less consistently than she draws on gender contrasts.
123. Tudanca (1997), 42–44, recognizes the urban-rural hostilities inherent in the Priscillianist controversy, but places them within a traditional historiographical context of fourth-century ruralization.
124. Sulp. Sev., *Chron.* 2.50.2–3.
125. For the allusions to Sallust's Catilinarian conspirators in the rogues gallery of Sulpicius, see Fontaine (1975).
126. Too much luck with the ladies also influenced the dislike of Pope Damasus: *Coll. Avell.* 1.9.
127. Prisc., *Tract.* 2.53 (Schepss 42.12): *damnanda damnentur, superflua non legantur.*
128. Prisc., *Tract.* 3.66 (Schepss 51.10–12): *damna quod ego nescio, damna quod ego non lego, damna quod studio pigriscentis otii non requiro.*
129. In general, see the compilation of McKenna (1938) and the analyses of Hillgarth (1980) and Díaz and Torres (2000).
130. Elvira 61 (= CCH 4: 255).
131. Prisc., *Tract.* 1.23. As Chadwick (1976), 20, rightly points out, this accusation of weather magic should probably be read in connection with

canon 4 of Caesaraugusta (CCH 294–95), which prohibits walking barefoot in the countryside, an act with potentially magical implications.

132. CIL 2²/5: 510a. See also the golden tablet inscribed in Greek with the names of Sodom, Gomorrah, and a series of angels, perhaps dating to the fourth century: *HEp.* 5: 944 = *AE* 1993: 1007.

133. Mart. Brac., *De Corr. Rust.* 16.4–5. The cult of the *lares viales* was almost exclusive to the three *conventus* of the Spanish northwest (see the map in Portela Filgueiras [1984], 164). The cult is hardly known elsewhere in the Roman world while its distribution in Gallaecia is very intense. It would thus appear that local pre-Roman beliefs were especially assimilable to an *interpretatio romana* as protective spirits of the highway.

134. Thus the baths of the high imperial villa at Torreblanca del Sol, which had been a *garum* factory in the fourth century, was by the sixth or the seventh century a church as shown by a fragmentary inscription: Puertas Tricas (1986–87), 150.

135. See Jordán and Matilla (1995), suggestive though unprovable.

136. Escrivà and Vidal (1995), 238–39. In this habit of resacralizing an old cult site, the Christians were following a time-honored Roman precedent, inasmuch as the adoption of Roman ways had often meant the deliberate supplanting of an older Iberian cult site with a specifically Roman shrine, as at Montaña Frontera, near Sagunto, where an indigenous cult site of some sort of harvest god was replaced by a shrine to Liber Pater as early as the first century B.C.: Corell (1988).

137. Clariana and Járrega (1990); unfortunately, the altar fragment was found in a zone without stratigraphy.

138. The problem can affect even excellent site reports, like Posac and Puertas (1989) on the Christian basilica of Vega del Mar, which dates the construction of the basilica to circa 500 not for any archaeological reason but because the presence of barbarians in the region before that would have made it impossible to build such a church. In fact, the only archaeological *terminus post quem* is given by some bronze coins of Valentinian II.

139. In general, Fernández Gómez et al. (1987).

140. Ibid.

141. A complete report on the reexcavation of Torre de Palma has been promised; in the meantime, see Maloney and Hale (1996) for the site as a whole, Maloney (1995) for the basilica, superseding Almeida (1972–74) entirely. The dates proposed on typological grounds in Maloney (1995) have been adjusted dramatically by the advent of reliable carbon 14 dating, with the result that the initial site reports must be read in conjunction with Maloney and Ringbom (2000).

142. We are not, however, justified in putting the name *Basilius* to this *domi-*

nus on the basis of an inscribed seal found in the excavations of the 1950s.

143. Maloney and Ringbom (2000).
144. Bendala et al. (1998).
145. Alfenim and Conceição Lopes (1995).
146. See pp. 133–36, above.
147. Alarção, Étienne, and Mayet (1995). On the other hand, the development of a second church on the site almost certainly belongs to a period after the villa itself had ceased to be inhabited. Perhaps in the seventh century, perhaps already in the Islamic period, a small basilica was installed on a part of the remains of the Antonine villa that had not been incorporated into the new plan of the site by the fourth-century architect.
148. We still lack a reliable corpus of rural sites with Christian architectural remains.
149. Pot., *De Laz.* 84–87.

Chapter 11. The Earlier Sixth Century and the Goths in Spain

1. See pp. 208–9, above.
2. There is no positive evidence for the view, stated by Bruck (1954) and repeated in standard histories, that Alaric supported the council mainly to curry favor with his orthodox subjects in the face of increasing hostility from the Frankish king Clovis.
3. Caesarius had been exiled to Bordeaux in 505 when the notary Licinianus charged him with treasonably plotting to place his diocese in Burgundian hands: *Vit. Caes.* 1.21. But Caesarius was necessary to the success of Alaric's great council, hence his recall from exile: Klingshirn (1994), 93–96.
4. Ibid., 97–104.
5. The plans for a new council, to be held at Toulouse in 507, emerge from Caes., *Ep.* 3, in which Caesarius rebukes Ruricius of Limoges for his failure to attend at Agde and urges him to come to the next council at Toulouse. The defeat of Alaric at Vouillé ensured that this second council never took place.
6. It is tempting to see the absence of the Spanish bishops as in some way connected to the "tyranny" of Petrus, but while the date of the council is fixed, that of Petrus's usurpation can only be approximate. Thus, though it is plausible that some connection existed, it can only be speculative.
7. The Frankish raid on Bordeaux recorded in the Copenhagen continuation of Prosper s.a. 498 (MGH AA 9: 331: *Franci Burdigalam obtinerunt et a potestate Gothorum in possessionem sui redegerunt capto Suatrio Gotho-*

rum duce) is sometimes thought to represent the start of these hostilites (by, e.g., Wood [1994], 47).

8. On Theodoric's foreign relations generally, see Moorhead (1992), 172–94. Theodoric suggested that causes of the dispute between Alaric and Clovis were really quite trivial. Cass., *Var.* 3.1: *non vos parentum fusus sanguis inflammat, non graviter urit occupata provincia. adhuc de verbis parva contentio est.* Ibid., 3.4: *impatiens sensus est ad primam legationem arma protinus commovere.* To Gundobad he appealed as a fellow senior statesman: ibid., 3.2.2: *nostrum est regios iuvenes obiecta ratione moderari.* Ibid.: *decet enim nos aspera verba dicere, ne affines nostri ad extremum debeant pervenire.*

9. To Alaric, Cass., *Var.* 3.1.4: *name ille me iure sustinebit adversum qui vobis nititur esse contrarius.* To Clovis, ibid., 3.4.4: *Iure patris vobis interminor et amantis. ille nos et amicos nostros patietur adversos qui talia monita, quod non poniamur, crediderit esse temnenda.*

10. Greg. Tur., *Hist.* 2.35: *Cuniunctique* [sc. *Alaricus et Chlodovecus*] *in insula Ligeris que erat iuxta vicum Ambaciensim terretorium urbis Toronicae simul locuti, comedetentes pariter et bibentes, promissa sibi amicitia, paxifici discesserunt.*

11. For Theodoric's anxieties, Cass., *Var.* 3.1.1–2: *cavete subito in aleam mittere quos constat tantis temporibus exercitia non habere. terribilis est hominibus conflictus si non sit assiduus et nisi usu praesumatur, concertandi subito fiducia non habetur.*

12. Greg. Tur., *Hist.* 2.37: *Maximus ibi tunc Arvernorum populus qui cum Apollinare venerat et primi qui erant ex senatoribus corruerunt.* The late and unreliable *Vita Aviti Peracorici* (cited by Orlandis [1987], 66) suggests that Gallo-Romans were pressed into service by the Goths, but the more contemporary evidence proves voluntary participation. The main source for Clovis's campaign against Alaric is Gregory of Tours, hostile to the Goths both because they were Arians and because they were Goths. Gregory portrays Clovis's campaign as an orthodox crusade against the heretic Alaric, a crusade welcomed by Alaric's subjects. Gregory's account is evocative and endowed with his customary narrative momentum, but also with his customary tendentiousness. It is not at all certain that Clovis was an orthodox Christian in 507, while both the king's magnanimity and the extent of his piety are exaggerated in order to glorify Gregory's patron, Saint Martin. On Clovis's conversion, see Wood (1985) and Shanzer (1998). For the campaign, Wood (1994), 45–48.

13. *Boglada* in *Cons. Caes.* 88a (= CCSL 173A: 28). Gregory's account runs as follows (*Hist.* 2.37): *Chlodovechus rex cum Alarico rege Gothorum in campo Vogladense decimo ab urbe Pictava miliaro convenit et confligentibus his eminus resistunt comminus illi. cumque secundum consuetudinem Gothi terga vertissent, ipse rex Chlodovechus victoriam Domino adiuvante obti-*

> *nuit . . . Porro rex cum fugatis Gothis Alaricum regem interfecisset.* Proc.,
> *Bell.* 5.12.35 erroneously locates this decisive battle at Carcassonne. The
> identification of Voglada as Vouillé was first made by Longnon (1878),
> 576–87, but is rejected by Gerberding (1987), 41, on not implausible
> grounds.

14. *Cons. Caes.* 88a (= CCSL 173A: 28): *His diebus pugna Gothorum et Fran-*
    corum Boglada facta. Alaricus rex in proelio a Francis interfectus est. regnum
    Tolosanum destructum est.

15. *Chron. Gall. a. 511* 86–87 (= Burgess [2001b], 99): *XV. Occisus Alaricus*
    rex Gothorum a Francis. Tholosa a Francis et Burgundionibus incensa et Bar-
    cinona a Gundefade Burgundionum capta. This suggests that Gundobad,
    marching into the Gothic kingdom from either Lyons or Vienne, had
    taken no part in the decisive battle at Vouillé, making instead for the
    Gothic king's residence and the inevitable division of the spoils.

16. Greg. Tur., *Hist.* 2.37; *Chron. Gall. a. 511* 87 (= Burgess [2001b], 99): *et*
    Geseleycus rex cum maxima suorum clade ad Ispanias regressus est; Isid., *HG*
    37: *Gisaleicus superioris regis filius ex concubina creatus Narbona princeps*
    efficitur. It is universally assumed, by, e.g., Thompson (1969), 8, that the
    Gallic chronicler's account of an attack on Barcelona is an error for Nar-
    bonne (see previous note for text). Not only is that emendation histori-
    cally unnecessary, but the corruption from *Narbo* or *Narbona* to *Barci-*
    nona in a Gallic source is palaeographically unlikely. Narbona was one
    of the best known cities of Gaul, Barcelona was Spanish and much less
    famous, so that *Barcinona* is by some distance the *lectio dificilior.* Indeed,
    if it is necessary to emend the reading of *Barcinona,* we would do better
    to read *Carcasona,* a much more obscure town than Barcelona, let alone
    Narbo, and a town at which Procopius (*Bell.* 5.12.35) has some confused
    testimony about fighting between Goths and Franks.

17. Greg. Tur., *Hist.* 2.37: *De hac pugna Amalaricus filius Alarici in Spaniam*
    fugit regnumque patris sagaciter occupavit. Gregory telescopes the narra-
    tive and retrojects to 507 Amalaric's sole accession to the Gothic royal
    title, but he is probably right to think that Amalaric fled Gaul to Spain
    just as Gesalic did.

18. Ibid.: *Chlodovechus vero filium suum Theudoricum per Albigensim ac Ruti-*
    nam civitatem ad Arvernus dirigit, qui abiens, urbes illas a finibus Gothorum
    usque Burgundionum terminum patris sui dicionibus subiugavit. Carcas-
    sonne features in none of the western sources, but Procopius imagines
    it to be the chief city of the Gothic kingdom and locates the decisive bat-
    tle between Alaric and Clovis there (*Bell.* 5.12.35). He also suggests
    (ibid., 5.12.41) that the Visigothic royal treasure was housed at Carcas-
    sonne and envisages (ibid., 5.12.44) King Theodoric himself breaking a
    Frankish siege of the city. The first two statements are demonstrably in
    error, while the second can be neither confirmed nor disproved, though

Theodoric the Ostrogoth did certainly come personally to Gaul in 508. It is hard to imagine Procopius's having introduced the minor city of Carcassonne into his account for no reason whatsoever. It is altogether more likely that he has preserved a genuine record of some action at Carcassonne that he has inadvertently mistaken for the main center of the campaigns.

19. It cannot have been the whole of the Visigothic royal treasure, because Theodoric the Ostrogoth had possession of a large part of it in later years as regent for his grandson. Clovis's winter quarters at Bordeaux lay directly on the route between Poitiers and Toulouse and Clovis had probably seized it in the immediate aftermath of Vouillé. Unlike Toulouse, however, Bordeaux lay within Aquitania proper and had formed part of the initial imperial grant to the Goths a century before. It is not entirely clear why both Clovis and his son Theuderic found it necessary to winter in Aquitania: either Novempopulana and Narbonensis were less secure than Aquitania, so that the Franks were forced to winter in the latter region, or the Aquitanian provinces required more attention and a heavier hand, hence the decision to winter there.

20. Greg. Tur., *Hist.* 2.38: *Chlodovechus vero apud Burdigalinsi urbe hiemem agens, cunctos thesauros Alarici a Tholosa auferens, Ecolisnam venit . . . tunc exclusis Gothis urbem suo dominio subiugavit. Post haec, patrata victoria, Turonus est regressus . . . Egressus autem a Turonus Parisius venit ibique cathedram regni constituit. Ibi et Theudericus ad eum venit.*

21. In 508, when Clovis had returned to the north from his winter sojourn in Bordeaux, he received from Anastasius the codicils of the consulate: Greg. Tur., *Hist.* 2.38.

22. Perhaps because of imperial attacks on the Italian coast (for which see Moorhead [1992], 182), the Ostrogothic call-up did not start until June 508, as shown by *Var.* 1.24, which gives 24 June as the date by which the force is to be assembled.

23. Cass., *Chron.* 1348–49: *Venantius iun. et Celer: His coss. contra Francos a domino nostro destinatur exercitus, qui Gallias Francorum depraedatione confusas victis hostibus ac fugatis suo adquisivit imperio; Vit. Caes.* 1.28: *Etenim, obsidentibus Francis ac Burgundionibus civitatem, iam enim Alarico rege a victoriosissimo rege Chlodoveo in certamine perempto, Theudericus Italiae rex Provinciam istam ducibus missis intravit.*

24. Theodoric's presence on the campaign is shown by ibid.: *Theudericus . . . Provinciam . . . intravit,* with the less reliable Proc., *Bell.* 5.12.44. For Ibba as the victor of Arles, Jord., *Get.* 302. Ibba at Narbonne: Cass., *Var.* 4.17.

25. In 509, the Gothic general Mammo campaigned, perhaps in Burgundian territory (Marc. Com., s.a. 508), and Theodoric also fortified the river Durance to protect his new border with the Burgundians (Cass., *Var.* 3.41.2).

26. As ibid., 5.43.2 shows, before 510/511 Gesalic was regarded as an ally by the Ostrogothic court.

27. Perhaps in 510, Gesalic caused the death of that same Goiaric who had been one of Alaric's chief ministers and undertaken the publication of his king's *Breviarium: Cons. Caes.* 91a (= CCSL 173A: 30): *His consulibus Gesalecus Goericum Barcinone in palatio interfecit.* In the following year, after Gesalic had been driven from Spain, a Gothic count Veila, who may have supported him, was likewise killed at Barcelona: *Cons. Caes.* 92a (= CCSL 173A: 30): *Comes vero Veila Barcinone occiditur.* We are perhaps seeing the traces of factional reprisals within the court. *Pace* García Iglesias (1975), 95–96, nothing links this violence to rivalry between Gesalic and Amalaric or between Visigoth and Ostrogoth.

28. Murray (1983).

29. See Cass., *Var.* 5.43, a hectoring chastisement for Thrasamund's having done even that much, with *Cons. Caes.* 91a (= CCSL 173A: 30): *quo anno idem Gesalecus ab Helbane Theodorici Italorum regis duce ab Hispania fugatus Africam petit.*

30. *Cons. Caes.* 94a (= CCSL 173A: 31): *His consulibus Gisalecus de Africa rediens ob metum Helbanis Aquitaniam petiit ibique latuit annum unum.* Isid., *HG* 38 does not note this initial battle between Gesalic and Ibba and has Gesalic go directly from Africa to Aquitania before encountering Ibba in the following year. While either source may simply have reversed the order of events, it is just as likely that each has recorded one part of a complicated series of brief campaigns between Gesalic and Theodoric's chief general.

31. Isid., *HG brev.* 38: *[Gesalicus] . . . Hispaniam reversus ab Ebbane Theudorici regis duce duodecimo a Barcinona urbe miliario commisso proelio superatus in fugam vertitur captusque trans fluvium Druentium Galliarum occiditur.* The long version is more judgmental: *trans flumen Druentium Galliarum interiit, sicque prius honorem, postea vitam amisit.* Gesalic's presence in Burgundian territory with a few supporters may account for a peculiar notice in the *Vita* of Caesarius of Arles, which records a Visigothic attack on the Ostrogothic prefect Liberius some time in this period. *Vit. Caes.* 2.10: *Quodam igitur tempore patricius Liberius insidiantibus Gothis quos Wisigothos dicunt lanciae vulnere in ventre usque ad vitalia perforatus est. Et quia trans Druentia periculum ipsum gestum fuerat, turbatis omnibus concurrentibusque post percussorem, ille sole remansit.* The whole story, which ends with Caesarius's intervention and Liberius's recovery, is told at *Vit. Caes.* 2.10–12, on which see Klingshirn (1994), 112.

32. There is a notice of uncertain value in Jord., *Get.* 302: *nam et Thiudem suum armigerum post mortem Alarici generi tutorem in Spaniae regno Amalarici nepotis constituit.* Regardless of the authenticity of the titles Jordanes gives Theudis, his account contains no chronological indicators.

33. Proc., *Bell.* 5.12.50–54.
34. Ibid., 5.13.4–8.
35. Ibid., 5.13.6.
36. Ibid., 5.13.10–12; *Cons. Caes.* 115a (= CCSL 173A: 37); Greg. Tur., *Hist.* 3.10. Isid., *HG* 40 adds nothing of value. Most Spanish scholars, e.g., Gurt and Godoy (2000), 444, follow the *Consularia.*
37. While it is usual to call upon the legal evidence to fill out the picture, doing so raises substantial problems. Not only is there the usual difficulty of trying to correlate normative sources with actual practice, there are also special problems with the date at which, and the places in which, different Gothic royal laws were in place. The legal texts issued by the early Gothic kings are the Paris Fragments traditionally known as the *Codex Eurici* (Paris Lat. 12161 [*CLA* 5: 626], edited by Zeumer in MGH LL 1 and in D'Ors [1960]); the *Lex Romana Visigothorum,* more generally known by its early modern name, the *Breviarium Alarici;* and the seventh-century compilations of the *Leges Visigothorum* in their several recensions. As Nehlsen (1982); (1984) shows, the Paris Fragments may actually date to Alaric II's reign. The *Breviarium,* promulgated on 2 February 506, certainly does. The Paris Fragments were new law, legislating for situations brought about by the change from imperial to royal government. The *Breviarium* was a re-edition and abridgment of the Theodosian Code for the changed circumstances of the post-imperial period, eliminating material that was superfluous and supplying *interpretationes* that clarified the obscurities of the original imperial constitutions (see Matthews [2000]; [2001]). Alaric shared Theodosius's explicit concern with the public interest: the commissioners who compiled the *Breviarium* worked for the *utilitates populi nostri* and the royal legislator envisaged a long life for his text, as well as its active use in court (*contra,* the view of Bruck [1954] that the *Breviarium* was merely a sop to the Gallo-Romans on the eve of war with Clovis). Despite old theories about the "personality of law" in Germanic societies (still retailed in Guterman [1990]), it is clear that both the Paris Fragments and the *Breviarium* were territorial laws directed to all the inhabitants of the Gothic kingdom (as long since argued by García Gallo, esp. [1936–41]; [1942–43] and by D'Ors [1956]). Gothic kings, in other words, ruled over a kingdom that contained both Goths and Romans who lived under a single administration, and they legislated equally for both populations. While it is clear that in the Gallic kingdom the population accepted the Gothic kings as the legal successors to the emperors, and were prepared to live according to their laws, the only evidence for this in Spain is the fact that Theudis, the only Gothic king definitely known to have legislated between 506 and the 570s, explicitly commanded his financial decree to be appended to the *Breviarium.* It is likely, then, that the *Breviarium* was

in use in those parts of Spain where Gothic rulership was firmly established, but its contents do not allow us to determine where those were,
or whether royal law was actively enforced by Gothic administrators.
The seventh-century Visigothic Code is more problematical still. Some
of what it designates as *leges antiquae* are clearly derived from, or identical to, the Paris Fragments and it has long been assumed that all the
leges antiquae that do not obviously derive from the Paris Fragments instead represent a code of Leovigild (what has come to be called his *codex
revisus* in the literature). However, as García Gallo (1974), 381–82 and
395–400, shows, Isid., *HG* 51 does not demonstrate that Leovigild issued a law code, nor does it allow us to identify the *leges antiquae* with
the legislation of Leovigild rather than unnamed kings both earlier and
later than him. Thus, because we do not know when these *antiquae* were
issued, we do not know when or where they applied. They are certainly
evidence for the seventh-century kingdom, but while many may indeed
be applicable to sixth-century regions under Gothic control, we cannot
tell which those are.

38. They did so some time between 507 and 531, as is shown by the fact
that, after Amalaric's death in 531, the Frankish kings needed to seize
the cities of Rodez and Beziers, as well as a castle near Lodève: Greg. Tur.,
Hist. 3.21–22.

39. Proc., *Bell.* 5.12.48–49.

40. Gurt and Godoy (2000), 446, citing a recently discovered silver coin
minted at a one-quarter *siliqua* standard, which is diagnostic of Ostrogothic coinage. See Tomasini (1964), 154; *MEC* 1: 48–49.

41. Liberius's remit included even military duties: Cass., *Var.* 11.1. The *Breviarium* suggests that the financial staff of the praetorian prefects survived under Gothic rule, eventually being absorbed into the old *res privata* as a new palatine bureau, the *domus dominica:* full references,
cautiously deployed, at García Moreno (1974), 21–42. The later Visigothic *comes patrimonii* is not attested until the reign of Reccared.

42. For Gemellus as vicar, Cass., *Var.* 3.17, and as *vir spectabilis,* without
specified office, in *Var.* 3.16–18; 3.41; 4.12; 4.19; 4.21.

43. Ibid., 5.35; 5.39, of which 5.39 is the earlier since it is addressed to the
two men at the start of their mission, seemingly before they had left Italy
for Spain.

44. Ibid., 5.39.

45. Ibid., 5.35.

46. Some, e.g., García Moreno (1989), 91–93, would see Ampelius as praetorian prefect over the Hispano-Roman population and Liuverit as the
military commander of the Gothic population. Nothing in the sources
warrants this interpretation and the existence of Liberius at Arles mili-

tates against Ampelius's having been praetorian prefect; there had never been a prefecture of Spain, and one only came into existence briefly at the end of the 520s when Theodoric's death caused the division of Gallic and Spanish provinces (see next note). There are no grounds for retrojecting those circumstances into the earlier 520s. The conviction that such a division of administrative competencies into Roman and Gothic spheres existed derives not from the evidence, but from a belief in the personality of law that would have required separate administrative hierarchies for Goth and Roman.

47. He was appointed in 528/529 and removed from office between 530 and 532. *Cons. Caes.* 113a (= CCSL 173A: 36): *His diebus, Stephanus Hispaniarum praefectus efficitur, qui tertio anno praefecturae suae in ciuitate Gerundensi in concilio discinctus est.* There is no evidence for the view of Jiménez Garnica (1983), 159, that he was removed from office by the vote of the primitive Germanic assembly of the Goths.

48. Respectively, *Var.* 5.39.15; 5.39.14; 5.39.6.

49. *Telonei:* ibid., 5.39.7–9. Tax on traders: ibid., 5.39.7, with García Moreno (1974), 55.

50. Castellanos (1998), 45–47, on Vincentius of Osca, and *LV* 10.3.1–2 for the royal laws on *termini* and *limites;* these laws are classed as *antiquae,* though of course we can never know where, or how effectively, they were enforced.

51. García Moreno (1974) remains the only reliable study of this material, and its conclusions are not always reflected in the author's later studies. The evidence is complicated by the fact that the seventh-century law codes share a vocabulary with, but not the institutional assumptions of, the fifth- and sixth-century texts, a fact consistently disguised in King (1972), though acknowledged in Thompson (1969), 114–52. Both studies are undermined by the assumption that Gothic control of Spain was total, and that Goths and Romans lived under parallel but different administrations.

52. Proc., *Bell.* 5.12.50–54; 6.30.15. Jord., *Get.* 302, with n. 33, above, for the position of Theudis under Theodoric.

53. The law, known from a single manuscript and highly lacunose, was promulgated on *die VIII. kalendas Decembrias anno XV regni,* i.e., 24 November 546, and is printed as an addendum to Zeumer's edition of the *Leges Visigothorum* (MGH LL 1, sect. 1: 467–69).

54. Ripoll (2000), 386–89; Velázquez and Ripoll (2000) for Toledo as Theudis's capital.

55. But not, as does Ripoll (2000), 392, on the basis of supposedly Gothic graves in the vicinity. See below.

56. CCH 4: 365. For the meaning of Carpetania in the sixth and seventh centuries, see Vallejo (1992), 39–43.

57. The councils at issue are those of Tarragona in 515 (CCH 4: 269–81), Gerona in 517 (CCH 4: 283–90), II Toledo in 527 (CCH 4: 345–66), and Lérida, possibly held in 546 (CCH 4: 297–311). Only Bishop Orontius of Elvira in Baetica, who attended the council at Tarragona, came from outside Carthaginiensis or Tarraconensis. The council of Valencia, held at an uncertain date between 546 and 549, similarly demonstrates Theudis's recognition in that city and its *territorium*: CCH 4: 314.

58. That the bishops gathered at Toledo appealed to the canons of the council of Agde likewise supports this interpretation; Agde had clearly been a council of the Gothic kingdom as it existed under Alaric II, and reference to it at Toledo might have been intended to point up the parallels.

59. García Moreno (1994); Ripoll (1998a).

60. E.g., Keay (1991a); (1996) by contrast with id. (1989).

61. Spanish scholars use separate adjectives, *visigodo* and *hispanovisigodo,* to distinguish between the "purely" Visigothic culture of the fifth and sixth centuries on the one hand, and that of the later sixth and seventh centuries on the other. For the extant seventh-century churches, see Dodds (1990) and Fontaine (1973).

62. Pp. 209–14, above.

63. For examples with reference to the Goths, see Kazanski (1993); Bierbrauer (1992); (1994); and the essays collected in Périn (1991) and Vallet and Kazanski (1993). For the same assumptions in a post-processual context, Greene (1987).

64. See esp. Shennan (1989); Brather (2000), with extensive references to the earlier literature, and id. (2002) for a valuable case study. Siegmund (2000) does not provide the theoretical alternative it attempts to.

65. Daim (1998), absolutely correct in theory, though failing to demonstrate the theory to be practically feasible.

66. Curta (2001) is the most sensitive case study of how the material artifacts preserved in the archaeological record can be read in terms of strategies of ethnic distinction. It will be possible to extend its methods to the evidence of the Spanish sixth century only if typologies of local pottery are refined and, more important, if it can be shown that the typologies of personal adornments now standardized by Ripoll (esp. [1985]; [1998a]; [1998b]) are not contaminated by a chronology drawn from the literary sources, which does not seem to be the case.

67. The ethnic assumptions guiding the first modern work on the subject, Zeiss (1934), have remained constant in its successors: Hübener (1970); (1974); (1991); König (1980); Ripoll (1998a); (1998b).

68. Duratón: Molinero (1948); König (1985); Ciezar (1990). Castiltierra: Werner (1942); (1946). El Carpio: Mergelina (1949); Ripoll (1985); (1993–94). Herrera de Pisuerga: Martínez Santa-Olalla (1933).

69. E.g., Almagro Basch (1975); Ardanaz (2000).

70. Most recently Ripoll (1998a).
71. The recently excavated cemetery of Cacera de las Ranas in the south of the Comunidad de Madrid has been rigorously published by Ardanaz (2000), but its chronology is drawn from the typological chronology developed in Ripoll (1985) and perfected in id. (1998a), on the basis of the cemeteries excavated unscientifically in the 1920s and 1930s.
72. Ripoll (1998a).
73. The attempt to distinguish "Mediterranean" from "Germanic" bones is not helpful, *pace* Ardanaz (2000), 288.
74. James (1977).
75. Schwarcz (2001).
76. Halsall (1992). In Spain, the remains of weapons at Cacera de las Ranas, for which see Ardanaz (2000), do suggest a surprising local continuity with the so-called Duero necropoles of the fourth century, on which see Fuentes Domínguez (1989).
77. Pérez Rodríguez-Aragón (1997), despite his acceptance of material ethnicity in so-called Gothic, Suevo-Vandalic, and Hunnic artifacts from Spanish sites, at least accepts that these finds cannot be taken as simple evidence for the presence of these ethnic groups in a particular place.
78. As by, e.g., García Moreno (1994), 559; similarly, the parallels between the material finds at El Corralón near Cartagena and those from Duratón do not necessarily imply a Gothic population in the area, as recognized by Antolinos and Sánchez (2000).
79. Though this interpretation is becoming an article of faith: Méndez and Rascón (1989a); (1989b) on the necropolis of the Camino de los Afligidos; Rascón (1995), 180–82; (1999); Sánchez Montes (1999). The extended review of the cemetery in Ripoll (1989) is usefully cautious.
80. Though even here, certain doubts have emerged and the horseshoe arches and architectonic features traditionally regarded as Visigothic may actually reflect the eighth- and ninth-century culture of the Mozarabs: Alba (1999).
81. It is very difficult to extract a strict *anno domini* chronology from the sources for sixth-century Spain. The defects of the *Consularia Caesaraugustana* have already been treated (see p. 207, above) and derive in part from the faulty chronology of Victor of Tunnuna; the faults in Victor's chronology are perpetuated in John of Biclar's continuation of Victor. For the last four years of his chronicle, Victor ceases to date by the postconsulate of Basilius and begins to use the regnal years of Justinian intead, but we cannot tell whether he counted the twenty-third year of the post-consulate of Basilius twice, once in that form and once as the thirty-seventh year of Justinian. As a consequence, we do not know whether Victor's final four entries correspond to the years 563–566 or 564–567. As a further consequence, we do not have a secure starting date for John's

continuation. Although John corrected Victor's error in giving Justinian an extra regnal year, his fortieth, he necessarily perpetuated the confusion of the final four entries in Victor, a confusion that persists throughout his continuation. His chronicle may thus run from 566 to 589 or from 567 to 590.

On this point, it is not possible to introduce the evidence of a series of regnal lists known as the *laterculi regum visigothorum* that appear in some MSS of the Visigothic law code (ed. Mommsen, MGH AA 13: 461–69; ed. Zeumer, MGH LL 1: 457–61). The *laterculi* do not link their lists to specific chronologies, which were instead introduced by authors who used *laterculi* as sources, e.g., Isidore. Although it is perfectly possible that one or another extant recension of the *laterculi,* or indeed some combination of them, preserves a historically accurate reckoning of the Gothic reigns, we have no way of knowing which of our texts, if any, this one might be.

The *Historia Gothorum* of Isidore is likewise problematical. It has long been accepted that the *Historia Gothorum Vandalorum Sueborum,* a history of the Goths with brief, appended histories of the Vandals and Sueves, survived in two forms. The short version runs to the death of Sisebut in 619 or 620, and is extant in the twelfth-century MS Paris, BN Lat. 4873, of which there is one copy, and the thirteenth-century Madrid BN 8696, which belongs to a different MS family. The long version runs to the fifth year of Suintila, which fell between 624 and 626, and contains the famous *Laus Spaniae* prologue, as well as a *Recapitulatio* (*HG* 66–70) called the *Laus Gothorum* in some MSS. This long version is much more common than the short, and has a considerably more complicated MS history. (For the MSS, see Rodríguez Alonso [1975], 121–63.) Unfortunately, the relationship between these two versions is difficult to fathom. The long version is not simply an expanded version of the short, nor is the short simply an abbreviated version of the long. The short version reads as continuous prose, the long is broken down annalistically into chapters. Each version contains important information lacking in the other (for the most striking divergences, see Collins [1994], 350–52). To explain this fact, Mommsen postulated an original Isidorian archetype of which both extant versions were mutilated debasements (MGH AA 11: 254). This is far from impossible, and other Isidorian works, for instance, the *De viris illustribus* and the *De natura rerum,* exist in several forms because of editorial intervention in the later seventh century (see Codoñer Merino [1964], 17–41, on the *DVI* and Fontaine [1960], 38–83, on the *DNR,* respectively). But in these works, and also in Isidore's chronicle, the same common core text is clearly visible amid the editorial interference.

This is much less the case with the versions of the *HG,* which may lead one to conclude that they are the work of two different hands. This is the suggestion of Collins (1994), which while unprovable is probably nonetheless correct. Collins postulates that what we call the short recension of Isidore's *HG* is in fact the lost *historiola* of Maximus of Zaragoza, which we know about from *DVI* 33. This *historiola* has traditionally been identified with the so-called *Consularia Caesaraugustana*, but that conclusion, as we have seen, is untenable. The short recension of the *HG*, by contrast, is a very strong candidate for this position, being generically a history, rather than a chronicle, and covering events through the reign of Sisebut, during which Maximus is known to have lived. The wholesale but inconsistent parallels between the two versions also make good sense in the context of Isidore's known compositional methods. The identification of Maximus as author of the short version of the *HG* makes it necessary to regard the dates given in both versions as potentially independent evidence for the chronology of sixth-century events. I.e., divergences between long and short versions cannot be dismissed as purely the effect of scribal corruption from a correct archetype.

The chronological framework of the two texts is parallel, as one would expect if Isidore was working from the original version of Maximus. Both versions correlate Spanish *aera* dates to imperial regnal years. These dates, in combination, provide the pegs for the Gothic regnal list. The *aera* and the *anni imperii* are both there for dating purposes. The Gothic reigns, by contrast, form part of the substantive historical material in the chronicle. There are, however, large differences between the chronologies of the two texts. These are comprehensively disguised in the Mommsen edition and in the tabulated chronology he prints at MGH AA 11: 246–51. In both versions of the *HG*, internal evidence suggests that imperial regnal years were counted as calendar years beginning on 1 January following the accession of the emperor, but there are serious miscalculations in the correlation of *aera* dates with imperial regnal years, often by one or more years. There is no consistent margin of error, nor is the number of years elapsed according to *aera* dates and according to imperial regnal dates consistent or progressive, which means that we cannot correct for it by eliminating doubled-up years.

By the same token, we cannot simply choose between *aera* and imperial regnal schema, because we do not know which dating scheme the author(s) considered primary. We do not know whence the sixth-century *aera* dates are derived; most of the fifth-century *aera* dates in the *HG* are derived from Hydatius, and not only incorporate the source's defects but introduce new errors of calculation as well (Gillett [1999], 18, who does not distinguish between the two versions of the *HG*). The same holds true for the imperial regnal years. We cannot tell whether the author(s) had access to independent reckonings of both *aera* dates and imperial regnal years, which were then imperfectly correlated; whether one system was derived from a complete reckoning of the other; or whether the author(s) had complete reckonings of neither *aera* nor imperial regnal dates, and therefore calculated some of the dates in each system from scraps available in one or both. On the whole, the last option seems likeliest given the absence of a discernable pattern to the discrepancies between the two systems.

As to Gothic regnal years, it seems clear that the author(s) of the *HG* had access to a Gothic *laterculus* similar but not identical to one of those still extant, but one that did not link Gothic regnal years to either the *aera* or the imperial regnal chronologies. The lengths of Gothic reigns given in the *HG* correspond consistently neither to *aera* years nor to imperial regnal dates, which means the correlation of a Gothic regnal list with *aera* and imperial dating systems must have been the work of the author(s) of the *HG*. There is no guarantee that this correlation was made correctly and the fact that in a few cases the number of regnal years fails to match calculations of either aera or imperial dates does not inspire confidence. The consequence of all this is fairly serious. Neither the *aera* dates nor the imperial regnal years of the *HG* can be accepted as accurate without some sort of confirmation in each instance, while for the lengths of Gothic reigns, the numbers given are neither more nor less reliable than in any other of the extant Gothic *laterculi*.

Because we cannot determine any pattern by which the *HG*'s regnal *laterculus* was tied to a fixed system of chronological reckoning, we have no way of checking its accuracy over time. Any one piece of information may be correct, as may any one correlation of *aera* date, imperial regnal date, or Gothic regnal length. Indeed, in a few cases, external evidence shows both the date and the chronological calculation to be correct. Regrettably, these demonstrable instances of accuracy prove nothing. As with other sources, we must take the *HG* as a package, which in this case means recognizing that its chronology lacks explicable system. Consequently, we can feel secure only on the point of its own relative chronology, which is more substantial and informative than most of what we have for sixth-century Spain. On the other hand, we cannot cite the *HG* as confirmatory evidence for our other chronological information, nor can we use its absolute chronology save where more reliable outside sources attest to the same thing.

82. Greg. Tur, *Hist.* 3.30: *Childeberthus rex in Hispaniam abiit. Qua ingressus cum Chlothachario, Caesaraugustanam civitatem cum exercitu vallant atque obsedent. At ille in tanta humilitate ad Deum conversi sunt ut induti ciliciis, abstinentis a cibis et poculis, cum tonica beati Vincenti martiris muros civitatis psallendo circuirent . . . Hii autem qui obsedebant . . . timentes se ab ea civitate removerunt. Tamen adquisitam maximam Hispaniae partem, cum magnis spoliis in Galliis redierunt.*

83. *Cons. Caes.* 130a (= CCSL 173A: 43): *Hoc anno Francorum reges numero V per Pampelonam Hispanias ingressi Caesaraugustam venerunt, quam obsessam per quadraginta novem dies omnem fere Tarraconensem prouinciam depopulatione attriuerunt;* Isid., *HGbrev.: Iste* [scil. *Theudis*] *Francorum reges quinque Caesaraugustam obsidentes omnemque fere Terraconensem provinciam bello depopulantes misso duce Theudisclo fortiter debellavit atque a regno suo non prece, sed armis exire coegit;* Isid., *HGprolix.* 41: *eo regnante dum Francorum reges cum infinitis copiis in Spanias convenissent et Tarraconensem provinciam bello depopularent, Gothi duce Theudisclo obicibus Spaniae interclusis Francorum exercitum multa cum admiratione victoriae prostraverunt.* There is nothing to suggest more than a single historical tradition at work here.
84. *Contra,* Larrañaga (1993); Azkarate (2001). It must, however, be admitted that the cemetery of Aldaieta in Álava province, published in Azkarate (1999), is suggestive, inasmuch as the typologies of its burials are much closer to those of Aquitaine and the Merovingian world more generally than they are to those of sixth-century Spain.
85. The corroboration of this date seemingly offered by the *Cons. Caes.* is worthless, given that the dates of its other annotations on Theudis are demonstrably wrong.
86. The best treatment of this episode remains Goubert (1947–51).
87. Proc., *Bell.* 4.5.6. and *Aed.* 6.7.14, often cited as proof of a Vandal garrison in the city (e.g., Gonzalbes [1981]; [1986]; [1989]; Vallejo [1993], 41–70), in fact suggests quite the contrary, that the site lay outside the Vandal kingdom. The *terminus post quem* for the taking of Ceuta is the capture of Carthage by Belisarius in September 533 (see PLRE 3: 191–92, for references), the *terminus ante quem* is *CJ* 1.27 of April 534, in which Ceuta is specifically named in Justinian's organization of the new African provinces. The first archaeological evidence for sixth- and seventh-century occupation is only just beginning to be published: Bernal and Pérez (2000), with references to the sparse earlier literature.
88. The date is unrecoverable. Bury (1923), 2: 146, places the attack in 544, Stein (1949), 561, places it in 547. The only certainty is that it followed the Frankish invasion of circa 541 and preceded Theudis's death, itself of uncertain date, but perhaps 548.
89. Isid., *HG* 42: *denique dum adversum milites qui Septem oppidum pulsis Gothis invaderant oceani freta transissent eundemque castrum magna vi certaminis expugnarent adveniente die dominico deposuerunt arma, ne diem sacrum proelio funestarent. hac igitur occasione reperta milites repentino incursu adgressum exercitum mari undique terraque conclusum adeo prostraverunt, ut ne unus quidem superesset qui tantae cladis excidium praetiterit.* The tenth-century Arabic history of Ahmad al-Razi, which is preserved only in its later Castilian version as the chronicle of *el Moro Rasis,* transmits a very different version of this attack, which is admitted as valid ev-

idence by Gonzalbes (1989). There is not, however, any way to evaluate the authenticity of al-Razi's information and the methodology of the first chroniclers of al-Andalus does not inspire confidence (see Collins [1989] and, *contra*, Kennedy [1995]).

90. Isid., *HG* 43; *Cons. Caes.* 133a (= CCSL 173A: 45). This murder began what Gregory of Tours characterizes as a loathsome Gothic habit of killing kings that displeased them: *Hist.* 3.30: *Sumpserant enim Gothi hanc detestabilem consuetudinem ut, siquis eis regibus non placuisset, gladio eum adpeterent et qui libuisset animo hunc sibi statuerunt regem.*

91. MGH LL 1: 467–69.

92. For the parallel evidence of church councils, see p. 266, above.

93. Horm., *Ep.* 26.

94. For the Méridan inscriptions, *ICERV* 418 = *CICM* 181; *ICERV* 425 = *CICM* 179; *ICERV* 426 = *CICM* 178. For Mértola, Alves Dias (1993), 112–14.

95. For Martin's career, see the introduction to Barlow's edition and Ferreiro (1981).

96. For Martin's insistence on hierarchy and church organization, see I Braga 6.

97. For the resounding silence about Martin in the Visigothic church, see Ferreiro (1986).

98. Both of Athanagild's daughters married Frankish kings, while Frankish princesses were married to the sons of Leovigild. See Isla (1990).

99. A point brought out forcefully in Thompson (1969), 323.

100. Isid., *HGbrev.: Interempto Theudi Theudisclus Gothis praeficitur regnans anno I hic pari coniuratorum manu inter epulas cenae gladio confossus extinguitur;* Isid., *HGprolix.* 44: *Interempto Theudi Theudisclus Gothis praeficitur, regnavit anno I mensibus VII qui dum plurimorum potentum conubia prostitutione publica macularet et ob hoc instrueret animum ad necem multorum, praeventus coniuratorum manu Spali inter epulas iugulatur confususque extinguitur; Cons. Caes.* 133a (= CCSL 173A: 45): *Thiudi mortuo Thiudisclus Gotthos regit an. I m. VII;* Greg. Tur., *Hist.* 3.30: *[Theudem] interfectum Theudegiselum levaverunt regem. his dum ad caenam cum amicis suis aepularet et esset valde laetus, caereis subito extinctis in recubitu ab inimicis gladio percussus interiit.*

101. *Cons. Caes.* 134a (= CCSL 173A: 45): *Thiudisclo mortuo Agila Gotthos regit annos V m. VI;* Isid., *HG* 45: *Extincto Theudisclo Agila rex creatur regnans annis V.*

102. Isid., *HG* 45: *iste adversus Cordubensem urbem proelium movens dum in contemptu catholicae religionis beatissimi martyris Aciscli iniuriam inferret hostiumque ac iumetorum horrore sacrum sepulchri eius locum ut profanatur polueret, inito adversus Cordubenses cives certamine poenas dignas sanctis inferentibus meruit. nam belli praesentis ultione percussus et filium ibi cum copia exercitus interfectum amisit et thesaurum omnem cum insignibus opibus*

perdidit. ipse victus ac miserabili fugatus Emeritam se recepit. Greg. Tur., *Hist.* 4.8 attests to the unpopularity of the king: *Regnante vero Agilane apud Hispaniam, cum populum gravissimo dominationis suae iugo adterriret, exercitus imperatoris Hispanias est ingressus et civitates aliquas pervasit.*

103. We would suspect the noble lineage of Athanagild, even without the confirmation provided by Ven. Fort., *carm.* 6.1.124–27. There is not, however, any reason to suppose with Vallejo (1993), 81, that Athanagild was an Amal attempting to assert the rights of that much-diminished *stirps regum.*

104. Isid., *HG* 46: *adversus quem* [viz., Agilanem] *interiecto aliquanto temporis spatio Athanagildus tyrannidem regnandi cupiditate arripiens, dum exercitum eius contra se Hispalim missum virtute militari prostrasset, videntes Gothi proprio se everti excidio et magis metuentes ne Spaniam milites auxili occasione invaderent, Agilanem Emerita interficiunt et Athanagildi se regimini tradiderunt.* See also Greg. Tur., *Hist.* 4.8.

105. Jord., *Get.* 302 is the only source to mention Liberius, who (as CIL 11: 382 shows) was around eighty-five at the time of the expedition. This passage of Jordanes comes at the very end of the *Getica* and there is no guarantee that the expedition had actually sailed when it was written. One might well doubt that Justinian placed a man in his eighties in charge of so important a mission and Liberius was certainly in Constantinople during a church council in 553 (Mansi 9: 197B, 198C). It seems unlikely that he ever got as far as Spain, whatever the emperor's initial plans might have been. As to the problem of date, if Liberius is accepted as the commander of the expedition, then the chronology of his career demands a date after spring 552 and before 553 (see Stein [1949], 820–21), but if we reject Liberius as the expedition's commander, then we are left with only a *terminus post quem* in the shape of Athanagild's rebellion, an event itself of uncertain date.

106. Moorhead (1994) is good on the basic opportunism of Justinianic policy.

107. N. 104, above; *Cons. Caes.* 144a (= CCSL 173A: 47): *Agilane mortuo Athanagildus, qui dudum tyranidem assumpserat, Gotthorum rex efficitur.*

108. For this plausible theory, Thompson (1969), 326–27.

109. The existence of this agreement is attested by Greg. Magn., *Ep.* 9: 229, in which the pope regrets to the Gothic king Reccared that no text of this pact has been preserved.

110. It is clear that the Byzantine province in southeastern Spain was only established much later. The Byzantine governing apparatus may not have been systematically organized until the 570s and always remained numerically small: Fuentes Hinojo (1998); *contra* Thompson (1969), 329–31. This is parallel to developments in Africa, for which see Pringle (1981). Vallejo (1999a) unravels the evidence for the precise administrative status of the province under Maurice. As established by Ripoll

(1996), even after imperial government was firmly installed in the southeast, nothing like a clearly demarcated *limes* existed between the Byzantine province and the rest of the peninsula, though the older views of García Moreno (1973) persist: Vallejo (1993), 376–77.

111. Ramos Fernández (1975) is the standard synthesis.

112. There is a good attempt at making sense of old and incomplete reports on the basilica in Márquez Villora and Poveda (2000).

113. The administrative organization of Byzantine Spain is controversial and the only grounds for considering Carthago Spartaria the capital of a Spanish province is the discovery there of the famous inscription of the *magister militum* Commentiolus: CIL 2: 3420 = *IHC* 176 = Abascal and Ramallo (1997), n. 208, on which see Prego (2000).

114. The possibility of its being Pliny's Ilunum is conjecture.

115. Abad Casal et al. (1993b) is a well-illustrated introduction.

116. Published in full at Abad Casal (1996), 80–82.

117. El Tolmo is the Madinat Iyih of the *pactus* and is mentioned as such by both al-Udri and al-Idrisi: Abad Casal et al. (1993a).

118. See the discussion of Ramallo (2000), 579–80.

119. Ramallo (1989) remains the basic introduction to the archaeology of Carthago Nova. For the epigraphy, p. 35, above.

120. See now Ramallo (2000), 586–87, *contra* San Martín Moro (1985); Ramallo and Méndez (1986).

121. Ramallo, Ruiz, and Berrocal (1996); Marín and de Miquel (1999).

122. Laiz, Pérez, and Ruiz (1987).

123. Ramallo, Ruiz, and Berrocal (1996); Ramallo and Ruiz (1996–97); Ramallo and Ruiz (2000).

124. Ramallo and Ruiz (1998), 38–42; Ramallo (2000), 601, for the coins.

125. Reynolds (1993), 21–25.

126. Martínez Rodríguez and Ponce (2000); Ramallo and Ruiz (2000), 313.

127. Reynolds (1993), 21–25. Ramallo (2000), 600, asserts the importance of sixth- and seventh-century Cartagena as a point for redistributing goods to its hinterland, but gives no evidence.

128. Most explicitly Thompson (1969), but generally including all the standard histories of the period, e.g., Orlandis (1987); García Moreno (1989).

129. Inter alia, Salvador (1986); Vallejo (1993); Ripoll (1996).

130. There is a large literature on the family of Isidore: see esp. Beltrán Torreira (1993), arguing definitively against Fontaine and Cazier (1983). Ripoll (1996), 255, sees in the flight of Isidore's family a sign that the Carthaginiensian nobility had resisted Byzantine occupation and that Cartagena had been occupied by force.

131. *Cons. Caes.* 6a (= CCSL 173A: 61): *Hic Athanagildus Hispalim ciuitatem Hispaniae provinciae Baeticae sitam bello impetitam suam fecit, Cordubam uero frequenti incursione admodum laesit.* The only pre-Leovigildian in-

scription from Spain to be dated by regnal year refers to the *anno Atanag-ildi septimo regis* (*ILERV* 284). Though now preserved only in transcription, the inscription came from Zaragoza.

132. Isid., *HG* 47: *decessit autem Athanagildus Toleto propria morte vacante regno mensibus V.*

133. Velázquez and Ripoll (2000), 538, envisage a civil war for the royal title during the five-month interregnum, reading more into the sources than is there.

134. Isid., *HG* 48: *post Athanagildum Liuua Narbonae Gothis regno praeficitur regnans annis tribus.* Ioh. Bicl., II Justini 3: *His temporibus Athanaildus rex Gothorum in Hispania vitae finem suscepit et Livva pro eo in regnum provehitur.*

135. See previous note.

136. For which see Vallejo (1999b).

137. For the following, see Ioh. Bicl. 11–79 (= CCSL 173A: 62–77) and Isid., *HG* 48–51; for the sack of Saint Martin's monastery near Sagunto, Greg. Tur., *Glor. conf.* 12.

138. Hillgarth (1966) remains the best treatment, but see now Arce (2001).

139. For the role of episcopal consent to the Gothic monarchy, see Stocking (2000), who rightly emphasizes the novelty and sense of experiment behind III Toledo.

140. Ioh. Bicl. 10 (= CCSL 173A: 61).

Chapter 12. The New World of the Sixth Century

1. The *nomina hispanarum sedium,* also called the *provinciale visigothicum,* is edited in CCSL 175: 421–28. The extant text is eighth-century, but it seems likely that it was based on a seventh-century original: David (1947), 1–4.

2. Roldán (1975), 19–110.

3. Interesting commentary in Fuentes Domínguez (1997b).

4. Particularly the evidence of Hil., *Ep.* 16 (Thiel) = PL 58: 17, but see chapters 3 and 5 in this volume.

5. Thus the *lex Irnitana* comes to us not from the forum of *Irni,* but rather from a metal worker's shop to which it had been transported at an unknown date in late antiquity: Fernández Gómez and del Amo (1990).

6. Extensive work on the typologies of the local ceramics that replaced African imports in the 550s is needed, but once they are clarified we will possess much better tools for dating sixth-century evidence.

7. It is becoming increasingly common to find the old rhetoric of the third-century crisis reapplied to the fifth century: see the various contributions of García Moreno and Rascón (1999). However, Gurt and Palet (2001) offers a stimulating and subtle alternative.

8. We know this because King Sisebut had the relics of Saint Zoilus trans-

ferred to the church of Saint Felix, an intramural church otherwise not known archaeologically: Rodríguez Neila (1988), 550, although Marfil (2000) believes that the church of Saint Felix was actually located in the extramural complex of Cercadilla.

9. *ILPG* 152, with plate 98 = *ILERV* 303 = CIL 2²/5: 652 = *HEp.* 6: 587: *In nomini dei nostri Iesu Christi consacrata ese eclesia sancti Stefani primi martyris y in locum Nativola a sancto Paulo Accitano pontifice die . . . anno . . . domini nostri gloriosissimi Wittirici regis era DCXLV. Item consacrata est eclesia sancti Iohannis Baptistae . . . Item consacrata est eclesia sancti Vincentii martyris Valentini a sancto Lilliolo Accitano pontifice die XI kalendas Februarias anno VIII gloriosissimi domini Reccaredi regis era DCXXXII. Haec sancta tria tabernacula in gloriam Trinitatis sanctissimae cohoperantibus sanctis aedificata sunt ab inlustri Gudiliuva cum operarios vernolos et sumptu propio.* The inscription is presently in Granada.

10. As early as the start of the fifth century, Jerome tells us of the Baetican aristocrat Lucinius whose Christian piety led him to donate on a grand scale both to local churches and to others in Jerusalem and Alexandria: *Ep.* 71.

11. *ILPG* 161 = *ILERV* 177: *recessit in pace die duodecimo [kal.] Maias anno [pri]mo domini nostri [Steph]ani episcopi,* speaking of the priest Nocidius of Elvira, dead in 589.

12. The council of Valencia attracted only six bishops and fully three of the council's six extant canons (Valencia 2–4 [CCH 4: 314–20]) are concerned both to preserve a bishop's possessions from casual looters and from relatives of the dead bishop who might lay claim to his property, and to regulate the conduct of an episcopal funeral. The council met on 4 December, some time between 546 and 549. The difficulty with dating it lies in the fact that the *aera* date of the council is given as 587, which is to say A.D. 549; but the formula *anno XV Theudi regis sub die II nonas Decembris* should probably mean 546 (CCH 4: 313–14). None of the attested MS variants resolve the contradiction, both numbers are equally likely to have experienced corruption, and the problem is insoluble.

13. *ILERV* 279 = *IRVT* 117: *Pius preclarus doctor alacerque facundus / Iustinianus caelebs pontifex sacer / noba templa construens vetustaque restaurans / ornabit festa dictis predicans in populis / virgines instituens monacosque guvernans / scripsit plura posteris profutura [permultis] hic miro maris insolam munimine sepsit / inque amaris circumfluentibus undis / silice disrupto predulcem repperit limfam / hic Vincentium gloriosum martirem Xri / sat pio quem coluit moderamine vivens / hunc devotus moriens reliquid eredem / undecim presentis quinquennia vite [peragens] / quattuor lustris visque quaternis mensibus / connumerandus sanctis ministrabit antestis.* Corell (1989) has shown that the traditional attribution to Bishop Justinian of a second inscription, *ILERV* 356 = *IRVT* 116, is impossible.

14. *ILERV* 277: 3–5: *in te libra morum in te modestia tenuit regnum / nitens elo-*

quio mitissimus pollebas in corde / gerens curam pauperum, pietate preditus ampla.

15. Roselló (1995), though the evidence is minimal. Mateu y Llopis (1949), 157, is probably correct in seeing the monastery surrounded with waters as lying at Valencia itself, in the delta of the Turia.

16. That the traditional ascription to an unknown deacon Paul is a pious fiction was shown by Maya Sánchez in the introduction to her edition. See chapter 10.

17. See Mateos (1999).

18. For the uncertainty of the date, see pp. 238–39, above.

19. For the same reason, the two side apses that flanked the central apse likewise had no communication with the nave, which was tripartite, its central aisle 15 meters across, each side aisle half that width. Unusually for a basilica of this era, the three naves were between them wider than the three apses. There is a three-dimensional reconstruction in Caballero and Mateos (1992), 41. On the liturgical aspects, Godoy (1995), 278–81.

20. This separation is demonstrated by the remains of this feature's foundation, which runs perpendicular to the arcades of the nave. Because only the foundation is preserved, it is impossible to tell whether an arcade or some sort of wall sat atop it: Mateos (1999), 82–85.

21. See Godoy (1995), 104–19, with Dodds (1990) for the later period.

22. Cruz Villalón (1985) is an exhaustive catalogue of these remains up to the date of its publication; it may be supplemented by Cruz Villalón (1995) and by the catalogue of the Visigothic collection of the MNAR: Álvarez and Barrera (1995). Mateos (1999), 192, discusses the literary evidence for intramural churches. The structure identified by Márquez and Hernández (1998) as a church near the provincial forum is too imperfectly known to allow for that conclusion.

23. It is also likely that towers were raised on either side of the central apse, communicating with the exterior of the basilica and the side apses, but still not with the interior. Mateos (1999), 160, identifies these reforms as those recorded in the *Vitas Patrum* of Bishop Fidelis, whose episcopate lasted from 560 to 570. Though plausible, the connection cannot be proven and the reforms might actually date to the seventh century not the sixth.

24. The fourth-century remains are treated in passing by Caballero and Mateos (1991), 544–46, and Mateos (1995b), 309–10, in both of which the early mausolea are said to have been destroyed in the middle of the fifth century, probably in the course of a barbarian raid. Until the excavation receives a thorough publication along the lines of Mateos (1999), we can only be certain that the fourth-century mausolea had fallen into disrepair by the middle of the sixth century when new construction on the site made use of their remains.

25. *VPE* 5.3.
26. It is much less good for residential structures, but see Barrientos (2001), for possible evidence.
27. We cannot date it with certainty: see p. 107, above.
28. Hauschild (1984–85); Avellà (1985). The date depends entirely upon knowing how long early fifth-century bronze coins remained in circulation, a matter of some controversy.
29. See most recently Marfil (2000).
30. Jiménez Cobo (2000), 50–51.
31. As demonstrated by the addition of a new layer of sand that raised and enlarged the fourth-century floor of the arena: see p. 95, above.
32. As suggested by the internal partitions with which they were now subdivided: Dias Diogo (1993). See the similar sixth- and seventh-century evidence from the site of the theater of Córdoba: Monterroso and Cepillo (2002).
33. Beltrán Lloris (1993).
34. The evidence for domestic architecture is complicated by the circumstances of its excavation, largely in rescue digs of the 1970s, which concentrated on mosaic remains and provides fairly minimal evidence for the chronology of the *domus* themselves. While most of the mosaics date from the late third and fourth centuries, and come from houses that are said to have been abandoned during the fifth century, the mosaics of the so-called Casa de Cupidos are dated typologically to a point well into the fifth century: Fernández Galiano (1984a); (1984b).
35. The only adequate chronological indicator for this desuetude is a coin of Theodosius II found in the layer of fill that was used to level the site of the public buildings after they were no longer being used. Given the very great length of time for which late Roman coins could circulate in Hispania, this coin is not as useful as it might be.
36. Rascón (1995), 172–81; (1999); Sánchez Montes (1999).
37. On which see TED'A (1990); (1994).
38. Sisebut, *Ep. Wis.* 6.
39. Keay (1991a).
40. Thus Carreté, Keay, and Millett (1995), which does so much to dispel the notion of Tarragona's fifth-century decadence, continues to insist upon the late sixth-century desolation of the site.
41. See Rocas at al. (1992); Llinàs et al. (1992); (1997).
42. Gurt and Godoy (2000), 449–51, gives an excellent, if impressionistic, account of the city in the sixth century.
43. For a summary of the chronology, Argente Oliver (1979), 125–26.
44. Ibid., 120–24.
45. The date is suggested by a *triens* of the Gothic king Wittiza: Ramos Sáinz and Castelo (1993).
46. Rubio (1988); (1991).

47. See Maloney and Hale (1996), though the lack of a stratigraphy from the site makes it difficult to be certain about dates.
48. Rodríguez Martín (1995a); (1995b).
49. Other examples include the villa of Pacs in Barcelona province: Balil (1987).
50. Clariana and Prevosti (1994). A similar progression can be observed at the less splendid Catalan villa of Puig Rodon, where the sixth century brought at least part of the site full circle: in the late second or early third century, an early imperial industrial patio, perhaps for making ceramics, was amortized and rebuilt as a fine dwelling room with a mosaic floor that seems to have continued in use throughout late antiquity. Then, during the second half of the fifth century and probably at the very end of it, the room was again turned to an industrial purpose, with kilns being installed on top of the high imperial mosaic: Casas (1986).
51. Vaquerizo (1990).
52. Carmona (1990).
53. Generally, Palol (1989).
54. In fact, the sequence of coins from the site runs as late as the reign of Achila II, the last Gothic king and one known to history solely from his coinage: Palol (1986). For the seventh-century coinage more generally, see Miles (1952) and *MEC* 1: 49–54.
55. The protofeudalism of the later seventh-century (or even earlier: Carrobles and Rodríguez [1988], 121–30; Tudanca [1997], 60–61) is a basic assumption of the literature on the period, rooted in the works of Barbero and Vigil, e.g., (1974) and (1978).
56. Nolla and Casas (1990); see also Gurt and Palet (2001).
57. Carreté, Keay, and Millet (1995); Reynolds (1993); the localized evidence from Celti tells the same story for the lower Guadalquivir valley, with local production taking up the slack of declining imports: Keay, Creighton, and Remesal (2000).
58. At the villa of Torre Llauder near Mataró, imported African pottery survived in some quantity until the middle of the sixth century: Clariana and Prevosti (1994) and on the pottery, Clariana and Járrega (1994).
59. Feijoo (2000a). The date is unclear because the ceramic typologies of the period are so badly understood.
60. The date depends upon how one assesses the Byzantine influences on the villa's typology, rather than firmly dateable finds.
61. On Pla de Nadal, see Juan and Pastor (1989a); (1989b).
62. Arrechea (1997); Olmo (1997).
63. The best treatment of the life can be found in the very similar Castellanos (1998) and (1999).
64. Braulio's Cantabria is a not very well-defined region, but it is certainly a much larger place than the modern-day province that bears its name. At one time or another in the *Vita Aemiliani* it seems to take in the whole

mountain area between Tarazona (Turiasso) in the east, and Amaia, near modern Villadiego, in the west (*BAGRW* 25: A2–D4).

65. *V. Aem.* 9: *relinquensque rura tentendit ad eremi loca.*

66. Ibid., 10: *villa Vergegio . . . non multo moratus tempore, vidit impedimento sibi fore hominum ad se concurrentium multitudinem.*

67. Ibid., 12: *Didymo etiam, qui tunc pontificatus gerebat in Tyrassona ministerium, cum hoc quoque fuisset delatum, insequitur hominem ordini ecclesiastico volens inserere, eius quippe erat in dioecesi. durum illi primum videri, ac grave refugere ac reniti et quasi de coelo traduci ad mundum, de quiete iam paene nacta ad offica laboriosa, vitamque contemplativam transferri ad activam.*

68. Ibid., 13: *Tunc a suscepto dudum ministerio relaxatus, ubi tunc vocatur eius oratorium reliquum vitae tempus peregit innoxius.*

69. For the location and discussion, Castellanos (1999), 28–30.

70. The recent translation of Fear (1997), 28, prejudges the case in calling Amaia a village.

71. *V. Aem.* 26.

72. Maximus and Columba: *V. Aem.* 16; Honorius: *V. Aem.* 17.

73. Fredegar 4.1.33; Greg. Tur., *Hist.* 4.8.

74. *Form. Vis.* 20.1–2: *Insigni merito et Geticae de stirpe senatus illius sponsae nimis dilectae illae.*

75. See García Moreno (1995).

Bibliography

Primary Sources

Ammianus Marcellinus. *Res Gestae.* W. Seyfarth, ed. 2 vols. Leipzig, 1978.

Antonine Itinerary. O. Cuntz, ed. *Itineraria Romana I: Itineraria Antonini Augusti et Burdigalense.* Leipzig, 1929.

Augustine of Hippo. *Epistulae nuper in lucem prolatae.* J. Divjak, ed. (CSEL 88). Vienna, 1981.

———. *Sermones.* C. Lambot, ed. (CCSL 41). Turnhout, 1961.

Ausonius. *The Works of Ausonius.* R. P. H. Green, ed. Oxford, 1991.

Braulio. *Vita Aemiliani. Sancti Braulionis Caesaraugustani Episcopi Vita S. Emiliani.* Luís Vázquez de Parga, ed. Madrid, 1943.

Caesarius Arelatensis. *Epistulae.* G. Morin, ed. (CC 103–4). Turnhout, 1953.

Cassiodorus. *Chronica.* In *Chronica minora* 2. Pp. 109–62.

———. *Variae.* Th. Mommsen, ed. (MGH AA 12). Berlin, 1894.

Chronica Caesaraugustana. See *Consularia Caesaraugustana.*

Chronica gallica a. 452. See Burgess (2001a).

Chronica gallica a. 511. See Burgess (2001b).

Chronica minora, saec. IV.V.VI.VII. Th. Mommsen, ed. 3 vols. (MGH AA 9, 11, 13). Berlin, 1892–98.

Chronicon Paschale. L. Dindorf, ed. Bonn, 1832.

Claudian. *Opera quae extant.* Th. Birt, ed. (MGH AA 10). Berlin, 1892.

Codex Eurici. In *Leges Visigothorum.* K. Zeumer, ed. (MGH LL 1). Hannover, 1902. Pp. 1–32.

Codex Justinianus. Paul Krueger, ed. (Corpus Iuris Civilis 2). Berlin, 1892.

Codex Theodosianus. Th. Mommsen, ed. *Theodosiani libri XVI cum constitutionibus Sirmondianis.* 3 vols. Berlin, 1905.

Collectio Avellana. Epistulae imperatorum pontificum aliorum Avellana quae dicitur collectio. O. Guenther, ed. (CSEL 35). Vienna, 1895.

Consentius of Minorca. *Epistulae.* In *Sancti Augustini Opera: Epistolae ex duobus codicibus nuper in lucem prolatae.* J. Divjak, ed. (CSEL 88). Vienna, 1981. Pp. 51–80.

Consularia Caesaraugustana. C. Cardelle de Hartmann, ed. (CSSL 173A). Turnhout, 2001.

Consularia Constantinopolitana. See Burgess (1993), 214–46.

Consularia Italica. In *Chronica minora* 1. Pp. 249–336.

Cyprian of Carthage. *Epistulae.* W. de Hartel, ed. (CSEL 3). Vienna, 1871.

Ennodius of Pavia. *Vita Epiphanii.* F. Vogel, ed. (MGH AA 7). Berlin, 1885. Pp. 84–109.

Epistulae Arelatenses. W. Gundlach, ed. (MGH Ep. 3). Berlin, 1903. Pp. 1–83.

Epistulae Wisigothicae. See Gil (1972), 1–49.

Eugenius of Toledo. *Carmina.* F. Vollmer, ed. (MGH AA 14). Berlin, 1905. Pp. 11–44.

Eutropius. *Breviarium.* C. Santini, ed. Stuttgart, 1979.

Evagrius Scholasticus. *Historia Ecclesiastica.* J. Bidez and L. Parmentier, eds. *Ecclesiastical History.* London, 1898.

Excerpta Sangallensia. In *Chronica minora* 1. Pp. 274–336.

Festus. *Breviarium.* J. Eadie, ed., *The Breviarium of Festus.* London, 1967.

Formulae Visigothicae. See Gil (1972), 70–112.

Fredegarius. *Chronica.* J. M. Wallace-Hadrill, ed. *The Fourth Book of the Chronicle of Fredegar, with his Continuations.* Edinburgh, 1960.

Gennadius Arelatensis. *De viris illustribus.* E. Richardson, ed. Leipzig, 1896.

Gregory the Great, Pope. *Registrum epistularum.* D. Norberg, ed. (CCSL 140–140A). Turnhout, 1982.

Gregory of Tours. *Libri historiarum X.* B. Krusch and W. Levison, eds. (MGH SRM 1.1). Hannover, 1951.

———. *Gloria confessorum.* B. Krusch, ed. (MGH SRM 1.2). Hannover, 1885.

———. *Gloria martyrum.* B. Krusch, ed. (MGH SRM 1.2). Hannover, 1885.

Herodian. C. R. Whittaker, ed. 2 vols. London, 1969.

Hilarius Arelatensis. *Vita Honorati.* S. Cavallin, ed. *Vitae SS. Honorati et Hilarii.* Lund, 1952.

Hilarus, Pope. *Epistulae.* A. Thiel, ed. *Epistulae romanorum pontificum.* Braunsberg, 1868. Pp. 126–70.

Historia Augusta. E. Hohl, ed. 2 vols. Leipzig, 1927.

Hormisdas, Pope. *Epistulae.* A. Thiel, ed. *Epistulae romanorum pontificum.* Braunsberg, 1868. Pp. 741–990.

Hydatius. See Burgess (1993), 9–124.

Innocent, Pope. *Epistulae.* PL 20: 463–608.

Isidore of Seville. *Historia Gothorum.* C. Rodríguez Alonso, ed. *Las historias de los Godos, Vandalos, y Suevos de Isidoro de Sevilla: estudio, edición crítica y tra-ducción.* León, 1975.

————. *De viris illustribus.* See Codoñer (1964).

Itineraria Antoniniana. See Antonine Itinerary.

Jerome. *Chronicon.* R. Helm, ed. *Eusebius Werke 17: Die Chronik des Hierony-mus.* (GCS 47). Berlin, 1956.

————. *De viris illustribus.* E. Richardson, ed. Leipzig, 1896.

————. *Epistulae.* I. Hilberg, ed., rev. M. Kamptner. 3 vols. in 4. (CSEL 54–56). Vienna, 1996.

John of Biclar. C. Cardelle de Hartmann, ed. (CSSL 173A). Turnhout, 2001.

Jordanes. *Getica.* Th. Mommsen, ed. (MGH AA 5.1). Berlin, 1882.

Julian. *Epistulae.* J. Bidez and F. Cumont, eds. *Iuliani Epistulae Leges Poematia Fragmenta Varia.* Paris, 1922.

Laterculus Veronensis. See Barnes (1982), 202–3.

Leges visigothorum. K. Zeumer, ed. (MGH LL 1, sect. 1). Hanover, 1902.

Leo I, Pope. *Epistulae.* PL 54: 593–1218.

Lex romana visigothorum. G. Haenel, ed. Berlin, 1849.

Marcellinus Comes. In *Chronica minora* 2. Pp. 37–103.

Marius of Avenches. See Favrod (1993).

Martin of Braga. *De correctione rusticorum.* C. Barlow, ed. *Martini episcopi Bra-carensis opera omnia.* New Haven, 1950. Pp. 183–203.

Merobaudes. *Fl. Merobaudis Reliquiae.* F. Vollmer, ed. (MGH AA 14). Berlin, 1905. Pp. 1–20.

Nomina hispanarum sedium. F. Glorie, ed. (CCSL 175). Pp. 421–28.

Notitia Dignitatum. O. Seeck, ed. *Notitia Dignitatum accedunt Notitia urbis Con-stantinopolitanae et latercula provinciarum.* Berlin, 1876.

Notitia Galliarum. F. Glorie, ed. (CCSL 175). Pp. 379–410.

Olympiodorus of Thebes. See Blockley (1983), 152–210.

Orientius. *Commonitorium.* R. Ellis, ed. *Poetae Christiani Minores.* (CSEL 16). Vienna, 1888. Pp. 205–43.

Orosius. *Historiarum aduersum paganos libri septem.* K. Zangemeister, ed. (CSEL 5). Vienna, 1882.

Pacian of Barcelona. *San Paciano, Obras.* L. Rubio Fernández, ed. Barcelona, 1958.

Panegyrici Latini. R. Mynors, ed. *XII Panegyrici Latini.* Oxford, 1964.

Passio Marcelli. See Lanata (1972).

Paulinus of Nola. *Epistulae.* W. de Hartel, ed. (CSEL 29). Vienna, 1894.

————. *Carmina.* W. de Hartel, ed. (CSEL 30). Vienna, 1894.

Paulinus of Perigueux. *Vita sancti Martini.* M. Petschenig, ed. *Poetae Christiani Minores.* (CSEL 16). Vienna, 1888. Pp. 17–159.

Philostorgius. *Historia Ecclesiastica.* J. Bidez, ed. (GCS 21). Berlin, 1913.

Phoebadius. *Contra Arianos.* R. Demeulenaere, ed. (CCSL 64). Turnhout, 1985. Pp. 23–54.

Pliny. *Historia Naturalis.* C. Mayhoff, ed. Leipzig, 1899–1906.

Polemius Silvius. *Laterculus.* In *Chronica minora* 1. Pp. 511–51.

Polybius. W. R. Paton, ed. and trans. 6 vols. London, 1922–27.

Possidius. *Vita Augustini.* H. T. Weiskotten, ed. Princeton, 1919.

Potamius of Lisbon. *De Lazaro.* In *Potamii episcopi Olisponensis opera omnia.* M. Conti, ed. (CCSL 69A). Turnhout, 1999. Pp. 165–75.

Priscillian of Avila. *Opera quae extant.* G. Schepps, ed. Vienna, 1889.

Priscus. See Blockley (1983), 222–378.

Procopius. *Opera.* J. Haury, ed. 4 vols. Leipzig, 1905–13.

Prosper of Aquitaine and Continuations. In *Chronica minora* 1. Pp. 341–500.

Provinciale visigothicum. See *Nomina hispanarum sedium.*

Prudentius. *Peristephanon.* E. Cunningham, ed. (CCSL 126). Turnhout, 1966. Pp. 251–389.

Ruricius. *Epistulae.* R. Demeulenaere, ed. (CCSL 64). Turnhout, 1985. Pp. 303–94.

Rutilius Namatianus. *De reditu suo.* J. Vessereau and F. Préchac, eds. Paris, 1933.

Salvian. *De gubernatione Dei.* C. Halm, ed. (MGH AA 1.1). Berlin, 1877.

Severus of Minorca. *Epistula.* See Bradbury (1996).

Sidonius Apollinaris. *Poèmes et Lettres.* A. Loyen, ed. 3 vols. Paris, 1960–70.

Sozomen. *Historia Ecclesiastica.* J. Bidez and G. C. Hanson, eds. (GCS 50). Berlin, 1960.

Strabo. H. L. Jones, ed. 8 vols. London, 1917–33.

Sulpicius Severus. *Chronicon.* C. Halm, ed. (CSEL 1). Vienna, 1866. Pp. 1–105.

———. *Vita Sancti Martini.* C. Halm, ed. (CSEL 1). Vienna, 1866. Pp. 107–37.

Symmachus. *Epistulae.* O. Seeck, ed. (MGH AA 6.1). Berlin, 1883.

Venantius Fortunatus. *Carmina.* F. Leo, ed. (MGH AA 4.1). Berlin, 1881.

Victor, Sextus Aurelius. *De Caesaribus.* Fr. Pichlmayr, ed. Leipzig, 1911.

Victor of Aquitaine. *Cursus paschalis.* In *Chronica minora* 1. Pp. 666–735.

Victor of Tunnuna. C. Cardelle de Hartmann, ed. (CCSL 173A). Turnhout, 2001.

Victor of Vita. *Historia persecutionis Africanae provinciae.* C. Halm, ed. (MGH AA 3.1). Berlin, 1879.

Vita Caesarii Arelatensis. S. Cavallin, ed. *Vitae SS. Honorati et Hilarii.* Lund, 1952.

Vitas Sanctorum Patrum Emeretensium. A. Maya Sánchez, ed. (CCSL 116). Turnhout, 1992.

Zosimus. *Historia Nova.* F. Paschoud, ed. 3 vols. in 5. Paris, 1970–89.

COLLECTIVE WORKS WITH NO LISTED EDITORS

I Actas Andalucía = *Actas del I coloquio de historia antigua de Andalucía.* 2 vols. Córdoba, 1993.

II Actas Andalucía = *Actas del II congreso de historia de Andalucía, Córdoba, 1991.* Córdoba, 1994.

I Actas Palencianas = *Actas del I congreso de historia de Palencia, tomo I: arte, aqueología y edad antigua.* Palencia, 1987.

II Actas Palencianas = *Actas del II congreso de historia de Palencia, tomo I: prehistoria, arqueología, e historia antigua.* Palencia, 1990.

II Actas Sorianas = *Actas del II symposium de arqueología soriana.* Soria, 1989.

I Actas Talavera = *Actas de las primeras jornadas de arqueología de Talavera de la Reina y sus tierras.* Toledo, 1993.

La casa urbana = *La casa urbana hispanorromana.* Zaragoza, 1991.

II Congreso Arq. Med. Esp. = *Actas del II Congreso de Arqueología Medieval Española.* 2 vols. Madrid, 1987.

III Congreso Arq. Med. Esp. = *Actas del III Congreso de Arqueología Medieval Española.* 2 vols. Oviedo, 1989.

IV Congreso Arq. Med. Esp. = *Actas del IV Congreso de Arqueología Medieval Española.* 2 vols. Alicante, 1993.

XIV Congreso Int. Arq. Clas. = *Actas del XIV Congreso Internacional de Arqueología Clásica: La ciudad en el mundo romano/Actes del Congrés Internacional d'Arqueologia Clàssica: La ciutat en el món romà (Tarragona 1993).* Tarragona, 1994.

Empereurs d'Espagne = *Les empereurs romains d'Espagne.* Paris, 1966.

"Excavacions arqueològiques Tarragona" (2000) = various authors, "Excavacions arqueològiques a la Plaça de la Font de Tarragona," in Ruiz (2000), 61–67.

Galicia: da romanidade á xermanización = *Galicia: da romanidade á xermanización. Problemas históricos e culturais (Actas do encontro científico en homenaxe a Fermín Bouza Brey (1901–1973), Santiago de Compostela, outubro 1992).* Santiago de Compostela, 1993.

Hispania el Legado = *Hispania, el legado de Roma. En el año de Trajano. (La Lonja—Zaragoza, Septiembre–Noviembre 1998).* Madrid, 1998.

Homenaje Saenz = *Homenaje a Saenz de Buruaga.* Badajoz, 1982.

Legio VII Gemina = *Legio VII Gemina.* León, 1970.

Mérida 1 = *Mérida. Excavaciones Arqueológicas: 1994–1995. Memoria.* Mérida, 1997.

Mérida 2 = *Mérida. Excavaciones Arqueológicas 2: 1996. Memoria.* Mérida, 1998.

Mérida 3 = *Mérida. Excavaciones Arqueológicas 3: 1997. Memoria.* Mérida, 1999.

Mérida 4 = *Mérida. Excavaciones Arqueológicas 4: 1998. Memoria.* Mérida, 2000.

Mérida 5 = *Mérida. Excavaciones Arqueológicas 5: 1999. Memoria.* Mérida, 2001.

Mérida: Patrimonio = *Mérida: Patrimonio de la Humanidad. Conjunto Monumental.* Mérida, 1999.

Miscel.lània Recasens = *Miscel.lània Arqueològica a Josep M. Recasens, Abril 1992.* Tarragona, 1992.

Necrópolis de Zaragoza = *Las Necrópolis de Zaragoza, Cuadernos de Zaragoza* 63. Zaragoza, 1991.

Plaza de la Seo = *La Plaza de la Seo, Zaragoza: Investigaciones histórico-arqueológicas.* Zaragoza, 1989.

RACH III = *III Reunió d'arqueologia cristiana hispànica (Maó, Menorca)*. Barcelona, 1994.
RACH IV = *IV Reunió d'arqueologia cristiana hispànica (Lisboa)*. Barcelona, 1995.
RACH V = *V Reunió d'arqueologia cristiana hispànica (Cartagena)*. Barcelona, 2000.

OTHER TITLES

Abad Casal, Lorenzo. (1996). "La epigrafía del Tolmo de Minateda (Hellín, Albacete) y un nuevo municipio romano del *conventus Carthaginiensis,*" *AEspA* 69: 77–108.

——, Sonia Gutiérrez Lloret, and Rubí Sanz Gamo. (1993a). "El proyecto de investigación arqueológica 'Tolmo de Minateda' (Hellín, Albacete): Nuevas perspectivas en el panorama arqueológico de sureste peninsular," in *Jornadas de Arqueología Albacetense en la Universidad Autónoma de Madrid*. Madrid. Pp. 147–76.

——, Sonia Gutiérrez Lloret, and Rubí Sanz Gamo. (1993b). "El Tolmo de Minateda (Hellín, Albacete) a la luz de las últimas excavaciones (1988–1992)," in *El Acequión (Albacete) y El Tolmo de Minateda (Hellín): Síntesis de las excavaciones*. Albacete. Pp. 29–51.

d'Abadal i de Vinyals, Ramon. (1960). *Del Reino de Tolosa al Reino del Toledo*. Madrid. Reprinted, in Catalan, in Abadal (1969), 27–56.

——. (1969). *Dels visigots als catalans 1: la Hispània visigòtica i la Catalunya carolíngia*. Barcelona.

Abascal Palazón, Juan Manuel. (1994). "Hallazgos arqueológicos y circulación monetaria: Disfunciones metodológicas en el estudio de la Hispania romana," in *Actas del IX Congreso Nacional de Numísmatica*. Elche. Pp. 143–58.

——, and Urbano Espinosa. (1989). *La ciudad hispano-romana: privilegio y poder*. Logroño.

——, and Sebastián F. Ramallo Asensio. (1997). *La ciudad de Carthago Nova*, vol. 3: *La documentación epigráfica*. Murcia.

——, Martín Almagro-Gorbea, and Alberto J. Lorrio Alvarado. (1997). "Las termas monumentales de Segóbriga," *Revista de Arqueología* 195: 38–45.

Adserias, M., J. M. Macias, J. J. Menchon, and J. M. Puche. (1997). "La transformació urbana de Tarragona al segle IV: Noves dades arqueològiques," in *Hispània i Roma: D'August a Carlemany, Congrés d'homenatge al Dr. Pere de Palol*. Girona. Pp. 923–38.

Aguarod Otal, Carmen, and Antonio Mostalac Carrillo. (1998). *La Arqueología de Zaragoza en la Antigüedad tardía*. (Historia de Zaragoza 4). Zaragoza.

Aguilar Sáenz, Antonio. (1991). "Excavaciones arqueológicas en la villa romana de 'La Sevillana' (Esparragosa de Lares, Badajoz): Campañas de 1987, 1988 y 1989," *Extremadura Arqueológica* 2: 445–56.

——, Pascal Guichard, and S. Lefebvre. (1992–93). "La ciudad antigua de Lacimurga y su entorno rural," *SHHA* 10–11: 109–30.

————, and Pascal Guichard. (1993). *Villas romaines d'Estrémadure: Doña Maria, La Sevillana et leur environment.* (Collection de la Casa de Velázquez 43). Madrid.

Alarção, Jorge de. (1990). "A urbanização de Portugal nas épocas de César e de Augusto," in Trillmich and Zanker (1990), 43–57.

————. (1998). *S. Cucufate.* (Roteiros da Arqueologia Portuguesa 5). Lisbon.

————, and Robert Étienne. (1977). *Fouilles de Conimbriga I: L'architecture.* Paris.

————, Robert Étienne, and F. Mayet. (1990). *Les villas romaines de São Cucufate (Portugal).* Paris.

————, Robert Étienne, and F. Mayet. (1995). "Os monumentos cristãos da villa de S. Cucufate," in *RACH IV,* 383–87.

Alba Calzado, Miguel. (1997). "Ocupación diacrónica del área arqueológica de Morería (Mérida)," in *Mérida 1,* 285–315.

————. (1998). "Consideraciones arqueológicas en torno al siglo V en Mérida: repercusiones en las viviendas y en la muralla," in *Mérida 2,* 361–85.

————. (1999). "El ámbito doméstico de época visigoda en Mérida," in *Mérida 3,* 387–418.

————. (2000). "Intervención arqueológica en el solar de la c/ Suárez Somonte, esquina con c/ Sáenz de Buruaga: Transición de un espacio doméstico y viario de época romana a la Tardoantigüedad," in *Mérida 4,* 277–303.

————. (2001). "Características del viario urbano de Emerita entre los siglos I y VIII," in *Mérida 5,* 397–423.

Albertini, Eugène. (1923). *Les divisions administratives de l'Espagne romaine.* Paris.

Albiach, Rosa, Àngels Badía, Matías Calvo, Carmen Marín, Josefina Piá, and Albert Ribera. (2000). "Las últimas excavaciones (1992–1998) del solar de l'Almoina: nuevos datos de la zona episcopal de *Valentia,*" in *RACH V,* 63–86.

Alfenim, Rafael A. E., and Maria da Conceição Lopes. (1995). "A basílica paleocristã/visigótica do Monte da Cegonha (Vidigueira)," in *RACH IV,* 389–99.

Alföldy, Géza. (1969). *Fasti Hispanienses.* Wiesbaden.

————. (1973). *Flamines provinciae Hispaniae Citerioris.* (Anejos del *Archivo Español de Arqueología* 6). Madrid.

————. (1975). *Die römischen Inschriften von Tarraco.* (Madrider Forschungen 10). 2 vols. Berlin.

————. (1977). *Res publica Leserensis (Forcall, Castellón).* Valencia.

————. (1984). "Drei städtische Eliten im römischen Hispanien," *Gerión* 2: 193–238.

————. (1985). *The Social History of Rome.* D. Braund and F. Pollock, trans. London.

———. (1987). *Römisches Städtwesen auf der neukastilischen Hochebene.* Heidelberg.

———. (1988). "Tarraco y la Hispania romana: cultos y sociedad," in Mayer (1988), 7–26.

———. (1992). "Una inscripción funeraria de Tarraco del Bajo Imperio," in *Miscel.lània Recasens,* 13–17.

———. (1994). "Evergetismo en las ciudades del imperio romano," in *XIV Congreso Int. Arq. Clas.,* 63–67.

———. (1995). "Der Status der Provinz Baetica um die Mitte des 3. Jahrhunderts," in Regula Frei Stolba and Michael Alexander Speidel, eds. *Römische Inschriften—Neufunde, Neulesungen und Neuinterpretationen. Festschrift für Hans Lieb zum 65. Geburtstag.* Basel. Pp. 29–42.

———. (1996). "Spain," in Bowman, Champlin, and Lintott (1996), 449–63.

———. (1997). *Die Bauinschriften des Aquäduktes von Segovia und des Amphitheaters von Tarraco.* (Madrider Forschungen 19). Berlin.

———. (1999). "Aspectos de la vida urbana en las ciudades de la Meseta Sur," in González Fernández (1999b), 467–85.

———. (2000a). *Provincia Hispania superior.* Heidelberg.

———. (2000b). "Spain," in Bowman, Garnsey, and Rathbone (2000), 444–61.

Almagro Basch, Martín. (1951). *Ampurias: Historia de la ciudad y guía de las excavaciones.* Barcelona.

———. (1952). *Las inscripciones ampuritanas griegas, ibéricas, y latinas.* Barcelona.

———. (1975). *La necrópolis hispano-visigoda de Segóbriga, Saelices (Cuenca).* Madrid.

———, and Pere de Palol. (1962). "Los restos arqueológicos paleocristianos y alto-medievales de Ampurias," *Revista de Gerona* 20: 27–41.

Almagro-Gorbea, Antonio, and Martín Almagro-Gorbea. (1994). "El anfiteatro de Segobriga," in Álvarez and Enríquez (1994), 139–76.

Almagro-Gorbea, Martín. (1998). "Emporiae, ciudad greco-romana," in *Hispania el Legado,* 417–21.

———, and Juan Manuel Abascal Palazón. (1999a). "Segóbriga en la antigüedad tardía," in García Moreno and Rascón (1999), 143–60.

———, and Juan Manuel Abascal Palazón. (1999b). *Segóbriga y su conjunto arqueológico.* Cuenca.

———, José M. Álvarez Martínez, José Maria Blázquez, and Salvador Rovira, eds. (2000). *El Disco de Teodosio.* Madrid.

Almeida, Fernando de. (1972–74). "Torre de Palma (Portugal): A basílica páleocristã e visigótica," *AEspA* 46–47: 103–12.

———. (1977). "*Civitas Igaeditanorum* et *Egitania: municipium* romain—ville epicopale wisigothique," in Duval and Frézouls (1977), 39–52.

Alonso Sánchez, Ángela, and José Maria Fernández Corrales. (2000). "El proceso de romanización de la Lusitania oriental: la creación de asentamientos militares," in Gorges and Nogales (2000), 85–100.

———, Enrique Cerrillo Martín de Cáceres, and José Maria Fernández Corrales. (1992–93). "Tres ejemplos de poblamiento rural romano en torno a ciudades de la via de la plata: *Augusta Emerita, Norba Caesarina y Capara,*" *SHHA* 10–11: 67–87.

Álvarez Martínez, José María, and Juan Javier Enríquez Navascués, eds. (1994). *Actas del Coloquio Internacional El Anfiteatro en la Hispania romana, Mérida 26–28 noviembre de 1992.* Mérida.

———, and José Luis de la Barrera Antón. (1995). *Guía breve de la collección visigoda.* Mérida.

Alves Dias, Manuela. (1993). "Epigrafia," in Torres and Macias (1993), 102–38.

Amaré Tafalla, Maria Teresa, ed. (2002a). *Astorga I: Contexto geográfico e histórico.* León.

———, ed. (2002b). *Astorga II: Escultura, glíptica y mosaico.* León.

Andreu Pintado, Javier. (2001). "*Thermae Cassiorum:* ocio y evergetismo en la *Olisipo* tardoantigua," in García Moreno and Rascón (2001), 239–53.

Antolinos Marín, Juan Antonio, and José Joaquín Vicente Sánchez. (2000). "La necrópolis tardoantigua de el Corralón (Los Belones, Cartagena)," in *RACH V,* 323–32.

Aquilué, Xavier. (1984). *El fòrum romà d'Empúries (excavations de l'any 1982): Una aproximació arqueològica al procés històric de la romanització al nord-est de la Península Ibèrica.* Barcelona.

———. (1992). "Comentari entorn a la presència de les ceràmiques de producció africana a Tàrraco," in Dupré (1992), 25–33.

———. (1993). *La seu del Col.legi d'Arquitectes: Una intervenció arqueológica en el centre històric de Tarragona.* Tarragona.

Aranegui Gascó, Carmen, ed. (1991). *Saguntum y el mar.* Valencia.

———. (1993). "Datos para el conocimiento de Sagunto en el siglo II," in Arce and Le Roux (1993), 139–46.

Arbeiter, Achim. (2002). "Centcelles: Puntualizaciones relativas al estado actual del debate," in Arce (2002b), 1–9.

———, with Dieter Korol. (1989). "Der Mosaikschmuck des Grabbaues von Centcelles und der Machtwechsel von Constans zu Magnentius," *MM* 30: 289–331.

Arce, Javier. (1978). "La crisis del siglo III d.C. en Hispania y las invasiones bárbaras," *Hispania Antiqua* 8: 257–69; reprinted in Arce (1988), 53–67.

———. (1979). *Caesaraugusta, ciudad romana.* Zaragoza.

———. (1980). "La *Notitia Dignitatum* et l'armée romaine dans la *diocesis Hispaniarum,*" *Chiron* 10: 593–608.

———. (1981). "Inestabilidad política en Hispania durante el siglo II d.C.," *AEspA* 54: 101–15; reprinted in Arce (1988), 33–52.

———. (1982). *El último siglo de la España romana (284–409).* Madrid.

―――――. (1985). "Notitia Dignitatum Occ. XLII y el ejército de la Hispania tardorromana," in Castillo (1985), 51–61.

―――――. (1986a). "El mosaico de 'las metamorfosis' de Carranque (Toledo)," *MM* 27: 365–74.

―――――. (1986b). "Epigrafía de la Hispania tardorromana de Diocleciano a Teodosio: problemas de historia y de cultura," in Angela Donati, ed. *La terza età dell'epigrafia*. Faenza. Pp. 211–27.

―――――. (1988). *España entre el mundo antiguo y el mundo medieval*. Madrid.

―――――. (1992a). "Las *villae* romanas no son monasterios," *AEspA* 65: 323–30.

―――――. (1992b). "Prudencio y Eulalia," *Extremadura Arqueológica* 3: 9–14; reprinted in Arce (2002d), 167–77.

―――――. (1993). "Los mosaicos como documentos para la historia de la *Hispania* tardía (siglos IV–V)," *AEspA* 66: 265–74.

―――――. (1994). "Constantinopla, Tarraco y Centcelles," *Boletín Arqueológico* 16: 147–65.

―――――. (1995). "El catastrofismo de Hydacio y los camellos de la Gallaecia," in Velázquez et al. (1995), 219–29.

―――――. (1997). "Emperadores, palacios y *villae* (a propósito de la villa romana de Cercadilla, Córdoba)," *Antiquité Tardive* 5: 293–302.

―――――. (1999). "La *Epistula* de Honorio a las tropas de *Pompaelo*: comunicaciones, ejército y moneda en Hispania (siglos IV–V d.C.)," in Centeno, García-Bellido, and Mora (1999), 461–68.

―――――. (2001a). "*Leovigildus rex* y el ceremonial de la corte visigótica," in Arce and Delogu (2001), 79–92.

―――――. (2001b). "*Ludi circenses* en Hispania en la Antigüedad Tardía," in Nogales and Sánchez-Palencia (2001), 273–83.

―――――. (2002a). "Nuevas reflexiones sobre la iconografía de la cúpula de Centcelles," in Arce (2002b), 11–20.

―――――, ed. (2002b). *Centcelles. El monumento tardorromano. Iconografía y arquitectura*. Rome.

―――――. (2002c). "La inscripción de Sabinianus y los *ludi circenses* en *Emerita* en la Antigüedad Tardía," in Arce (2002d), 137–46.

―――――. (2002d). *Mérida tardorromana (300–580 d.C.)*. (Cuadernos Emeritenses 22). Mérida.

―――――, and Patrick Le Roux, eds. (1993). *Ciudad y comunidad cívica en Hispania, siglos II y III d.c. (Actes du colloque organisé par la Casa de Velázquez et par le Consejo Superior de Investigaciones Científicas, Madrid, 25–27 janvier 1990)*. (Collection de la Casa de Velázquez 40). Madrid.

―――――, Luis Caballero, and Miguel Ángel Elvira. (1997). "El edificio octogonal de Valdetorres de Jarama (Madrid)," in Teja and Pérez (1997), 321–37.

―――――, and Paolo Delogu, eds. (2001). *Visigoti e Longobardi: Atti del Seminario (Roma 28–29 aprile 1997)*. Florence.

Ardanaz Arranz, Francisco. (2000). *La necrópolis visigoda de Cacera de las Ranas (Aranjuez, Madrid)*. Madrid.

Argente Oliver, José Luis. (1979). *La villa tardorromana de Baños de Valdearados (Burgos).* (Excavaciones Arqueológicas en España 100). Madrid.
———, ed. (1993). *Tiermes: Campaña de excavaciones 1993.* Soria.
———, Inmaculada Argente Oliver, Carlos de la Casa Martínez, Adelia Díaz
Díaz, Victor Férnandez Martínez, Alfonso González Uceda, and Elías Terés
Navarro. (1984). *Tiermes II (Campañas de 1979 y 1980): Excavaciones realizadas en la ciudad romana y en la necrópolis medieval.* (Excavaciones Ar-
queológicas en España 128). Madrid.
———, and Adelia Díaz Díaz, eds. (1994). *Tiermes IV: La Casa del Acueducto
(Domus alto imperial de la ciudad de Tiermes, Campañas 1979–1986).* (Ex-
cavaciones Arqueológicas en España 167). Madrid.
Arrechea Silvestre, Horacio. (1997). "Sobre las circunscripciones menores en
el reino visigodo de Toledo," in Méndez et al. (1997), 239–45.
Astin, A. E. (1967). *Scipio Aemilianus.* Oxford.
Avellà, L. C. (1985). "Ausgrabungen in der Torre de Minerva, Tarragona: Die
Münzenfunde von 1979," *MM* 26: 122–24.
Ayerbe Vélez, Rocío. (1999). "Intervención arqueológica en el solar de la c/
Suárez Somonte, n. 66: Restos de una *domus* y de un *cardo* porticado," in
Mérida 3, 169–96.
———, and Juana Márquez Pérez. (1998). "Intervención arqueológica en el
solar de la calle Cabo Verde: espacio funerario del sitio del Disco," in *Mérida
2,* 135–66.
Azkarate Garai-Olaun, Augustin. (1999). *La necrópolis tardoantigua de Aldaieta
(Nanclares de Gamboa, Alava) I: Memoria de la excavación e inventario de hal-
lazgos.* Vitoria.
———. (2001). "Nuevas perspectivas sobre la tardoantigüedad en los Piri-
neos occidentales a la luz de la investigación arqueológica," in Arce and
Delogu (2001), 37–55.
Bajo Álvarez, Fe. (1995). *Los últimos hispanorromanos: el Bajo Imperio en la
Península Ibérica.* Madrid.
Bakker, L. (1993). "Die Siegesaltar zur Juthungenschlacht von 260 n. Chr. Ein
spektakulärer Neufund aus Augusta Vindelicium/Augsburg," *Archäologische Nachrichten* 24: 274–77.
Balil, Alberto. (1957). "Las invasiones germánicas en Hispania," *Cuadernos de
trabajos de la Escuela Española de Historia y Arqueología en Roma* 9: 97–143.
———. (1959–60). "La defensa de Hispania en el Bajo Imperio," *Zephyrus*
10–11: 179–97.
———. (1964). "Los gobernadores de Hispania en el Bajo Imperio," *AEspA*
37: 191–95.
———. (1965). "Aspectos sociales del Bajo Imperio," *Latomus* 24: 886–904.
———. (1967). "De Marco Aurelio a Constantino: una introducción a la España del Bajo Imperio," *Hispania* 27: 245–341.
———. (1970). "La defensa de Hispania en el Bajo Imperio: amenaza exterior y inquietud interna," in *Legio VII Gemina,* 601–20.

————. (1987). "La villa romana de Pacs (Penedès, Barcelona)," *Boletín del Seminario de Estudios de Arte y Arqueología* 53: 181–89.

————, and R. Martín Valls. (1979). *Tesorillo de antoninianos en Honcalada (Valladolid)*. Valladolid.

Barbero de Aguilera, Abilio. (1963). "El priscilianismo: ¿herejía o movimiento social?" *Cuadernos de Historia de España* 37: 5–41.

————, and Marcelo Vigil Pascual. (1971). "La organización social de los Cántabros y sus transformaciones en relación con los origines de la Reconquista," *Hispania Antiqua* 1: 197–232; reprinted in Barbero and Vigil (1974), 139–95.

————, and Marcelo Vigil Pascual. (1974). *Sobre los origines sociales de la Reconquista*. Barcelona.

————, and Marcelo Vigil Pascual. (1978). *La formación del feudalismo en la Península Ibérica*. Madrid.

Barker, Graeme, and John Lloyd, eds. (1991). *Roman Landscapes: Archaeological Survey in the Mediterranean Region*. (Archaeological Monographs of the British School at Rome 2). London.

Barnes, T. D. (1975). "Patricii under Valentinian III," *Phoenix* 29: 159–63.

————. (1981). *Constantine and Eusebius*. Cambridge, MA.

————. (1982). *The New Empire of Diocletian and Constantine*. Cambridge, MA.

————. (1993). *Athanasius and Constantius: Theology and Politics in the Constantinian Empire*. Cambridge, MA.

————. (1996a). "Emperors, Panegyrics, Prefects, Provinces and Palaces (284–317)," *JRA* 9: 532–52.

————. (1996b). "The Franci before Diocletian," in Giorgio Bonamente and François Paschoud, eds. *Historiae Augustae Colloquium Genevense 2*. Macerata. Pp. 11–18.

Barraca de Ramos, Pilar. (1997). "Poblamiento al sur del Duero en época tardía," in Teja and Pérez (1997), 353–59.

Barrachina, A., E. Hernández, M. López Piñol, A. Mantilla, and E. Vento. (1984). "Excavaciones en el Grau Vell de Sagunt. 1983," *Saguntum* 18: 205–28.

Barral i Altet, X. (1995). "La cristianización de las ciudades romanas de Hispania," *Extremadura Arqueológica* 3: 51–55.

Barrientos Vera, Teresa. (1997). "Baños romanos en Mérida: estudio preliminar," in *Mérida 1*, 259–84.

————. (1998a). "Intervención arqueológica en el solar de la c/ Ventosilla, n. 11," in *Mérida 2*, 73–101.

————. (1998b). "Intervención arqueológica en el solar de la calle San Salvador, esquina Holguín: un ejemplo de la evolución del viario urbano emeritense," in *Mérida 2*, 103–33.

————. (2000a). "Intervención arqueológica realizada en la esquina de las calles Francisco Almaraz y Forner y Segarra: nuevos datos del viario romano en la zona norte," in *Mérida 4*, 59–81.

———. (2000b). "Intervención arqueológica en el solar no. 32 de la c/ Parejos: Un ejemplo de reutilización de estructuras desde época altoimperial hasta la tardoantigüedad," in *Mérida 4*, 221–75.

———. (2001). "Secuencia ocupacional en las proximidades de la muralla romana: Intervención arqueológica realizada en el solar no. 38 de la calle Muza," in *Mérida 5*, 85–118.

Bartholomew, P. (1982). "Fifth-century Facts," *Britannia* 13: 261–70.

Bea Castaño, David, and Albert Vilaseca Canals. (2000). "Dues necròpolis de segle V d. N.E. a Tarragona: excavacions al carrer de Prat de la Riba i al Mas Rimbau," in Ruiz (2000), 155–64.

Bejarano Osorio, Ana. (1998). "Tipología de las sepulturas en las necrópolis tardorromanas-cristianas de Mérida: evolución de los espacios funerarios," in *Mérida 2*, 341–59.

Beltrán, A. (1954). "La inscripción romana de Siresa," *Caesaraugusta* 4: 133–39.

———, and F. Beltrán Lloris. (1991). *El anfiteatro de Tarraco: Estudio de los hallazgos epigráficos*. Tarragona.

Beltrán Lloris, Miguel. (1993). "El teatro de Caesaraugusta: Estado actual de conocimiento," *CAR* 2: 93–118.

———, and Guillermo Fatás Cabeza. (1998). *César Augusta, ciudad romana*. (Historia de Zaragoza 2). Zaragoza.

Beltrán Martínez, Antonio. (1976). "La Antigüedad," in *Historia de Zaragoza*. Zaragoza. Pp. 11–90.

Beltrán Torreira, Federico-Mario. (1993). "San Leandro de Sevilla y sus actitudes político-religiosas (nuevas observaciones sobre su historia familiar)," in *I Actas Andalucía*, 2: 335–48.

Bendala Galán, Manuel. (1990). "El plan urbanístico de Augusto en Hispania: precedentes y pautas macroterritoriales," in Trillmich and Zanker (1990), 25–42.

———. (1994). "La ciudad en la Hispania romana," in *XIV Congreso Int. Arq. Clas.*, 115–23.

———. (1998). "La paz augustea y la romanización," in *Hispania El Legado*, 127–37.

———, and Negueruela Martínez. (1980). "Baptisterio paleocristiano y visigodo en los Reales Alcazares de Sevilla," *NAH* 10: 335–79.

———, Raquel Castelo Ruano, and Raúl Arribas Domínguez. (1998). "La villa romana de El Saucedo (Talavera la Nueva, Toledo)," *MM* 39: 298–310.

Berges, P. M. (1969–70). "Informe sobre Els Munts," *Boletín Arqueológico* 69–70: 140–50.

———. (1970). "Las ruinas de Els Munts (Altafulla, Tarragona)," *Información Arqueológica (Barcelona)* 3: 81–87.

Bernal Casasola, Darío. (1997). "Ánforas del bajo imperio en *Baetica* y *Tingi-*

tania: estado de la cuestión y primeras aportaciones arqueológicas," in Teja and Pérez (1997), 361–76.

———, and José Manuel Pérez Rivera. (2000). "La ocupación bizantina de *Septem.* Análisis del registro arqueológico y propuestas de interpretación," in *RACH V,* 121–33.

Berrocal Caparrós, M. Carmen, and M. Dolores Laiz Reverte. (1995). "Tipología de enterramientos en la necrópolis de San Antón, en Cartagena," in *RACH IV,* 173–82.

Berto Martí, Encarna. (1991). "El yacimiento subacuatico," in Aranegui (1991), 69–78.

Bierbrauer, Volker. (1992). "Die Goten vom 1.-7. Jahrhundert n. Chr.: Siedelgebiete und Wanderbewegungen aufgrund archäologischer Quellen," *Peregrinatio Gothica* 2: 9–43.

———. (1994). "Archäologie und Geschichte der Goten vom 1.-7. Jahrhundert," *Frühmittelalterliche Studien* 28: 51–171.

Birley, Anthony R. (1988). *Septimius Severus: The African Emperor.* 2nd ed. New Haven.

———. (1997). *Hadrian: The Restless Emperor.* London.

Bischoff, Bernard, and W. Koehler. (1939). "Eine illustrierte Ausgabe der spätantiken ravennater Annalen," in W. Koehler, ed. *Medieval Studies in Honor of A. Kingsley Porter.* Cambridge. Pp. 125–38.

Blagg, Thomas, and Martin Millett, eds. (1990). *The Early Roman Empire in the West.* Oxford.

Blasco, Juli, Vicent Escrivà Torres, Albert Ribera i Lacomba, and Rafaela Soriano Sánchez. (1994). "Estat actual de la investigació arqueològica de l'Antiguitat Tardana a la ciutat de València," in *RACH III,* 185–99.

Blázquez, José Maria. (1964). *Estructura económica y social de Hispania durante la anarquía militar y el bajo imperio.* Madrid; reprinted in Blázquez (1978), 485–618.

———. (1974). "Der Limes im Spanien des vierten Jahrhunderts," in *Actes du IXème congrés international d'études sur les frontières romaines.* Bucharest. Pp. 485–502.

———. (1976). "Rechazo y asimilación de la cultura romana en Hispania (siglos IV–V)," in *VIème congrès international des études classiques.* Bucharest and Paris. Pp. 63–94.

———. (1978). *Economía de la Hispania romana.* Bilbao.

———. (1980). "Der Limes Hispaniens im 4. und 5. Jahrhundert: Forschungsstand," in *Roman Frontier Studies XII.* Oxford. Pp. 345–94.

———. (1987). "Arte y mitología en los mosaicos palentinos," in *I Actas Palencianas,* 361–406.

———, and M. P. García-Gelabert. (1993). "Castulo en el bajo imperio," in *I Actas Andalucía,* 2: 289–303.

Blockley, R. C. (1983). *The Fragmentary Classicising Historians of the Later Ro-*

man Empire: Eunapius, Olympiodorus, Priscus and Malchus, vol. 2: *Text, Translation and Historiographical Notes.* Liverpool.

Bona, J., and J. Nuñez. (1985). "Avance al estudio del mosaico romano localizado en la calle Tudela 13 de Tarazona (Zaragoza)," *Turiaso* 6: 63–83.

Bonnet, Charles, and Julia Beltrán de Heredia. (2000a). "El primer grupo episcopal de Barcelona," in Ripoll and Gurt (2000), 467–90.

———, and Julia Beltrán de Heredia. (2000b). "Nuevas intervenciones arqueológicas en el Museo de Historia de la Ciudad: una iglesia de época visigótica en el grupo episcopal de Barcelona," in *RACH V,* 135–44.

Bourgeois, C. (1980). "Les Vandales, les vandalisme, et l'Afrique," *Antiquités Africaines* 16: 213–28.

Bowersock, G. W., Peter Brown, and Oleg Grabar, eds. (1999). *Late Antiquity: A Guide to the Postclassical World.* Cambridge, MA.

Bowes, Kim. (2001). "'. . . *Nec sedere in villam*': Villa Churches, Rural Piety and the Priscillianist Controversy," in Thomas S. Burns and John W. Eadie, eds. *Urban Centers and Rural Contexts in Late Antiquity.* East Lansing. Pp. 323–48.

———, and Michael Kulikowski, eds. (forthcoming). *Hispania in Late Antiquity: Twenty-First-Century Approaches.*

Bowman, Alan K. (1996). "Provincial Administration and Taxation," in Bowman, Champlin, and Lintott (1996), 371–96.

———, Edward Champlin, and Andrew Lintott, eds. (1996). *The Cambridge Ancient History X: The Augustan Empire, 43 B.C.–A.D. 69.* 2nd ed. Cambridge.

———, Peter Garnsey, and Dominic Rathbone, eds. (2000). *The Cambridge Ancient History XI: The High Empire, A.D. 70–192.* 2nd ed. Cambridge.

Bradbury, Scott. (1996). *Severus of Minorca: Letter on the Conversion of the Jews.* Oxford.

Brather, Sebastian. (2000). "Ethnische Identitäten als Konstrukte der frühgeschichtlichen Archäologie," *Germania* 78: 139–77.

———. (2002). "Ethnic Identities as Constructions of Archaeology: The Case of the *Alamanni,*" in Gillett (2002), 149–76.

Bravo Castañeda, Gonzalo. (1983). "Las revueltas campesinas del alto valle del Ebro a mediados del siglo V d.C. y su relación con otros conflictos sociales contemporaneos (una revisión sobre bagaudas)," *Cuadernos de Investigación* 9: 219–30.

———. (1984). "Acta Bagaudica (I): Sobre quiénes eran 'bagaudas' y su posible identificación en los textos tardíos," *Gerión* 2: 251–64.

———. (1997). "Prosopographia theodosiana (II): El presunto 'Clan Hispano' a la luz del análisis prosopográfico," in Teja and Pérez (1997), 21–30.

———. (2000). "Cristianización y conflictos sociales en el valle medio del Ebro," in Santos and Teja (2000), 325–38.

Brennan, P. S. (1995). "The *Notitia Dignitatum,*" in C. Nicolet, ed. *Les littéra-*

tures techniques dans l'antiquité romaine. (Entretiens Hardt 42). Geneva. Pp. 147–78.

Bruck, Eberhard F. (1954). "Caesarius von Arles und die Lex Romana Visigothorum," in *Über römisches Recht im Rahmen der Kulturgeschichte.* Berlin. Pp. 146–63.

Brunt, P. A. (1959). "The Revolt of Vindex and the Fall of Nero," *Latomus* 18: 531–59; reprinted in Brunt (1990), 9–32.

———. (1963). "Augustan Imperialism," *JRS* 53: 170–76; reprinted in Brunt (1990), 96–109.

———. (1965). "Reflections on British and Roman Imperialism," *Comparative Studies in Society and History* 7/3: 267–88; reprinted in Brunt (1990), 110–33.

———. (1976). "The Romanization of the Local Ruling Classes in the Roman Empire," in *Assimilation et résistance à la culture gréco-romaine dans le monde ancien.* Paris. Pp. 161– 73; reprinted in Brunt (1990), 267–81.

———. (1978). "Laus imperii," in P. D. A. Garnsey and C. R. Whittaker, eds. *Imperialism in the Ancient World.* Cambridge. Pp. 159–91; reprinted in Brunt (1990), 288–323.

———. (1990). *Roman Imperial Themes.* Oxford.

Burgess, R. W. (1987). "The Third Regnal Year of Eparchius Avitus: A Reply," *CP* 82: 335–45.

———. (1989). "Hydatius: A Late Roman Chronicler in Post-Roman Spain." Diss. Oxon.

———. (1992). "From *Gallia romana* to *Gallia gothica:* The View from Spain," in Drinkwater and Elton (1992), 19–27.

———. (1993). *The Chronicle of Hydatius and the Consularia Constantinopolitana: Two Contemporary Accounts of the Final Years of the Roman Empire.* Oxford.

———. (1995). "Hydatius and the Final Frontier: The Fall of the Roman Empire and the End of the World," in Mathisen and Sivan (1995), 321–32.

———. (2001a). "The Gallic Chronicle of 452: A New Critical Edition with a Brief Introduction," in Mathisen and Shanzer (2002), 52–84.

———. (2001b). "The Gallic Chronicle of 511: A New Critical Edition with a Brief Introduction," in Mathisen and Shanzer (2002), 85–100.

Burns, T. S. (1992). "The Settlement of 418," in Drinkwater and Elton (1992), 49–63.

———. (1994). *Barbarians within the Gates of Rome: A Study of Roman Military Policy and the Barbarians, ca. 375–425 A.D.* Bloomington.

Burrus, Virginia. (1995). *The Making of a Heretic: Gender, Authority and the Priscillianist Controversy.* Berkeley and Los Angeles.

Burton, G. P. (1975). "Proconsuls, Assizes and the Administration of Justice under the Empire," *JRS* 65: 92–106.

———. (1979). "The *curator rei publicae:* Towards a Reappraisal," *Chiron* 9: 465–87.

Bury, J. B. (1923). *A History of the Later Roman Empire from the Death of Theodosius I to the Death of Justinian.* 2 vols. London.

Caamaño Gesto, José Manuel. (1989). "Estampillas de la *Cohors I Celtiberorum*, halladas en el campamento romano de Cidadela," *Gallaecia* 12: 177–90.

———, and Carlos Fernández Rodríguez. (2000). "Excavaciones en el campamento de Cidadela (A Coruña)," *Brigantium* 12: 199–207.

Caballero Zoreda, Luís, and Pedro Mateos Cruz. (1991). "Excavaciones en Santa Eulalia de Mérida," *Extremadura Arqueológica* 2: 525–46.

———, and Pedro Mateos Cruz. (1992). "Trabajos arqueológicos en la iglesia de Santa Eulalia de Mérida," *Extremadura Arqueológica* 3: 15–49.

———, and Pedro Mateos Cruz. (1995). "Excavaciones arqueológicas en la basílica de Santa Eulalia de Mérida," in *RACH IV,* 297–307.

Caballos Rufino, Antonio. (1990). *Los senadores hispanorromanos y la romanización de Hispania (siglos I–III).* Écija.

———. (1999). "Preliminares sobre los caballeros romanos originarios de las provincias hispanas, siglos I–III d.C.," in Rodríguez Neila (1999), 103–44.

Cameron, Alan. (1970). *Claudian: Poetry and Propaganda at the Court of Honorius.* Oxford.

———. (1976). "Theodorus *Triséparchos,*" *GRBS* 17: 269–86.

Cameron, Averil.. (1983). "Constantinus Christianus," *JRS* 73: 184–90.

———. (1993). *The Later Roman Empire.* Cambridge, MA.

———, ed. (1998). *The Cambridge Ancient History XIII: The Late Empire, A.D. 357–425.* Cambridge.

Campos Carrasco, Juan. (1993). "La estructura urbana de la Colonia Iulia Romula Hispalis en época imperial," *AAC* 4: 181–219.

———, and Julián González. (1987). "Los foros de Hispalis Colonia Romula," *AEspA* 60: 123–58.

Carcopino, Jérôme. (1943). *Le Maroc antique.* Paris.

Carmona Berenguer, Silvia. (1990). "La necropolis tardorromana de El Ruedo, Almedinilla, Córdoba," *AAC* 1: 155–72.

Carr, Karen Eva. (2002). *Vandals to Visigoths: Rural Settlement Patterns in Early Medieval Spain.* Ann Arbor.

Carrasco, Marta, and Maria Ángel Elvira. (1994). "Marfiles coptos en Valdetorres de Jarama (Madrid)," *AEspA* 67: 201–8.

Carreté i Nadal, Josep-Maria, and Xavier Dupré i Raventós. (1994). "La fase tardoantiga de l'Audiència de Tarragona," in *RACH III,* 157–66.

———, Simon Keay, and Martin Millett. (1995). *A Roman Provincial Capital and Its Hinterland: The Survey of the Territory of Tarragona, Spain, 1985–1990.* (Journal of Roman Archaeology Supplementary Series 15). Ann Arbor.

———, M. del Mar Llorens, Jaume Nassó, and Pilar Sada. (1999). "El món de la mort a Tàrraco: un proyecto integral de restauración, conservación y dinamización de la Necrópolis de Tarragona," *XXV CNA:* 65–72.

Carrié, J.-M. (1994). "Dioclétien et la fiscalité," *Antiquité Tardive* 2: 33–64.

Carrillero, M., O. Garrido, B. Nieto, and B. Padial. (1995). "La villa romana de Las Viñas (Cuevas del Becerro, Málaga) y el poblamiento rural romano en la depresión de Ronda," *Florentia Iliberritana* 6: 89–108.

Carrillo Díaz-Pinés, José Ramón. (1991). "El poblamiento romano en las Subbéticas cordobesas," *AAC* 2: 225–53.

———. (1993). "Los estudios sobre las villas romanas de Andalucía: una revisión historiográfica," *AAC* 4: 233–57.

———, Carlos Márquez Moreno, Juan F. Murillo Redondo, and Ángel Ventura Villanueva. (1995a). "Arqueología de Córdoba: La Colonia Patricia altoimperial," *Revista de Arqueología* 172: 34–45.

———, Carlos Márquez Moreno, Juan F. Murillo Redondo, and Ángel Ventura Villanueva. (1995b). "Arqueología de Córdoba: De época tardorromano a la conquista cristiana," *Revista de Arqueología* 173: 48–57.

Carrobles Santos, Jesús. (1999). "La ciudad de Toledo en la antigüedad tardía," in García Moreno and Rascón (1999), 193–200.

———, and Sagrario Rodríguez Montero. (1988). *Memoria de las excavaciones de urgencia del solar del nuevo mercado de abastos (Poligono Industrial, Toledo): Introducción al estudio de la ciudad de Toledo en siglo IV d.C.* Toledo.

Carvalho, Pedro C. (1998). *O forum de Aeminium.* Lisbon.

Cary, M. (1949). *The Geographic Background of Greek and Roman History.* Oxford.

Casa Martínez, Carlos de la, Manuela Doménech Esteban, José María Izquierdo Bertiz, and Elías Terés Navarro. (1994). *Tiermes III: Excavaciones realizadas en la Ciudad Romana y en las Necrópolis Medievales (Campañas de 1981–1984).* (Excavaciones Arqueológicas en España 166). Madrid.

Casabona Sebastián, J. F. (1990). "La excavación de Sepulcro 1–15 Zaragoza," *Arqueología Aragonesa* 16: 185–90.

Casas, J. (1982–83). "Les bornes mil.liàres de Palau Sacosta i Sarrià de Ter (Girona)," *Annals de l'Institut d'Estudis Gironins* 26: 131–38.

———. (1986). "Excavaciones en la vil.la romana de Puig Rodon (Corçà, Baix Empordà)," *Estudis sobre Temes del Baix Empordà* 5: 15–77.

Castellanos, Santiago. (1998). *Poder social, aristocracias y hombre santo en la Hispania Visigoda: La Vita Aemiliani de Braulio de Zaragoza.* Logroño.

———. (1999). *Hagiografía y sociedad en la Hispania visigoda: La Vita Aemiliani y el actual territorio riojano (siglo VI).* Logroño.

Castellvi, G. (1995). "Clausurae (Les-Cluses, P.-O.): forteresses-frontières du Bas-Empire romain," in A. Rouselle, ed. *Frontières terrestres, frontières celestes dans l'Antiquité.* Perpignan. Pp. 81–117.

Castillo, Arcadio del, ed. (1985). *Ejército y sociedad.* León.

Castillo, Carmen. (1988). "Los pontífices de la Bética," in Mayer (1988), 83–93.

———. (1999). "Ciudades privilegiados en Hispania: veinticinco años de estudio (1972–1996)," in González Fernández (1999b), 269–78.

Castillo Maldonado, Pedro. (1999). *Los mártires hispanorromanos y su culto en la Hispania de la Antigüedad Tardía.* Granada.

Cavada Nieto, Milagros. (1994). *La crisis económico-monetaria del s. III:¿un mito históriográfico? Avance del resultado de los análisis metalográficos sobre dos tesorillos de la provincia de Lugo.* Santiago de Compostela.

Centeno, R. M. S., M. P. García-Bellido, and G. Mora, eds. (1999). *Rutas, ciudades y moneda en Hispania.* (Anejos del *Archivo Español de Arqueología* 20). Madrid.

Cepas Palanca, Adela. (1997). *Crisis y continuidad en la Hispania del siglo III.* (Anejos del *Archivo Español de Arqueología* 17). Madrid.

Cerrillo Martín de Cáceres, Enrique. (1983). *La villa romana de Los Términos, Monroy (Cáceres).* Cáceres.

———. (1995). "Reflexiones sobre las *villae* romanas en *Hispania*," in Noguera (1995), 17–26.

———, Gregorio Herrera, Juana Molano Brías, Manuel de Alvarado Gonzalo, Jesús Castillo Castillo, and Miguel Hernández López. (1991). "Excavaciones arqueológicas en la villa romana de 'Los Términos,' Monroy, Cáceres: actuaciones y propuestas de futuro (1984–1990)," *Extremadura Arqueológica* 2: 379–86.

Chadwick, Henry. (1976). *Priscillian of Avila.* Oxford.

Chastagnol, André. (1966). "Les espagnols dans l'aristocratie gouvernementale à l'époque de Théodose," in *Empereurs d'Espagne,* 269–92.

———. (1976). "Les inscriptions constantiniennes du cirque de Mérida," *MEFRA* 88: 259–76.

———. (1978). *L'album municipal de Timgad.* (Antiquitas 3: 22). Bonn.

Chic García, Genaro. (1999). "Comercio, fisco y ciudad en la provincia romana de la Bética," in González Fernández (1999), 33–59.

Chicarro, C. (1972–74). "Epigrafía de Munigua (Mulva, Sevilla)," *AEspA* 45–47: 337–410.

Christol, Michel. (1987). "Rome et les tribus indigènes en Maurétanie Tingitane," *L'Africa Romana* 5: 305–37.

———. (1997). *L'empire romain du IIIe siècle: histoire politique 192–325 après J.-C.* Paris.

———, and Pierre Sillières. (1980). "Constantin et la péninsule ibérique," *REA* 82: 70–80.

———, and Olivier Masson, eds. (1997). *Actes du Xe congrès international d'épigraphie grecque et latine, Nimes, 4–9 Octobre 1992.* Paris.

Ciezar, P. (1990). "Sériation de la nécropole wisigothique de Duratón (Ségovie, Espagne)," *Histoire et Mesure* 5: 107–44.

Cimma, M. R. (1989). *L'episcopalis audientia nelle costituzioni imperiali da Costantino a Giustiniano.* Turin.

Clariana i Roig, Joan Francesc. (1996). *Iluro: Ciutat Romana.* 2nd ed. Mataró.

———, and Ramón Járrega Domínguez. (1990). "Aportación al conocimiento de unas estructuras arquitectónicas del yacimiento arqueológico de Can Modolell (Cabrera de Mar, Barcelona)," *AEspA* 63: 330–44.

———, and Ramón Járrega Domínguez. (1994). "Estudi de la fase baix imperial de la vil.la romana de Torre Llauder (Mataró, El Maresme)," *Laietana* 9: 253–89.

———, and Maria Prevosti. (1994). "Un exemple de ruralització a l'Antiguitat Tardana: la vil.la de Torre Lauder," in *RACH III*, 117–26.

Clarke, C., ed. (1990). *Reading the Past in Late Antiquity.* Sydney.

Clarke, G. W. (1971). "Prosopographical Notes on the Epistles of Cyprian I: The Spanish Bishops of Epistle 67," *Latomus* 30: 1141–45.

Clover, F. M. (1971). *Flavius Merobaudes: A Translation and Commentary.* Philadelphia.

Codoñer Merino, Carmen. (1964). *El De viris illustribus de Isidoro de Sevilla: estudio y edición crítica.* Salamanca.

Collins, Roger. (1989). *The Arab Conquest of Spain.* Oxford.

———. (1994). "Isidore, Maximus and the *Historia Gothorum*," in A. Scharer and G. Scheibelreiter, eds. *Historiographie im frühen Mittelalter.* Vienna and Munich. Pp. 354–58.

———. (1995). *Early Medieval Spain: Unity in Diversity, 400–1000.* 2nd ed. New York.

Conti, Marco. (1998). *The Life and Works of Potamius of Lisbon.* (Instrumenta Patristica 32). Turnhout.

Cooley, Alison E., ed. (2002). *Becoming Roman, Writing Latin? Literacy and Epigraphy in the Roman West.* Portsmouth, RI.

Corbier, Mireille. (1991). "City, Territory, and Taxation," in John Rich and Andrew Wallace-Hadrill, eds. *City and Country in the Ancient World.* London. Pp. 211–39.

Corell, Josep. (1988). "El culto a *Liber Pater* en el sur del *conventus Tarraconensis* según la epigrafía," in Mayer (1988), 125–43.

———. (1989). "Inscripción del obispo Anesio atribuida erróneamente a Justiniano," *Saitabi* 39: 63–72.

———. (1997). *Inscripcions romanes de Valentia i el seu territori.* Valencia.

Cornell, Tim, and John Matthews. (1982). *Atlas of the Roman World.* New York.

Cortijo Cerezo, Maria Luisa. (1993a). *La administración territorial de la Bética romana.* Córdoba.

———. (1993b). "Algunos aspectos sobre el medio rural en la Bética romana: pagi y vici," *Hispania Antiqua* 17: 197–214.

Courcelle, Pierre. (1964). *Histoire littéraire des grandes invasions germaniques.* 3rd ed. Paris.

Courtois, Christian. (1955). *Les Vandales et l'Afrique.* Paris.

Croke, Brian, and A. M. Emmett, eds. (1983). *History and Historians in Late Antiquity.* Sydney.

Cruz Villalón, Maria. (1985). *Mérida visigoda: la escultura arquitectónica y litúrgica.* Badajoz.

————. (1995). "Mérida entre Roma y el Islam: nuevos documentos y reflexiones," in Velázquez et al. (1995), 185–217.

Curchin, Leonard A. (1983). "Personal Wealth in Roman Spain," *Historia* 32: 227–44.

————. (1985). *"Vici* and *pagi* in Roman Spain," *REA* 87: 327–43.

————. (1990a). *The Local Magistrates of Roman Spain.* (Phoenix Supplementary Volume 28). Toronto.

————. (1990b). *Roman Spain: Conquest and Assimilation.* London.

————. (1994). "Juridical Epigraphy and Provincial Administration in Central Spain," in González Fernández (1994), 87–102.

Curta, Florin. (2001). *The Making of the Slavs: History and Archaeology of the Lower Danube Region c. 500–700.* Cambridge.

Daim, Falko. (1998). "Archaeology of Ethnicity and the Structures of Identification: The Example of the Avars, Carantanians and Moravians in the Eighth Century," in Pohl and Reimitz (1998), 71–93.

David, Pierre. (1947). *Études historiques sur la Galice et le Portugal du VIe au XIIe siècle.* Lisbon and Paris.

De Clerq, Victor C. (1954). *Ossius of Cordova: A Contribution to the History of the Constantinian Period.* Washington, DC.

del Amo, M. D. (1979–89). *Estudio crítico de la necrópolis paleocristiana de Tarragona.* 3 vols. Tarragona.

Demougeot, Emilienne. (1951). *De l'unité à la division de l'empire romain.* Paris.

————. (1956). "Une lettre de l'empereur Honorius sur l'*hospitium* des soldats," *RHDFE* 34: 25–49.

Dias Diogo, A. M. (1993). "O teatro romano de Lisboa: Notícia sobre as actuais escavações," *CAR* 2: 217–24.

Díaz Martínez, Pablo C. (1993). "El imperio, los barbaros y el control sobre la Bética en el siglo V," in Rodríguez Neila (1993), 317–25.

————. (2000). "El reino suevo de *Hispania* y su sede en *Bracara*," in Ripoll and Gurt (2000), 403–23.

————, and Juana M. Torres. (2000). "Pervivencias paganas en el cristianismo hispano (siglos IV–VII)," in Santos and Teja (2000), 236–61.

Díaz y Díaz, Manuel C. (1979). *Libros y librerías en la Rioja altomedieval.* Logroño.

Dodds, Jerilynn D. (1990). *Architecture and Ideology in Early Medieval Spain.* University Park, PA.

Domenech i Montaner, Lluis. (1931). *Centcelles: Baptisteri i celle-memoria de la primitiva esglesia-metropolitana de Tarragona.* Barcelona.

Domergue, Claude. (1990). *Les mines de la péninsule ibérique dans l'antiquité romaine.* Rome.

Domínguez-Monedero, A. J. (1983). "Los ejércitos regulares tardorromanos en la Península Ibérica y el problema del pretendido *limes hispanus*," *Revista de Guimarães* 93: 107–31.

D'Ors, Álvaro. (1956). "La territorialidad del Derecho de los visigodos," in *Es-*

tudios visigóticos I. (Cuadernos del Instituto Jurídico Español 5). Rome and Madrid. Pp. 91–124.

———. (1960). *El Codigo d'Eurico: Edición, Palingenesia, Indices.* (Cuadernos del Instituto Jurídico Español 12). Madrid.

———. (2001). "Un aviso sobre la 'ley municipal,' *lex rescripta*," *Mainake* 23: 97–100.

Drinkwater, J. F. (1983). *Roman Gaul.* London.

———. (1987). *The Gallic Empire: Separatism and Continuity in the North-Western Provinces of the Roman Empire, A.D. 260–274.* (Historia Einzelschriften 52). Stuttgart.

———. (1989). "Patronage in Roman Gaul and the Problem of the Bagaudae," in Wallace-Hadrill (1989), 189–203.

———. (1992). "The Bacaudae in Fifth-century Gaul," in Drinkwater and Elton (1992), 208–17.

———. (1994). "Silvanus, Ursicinus and Ammianus: Fact or Fiction?" in C. Deroux, ed. *Studies in Latin Literature and Roman History VII.* (Collection Latomus 227). Brussels. Pp. 568–76.

———. (1998). "The Usurpers Constantine III (407–411) and Jovinus (411–413)," *Britannia* 29: 269–98.

———, and Hugh Elton, eds. (1992). *Fifth-century Gaul: A Crisis of Identity?* Cambridge.

Duchesne, Louis. (1887). "Le Concile d'Elvire et les flamines chrétiens," in *Melanges Renierr: Bibliothèque de l'École des Hautes Études* 73. Paris. Pp. 159–74.

Dupré i Raventós, Xavier, ed. (1992). *Miscel.lània arqueòlogica a Josep M. Recasens, Abril 1992.* Tarragona.

———. (1994). "Los arcos honoríficos de *Tarraco*," in *XIV Congreso Int. Arq. Clas.*, 177–88.

———, M. J. Massó i Carballido, M. L. Palanques i Salmerón, and P. A. Verduchi Brunori. (1988). *El circ Romà de Tarragona I: les voltes de Sant Ermenegild.* Barcelona.

Durán Cabello, Rosalía-María. (1991). "La técnica constructiva de la llamada 'Casa-basílica' de Mérida," in *La casa urbana*, 359–69.

———. (1998). *La última etapa del teatro romano de Mérida: La uersura oriental y los sellos latericios.* (Cuadernos Emeritenses 14). Mérida.

———. (1999). "Mérida en la antigüedad tardía," in García Moreno and Rascón (1999), 161–80.

Durliat, Jean. (1990). *Les finances publiques de Dioclétien aux Carolingiens (284–889).* (Beihefte der *Francia* 21). Sigmaringen.

Duthoy, R. (1979). "*Curatores rei publicae* en Occident durant le Principat," *Ancient Society* 10: 171–239.

Duval, P.-M., and E. Frézouls, eds. (1977). *Thèmes de recherches sur les villes antiques d'Occident, Strasbourg 1–4 Octobre 1971.* Paris.

Edmondson, Jonathan C. (1990). "Romanization and Urban Development in Lusitania," in Blagg and Millett (1990), 151–78.

———. (1999). "The Epigraphy and History of Roman *Hispania:* The New Edition of *CIL* II," *JRA* 12: 649–66.

———. (2002). "Writing Latin in the Province of Lusitania," in Cooley (2002), 41–60.

Elliot, J. H. (1964). *Imperial Spain, 1469–1716.* New York.

Elton, Hugh. (1995). "Defining Romans, Barbarians, and the Roman Frontier," in Mathisen and Sivan (1995), 126–35.

———. (1996). *Warfare in Roman Europe, AD 350–425.* Oxford.

Elvira, Maria Ángel, and C. Puertas. (1988). "El conjunto escultórico de Valdetorres de Jarama," *Goya* 208: 194–99.

Escacena Carrasco, José Luis, and Aurelio Padilla Monge. (1992). *El poblamiento romano en las margenes del antiguo estuario del Guadalquivir.* Écija.

Escribano Paño, María Victoria, and Guillermo Fatás Cabeza. (2001). *La antigüedad tardía en Aragón (284–714).* Zaragoza.

Escrivà Torres, Vicent, and Rafaela Soriano Sánchez. (1989). "El área cementerial asociada a la Basílica de la Almoina," in *III Congreso Arq. Med. Esp.,* 2: 103–9.

———, and Rafaela Soriano Sánchez. (1990). "El área episcopal de Valentia," *AEspA* 63: 347–54.

———, and Xavier Vidal Ferrús. (1995). "La Partida de Mura (Llíria, Valencia): un conjunto monumental de época flavia," *Saguntum* 29: 231–39.

Estefania, Dulce. (1958). "Notas para la delimitación de los Conventos jurídicos en Hispania," *Zephyrus* 9: 51–58.

Estévez Morales, José Antonio. (2000a). "Intervención arqueológica en el solar de la c/ Hernando de Bustamante, no. 7: Espacios de uso público (vía) y privado de época romana," in *Mérida 4*, 83–113.

———. (2000b). "Seguimiento arqueológico de la obra de construcción de un colector de aguas en la Avda. Juan Carlos I: Intervención arqueológica en un área funeraria y de tránsito (calzada)," in *Mérida 4*, 359–83.

Étienne, Robert. (1958). *Le culte impérial dans la Péninsule Ibérique.* Paris.

———. (1966a). "Les sénateurs espagnols sous Trajan et Hadrien," in *Empereurs d'Espagne,* 55–82.

———. (1966b). "Ausone et l'Espagne," in *Mélanges d'archéologie et d'épigraphie et d'histoire offerts à Jérôme Carcopino.* Paris. Pp. 319–32.

———. (1982). "Mérida, capitale du vicariat des Espagnes," in *Homenaje Saenz,* 201–7.

Euzennat, M. (1989). *Limes de Tingitane I: La frontière meridionale.* Paris.

Fanning, Stephen. (1992). "Emperors and Empires in Fifth-century Gaul," in Drinkwater and Elton (1992), 288–97.

Favrod, Justin. (1993). *La chronique de Marius d'Avenches (455–581): Texte, traduction et commentaire.* 2nd ed. Lausanne.

Fear, A. T. (1996). *Rome and Baetica: Urbanization in Southern Spain, c. 50 BC–AD 150*. Oxford.

———. (1997). *Lives of the Visigothic Fathers*. (Translated Texts for Historians). Liverpool.

Feijoo Martínez, Santiago. (2000a). "Intervención arqueológica en la zanja para canalización de aguas de la c/ Nerja: Unas termas de época visigoda extramuros de la ciudad," in *Mérida 4*, 333–57.

———. (2000b). "Generación y transformación del espacio urbano romano de *Augusta Emerita* al exterior de la muralla," in *Mérida 4*, 571–81.

Fernández Castro, Maria Cruz. (1982). *Villas romanas en España*. Madrid.

———. (1995). *Iberia in Prehistory*. Oxford.

Fernández Corrales, J. M. (1988). *El asentamiento romano en Extremadura y su analisis espacial*. Cáceres.

Fernández-Galiano Ruiz, Dimas. (1984a). *Complutum I: Excavaciones*. Madrid.

———. (1984b). *Complutum II: Mosaicos*. Madrid.

———. (1992a). "Cadmo y Harmonía: Imagen, mito y arqueología," *JRA* 5: 162–77.

———. (1992b). "Monasterios paganos: una propuesta," *AEspA* 65: 331–34.

———. (1992c). *Las villas hispanorromanas*. (Cuadernos de Arte Español 26). Madrid.

———. (1998). "La villa romana de Carranque," in *Hispania el Legado*, 487–89 and 657–58.

———, ed. (2001). *Carranque, centro de Hispania romana (Alcalá de Henares, 27 Abril–23 Septiembre 2001)*. Alcalá de Henares.

Fernández Gómez, F. (1991). "Nuevos fragmentos de leyes municipales y otros bronces epigráficos de la Bética en el Museo Arqueológico de Sevilla," *ZPE* 86: 121–36.

———, J. Alonso de la Sierra Fernández, and M. Gracia Lasso de la Vega. (1987). "La basilica y necrópolis paleocristianas de Gerena (Sevilla)," *NAH* 29: 103–99.

———, and M. del Amo y de la Hera. (1990). *La Lex Irnitana y su contexto arqueológico*. Seville.

Fernández Martínez, V. (1980). "Informe de la 5a campaña de excavaciones arqueológicas en Tiermes (Montejo de Tiermes, Soria), realizada en el verano de 1979: Muralla tardorromana," *Celtiberia* 60: 276–79.

Fernández Ochoa, Carmen. (1994a). "Las industrias de salazón en el norte de la península," *AEspA* 67: 115–34.

———. (1994b). *Una industria de salazones de época romana en la Plaza del Marqués (Gijón, Asturias)*. Gijón.

———, ed. (1996). *Los finisterres atlánticos en la antigüedad: época prerromana y romana (Coloquio internacional): Homenaje a Manuel Fernández-Miranda*. Gijón.

———. (1997). *La muralla romana de Gijón (Asturias)*. Gijón.

————. (1999). "La ciudad en la antigüedad tardía en la cornisa cantábrica," in García Moreno and Rascón (1999), 73–86.

————, and Ángel Morillo Cerdán. (1991). "Fortificaciones urbanas de época bajoimperial en Hispania: una aproximación a su crítica 1," *Cuadernos de Prehistoria y Arqueología de la Universidad Autónoma de Madrid* 18: 227–59.

————, and Ángel Morillo Cerdán. (1992). "Fortificaciones urbanas de época bajoimperial en Hispania: una aproximación a su crítica 2," *Cuadernos de Prehistoria y Arqueología de la Universidad Autónoma de Madrid* 19: 319–60.

————, and Ángel Morillo Cerdán. (1994a). "La ruta marítima del cantábrico en época romana," *Zephyrus* 46: 225–31.

————, and Ángel Morillo Cerdán. (1994b). *De Brigantium a Oiasso: Una aproximación al estudio de los enclaves marítimos cantábricos en época romana.* Madrid.

————, and Ángel Morillo Cerdán. (1997). "Urban Fortifications and Land Defence in Later Roman Spain," in *Roman Frontier Studies 1995: Proceedings of the XVIth International Conference on Roman Frontier Studies.* Oxford. Pp. 343–46.

————, and Ángel Morillo Cerdán. (1999). *La tierra de los astures: Nuevas perspectivas sobre la implantación romana en la antigua Asturias.* Gijón.

————, and Ángel Morillo Cerdán. (forthcoming). "Walls in the Urban Landscape of Late Roman Spain: Defence and Imperial Strategy," in Bowes and Kulikowski (forthcoming)

————, and Mar Zarzalejos Prieto. (2001). "Las termas públicas de las ciudades hispanas en el Bajo Imperio," in García Moreno and Rascón (2001), 19–35.

————, Paloma García Díaz, and Alexandra Uscatescu Barrón. (1992). "Gijón en el periodo tardoantiguo: cerámicas importadas de las excavaciones de Cimadevilla," *AEspA* 65: 105–49.

Fernández Ubiña, José. (1981). *La crisis del siglo III en la Bética.* Granada.

————. (1997). "El *Libellus Precum* y los conflictos religiosos en la Hispania de Teodosio," in Teja and Pérez (1997), 59–68.

Ferreiro, Alberto. (1981). "The Missionary Labors of St. Martin of Braga in Sixth-century Galicia," *Studia Monastica* 23: 11–26.

————. (1986). "The Omission of St. Martin of Braga in John of Biclaro's Chronica and the Third Council of Toledo," *Ant. Crist.* 3: 145–50.

————, ed. (1998). *The Visigoths: Studies in Culture and Society.* Leiden.

Février, Paul-Albert. (1974). "Permanence et héritages de l'Antiquité dans la topographie des villes de l'Occident durant le Haut Moyen Âge," *Settimane di Studi* 21: 41–138. Reprinted in idem, *La Méditerranée.* Aix-en-Provence, 1996. Pp. 379–494.

Figuerola, Miguel. (1999). "La circulación del AE2 Teodosiano en la Vía de la Plata," in Centeno et al. (1999), 367–79.

Flórez, Enrique. (1789). *España Sagrada IV.* Madrid.

Fontaine, Jacques. (1973). *L'art préroman hispanique.* Paris.

———. (1975). "L'affaire priscillen ou l'ère des nouveaux Catilina: observations sur le 'sallustianisme' de Sulpice Sévère," in P. T. Brannan, ed. *Classica et Iberica: A Festschrift in Honor of the Rev. Joseph M.-F. Marique, S.J.* Worcester, MA. Pp. 355–92.

———, and Pierre Cazier. (1983). "Qui a chassé de Carthaginoise Severianus et les siens? Observations sur l'histoire familiale d'Isidore de Séville," in *Estudios de Homenaje a Don Claudio Sánchez Albornoz en sus 90 años.* Buenos Aires. Pp. 349–400.

Fornell Muñoz, Alicia. (2001). "Ocio a través de las termas y los mosaicos encontrados en las *villae* de la *Hispania* meridional," in García Moreno and Rascón (2001), 39–58.

Franchi dei Cavalieri, Pío. (1959). "Las actas de San Fructuoso de Tarragona," *Boletín Arqueológico* 65–68: 3–70, first pub. in *Note Agiographiche, Studi e Testi* 8 (1935), 128–99.

Frézouls, E. (1980). "Rome et la Maurétanie Tingitane: un constat d'échec?" *Antiquités Africaines* 16: 65–93.

Fuentes Domínguez, Ángel. (1989). *La necrópolis tardorromana de Albalate de las Nogueras (Cuenca) y el problema de las denominadas "necrópolis del Duero."* Cuenca.

———. (1991). "Urbanismo privado y casas en Valeria," in *La casa urbana.* Pp. 265–80.

———. (1996). "La romanidad tardía en los territorios septentrionales de la Península Ibérica," in Fernández Ochoa (1996), 213–22.

———. (1997a). "Los ejércitos y otros sintomas de la descomposición social: Fin del Imperio romano," in *La Guerra en la Antigüedad: Una aproximación al origen de los ejércitos en Hispania (Madrid, 29 de Abril–29 de Junio 1997).* Madrid. Pp. 357–71.

———. (1997b). "Aproximación a la ciudad hispana de los siglos IV y V," in Teja and Pérez (1997), 477–96.

Fuentes Hinojo, Pablo. (1998). "Sociedad, ejército y administración en la provincia bizantina de *Spania,*" *SHHA* 16: 301–30.

Galsterer, Hartmut. (1971). *Untersuchungen zum römischen Stadtwesen auf der iberische Halbinsel.* Berlin.

———. (2000). "Local and Provincial Institutions and Government," in Bowman, Garnsey, and Rathbone (2000), 344–60.

Galvao-Sobrinho, Carlos R. (1995). "Funerary Epigraphy and the Spread of Christianity in the West," *Athenaeum* 83: 431–62.

García de Castro, F. J. (1995). "La trayectoria histórica de *Hispania* romana durante el siglo IV D.C.," *Hispania Antiqua* 19: 327–61.

García y Bellido, Antonio. (1960). *Colonia Aelia Augusta Italica.* Madrid.

———. (1967). *Les religions orientales dans l'Espagne romaine.* Leiden.

———. (1976). "El ejército romano en Hispania," *AEspA* 49: 59–101.

García Entero, Virginia. (2001). "Reflexiones en torno a las termas de las villae hispanorromanas: el material constructivo: cronología y dispersión geográfica," in García Moreno and Rascón (2001), 59–78.

García Fernández, Estela. (2001). *El municipio latino: Origen y desarollo constitucional.* (Anejos de *Gerión* 5). Madrid.

García Gallo, Alfonso. (1936–41). "Nacionalidad y territorialidad del derecho en la época visigoda," *AHDE* 13: 168–264.

———. (1942–43). "La territorialidad de la legislación visigoda: respuesta al Prof. Merêa," *AHDE* 14: 593–609.

———. (1974). "Consideración crítica de los estudios sobre la legislación y la costumbre visigodas," *AHDE* 44: 343–464.

———. (1983). "El proceso de San Marcelo de León," in *Estudios en Homenaje a Don Claudio Sánchez Albornoz en sus 90 años.* Buenos Aires. 1: 281–90.

García Iglesias, Luís. (1975). "El intermedio ostrogodo en Hispania (507–549 D.C.)," *Hispania Antiqua* 5: 89–120.

García Merino, Carmen. (1995). *Uxama I. Campañas de 1976 y 1978. Casa de la Cantera. Casa del Sectile. El Tambor.* (Excavaciones Arqueológicas en España 170). Madrid.

———, and Margarita Sánchez Simón. (1998). *Uxama II. La Casa de la Atalaya.* Valladolid.

García Moreno, Luís A. (1973). "Organización militar de Bizancio en la Península Ibérica (ss. VI–VII)," *Hispania* 33: 5–22.

———. (1974). "Estudios sobre la organización administrativa del reino visigodo de Toledo," *AHDE* 44: 1–155.

———. (1976). "Hidacio y el ocaso del poder imperial en la península ibérica," *RABM* 79: 27–42.

———. (1977–78). "La christianización de la topografía de las ciudades de la Península Ibérica durante la antigüedad tardía," *AEspA* 50–51: 311–21.

———. (1982). "Mérida y el reino visigodo de Tolosa (418–507)," in *Homenaje Saenz,* 227–40.

———. (1985). "La invasión del 409 en España," in Castillo (1985), 63–86.

———. (1989). *Historia de España Visigoda.* Madrid.

———. (1994). "La Andalucía de San Isidoro," in *II Actas Andalucía,* 554–79.

———. (1995). "En las raíces de Andalucía (ss. V–X): los destinos de una aristocracia urbana," *AHDE* 65: 849–78.

———. (2001). "Materno Cinegio, cristianísimo colaborador del hispano Teodosio el Grande," in Fernández-Galiano (2001), 53–67.

———, and Sebastián Rascón Marqués, eds. (1999). *Complutum y las ciudades hispanas en la antigüedad tardía (Actas del I Encuentro Hispania en la Antigüedad Tardía, Alcalá de Henares, 16 de Octubre de 1996).* (Acta Antiqua Complutensia 1). Alcalá de Henares.

———, and Sebastián Rascón Marqués, eds. (2001). *Ocio y espectáculo en la*

Antigüedad Tardía (Actas del II Encuentro Hispania en la Antigüedad Tardía, Alcalá de Henares, 15 a 17 de Octubre de 1997). (Acta Antiqua Complutensia 2). Alcalá de Henares.

García Noguera, M., and J. A. Remolà Vallverdú. (2000). "Noves intervencions a les necròpolis tardoantigues del marge esquerre de riu Francolí," in Ruiz (2000), 165–80.

García Villanueva, I., and M. Rosselló Mesquida. (1992). "Las ánforas tardorromanas de Punta de l'Illa de Cullera," *Trabajos Varios del SIP* 89: 639–61.

Garnsey, Peter. (1988). *Famine and Food Supply in the Graeco-Roman World.* Cambridge.

Gascou, J. (1979). "L'emploi du terme *res publica* dans l'epigraphie latine d'Afrique," *MEFRA* 91: 383–98.

———. (1982a). "La politique municipale de Rome en Afrique du Nord I: De la mort d'Auguste au début du IIIe siècle," *ANRW* II 10.2: 136–229.

———. (1982b). "La politique municipale de Rome en Afrique du Nord II: Après la mort de Septime-Sévère," *ANRW* II 10.2: 230–320.

Gaudemet, Jean. (1959). *L'église dans l'empire romain (IVe–Ve siècles)*. Paris.

Gautier, E.-F. (1951). *Genséric, roi des Vandales*. Paris.

Gerberding, R. A. (1987). *The Rise of the Carolingians and the Liber Historiae Francorum*. Oxford.

Geuenich, Dieter. (1997). *Geschichte der Alemannen*. Stuttgart.

Gil, Juan. (1972). *Miscellanea Wisigothica*. Seville.

———. (1984). "Interpretaciones latinas," *Habis* 15: 185–97.

———, and Julián González Fernández. (1977). "Inscripción sepulcral de un noble visigodo de Igabrum," *Habis* 8: 455–61.

Gil Farrés, O. (1966). *La moneda hispánica en la edad antigua*. Madrid.

Gil Mantas, Vasco. (1993). "A cidade luso-romana de Ossonoba," in Rodríguez Neila (1993), 1: 515–37.

Gillett, Andrew. (1995). "The Birth of Ricimer," *Historia* 44: 80–84.

———. (1999). "The Accession of Euric," *Francia* 26.1: 1–40.

———, ed. (2002). *On Barbarian Identity: Critical Approaches to Ethnicity in the Early Middle Ages*. Turnhout.

———. (2003). *Envoys and Political Communication in the Late Antique West, 411–533*. Cambridge.

Godoy Fernández, Cristina. (1995). *Arqueología y liturgia: Iglesias hispánicas (siglos IV al VIII)*. Barcelona.

Goffart, Walter. (1974). *Caput and Colonate: Towards a History of Late Roman Taxation*. Toronto.

———. (1980). *Barbarians and Romans, A.D. 418–584: The Techniques of Accommodation*. Princeton.

Goldsworthy, Adrian. (1996). *The Roman Army at War, 100 BC–AD 200*. Oxford.

Gómez Santa Cruz, J. (1989). "Aproximación al poblamiento rural hispanoromano en la provincia de Soria," in *Actas Sorianas II*: 937–56.

Gonzalbes Cravioto, Enrique. (1981). "El problema de la Ceuta bizantina," *Les Cahiers de Tunisie* 115–16: 23–53.

———. (1986). *Los bizantinos en Ceuta (siglos VI–VII)*. Ceuta.

———. (1989). "El ataque del rey visigodo Teudis contra *Septem*," *Cuadernos del Archivo Municipal de Ceuta* 5: 41–54.

González, José Maria Esteban, Ángel Muñoz Vicente, and Francisco Blanco Jiménez. (1993). "Breve historia y criterios de intervención en el área urbana del teatro romano de Cádiz," *CAR* 2: 141–56.

González-Conde, M. P. (1987). *Romanidad e indigenismo en Carpetania*. Alicante.

González Fernández, Julián. (1986). "The Lex Irnitana: A New Flavian Municipal Law," *JRS* 76: 147–243.

———. (1988). "Divinidades prerromanas en Andalucía," in Mayer (1988), 271–82.

———. (1990). *Bronces jurídicos romanos de Andalucía*. Seville.

———. (1993). "*Lex Villonensis*," *Habis* 23: 97–119.

———, ed. (1994). *Roma y las provincias: realidad administrativa e ideología imperial*. Madrid.

———. (1999a). "Nuevos fragmentos de la *lex Flavia municipalis* pertenecientes a la *Lex Villonensis* y a otros municipios de nombre desconocido," in idem (1999b), 239–45.

———, ed. (1999b). *Ciudades privilegiadas en el occidente romano*. Seville.

———, and Javier Arce, eds. (1988). *Estudios sobre la Tabula Siarensis*. Madrid.

González Román, Cristóbal. (1991a). "Elite social y religión en la Colonia Augusta Gemella Tucci," in Mayer (1988), 283–94.

———, ed. (1991b). *La Bética en su problemática histórica*. Granada.

———. (2000). "Colonización y municipalización en la Oretania," in Salvador (2000a), 47–74.

Gorges, Jean-Gérard. (1979). *Les villas hispano-romaines*. Paris.

———. (1992). "Archéologie et economie des campagnes hispano-romaines: vingt-cinq ans de bibliographie commentée (1968–1992)," *MCV* 28: 93–142.

———, and Francisco Germán Rodríguez-Martín. (1997). "Nuevo miliario de Magnencio hallado en la villa romana de Torre Águila (Montijo, Badajoz): epigrafía y territorio," *Anas* 10: 7–24.

———, and Trinidad Nogales Basarrate. (2000). *Sociedad y cultura en Lusitania romana. IV Mesa redonda internacional*. Mérida.

Goubert, Pierre. (1947–51). "Ceuta byzantine ou wisigothique? Notes d'histoire et d'archéologie," in *Miscel.lània Puig i Cadafalch*. 2 vols. Barcelona. 1: 337–43.

Gozalbes Fernández de Palencia, Manuel. (1999). *Los hallazgos monetarios del Grau Vell (Sagunt, València)*. Valencia.

Granados, J. Oriol. (1987). "La transformación de la colonia Barcino," in *II Congreso Arq. Med. Esp.*, 2: 353–61.

———. (1995). "Notes per a l'estudi de la Basílica i del conjunt episcopal paleocristià de Barcelona: Valoració de la primera fase," in *RACH IV*, 121–32.

———, and I. Rodà. (1994). "Barcelona en la Baixa Romanitat," *III Congrés d'Historia de Barcelona: La ciutat i el seu territori, dos mil anys d'història (Barcelona, 20, 21 i 22 d'octubre de 1993)*. Barcelona. Pp. 25–46.

Greene, Kevin. (1987). "Gothic Material Culture," in Ian Hodder, ed. *Archaeology as Long-Term History*. Cambridge. Pp. 117–31.

Grierson, Philip, and Mark Blackburn. (1986). *Medieval European Coinage with a Catalogue of the Coins in the Fitzwilliam Museum, Cambridge,* vol. I: *The Early Middle Ages (5th–10th centuries)*. Cambridge.

Grosse, R. (1947). *Fontes Hispaniae Antiquae, volumen IX*. Barcelona.

Gruen, Erich S. (1992). *Culture and National Identity in Republican Rome*. Ithaca.

Grünhagen, Wilhelm. (1982). "Cronología de la muralla de Munigua," in *Homenaje Saenz*, 315–28.

———, and Theodor Hauschild. (1983). "Excavaciones en Munigua: Campañas de 1977 a 1980," *NAH* 17: 321–32.

Güell, Manuel, Isabel Peña, Olga Tobías, and Mercedes Tubilla. (1993). "La restitución arquitectónica de la Plaza de Representación (el denominado "Foro Provincial")," in Mar (1993), 157–90.

Guiral Pelegrín, Carmen, and Antonio Mostalac Carrillo. (1991). "Pinturas romanas," in Aranegui (1991), 64–68.

Gurt i Esparraguera, Josep Maria. (1985). *Clunia III: Hallazgos monetarios. La romanización de la Meseta Norte a través de la circulación monetaria en la ciudad de Clunia*. Madrid.

———, Gisela Ripoll López, and Cristina Godoy Fernández. (1994). "Topografía de la antigüedad tardía hispana: Reflexiones para una propuesta de trabajo," *Antiquité Tardive* 2: 161–80.

———, and Cristina Godoy Fernández. (2000). "*Barcino,* de sede imperial a *urbs regia* en época visigoda," in Ripoll and Gurt (2000), 425–66.

———, and Josep Maria Palet i Martínez. (2001). "Pervivencias y cambios estructurales durante la Antigüedad tardía en el Nordeste de la Península Ibérica," in Arce and Delogu (2001), 9–36.

Guterman, Simeon L. (1990). *The Principle of the Personality of Law in the Germanic Kingdoms of Western Europe from the Fifth to the Eleventh Century*. New York.

Gutiérrez Lloret, S. (1988). "El poblamiento tardorromano en Alicante a través de los testimonios materiales: estado de la cuestión y perspectivas," *Ant. Crist.* 5: 323–37.

———. (1993). "De la *civitas* a la *madina:* destrucción y formación de la ciudad en el sureste de Al-Andalus. El debate arqueológico," in *IV Congreso Arq. Med. Esp.,* 1: 13–35.

Haley, Evan. (1994). "A Palace of Maximianus Herculius at Corduba?" *ZPE* 101: 208–14.

————. (1997). "Town and Country: The Acculturation of Spain," *JRA* 10: 495–503.

Halsall, Guy. (1992). "The Origins of the *Reihengräberzivilisation:* Forty Years On," in Drinkwater and Elton (1992), 196–207.

Hamdoune, C. (1994). "Note sur le statut colonial de Lixus et de Tanger," *Antiquités Africaines* 30: 81–87.

Harl, Kenneth W. (1996). *Coinage and the Roman Economy, 300 B.C. to A.D. 700.* Baltimore.

Harries, Jill. (1992). "Sidonius Apollinaris, Rome and the Barbarians: A Climate of Treason?" in Drinkwater and Elton (1992), 298–308.

————. (1994). *Sidonius Apollinaris and the Fall of Rome.* Oxford.

————. (1999). *Law and Empire in Late Antiquity.* Cambridge.

Harris, W. V. (1979). *War and Imperialism in Republican Rome, 327–70 BC.* Oxford.

————, ed. (1984). *The Imperialism of Mid-Republican Rome.* Rome.

Harrison, Richard J. (1988). *Spain at the Dawn of History: Iberians, Phoenicians and Greeks.* London.

Hartmann, F. (1982). *Herscherwechsel und Reichkrise: Untersuchungen zu den Ursachen und Konsequenzen der Herrscherwechsel im Imperium Romanum der Soldatenkaiserzeit (3. Jahrhundert n. Chr.).* Frankfurt-am-Main.

Hauschild, Theodor. (1983). *Arquitectura romana de Tarragona.* Tarragona.

————. (1984). "Munigua: Vorbericht über die Grabungen in Haus 1 und Haus 6, Kampagne 1982," *MM* 25: 159–80, with plates 36–49.

————. (1984–85). "Excavaciones en la muralla romana de Tarragona: Torre de Minerva (1979) y Torre del Cabiscol (1983)," *Butlletí Arqueòlogic* 5, nos. 6–7: 11–38.

————. (1993a). "Traditionen römischen Stadtbefestigungen der Hispania," in Hauschild (1993b), 217–31.

————, ed. (1993b). *Hispania Antiqua: Denkmäler der Römerzeit.* Mainz.

————. (1994a). "Hallazgos de la época visigoda en la parte alta de Tarragona," in *RACH III,* 151–56.

————. (1994b). "Murallas de *Hispania* en el contexto de las fortificaciones del área occidental del imperio romano," in *XIV Congr. Int. Arq. Clas.,* 223–32.

————, and Erika Hausmann. (1991). "Casas romanas en Munigua," in *La casa urbana.* Pp. 329–35.

Häussler, Ralph. (2002). "Writing Latin—From Resistance to Assimilation: Language, Culture and Society in N. Italy and S. Gaul," in Cooley (2002), 61–76.

Heather, Peter. (1991). *Goths and Romans, 332–489.* Oxford.

————. (1992). "The Emergence of the Visigothic Kingdom," in Drinkwater and Elton (1992), 84–94.

————. (1995). "The Huns and the End of the Roman Empire in Western Europe," *EHR* 110: 4–41.

————. (1996). *The Goths*. Oxford.

Hernández Hervás, Emilia, Montserrat López Piñol, Ignacio Pascual Buyé, and Carmen Aranegui. (1993). "El teatro romano de Sagunto," *CAR* 2: 25–42.

————, Montserrat López Piñol, and Ignacio Pascual Buyé. (1995). "La implantación del Circo en el área suburbana de Saguntum," *Saguntum* 29: 221–30.

Hernández Ramírez, Julián. (1998). *Augusta Emerita: Estructura urbana*. Badajoz.

Hernández Vera J. A., and J. Núñez Marcén. (1998). "Nuevos datos para el conocimiento del foro de *Caesaraugusta*," *Empúries* 51: 93–104.

Hess, Hamilton. (1958). *The Canons of the Council of Sardica, A.D. 343*. Oxford.

Hidalgo Prieto, Rafael. (1994). "Mosaicos de la villa romana de El Ruedo (Almedinilla, Córdoba)," in *VI Coloquio internacional sobre mosaico antiguo: Palencia-Mérida, Octubre 1990*. Madrid. Pp. 15–22.

————. (1996). *Espacio publico y espacio privado en el conjunto palatino de Cercadilla (Córdoba): el aula central y las termas*. Córdoba.

————. (1999). "La incorporación del esquema palacio-circo a la imagen de la *Corduba* bajoimperial," in González Fernández (1999), 377–96.

————, and Ángel Ventura Villanueva. (1994). "Sobre la cronología e interpretación del palacio de Cercadilla en Corduba," *Chiron* 24: 221–40.

Hiernard, Jean. (1978). "Recherches numismatiques sur Tarragone au IIIe siècle après Jésus-Christ," *Numisma* 28: 307–21.

Hillgarth, J. N. (1966). "Coins and Chronicles: Propaganda in Sixth-century Spain and the Byzantine Background," *Historia* 15: 483–508.

————. (1980). "Popular Religion in Visigothic Spain," in James (1980), 3–60.

Hoffmann, Dietrich. (1969–70). *Die spätrömische Bewegungsheer und die Notitia Dignitatum*. (Epigraphische Studien 9). 2 vols. Dusseldorf.

Hoyo Calleja, J. del. (1988). "Relación culto-estrato social en la Hispania romana," in Mayer (1988), 303–8.

————. (1995). "Duratón, municipio romano: A propósito de un fragmento inédito de ley municipal," *ZPE* 108: 140–44.

————. (1998). "Nuevo documento metróaco hallado en la provincia de Segovia," *Gerión* 16: 345–82.

Hübener, Wolfgang. (1970). "Zur Chronologie der westgotenzeitlichen Grabfunde in Spanien," *MM* 11: 187–211.

————. (1974). "Problemas de las necrópolis visigodas españolas desde el punto de vista centroeuropeo," *Miscelánea Arqueológica* 1: 361–78.

————. (1991). "Temoins archéologiques des Wisigoths en Espagne," in Périn (1991), 133–39.

Humphrey, J. H. (1986). *Roman Circuses: Arenas for Chariot Racing*. London.

Isaac, Bernard. (1988). "The Meaning of 'limes' and 'limitanei' in Ancient Sources," *JRS* 78: 125–47.

Isla Frez, Amancio. (1990). "Las relaciones entre el reino visigodo y los reyes merovingios a finales del siglo VI," *En la España Medieval* 13: 11–32.

Jacques, François. (1984). *La privilège de liberté: politique impériale et autonomie municipale dans les cités de l'Occident.* Paris.

Jaczynowska, M. (1970). "Les organisations des iuvenes et l'aristocratie municipale au temps de l'empire romain," in *Recherches sur les structures sociales dans l'antiquité classique.* Caen. Pp. 265–74.

James, Edward. (1977). *The Merovingian Archaeology of South-West Gaul.* (British Archaeological Reports, International Series 22). Oxford.

———, ed. (1980). *Visigothic Spain: New Approaches.* Oxford.

Járrega Domínguez, Ramón. (1991). "Consideraciones sobre la cronología de las murallas tardorromanas de Barcelona: ¿un fortificación del siglo V?" *AEspA* 64: 326–35.

Jiménez Cobo, Martín. (2000). *Jaén romano.* Córdoba.

Jiménez Garnica, Ana Maria. (1983). *Origines y desarrollo del reino visigodo de Tolosa (a. 418–507).* Valladolid.

Jiménez Salvador, José Luis. (1993). "Teatro y desarrollo monumental urbano en Hispania," *CAR* 2: 225–38.

———. (1994). "El templo romano de la calle Claudio Marcelo en Córdoba y su importancia dentro del programa monumental de *Colonia Patricia* durante el alto imperio," in *XIV Congreso Int. Arq. Clas.,* 245–51.

———. (1998). "La multiplicación de plazas públicas en la ciudad hispanorromana," *Empúries* 51: 11–30.

Johnson, Stephen. (1983). *Late Roman Fortifications.* London.

Jones, A. H. M. (1964). *The Later Roman Empire, 284–602.* 3 vols. Oxford.

Jordán Montes, Juan Francisco, and Gónzalo Matilla Séiquer. (1995). "Poblamiento rural tardoantiguo y monasterios visigodos en el curso bajo del Río Mundo (Hellín y Tobarra, provincia de Albacete)," in Noguera (1995), 323–37.

Jorge, Ana Maria C. M. (2002). *L'épiscopat de Lusitanie pendant l'Antiquité tardive (IIIe–VIIe siècles).* (Trabalhos de Arqueologia 21). Lisbon.

Juan Navarro, Empar, and Ignacio Pastor Cubillo. (1989a). "El yacimiento de época visigótica de Pla de Nadal," *Archivo de Prehistoria Levantina* 19: 357–73.

———, and Ignacio Pastor Cubillo. (1989b). "Los visigodos en Valencia. Pla de Nadal. ¿una villa aulica?" *Boletín de Arqueología Medieval* 3: 137–79.

Junyent, E., and Arturo Pérez Almoguera. (1994). "El Bajo Imperio ilerdense: las excavaciones de la Paería," in *RACH III,* 127–50.

Kazanski, Michel. (1993). *Les Goths.* Paris.

Keay, Simon. (1989). *Roman Spain.* Berkeley and Los Angeles.

———. (1990). "Processes in the Development of the Coastal Communities of Hispania Citerior in the Republican Period," in Blagg and Millett (1990), 120–50.

———. (1991a). "New Light on the *colonia Iulia Urbs Triumphalis Tarraco* (Tarragona) during the Late Empire," *JRA* 4: 387–97.

———. (1991b). "The *Ager Tarraconensis* in the Late Empire: A Model for the Economic Relationship of Town and Country in Eastern Spain?" in Barker and Lloyd (1991), 79–87.

———. (1996). "Tarraco in Late Antiquity," in N. Christie and S. T. Loseby, eds. *Towns in Transition.* Aldershot. Pp. 18–44.

———, John Creighton, and José Remesal Rodríguez. (2000). *Celti. Peñaflor: The Archaeology of a Hispano-Roman Town in Baetica.* Southampton and Oxford.

Kennedy, Hugh. (1995). *Muslim Spain and Portugal.* London.

Kent, J. P. C. (1994) *The Roman Imperial Coinage X: The Divided Empire and the Fall of the Western Parts, AD 395–491.* London.

Kienast, Dietmar. (1996). *Römische Kaisertabelle. Grundzüge einer römischen Kaiserchronologie.* 2nd ed. Darmstadt.

Kienast, W. (1984). "Gefolgswesen und Patrocinium im spanischen Westgotenreich," *HZ* 239: 23–75.

King, P. D. (1972). *Law and Society in the Visigothic Kingdom.* Cambridge.

Klingshirn, William E. (1994). *Caesarius of Arles: The Making of a Community in Late Antique Gaul.* Cambridge.

König, Gerd G. (1980). "Archäologische Zeugnisse westgotischer Präsenz im 5. Jahrhundert," *MM* 21: 220–47.

———. (1985). "Duratón," *RGA* 6: 284–94.

König, I. (1981). *Die gallischen Usurpatoren von Postumus bis Tetricus.* (Vestigia: Beiträge zur Alten Geschichte 31). Munich.

Koppel, Eva María. (1988). *La Schola del Collegium Fabrum de Tarraco y su decoración escultórica.* Bellaterra.

Kornemann, E. (1901). "Collegium," *P-W* 4: 380–480.

Krause, Jens-Uwe. (1987). *Spätantike Patronatsformen im Westen des römischen Reiches.* Munich.

Kulikowski, Michael. (1998). "The *Epistula Honorii,* Again," *ZPE* 122: 247–52.

———. (2000a). "The Career of the *comes Hispaniarum* Asterius," *Phoenix* 54: 123–41.

———. (2000b). "Barbarians in Gaul, Usurpers in Britain," *Britannia* 31: 325–45.

———. (2000c). "The *Notitia Dignitatum* as an Historical Source," *Historia* 49: 358–77.

———. (2001). "The Visigothic Settlement in Aquitania: The Imperial Perspective," in Mathisen and Shanzer (2001), 26–38.

———. (2002). "Fronto, the Bishops, and the Crowd: Episcopal Justice and Communal Violence in Fifth-century Tarraconensis," in *Early Medieval Europe* 11: 297–320.

Lacarra, J. M. (1945). "Textos navarros del códice de Roda," *Estudios de la Edad Media en la Corona de Aragon* 1: 193–283.

Laeuchli, Samuel. (1972). *Power and Sexuality: The Emergence of Canon Law at the Synod of Elvira*. Philadelphia.

Laffi, U. (1966). *Adtributio e contributio*. Pisa.

Laiz Reverte, Maria D., and Elena Ruiz Valderas. (1988). "Área de *tabernae* tardorromanas de Cartagena," *Ant. Crist.* 5: 425–33.

———, L. M. Pérez Adán, and Elena Ruiz Valderas. (1987). "Nuevas hallazgos bizantinos en Cartagena," *AEspA* 60: 281–85.

Lana, I. (1962). *Due capitoli prudenciani: la biografia; la cronologia delle opere*. Rome.

Lanata, G. (1972). "Gli atti del processo contro il centurione Marcello," *Byzantion* 42: 509–22.

Lane Fox, Robin. (1986). *Pagans and Christians*. Harmondsworth.

Larrañaga Elorza, Koldo. (1989). "En torno al caso del obispo Silvano de Calagurris: consideraciones sobre el estado de la iglesia del alto y medio Ebro a fines del imperio," *Veleia* 6: 171–91.

———. (1993). "El pasaje del pseudo-Fredegario sobre el dux francio de Cantabria," *AEspA* 66: 177–206.

Lee, A. D. (1993). *Information and Frontiers*. Cambridge.

León, Pilar, ed. (1993a). *Colonia Patricia Corduba: una reflexión arqueológica*. Córdoba.

———. (1993b). "Hacia una nueva visión de la Córdoba romana," in León (1993a), 17–36.

Le Roux, Patrick. (1982). *L'armée romaine et l'organisation de les provinces ibériques d'Auguste à l'invasion de 409*. Paris.

———. (1992–93). "*Vicus* et *castellum* en Lusitanie sous l'Empire," *SHHA* 10–11: 152–60.

———. (1994). "Cités et territoires en Hispanie: l'épigraphie des limites," *MCV* 30: 37–51.

Liebeschuetz, J. H. W. G. (2001). *The Decline and Fall of the Roman City*. Oxford.

Lintott, Andrew. (1993). *Imperium Romanum: Politics and Administration*. London.

Llanos, A. (1978). *Carta arqueológica de Alava*. Madrid.

Llinàs i Pol, J., S. Manzano i Vilar, A. M. Puig i Griessenberger, and X. Rocas i Gutiérrez. (1992). "Noves aportacions al coneixement de les necròpolis emporitanes," *Annals de l'Institut d'Estudis Empordanesos* 25: 351–81.

———, S. Manzano i Vilar, A. M. Puig i Griessenberger, and X. Rocas i Gutiérrez. (1997). *L'excavació de la carretera de Sant Martí: un sector de l'entorn d'Empúries des de la baix república fins a l'antiguitat tardana*. (Estudis Arqueològics 3). Gerona.

Lomas Salmonte, Francisco Javier. (1993). "Panorama cultural y espiritual de la Bética en el siglo IV," in Rodríguez Neila (1993), 269–87.

Longnon, Auguste. (1878). *Géographie de la Gaule au VIe siècle.* Paris.

López Piñol, Montserrat. (1991). "El nivel de abandono del Grau Vell: las sigillatas de producción africana," in Aranegui (1991), 103–6.

López i Vilar, Jordi. (1993). "Excavacions al Pla de Sant Miguel," in Mar (1993), 245–55.

———. (1997). "Un nuevo conjunto paleocristiano en las afueras de Tarraco," *Revista de Arqueología* 197: 58–64.

———. (2000). "Excavacions al solar de Parc Central," in Ruiz (2000), 191–96.

Loyen, André. (1943). *Recherches historiques sur les panégyriques de Sidoine Apollinaire.* Paris.

———. (1963). "Résistants et collaborateurs en Gaule à l'époque des Grandes Invasions," *Bulletin de l'Association Guillaume Budé* 23: 437–50.

Luzón, J. M. (1975). *La Itálica de Adriano.* Seville.

———, ed. (1982). *Itálica (Santiponce, Sevilla).* Madrid.

Macias Solé, Josep Maria. (2000). "L'urbanisme de Tàrraco a partir de les excavacions de l'entorn del fòrum de la ciutat," in Ruiz (2000), 83–106.

Mackie, Nicola. (1983). *Local Administration in Roman Spain, AD 14–212.* Oxford.

———. (1990). "Urban Munificence and the Growth of Urban Consciousness in Roman Spain," in Blagg and Millett (1990), 179–92.

MacMullen, Ramsay. (1963). *Soldier and Civilian in the Later Roman Empire.* Cambridge, MA.

———. (1964). "Imperial Bureaucrats in the Roman Provinces," *HSCP* 68: 305–16.

———. (1965). "The Celtic Renaissance," *Historia* ; reprinted in MacMullen (1990), 41–48.

———. (1966). *Enemies of the Roman Order.* Cambridge, MA.

———. (1974). *Roman Social Relations, 50 B.C. to A.D. 284.* New Haven.

———. (1982). "The Epigraphic Habit in the Roman Empire," *AJP* 103: 233–46.

———. (1984). *Christianizing the Roman Empire, 100–400.* New Haven.

———. (1990). *Changes in the Roman Empire: Essays in the Ordinary.* Princeton.

Maguire, Henry. (1999). "The Good Life," in Bowersock, Brown, and Grabar (1999), 238–57.

Maloney, Stephanie J. (1995). "The Early Christian Basilican Complex of Torre de Palma (Monforte, Alto Alentejo, Portugal)," in *RACH IV,* 449–58.

———, and John R. Hale. (1996). "The Villa of Torre de Palma (Alto Alentejo)," *JRA* 9: 275–94.

———, and Asa Ringbom. (2000). "14C Dating of Mortars at Torre de Palma, Portugal," in *RACH V,* 151–55.

Mangas Manarrés, Julio. (1996). *Aldea y ciudad en la antigüedad hispana.* Madrid.

————. (2000). "Leyes de las ciudades romanas de la Bética," in Salvador (2000), 75–93.

————. (2001). *Leyes coloniales y municipales de la Hispania romana.* Madrid.

Mann, J. C. (1974). "The Frontiers of the Principate," *ANRW* 2.1: 508–33.

Mar, Ricardo, ed. (1993). *El monuments provincials de Tàrraco: noves aportacions al seu coneixement.* (Documents d'Arqueologia Clàssica 1). Tarragona.

————, and Joaquín Ruiz de Arbulo. (1990). "El foro de Ampurias y las transformaciones augusteas de los foros de la Tarraconense," in Trillmich and Zanker (1990), 144–63.

————, and Joaquín Ruiz de Arbulo. (1993). *Ampurias Romana: Historia, Arquitectura y Arqueología.* Sabadell.

————, and Joaquín Ruiz de Arbulo. (1999). "Veinte años de arqueología urbana en Tarragona," *XXV CNA,* 240–48.

————, Mercedes Roca, and Joaquín Ruiz de Arbulo. (1993). "El teatro romano de Tarragona: Un problema pendiente," *CAR* 2: 11–23.

————, Jordi López i Vilar, O. Tobías, I. Peña, and L. Palahí. (1996). "El conjunto paleocristiano del Francolí en Tarragona: Nuevas aportaciones," *Antiquité Tardive* 4: 320–24.

Marcet, R., and Enric Sanmartí i Grego. (1989). *Empúries.* Barcelona.

Marcillet-Jaubert, J. (1968). *Les inscriptions d'Altava.* Aix-en-Provence.

Marco Simón, F. (1988). "La individuación del espacio sagrado: testimonios cultuales en el noroeste hispánico," in Mayer (1988), 317–24.

Marfil Ruiz, Pedro. (2000). "La sede episcopal cordobesa en época bizantina: evidencia arqueológica," in *RACH V,* 157–75.

Marín Baño, Carmen, and Luis E. de Miquel Santed. (1999). "Estudio preliminar de una domus antoniniana en Carthago Nova (Calles Jara, Palas y Cuatro Santos)," *XXV CNA,* 280–85.

Marín Jordá, Carmen, and Albert Ribera i Lacomba. (1999). *Las termas romanas de l'Almoina.* (Quaderns de Difusió Arqueològica 3). Valencia.

————, Josefina Piá Brisa, and Miquel Rosseló i Mesquida. (1999). *El foro romano de Valentia.* (Quaderns de Difusió Arqueològica 4). Valencia.

Mariner, S. (1973). *Inscripciones romanas de Barcelona lapidarias y musivas.* Barcelona.

Marot, Teresa. (1997). "Algunas consideraciones sobre la significación de las emisiones del usurpador Máximo en *Barcino,*" in Teja and Pérez (1997), 569–80.

————. (1999a). "La ciudad de *Barcino* durante los siglos V y VI: nuevas aportaciones sobre el circulante," in Centeno et al. (1999), 415–22.

————. (1999b). "Invasions i accions militars a la península ibèrica durant l'antiguitat tardana (segles VI–VII): el testimoni de la moneda," in *III Curs d'Historia monetària de Hispània: Moneda i exèrcits, 25 i 26 de novembre de 1999.* Barcelona. Pp. 145–67.

Márquez Moreno, Carlos. (1993). *Capiteles romanos de Colonia Patricia Corduba.* Córdoba.

————. (1998a). *La decoración arquitectónica de Colonia Patricia: una aproximación a la arquitectura y urbanismo de la Córdoba romana.* Córdoba.

————. (1998b). "Acerca de la función e inserción urbanística de las plazas en *Colonia Patricia,*" *Empúries* 51: 63–76.

————. (1999). "Colonia Patricia Corduba, paradigma urbano en la Bética," in González Fernández (1999b), 351–63.

————, Rafael Hidalgo Prieto, and Pedro Marfil Ruiz. (1991). "El complejo monumental tardorromano de Cercadilla en colonia patricia Corduba," *L'Africa Romana* 9: 1039–47.

Márquez Pérez, Juana. (1998). "Nuevos datos sobre la dispersión de las áreas funerarias de Emerita Augusta," in *Mérida 2,* 291–301.

————, and Miguel Hernández López. (1998). "Intervención en un solar de la c/ Almendralejo, interior del Parador Nacional," in *Mérida 2,* 193–210.

Márquez Villora, Juan Carlos, Jaime Molina Vidal, and M. José Sánchez Fernández. (1999). "La factoría de salazones del Portus Ilicitanus (Santa Pola, Alicante): Nuevos descubrimientos y estado de la cuestión," *XXV CNA,* 360–64.

————, and Antonio M. Poveda Navarro. (2000). "Espacio religioso y cultura material en *Ilici* (ss. IV–VII d.C.)," in *RACH V,* 185–98.

Martin, Jochen. (1995). *Spätantike und Völkerwanderung.* 3rd ed. (Oldenbourg Grundriss der Geschichte 4). Munich.

Martínez Rodríguez, Andrés, and Juana Ponce García. (2000). "Lorca como centro territorial durante los siglos V–VII d.C.," in *RACH V,* 199–209.

Martínez Santa-Olalla, J. (1933). *Excavaciones en la necrópolis visigoda de Herrera de Pisuerga (Palencia).* Madrid.

Martins, Manuela, and Manuela Delgado. (1996). "*Bracara Augusta:* uma cidade na periferia do Império," in Fernández Ochoa (1996), 121–27.

Mas García, Julio, ed. (1986). *Historia de Cartagena,* tomo V: *El medievo y la cultura mediterránea: El sureste ibérico en la alta Edad Media (siglos V–XIII).* Murcia.

Mateos Cruz, Pedro. (1992). "El culto a santa Eulalia y su influencia en el urbanismo emeritense (siglos IV–VI)," *Extremadura Arqueológica* 3: 57–79.

————. (1994–95). "Reflexiones sobre la trama urbana de Augusta Emerita," *Anas* 7–8: 233–53.

————. (1995a). "Arqueología de la tardoantigüedad en Mérida: estado de la cuestión," in Velázquez et al. (1995), 125–50.

————. (1995b). "Identificación del *Xenodochium* fundado por Masona en Mérida," in *RACH IV,* 309–16.

————. (1999). *La basílica de Santa Eulalia de Mérida: Arqueología y urbanismo.* (Anejos del *Archivo Español de Arqueología* 19). Madrid.

————. (2000). "*Augusta Emerita,* de capital de la *Diocesis Hispaniarum* a sede temporal visigoda," in Ripoll and Gurt (2000), 491–520.

————, and Miguel Alba Calzado. (2000). "De *Emerita Augusta* a Marida," in

Luis Caballero Zoreda and Pedro Mateos Cruz, eds. *Visigodos y Omeyas: Un debate entre la Antigüedad Tardía y la alta Edad Media.* Madrid. Pp. 143–68.

Mateu y Llopis, Felipe. (1949). "Las inscripciones del obispo Justiniano y la Catedral visigótica de Valencia," *Anales del Centro de Cultura Valenciana* 17: 139–67.

Mathisen, Ralph W. (1984). "Emigrants, Exiles and Survivors: Aristocratic Options in Visigothic Aquitania," *Phoenix* 38: 159–70.

———. (1985). "The Third Regnal Year of Eparchius Avitus," *Classical Philology* 80: 326–35.

———. (1991). "The Third Regnal Year of Eparchius Avitus: The Interpretation of the Evidence," in id., *Studies in the History, Literature, and Society of Late Antiquity.* Amsterdam. Pp. 163–66.

———, ed. (2001). *Law, Society and Authority in Late Antiquity.* Oxford.

———, and Hagith S. Sivan, eds. (1995). *Shifting Frontiers in Late Antiquity.* Aldershot.

———, and Hagith S. Sivan. (1998). "Forging a New Identity: The Kingdom of Toulouse and the Frontiers of Visigothic Aquitaine," in Ferreiro (1998), 1–62.

———, and Danuta Shanzer, eds. (2001). *Society and Culture in Late Antique Gaul: Revisiting the Sources.* Aldershot.

Matthews, J. F. (1975). *Western Aristocracies and Imperial Court, 364–425.* Oxford.

———. (2000). "Roman Law and Barbarian Identity in the Late Roman West," in Mitchell and Greatrex (2000), 31–44.

———. (2001). "Interpreting the *interpretationes* of the *Breviarium*," in Mathisen (2001), 11–32.

Mattingly, D. J., ed. (1997). *Dialogues on Roman Imperialism.* London.

Mayer Olivé, Marc, ed. (1988). *Religio Deorum: Actas del Coloquio Internacional de Epigrafía, Culto y Sociedad en Occidente.* Barcelona.

———. (1992). "Numi Emili Dexter: Un col.laborador barceloní de l'emperador Teodosi," *Revista de Catalunya* 64: 41–50.

———. (1993). "Màxim, l'emperador de la Tarraconense," *Revista de Catalunya* 72: 55–69.

———. (1996). *Gal.la Placídia i la Barcelona del segle V.* Barcelona.

———. (1997). "La epigrafía de Hispania del último cuarto de siglo," in Christol and Masson (1997), 431–38.

———, and Dimas Fernández-Galiano Ruiz. (2001). "Epigrafía de Carranque," in Fernández-Galiano (2001), 119–34.

McKenna, S. (1938). *Paganism and Pagan Survivals in Spain up to the Fall of the Visigothic Kingdom.* Washington, DC.

Medrano Marqués, Manuel M. (1990). *Analisis estadistico de la circulación monetaria bajoimperial romana en la Meseta Norte de España.* Zaragoza.

Meigne, M. (1975). "Concile ou collection d'Elvire?" *RHE* 70: 361–87.

Melchor Gil, Enrique. (1993). "Construcciones cívicas y evergetismo en Hispania romana," *Espacio, Tiempo y Forma, Serie II, Historia Antigua* 6: 443–66.

———. (1999). "Elites municipales y mecenazgo cívico en la Hispania romana," in Rodríguez Neila (1999), 219–63.

———, and Juan Francisco Rodríguez Neila. (2002). "Sociedad, espectáculos y evergetismo en Hispania," in Nogales (2002), 135–56.

Mendes-Pinto, José Marcelo S. (1999). "Circulação monetária em torno a *Cale* no Baixo-Império," in Centeno et al. (1999), 401–13.

Méndez Madariaga, Antonio, and Sebastián Rascón Marqués. (1989a). "Complutum y el bajo Henares en época visigoda," in *III Congreso Arq. Med. Esp.,* 2: 96–102.

———, and Sebastián Rascón Marqués. (1989b). *Los visigodos en Alcalá de Henares.* (Cuadernos de Juncal 1). Alcalá de Henares.

———, Teresa Montoro, and Dolores Sandoval, eds. (1997). *Monográfico: Jornades internacionales "Los Visigodos y su Mundo," Ateneo de Madrid, Noviembre de 1990.* Madrid.

Mentxaka, Rosa. (1993). *El senado municipal en la Bética hispana a la luz de la Lex Irnitana.* (Anejos de *Veleia,* Series Minor 5). Vitoria-Gasteiz.

Merêa, Paulo. (1948). *Estudos de direito visigótico.* (Acta Universitatis Conimbrigensis). Coimbra.

Mergelina, C. de. (1949). "La necrópolis de Carpio de Tajo: Notas sobre ajuar en sepulturas visigodas," *BSAA* 15: 145–54.

Meyer, Elizabeth A. (1990). "Explaining the Epigraphic Habit: The Evidence of Epitaphs," *JRS* 80: 74–96.

Meyer, Katharina E. (2001). "Die Häuser 1 und 6," in Meyer, Basas, and Teichner (2001), 1–150.

———, Carlos Basas, and Felix Teichner. (2001). *Mulva IV.* (Madrider Beiträge, Band 27). Mainz.

Migl, J. (1994). *Die Ordnung der Ämter.* Frankfurt.

Miles, G. C. (1952). *The Coinage of the Visigoths of Spain: Leovigild to Achila II.* New York.

Millar, Fergus. (1977). *The Emperor in the Roman World.* London.

———. (1986). "Italy and the Roman Empire: Augustus to Constantine," *Phoenix* 40: 295–318.

Mitchell, Stephen, and Geoffrey Greatrex, eds. (2000). *Ethnicity and Culture in Late Antiquity.* London.

Molinero Pérez, A. (1948). *La necrópolis visigoda de Duratón (Segovia): Excavaciones del Plan Nacional de 1942 y 1943.* (Acta Arqueológica Hispánica 4). Madrid.

Montalvo Frías, Ana María. (1999). "Intervención arqueológica en un solar de la barriada Santa Catalina: una aproximación al conocimiento del área Norte de Augusta Emerita," in *Mérida 3,* 125–51.

———, María Eulalia Gijón Gabriel, and F. Javier Sánchez-Palencia. (1997). "Circo romano de Mérida: Campaña de 1995," in *Mérida 1,* 244–58.

Montenegro Duque, Ángel. (1983). "Los problemas jerárquicos del cristian-ismo hispano durante el siglo IV y las raices del Priscilianismo," in *Estudios en Homenaje a Don Claudio Sánchez Albornoz en sus 90 años.* Buenos Aires. 1: 223–40.

―――, José Maria Blázquez, and J. M. Solana Sáinz. (1986). *Gredos Historia de España 3: España Romana.* Madrid.

Montero Vallejo, Manuel. (1996). *Historia del urbanismo en España I: Del Ene-olítico a la Baja Edad Media.* Madrid.

Monterroso Checa, Antonio. (2002a). "La secuencia estratigráfica: evolución histórica del teatro de *Colonia Patricia,*" in Ventura et al. (2002), 133–46.

―――. (2002b). "El teatro como cantera: Historia de un saqueo," in Ventura et al. (2002), 147–60.

―――, and Jorge Juan Cepillo Galvín. (2002). "La ocupación medieval y fos-ilizaciones actuales," in Ventura et al. (2002), 161–72.

Montes Moreira, A. (1969). *Potamius de Lisbonne et la controverse arienne.* Lou-vain.

Moorhead, John. (1992). *Theoderic in Italy.* Oxford.

―――. (1994). *Justinian.* London.

Mora, Gloria. (1981). "Las termas romanas en Hispania," *AEspA* 54: 37–89.

Morand, Isabelle. (1994). *Idéologie, culture et spiritualité chez les propriétaires de l'Hispanie romaine.* Paris.

Moreno, M., J. Murillo, A. Ventura, and S. Carmona. (1997). "Nuevos datos sobre el abastecimiento de agua a la Córdoba romana e islámica," *Arte y Arqueología* 1997: 13–23.

Mostalac Carrillo, Antonio. (1994). *Los sarcófagos romano-cristianas de la pro-vincia de Zaragoza: análisis iconográfico e iconológico.* Zaragoza.

―――, and Jesus Angel Pérez Casas. (1989). "La excavación del foro de Cae-saraugusta," in *Plaza de la Seo,* 81–155.

Mrozek, Stanislaw. (1973). "À propos de la répartition chronologique des in-scriptions latines dans le Haut-Empire," *Epigraphica* 35: 113–18.

Muhlberger, Steven. (1983). "The Gallic Chronicle of 452 and Its Authority for British Events," *Britannia* 14: 22–33.

―――. (1990). *The Fifth-Century Chroniclers.* Leeds.

Murillo, J. F., A. Ventura, S. Carmona, J. R. Carrillo, R. Hidalgo, J. L. Jiménez, M. Moreno, and D. Ruiz. (2001). "El circo oriental de *Colonia Patricia,*" in Nogales and Sánchez-Palencia (2001), 57–74.

Murray, Alexander Callander. (1983). *Germanic Kinship Structure: Studies in Law and Society in Antiquity and the Early Middle Ages.* Toronto.

Musurillo, Herbert. (1972). *Acts of the Christian Martyrs.* Oxford.

Navarro Caballero, M., and M. A. Magallón Botaya. (1999). "Las ciudades del prepirineo occidental y central en época alto-imperial: sus habitantes y su *status,*" in González Fernández (1999b), 61–86.

Nehlsen, Hermann. (1982). "Alarich II. als Gesetzgeber—Zur Geschichte der *Lex Romana Visigothorum,*" in G. Lanwehr, ed. *Studien zu den germanischen*

Volksrechten: Gedächtnisschrift für Wilhelm Ebel. Frankfurt-am-Main. Pp. 143–204.

———. (1984). "Codex Euricianus," *RGA* 5: 42–47.

Nelis-Clément, Jocelyne. (2000). *Les beneficiarii: militaires et administrateurs au service de l'empire (1er s. a.C.–VIe s. p.C.).* Bordeaux.

Neri, Valerio. (1997). "Usurpatore come tiranno nel lessico politico della tarda antichità," in François Paschoud and Joachim Szidat, eds. *Usurpationen in der Spätantike.* Stuttgart. Pp. 71–86.

Nodar Becerra, Raquel. (1997a). "Intervención en el solar de la c/ Carderos, n. 11," in *Mérida 1,* 20–28.

———. (1997b). "Intervención en un solar de la c/ S. Lázaro, no. 68," in *Mérida 1,* 30–36.

Noethlichs, K. L. (1982). "Zur Entstehung der Diözesen als Mittelinstanz des spätrömischen Verwaltungssystems," *Historia* 31: 70–81.

Nogales Basarrate, Trinidad. (2000). *Espectáculos en Augusta Emerita.* (Monografías Emeritenses 5). Badajoz.

———, ed. (2002). *Ludi romani: Espectáculos en Hispania Romana (Museo Nacional de Arte Romana, Mérida, 29 de Julio–13 de octubre, 2002).* Mérida.

———, and Francisco Javier Sánchez Palencia, eds. (2001). *El circo en Hispania romana.* Mérida.

Noguera Celdrán, José Miguel, ed. (1995). *Poblamiento rural romano en el sureste de Hispania (Actas de las Jornadas celebradas en Jumilla del 8 al 11 de noviembre de 1993).* Murcia.

Nolla i Brufau, J. M. (1984). *Carta arqueologica de les Comarques de Girona.* Girona.

———. (1988). "Gerunda: dels orígens a la fi del món antic," *Fonaments* 7: 69–108.

———. (1992). "L'abandonament de la neàpolis emporitana: Estat de la qüestió i noves dades," in Dupré (1992), 83–89.

———. (1993). "Ampurias en la Antigüedad Tardía," *AEspA* 66: 207–24.

———. (1995). "Els cementiris tardo-antics de la neàpolis emporitana," in *RACH IV,* 99–105.

———, and J. Casas. (1990). "El material ceràmic d'importació de la vil.la romana de Puig Rodon (Corçà, Empordà)," *Cypsela* 8: 193–218.

———, and F. J. Nieto Prieto (1979). "Acerca de la cronología de la muralla romana tardía de Gerunda: la terra sigillata de 'Casa Pastors,'" *Faventia* 1–2: 263–83.

———, and F. J. Nieto Prieto. (1982). "Una factoria de salaó de peix a Roses," *Fonaments* 3: 187–200.

———, Josep Burch, Jordi Sagrera, David Vivó, Xavier Aquilué, Pere Castanyer, Joaquim Tremoleda, and Marta Santos. (1996). "Les esglésies de Santa Margarida i Santa Magdalena d'Empúries (L'Escala, Alt Empordà)," *III Jornades d'Arqueologia de les Comarques de Girona.* Santa Coloma de Farrers. Pp. 225–41.

Norman, A. F. (1958). "Gradations in Later Municipal Society," *JRS* 48: 79–82.

O'Flynn, John Michael. (1983). *Generalissimos of the Western Roman Empire.* Edmonton, Alberta.

Ojeda Torres, Juan Matías. (1999). "Luces y sombras del estado burocrático. La administración de las provincias hispanas durante el alto imperio: el caso de la Bética," in Rodríguez and Navarro (1999), 145–66.

Okamura, Lawrence. (1988). "Social Disturbances in Late Roman Gaul: Deserters, Rebels and Bagaudae," in Toru Yuge and Masaoki Doi, eds. *Forms of Control and Subordination in Antiquity.* Tokyo. Pp. 288–302.

Olmo Enciso, Lauro. (1997). "Nuevas perspectivas para el estudio de la ciudad en la época visigoda," in Méndez et al. (1997), 259–69.

Oost, S. I. (1968). *Galla Placidia Augusta: A Biographical Essay.* Chicago.

Orlandis, José. (1987). *Gredos Historia de España 4: Época visigoda (409–711).* Madrid.

Ortiz Palomar, M. E. (1992). "Avances metodológicos en el estudio del vidrio antiguo en Aragón: analítica y tratamiento," *Arqueología Aragonesa* 18: 115–20.

Ortiz de Urbina Álava, Estíbaliz. (1999). "La *res publica* en las comunidades hispanas a partir de la formula epigráfica *omnibus honoribus functus*," in González Fernández (1999), 127–46.

———. (2000). *Las comunidades hispanas y el derecho latino.* Vitoria-Gasteiz.

Osuna Ruiz, M. (1976). *Ercavica I.* Cuenca.

Page, D. L. (1941). *Select Papyri III: Literary Papyri (Poetry).* London.

Palma García, Félix. (1999a). "Intervención arqueológica en el solar de la calle John Lennon, n. 28 de Mérida. Una propuesta de integración," *XXV CNA,* 325–31.

———. (1999b). "Las casas romanas intramuros en Mérida: estado de la cuestión," in *Mérida 3,* 347–65.

———. (2000). "Intervención arqueológica en el solar de la c/ John Lennon, no. 28: Hallazgo de un foso de época almohade entorno a la alcazaba árabe," in *Mérida 4,* 161–220.

———. (2001). "Ampliación al conocimiento del trazado viario romano de Mérida: Intervención arqueológica en el solar no. 6 de la c/ Lope de Vega," in *Mérida 5,* 225–41.

———, and Ana Bejarano Osorio. (1997). "Excavación del Mausoleo de la 'Casa del Anfiteatro,'" in *Mérida 1,* 44–52.

Palol, Pere de. (1958). "Las excavaciones de San Miguel de Arroyo," *BSAA* 24: 209–17.

———. (1964). "Cuchillo hispanorromano del siglo IV d. J.C.," *BSAA* 30: 67–102.

———. (1970). "Necrópolis hispanorromanos del siglo IV en el valle del Duero III: los vasos y recipientes de bronce," *BSAA* 36: 205–36.

———. (1986). "Las excavaciones del conjunto de El Bovalar, Seros (Segria, Lérida) y el reino de Akhila," *Ant. Crist.* 3: 513–26.

————. (1987). "Palencia al final del mundo antiguo," in *I Actas Palencianas*, 1: 345–59.

————. (1989). *El Bovalar (Seròs, Segrià): conjunt d'època paleocristiana i visigótica.* Barcelona and Lleida.

————. (1992a). "Una ampulla del santuari de Sant Menes, d'Egipte, a les col.leccions emporitanes del Museu de Girona," in Dupré (1992), 91–95.

————. (1992b). "Transformaciones urbanas en Hispania durante el Bajo Imperio: los ejemplos de Barcino, Tarraco y Clunia. Trascendencia del modelo en época visigoda: Toledo," in *Felix Temporis Reparatio, Atti del Convegno Archeologico Internazionale: Milano capitale dell'Impero Romano, Milano 8–11 Marzo 1990.* Milan. Pp. 381–94.

Pampliega Nogués, J. (1996–97). "El *doulos*-Evervulfo: Un siervo en el séquito doméstico de Ataúlfo," *Annals de l'Institut d'Estudis Gironins* 37: 983–89.

Paschoud, François. (1986). *Zosime: Histoire nouvelle III, 1 (Livre V).* Paris.

————. (1989). *Zosime: Histoire nouvelle III, 2 (Livre VI et index).* Paris.

Pascual Buyé, Ignacio. (2001). "El circo romano de Sagunto," in Nogales and Sánchez-Palencia (2001), 155–74.

Pastor Muñoz, Mauricio. (1988). "Religión y culto en el *Municipium Florentinum Iliberritanum*," in Mayer (1988), 369–87.

————, and Angela Mendoza Eguaras. (1987). *Inscripciones latinas de la provincia de Granada.* Granada.

Pauliatti, Agatina, and Patrizio Pensabene. (1993). "La decorazione architettonica dei monumenti provinciali di Tarraco," in Mar (1993), 25–105.

Paz Peralta, J. (1991). *Cerámica de mesa romana de los siglos III al VI d.C. en la provincia de Zaragoza.* Zaragoza.

Peña Rodríguez, Isabel. (2000). "Intervenciones del Servei Arqueològic de la URV en el sector oeste de la plaza de representación de Tárraco," in Ruiz (2000), 17–26.

Pérez Almoguera, Arturo. (1996). "La ciutat d'Ilerda de la conquesta romana al Baix Imperi (s. II a.C.–V d.C.)," *Fonaments* 9: 145–201.

Pérez Centeno, M. del Rosario. (1999). *Ciudad y territorio en la Hispania del siglo III d.C.* Valladolid.

Pérez Losada, Fermín. (2002). *Entre a cidade e a aldea: Estudio arqueohistórico dos "aglomerados secundarios" romanos en Galicia.* (*Brigantium* 13). La Coruña.

Pérez Rodríguez-Aragón, Fernando. (1990). "Nuevas investigaciones en torno a la antigua ciudad de Saldania," in *II Actas Palencianas*, 275–98.

————. (1996). "Más allá del 'necrópolis del Duero': Hacia un nuevo panorama de la Antigüedad Tardía en el cuadrante noroeste peninsular," in Fernández Ochoa (1996), 223–27.

————. (1997). "Elementos de tipo bárbaro oriental y danubiano de época bajoimperial en Hispania," in Teja and Pérez (1997), 629–47.

————, and José Antonio Abasolo Álvarez. (1987). "Acerca de Saldania romana," in *I Actas Palencianas*, 559–71.

Périn, Patrick, ed. (1991). *Gallo-Romains, Wisigoths et Francs en Aquitaine, Septimanie et Espagne*. Rouen.

Pessoa, Miguel. (1991). "Villa romaine de Rabaçal, Penela (Coimbra-Portugal): Realités et perspectives," *Conimbriga* 30: 109–19.

———. (1995). "Villa romana do Rabaçal, Penela (Coimbra-Portugal): Notas para o estudo da arquitectura e mosaicos," in *RACH IV,* 471–91.

Petrikovits, Harald van. (1971). "Fortifications in the Northwestern Roman Empire from the Third to the Fifth centuries A.D.," *JRS* 61: 178–218.

Piñol Masgoret, Lluis. (1993). "Intervencions arqueològiques al carrer Merceria, 11: Noves aportacions al coneixement del Fòrum Provincial de Tàrraco," in Mar (1993), 257–68.

———. (2000). "El circ romà de Tarragona: Qüestions arquitectòniques i de funcionament," in Ruiz (2000), 53–60.

Placanica, A. (1997). *Vittore da Tunnuna: Chronica. Chiesa e impero nell'età di Giustiniano*. Florence.

Pohl, Walter, and Helmut Reimitz, eds. (1998). *Strategies of Distinction: The Construction of Ethnic Communities, 300–800*. Leiden.

Ponsich, Michel. (1970). *Implantation rurale antique sur le bas-Guadalquivir, 2: La Campana-Palma del Río-Posadas*. Madrid.

———. (1974). *Implantation rurale antique sur le bas-Guadalquivir, 1: Seville-Alcalá del Río-Lora del Río-Carmona*. Madrid.

———. (1982). "Tanger antique," *ANRW* 2.10.2: 787–816.

———. (1987). *Implantation rurale antique sur le bas-Guadalquivir, 3: Bujalance-Montoro-Andújar*. Madrid.

———. (1991). *Implantation rurale antique sur le bas-Guadalquivir, 4: Écija, Dos Hermanas, Los Palacios y Villafranca, Lebrija, Sanlúcar de Barrameda*. Madrid.

Portela Filgueiras, Maria Isabel. (1984). "Los dioses Lares en la Hispania romana," *Lucentum* 3: 153–80.

Posac Mon, C., and R. Puertas Tricas. (1989). *La basilica paleocristiana de Vega del Mar (San Pedro de Alcántara, Marbella)*. Marbella.

Potter, D. S. (1990). *Prophecy and History in the Crisis of the Roman Empire: A Historical Commentary on the Thirteenth Sibylline Oracle*. Oxford.

Prego de Lis, Augusto. (2000). "La inscripción de *Comitiolus* del Museo Municipal de Arqueología de Cartagena," in *RACH V,* 383–90.

Prevosti, Marta. (1981a). *Cronologia i poblament a l'àrea rural de Baetulo*. Badalona.

———. (1981b). *Cronologia i poblament a l'àrea rural d'Iluro*. Mataró.

———. (1991). "The Establishment of the Villa System in the Maresme (Catalonia) and Its Development in the Roman Period," in Barker and Lloyd (1991), 135–41.

Pringle, David. (1981). *The Defence of Byzantine Africa from Justinian to the Arab Conquest*. Oxford.

Puerta, C., M. A. Elvira, and T. Artigas. (1994). "La colleción de esculturas hallada en Valdetorres de Jarama," *AEspA* 67: 179–200.

Puertas Tricas, R. (1986–87). "Los hallazgos arqueológicos de Torreblanca del Sol (Fuengirola)," *Mainake* 8–9: 145–200.

Raddatz, Klaus. (1973). *Mulva I: Die Grabungen in der Nekropole in den Jahren 1957 und 1958.* (Madrider Beiträge 2). Mainz.

Ramallo Asensio, Sebastián F. (1989). *La ciudad de Carthago Nova: la documentación arqueológica.* Murcía.

———. (1999). "El programa epigráfico y arquitectónico del teatro romano de Cartagena: Un ejemplo de monumentalización precoz en Hispania," in González Fernández (1999b), 397–410.

———. (2000). "*Carthago Spartaria,* un núcleo bizantino en *Hispania,*" in Ripoll and Gurt (2000), 579–611.

———. (2002). "La arquitectura del espectáculo en Hispania: teatros, anfiteatros y circos," in Nogales (2002), 91–117.

———, and R. Méndez Ortiz. (1986). "Fortificaciones tardorromanas y de época bizantina en el sureste," in Mas (1986), 79–98.

———, Elena Ruiz Valderas, and M. C. Berrocal Caparrós. (1996). "Contextos cerámicos de los siglos V–VII en Cartagena," *AEspA* 69: 135–90.

———, and Elena Ruiz Valderas. (1996–97). "Bizantinos en Cartagena: una revisión a la luz de los nuevos hallazgos," *Annals de l'Institut d'Estudis Gironins* 38: 1203–19.

———, and Elena Ruiz Valderas. (1998). *El teatro romano de Cartagena.* Murcia.

———, and Elena Ruiz Valderas. (2000). "Cartagena en la arqueología bizantina en *Hispania:* estado de la cuestión," in *RACH V,* 305–22.

Ramírez Sádaba, José Luis, Agustin Velázquez Jímenez, and Eulalia Gijón Gabriel. (1993). "Un nuevo pedestal de Galieno encontrado en Mérida," *Anas* 6: 75–84.

———, and Eulalia Gijón Gabriel. (1994). "Las inscripciones de la necrópolis del Alabarregas (Mérida) y su contexto arqueológico," *Veleia* 11: 117–67.

———, and Pedro Mateos Cruz. (2000). *Catalogo de las inscripciones cristianas de Mérida.* (Cuadernos Emeritenses 16). Mérida.

Ramos Fernández, R. (1975). *La ciudad romana de Ilici: estudio arqueológico.* Alicante.

Ramos Folques, Alejandro. (1960). *Las invasiones germánicas en la provincia de Alicante (siglos III y V de J.C.).* Alicante.

Ramos Sáinz, Maria Luisa, and Raquel Castelo Ruano. (1993). "Excavaciones en la villa romana de Saucedo: últimos avances en relación al hallazgo de una basilica paleocristiana," in *Actas Talavera I,* 115–38.

Raña Trabado, J. C. (1988). "Priscus Attalus y la Hispania del s. V," in *Actas del primero congreso peninsular de historia Antigua.* 3 vols. Santiago. 3: 277–85.

Rascón Marqués, Sebastián. (1995). *La ciudad hispanorromana de Complutum.* (Cuadernos de Juncal 2). Alcalá de Henares.

———. (1999). "La ciudad de Complutum en la tardoantigüedad: restauración y renovación," in García Moreno and Rascón (1999), 51–72.

Rebuffat, R. (1974). "Enceintes urbaines et insecurité en Maurétanie Tingitane," *MEFRA* 86: 501–22.

Reinhart, W. (1952). *Historia general del reino hispánico de los Suevos.* Madrid.

Remesal Rodríguez, José. (1997). *Heeresversorgung und die wirtschaftlichen Beziehungen zwischen der Baetica und Germanien.* Stuttgart.

Revilla, V. (1994). "El alfar romano de Tomoví. Producción anfórica y agricultura en el área de Tarraco," *Butlletí Arqueòlogic* 16: 111–12.

Revuelta Carbajo, Raúl. (1997). *La ordenación del territorio en Hispania durante la Antigüedad Tardía.* Madrid.

Reynolds, Paul. (1993). *Settlement and Pottery in the Vinalopó Valley (Alicante, Spain) A.D. 400–700.* (British Archaeological Reports, International Series 588). Oxford.

Ribera i Lacomba, Albert. (1998). "The Discovery of a Monumental Circus at *Valentia* (Hispania Tarraconensis)," *JRA* 11: 317–37.

———. (2001). "El circo romano de *Valentia* (Hispania Tarraconensis)," in Nogales and Sánchez-Palencia (2001), 175–96.

———, and Rafaela Soriano Sánchez. (1987). "Enterramientos de la Antigüedad tardía en Valentia," *Lucentum* 6: 139–64.

———, and Rafaela Soriano Sánchez. (1996). "Los cementerios de época visigoda," *Saitabi* 46: 195–230.

Richardson, J. S. (1986). *Hispaniae: Spain and the Development of Roman Imperialism.* Cambridge.

———. (1996). *The Romans in Spain.* Oxford.

Richmond, Ian. (1931). "Five Town Walls in Hispania Citerior," *JRS* 21: 86–100.

Ripoll López, Gisela. (1985). *La necrópolis visigoda de El Carpio de Tajo (Toledo).* Madrid.

———. (1989). "Acerca de 'Los visigodos en Alcalá de Henares,'" *Espacio, Tiempo y Forma* 2: 458–71.

———. (1993–94). "La necrópolis visigoda de El Carpio de Tajo: Una nueva lectura a partir de la topochronología y los adornos personales," *Butlletí de la Reial Acadèmia Catalana de Belles Arts de Sant Jordi* 7–8: 187–250.

———. (1996). "Acerca de la supuesta frontera entre el *Regnum Visigothorum* y la *Hispania* bizantina," *Pyrenae* 27: 251–67.

———. (1998a). *Toréutica de la Bética (siglos VI y VII d.C.).* Barcelona.

———. (1998b). "The Arrival of the Visigoths in Hispania: Population Problems and the Process of Acculturation," in Pohl and Reimitz (1998), 153–87.

———. (2000). "*Sedes regiae* en la *Hispania* de la Antigüedad Tardía," in Ripoll and Gurt (2000), 371–401.

———, and Isabel Velázquez. (1995). *La Hispania visigoda: del rey Ataúlfo a Don Rodrigo.* Madrid.

———, and Josep M. Gurt, eds. (2000). *Sedes regiae (ann. 400–800)*. Barcelona.

Ritterling, E. (1903). "Zum römischen Heerwesen des ausgehenden dritten Jahrhunderts," *Beiträge zur alten Geschichte und griechisch-römischen Alterthumskunde: Festschrift zu Otto Hirschfelds sechzigstem Geburtstage*. Berlin. Pp. 345–49.

Robert, Louis. (1960). *Hellenica XI–XII*. Paris.

Roberts, Michael. (1992). "Barbarians in Gaul: The Response of the Poets," in Drinkwater and Elton (1992), 97–106.

Rocas, X., S. Manzano, and A. M. Puig. (1992). "L'excavació d'urgència a la carretera de Sant Martí d'Empúries a la carretera d'Orriols a l'Escala," in *Primeres Jornades d'Arqueologia de les Comarques de Girona*. Sant Feliu de Guixols. Pp. 125–36.

Rodà, Isabel. (1988). "Consideraciones sobre el sevirato en Hispania: Las dedicatorias *ob honorem seviratus* en el *conventus Tarraconensis*," in Mayer (1988), 399–404.

Rodríguez Alonso, Cristóbal. (1975). *Las historias de los Godos, Vandalos, y Suevos de Isidoro de Sevilla: estudio, edición crítica y traducción*. (Fuentes y Estudios de Historia Leonesa 13). León.

Rodríguez Colmenero, Antonio. (1997). *Aquae Flaviae I: Fontes epigráficas da Gallaecia meridional interior*. 2nd ed. Chaves.

———. (1999). *Aquae Flaviae II: O tecido urbanístico da cidade romana*. Chaves.

Rodríguez Martín, Francisco Germán. (1988). "La villa romana de la dehesa de Torre Águila en Barbaño, Montijo, Badajoz," *Extremadura Arqueológica* 1: 201–19.

———. (1995a). "La villa romana de Torre Águila (Barbaño-Montijo, Badajoz)," *JRA* 8: 312–16.

———. (1995b). "La villa romana de Torre Águila: Un asentamiento rural en la cuenca media del Guadiana," *Revista de Arqueología* 176: 46–55.

Rodríguez Neila, Juan Francisco. (1975). "Notas sobre la 'contributio' en la administración municipal de la Bética romana," *Archivo Hispalense* 135: 55–61.

———. (1988). *Historia de Córdoba: Del amanecer prehistórico al ocaso visigodo*. Córdoba.

———. (1992). *Confidentes de César: los Balbos de Cádiz*. Madrid.

———, ed. (1993). *Actas del I coloquio de historia antigua de Andalucía, Córdoba 1988*. 2 vols. Córdoba.

———. (1999). "Elites municipales y ejercicio del poder en la Bética romana," in Rodríguez Neila and Navarro (1999), 25–102.

———, and Francisco Javier Navarro Santana, eds. (1999). *Elites y promoción social en la Hispania romana*. Pamplona.

Rodríguez Oliva, Pedro. (1993). "Nuevas investigaciones sobre el teatro romano de Málaga," *CAR* 2: 183–94.

————. (1994). "Transformaciones urbanas en las ciudades de la *Baetica* durante el alto imperio," in *XIV Congreso Int. Arq. Clas.,* 347–56.

Rojas Rodríguez-Malo, Juan Manuel. (1996). "Paseo de la Rosa, 76 (La piscina romana de Cabrahigos)," in Sánchez-Palencia (1996), 67–81.

————, and J. Ramón Villa González. (1996). "Consejería de Obras Públicas," in Sánchez-Palencia (1996), 225–37.

Roldán Hervas, José Manuel. (1974). *Hispania y el ejército romano: Contribución a la historia social de la España antigua.* Salamanca.

————. (1975). *Itineraria Hispana: fuentes antiguas para el estudio de las vías romanas en la península ibérica.* Valladolid.

————. (1976). "El ejército romano y la romanización de la Península Ibérica," *Hispania Antiqua* 6: 125–45.

————. (1993). *Los hispanos en el ejército romano de época republicana.* Salamanca.

Rosselló Mesquida, Miguel. (1995). "Punta de l'Illa de Cullera (Valencia): un posible establecimiento monástico del s. VI d.C.," in *RACH IV,* 151–61.

————, and Rafaela Soriano Sánchez. (1998). "Los restos arqueológicos exhibidos," in *La cripta arqueológica de la Cárcel de San Vicente.* Valencia. Pp. 41–55.

Rostovtzeff, Michael. (1957). *Social and Economic History of the Roman Empire.* 2nd ed. P. M. Fraser, ed. Oxford.

Roueché, Charlotte. (1997). "Benefactors in the Late Roman Period: The Eastern Empire," in Christol and Masson (1997), 353–68.

Rovira i Soriano, Jordi. (1993). "Alguns aspectes per a la contextualització històrica de Fòrum Provincial de Tàrraco," in Mar (1993), 195–228.

Rubio Muñoz, Luis-Alonso. (1988). "Excavaciones en la villa romana de Pesquero," *Extremadura Arqueológica* 1: 187–200.

————. (1991). "Precisiones cronológicas en cuanto al inicio y fin de la ocupación de la villa romana de Pesquero," *Extremadura Arqueológica* 2: 431–44.

Ruiz de Arbulo, Joaquín. (1993). "Edificios públicos, poder imperial y evolución de las élites urbanas en *Tarraco* (s. II–IV d.C.)," in Arce and Le Roux (1993), 93–113.

————, ed. (2000). *Tàrraco 99: Arqueología d'una capital provincial romana (Tarragona 15, 16, i 17 d'abril de 1999).* Tarragona.

————, and Ricardo Mar. (2001). "El circo de Tarraco: Un monumento provincial," in Nogales and Sánchez-Palencia (2001), 141–54.

Sagredo San Eustoquio, Luis. (1987). "Sobre la supuesta invasión del siglo III d.C. en la Meseta Norte. Palencia," in *I Actas Palencianas,* 531–58.

Salinas de Frías, M. (1992–93). "El poblamiento rural antiguo de la provincia de Salamanca: modelos e implicaciones históricas," *SHHA* 10–11: 177–88.

Salvador Ventura, Francisco. (1986). "Reflexiones sobre las causas de la intervención bizantina en la península," *Ant. Crist.* 3: 69–73.

———. (1998). *Prosopografía de Hispania Meridional, III: Antigüedad tardía (300–711).* Granada.

———, ed. (2000a). *Hispania Meridional durante la Antigüedad.* Jaén.

———. (2000b). "Los siglos VI y VII en el sur de Hispania: De periodo de autonomía ciudadana a pilar del reino hispano-visigodo," in id. (2000a), 183–203.

Sánchez Fernández, María José. (1991). "La factoría de salazón de pescado, Santa Pola (Alicante)," in Aranegui (1991), 117–18.

———, Elena Blasco, and Araceli Guardiola. (1986). *Portus Illicitanus: Datos para una síntesis.* Alicante.

Sánchez-Lafuente Pérez, Jorge. (1994). "Algunos testimonios de uso y abandono de anfiteatros durante el Bajo Imperio en Hispania: El caso segobricense," in Álvarez and Enríquez (1994), 177–83.

Sánchez León, Juan Carlos. (1996a). *Les sources de l'histoire des Bagaudes: Traduction et Commentaire.* Paris.

———. (1996b). *Los Bagaudas: rebeldes, demonios, y mártires. Revueltas campesinas en Galia e Hispania durante el Bajo Imperio.* Jaén.

Sánchez Montes, Ana Lucía. (1999). "La antigüedad tardía en Complutum: la época hispanovisigoda," in García Moreno and Rascón (1999), 249–65.

Sánchez-Palencia, F. J., ed. (1996). *Toledo: Arqueología en la ciudad.* Toledo.

———, and M. J. Sáinz Pascual. (1988). *El circo romano de Toledo: estratigrafía y arquitectura.* Toledo.

———, and M. J. Sáinz Pascual. (2001). "El circo de *Toletum*," in Nogales and Sánchez-Palencia (2001), 97–115.

———, Ana Montalvo, and Eulalia Gijón. (2001). "El circo romano de *Augusta Emerita*," in Nogales and Sánchez-Palencia (2001), 75–95.

———, S. Martínez Lillo, A. de Juan García, M. J. Sáinz-Pascual, R. Izquierdo Benito, J. Pereira Sieso, and L. Olmo. (1996). "Circo romano," in Sánchez-Palencia (1996), 25–28.

Sánchez Real, José. (1957). "Las invasiones germánicas," *Boletín Arqueológico* 57: 6–12.

———. (1969). "Exploración en el jardín de la Catedral de Tarragona," *MM* 10: 276–95.

Sánchez Sánchez, Gilberto. (1997). "Intervención en un solar de la c/ Constantino, n. 25," in *Mérida 1*, 178–86.

———. (2000). "Intervención arqueológica en el solar de la c/ Almendralejo, no. 2, c.v. a la c. Morería. Nuevas aportaciones al conocimiento de la red viaria en *Augusta Emerita*," in *Mérida 4*, 115–36.

———. (2001). "Ejemplo de continuidad en un espacio funerario de Mérida: Intervención arqueológica en un solar s/n de la c/ Travesía Marquesa de Pinare," in *Mérida 5*, 49–82.

Sanmartí i Grego, Enric, ed. (1984). *El forum romà d'Empuries (Excavacions de l'any 1982): Una aproximació arqueológica al proces históric de la romanització al nord-est de la Peninsula Ibérica.* Barcelona.

————, Pere Castañer i Masoliver, and Joaquim Tremoleda i Trilla. (1990). "Emporion: un ejemplo de monumentalización precoz en la Hispania republicana. (Los santuarios helenísticos de su sector meridional)," in Trillmich and Zanker (1990), 117–44.

San Martín Moro, P. (1985). "Nuevas aportaciones al plano arqueológico de Cartagena," *Boletín del Museo de Zaragoza* 4: 131–49.

Santero Santurino, José Maria (1978). *Asociaciones populares en Hispania romana.* Seville.

Santos, Juan, and Ramón Teja, eds. (2000). *El Cristianismo: Aspectos históricos de su origen y difusión en Hispania (Actas del Symposium de Vitoria-Gasteiz (25 a 27 Noviembre de 1996).* Vitoria-Gasteiz.

Sanz Serrano, Rosa. (1986). "Aproximación al estudio de los ejércitos privados en Hispania durante la antigüedad tardía," *Gerión* 4: 225–64.

Saquete Chamizo, José Carlos. (1997). *Las elites sociales de Augusta Emerita.* (Cuadernos Emeritenses 13). Mérida.

————. (2000). "Septimius Acindynus, corrector Tusciae et Umbriae: Notes on a New Inscription from Augusta Emerita (Mérida, Spain)," *ZPE* 129: 281–86.

————, José Luis Mosquera Müller, and Juana Marquez Pérez. (1993). "Aemilius Aemilianus, un nuevo gobernador de Lusitania," *Anas* 4–5: 31–43.

Sayas Abengochea, J. J. (1985). "Los vascones y la bagaudia," in J. Santos Yanguas, ed. *Asimilación y resistencia a la romanización en el norte de Hispania.* Vitoria. Pp. 189–236.

Scharf, Rolf. (1993). "Iovinus, Kaiser in Gallien," *Francia* 20: 1–13.

Schlunk, Helmut. (1988). *Die Mosaikkuppel von Centcelles.* 2 vols. Mainz.

Schmidt, Ludwig. (1933). *Geschichte der deutschen Stämme bis zum Ausgang der Völkerwanderung: Die Ostgermanen.* 2nd ed. Munich.

————. (1942). *Geschichte der Wandalen.* 2nd ed. Munich.

Schulten, Adolf. (1936). "Narbasi," P-W 16.2: 1700. Stuttgart.

Schwarcz, Andreas. (2001). "The Visigothic Settlement in Aquitania: Chronology and Archaeology," in Mathisen and Shanzer (2001), 15–25.

Seeck, Otto. (1913). *Geschichte des Untergangs der antiken Welt 5.* Berlin.

————. (1919). *Regesten der Kaiser und Päpste für die Jahre 311 bis 476 n. Chr.* Stuttgart.

————. (1920). *Geschichte des Untergangs der antiken Welt 6.* Stuttgart.

Segura Arista, M. L. (1988). *La ciudad ibero-romana de Igabrum (Cabra, Córdoba).* Córdoba.

Selb, W. (1967). "Episcopalis audientia von der Zeit Konstantins bis zur Nov. XXXV Valentinians III.," *ZSS, Röm. Abt.* 84: 162–217.

Serra Ràfols, J. de C. (1927–31). "Les muralles ibèriques i romanes de Girona," *Anuari de l'Institut d'Estudis Catalans* 9: 69–84.

Serra-Vilaró, J. (1948). *La necrópolis de San Fructuoso.* Tarragona.

Seston, William. (1946). *Dioclétien et la Tétrachie I: les guerres et les réformes.* Paris.

Shanzer, Danuta. (1998). "Dating the Baptism of Clovis: The Bishop of Vienne vs. the Bishop of Tours," *EME* 7: 29–57.

Shennan, Stephen. (1989). "Introduction: Archaeological Approaches to Cultural Identity," in id., ed. *Archaeological Approaches to Cultural Identity.* London. Pp. 1–32.

Sherwin-White, A. N. (1973). *The Roman Citizenship.* 2nd ed. Oxford.

Siegmund, Frank. (2000). *Alemannen und Franken.* (Ergänzungsbände zum Reallexikon der Germanischen Altertumskunde 23). Berlin.

Sienes Hernando, Milagros. (1999). "Las imitaciones de monedas de bronce del siglo IV d.C. en la Península Ibérica. El caso del AE2 *REPARATIO REIPUB*," in Centeno et al. (1999), 381–86.

Sillières, Pierre. (1993). "La péninsule ibérique," in Philippe Leveau, Pierre Sillières, and Jean-Pierre Vallat, eds. *Campagnes de la Méditerranée romaine: occident.* Paris. Pp. 201–49.

Sivan, Hagith. (1985). "An Unedited Letter of the Emperor Honorius to the Spanish Soldiers," *ZPE* 61: 273–85.

Soriano Sánchez, Rafaela. (1990). *La arqueología cristiana en la ciudad de Valencia: De la leyenda a la realidad.* València.

———. (1994). "Las excavaciones arqueológicas de la Cárcel de San Vicente (Valencia)," *Saguntum* 27: 173–86.

———. (1995). "Los restos arqueológicos de la sede episcopal valentina: avance preliminar," in *RACH IV,* 133–40.

Sotomayor, Manuel. (1991). "Consideraciones sobre las fuentes para el estudio del cristianismo primitivo en Andalucía," in González Román (1991b), 299–311.

———. (1994). "Andalucía: romanidad y cristianismo en la época tardoantigua," in *II Actas Andalucía,* 537–53.

———. (2000). "El concilio de Elvira en el contexto de la *Collección Canónica Hispana,*" in Santos and Teja (2000), 189–99.

Spaul, John. (1997). "Across the Frontier in Tingitana," in *Roman Frontier Studies 1995: Proceedings of the XVIth International Congress of Roman Frontier Studies.* Oxford. Pp. 253–58.

Spitzl, T. (1984). *Lex municipii Malacitani.* Munich.

Stein, Ernst. (1949). *Histoire du Bas-Empire II: De la disparation de l'empire d'occident a la mort de Jutinien (476–565).* J.-R. Palanque, ed. Paris.

———. (1959). *Histoire du Bas-Empire I: De l'état romain à l'état byzantin (284–476).* J.-R. Palanque, ed. Paris.

Stevens, C. E. (1933). *Sidonius Apollinaris and His Age.* Oxford.

———. (1957). "Marcus, Gratian, Constantine," *Athenaeum* 35: 316–47.

Stocking, Rachel L. (2000). *Bishops, Councils, and Consensus in the Visigothic Kingdom, 589–633.* Ann Arbor.

Stroheker, K. F. (1948). *Der senatorische Adel im spätantiken Gallien.* Tübingen.

———. (1963). "Spanische Senatoren der spätrömischen und westgotischen Zeit," *MM* 4: 107–32; reprinted in Stroheker (1965), 54–87.

———. (1965). *Germanentum und Spätantike.* Zurich.

———. (1972–74). "Spanien im spätrömischen Reich (284–475)," *AEspA* 40–42: 587–605.

Stylow, Armin U. (1999). "Entre edictum y lex: A propósito de una nueva ley municipal flavia del término de Écija," in González Fernández (1999), 229–37.

———. (2000). "Nuevo gobernador de la Bética del siglo IV," *Gerión* 18: 425–27.

Sundwall, Johannes. (1915). *Weströmische Studien.* Berlin.

Superbiola Martínez, J. (1987). *Nuevos concilios hispano-romanos de los siglos III y IV: La colleción de Elvira.* Málaga.

Syme, Ronald. (1958). *Tacitus.* 2 vols. Oxford.

———. (1964). "Hadrian and Italica," *JRS* 54: 142–49; reprinted in Syme (1980), 2: 617–28.

———. (1970). "The Conquest of Northwest Spain," in *Legio VII,* 83–107; reprinted in Syme (1980), 2: 825–54.

———. (1971). *Emperors and Biography: Studies in the Historia Augusta.* Oxford.

———. (1980). *Roman Papers.* Ernst Badian, ed. 2 vols. Oxford.

Taracena, B. (1950). "La invasiones germánicas en España durante la segunda mitad del siglo III de J.C.," in *Primer Congreso Internacional de Pireneistas del Instituto de Estudios Pirenaicos.* Zaragoza. Pp. 4–13.

Tarradell, Miguel. (1955). "Sobre las invasiones germánicas del siglo III de J.C. en la península ibérica," *Estudios Clásicos* 3: 95–110.

———. (1977). "Les villes romaines dans l'*Hispania* de l'Est," in Duval and Frézouls (1977), 97–98.

Tarrats Bou, Francesc, Josep M. Macias i Solé, Esther Ramon Sariñena, and Josep A. Remolà Vallverdú. (1998). "Excavacions a l'àrea residencial de la vil.la romana dels Munts (Altafulla, Tarragonès)," *Empúries* 51: 197–225.

TED'A. (1987). *Els enterraments del Parc de la Ciutat i la problemàtica funerària de Tàrraco.* Tarragona.

———. (1989a). *Un abocador del segle V d.c. en el fòrum provincial de Tàrraco.* Tarragona.

———. (1989b). "El foro provincial de Tarraco, un ejemplo arquitectónico de época flavia," *AEspA* 62: 141–91.

———. (1990). *L'amfiteatre romà de Tarragona, la basílica visigòtica i l'església romànica.* Tarragona.

———. (1994). "Novas aportacions a l'estudi de la basílica chrisiana de l'amfiteatre de Tàrraco," in *RACH III,* 167–84.

Teichner, Felix. (2001). "Das Haus 2," in Meyer, Casas, and Teichner (2001), 209–332.

Teitler, H. C. (1992). "Un-Roman Activities in Late Antique Gaul: The Cases of Arvandus and Seronatus," in Drinkwater and Elton (1992), 309–18.

Teja, Ramón. (1973). "Las corporaciones romanas municipales en el Bajo Imperio: alcance y naturaleza," *Hispania Antiqua* 3: 153–77.

———. (1990). "La carta 67 de S. Cipriano a las comunidades cristianas de León-Astorga y Mérida," *Ant. Crist.* 7: 115–24.

———. (1994). "Los juegos de anfiteatro y Cristianismo," in Álvarez and Enríquez (1994), 69–78.

———. (2000). "Una mirada a los estudios sobre el Cristianismo antiguo en España," in Santos and Teja (2000), 29–36.

———. (2002). "Espectáculos y mundo tardío en Hispania," in Nogales (2002), 163–70.

———, and Cesáreo Pérez, eds. (1997). *Congreso Internacional La Hispania de Teodosio, Segovia-Coca. Octubre, 1995.* 2 vols. Salamanca.

Thomas, Edmund, and Christian Witschel. (1992). "Constructing Reconstruction: Claim and Reality of Roman Rebuilding Inscriptions from the Latin West," *PBSR* 60: 135–77.

Thompson, E. A. (1952). "Peasant Revolts in Late Roman Gaul and Spain," *Past and Present* 2: 11–23; reprinted in M. I. Finley, ed. *Studies in Ancient Society.* London, 1974. Pp. 304–20.

———. (1969). *The Goths in Spain.* Oxford.

———. (1980). "Barbarian Invaders and Roman Collaborators," *Florilegium* 2: 71–88.

———. (1982a). "Zosimus 6.10.2 and the Letters of Honorius," *CQ* 32: 445–62.

———. (1982b). *Romans and Barbarians: The Decline of the Western Empire.* Madison.

Tomasini, W. F. (1964). *The Barbaric Tremissis in Spain and Southern France, Anastasius to Leovigild.* New York.

Torrent, A. (1970). *La iurisdictio de los magistrados municipales.* Salamanca.

Torres, Casimiro. (1957). "Un rector de la ciudad de Lugo en el siglo V," *Cuadernos de Estudios Gallegos* 12: 158–66.

———. (1977). *Galicia Sueva.* La Coruña.

Torres, Cláudio, and Santiago Macias, eds. (1993). *Museu de Mértola: Basílica Paleocristã.* Mértola.

Tovar, Luis Carlos Juan. (1997). "Las industrias cerámicas hispanas en el Bajo Imperio: Hacia una sistematización de la Sigillata Hispánica Tardía," in Teja and Pérez (1997), 543–68.

Tranoy, A. (1981). *La Galice romaine.* Paris.

Trillmich, Walter. (1993). "'Foro provincial' und 'Foro municipal' in den Hauptstädten der drei hispanischen Provinzen: eine Fiktion," in Arce and Le Roux (1993), 115–24.

———, and Paul Zanker, eds. (1990). *Stadtbild und Ideologie: Die monumentalisierung hispanischer Städte zwischen Republik und Kaiserzeit.* Munich.

Tsirkin, J. B. (1987). "The Crisis of Antique Society in the Third Century," *Gerión* 5: 253–70.

Tudanca Casero, Juan Manuel. (1997). *Evolución socioeconómica del alto y medio valle del Ebro en época bajoimperial romana.* Logroño.

Vallejo Girvés, Margarita. (1992). *Fuentes históricas para el estudio de Complutum romano y visigodo.* Alcalá de Henares.

———. (1993). *Bizancio y la España tardoantigua (ss. V–VIII): un capítulo de historia mediterránea.* Alcalá de Henares.

———. (1999a). "Byzantine Spain and the African Exarchate: An Administrative Perspective," *JÖB* 49: 13–23.

———. (1999b). "'Un asunto de chantaje': la familia de Atanagildo entre Metz, Toledo y Constantinopla," *Polis* 11: 261–79.

Vallet, Françoise, and Michel Kazanski, eds. (1993). *L'armée et les barbares du IIIe au VIIe siècle.* Paris.

Van Dam, Raymond. (1985). *Leadership and Community in Late Antique Gaul.* Berkeley.

———. (1986). "'Sheep in Wolves' Clothing': The Letters of Consentius to Augustine," *Journal of Ecclesiastical History* 37: 515–35.

Vaquerizo Gil, Desiderio. (1990). "La villa romana de El Ruedo (Almedinilla, Córdoba)," *AEspA* 63: 295–316.

———. (1994a). "El Hypnos de Almedinilla (Córdoba)," *MM* 35: 359–79.

———, ed. (1994b). *Arqueología Cordobesa: Almedinilla.* Córdoba.

———, and José Ramón Carrillo Díaz-Pínes. (1995). "The Roman Villa of El Ruedo," *JRA* 8: 121–52.

———, and José Miguel Noguera. (1997). *La villa romana de El Ruedo (Almedinilla, Córdoba): Decoración escultórica e interpretación.* Murcia.

Vegas, M. (1988). *Mulva II: Die Südnekropole von Munigua, Grabungskampagnen 1977 bis 1983.* Mainz.

Velázquez, Agustín. (1998). "Colonia Augusta Emerita," in *Hispania el Legado,* 397–404.

———, Enrique Cerrillo Martín de Cáceres, and Pedro Mateos Cruz, eds. (1995). *Los últimos romanos en Lusitania.* (Cuadernos Emeritenses 10). Mérida.

Velázquez, Isabel, and Gisela Ripoll López. (2000). "*Toletum,* la construcción de una *urbs regia,*" in Ripoll and Gurt (2000), 521–78.

Ventura Villanueva, Ángel. (1991). "Resultados del seguimento arqueológico en el solar de c/ Angel de Saavedra, no. 10, Córdoba," *AAC* 2 (1991), 253–90.

———. (1993). *El abastacimiento de agua a la Córdoba romana I: el acueducto de Valdepuentes.* Córdoba.

———. (1996). *El abastacimiento de agua a la Córdoba romana II: acueductos, ciclo de distribución y urbanismo.* Córdoba.

———, and Silvia Carmona Berenguer. (1992). "Resultados sucintos de la excavación arqueológica de urgencia en los solares de la calle Blanco Belmonte Numeros 4–6 y Ricardo de Montis 1–8, Córdoba. El trazado del Cardo Maximo de la Colonia Patricia Corduba," *AAC* 3: 199–242.

————, José M. Bermúdez, Pilar León, Isabel M. López, Carlos Márquez, and Juan J. Ventura. (1993). "Análisis arqueológico de la Córdoba romana: resultados e hipótesis de la investigación," in León (1993a), 87–118.

————, and Armin U. Stylow. (1993). "Consideraciones en torno al patronato provincial (siglos I a V. d.C.)," in Rodríguez Neila (1993), 505–14.

————, Carlos Márquez Montero, Antonio Monterroso Checa, and Miguel A. Carmona Berenguer, eds. (2002). *El teatro romano de Córdoba: Catálogo de la exposición.* Córdoba.

Veyne, Paul. (1976). *Le pain et le cirque.* Paris; heavily abbreviated translation by B. Pearce as *Bread and Circuses.* Harmondsworth, 1992.

Vianney, J., and M. Arbeola. (1987). "El anfiteatro romano de Tarragona: Estado de la cuestión," *XVIII CNA.* Zaragoza. Pp. 903–21.

Vicens Vives, J. (1986). *Atlas de Historia de España.* 13th ed. Barcelona.

Vigil Pascual, Marcelo, and Abilio Barbero de Aguilera. (1967). "Sobre los orígenes sociales de la Reconquista," *BRAH* 15: 271–339; reprinted in Barbero and Vigil (1974), 11–98.

Vilaseca i Canals, Albert, and Jordi Diloli i Fons. (2000). "Excavacions a l'àrea del fòrum provincial: Plaça del Rei, núm. 4, i Casa-Museu Castellarnau," in Ruiz (2000), 47–52.

Vilella Masana, Josep. (1989). "Hispaniques et non-Hispaniques: motifs et itinéraires des voyages et correspondances dans l'Antiquité tardive (IVe–VIe s.)," *Ktema* 14: 139–58.

————. (1992). "Rang i procedència geogràfica dels vicaris i governadors de la Diòcesis Hispaniarum (300–409)," *Fonaments* 8: 79–98.

————. (2000). "El *corpus* prosopográfico del cristianismo hispano antiguo," in Santos and Teja (2000), 145–60.

Villaverde Vega, Noé. (2000). "La iglesia de *Tingitana* (ss. IV–VII): dos *carmina latina epigraphica* y nuevas lecturas en epitafios cristianos," in *RACH V,* 291–302.

————. (2001). *Tingitania en la Antigüedad Tardía (siglos III–IV). Autoctonía y romanidad en el extremo occidente mediterráneo.* Madrid.

Vittinghoff, F. (1970). "Die Entstehung von städtischen Gemeinwesen in der Nachbarschaft römischer Legionslager: ein Vergleich Leons mit Entwicklungslinien im Imperium Romanorum," in *Legio VII Gemina,* 339–52.

Vives, José. (1938). "Die Inschrift an der Brücke von Merida und der Bischof Zenon," *Römische Quartalschaft für christliche Altertumskunde* 46: 57–61.

————. (1963). *Concilios visigóticos e hispano-romanos.* Barcelona and Madrid.

————. (1971–72). *Inscripciones latinas de la España romana.* 2 vols. Barcelona.

Vogler, Chantal. (1979). *Constance II et l'administration impériale.* Strasbourg.

von Hesberg, Henner. (1993). "Römische Grabbauten in den hispanischen Provinzen," in Hauschild (1993b), 159–82.

Wacher, John. (1998). "The Dating of Town-Walls in Roman Britain," in J.

Bird, ed. *Form and Fabric: Studies in Rome's Material Past.* Oxford. Pp. 41–50.

Wallace-Hadrill, Andrew, ed. (1989). *Patronage in Ancient Society.* London.

Waltzing, J. P. (1895–1900). *Étude historique sur les corporations professionelles chez les Romains depuis les origines jusqu'à la chute de l'empire d'Occident.* 4 vols. Brussels.

Ward-Perkins, Bryan. (1998). "The Cities," in Cameron (1998), 371–410.

Warland, Rainer. (2002). "Die Kuppelmosaïken von Centcelles als Bildprogramm spätantiker Privatrepräsentation," in Arce (2002), 21–35.

Watson, Alaric. (1999). *Aurelian and the Third Century.* London.

Way, Ruth. (1962). *A Geography of Spain and Portugal.* London.

Werner, J. (1942). "Die Ausgrabung des westgotischen Gräberfeldes von Castiltierra (Prov. Segovia) in Jahre 1941," *Forschungen und Fortschritte* 11–12: 108–9.

———. (1946). "Las excavaciones del Seminario de Historia Primitiva del Hombre en 1941, en el cementerio visigodo de Castiltierra (Segovia)," *Cuadernos de Historia Primitiva del Hombre* 1: 46–50.

Whittaker, C. R. (1994). *Frontiers of the Roman Empire.* Baltimore.

Wiegels, R. (1985). *Die Tribusinschriften des römisches Hispanien: Ein Katalog.* Berlin.

Wightman, Edith Mary. (1985). *Gallia Belgica.* London.

Williams, Stephen. (1985). *Diocletian and the Roman Recovery.* New York.

Witschel, Christian. (1999). *Krise—Rezession—Stagnation? Der Westen des römischen Reiches im 3. Jahrhundert n. Chr.* Frankfurt-am-Main.

Wolfram, Herwig. (1988). *History of the Goths.* Thomas J. Dunlap, trans. Berkeley and Los Angeles.

Wood, Ian. (1985). "Gregory of Tours and Clovis," *Revue Belge de Philologie et d'Histoire* 63: 249–72.

———. (1994). *The Merovingian Kingdoms, 450–751.* London.

Woolf, Greg. (1998). *Becoming Roman.* Cambridge.

Zeiss, H. (1934). *Die Grabfunde aus dem spanischen Westgotenreich.* Berlin and Leipzig.

Index

barbarian settlement, 47, 83; of A.D. 411,
in Spain, 163–67; Gothic, in Gaul,
170–72, 194–95
Barcelona, 219–20, 306; Athaulf and,
168–69; curia of, 24, 48–49; epigra-
phy of, 32–33; *fabri* in, 56; mint of,
158, 163; as residence of Gesalic,
Amalaric, 258–61, 265; as residence
of Maximus, 120–21
Barcelona, monuments of: churches,
233; *domus,* 122, 297; *episcopium,*
233; walls, 103, 158, 163, 233
Barcino. *See* Barcelona
Basilides, bishop, 216–17
Basilius, bacaudic chief, 185
Basques, 185, 285
Basti, 284
baths, 100–101, 250. *See also under*
Braga; Complutum; Gijón; Jaén; Lis-
bon; Mérida; Segobriga; Tarragona;
Toledo; Valencia; Zaragoza
Baza. *See* Basti
Beja, 90, 122
Belgica, 156
Belisarius, 272–73
Benalúa, 121
Besso, a Frank, 261
Boniface, *comes,* 174–75, 176
Bonosus, 338n. 49
Bordeaux, 258
Bracara Augusta. *See* Braga
Braga, 9, 173, 188; baths in, 101; as cap-
ital of Gallaecia, 71, 120; epigraphy
of, 35
Braulio, bishop of Zaragoza, 304–6
Breviarium, of Alaric, 399–400n. 37; law
of Theudis and, 265, 273–74
Britain, 156–57, 159, 171; town walls
in, 108
Briviesca, 47–48
Burdigala. *See* Bordeaux
Burdunelus, usurper in Spain, 206–9,
257
Burgo de Osma. *See* Uxama
Burgundians, 160, 178; and Clovis,
257–60, 397n. 25; and Theoderic II,
188, 191
burial: *ad sanctos,* 225–26, 229, 236,

251, 291; intramural, 212, 231–32,
294
Byzantines: in Baetica and Carthaginiensis, 276–82, 409n. 110; in Tingitania,
272–73

Cacera de las Ranas, cemetery of, 403n.
71
Cáceres, walls of, 102
Cádiz, 73, 169, 177, 319n. 8; theater of,
95
Caelestinus, Q. Attius Granius, *consularis
Baeticae,* 43
Caesar, G. Julius, 4–5; *coloniae* founded
by, 7, 98, 114, 279
Caesaraugusta. *See* Zaragoza
Caesarius, bishop of Arles, 257, 394n. 3
Calagurris. *See* Calahorra
Calahorra, 47–48
Cale. *See* Oporto
campi Pallentini, 158. *See also* Palencia
Canama, 28–29
Can Modolell, *mithraeum* of, 250
Cantabri, 4
Cantabri, family of Conimbriga, 46,
199–200
Cantabria, Roman region, 75, 284, 304–
6, 415n. 64
Cantabria, Spanish *autonomía,* 14, 123;
Roman population of, 132
capitatio. See taxation
Caracalla, emperor, 71
Carcaso. *See* Carcassonne
Carcassonne, 258, 396n. 18
Carinus, 69; dedication to, 33
Carolingian Spain, 300
Carpetania, 266
Carranque, villa of, 145–48
Cartagena: Byzantine, 277–81, 410n.
113; as capital of Carthaginiensis, 71,
120, 279; epigraphy of, 35, 279; size
of, 128; Vandals and, 177–78
Cartagena, monuments of: cemeteries,
229; theater, 95, 279–81; walls, 279
Carthage, 73, 217
Carthaginians, in Spain, 2–3
Carthaginiensis: Balearic separated from,
82; Byzantines in, 276–82; Diocle-

The series Ancient Society and History offers books, relatively brief in compass, on selected topics in the history of ancient Greece and Rome, broadly conceived, with a special emphasis on comparative and other nontraditional approaches and methods. The series, which includes both works of synthesis and works of original scholarship, is aimed at the widest possible range of specialist and nonspecialist readers.

Published in the Series:

Eva Cantarella, *Pandora's Daughters: The Role and Status of Women in Greek and Roman Antiquity,* translated by Maureen B. Fant

John E. Stambaugh, *The Ancient Roman City*

Géza Alföldy, *The Society History of Rome,* translated by David Braund and Frank Pollock

Giovanni Comotti, *Music in Greek and Roman Culture,* translated by Rosaria V. Munson

Mark Golden, *Children and Childhood in Classical Athens*

Thomas Cole, *The Origins of Rhetoric in Ancient Greece*

Stephen L. Dyson, *Community and Society in Roman Italy*

Suzanne Dixon, *The Roman Family*

Alison Burford, *Land and Labor in the Greek World*

Steven H. Lonsdale, *Dance and Ritual Play in Greek Religion*

J. Donald Hughes, *Pan's Travail: Environmental Problems of the Ancient Greeks and Romans*

C. R. Whittaker, *Frontiers of the Roman Empire: A Social and Economic Study*

Nancy Demand, *Birth, Death, and Motherhood in Classical Greece*

Elaine Fantham, *Roman Literary Culture: From Cicero to Apuleius*

Kenneth W. Harl, *Coinage in the Roman Economy, 300 B.C. to A.D. 700*

Christopher Haas, *Alexandria in Late Antiquity: Topography and Social Conflict*

James C. Anderson, jr., *Roman Architecture and Society*

Matthew R. Christ, *The Litigious Athenian*

Gregory S. Aldrete, *Gestures and Acclamations in Ancient Rome*

H. A. Drake, *Constantine and the Bishops: The Politics of Intolerance*

Tim G. Parkin, *Old Age in the Roman World: A Cultural and Social History*

Thomas S. Burns, *Rome and the Barbarians, 100 B.C.–A.D. 400*